Manufacturing Systems Economics

THE LIFE-CYCLE COSTS AND BENEFITS OF INDUSTRIAL ASSETS

R. F. de la Mare

University of Bradford

HOLT, RINEHART AND WINSTON
London · New York · Sydney · Toronto

Holt, Rinehart and Winston Ltd: 1 St Anne's Road,
Eastbourne, East Sussex BN21 3UN

131785b

British Library Cataloguing in Publication Data

de la Mare, R.
  Manufacturing systems economics.
  1. Business enterprises 2. New products
  3. Product life cycle
  I. Title
  658.5'75   HD69.N4
ISBN 0-03-910363-3

Printed in Northern Ireland at The Universities Press (Belfast) Ltd.

Last digit is print number: 9 8 7 6 5 4 3 2 1

Manufacturing Systems Economics

Contents

PREFACE   xi

PART ONE   MANUFACTURING SYSTEMS ECONOMICS IN CONTEXT   1

1   Physical Asset Management and International Competition   3

1.1   The national importance of manufacturing   3
1.2   Economic growth and increased productivity   6
1.3   The significance of technological innovation   8
1.4   The need for a life-cycle approach to product innovation   11
1.5   Bibilography   12

2   The Rudiments of Microeconomic Theory   13

2.1   Human behavioural effects on prices   13
2.2   Supply and demand schedules and price equilibrium   14
2.3   The utility of demand   16
2.4   The price elasticity of demand   22
2.5   Income-elasticity and cross-elasticity of demand   23
2.6   The production function   25
2.7   The cost of production   30
2.8   Revenue from sales   33
2.9   Profit from sales   33
2.10   The opportunity cost of limiting resources   37
2.11   Summary   40
2.12   Bibliography   41
2.13   Questions   41

3   The Need for a Corporate Objective   44

3.1   A philosophy of the firm   44
3.2   The need for a corporate strategy   45
3.3   The nature of corporate planning   46
3.4   Formulating a corporate objective   47
3.5   Forecasting the 'profit gap'   51
3.6   Summary   56
3.7   Bibliography   56

PART TWO   THE INVESTMENT DECISION   57

4   On the Search for New Manufacturing Opportunities   59

4.1   The need for new product strategy   59
4.2   The need for an R & D strategy   63
4.2   Capability analysis   65
4.4   The management of technological innovation   66
4.5   Summary   69
4.5   Bibliography   69

5   The Choice of Investment Appraisal Criterion   71

5.1   *The principles of compound interest*   72
5.2   *Investment on a mortgage basis*   73
5.3   *The discounting technique*   74
5.4   *The discounted cash flow rate of return on investment*   76
5.5   *Appraising the economic merits of projects using NPV and DCFRR criteria*   79
5.6   *Discounting annuities*   82
5.7   *Two special cases involving annuities*   83
5.8   *Alternative means of measuring the economic worth of prospective investment projects*   84
5.9   *The superiority of the discounting technique*   87
5.10 *An economic life-cycle model*   88
5.11 *Cost benefit analysis*   89
5.12 *Summary*   89
5.13 *Bibilography*   90
5.14 *Questions*   90

6   Choosing Between Competing Projects   94

6.1   *The time preference for money*   94
6.2   *The economics of mutually exclusive projects*   100
6.3   *The choice of projects when capital is rationed*   106
6.4   *Rule-of-thumb techniques*   108
6.5   *Cash rationing between projects using mathematical programming techniques*   109
6.6   *Conclusions*   118
6.7   *Bibliography*   119
6.8   *Questions*   120

7   On the Systematic Search for Relevant Information   123

7.1   *An evaluation of the business and economic environment*   124
7.2   *Determining market size*   127
7.3   *Determining product price*   141
7.4   *Determining market share*   147
7.5   *Capital cost estimating*   149
7.6   *Estimating working capital requirements*   166
7.7   *Operating cost estimating*   169
7.8   *A special costing problem involving the use of existing facilities*   172
7.9   *Terotechnology and the life cycle costs of asset ownership*   173
7.10 *The duration of a project's building programme and its economic life*   180
7.11 *Company taxation*   181
7.12 *Project optimization*   187
7.13 *Summary*   188

8   The Cost of Capital   190

8.1   *The cost of short-term sources of finance*   190
8.2   *The cost of medium- and long-term debt*   192
8.3   *The cost of equity sources of finance*   193
8.4   *The combined cost of long-term debt and equity capital*   196
8.5   *The influence of short-term debt on a firm's overall cost of capital*   199
8.6   *The effect of inflation on a firm's overall cost of capital*   199
8.7   *Summary*   201
8.8   *Bibliography*   202

9   Uncertainty and Risk   203

9.1   *The existence of uncertainty*   203
9.2   *Allowing for risk in practice*   205
9.3   *Sensitivity analysis*   208
9.4   *Making investment decisions under conditions of complete uncertainty*   211
9.5   *The maximin and the maximax rules*   212

9.6   The minimax regret rule   213
9.7   The Laplace method   214
9.8   The Hurwicz rule   214
9.9   Summary of the elementary rules for dealing with investment under conditions of uncertainty   215
9.10 Some basic probability concepts   216
9.11 A practical approach to the use of probability theory in capital budgeting   226
9.12 Risk analysis using utility theory   236
9.13 Conclusions   242
9.14 Bibliography   242
9.15 Questions   243

10   The Economics of Research and Development   246

10.1 The costs and benefits of R & D   246
10.2 The appraisal of R & D projects   248
10.3 Sequential decision making   253
10.4 The techniques of technological forecasting   257
10.5 The corporate significance of technological innovation   261
10.6 Summary   262
10.7 Bibliography   262
10.8 Questions   264

11   A Total Systems Approach to Investment in Manufacturing Assets   267

11.1 A misplaced emphasis on capital budgeting   267
11.2 The management of risk   272
11.3 The organization of capital budgeting   273
11.4 The strategic implications of capital investment   275
11.5 Summary   276
11.6 Bibliography   276

12   A Capital Budgeting Game   278

12.1 The development of the model   278
12.2 Project 'Unowat'   282

PART THREE   THE OPTIMAL EMPLOYMENT OF EXISTING ASSETS   293

13   The Control of Existing Resources Using Accounting Information   295

13.1 The basic need for cost control   295
13.2 The elements of corporate control   297
13.3 Responsibility costing   298
13.4 Budgetary control   299
13.5 The rudiments of short-term budgeting   301
13.6 Standard costing and variance analysis   305
13.7 The elements of job costing   309
13.8 Marginal costing   315
13.9 The need for a comprehensive management information system   317
13.10 Summary   317
13.11 Bibliography   317
13.12 Questions   318

14   Economic Appraisal Using Network Analysis   323

14.1 The basic logic of network diagrams   324
14.2 Network analysis   327
14.3 Allowing for uncertainty in network analysis   333
14.4 The economic implications of network analysis   334

14.5   Summary   337
14.6   Bibliography   337

15   Inventory Cost Control   339

15.1   The purpose of stocks   339
15.2   The various categories of inventory costs   340
15.3   The physical implications of stock control   343
15.4   The classical inventory model   344
15.5   An inventory model with stock-out costs   349
15.6   An inventory model involving production runs   351
15.7   A multiple product batch sequence model   353
15.8   A constrained inventory model   355
15.9   Inventory problems under conditions of risk and uncertainty   358
15.10 Summary   361
15.11 Bibliography   361
15.12 Questions   361

16   Minimizing the Cost of Queueing   365

16.1   The fundamental reasons for queues   365
16.2   The physical behaviour of queues   367
16.3   The economic implications of queues involving a single channel, single phase service 368
16.4   The economic implications of queues involving a multi-channelled single phase service 370
16.5   Dealing with more complex queueing situations   371
16.6   Summary   373
16.7   Bibliography   373

17   Optimizing the Use of Existing Resources Using Mathematical
     Programming Techniques   375

17.1   The algebraic method of solving linear programming problems   375
17.2   A description of the simplex algorithm   380
17.3   Solving minimization problems using the simplex algorithm   385
17.4   Formulating linear programming models   388
17.5   An introduction to transportation linear programming   392
17.6   Transportation linear programming—the stepping-stone method   393
17.7   Transportation linear programming—Vogel's approximation method   397
17.8   Transportation linear programming—the modified distribution method   399
17.9   Dealing with degeneracy in TLP problems   401
17.10 Unequal supply and demand in TLP problems   402
17.11 The practical application of transportation linear programming   403
17.12 Dealing with non-linearity   404
17.13 The Hungarian assignment technique   406
17.14 Summary   408
17.15 Bibliography   409
17.16 Questions   410

18   Case Study I   421

PART FOUR   THE DISPOSAL OF MANUFACTURING ASSETS

19   The Replacement and Retirement of Manufacturing Assets   427

19.1   The fundamental objects of replacement and retirement analysis   427
19.2   The economic life of an asset   429
19.3   The value of an existing asset   433
19.4   The principle of sunk cost   440
19.5   Taxation effects in replacement economics   442
19.6   A dynamic programming approach to replacement analysis   449

19.7 The problem of uncertainty in replacement analysis   454
19.8 The influence of process innovation on plant replacement decisions 457
19.9 Some common errors in replacement studies   462
19.10 Summary   463
19.11 Bibliography   464
19.12 Questions   464

20 Case Study II   470

21 Case Study III   475

APPENDICES

A   *Opportunity Costs and Lagrange Multipliers*   483

B   *The Rudiments of Accounting*   487

C   *Solutions to the Capital Budgeting Game of Chapter 12*   494

D   *Solutions to the Case Studies*   502

E   *Answers to Odd-Numbered Questions*   513

F   *Some Technical Problems with the Discounted Cash Flow Technique*   522

G   *Tables of Discount Factors*   535

NAME INDEX   541

SUBJECT INDEX   543

Preface

Although a proper understanding of wealth creation is fundamental to a thorough education in technology and business management, it would appear that few textbooks cover the corporate economic implications of manufacturing in a comprehensive way. Textbooks dealing with economic theory are literally legion and books concerned with the capital investment decision abound but very few books deal with the manufacturing process from a perspective which clearly recognizes that new products, processes and plants need inventing, designing, appraising and selecting, manufacturing, selling and ultimately retiring if a firm is to survive and prosper in the long term. This book is designed to fill that 'gap'; an objective which determines its scope, content and presentation.

With regards to *scope*, this book maintains that a profitable manufacturing sector is essential for sustaining the high standards of living and employment currently enjoyed by several developed nations. As such, its focus on manufacturing extends beyond any parochial considerations which might apply in a production engineering or production management context. Instead, this book exposes the reader to the idea of a firm as a marketing entity in which market forces which comprise opportunities and threats provide the orientation of the company as a whole, recognizing that customers only reward those firms whose products and services constitute a useful rendering of economic service. The invention, selection and funding of products which provide this competitive advantage cannot therefore be left to chance. Instead each firm should identify that particular 'niche' which it wants and believes it can attain in the market and it should then devise its R and D and product strategies so that it enhances that distinctiveness which clearly sets it and its products apart from the competitive rivalry which pervades the market. Such matters as these form the background to this book to ensure that subsequent matters of economic concern are interpreted in a realistic way.

Since the development and manufacture of new products involves using scarce company resources and pre-empts their alternative employ, it is imperative that the corporate economic implications of a new product strategy should be thoroughly evaluated to ensure that it is soundly based and compatible with the firm's economic goals. Indeed, one of the major assertions of this book is that any *manufacturing* process which is devised to create wealth must be examined from a total *system* viewpoint if its *economics* are to be properly appraised and it is this emphasis which gives rise to the main title of this book.

Due to product obsolescence and problems of physical impairment, the profits accruing to a firm's existing stock of plant and machinery eventually erode with time causing their replacement and (or) retirement, when their economic life cycles are spent. To make sensible capital investment, replacement and retirement decisions, therefore, we are obliged to study the economic benefits and costs of physical assets throughout their economic life cycles and it is this focus which results in the sub-title of this book. Actually, a philosophy concerned with life-cycle costs and benefits is used to underpin and unify all of the economic issues which appear herein.

The over-all scope of this book therefore is to demonstrate *why* it is so important to appraise the economic merits of any manufacturing endeavour throughout its life cycle—from its inception to selection, design and commissioning, operation and maintenance through to its eventual replacement and retirement—and show *how* this appraisal can be accomplished, using a life-cycle economic approach.

In selecting the *contents* of this book, we have taken into account the needs of the reader wanting to practise the general principles of manufacturing economy (interpreted in its widest context), and that certain common economic concepts exhibit basic weaknesses which are likely to remain unresolved. We have avoided the 'cook book' approach. Instead we have endeavoured to expose and explain both the strengths and the weaknesses of current economic thought so that the reader can fully appreciate these matters.

The reader of this book requires no previous knowledge of business studies or engineering economics whatsoever. In this respect the book is self-contained and although we liberally use accounting terminology, the meaning of which might appear somewhat obscure to the reader unacquainted with such jargon, nevertheless this book provides a proper accounting appendix to ensure that their meaning is not used in an undisciplined way.

With regard to mathematical expertise, a comprehensive understanding of this book requires little more than a working knowledge of algebra and graph theory. Where slightly more complicated matters arise, which require a mathematical treatment, they are either explained in several different ways or else they are confined to appendices for the more mathematically sophisticated reader. Moreover, despite our dealing with matters of risk and uncertainty in depth, no prior knowledge of probability theory is required excepting a layman's understanding of 'odds' and 'chance'.

Since the major thrust of this book concerns money matters, limitations of space preclude a thorough treatment of human behaviour matters here, although their importance, especially in the context of purchasing and working behaviour, human inventiveness and risk taking, is fully recognized. In this respect it is well to qualify that there is no economic substitute for a decisive and enlightened management working in harmony with a diligent and intelligent workforce, where the efficiency of any manufacturing enterprise is concerned but such matters as these lie beyond the scope of this book.

As regards *presentation*, this book is arranged in four major parts plus several appendices. Part I forms a general introduction in which the national importance of manufacturing is emphasized and it is also the 'foundation' upon which a comprehensive coverage of manufacturing systems economics is subsequently developed. Parts II, III and IV, dealing with the investment decision, the optimal employment of existing assets, and the disposal of manufacturing assets, collectively represent the life-cycle economic approach to manufacturing asset management which is the theme of this book.

For a pedagogical text to be useful, it is necessary for it to commence with basic yet highly restrictive models to teach points of principle and then to systematically relax these restrictions as the book progresses and the reader gains confidence in dealing with more complex, real issues. This book is no stranger to this most basic of teaching principles. In this respect it should be stressed that a proper understanding of manufacturing systems economics only comes from a full reading of this book. As such, the chapters are systematically arranged so that the substance of successive chapters builds on that of preceding chapters. To enhance correspondence between chapters we use a numerical code. For example; reference to Table 10.2.3 means that the particular table of interest is the third (3) table located in the second (2) section of Chapter 10. Using such a code means that we do not have to repeat previous material and we can link current reading with future reading.

As the principles and concepts promulgated by this book apply in all free-market economies, currency of no particular denomination is used throughout this text so revenues and costs are referred to in 'money units', henceforth abbreviated to 'munits'.

Since the substance of this book is virtually boundless, the greatest difficulty lay in knowing what to omit. To counter any deficiencies which might arise from the limitations of space we therefore provide comprehensive reference lists, incorporating books and papers, at the ends of every chapter so readers should experience little difficulty in pursuing each topic beyond the scope presented here. Questions are also provided at the ends of most chapters to reinforce their lessons and answers to odd-numbered questions are provided in an appendix.

To develop the theoretical treatise of this text into a practical aid to decision-making, the principles, concepts and techniques of this book are reinforced using case studies (and their solutions) which become progressively more difficult through the book. Furthermore, a short, realistic yet extremely effective game, which has been used on many occasions to emphasize the iterative nature of the capital budgeting decision, is also used for the same purpose. Permission to reproduce this material here is given by Mr N. Le Page (formerly of ICI Mond Division), Mr A. P. Hall (my colleague at the Bradford Management Centre) and the Cranfield Case Clearing House.

Besides my great debt to these authors, I am also grateful to several publishers: the Instutution of Chemical Engineers, the University of Bradford and colleagues for permission to reproduce several tables, graphs and examination questions. My thanks are also due to friends and colleagues too numerous to mention who have encouraged, assessed and made possible my writing this book and to secretaries who diligently and enthusiastically produced the typescript.

Last, but certainly not least, I would like to thank those many hundreds of undergraduate, postgraduate and post-experience students previously at the University of Bradford, the Bradford Management Centre and the Norwegian Institute of Technology who, over the years, have been willing candidates for evaluating the substance contained herein. Based on their collective experiences we expect this book to be of value to engineers and managers alike, who are working or expect to be working in the manufacturing and process industries in particular and in industry in general. In this regard the book should be suitable for business study courses proper and those business courses which have become an integral part of so many engineering degree courses. It should also be of direct relevance to practising engineers who wish to understand how their engineering endeavours relate to matters of economics and to practising managers seeking to expand their knowledge of such matters.

R. F. DE LA MARE

To
Catherine, Alex and Maureen

whose love is a constant source of inspiration

PART I
Manufacturing Systems Economics in Context

1. *Physical Asset Management and International Competition*

'The age of chivalry is gone; that of sophisters, economists and cal- culators has succeeded.'

Edmund Burke

The economic miracle of our age has been the vigour with which the previously vanquished economies of West Germany and Japan have risen from the ashes of war to become two of the most affluent societies in the world. Poorly endowed with natural resources, they have achieved this result through the execution of sound manufacturing strategies clearly devised to produce high quality–high technology products requiring substantial research and development (R & D) expenditure and massive investment in new capital plant and machinery. As an introduction to this book, this chapter traces the effects of such a strategy on the market competitiveness, profitability, productivity and innovative capacity of similarly endowed nations wishing to retain their standards of living and high levels of employment. Although these matters are extremely complicated and interdependent, the crux of such matters rests firmly and squarely on the ability of firms to develop products which are judged by customers to offer a pleasing, useful and economic service. To this end, therefore, products must possess life-cycle cost characteristics which are competitive and acceptable to potential owners. They also have to offer sufficient economic reward to their manufacturers to warrant the investment and risks involved with their production.

1.1 THE NATIONAL IMPORTANCE OF MANUFACTURING

The importance of manufacturing to the prosperity of industrial nations and its effect on their general standards of living cannot be overstressed. As the details of Table 1.1.1 show, manufacturing industries generate a substantial proportion of the wealth of most developed countries and employ a large part of their working populations. Furthermore, the effects of manufacturing permeate the entire fabric of most industrial societies providing the major outlets for their raw materials and energy industries, the basis of their transport and distribution industries, products for their wholesale and retail trade, machinery for their agricultural, clothing and building industries and, of course, a major market for their financial and service industries. So although the proportion of the workforce employed in manufacturing has fallen slightly over the past twenty years; for most developed nations, nevertheless the success of their non-manufacturing industries is very much influenced by the strength of their manufacturing sectors. For example, Gershuny (1978) suggests that half of those employed by the non-manufacturing sector in the UK rely for their jobs on links with its manufacturing industry. Furthermore, a slow erosion in the proportion

Table 1.1.1 *The importance of manufacturing to national economies*

Year	Belgium I	Belgium II	France I	France II^a	West Germany I	West Germany II	Italy I	Italy II	Japan I	Japan II	Netherlands I	Netherlands II	Sweden I	Sweden II	UK I	UK II	USA I^b	USA II
1950	32.7	–	–	41.7	–	39.7	–	28.8^d	–	–	30.2	31.9	–	27.6	34.7	37.7	34.4	29.2
1960	33.5	30.5	27.9	40.3	34.7	42.2	26.6	27.2	21.3	28.9	28.6	34.5	32.1^c	26.8	35.8	36.1	33.6	28.4
1970	32.7	32.1	27.8	31.3	37.4	42.7	31.7	28.8	27.0	35.9	26.2	29.0	27.6	26.8	34.7	32.4	32.3	25.7
1975	30.1	27.9	27.9	29.6	35.9	38.6	32.6	–	25.8	33.8	24.0	–	28.0	28.9	30.9	28.9	29.0	23.0
1978^e	29.5	26.8	27.6	29.1	35.6	37.6	32.4	28.0	25.8	33.2	23.9	27.8	27.6	28.3	29.8	28.0	28.8	22.0

Source: after OECD.

I. Proportions of total employment in manufacturing in various countries (%). These statistics make allowance for discontinuities in official labour statistics due to changes in industrial classification.

II. Manufacturing output as a proportion of Gross Domestic Product at current prices excepting UK and Italy where at factor cost.

^a Manufacturing, mining, quarrying, gas, electricity and water.
^b Industrial employment.
^c 1961 data.
^d 1951 data.
^e More up-to-date information is available but has been excluded due to the mass unemployment currently experienced in the Western World.

of a nation's workforce employed in manufacturing should not be interpreted as a decline in the importance of manufacturing, since it is in the very nature of modern technology for machines and systems to replace or supplement human effort in the quest for higher productivity and more economic production. The maintenance of a profitable, vigorous and buoyant manufacturing sector is therefore essential for the sustained prosperity of any developed nation.

The manufacturing sectors of many countries also play a key role in international trade, because manufactured exports provide a major source of international currency to purchase food and raw materials from countries better endowed with natural resources. Exports also provide the means of affording the luxury products and technologies of other nations, two factors which play an ever increasing part in motivating less developed countries to expand their own manufacturing capabilities. Furthermore, the removal of restrictions to free international trade made possible within common markets, such as the European Economic Community (EEC) and

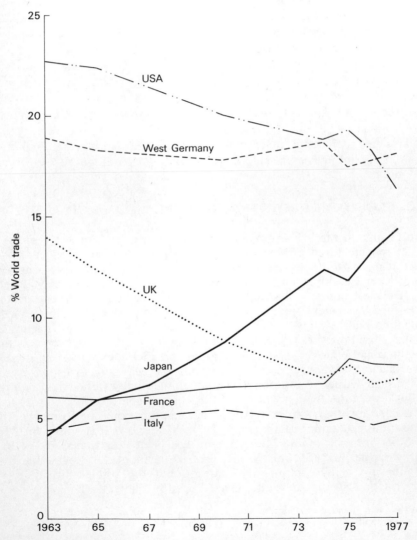

Figure 1.1.1 *Share of world engineering–product exports. Source:* Bulletin of Statistics on World Trade in Engineering Products, UN (1979), S.I.C. Section 7 (basis: *value of exports in US dollars, fob*).

encouraged by the General Agreement on Tariffs and Trade (GATT)* has meant that many countries now have ready access to each others domestic markets, so much so that the distinction between 'domestic' and 'export' markets is becoming blurred and somewhat obsolete. Each nation's manufacturers therefore compete with their international rivals for profit, growth and market share, the rewards going to those who can satisfy customer tastes and preferences. As a result of the growing affluence of developed nations these past twenty years, this direct competition has tended to increase the proportion of manufactured products both exported and imported by each major industrial nation, some being more successful and better equipped for this competitive rivalry than others. This point is amply demonstrated by Figure 1.1.1, which illustrates the significant decline in the international manufacturing competitive performance of the United Kingdom compared with the exceptional improvement in performance by Japan. Indeed, it is a sobering thought to consider that the former of these two great nations, once the richest country in the world and the centre of a massive economic empire could lose its competitive edge so rapidly whereas the latter, once a defeated and dejected people, were able, in 30 years, to establish themselves as world leaders in shipbuilding, steelmaking, and in the manufacture of motor vehicles, instruments, optics and electronics, all at the highest of international standards and all in the van of excellent product design, development, manufacture and marketing. The reasons for these stark differences are manifold, but they relate primarily to the recognition that countries relatively poor in raw materials and especially those needing to import a substantial proportion of their food can only achieve and maintain a high standard of living for their people by developing sound manufacturing and marketing strategies and to that end they have to educate, train and harness their human resources accordingly.

1.2   ECONOMIC GROWTH AND INCREASED PRODUCTIVITY

A nation's ability to capture and retain a consistent or increasing share of the world market for manufactured products has considerable economic implications. In the first place it means that the largest economic sizes of plant incorporating the best technologies can be employed in the confidence that their capacities will be filled, yielding 'technical benefits of scale' and providing the user with cost advantages. Secondly, such investments permit productivity gains to be realized by replacing or supplementing human effort with machine power and artificial intelligence. These investments also afford an ideal opportunity to improve productivity by reorganizing work methods and removing restrictive working practices, and such opportunities as these are facilitated when a nation's own domestic economy is also fast growing, since it is usually easier to capture market share nationally rather than internationally. In this respect the economy of the UK has been laggard compared with its other EEC rivals and together with its relatively poor international performance, this has had very serious economic repercussions. Table 1.2.1 shows that within the EEC the economic performance of the UK economy has been outstripped by all but one community partner and that relative to all of its partners it is stagnating. Coupled with a poor productivity rating, this has reduced the profitability of its entire manufacturing industry to the pitiful level shown by Table 1.2.2.

---

* The theory of international trade suggests that it is in the mutual economic interests of countries to trade freely without tariffs and quota restrictions, thereby permitting each country to specialize in the production of goods and services in which it possesses a 'comparative advantage'. Of course, such a philosophy does contain major political implications. An excellent introductory account of international trade economics is given in Samuelson (1976).

Table 1.2.1 *Gross domestic product (GDP) per capita for several industrialized nations relative to that of the United Kingdom (UK = 100)*

Country	1966	1977
UK	100	100
West Germany	109	129
France	99	124
Italy	69	77
Netherlands	97	117
Belgium	93	119
Denmark	115	129

Source: Statistical office of the EEC, 1978, indices of GDP per capita at market prices shown at purchasing power parities.

Both change and growth in industry depend on the level of investment in new plant and machinery which can be made effective in the manufacture and sale of products, which possess competitive advantages. This in turn depends in large measure on the availability of finance through profits retained from existing plants, processes and products. Declining profitability therefore reduces a nation's ability to finance the next generation of new product ideas (through research and development) and regenerate its stock of capital assets and, of course, such dwindling profits also deter external investment in manufacturing by banks and other financial institutions. The concomitant long-term effect of deteriorating profitability is that a nation's productivity can also deteriorate relative to its more profitable rivals and this in turn has a cascade effect, which is amply illustrated by the extremely poor productivity performance of the UK, as shown by Table 1.2.3.

Of course productivity improvements can be made in the face of dwindling profits providing there exists the human will to realize such improvements. To achieve this end it is necessary for pride (in the product being manufactured) and the total commitment of the workforce (to make products better than those of competitors) to predominate over entrenched restrictive working practices and antipathy or even suspicion of technological and organizational change. In effect, therefore, a Luddite mentality must not prevail if a nation's workforce is to prosper in the long run but instead it must be fired by the passion to excel in the manufacture of products which it must carefully select and fund accordingly.

Table 1.2.2 *International comparisons of the profitability of each nation's manufacturing sector. Net after tax rate of return[a] (% pa)*

	Canada	USA	Japan	West Germany	UK
1963–7	18.5	31.7	26.7	18.7	13.6
1968–71	15.5	21.6	28.4	19.0	10.7
1971–5	17.0	17.4	15.7	12.5	5.6
1975	14.5	14.5	13.9	11.0	2.1
1976	13.3	18.1	na	13.5	2.5
1977	12.5	19.0	na	13.3	3.9

Source: Department of Industry, London, 1979.
[a] Defined as the ratio of the net operating profit (after tax) to the net asset value of fixed assets excluding land.

Table 1.2.3 *The productivity rating[a] of several nations relative to the UK*

	1970	1973	1975	1977
UK	100	100	100	100
Belgium	156	146	160	na
France	177	185	197	205
West Germany	153	146	151	165
Italy	138	117	111	120[b]
Netherlands	178	173	182	na
Japan	215	238	233	263
USA	340	336	338	360

Source: after National Institute of Economic and Social Research Review, February 1979.
[a] Defined as the value added per employee measured in US dollars at purchasing power parity rates of exchange in 1970 terms.
[b] 1976 data.

1.3   THE SIGNIFICANCE OF TECHNOLOGICAL INNOVATION

It is interesting to reflect that at the beginning of this century there was no television, radio, radar, motor car, aeroplane, jet engine, antibiotics, genetic engineering, synthetic detergents, chemical herbicides, fungicides and pesticides, man-made plastics and fibres, stainless steel, computers, robots, lasers, nuclear energy and space vehicles – just to mention a *few* of the technological innovations which have been realized during the past hundred years and many within the last 40 years – and change continues! Indeed, continuous innovation has of necessity become a way of corporate life since it is only through technological and marketing innovation that a firm can achieve that competitive advantage which clearly distinguishes it and its products amongst the rivalry which pervades the international marketing scene. Manufacturing companies, therefore, have to accommodate the inevitable obsolescence of products and processes, by anticipating and meeting market change. They achieve this in three ways:

through incremental improvements to their products, plants, processes and working methods;
by exploiting their existing expertise in different marketing areas; and
through radical innovations incorporating new technologies, processes and products.

The majority of technological progresses derive from the former of these methods, which usually involves the least risk alternative, whereas the latter can often be highly profitable, if properly executed, but often involves a high degree of risk. Irrespective of which method or combination of methods is used, however, technological innovation requires a commitment both at the national and corporate level for invention and the development of innovations which then become the nation's 'seed corn' for its future prosperity. Evidence shows there is a direct link between a firm's past level of investment in product and process innovation and its ability to afford subsequent R & D and capital projects and this of course holds true at the national level also*. More often than not organizations with established records for technological innovation are able to recruit and retain a cadre of high level

---

* This evidence is presented in Chapter 4.

professional engineers and scientists many of whom then penetrate the echelons of higher management and, in so doing, enhance the firm's innovative capacity and acceptance of change. Conversely, of course, companies unable to recruit their own inhouse R & D capability might ultimately find that they lack the corporate expertise to recognize and anticipate the need and nature for such change. It follows, therefore, that a commitment of resources to generate future innovations is essential at *all* times for *all* companies, even when profitability is low and competitive pressures severe.

Continual manufacturing innovation needs incubation in a political climate which is conducive to change requiring benign government policies towards innovation. This requires several important ingredients. In the first place it requires the officers of government to be adept at making decisions of a technological as well as of a political nature, realizing of course that for industrialized societies these two types of decision are related. Secondly, it requires the objectives of a national strategy towards innovation to be identified clearly emphasizing those general marketing areas in which the nation has, or must have, the talent and resources to excel. This is necessary because any government-sponsored technological innovation must enhance rather than deter the profitability of privately sponsored innovation so that the total national commitment to innovation is seen to be in the common good of the entire nation. Unfortunately, there is ample evidence that government-sponsored research and development can often *distort* R & D priorities starving manufacturing industries of the funds and talent necessary to support viable manufacturing enterprises. Perhaps the most classic case of this distortion was the massive investment in the Concorde aircraft project which, although technically superb, must have been one of the greatest economic disasters of all times. Essentially what is required of government however is a fiscal and monetary policy which encourages economic growth and investment, coupled with the introduction of legislation and social services which support product innovation, relevant education, retraining and redeployment and a flexible attitude towards work. It would appear that the governments of several nations have succeeded in devising such schemes and have successfully encouraged healthy attitudes towards change in their societies. By contrast others have not, with the result that much of their societies still possess archaic attitudes towards change which result in internecine labour disputes and a general loss of international competitiveness and confidence.

A definitive policy towards technological innovation is required for another major reason. The major industrial nations compete for markets against each other but also to an ever increasing extent with manufacturers from developing nations. Despite a current low share of the world export market for manufactured products, several of these nations have demonstrated their ability to penetrate markets rapidly so that, coupled with their potential, they represent a considerable threat to the sustained high standards of living currently enjoyed by some nations, especially in a world which is increasingly becoming raw material resource limiting. Of course the industrialized nations have a moral obligation to ensure that the living standards of the poorer nations are raised substantially *anyway* but, as manufacturing processes and techniques become standardized, these nations will implement these schemes and with modern plants and cheap labour they will possess a comparative cost advantage permitting them *to take* market share where *conventional* products are concerned. To contain this change at a rate which is politically acceptable to those involved, the developed nations have to invent and exploit new products and processes which involve high levels of human skill, knowledge and inventiveness: in other words they have to innovate to survive.

It is difficult to assess a nation's capacity to innovate, but there seems to be a growing consensus of opinion that a nation's ability to gain international market

Table 1.3.1 *Proportion of industrial R & D expenditure and the share of foreign based US patents lodged by seven OECD countries, 1963–76. (Units % to the nearest decimal point)*

	Total industry performed R & D		Industry financed R & D			Share of US patenting		
	1967	1975	1967	1975	1963	1967	1973	1976
France	18.3	15.0	13.0	11.9	13.1	14.0	12.0	11.8
W. Germany	23.6	25.6	25.1	25.1	35.6	33.5	31.1	29.6
Italy	4.2	4.9	5.3	5.6	5.3	4.4	4.3	3.7
Japan	19.9	28.8	25.8	35.4	6.8	13.3	28.3	31.7
Netherlands	4.5	3.6	5.3	4.1	5.0	4.5	3.9	3.6
Sweden	2.8	3.4	2.6	3.3	6.0	5.1	4.4	5.2
UK	26.7	18.6	22.9	14.6	28.1	25.2	16.1	14.5

Source: OECD (1980) and OTAF (1977) R & D expenditures calculated at 1970 prices using OECD R & D exchange rates.

share is highly correlated with its investment in R & D. This point is well demonstrated by Pavitt (1980). Although there exists no special indicator which enables a systematic comparison across the R & D activities of various countries nevertheless one measure of a nation's innovative ability is its share of foreign-based patents registered in the USA, which is generally recognized as the most vigorous and competitive market in existence. Such statistics are given in Table 1.3.1, which reflects the same consistent pattern which we have come to expect from previous sections of this chapter, namely the vigorous increase in R & D activity by Japan, the sustained high level of activity by West Germany and the inevitable decline in R & D expenditure by the UK relative to its industrial competitors.

To survive and prosper, therefore, it is essential for advanced industrial societies to move up market and sell products on the basis of non-price factors, it now being appreciated more than ever before that the life-cycle costs of owning physical assets, whether customer-durable or industrial capital equipment, depend only to some extent on their initial purchase prices. This philosophy applies whether one is concerned with relatively ordinary equipment such as television sets, washing machines, portable power tools or fork lift trucks or more sophisticated industrial equipment such as textile machinery and heavy duty capital plant. Indeed, several well publicised studies by Rothwell (1980), Sciberras (1979) and Stout (1977) demonstrate only too vividly that customers are often willing to pay a premium to avoid problems involved with unreliability and after sales service and the evidence suggests that, given the increasing complexity of modern production systems, the demand for higher technical quality and reliability is likely to continue. Several of

Table 1.3.2 *The relative value of exports to imports[a] for several industrial nations*

	Exports		Imports		Exports/Imports	
	1970	1977	1970	1977	1970	1977
UK	100	138	165	290	0.61	0.48
France	99	220	125	246	0.79	0.89
West Germany	121	297	114	262	1.06	1.13

Source: NEDO, 1979.
[a] US $ per tonne at exchange parity prices.

the industrialized nations have been quick to recognize this need and have devised their product design strategies accordingly, not only at the corporate level but at the national level too, concentrating their resources in the manufacture of high technology–high value added products. Others, however, have yet to respond in the same way, the UK being the most notable example. Table 1.3.2 provides some statistics which highlight this subtlety showing how West Germany has definitely moved up market, how France is succeeding in this direction, but that the UK seems to be adopting the opposite approach, namely selling low and buying high value added products.

1.4 THE NEED FOR A LIFE-CYCLE ECONOMIC APPROACH TO PRODUCT INNOVATION

Within the confines of only a few pages, therefore, we have come full-circle to realize that the prosperity of nations poorly endowed with natural resources depends in large measure on their ability to develop new products and processes to sell in competitive world markets. To achieve this, they *have to* invest in product innovation and new capital machinery, which provides the *potential* for realizing production economies, always cognizant that this advantage eventually erodes with the passage of time as better products and processes make their predecessors obsolete. However, investment requires savings and constraints in current consumption to realize future benefits greater than would otherwise be forthcoming. Throughout society this requires respect for *savings* and *profit*, which must be interpreted as the life-line to corporate survival rather than a political symbol of the exploitation of the masses. Furthermore, in societies which are already highly industrialized, adequate profits must be seen as the only conceivable long-term means of securing high levels of worthwhile employment in a world which is becoming increasingly competitive.

In itself the building of new capital plants is not enough: the benefits of such assets have to be realized through skilful management fostering a working climate in which people can work together in harmony, resolving their differences agreeably and enhancing their skills through collaboration and a continuous process of further education and training.

At government level the same objects obtain, it being the duty of government to create an environment in which companies can prosper and to regulate such companies by a variety of fiscal, monetary and statutory means to ensure the greatest overall welfare for its citizens. Furthermore it behoves government to create those instruments which help its citizens work together with minimum discord in a culture which recognizes the need to reward talent and hard work.

On the face of things it would therefore appear that corporate survival and the perpetuation of a high standard of living are closely related and extremely complicated matters but the *kernel* of such matters is relatively simple, namely the offering of products which are judged by society in general and customers in particular to serve a useful social and economic service. All these other matters such as international competitiveness, profitability, productivity, R & D and investment strategies are but physical manifestations of how successful or otherwise companies and nations are in this single endeavour – devising, developing, manufacturing and selling worthwhile products. To this most singular end it follows that products must possess the appropriate aesthetic appeal and function properly but in addition they must be economically competitive both from the point of view of their *cost of ownership* and from the *economic benefits* accruing to their manufacturers. It is these latter economic considerations which we now examine throughout this book.

1.5 BIBLIOGRAPHY

General texts

Rosenberg, N. (Ed.), *The Economics of Technological Change*, Penguin Modern Economic Readings, Penguin, London, 1971. This collection of papers forms suitable background reading for this chapter in particular but also provides excellent supplementary reading for the remainder of this book in a more general context.

Samuelson, P., *Economics*, McGraw-Hill, 1976. This is surely one of the best received books ever written in economics. It includes both micro and macro economics and forms an excellent reference for any student of economic theory.

Specific texts

Gershuny, J., *After Industrial Society?* MacMillan, London, 1978.

Pavitt, K., 'Industrial R & D and the British Economic Problem', *R & D Management 10*, Special Issue, 1980.

Rothwell, R., '*Innovation in Textile Machinery*', in *Technical Innovation and British Economic Performance* (Ed.) K. Pavitt, MacMillan, London, 1980.

Sciberras, E., *Technical Change in the US Consumer Electronics Industry*, Science Policy Research Unit, University of Sussex, 1979.

Stout, D., *International Price Competitiveness Non-price Factors and Export Performance*, National Economic Development Office, London, 1977.

2. *The Rudiments of Microeconomic Theory*

'Every individual endeavours to employ his capital so that its produce may be of greatest value. He generally neither intends to promote the public interest, nor knows how much he is promoting it. He intends only his own security, only his own gain. And he is in this led by an INVISIBLE HAND *to promote an end which was no part of his intention. By pursuing his own interest he frequently promotes that of society more effectively than when he really intends to promote it.'*

Adam Smith, *The Wealth of Nations*, 1776

To understand properly the marginal jargon which pervades this book, we need to appreciate some of the principles and concepts which are fundamental to economic theory. This chapter is concerned with a branch of economics known as 'microeconomics' and confines its attention to the economics of the firm working in a single market. It explores the basis for deriving the price of a product and the conditions which affect the profit accruing from its sale. Ideas relating to the working of the total national economy containing that firm are not considered here, but are developed elsewhere in this book. Initially some of the ideas which are contained in this chapter might appear academic and incongruous with the rest of the book, which attempts to be practically orientated. The reason for developing such ideas is that they are needed later to help resolve some of the more controversial and complex issues concerning management decisions, especially those involving the economics of manufacturing processes and the life-cycle costs of physical assets. Throughout this chapter we refer to the output of a firm as its product, without specifying the precise nature of that product. This abstraction is quite purposeful since we are endeavouring to develop points of principle. Unless otherwise stated reference to products could signify consumer goods (such as television sets and refrigerators), industrial capital goods (such as machine tools and chemical plants) or industrial services (such as the supply of gas or electricity). Towards the end of this chapter, we conveniently assume that the objectives of our make believe company represent the interests of a hypothetical entrepreneur. Such an assumption is needed to help develop our academic notions of how a firm might be expected to operate. It should be noted however that all of these academic niceties are challenged in subsequent chapters.

2.1 HUMAN BEHAVIOURAL EFFECTS ON PRICES

In free-enterprise markets, which are not regulated by government pricing policies, prices are determined by the supply and demand for products. Since the manufacture of products necessitates the use of resources which, in microeconomic theory, are called factors of production, involving:

(i) land for agriculture, minerals extraction and factories;
(ii) labour for manual, executive and creative work; and
(iii) capital for investment in machines and buildings,

it follows that supply represents a condition of scarcity for these factors. Without scarcity there would be plenty and the factors of production would be freely available at no cost to satisfy all human wants. By contrast, demand represents the want, for the product, which is backed by purchasing power. Without demand a product would have no price irrespective of the conditions affecting the scarcity of its factors of production. To some extent, therefore, the forces which influence the price of a product are analogous to the operation of scissors. Just as the scissors require two blades for cutting, so too the quantity bought and price paid for a product depend inextricably on the supply and demand for that product.

  To say that people have needs and wants which they like to satisfy might of itself seem trite, except when we remember that the task facing a manufacturer is to interpret these desires and translate them into products which will be bought at adequate prices. As a basis to all purchasing behaviour, therefore, we must always remember that people have physiological needs – for sustenance, shelter and psychological needs – to socialize, and achieve status and self-fulfilment. How its products satisfy or partly satisfy some of these basic needs is a problem which each firm has to resolve, since customers only reward those firms whose products and services are deemed to constitute a useful rendering of economic service.

2.2 SUPPLY AND DEMAND SCHEDULES AND PRICE EQUILIBRIUM

In classical economic theory, the condition of 'pure and perfect' competition defines a hypothetical market state where there is a sufficient number of producers and customers, each of limited commercial size, that none can influence the price of a product by their own individual actions. Furthermore, it assumes that complete knowledge relating to the costs of production and pricing is freely available to all, that there is complete mobility of the factors of production and customers and, lastly, that the size (scale) of production facilities is infinitely divisible. With these rather unrealistic assumptions, we shall now investigate the mechanics of pricing to determine the economic conditions which *could* prevail in such a market.

Table 2.2.1 *Hypothetical supply and demand schedules for an imaginary product X*

Price per item munits	Quantity demanded per month (items)	Quantity supplied per month (items)
1	140	10
2	110	40
3	90	55
4	70	70
5	55	80
6	40	90
7	30	100
8	20	105
9	15	110
10	10	115

Given that customers' incomes are fixed, at least in the very short term, experience suggests that as the price of a normal product falls so more of that product is purchased and, of course, the converse holds true too. Due to the lower product price, existing customers find they have surplus disposable income and some will buy more of that product. Furthermore the lower price encourages others, who previously could not afford that product, to buy. If we also assume that the stock of capital plant and equipment is also fixed in the short term, it follows that the higher the price paid for a product, the greater is the motivation of firms to produce more. We shall need to justify both of these hypotheses. Before doing so, however, it might be instructive to consider the implications of what has just been stated. Table 2.2.1

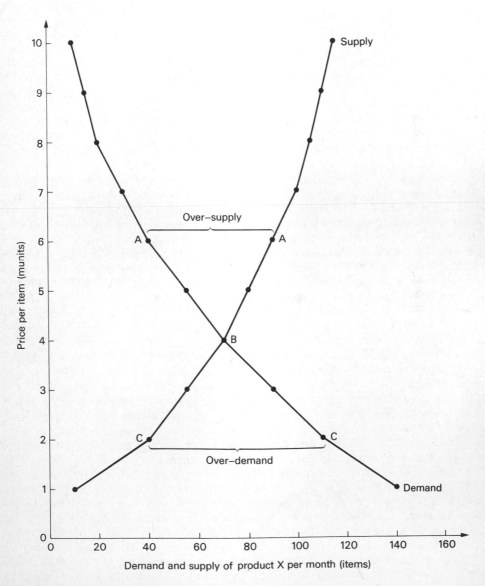

Figure 2.2.1 *Hypothetical supply and demand schedules for an imaginary product X.*

illustrates the supply and demand schedules for an imaginary product X, over an arbitrarily specified time period of one month. The prices stated relate to the discrete quantities which are bought and sold at those particular prices. The data of Table 2.2.1 are also shown graphically in Figure 2.2.1 which illustrates how the supply and demand curves intersect at point B, where customers and producers are able to transact 70 items per month at a price of 4 munits each. The market condition depicted by point B is said to be a condition of 'price equilibrium': it is the price towards which this hypothetical market would develop if it originated at some other price. For example, if the market price originated at point A with a price of six munits, then the market would be in a state of 'over-supply' since the producers would like to sell 90 items, whereas the customers would only be willing to buy 40 items per month, at that price. Recognizing this over-supply and the ensuing and expensive stockpiling problems which would result from such a level of production, firms would be motivated to reduce their level of production and sell at a lower price which would then entice customers to buy more. In theory, therefore, this behaviour would continue until point B was reached. Similarly, originating at point C with a price of 2 munits the market would be in a position of 'over-demand'. Perceiving this demand, producers would be motivated to increase their production, but only at a higher price and, again in theory, this process would continue until point B was reached.

2.3   THE UTILITY OF DEMAND

To progress further we are obliged to study the somewhat abstract concept of utility. Individuals have their own particular tastes and preferences for products as determined by a host of physiological, psychological, environmental and sociological factors, and it seems reasonable to suppose that each person endeavours to satisfy or partly satisfy his own tastes and preferences in a way which gives the greatest overall satisfaction to that individual. In economic terms, this overall satisfaction is known as utility. This concept will help us unravel some complex business problems in later chapters. In very simple terms, therefore, we can imagine the individual evolving to a position by trial-and-error, whereby trading off one product for others he is able to reach a position of maximum satisfaction (utility), for a given fixed income. If we confine our attention to the purchase of two products, X and Y only, then it follows that the amount of utility a customer enjoys depends upon the amounts of X and Y he buys. For example, it is conceivable that quite different amounts of X and Y provide the same overall utility. Furthermore, we can imagine that for this constant amount of utility he would be willing to sacrifice one unit of X for one unit of Y if both were already being consumed in plenty but would become increasingly reluctant to such trading if one of these products became scarce in his consumption package. If X and Y were apples and oranges, the consumer might be prepared to forego oranges for apples on a one-for-one basis if he already had 50 of each but, as his consumption of oranges reduced, he might require two, three or perhaps four apples to compensate for each orange foregone in order to maintain his same overall degree of satisfaction. In other words, as the quantity of oranges diminished, so he would place an increasing premium on their value and a decreasing value on additional apples. If it were possible to measure these combinations of apples and oranges which gave the same utility directly, their plotting would result in a graph similar to that shown below in Figure 2.3.1 where the resultant curves are known as 'indifference curves' because they form the locus of points for combinations of X and Y, between which the consumer would be indifferent. It naturally follows that for a constant consumption of one of these products, the consumer's utility would increase

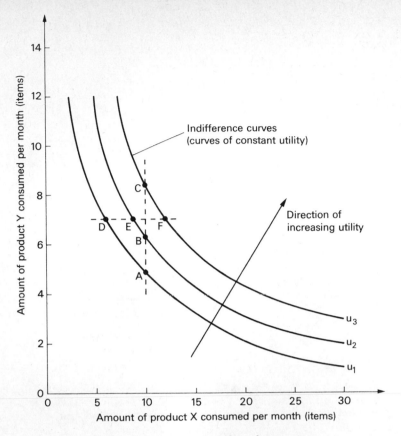

Figure 2.3.1 *A two product indifference map for a hypothetical consumer.*

with increasing consumption of the other product. Such a situation is depicted by the dotted lines in Figure 2.3.1, where the line ABC joins combinations of ten units of X but increasing quantities of Y; whereas the line DEF joins combinations of seven units of Y but increasing quantities of X. Logically therefore the indifference curves U_1, U_2 and U_3 are drawn in ascending order of utility such that:

$$U_3 > U_2 > U_1$$

(where the mathematical symbol $>$ means greater than).

We shall now endeavour to explain why the demand schedule for most products is of the form given by Figure 2.2.1. To do this we need three additional pieces of information: the prices of products X and Y, which we shall conveniently assume constant and unaffected by the individual consumer's buying habits, and the total income which that customer has available to spend on X and Y in some arbitrarily assumed time period, say one month. If we denote the price per item of X by p_X, that of Y by p_Y and the income by I, then it naturally follows that the most of X that the customer can purchase is I/p_X. For example, if his income is 100 munits per month and the price of X is 4 munits each, then a maximum of 25 items of X can be purchased. Similarly, the most of Y that can be bought is I/p_Y and if each item of Y costs 10 munits then only ten items of Y can be purchased. It naturally follows that any combination of X and Y which can be purchased is governed by the customer's

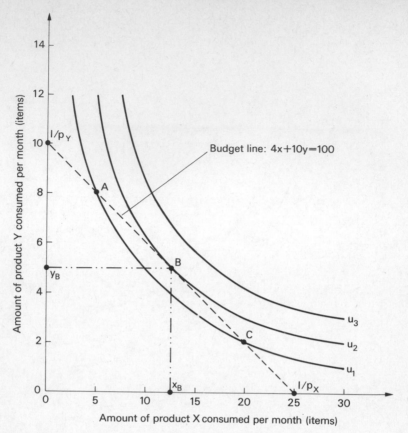

Figure 2.3.2   *Consumers' indifference map and budget line for products X and Y.*

income constraint as represented by the following mathematical relationship:

$$x \cdot p_X + y \cdot p_Y = I$$

where x and y denote the quantities of products X and Y which can actually be bought in combination. Using our previous price and income data this equation becomes:

$$4x + 10y = 100$$

This relationship, which we call the budget line, is shown superimposed on the indifference curves of Figure 2.3.1 to form the dotted sloping line shown in Figure 2.3.2 with intercepts on the X and Y axes of I/p_X and I/p_Y respectively. Given these conditions, it follows that the consumer can obtain the same utility (U_1) with monthly purchases of five items of X and eight items of Y at point A, and 20 items of X and two items of Y at point C, for his total fixed income of 100 munits. However, it will also be seen that, as the customer proceeds along his budget line between points A and C, his utility increases and reaches a maximum at point B when his utility is U_2*. The optimum combination of products X and Y is shown by

---

* Mathematically, it can be shown that this situation prevails when the budget line AC is tangential to the indifference curve of utility U_2, at point B.

the dotted lines with a product combination of:

$$x_B = 12.5$$

$$y_B = 5$$

and it is towards such a combination that microeconomic theory presumes that most rational consumers would proceed, given the limited assumptions formulated at the beginning of this chapter.

If both the consumer's income and the price of product Y remain unchanged, but the price of product X changes, we would discover that the quantities of X and Y which would be brought so as to yield the greatest utility would also change. This is demonstrated by Figure 2.3.3, where the price per item of X has been systematically decreased from its initial price of p_{X_1} to p_{X_2}, and on to p_{X_5} and it is seen that as the price decreases so the optimum quantity of X increases. Using mathematical notation and referring to the information provided by Figure 2.3.3, we see that,

for $p_{X_1} > p_{X_2} > p_{X_3} > p_{X_4} > p_{X_5}$,

then $x_1 < x_2 < x_3 < x_4 < x_5$.

Replotting the optimal results of Figure 2.3.3 according to the details of Figure 2.3.4, we obtain the downward sloping demand curve for the individual consumer.

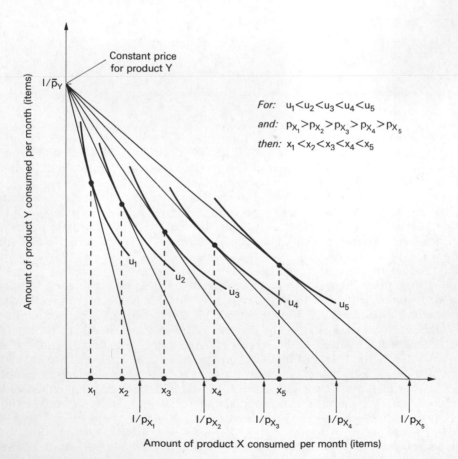

Figure 2.3.3 *Changing pattern of demand in response to a price decrease in product X.*

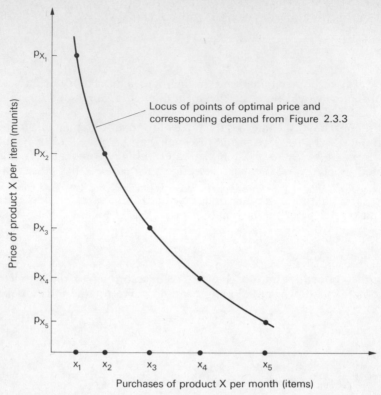

Figure 2.3.4   *Individual consumer's demand curve for product X.*

By amalgamating such demand curves for all customers of product X we derive the aggregate demand curve for product X which, of course, is downwards sloping to the right, as we prescribed at the outset of this chapter. Although it is difficult to derive individual indifference curves for each customer, we are able to measure their aggregate total demand curve. What utility theory has done, therefore, is help us understand the human behavioural aspects of demand in a little more detail, and this has led us to the notion that individuals attempt to optimize their purchasing strategies. Two further points should be considered briefly before we leave this section. The first concerns changes to the customer's income expendable on products X and Y, and the second point concerns changes to his purchases of product Y resulting from price changes to product X. To some extent the latter consideration is contained within the former, so we need to consider both points together. If the total income which a customer can spend on products X and Y increases with time (due to real salary rises, taxation cuts, or the disposal of less income on other products) and if we assume that it systematically increases during a time span of, say, three months so that his income in the third month (I_3) is greater than that in the second month (I_2) which is greater than his initial income (I_1) then his budget lines would correspond with those shown in Figure 2.3.5, their slopes remaining constant and equal to minus $p_{\bar{X}}/p_{\bar{Y}}$. For normal products the optimal purchases of both X and Y, resulting in maximum utility, would increase as shown by Figure 2.3.5 and such increases would result in a total shift in the aggregate market demand curve to the right, as shown by Figure 2.3.6. The second point is already contained in Figure 2.3.3, whereby it is seen that increases in the price of product X have brought about

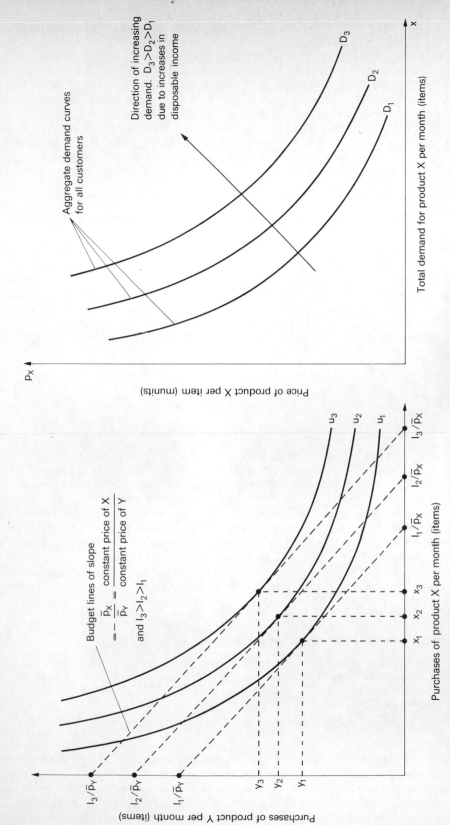

Figure 2.3.5 *Individual's increasing consumption of products X and Y arising from an increase in income.*

Figure 2.3.6 *Shift in aggregate demand resulting from an increase in disposable income*

Price of product X per item (munits)

Total demand for product X per month (items)

D_3

D_2

D_1

Direction of increasing demand. $D_3 > D_2 > D_1$ due to increases in disposable income

Aggregate demand curves for all customers

p_X

x

Purchases of product Y per month (items)

Purchases of product X per month (items)

u_3

u_2

u_1

$I_3/\bar{p}_X$

$I_2/\bar{p}_X$

$I_1/\bar{p}_X$

x_3

x_2

x_1

y_3

y_2

y_1

$I_3/\bar{p}_Y$

$I_2/\bar{p}_Y$

$I_1/\bar{p}_Y$

Budget lines of slope

$$= -\frac{\bar{p}_X}{\bar{p}_Y} = \frac{\text{constant price of X}}{\text{constant price of Y}}$$

and $I_3 > I_2 > I_1$

changes in the purchases of product Y. This phenomenon results from the fact that decreases in the price of product X effectively increase the disposable income for the joint purchase of X and Y. For normal products the tendency of this apparent increase in disposable income is to increase the quantity purchased of *both* products. However, the precise response of the purchases of product Y will depend on the strength of its substitution effect for product X – an aspect which is covered in more detail in Section 2.5. It is conceivable that the consumption of Y could increase, decrease or indeed remain constant depending on the precise shape of that customer's indifference curves.

2.4 THE PRICE ELASTICITY OF DEMAND

In subsequent chapters we need to estimate the effects of various pricing policies on the total cash receipts of a firm. Quite obviously, if we knew the market demand schedule facing the company, we could measure this response directly. Another way of evaluating these effects can be obtained by having some idea of the magnitude of a product's 'price elasticity of demand', which is defined as: 'the percentage change in the quantity of product bought in response to a percentage change in its price, when that price change is small'. For product X, this definition can be written as follows:

$$^{e}p_{X} = \frac{\dfrac{\Delta x}{x}}{\dfrac{\Delta p_{X}}{p_{X}}}$$

where Δ = a small change in the variable following it, either x or p_{X}, and $^{e}p_{X}$ stands for the price elasticity of demand for product X. For most products, a small positive change in the price of X, denoted Δp_{X}, results in a small negative change in the quantity bought (denoted Δx) so the value $^{e}p_{X}$ is usually negative. Quite frequently, economists drop reference to this negativity for ease of expression, the fact that it is really negative being known and understood; in other words they refer to the absolute value of $^{e}p_{X}$ without any negative sign by taking its modulus which is represented by $|^{e}p_{X}|$ in symbolic notation.

According to the values assumed by $|^{e}p_{X}|$ it is possible to denote three different categories of elasticity, where a product is known to be:

  (i) price inelastic if its value $|^{e}p_{X}|$ is less than unity,
 (ii) price unit elastic if its value $|^{e}p_{X}|$ is equal to unity,
(iii) price elastic if its value $|^{e}p_{X}|$ is greater than unity.

Diagrammatically these classifications can be represented by the limiting regions of the demand curves of Figure 2.4.1, the case of unit elasticity being a very special case requiring the mathematical formula shown in that diagram. The significance of the price elasticity of demand and the actual values it assumes only become apparent when we consider possible changes to the prices of a product. It can be shown that:

If	*Then*
(a) Demand is price inelastic $0 < |^{e}p_{X}| < 1$	Total cash receipts move in the same direction as a price change.
(b) Demand is price elastic $1 \leq |^{e}p_{X}| \leq \infty$	Total cash receipts move in the opposite direction to a price change.
(c) Demand is price unit elastic $|^{e}p_{X}| = 1$	Total cash receipts are price invariable.

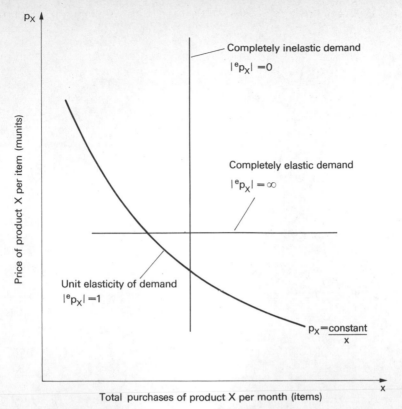

Figure 2.4.1 *Limits of the price elasticity of demand for product X.*

The total cash receipts of a firm are therefore sensitive to the price elasticity of demand for its products. It follows that a firm should only implement price changes after considering carefully the likely reactions of its competitors and the response of its customers since it is conceivable that a price reduction, to stimulate sales, would in fact reduce cash receipts (if the product was price inelastic) and increase total production costs and reduce profits; presumably the last thing any firm would wish to do!

2.5 INCOME-ELASTICITY AND CROSS-ELASTICITY OF DEMAND

As already mentioned in Section 2.3, the sales of a product are also affected by changes in the income of customers and the prices of other products. The former of these effects can be measured by a product's income elasticity of demand, which is defined as: 'the percentage change in the quantity of product bought in response to a percentage change in the income of its customers, when that income change is small'. For product X this definition can be written as follows:

$$e_I = \frac{\dfrac{\Delta x}{x}}{\dfrac{\Delta I}{I}}$$

where e_I is the income elasticity of demand, and I is the income of customers.

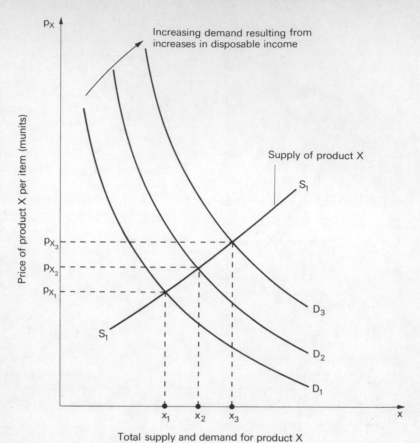

Figure 2.5.1   *Price–volume reactions to changes in demand.*

For most normal products an increase in customers' expendable income results in an increase in the sales of that product due to a shift of the demand curve to the right, as previously explained in Section 2.3, and illustrated in Figure 2.3.6. In these circumstances, prices are sensitive to the reactions of producers and the aggregate level of supply of the product. If firms were unable to increase their aggregate production capacity in the short term then prices would rise as shown by Figure 2.5.1. In the longer term, however, it is conceivable that higher prices would motivate firms to build additional production capacity. This would cause the supply curve to shift to the right and depress the ultimate product price. It should be noted however that not all products are normal. Some products can be described as inferior because they do not respond to changes in income in the way suggested above. Instead they respond in the reverse direction so that an increase in income results in a decline in their sales and a shift of their demand curves to the left instead. A good example of an inferior product is hamburgers because customers substitute better cuts of meat as their incomes rise. The actual value of the income elasticity of demand for a product can therefore be positive or negative depending on whether that product is considered a normal or an inferior product. It therefore behoves the management of a firm to recognize and indeed forecast the response of their sales to changes in customer income, since the physical manifestation of this concept is for customers to prefer better quality, more reliable and more stylish products as their real incomes improve.

The second concept, that of cross-elasticity of demand, concerns the effect of a price change in one product and its influence on the sales of the particular product of interest, in our case product X. Some products obviously vie with one another in that a price increase in one product causes its sales to decline and the sales of its competitor to increase. Such products are known as substitutes. Margarine and butter are excellent examples. Other products do not exhibit this competitive effect, but instead have a complementary influence on each other's sales so that a price increase in one product causes a corresponding decrease in the sales of the other product. For example, increases in the prices of motor vehicles can reduce their sales and this can lead to a reduction in the sales of motor gasoline too, even though the price of gasoline remains unchanged.

The cross elasticity of demand for a product X is defined as: 'the percentage change in the quantity of X demanded in response to a percentage change in the price of some other product Y, when that price change is small'. For product X this can be written as:

$$e_{cx} = \frac{\frac{\Delta x}{x}}{\frac{\Delta p_y}{p_y}}$$

The sign of e_{cx} obviously depends on whether the products X and Y are substitute or complementary products. The business significance of this concept is that a company cannot consider its own sales of product in isolation to what happens in the general market place. Instead, it must devise its product strategy to take advantage of complementary benefits from the market and mitigate any adverse substitutive effects to minimize the risks facing the company. In later chapters, we shall develop these ideas further into a more practical framework.

2.6 THE PRODUCTION FUNCTION

So far in this chapter we have dealt exclusively with problems of demand. Now we turn our attention to the supply curve and the reason for its upward sloping to the right shape previously shown by Figure 2.2.1. As with our treatment of demand, we shall develop our understanding of supply through an appreciation of how an individual, in this case a firm rather than customer, responds to changing circumstances, and we shall commence by studying the physical relationship between the quantity of resources which a manufacturer uses in his production process and the resultant quantity of product made.

To develop the following ideas with some sense of realism, it is convenient to imagine a factory comprising several job centres, each containing a machine requiring skilled technicians for their controlled and proper operation. For the sake of simplicity, let us imagine that there are five different job centres involving a milling machine, borer, automatic welding apparatus, a horizontal lathe and painting equipment. It is conceivable that one technician could operate all of these machines and produce on-grade product. However, it is fairly obvious that his productivity, measured by the number of items of final product produced per man hour, would be rather low, because much of his effort would be unproductive, involving the transfer of partly completed product from one job centre to the next. Furthermore, as he proceeded along the production line he would need to become reacquainted with the special features and requirements of each machine so that some job relearning would be necessary. With further recruitment of qualified technicians it is conceivable that productivity would improve due to two effects:

 (i) the increase in job specialization made possible by technicians being able to spend more time on given machines, thereby allowing them to become expert in their use; and
(ii) co-operation between technicians with the handling of heavy or awkward equipment and their joint solving of production problems.

As a consequence, productivity would increase until there was one technician per machine. Further recruitment might still be justified to cover meal breaks, absenteeism and holidays, and the transfer of partly finished product between machines. Such recruitment would obviously result in more product being produced per unit of time but it is likely that the productivity of this extra recruitment would *not* be so high because of its less specialized application. Further recruitment would *ultimately* result in such congestion on the factory floor that the level of production would deteriorate.

Table 2.6.1 is a numerical presentation of what has just been described. It shows the number of technicians employed per unit time by the factory and the corresponding number of items of product made in that unit time (which has quite arbitrarily been taken as one month), and these data are also shown in Figure 2.6.1. In both cases the output of the factory is known as the total physical product (TPP) in economic jargon.

Two rather interesting measures of productivity can be derived from this figure and table. The first concerns the idea of the average physical product (APP) of labour. This is defined as the total physical product per unit technician input and is derived from the expression:

$$\mathrm{APP} = \frac{\text{Total physical product per unit time}}{\text{Numbers of technicians employed per unit time}} = \frac{x}{n}$$

Statistics for the average physical product are given in Table 2.6.1. Graphically these statistics can be obtained by drawing a line from the origin of Figure 2.6.1 to the TPP curve and then dividing the resultant ordinate (x) by the value of the abscissor (n) as shown in Figure 2.6.1.

Table 2.6.1 *A numerical example of the production function*

Number of technicians employed per month (n)	Total physical product (TPP) – items per month (x)	Average physical product (APP) APP $= x/n$	Marginal physical product (MPP) MPP $= \Delta x/\Delta n$	Stage
0	0	0	0	I
1	10	10	10	Increasing
2	30	15	20	returns
3	60	20	30	
4	100	25	40	
5	125	25	25	II
6	145	24.17	20	Diminishing
7	155	22.14	10	returns
8	160	20.00	5	
9	160	17.78	0	III
10	159	15.90	−1	Decreasing
11	157	14.27	−2	returns
12	154	12.83	−3	

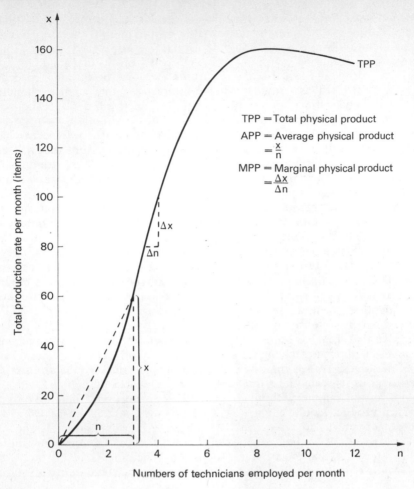

Figure 2.6.1 *The total physical product of a hypothetical factory. Note: all other inputs besides labour are assumed constant.*

The second measure of productivity concerns the marginal physical product (MPP) of labour. This is defined as the change in the total physical product resulting from a small change in the numbers of technicians employed. In economic parlance therefore the word marginal denotes a small change, and it is commonplace to consider a change brought about by one extra unit of the resource input. In business terminology the words incremental and marginal often have the same meaning. The marginal physical product of labour (MPP) is derived from the expression:

$$MPP = \frac{\text{A small change in the total physical product per unit time}}{\text{A small change in the number of technicians employed per unit time}} = \frac{\Delta x}{\Delta n}$$

Statistics for the marginal physical products are also given in Table 2.6.1. Graphically, the MPP is measured by the instantaneous slope of the TPP curve at the point of interest, according to the ratio $\frac{\Delta x}{\Delta n}$ as shown in Figure 2.6.1.

The outcome of the above numerical and graphical analysis is that the shape of the total physical product curve can be divided into three different stages, which are also tabulated in Table 2.6.1. These three stages depict increasing, diminishing and decreasing returns to the quantity of variable input, in this case the number of technicians. Quite obviously no company should be operated under Stage III conditions since it would be getting negative benefits from its marginal employment of technicians. Although Stage I looks rewarding, because the output per technician as measured by its APP is rising, it will be appreciated that such a phenomenon results from the underutilization of the machines at each job centre. The management of such a firm would not normally permit such a situation to be prolonged indefinitely. By contrast, Stage II represents what we all intuitively expect to happen, and what we frequently observe in everyday life to such an extent that it has given rise to a law, known as the Law of Diminishing Returns. This law is fundamental to microeconomics and can rightfully take its place alongside the well known physical laws of thermodynamics. The law states that if the input of any *one* resource is increased by equal increments per unit of time, while the inputs of all of the *other* resources are held constant, the total output of product per unit time will eventually increase by successively smaller increments. The law of diminishing returns applies to each of the input resources considered separately. Alternatively, it applies if *all* resources are increased but *one* is increased at a *faster* rate relative to the others.

Some readers might disagree with the outcome of the above analysis by arguing that for many real situations, doubling the number of men and their machines often leads to a doubling of output. In other words, they argue that output is proportional to input. For example, ten men with spades can accomplish ten times the work of one man given that they have ample room to manoeuvre. This is so, but in this case two resources of input are changing simultaneously, the number of men and the number of machines. To accommodate this situation we refer to the size of a firm's total operations as its scale of production. If this scale (size) is changed with respect to the major resource inputs without changing their proportions, then the output, the total physical product, could change as indicated by Table 2.6.2, and during that change constant returns to scale could be realized. However, diminishing returns would ultimately result leading to the well known Law of Diminishing Returns to Scale. This law states that 'successive proportional increments in *all* inputs simultaneously will eventually result in less than proportionate increments of output'.

Table 2.6.2 *The effect of returns to scale on the total physical product of a production process*

Number of machines employed per month	Number of technicians employed per month	Total physical product (TPP) number of items produced per month	Stage
0	0	0	
1	1	4	I
2	2	10	Increasing
3	3	18	returns
4	4	28	to scale
5	5	35	II
6	6	42	Constant
7	7	49	returns to
8	8	56	scale
9	9	60	III
10	10	63	Diminishing
11	11	65	returns to
12	12	66	scale

The precise range over which increasing, constant and diminishing returns to scale apply depends on the precise nature of the production system. Given our man/spade example, it is conceivable that two men could do more than twice the work of one due to their mutual co-operation, and it is possible that 20 could do ten times the work of two men. Above that number, however, it is also conceivable that supervision and communication problems could become a major constraint to the effectiveness of the work-force and result in diminishing returns to scale. The reason for diminishing returns is therefore due to some deterioration in the quality of the input(s), possibly due to some physical restriction (such as space) or the quality of management.

Researchers have tested the validity of these hypotheses using total market (aggregate) supply data and have found that production functions of the form:

$$Q = aI_1^{b_1} \cdot I_2^{b_2} \cdots I_i^{b_i} \cdot I_n^{b_n}$$

(where Q = the aggregate output per unit time, I_i = the aggregate input per unit time of resource i (where $i = 1, n$), b_i = the empirical constant for input i, and a = an overall empirical constant) are often well able to explain the relationship between resource input and product output. If we substitute the symbol K for the sum of the values of b_i in the previous equation such that:

$$K = b_1 + b_2 + b_i + \ldots + b_n$$

then it will be realized that the absolute value of K determines the nature of the production function because:

$K > 1$ signifies increasing returns to scale,
$K = 1$ signifies constant returns to scale,
$K < 1$ signifies diminishing returns to scale.

Where the symbols $>$ and $<$ mean greater than and less than respectively.

Examples of the use of such an equation are readily available in the economic literature. For example, during the period 1899–1922 it was found that output of the manufacturing sector of the UK economy could be represented quite accurately by the relationship

$$P = 1.01 C^{0.75} I^{0.25}$$

where P = the index of total manufacturing output, C = the index of fixed capital investment, I = the index of employment. This example shows constant returns to scale and yet diminishing returns with respect to changes in the individual inputs. Researchers have also found evidence of increasing and diminishing returns to scale and the interested reader is referred to the references at the end of this chapter for further reading.

Unfortunately, there is little documented evidence available concerning the production functions of individual firms. This is hardly surprising since its publication would be tantamount to disclosing their market competitiveness for all to scrutinize! Moreover, to establish such a relationship would require proper experimentation and change to that firm's inputs over a time period which could accommodate the effects of productivity improvements and technological innovation. Because of the disruption this would cause, it is doubtful if a firm could justify such experiments, even though the results might help to increase its future profits. Despite this shortcoming, the fact that aggregate supply is often well explained by such equations is all important, since it gives credibility to the concepts which have been promulgated here. It therefore behoves the management of each firm to anticipate the effects of increasing, constant, diminishing and decreasing returns even if they are unable or unwilling to measure them directly.

2.7 THE COST OF PRODUCTION

Although several different categories of cost appear in this book, it is convenient to start our study of costs by considering fixed and variable costs only. In the short term some costs, such as depreciation expenses, ground rent, insurance premiums, and the salary of the chief executive can be considered fixed in that they *do not* vary with the level of output, whereas other costs, involving raw materials and energy, can be considered 'variable' because they *do* vary with the level of output, from a production process. In effect, therefore, the total costs of production can be considered the sum of two different types of costs, variable costs and fixed costs, according to the following relationship

$$TC = TFC + TVC$$

where TC = total costs, TFC = total fixed costs, and TVC = total variable costs.

To proceed further, we need to reconsider the relationship between the inputs and outputs of a factory, given by Table 2.6.1 and Figure 2.6.1. Let us assume that the effective monthly costs of the firm's job centres, including the salary of the manager and any other fixed costs, are 10 000 munits per month. Let us also assume that the company's need for skilled technicians is too small in relation to the whole market for it to influence their wage rate, so the company is obliged to pay the going market rate, which is quite independent of its production rate. If a technician's salary is 1000 munits per month, it follows that the total variable costs (TVC) of production are given by the relationship

$$TVC = \text{rate per technician} \times \text{number of technicians}$$
$$= \bar{r} \cdot n$$
$$= 1000n$$

where $\bar{r}$ = a technician's constant salary, and n the number of technicians employed per month. The corresponding numerical values of the total costs, total fixed costs and total variable costs for our hypothetical company are given in Table 2.7.1 along with the level of output previously assumed in Table 2.6.1.

Several interesting cost statistics can be derived from this table. The first concerns the average costs of production, where an average cost is defined as the total cost per

Table 2.7.1 *Total production costs*

Production level (output per month) (x)	Number of technicians employed per month (n)	Total variable cost (TVC) = 1000n	Total fixed cost (TFC) = 10 000	Total cost (TC) = TVC+TFC
0	0	0	10 000	10 000
10	1	1 000	10 000	11 000
30	2	2 000	10 000	12 000
60	3	3 000	10 000	13 000
100	4	4 000	10 000	14 000
125	5	5 000	10 000	15 000
145	6	6 000	10 000	16 000
155	7	7 000	10 000	17 000
160	8	8 000	10 000	18 000
160	9	9 000	10 000	19 000
159	10	10 000	10 000	20 000
157	11	11 000	10 000	21 000
154	12	12 000	10 000	22 000

Table 2.7.2 *Average and marginal production costs*

Production level (output per month) x	Average fixed cost $(AFC) = TFC/x$	Average variable cost $(AVC) = TVC/x$	Average total cost $(ATC) = TC/x$	Marginal cost $= \Delta TC/\Delta x$
0	∞	0	∞	—
10	1 000.0	100.0	1 100.0	100.0
30	333.3	66.7	400.0	50.0
60	166.7	50.0	216.7	33.3
100	100.0	40.0	140.0	25.0
125	80.0	40.0	120.0	40.0
145	69.0	41.4	110.4	50.0
155	64.5	45.2	109.7	100.0
160	62.5	50.0	112.5	200.0
160	62.5	56.3	118.8	∞
159	62.9	62.9	125.8	⎫ negative
157	63.7	70.1	133.8	⎬ marginal
154	64.9	77.9	142.9	⎭ costs

unit of time divided by the number of items produced in the same time. According to this definition, we can derive three average costs:

$$\text{Average total cost (ATC)} = \frac{\text{Total cost}}{\text{level of output}} = \frac{TC}{x}$$

$$\text{Average fixed cost (AFC)} = \frac{\text{Total fixed cost}}{\text{level of output}} = \frac{TFC}{x}$$

$$\text{Average variable cost (AVC)} = \frac{\text{Total variable cost}}{\text{level of output}} = \frac{TVC}{x}$$

Since $TC - TFC + TVC$, it follows that $ATC = AFC + AVC$.

All three of these average costs are shown in Table 2.7.2, where it is seen that the average fixed costs (AFC) decline throughout most of the range of output and only increase at the highest levels of production. By contrast, the average variable costs (AVC) and the average total costs (ATC) at first decline and then increase rapidly as a firm increases its level of output from a plant of given capacity. It is because of these rising average costs that traditional economics assumes that the supply curve is upward sloping to the right, as depicted by Figure 2.2.1, the rationale being that an increasing price is needed to cover these rising costs. The second type of cost which interests us is that concerning the marginal cost (MC) defined as the increase in total cost (TC) resulting from a small change in the output of the factory. It is measured by the relationship

$$MC = \frac{\Delta \text{ Total cost}}{\Delta \text{ output}} = \frac{\Delta TC}{\Delta x}$$

Since the total fixed costs (TFC) do not of themselves vary with the level of output, it naturally follows that the marginal cost is also given by the relationship:

$$MC = \frac{\Delta \text{ total variable costs}}{\Delta \text{ output}} = \frac{\Delta TVC}{\Delta x}$$

The corresponding values of the marginal cost are also shown in Table 2.7.2 and it will be noticed that they first decline and then increase. A careful examination of Table 2.7.2 shows that when the marginal costs are declining and are less than the average variable and average total costs, these two averages also decline. Conversely, when the marginal costs are increasing and are greater than these average costs then the latter also increase. Such a phenomenon is to be expected and leads us to recognize that at their minima, both the ATC and the AVC are equal to the marginal costs.

Most of these costs relationships are shown in Figure 2.7.1 which has been truncated at an output level of 160 items per month to preclude the stage of

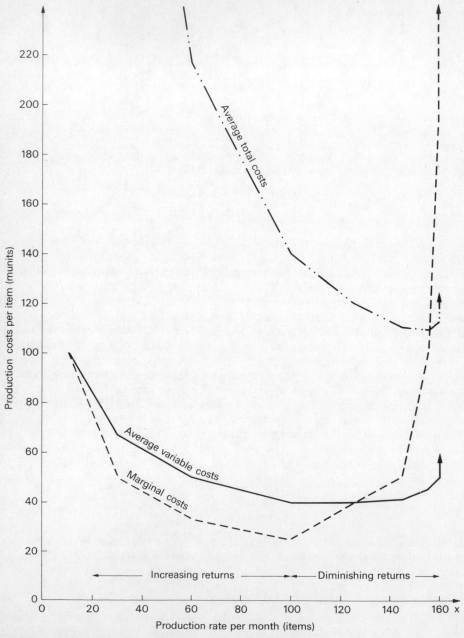

Figure 2.7.1   *Production costs as a function of production rate.*

decreasing returns. This has been done because Stage III displays negative marginal costs, meaning that the output could be increased and yet the total costs decreased by a reduction in the number of technicians employed.

2.8 REVENUE FROM SALES

When a firm sells a product it either receives the price paid by the customer or the promise of such payment in due course if credit facilities are extended to the customer. The total revenue which a firm can ultimately expect to receive from the sale of its products is therefore defined by the expression, total revenue = price per item sold × the quantity of items sold per unit time. It can be represented by the relationship:

$$TR = p_X \cdot x$$

where TR = the total revenue per unit time, p_X = the price per item of product X which *could* vary with the number of items sold, and x denotes the number of items sold per unit time. In line with our previous definitions, it follows that the average revenue (AR) and marginal revenue (MR) are defined by the relationships

$$AR = \frac{TR}{x} = \frac{p_X \cdot x}{x} = p_X$$

$$MR = \frac{\Delta TR}{\Delta x}$$

If we assume that the output of the firm is small relative to the size of the market into which it sells its products, it follows that the price facing the company is constant, and independent of the amount of product it sells. Since the average revenue is equal to the price (as previously demonstrated), it follows that the average revenue must be constant, and for that to hold true the marginal revenue must also be constant and equal the price. For pure and perfect competition we therefore have

$$AR = MR = \bar{p}_X$$

where $\bar{p}_X$ denotes the fact that the price of product X is constant.

2.9 PROFIT FROM SALES

We can now explore the relationship between the profit of a firm and its level of production. In economic theory the total profit (TP) of a firm is the difference between the total revenue and the total cost, as given by the relationship:

$$TP = TR - TC$$

It should be stressed that this relationship assumes that the total quantities of items produced and sold are the same so that no inventory is accumulated. According to the argument of Section 2.8, it follows that the total revenue of a firm engaged in pure and perfect competition increases proportionally with increases in output. This relationship is shown in Figure 2.9.1 where it is seen that the total revenue is represented by a straight line of slope equal to the constant price of the product, passing through the origin of the graph. By contrast, the total cost function is depicted by a curve, which intercepts the ordinate at a value equal to the total fixed

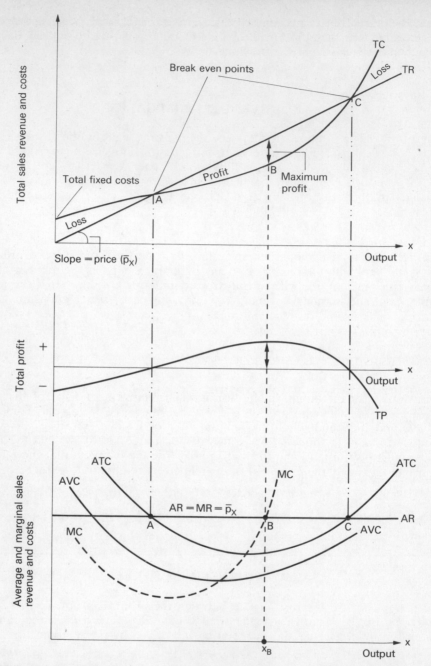

Figure 2.9.1 *Relationships between costs, sales revenues and profits for a firm in perfect competition.*

cost, and then increases as the quantity of product increases, first at a slow rate and then more rapidly. An examination of Figure 2.9.1 shows there are three regions of profit: two where the profit is negative, signifying an economic loss, and one where the profit is positive bounded by two 'break even points', where the profit is zero. Quite obviously firms wish to operate at a profit, otherwise they need access to funds to subsidize their operations. Between the break even points A and C it will be noticed that the profit reaches a maximum at point B. The bottom part of Figure 2.9.1 explores the same behaviour of profits, revenues and costs, but on an incremental basis. It shows that the same break even points at A and C prevail and that the condition of maximum profit is reached at point B, when the output level is x_B and the marginal cost (MC) of production is equal to the marginal revenue (MR) from sales. How do we explain this? If we remember that marginal means a small change in the variable of interest, brought about by a small change in the level of output x by, say, one item, then the following logic holds:

(a) if the marginal revenue is greater than the marginal cost, the profit will increase from an increase in output;
(b) if the marginal revenue is less than the marginal cost then the profit will decrease from an increase in output.

Neither of the above conditions results in a maximization of profit. By definition, therefore, the only condition which can prevail for the profit to be at a maximum must be when the marginal cost is equal to the marginal revenue, such that

$$MC = MR$$

Mathematical proof of the validity of this relationship is given in Section 2.10.

We have now arrived at the point which is the *raison d'être* for this entire chapter, namely a realization of the kinds of conditions which influence a company's operations and profitability. To galvanize our understanding we need to make one last assumption; that our hypothetical company is owned and managed by an entrepreneur. Given our rather limited assumptions of pure and perfect competition, we have already seen from Section 2.3 that customers are able to maximize their utility by changing their pattern of purchases, restricted by their own disposable income, and the prices which they pay for products. We have also assumed that each individual is unable to influence a price by his own purchases, but is able to do so in concert with all other buyers through the demand–supply–price relationship. The price which all buyers are willing to pay for a product therefore reflects their aggregate condition of maximum utility. If we now turn our attention to the firm, and more specifically to the activities of its entrepreneur, it will be realized that he bids for resources (factors of production) in such a way that he maximizes his own utility subject to the disposable income limitations of his company. Other entrepreneurs also bid for factors of production and collectively they affect the prices paid for such factors through the demand–supply–price relationship. But an entrepreneur also bids for factors anticipating the revenue which he expects to receive from the sale of the firm's products. It is reasonable to assume that, if he were able, he would attempt to maximize the profit from such a transaction because, in so doing, he could maximize his own income and utility. The activities of the entrepreneur are therefore twofold. He acts as a customer, along with all other customers, bidding for those scarce resources which constitute his own factors of production in a market-place where the price mechanism, as determined by aggregate supply and demand, ensures that customers both individually and collectively are able to attain their optimum degree of satisfaction. However, he also acts as a supplier of products attempting to maximize his own utility but likewise being constrained by the price mechanism which determines the price of his products. The same rationale holds for all suppliers of products and factors alike. It would therefore appear that through his own selfish pursuit of maximizing profits, the entrepreneur contributes to the total economy in such a way that leads to the maximization of overall welfare (satisfaction, utility). Such thinking is basic to the philosophy of free-enterprise economics, and is the keystone to the doctrine of capitalism. Put another way, this doctrine suggests that through their democratic vote to buy products, customers are able to influence the prices paid for products and factors in such a way that human satisfaction is maximized at any point in time. As demonstrated, this free-enterprise market works in such a way that the factor price equates factor supply and demand such that it is equal to the revenue obtained from the last marginal unit of product sold.

Motivated by the desire to maximize profits, it follows that entrepreneurs employ new techniques, technologies and combinations of factors in such a way that long-term costs are minimized and long-term profits maximized. Such activity obviously has a direct bearing on the prices paid for the factors of production in the long term. By the same token, however, it follows that such activity also leads to the most efficient use of factors because the free-market economy incorporates a self-regulatory mechanism which ensures that excessive profits or losses cannot endure. Profits greater than those considered normal (for a given type of business with a given perceived level of risk) obviously attract profit-hungry entrepreneurs into that market. As a result, the supply of that product increases and its price falls until a reasonable level of profit is attained by each company. Similarly, profits lower than those considered adequate result in the closure of firms, a reduction in the supply of the product and an increase in its price until normal profits are realized by each company. Quite obviously the outcome of such logic means that companies and products unable to make an adequate profit in the long run are forced to retire from the market, due to competitive pressures.

The essential tenet of the previous discussion is that, looking after one's own selfish ends, the welfare of the economy as a whole is optimized. Unfortunately, this philosophy says nothing about the aspirations of people who do not have money to back their needs. Neither does it cater for the indirect consequences of profit maximization, such as social welfare problems resulting from unemployment or atmospheric, environmental and noise pollution. Some of the assumptions of pure and perfect competition are naïve. For example, barriers exist which preclude new firms from entering lucrative markets. The most obvious ones are the lack of technical know-how and management skill, and a firm's inability or reluctance to borrow funds to finance plants of sufficient scale to be competitive. Moreover, companies already in such a market naturally try to prevent newcomers entering the market through a variety of commercial strategies and tactics, since it is in their interests to retain as large a market-share as possible to control their own destiny. Monopolies and oligopolies have existed for long times and there is evidence to suggest that their existence has not resulted in the maximization of overall economic welfare, but only the welfare of their owners. To resolve these deficiencies, governments have devised laws and codes of conduct to regulate the operations of firms in ways which are meant to achieve greater overall social and economic welfare. The most obvious examples of governmental interference are laws against trade restrictions and monopolies. In some cases companies have been legally forced to divest large parts of their operating assets to comply with these laws. More recent examples of such regulation are the health and safety laws which have gained international prominence and have forced companies to take a more professional approach to maintain the health and safety welfare not only of their employees but also of their customers. Whether this benign interference resolves the deficiencies of the market-place or exacerbates them is difficult to tell. Protagonists exist for the abolition of governmental interference, whereas others promote greater regulation, the strength and direction of their arguments being determined by their political affiliation. The fact remains however that governments do regulate the operations of companies by a variety of fiscal, monetary and legislative measures. If we assume that these actually redress the deficiencies of the market-place then we are led to believe that overall economic and social welfare is optimized by each company seeking to maximize its profits as a major strategic objective. Alternatively, if we do not believe that government interference eradicates these imperfections, then we are left with the axiom that each company should still seek to maximize its profits, not as a means of achieving overall economic welfare, but rather as a way of maximizing its own efficiency in the employment of resources. Whether or not such a principle can be applied in practice is a matter which we shall explore in Chapter 3.

2.10   THE OPPORTUNITY COST OF LIMITING RESOURCES

The basic principles and concepts which have been discussed in the previous sections of this chapter can be reinforced with the aid of a simple mathematical model, which will also help us to understand the principle of opportunity costs.

Let us imagine that a firm receives 100 munits for each item of product it sells, and that it can sell as many items as it likes in a given time period, say one month. If we represent this number of items by the variable x then it follows that the total revenue (TR) realized during one month is given by the expression:

$$TR(x) = 100x \qquad (2.10.1)$$

If the total fixed costs (TFC) during a month are 70 munits and the total variable costs are given by the expression

$$TVC(x) = 0.5x^2 + 20x$$

then it follows that the total costs (TC) incurred during a month must be given by the expression

$$TC(x) = 0.5x^2 + 20x + 70 \qquad (2.10.2)$$

The total profits (TP) realized during a month are therefore given by the difference between equations 2.10.1 and 2.10.2, namely

$$TP(x) = 80x - 0.5x^2 - 70 \qquad (2.10.3)$$

One way of discovering the level of sales which maximizes the total profit, for this example, involves computing the profit for various values of x according to equation 2.10.3. Such values are shown in Table 2.10.1, where we see that an output sales level of 80 items per month yields the maximum profit of 3130 munits per month. Since no higher profit can be realized, it follows that this constitutes the global maximum profit and the corresponding sales level of 80 items per month comprises the global optimum sales level.

Another way of achieving the same result is to use differential calculus. This method has the added advantage that it allows us to explore the economic implications of this example in greater depth. If we differentiate equation 2.10.3 with respect to x we get

$$\frac{dTP(x)}{dx} = 80 - x \qquad (2.10.4)$$

From classical calculus it is known that the condition for a global maximum is given when the first derivative of a function equals zero and the second derivative is negative at the optimum value. Differentiating equation 2.10.4 with respect to x we get

$$\frac{d^2TP(x)}{dx} = -1$$

Table 2.10.1 *Calculation of opportunity costs*

Production and sales level x items per month	Total revenue per month TR(x)	Total cost per month TC(x)	Total profit per month TP(x)	Incremental profit per month ΔTP(x)	Incremental cost per month ΔTC(x)	Incremental opportunity cost ΔTP(x)/ΔTC(x)	Marginal opportunity cost (according to Appendix A)
0	0	70	−70	–	–	–	4.00
10	1 000	320	680	750	250	3.00	2.33
20	2 000	670	1330	650	350	1.86	1.50
30	3 000	1120	1880	550	450	1.22	1.00
40	4 000	1670	2330	450	550	0.82	0.67
50	5 000	2320	2680	350	650	0.54	0.43
60	6 000	3070	2930	250	750	0.33	0.25
70	7 000	3920	3080	150	850	0.18	0.11
80	8 000	4870	3130[a]	50	950	0.05	0.00
90	9 000	5920	3080	−50	1050	−0.05	−0.09
100	10 000	7070	2930	−150	1150	−0.13	−0.17

[a] 3130 denotes the maximum profit.

showing that the second derivative is always negative, so that the condition for a global maximum profit prevails when

$$\frac{dTP(x)}{dx} = 80 - x = 0$$

when $x^* = 80$, and where x^* signifies the production and sales rate which maximize the profit per month, assuming that no inventory accumulation occurs. This value is, of course, consistent with that obtained from Table 2.10.1, which also incorporates values of the total revenues and costs at different production/sales output levels showing that the optimum sales revenue and total costs are 8000 and 4870 munits per month respectively.

If an output level of 80 items per month truly reflects the condition of maximum profit, then it follows from Section 2.9 that the corresponding marginal revenue should equal the marginal cost. As we are dealing with continuous revenue and cost functions, it naturally follows that these marginals are given by the first derivatives of equations 2.10.1 and 2.10.2 respectively. Differentiating equation 2.10.1 with respect to x we get

$$\text{marginal revenue (MR)} = \frac{dTR(x)}{dx} = 100 \qquad (2.10.5)$$

and from equation 2.10.2 we get

$$\text{marginal cost (MC)} = \frac{dTC(x)}{dx} = x + 20 \qquad (2.10.6)$$

Substituting the value ($x^* = 80$) into equation 2.10.6 therefore shows that both the marginal cost given by 2.10.6, and the marginal revenue given by 2.10.5 equal 100 munits per item, thereby proving that the condition of maximum profit occurs when the marginal cost and marginal revenue equate.

In real-life situations, firms are often constrained from earning more profit by a limitation on the availability of some resource such as cash, space or skilled manpower. In these circumstances they have to make do with the resources at their disposal, cognizant of the fact that they are *foregoing* the opportunity to make extra profit and an implied or imputed cost results from the rationing of resources. In economic jargon, these imputed costs are known as opportunity costs. In simple terms, therefore, an opportunity cost is the maximum value one would be willing to pay to procure a certain extra quantity of a particular resource†. Faced with this situation, management should determine the actual monetary cost of procuring extra resources, and compare this cost with their opportunity cost. Such an analysis would suggest that extra resources should be recruited by the firm if their actual costs were sufficiently smaller than their opportunity costs to warrant any extra risks involved with their purchase.

To understand this new principle properly let us develop the numerical example of this section further to demonstrate what happens to profits if some resource is profit-limiting. For the sake of an example, let us assume that our hypothetical firm needs to finance all of its monthly production with money available at the beginning of the month, prior to receiving any monies from subsequent sales. If we assume that the cash ration is limited to 3070 munits, then it follows from Table 2.10.1 that the maximum production level which can be sustained is 60 items per month, 20 items per month *less* than the optimum production/sales level. The profit corresponding

---

† As this book proceeds so we shall discover other situations where opportunity costs are incurred, necessitating slightly different definitions to the one given here.

with this smaller output level is 2930 munits per month which is also smaller than the maximum profit level of 3130 by 200 munits per month. Effectively, therefore, the cash restriction means that the company is foregoing extra profits of 200 munits per month simply by restricting its cash to 3070 compared with its optimum cash needs of 4870 munits per month. In very simple terms this means that the average opportunity cost of funds to this firm is

$$\frac{200}{(4870-3070)}=\frac{200}{1800}=0.11 \text{ munits per month per munit borrowed}$$

In these circumstances the firm would be advised to borrow money at an interest rate less than 0.11 because this money would finance extra profits. For example, if the firm could borrow the extra 1800 munits needed to finance the optimum production level at a cost of 0.10 (munits per month per munit borrowed), then the total debt charge would be 180 munits per month allowing the firm to make an extra profit of 20 munits per month. Unfortunately, the above analysis is rather simple-minded in that it only considers the average opportunity cost and does not take account of the fact that, in this example, the profit is not directly proportional to the firm's output level of sales. A better measure of the changing value of this opportunity cost is presented in the penultimate column of Table 2.10.1 where we see that the incremental opportunity cost, given by the expression $\frac{\Delta TP(x)}{\Delta TC(x)}$, di-minishes rapidly as the optimum sales level is approached. Unfortunately, these statistics are also rather crude being limited to relatively large changes in $\Delta TP(x)$ and $\Delta TC(x)$. If we explore the changes in profit brought about by borrowing one more munit per month (that is, the truly marginal analysis), then we find that the marginal opportunity cost of funds, in this example, corresponds with the values given in the last column of Table 2.10.1 These values are the mathematical limits of the opportunity costs developed from the mathematical relationships given in Appendix A. In Table 2.10.1 we see that the marginal opportunity cost of funds declines from 4.00 at zero output to nought at the optimum level of 80 items per month. The fact that we would not be willing to pay any money to finance production in excess of 80 items per month is, of course, self-evident because the total profit would decline as shown by Table 2.10.1. The corollary is that, beyond the optimum sales level, the opportunity cost must be negative. This is borne out by the analysis shown in the last two columns of the table. Faced with such a situation it therefore follows that a firm should only finance extra output if the marginal cost of borrowing funds is less than the corresponding marginal opportunity cost. For example, if the marginal cost of funds was 0.11, the firm should only finance sales up to 70 items per month since borrowing more funds to finance extra production would *reduce* profits.

Although we have developed this notion of an opportunity cost via a rather trivial mathematical example, the idea nevertheless is fundamental to all microeconomic theory. Whenever resources are employed in one particular end use, it naturally follows that they are precluded from *some alternative* end use so that an opportunity cost is incurred, equal to the benefit forgone from the best alternative use of those resources. We shall develop this principle in later chapters where we shall use it as an operational, decision-making tool.

2.11   SUMMARY

Our particular treatment of microeconomic theory in this chapter is not meant to provide the avid reader with a comprehensive understanding of the subject; that can only come from reading books specializing in economic theory. Instead, this chapter is meant to provide sufficient understanding of the principles, concepts and the jargon of economics so that the reader can interpret the remainder of this book properly in a practical sense. Our main purpose for including this chapter however is to develop the principle that a firm should attempt to maximize its profits as an ongoing corporate objective, and to explore some of the social implications of that objective. In the next chapter we shall challenge the validity of this principle from a practical point of view. As well as dealing with such basic ideas as profits, revenues and costs, this chapter also deals with the concept of opportunity cost, and a numerical example is developed to illustrate the usefulness of this concept. In later chapters we shall refer to this concept again, and to that end we include a comprehensive mathematical treatment of the subject in Appendix A.

2.12   BIBLIOGRAPHY

The recommended general text books for Chapter 1 also provide excellent background reading for this chapter.

2.13   QUESTIONS

2.13.1   The price (P) of a product is related to the quantity (Q) sold per unit time by the expression $Q = 1000 - 4P$: and the total cost of production (C) is given by the relationship $C = 6000 + 50Q$. Assuming there is no inventory accumulation, determine the sales levels and prices which maximize the total profit and the total sales revenue per unit of time.

2.13.2   The economic model of perfect competition is used to describe a marketing situation which manufacturing firms may experience. Discuss the assumptions underlying this model and whether they may be taken as reasonable approximations to real-life circumstances.

2.13.3   The capacity of a cement works is 40 tonnes per day. Current policy is to run the plant to capacity. The managing director has asked for a joint market research–industrial engineering study to be made to investigate the merits of this policy. The study gave the following information

   1. $P = 50 - Q$ (for $0 < Q \leqslant 40$) where P is the price (£/tonne), and Q is the quantity (tonnes per day) of cement demanded by customers.
   2. The cost of production is £300 per day plus £10 per tonne of cement produced.

   If you were the manager in charge of this team, what production/marketing policy would you recommend to the MD? The MD would like to know the production level at which the factory would break even, and the average and marginal costs and revenues. Advise him accordingly. (Note: all cement produced is sold: there is no inventory accumulation.)

2.13.4   What is meant by the concept economies of scale in the manufacturing industry? Explain carefully the sources of these economies both in the operation of existing plants and in relation to the choice of size for new plants. Give details of any factors which may ultimately prevent further economies of scale from being achieved.

2.13.5   A cement manufacturer finds that the marginal cost (MC) for producing cement from one kiln is approximated by the expression:

$$MC = 3X^2 - 20X + 35 \quad (\$/\text{tonne})$$

where X denotes the number of tonnes of cement produced by a kiln per hour. The fixed production costs are $250 per hour per kiln. All of the cement can be sold for $100 per tonne. Currently, each kiln is operated at a throughput of 5 tonnes per hour because this rate gives the minimum average variable cost. Prove that this production policy is suboptimal.

Two operators are required per tonne of cement produced and in the future it is likely that recruitment problems will limit the availability of operators to 16 per kiln. If such a problem should arise, how much should the company be willing to pay to remove such a constraint?

2.13.6   Prove from first principles that sales revenue responds to changes in price according to the value of the product's price elasticity of demand.

2.13.7   A company currently produces and sells 10 000 tonnes per annum of a product which sells for £5 per tonne. Market research has shown that the price elasticity of demand for this product is equal to two. Moreover, the marginal cost of production is £1 per tonne and the fixed costs are £10 000 per annum. If the current sales policy is suboptimal, what policy would you recommend in its stead?

2.13.8   Determine the necessary boundary conditions which must apply for the optimal price (P^*) of a product to be given by the following relationship:

$$P^* = \left(\frac{\varepsilon}{\varepsilon - 1}\right) V$$

where ε = price elasticity of demand, and V = constant unit variable cost. Show that $P^* = V + 1/B$ when the market sales are given according to the following relationship:

$$M = A \cdot \exp[-BP]$$

where M = potential market sales, P = price, and $A > 0$ and $B > 0$ are constants.

2.13.9   A chemical trader sells a chemical cleaning compound according to the following economic data and constraints:

Product selling price	¥100/tonne
Buying-in cost	¥50/tonne
Fixed cost	¥100/week
Working capital	25 per cent of sales revenue
Space requirements	0.2 cubic metres per ¥1 of cost of goods sold
Working capital constraint	¥700 per week
Warehousing effective maximum storage space	200 cubic metres

The direct labour handling costs are proportional to the square of the tonnage handled and amount to ¥1 per week when the quantity retailed is 1 tonne per week. How much product would you recommend the retailer to sell, and what price should he be willing to pay, if any, to remove the limits of working capital and/or space?

2.13.10 The manager of a manufacturing company would like to optimize his operations. Unfortunately, he believes that the availability of cash to finance working capital may restrain the company from achieving the maximum potential profit. Demonstrate that, for the operations of his company as defined below, he should consider borrowing money from a bank when:

$$\frac{n(p-v)}{C} > i$$

where n = a variable and is the number of units of a product which is manufactured and sold each month, p = a constant and is the unit price of the product, v = a constant and is the unit variable cost of manufacturing, storing and delivering product, C = the total cash which the company reckons could be made available, from internal sources, for financing working capital, i = the bank interest rate (per cent per month) and it is known that working capital requirements are directly proportional to the level of sales. Use the Lagrange Multiplier as a means of deriving your proof, and define the meaning of the multiplier in mathematical terms.

3. The Need for a Corporate Objective

'Would you tell me, please, which way I ought to go from here?' 'That depends a good deal on where you want to get to,' said the Cat. 'I don't much care where–' said Alice. 'Then it doesn't matter which way you go,' said the Cat.
Lewis Carroll, *Alice's Adventures in Wonderland*, 1865

In this chapter we re-examine the hypothesis that a firm should attempt to maximize its profits and show that such an objective does not really stand the test of time and experience. Instead, it is suggested that a much more reasonable aim for a firm is to provide an adequate return on its investment. To formulate such an idea, we are obliged to consider the activities of the firm as a corporate whole (a total system) and we conclude that some form of corporate planning is necessary if a firm is intent on achieving such an objective. Because most products have a limited life known as the 'product life cycle', corporate planning invariably demonstrates that a profit gap will ultimately develop between the firm's profit needs and its profit potential. To close that gap, new and better products have to be invented and developed along with better processes and machines for their production. Furthermore, more cost-effective methods for their promotion, distribution and sale have to be found. To conclude this chapter we demonstrate that the magnitude of the life-cycle costs of its products and the life-cycle benefits of its own capital assets, should be a great concern to every company intent on staying in business.

3.1 A PHILOSOPHY OF THE FIRM

Throughout this chapter the reader is exposed to the idea of the firm as a marketing entity in which market forces which comprise opportunities and threats provide the orientation for the design of the company as a whole. As an organizational concept, marketing goes beyond the parochial considerations of selling, distributing, advertising and market research, although these aspects are obviously incorporated within marketing. Instead, marketing has to become a way of life for most companies because it is only through marketing that the firm can achieve its aims and objectives. As already mentioned, in a free-market economy customers reward only those firms whose goods and services are judged to constitute a useful rendering of economic service. The fact that the customer cannot be controlled, although he can be influenced, is all important. Profitability, therefore, is not under the absolute control of the company, but is the result – the end result – of matching products with customer wants and needs. Only products, and to some extent their prices, are under the *direct* control of the company and it is through its products and the way in which they are offered that a company attempts to seek for itself that competitive advantage which clearly distinguishes it amongst the competitive rivalry which pervades the market-place.

44

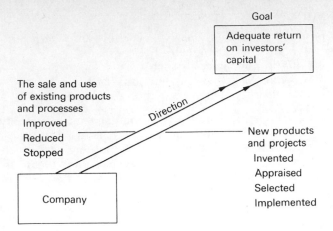

Figure 3.1.1 *The firm as a target seeking organization.*

It is in this light then that we recognize the firm as a means-end system: it has resources and it seeks market ends. In fact, we can think of the firm as a target seeking organization, as shown by Figure 3.1.1, continuously striving to adapt and adjust itself to the attainment of some end purpose. If this is true, then it is immediately clear that the capacity to achieve its end purpose through its ability to adapt and adjust must be very carefully considered, since these objectives will determine the way in which the corporate resources have to be combined, in the form of operating systems, to produce that competitive distinctiveness which leads to the desired end result. Usually these strategic objectives can only be obtained through decisive instrumental action, purposefully designed for the ends sought in the market-place.

3.2 THE NEED FOR A CORPORATE STRATEGY

Many companies have prospered and continue to prosper without any explicit corporate plan or strategy, and have no real sense of where they are going other than to seek profitable opportunities. For example, a shopkeeper wishing to make money would undoubtedly formulate corporate plans largely single-handed and in part subconsciously. He would consider such factors as local wages and population trends, the siting of a proposed housing estate, the influence of holidays on his business, the helpfulness of his bank manager and 'the prospect of marrying his ageing competitor's only daughter'. With this sort of thinking he would decide upon his strategy to make the best use of the most likely turn of future events. This, after all, is the way in which many business tycoons built up their businesses to become household names.

Nowadays, however, the nature of business, especially in the consumer durable and capital goods markets, is much more competitive and complex than it used to be. Greater competition has arisen from

(i) there being fewer but larger companies, each pursuing a policy of growth to achieve benefits of scale, and greater stability by way of larger markets,
(ii) a much more professional management ethic, and
(iii) the international character of competition.

Whereas greater complexity has resulted from

(iv) extensive product, process and marketing innovation which has accelerated as firms have attempted to differentiate their products,
(v) greater instability in raw materials supply,
(vi) seemingly more complicated labour relations, and
(vii) much more restrictive legislation regulating corporate activity.

To accommodate competitive pressures a company must carefully decide what aims it wants to achieve or must achieve in order to survive, and it needs to formulate its plans accordingly. Of course there is nothing very special in this idea, after all planning is done by any competent exploration team embarking on a hazardous venture and company planning is only slightly different from that required for a military campaign.

Uppermost in such planning there is the need to form a strategy. In the context of a business organization a strategy can be considered a plan which determines how that firm can best achieve its desired aims when considering the opposing forces exerted by its competitive environment and its own limited capabilities. Carried to its logical conclusion such a strategy is tantamount to deciding the precise niche which a company wants in the market-place, and the means of achieving that niche. The correct strategy therefore will establish the proper relationship between the distinctive capabilities of a firm and the problems and opportunities which beset it in the market-place, so that the search for this correct interrelationship is at the very heart of strategy formulation. Without a proper strategy it is highly likely that a firm will languish and ultimately die. It behoves each firm therefore to develop a master-plan which should incorporate the following elements.

(i) An explicit definition of the kind of business that firm really wants to become, and the market niche it wishes to attain with the resources it intends to marshal;
(ii) An explicit statement of the levels of performance it must achieve if (i) above is to be realized;
(iii) The specification of a plan of action involving a search for efficient means of implementing such a strategy; and
(iv) A reappraisal of (i) and (ii) in light of evidence concerning the company's own competence and the nature of its competition and external constraints.

In essence, therefore, a corporate strategy is formulated according to a continually iterative process whereby realistic corporate objectives cannot be established until due consideration has been given to alternative strategies, forecasts of the outcomes of future plans, an appraisal of the firm's capability, and an assessment of the competition and vice versa.

The influence of strategy can be seen all around us. For example, ever since its incorporation as the Computer Tabulating Recording Co, IBM has demonstrated the significance of a soundly conceived and formulated strategy. Recognizing its niche as a data systems business when its competitors were preoccupied with individual pieces of equipment, IBM developed a set of policies which resulted in its domination of the office equipment industry. By contrast Packard, which in the 1930s was to the motor car industry what IBM is to the computer industry today, had disappeared as an independent producer by the early 1950s because of its strategic myopia.

3.3 THE NATURE OF CORPORATE PLANNING

Growth in the size of many companies has meant that daily executive decision making is beyond the scope and capability of any centralized, head office executive.

To overcome this problem, companies have tended to decentralize their decision making so that executives in smaller units of the company are delegated the responsibility for resolving short- and possibly medium-term problems. To retain control, each operating unit of the corporation is held responsible for developing plans for its short-term activities in the form of budgets which *could* be added together to form a total plan for the corporation.

Such a concept of planning is fraught with all sorts of problems! First, such plans tend to confine the company's thinking to the boundaries of its existing organization, structure and activities. Second, it does not take cognizance of the fact that the separate divisions of the company can be of mutual support, and this enhancement can be a considerable source of corporate strength. In business jargon this effect is known as synergy. Third, divisional managers are invariably too busy resolving immediate problems to spare the time required to plan properly for the long term. As a result, such plans that are made this way do not constitute corporate planning proper. Instead, corporate planning, which is defined as an organized effort to plan the development of all the resources at the company's disposal in a co-ordinated fashion and as far into the future as is sensible, with the object of realizing the company's objective(s), should be done away from the immediate everyday pressures of a business. Ideally this planning should be carried out by the firm's chief executive if he has the time, inclination and talent. Quite often, however, it is delegated to other executives reporting directly to him, preferably without direct line responsibility so they can give the job the attention which it deserves.

3.4 FORMULATING A CORPORATE OBJECTIVE

Three essential questions need answering if a corporate plan is to be worthwhile:

  (i) What is the firm's current level of performance?
 (ii) What objectives does it wish to achieve?
(iii) How will it attain such objectives?

The first question requires the corporate planner to be knowledgeable in many matters relating to the company's performance and the nature of its competitive environment. Furthermore, he must continually question the nature of the company's business, because the answer to the question 'What business are we in?' strikes at the very core of a company's strategy. For example, some motor car manufacturers have realized that their distinctive competence lies not so much with the manufacture of cars as with making and selling vehicles in general and they have revised their strategies accordingly. Similarly, some famous mining firms have realized that their real skills lie not so much with mining as with their ability to finance and develop large natural resources, and they too have changed their former strategies often to the point of completely revitalizing their businesses.

The second question is one of the most important questions which a firm ever has to answer. Years ago it was thought that the objectives of the managers of a business should be the maximization of the wealth of the shareholders whose interests the managers were supposed to protect. However, most critics agree that the estrangement of the shareholders and the managers invalidates such an objective. Admittedly, the activities of the company are reported to the shareholders and, in theory at least, they have the power to remove the management if they are dissatisfied with their performance. In most circumstances, however, because of the wide spread of shareholding and inadequacies of information available to the shareholders, the management of a company are the dominant decision makers and many operate the company in their own rather than in the shareholders' interests. As a result, some managers attempt to enhance their own technical prestige by promoting company research and development, while others seek to make their jobs more secure by increasing the company's market share. In reality, therefore, the actual behaviour of the company is some complicated amalgam of the aspirations of the individual managers and their political force within the management structure.

Cyert and March (1963) have studied these behavioural characteristics of the firm in depth and suggest that nowadays a firm is really a coalition of various interest groups – shareholders, managers, employers, trade unions, customers, suppliers, the local community, and the government, each endeavouring to attain some end purpose through their association with that firm, whose activities they attempt to influence by their bargaining power. If this is true, then it will be realized that a company can have a portfolio of objectives. For example, it might wish to

  (i) increase the absolute level of its sales revenue,
 (ii) increase its market share,
(iii) become a technological leader,
 (iv) become a price leader,
  (v) be known as a good employer,
 (vi) gain a good public image,
(vii) achieve a satisfactory profit.

The basic question which we have to answer here is 'Which of these objectives, if any, is paramount'? Quite obviously all groups in the coalition can only achieve, or partly achieve, their aspirations if the company is to survive in the long term. Survival, therefore, is the absolute minimum of corporate objectives. Cognizant of this fact, Argenti (1968) suggests that three fundamental questions with three unique answers are needed to elucidate the primary corporate objective, namely

(i)	Under what conditions would a firm NOT wish to achieve a particular objective?	None
(ii)	Why would a firm wish to achieve that particular objective?	In order to survive
(iii)	Would the firm fail to survive if it consistently did not achieve a particular objective?	Yes

Quite rightly, he suggests that if the answers to these questions do not provide the answers listed above then, at best, the objective is secondary or simply a constraint. To illustrate this point let us test the validity of a firm wanting to increase its market share. Such a motive is quite understandable since a large share allows a firm to control its marketing better, and by the same token provides it with benefits of scale. However, the attainment of too large a market share could result in the firm contravening anti-monopoly legislation. Such an objective therefore would not pass the test of (i) above. The only objective which consistently stands the test of all three questions is to make an adequate profit. Such an outcome is hardly surprising since failure to achieve this end would mean that a firm could not afford to pay its shareholders an ample dividend and, at the same time, retain sufficient monies to replenish and improve its stock of capital assets and products. It would also result in a loss of confidence by potential financiers causing difficulties with raising funds to support lucrative projects and eventually result in the long-term demise of that firm with its attendant social and political repercussions. In other words such a company would be caught in an economic downward spiral in its fortunes. By contrast, a company consistently making an adequate profit could afford to recruit talented people, take advantage of new technology and raise funds to replenish and improve its stock of productive machinery, so as to improve its productivity and remain competitive.

The discerning reader will have noticed that little so far has been said about maximizing profits. Instead the emphasis has been placed on a firm making an adequate profit. Much of the reason for this change in emphasis comes from the fact that both academe and the business world are considerably disenchanted with the profit maximization concept for a variety of reasons. In the first place, it is an easy matter to draw the graphs of Chapter 2 to demonstrate the conditions in which profits *could* be maximized, but it is quite another matter to know how to accomplish this end in reality. The main reason for this difficulty lies in the fact that the business world is dynamic and forever changing, so the information needs of Chapter 2 are seldom realized. Furthermore, we understand how the maximum terminal speed of a free-falling object is governed by the laws of gravity, the shape and nature of the object and atmospheric conditions, but we really have no conception of what constitutes a maximum profit other than the fact that it should be as much as possible under the conditions which the firm finds itself. This will depend on the people comprising the firm and their individual needs and aspirations, some of which will not be satisfied by pecuniary reward. Take the hypothetical case of two entrepreneurs being the sole employees of their own companies, each of equal business acumen, energy, drive, enthusiasm and all those other characteristics which make for a top class businessman. To complete the assumptions, let us also assume that both have access to the same resources. One entrepreneur might be satisfied with a reward of 100 000 munits, if this was more than he could gain by hiring himself out as an employee providing, of course, it met his financial obligations and requirements. This entrepreneur might be quite happy to spend a considerable amount of time over each and every business transaction if this also allowed him to satisfy, in whole or in part, his social, ego and self-fulfilment needs. By contrast, the other entrepreneur might need an annual reward of 200 000 munits in order to meet his obligations, and might satisfy his psychological needs outside his business endeavours. This trivial example therefore highlights the point that we cannot formulate what constitutes a maximum profit, but we do have a good idea of what constitutes an adequate or satisfactory profit because the long-term return which a company provides for its shareholders, by way of dividend payments and share price enhancement, is to a large extent a direct measure of this adequacy. To illustrate this point consider the case of a shareholder buying a share for 100 munits and receiving a gross dividend payment of 4 munits at the end of a year. In this particular case the dividend yield defined by the expression:

$$\text{dividend yield} = \frac{\text{dividend payment per share} \cdot 100\%}{\text{market value of that share}}$$

would be 4 per cent per annum. Furthermore, if the stock market price of the company's shares rose to 106 munits by the end of the year then the growth rate in the valuation of those shares would be 6 per cent per annum. Continued payment of a 4 per cent dividend yield, based upon a market value growing by 6 per cent per annum would mean that the shareholder was receiving a gross return of 10 per cent per annum (4+6 per cent) on his original investment. Of course, income taxes might be payable on these dividends, and the shareholder might also have to pay capital gains tax on the resale of his shares, but such matters as these are beyond the control of a firm. In the case of our hypothetical company, therefore, the 10 per cent return on the shareholder's original investment would be the all important statistic. Providing a firm's dividend policy has been fairly stable, and there have been no gross vacillations in the market value of its shares, then its return on investment, computed by these means, must by definition have been adequate. Had this not been the case then either the value of the shares would have declined markedly showing the shareholders' dissatisfaction with too low a return, or else the dividend yield would have declined, showing the managers' and employees' dissatisfaction with too high a dividend payout. To some extent, therefore, we recognize that an adequate return is evolutionary; it either survives the test of time or it moves with the times and circumstance.

Actually the 10 per cent rate of return which we have just used is quite close to the average return of companies over the past 20–30 years, and it is certainly accurate enough for our purposes. However, it should be noted that many researchers have investigated such returns in detail, and notable amongst these studies is that by Merrett and Sykes (1963). Having access to the particular details concerning its own past dividend payments and share prices means that each company can calculate its own past return quite readily, and provided such a return was and still is deemed to be satisfactory, when compared with the returns of similar companies experiencing similar risks*, it can be used for forecasting purposes. One further piece of information is necessary to accomplish this end, namely the ratio of a firm's net profit after tax to its total dividend payment. Such a statistic is known as the dividend cover: it is a measure of the amount of earnings which a company likes to retain for its own internal growth and acts as a buffer to ensure that the dividends can be paid under most conditions of risk. The dividend cover of most companies lies in the range 1.4–2.5 but for demonstration purposes only we shall assume a value of 1.5. If we further assume that the market capitalization of a company's shares is currently 1 000 000 munits, then the forecast of that company's adequate profit requirements would be as shown in Table 3.4.1.

Table 3.4.1 *Forecasting a firm's adequate profit targets (in munits)*

	1982	1983	1984	1985	1986	1987
Market capitalization of company's shares (rising by 6 per cent pa)	1 000 000	1 060 000	1 123 600	1 191 015	1 262 477	1 338 226
Gross dividend (4 per cent yield before personal taxes)	40 000	42 400	44 944	47 641	50 499	53 529
Net corporate profit (after corporation tax) to allow for a 1.5 dividend cover	60 000	63 600	67 416	71 462	75 749	80 294
Profit targets	60 000	64 000	67 000	71 000	76 000	80 000

Profit forecasts devised by these means are not meant to be precise targets because it is realized that no company can control its profits accurately. Furthermore, it is recognized that the market capitalization of a company's shares depends on many factors outside of its control. Instead, these targets are meant to act as marker buoys in that they are something to aim for. During some years they may be surpassed, whereas in other years the firm's performance may fall short of these expectations. Their real benefit is that they help to stimulate corporate activity into seeking, devising, planning and implementing means to regenerate the company's

* Of necessity we have to postpone a comprehensive study of risk and its implications until Chapter 9.

profit performance and potential, thereby enhancing the chances of its meeting an adequate return, not necessarily in any particular year but on average.

3.5 FORECASTING THE PROFIT GAP

Establishing reasonable profit targets for the future activities of a company is one matter, calculating how much profit a company is likely to make from its existing inventory of resources, skills, products and processes is quite another matter, which requires forecasting the future, a discipline which is fraught with difficulties, uncertainties and their attendant risks. Exactly how far ahead it is prudent for a company to forecast depends very much on the nature of its business. Some companies are involved with products whose life-cycles last only 1–2 years so that it is doubtful if they would benefit much from 5–10 year forecasting. On the other hand, other companies are involved with expensive research and development programmes where the gestation period of a product can be as much as 5–7 years, followed by extensive capital investment. Such products would probably warrant long-term forecasting of perhaps 10–15 years. Some sceptics contend that forecasting is an absolute waste of time in that the outcome seldom matches the results of the forecasts. Unfortunately, the latter part of their argument is often true, but this does not invalidate the usefulness of forecasting, the real benefit of which is that it attempts, in a disciplined way, to map out those conditions which are likely to put the company in jeopardy, and those which could provide great opportunity, so that the company's strategy can be formulated accordingly. We shall deal with forecasting problems in Chapter 7 and we do not intend to dwell at length on the philosophy and mechanics of corporate planning since such matters are best dealt with by specialized books, several of which are listed in the references. What is important to grasp at this stage, however, is the fact that such forecasts invariably show that a company cannot expect to fulfil its profit target in years to come, based solely on its existing products, processes, stock of capital plant and skills. Instead a profit gap develops which has to be filled. The reasons for such a gap developing are quite easy to understand. Faced with severe competition firms experiment and innovate, the result being that new products supersede old ones, as do processes and plants for their manufacture. As a result, most products have a limited life and exhibit life-cycle characteristics similar to those shown by curve I in Figure 3.5.1 with the following phases:

 (i) a development phase, when monies are spent inventing and/or developing the product or process, possibly involving expenditure on capital plant as well as on R & D;
 (ii) an introduction phase, when the product is introduced to the market, possibly at an initial loss while it is established;
(iii) a growth phase, when the sales volume increases rapidly, generating a substantial profit well ahead of competitive retaliation;
(iv) a maturity phase, where the rate of sales growth declines either because market saturation is approached, or because other companies compete for market share. During this phase it is common for the profits to erode as the necessary technological expertise spreads and the attractiveness of the industry becomes more obvious to potential outside entrants, some of whom then become competitors;
 (v) a declining phase, when the sales volume and profit erode due to competitive pressures arising out of the availability of equally good, if not better, products and aggressive pricing policies by competitors.

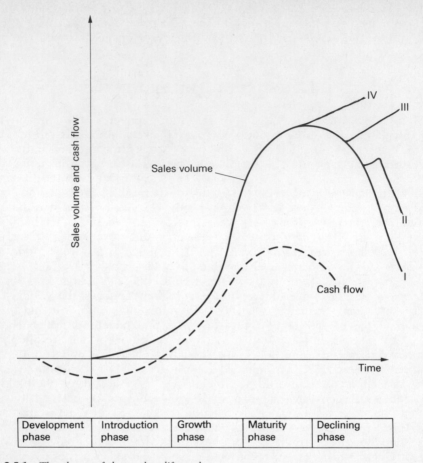

| Development phase | Introduction phase | Growth phase | Maturity phase | Declining phase |

Figure 3.5.1 *The phases of the product life-cycle.*

The extent of these life-cycles can vary enormously ranging from a few months for the 'Hula-hoop' to decades for the ordinary pencil. More typical examples of consumer durable products exhibiting such life-cycle characteristics are black and white television sets, and the thermionic valves initially used in their construction.

Undoubtedly some products exhibit different features. For example, some follow the previous example but, due to retaliatory and defensive tactics, their life-cycles are prolonged, as shown by curve II in Figure 3.5.1; some existing models of British motor cars are excellent examples in this category. Others exhibit a resounding come back as shown by curve III, the most prominent example being coal. The last category of products, depicted by curve IV, continue to grow according to the fluctuations of the economy(ies) containing them. This category applies to products which become diverse in their end use and are extremely important to an economy. Excellent examples are steel, cement, caustic soda and chlorine – in other words the commodity products.

The corporate implications of the product life-cycle are considerable and are best illustrated by Figure 3.5.2, which shows how a firm has to cleverly phase the introduction of new and/or improved products if it wants to achieve a satisfactory and possibly growing profit as previously suggested. This picture also illustrates the possibility of the firm having to meet a continuing and increasing R & D and capital investment commitment.

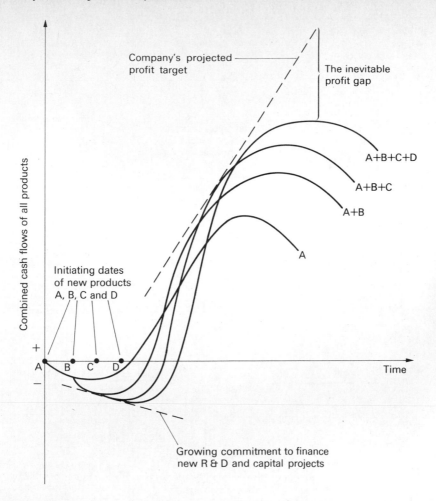

Figure 3.5.2 *The phasing of new products to meet a growing profit target.*

   The simple message which comes from this analysis therefore is that a firm has to invest in new products and eventually in new assets if it intends to survive in the long term: 'it has to spend money to make money'! Of course there are other ways of filling the inevitable profit gap, by way of better marketing (with the view to increasing sales revenue) and schemes devised to cut costs, as illustrated by Figure 3.5.3. However such endeavours are eventually constrained by the product's commercial life-cycle. On the one hand, therefore, each firm attempts to increase its own life-cycle benefits (profit) from the sale of its products, whereas, on the other hand, it attempts to match if not excel the life-cycle benefits arising from the purchase of its competitors' products. Both considerations are linked, but the right balance requires a form of genius. Quite obviously the benefit to the customer depends on many factors relating to the product (such as its aesthetic qualities, and its robustness and reliability) but one factor which invariably applies to the purchasing decision is the customers' evaluation of that product's life-cycle costs (LCC) of ownership. Such a concept extends beyond any parochial considerations of price, and allows for the maintenance, replacement and retirement costs of the product. Herein lies the central theme of this book, namely that concern for the life-cycle benefits of its own

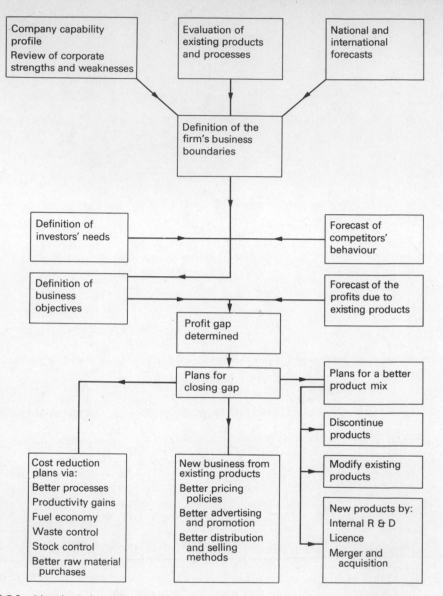

Figure 3.5.3 *Identifying the profit gap and evaluating alternative means for closing that gap.*

assets and the life-cycle costs of ownership of its products must be central to the theme and philosophy of any company.

The search for new and improved products and the means for making them more profitable cannot be left to chance. Instead procedures must be devised for their discovery, and when they are found they have to be thoroughly appraised to see if they

  (i) help fulfil the firm's strategic and profit objectives,
 (ii) can be afforded,
(iii) fit into the firm's portfolio of products and projects, thereby enhancing its corporate distinctiveness through some synergistic benefits, and
(iv) are of a risk class which can be accommodated by the firm.

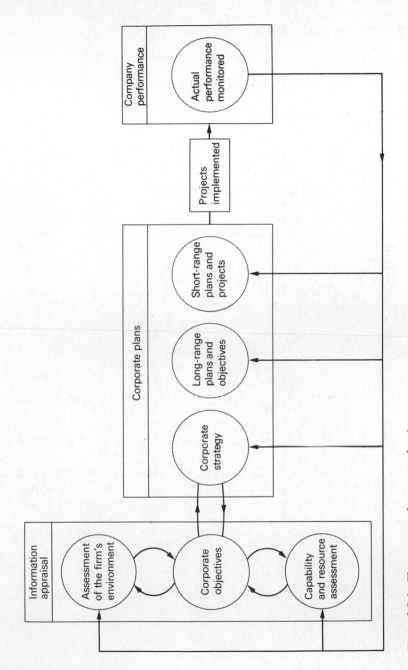

Figure 3.5.4 *The structure of corporate planning.*

Furthermore, once a decision has been made for their implementation, the same
dedication of purpose must ensue, and each product and project must be professionally controlled throughout each phase of its life-cycle, its actual performance being
monitored and fed back into the corporate planning activity so that future generations of decision makers can learn from the successes and mistakes of the past. Such
notions of corporate planning are contained in Figure 3.5.4.

3.6 SUMMARY

In the foregoing material we challenged the philosophy, previously developed in
Chapter 2, that each firm should endeavour to maximize its profits, and we found
that such an objective did not properly reflect the behaviour of most firms. Instead,
it appears that a more reasonable aim for a company is to yield an adequate return
on its shareholders' investments and it is towards the realization of that objective
that a firm's scarce resources should be marshalled. Because of the influence which
the product life cycle has on the profitability of a firm, it is suggested that forecasts
should be made of the extent and the timing of the inevitable profit gap which
develops between the profit needs of a firm and its profit potential. It is also
suggested that an imaginative but purposeful search for ways of closing that profit
gap should be made. To that end each firm should develop new and improved
products which exhibit life-cycle cost (LCC) characteristics which are competitive
with those of its competitors, and they should invest in plant, machinery, buildings
and processes which offer the firm adequate life-cycle benefits (LCB) too.

3.7 BIBLIOGRAPHY

General text

Argenti, J., *Corporate Planning*, Allen & Unwin, 1968. This book is especially well
   known in management circles because it is so profound and yet so easy to read
   and understand.
Cyert, R. M. and March, J. G., *A Behavioural Theory of the Firm*, Prentice-Hall,
   1963. Based on the results of original research, this book challenges the
   previously held and orthodox view that the managers of a firm should maximize
   the profits accruing to the shareholders.

Specific text

Merrett, A. J. and Sykes, Allen, 'Returns on equities and fixed interest securities
   1913–1963,' *District Bank Review*, December 1963 and June 1966.

PART II
The Investment Decision

In Part I we discussed the corporate goals and strategy of the firm and developed the idea that a profit gap would eventually develop between the firm's profit expectations and its performance due to the life-cycle characteristics of its products. It was suggested that plans were needed to resolve this problem, and that the only reasonable means of closing such a gap lay with the search for and implementation of lucrative projects, which would meet both its strategic and economic requirements. It was emphasized that although some of these projects could involve substantial economies in the sale and manufacture of existing products using existing assets, and might result in extensions to their economic lives, ultimately each firm would have to introduce new products and/or new capital plant in order to enhance its otherwise dwindling profits.

In Part II we shall develop and discuss the rationale for appraising the economic merits of new projects necessitating capital investment. Normal scientific convention suggests that in order to appraise the economic merits of alternative courses of action, one should gather the relevant cognitive facts prior to establishing the criterion (or set of criteria) for their evaluation. For pedagogical reasons, we reverse this procedure to demonstrate that the very nature of the criteria used in such appraisals dictates the kind of information which is required. Several of the more commonly used criteria for assessing the economic merits of capital proposals are shown to be deficient. In their stead, other criteria, based on the discounted cash flow technique, are developed and recommended, but only after an exhaustive check of their relative strengths and weaknesses in the context of real decision making. Furthermore, the information requirements for appraising the economic merits of a new capital project are discussed at length with a view to developing a better appreciation of the uncertainty and consequential risk involved with any capital investment enterprise.

We conclude Part II with an economic decision-making game which has been specially devised to simulate real investment decisions involving a manufacturing project which develops in a realistic way. This game incorporates problems of material corrosion, various production and sales strategies, health regulation requirements and a host of other important issues.

57

4. *On the Search for New Manufacturing Opportunities*

'Marketing innovation is the purpose of marketing – to cause change before you become a victim of it. It is far better to plan and manage change and make it happen.'

Arnold Corbin

New products and/or processes for their manufacture are fundamental to the long-term health of any manufacturing firm. But preceding any decision to finance and develop the fruits of its own or others' inventiveness, it is important that each firm should first take stock of its own strengths and weaknesses to discern those features (that distinctiveness) which clearly sets it and its product apart from its rivals. Such a uniqueness, or lack thereof, is the key to how that firm should use its resources in the search for and development of new products and processes and the clue as to how it should formulate its R & D and marketing policies. Only when such ideas have been challenged and questioned should a firm then devise means for closing its inevitable profit gap.

The purpose of this chapter is to illustrate the importance of these strategic issues and the ways in which they influence, or should influence, the choice of a firm's portfolio of projects. We conclude this chapter by considering the types of criteria which are necessary for evaluating the merits of a new project, thereby making way for subsequent chapters, which deal exclusively with the economic merits of projects.

4.1 THE NEED FOR NEW PRODUCT STRATEGY

The product life-cycle concept not only applies to individual products and companies, but embraces complete industries, since they comprise the aggregation of the sales of individual firms and products. So there exist embryonic industries (such as those associated with robotics), growth industries (such as microprocessors and plastics), mature industries (such as steel and cement) and declining industries (such as cotton and wool). Figure 4.1.1 illustrates the relative positioning of several of these industries on a typical sigmoidal, life-cycle curve.

Because of the profit implications of the product life-cycle, it behoves each firm to consider carefully and regularly reappraise its marketing strategy according to its own performance and its perception of external events. Foremost in such considerations is the need to identify clearly the general field of business which it wants to pursue. Such a consideration has its direct military counterpart in that a field marshal has to decide the general arena of engagement, and, like its military analogue, such a decision affects and is affected by the firm's strengths and weaknesses, relative to those of its rivals, and the hostile or benign nature of the environment. Besides concern for the general arena of business, however, a firm must carefully select that

59

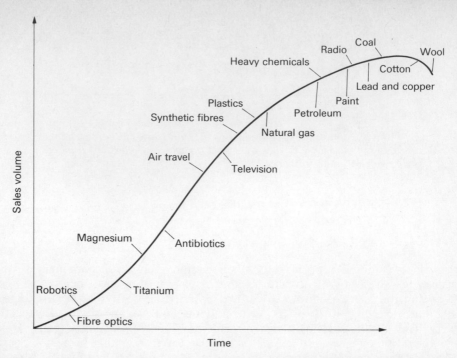

Figure 4.1.1   *A schematic presentation of the relative positions of several products in their life-cycles.*

market sector where its skills can be put to best advantage, and it must understand the demand factors behind growth or decay in differentiated segments of those market sectors. These causal factors include such considerations as

  (i) government spending on defence, education and transportation,
 (ii) fast growing markets associated with particular demographic and economic classes,
(iii) localized needs due to special geographical factors, such as new townships and large-scale projects, and
(iv) climatic effects.

   In other words there is a need for each firm to identify clearly the end use of its products by understanding the wants and needs of its prospective customers, and such a realization must constitute the bed-rock of any subsequent strategy which will incorporate all of those marketing elements shown in Figure 4.1.2.

   Quite clearly then, each firm should try to identify the current life-cycle phases of its existing products with a view to forecasting the likely duration of their individual profits. The outcome of these forecasts will determine the extent of the profit gap which has to be filled by the introduction of new and improved processes and products, and the retirement of old ones. It would be foolhardy to think that such forecasting is easy, because it is not: case after case has demonstrated that it is extremely difficult to estimate reliably how much growth potential a product really has. Metaphorically speaking, many companies have 'lost their shirts' backing so-called growth products, only to discover that industry in aggregate had too much production capacity for too little demand, thereby forcing all but the strongest companies to fail with substantial diseconomies to all concerned. Perhaps one of the most significant examples of this problem was that concerning the electronics

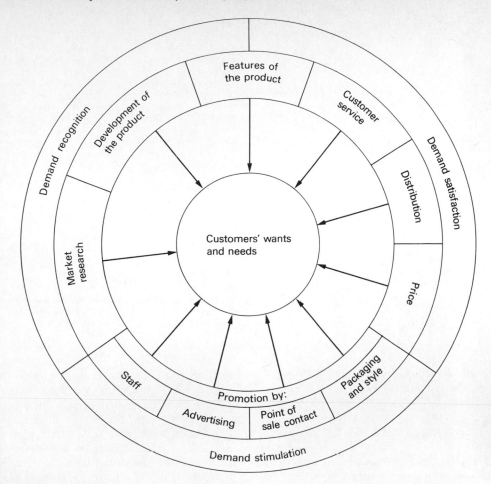

Figure 4.1.2   *The elements of a marketing strategy.*

industry during the early 1970s when many companies making television receivers, transistors and integrated circuits were forced to abandon or curtail production.

A firm has two ways of manipulating its product strategy – through innovative marketing and technology – with the array of possible options shown in Table 4.1.1.

Some of these options could be classified as short-term measures, involving better means for promoting, distributing and advertising existing products, including ways for realizing economies in manufacture. Others could be classed as long-term measures involving R & D expenditure, and possibly substantial investment in capital plant. It is not our intention to deal with short-term measures which dealt with in Part III. Instead, we shall deal with the long-term measures because they involve considerable diversification.

How a company should diversify is a moot point and there seems no one answer, since companies vary widely in their approach to the problem. Some companies accept any product so long as its financial prospects are good and will even commit themselves to mergers if what appears to be a good deal comes along, irrespective of the compatibility of their products. These firms are known as conglomerates: for them synergy means financial reinforcement. By stark contrast other companies adhere to one central theme which is either product, market or technology orientated. For them synergy means reinforcing know-how. The search for synergy is by

Table 4.1.1 *Marketing and technological options available to a firm*

Technological newness Market newness	No technological change	Technology improved to utilize more fully the firm's existing technological expertise	New technology to acquire corporate skills in new areas of tech- nology
No change to existing market	–	Reformulation to optimize the quality and design of existing products.	Replacement to develop new methods of produc- tion and fabrication, employing techniques not currently employed by the firm
Existing market strengthened to better exploit the product's and the marketing department's strengths	Remerchandising to increase sales of existing products to existing customers	Product improvement to improve the merchand- isability and utility of existing products	Extension to existing product lines to broaden the range of products currently offered using new technology
Absolutely new market designed to increase the range and numbers of customers	New use to discover new classes of customers to purchase the firm's existing products	Market extension to penetrate new market areas with a consider- ably modified product	Diversification to increase the number and classes of customers served by developing new technological expertise

no means an academic exercise. It can definitely constitute a strategic asset in a given competitive arena. For example, several of the smaller computer companies have captured a substantial share of the market because they have developed their skills in quite different ways from some of their 'giant' competitors. These vast differences in philosophy preclude a full treatment of such issues here, and are probably best dealt with using detailed and specific case histories. What is important, however, is to realize that product planning is at the very heart of business planning. It is a continuous process embracing the selection, development and implementation of the company's portfolio of products and it is the foundation of all the company's business. As such it is too important a matter to be delegated and must of necessity be one of the key areas of concern to the firm's chief executive, especially as its consequences penetrate the entire fabric of the company's functions involving marketing, R & D and product design, supply and production, costs at all stages, and personnel resources and finance. Some measure of this importance can be gleaned from the analyses of industrial market surveys of firms showing their reliance on relatively new products. A typical example of these analyses is shown in Figure 4.1.3.

The extent to which the various functions of a business are actually involved with product planning depends on its attitude to technical and marketing leadership and its propensity to taking risks. Two extreme situations can be identified: the desire to be market leader, and the desire to be the follower. Quite often the former entails using new and costly technology in the development of the product and/or in its method of production. This strategy involves high risks, but also the chance of high pay-offs, especially if the product or process gains market acceptance and can be protected by patent rights. Such a policy is obviously offensive. By contrast, the market follower is usually content to await some innovation and then endeavours to copy or imitate it. This strategy is obviously defensive, and usually entails less costly development, smaller risks, but smaller rewards too. Such extremes suggest that we need to consider the implications of alternative R & D strategies in greater depth if we are to understand the fuller economic implications of a product strategy.

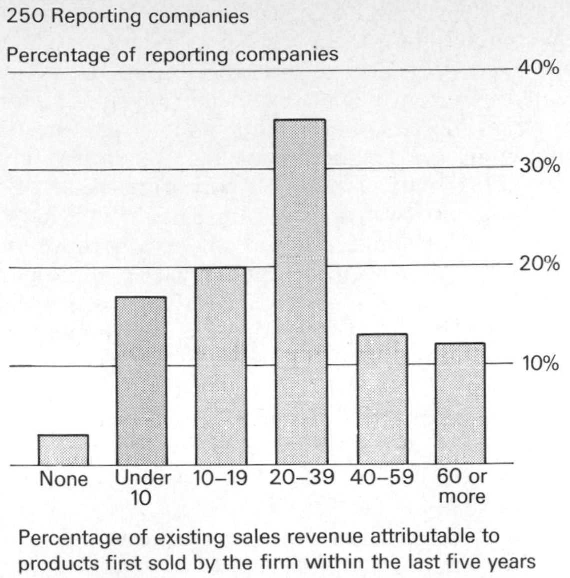
250 Reporting companies
Percentage of reporting companies
40%
30%
20%
10%
None
Under 10
10–19
20–39
40–59
60 or more
Percentage of existing sales revenue attributable to products first sold by the firm within the last five years

Figure 4.1.3 *Manufacturers' dependence on new products.*

4.2 THE NEED FOR AN R & D STRATEGY

Technological innovation is the process of using scientific and/or engineering discovery for commercial ends. It involves four major phases, usually but not always in the following sequence:

(i) the scientific search for knowledge,
(ii) the translation of that knowledge into some physical reality through engineering,
(iii) the entrepreneurial introduction of some product or process to society, and
(iv) the managerial optimization of its employment and its use of resources.

Each of these phases requires substantially different skills, knowledge and resources, making it essential for the whole process to be very carefully managed from beginning to end. To some extent the process of technological innovation can be likened to a chain with each of its phases represented by a link. Too weak a link, due to inadequate attention to detail possibly caused by an inadequate or poor distribution of resources, could cause the entire process to fail, whereas just sufficient strength in each and every link could provide success.

According to Bright (1968), the process of translating technical knowledge into economic reality can take up to ten years, and in some cases over 25 years. It usually involves the following steps:

(i) the search for ways of satisfying a definite need, a scientific suggestion, discovery or observation,
(ii) the development of a theory or a design concept,
(iii) laboratory verification of the theory or design concept,
(iv) laboratory demonstration of the intended application,
(v) field and/or full-scale trials,
(vi) commercial introduction, and
(vii) widespread adoption, possibly leading to proliferation.

Technological innovation can have both beneficial and detrimental effects. On the one hand, new opportunities for the profitable adaptation of technology are constantly available but need recognizing and developing to the point of satisfying customer desires. But this often means displacing inferior and/or more expensive products from the market-place. On the other hand, therefore, scientific advances are increasingly threatening the technological base of entire industries, as well as individual companies. This emphasizes the corporate need to keep abreast of relevant technology and devise appropriate strategies. But what constitutes a relevant technological threat is no longer easy to discern because such a threat often originates completely outside the normal supplier-user environment of a traditional industry making the significance of a discovery rather obscure. Perhaps one of the most poignant examples of the threat from outside was the very dramatic and swift change made by the Swiss watch making industry (which had traditional skills in mechanical engineering) into the production of electronic watches to counter the Japanese challenge to that industry. Similarly, traditional industries such as those involved with wood, cotton, wool and to some extent non-ferrous metals, have been under siege these last 20 years because of product innovations by the petro-chemical industry. Other famous examples such as the invention of xerography and Polaroid photography add weight to the evidence that it is not unusual for innovative threats to emanate outside a firm's traditional industry. One wonders what the effect will be on traditionally labour-intensive industries of microprocessor and robot technology in years to come!

How a firm should best devise its R & D strategy very much depends on the life-cycles of its products and those of its rivals, as well as on its own strengths and skills and the extent of its R & D capability. Short life-cycle products call for fast, responsive R & D work which can only be realized using multifunctional teams and an 'organic' form of management. Such products do not allow a firm to organize its R & D, product design, production engineering, manufacturing and marketing sequentially. Instead, these functions have to be developed concurrently – the accent being on speed and effectiveness, rather than on scientific and/or engineering rigour. Strength in this direction coupled with the desire to compete in markets with products of short duration would suggest that an offensive strategy was most appropriate. If, however, a firm's strengths lies in its ability to respond and adapt quickly to innovations in products with long life-cycles, then such a strength could equally) well be employed in a defensive role. By contrast, an offensive strategy involved with products of long duration justifies economy and efficiency rather than speed in the execution of innovations with the corporate functions being developed sequentially. These cases normally require significant R & D expenditure involving specialized R & D resources and long gestation periods.

Two other forms of strategy exist. One involves developing innovations to satisfy market gaps which remain unfilled by the market leaders, either because they have not been recognized or because they are too small to warrant the leaders' consideration; such a strategy is often more beneficial than a head-on confrontation with the market leader, as many computer companies have discovered in their dealings with IBM. Similar gaps in the product range of major American aircraft manufacturers have been successfully exploited by small European companies, whereas the larger companies, which have attempted to mount a direct challenge without the strength of a large home market, have failed. Another form of strategy involves developing a technology which cannot be exploited by the market leader without prejudicing its sales. Such a strategy only applies in saturated or slowly growing markets. However, it can yield handsome returns to the innovators, as the manufacturers of stainless steel razor blades and long-life electric light bulbs discovered to the cost of their major competitors.

In reality many multi-product companies develop a mixture of research strategies to meet the needs of their product range. Furthermore, cognizant of the fact that many existing technologies only provide diminishing returns to their use, they like to develop more than just a passing acquaintance with most new technologies so they can be in a position to develop them rapidly when the occasion permits.

4.3 CAPABILITY ANALYSIS

One of the most important tasks concerned with formulating any strategy is to assess what sets that firm apart from its rivals – what constitutes its distinctive competence? The preservation and possibly the enhancement of this distinctive 'something' is the clue as to how the firm should invest its money. For example, if it has a good reputation for solving technical problems then investment in research and marketing would be called for. If its reputation comes from speedy product delivery, then perhaps more flexible production and more exacting inventory control might be the key to its strategic success. Such a self-analysis is most important because the identification of a technological opportunity does not necessarily imply there is sufficient capacity or capability in the firm for its successful realization. Instead, it is possible that the firm's technological competence might have eroded due to the relentless march of industrial innovation unless, of course, proper recruiting, retraining and redeployment plans had been implemented.

Some of the most important factors which need to be considered when appraising a firm's R & D strengths are:

(i) the size of its R & D department and the capability of its personnel,
(ii) those technologies in which it has definite proven expertise,
(iii) the extent to which it is used to working at the frontiers of technology,
(iv) its past performance as measured by its creation of new products and processes which have been implemented,
(v) the emphasis which it usually places on research as opposed to development,
(vi) the typical length of the firm's product life-cycles and their usual R & D gestation periods, and
(vii) the relative strength of the R & D department to the firm's other functions and their compatibility.

Quite clearly this last point involves organizational matters which have a fundamental bearing on the type of strategy a company might successfully pursue. For example strength in R & D could compensate for weaknesses in production making possible an offensive strategy, whereas the converse might suggest that a defensive strategy is more appropriate. Ansoff and Stewart (1967) have studied these matters in detail and have proposed a systematic means for analysing the technological capability profile of a firm based on five criteria similar in many respects to those listed above.

One might be excused for thinking that the smaller a firm the greater its reliance on a defensive innovative strategy. Published evidence suggests that this is not so. For example, Jewkes (1958) and Cooper (1966) found that it is possible for a small firm to pursue an offensive policy even in markets dominated by a few large manufacturers. The most important reason for this involves behavioural factors, innovative success being closely allied with the entrepreneurial skills of the executive who is identified as the product or process champion. Many of the revolutionary innovations of the last few decades have come from smaller companies, such as Texas Instruments, Polaroid and Xerox.

Besides in house skills, each firm has to appraise its ability to capitalize on know-how and expertise which are readily available in the market-place, either through hiring consultants and/or licensing technology. Such a strategy is known as an absorptive strategy and, if properly pursued and executed, can be a very profitable way of circumventing known deficiencies in a firm's capability, and provides that necessary respite to rectify those deficiencies. It must be clearly recognized that internal investment in R & D and technological innovation are not necessarily the same thing, because little corporate benefit would result from developing some technology internally which could be more cheaply purchased elsewhere. With this in mind, it must be realized that the invented-here syndrome is often tantamount to corporate myopia, so a policy of in-house R & D expenditure must always be challenged. Perhaps the most successful application of an absorptive strategy was that pursued by Japan throughout the 1950s and 1960s. Mueller (1964) illustrates the wisdom of using other firms' R & D results by his analysis of du Pont's innovative strategy between 1920 and 1950. He discovered that only 40 per cent of its most important products, approximately 45 per cent of its sales revenue, were based on inventions by du Pont's scientists and engineers. This experience shows that a proper appraisal of a firm's capabilities is very important, since licensing can be used very effectively.

4.4 THE MANAGEMENT OF TECHNOLOGICAL INNOVATION

Technological expertise is one of the key assets which a company possesses, but it is the manner in which this expertise is directed and developed to meet market requirements which determines whether or not the company will continue profitably. Any technological progress made by a company only assumes commercial significance when it results in the offering of products to the market. To this end, therefore, the greater part of an organization's R & D spending must be objectively orientated. The Micawber attitude of 'waiting to see what turns up' must not be permitted, though a certain proportion of background and exploratory research is essential to maintain a healthy R & D function. It must also be recognized that serendipity (the faculty of making fortunate but unexpected discoveries by accident) definitely plays a part in technological innovation, but no company can afford to embark on a costly research programme in the hope that something will be found. Instead, an R & D department must be sensitive to, or made aware of, changing product demands in the market-place, and it is essential that the firm's uniquely differentiated skills should be directed towards the continued improvement of the business and the achievement of its market objective.

One of the major tasks for the management of any firm, therefore, is the purposeful search for lucrative ideas to produce existing products more economically and create new ones. Many disparate sources of information which might contain the germ of a new product or process idea are available. Some will originate outside the firm, for example from trade journals, customer contacts, scientific seminars and news events. Others are internally generated by laboratory discoveries and suggestion schemes, or they result from brain-storming sessions purposefully designed to extract and tap the creative skills of people associated with the firm. Irrespective of its sources, however, it is essential to a firm's survival that it develops a catalogue of good (if not excellent) ideas for its future business. Exactly how it should go about developing this catalogue is a very complex matter, but one thing must always be appreciated: the skills needed for invention and innovation are delicate and need to be fostered carefully. They require managing in a way which is distinctly different

Table 4.4.1 *Screening factor check list*

A *Corporate objectives and strategy* 1 Compatibility with existing strategy and-long range plan. 2 Does potential warrant a change in current strategy? 3 Company image. 4 Effects of synergy. **B** *Research and development* 1 Consistency with existing R & D strategy. 2 Does potential warrant a change in R & D strategy? 3 Can it be undertaken internally? 4 Would it be better to buy the technological know-how? 5 What is the chance of technical success? 6 Rate of technological change. 7 Scope for selling technology. 8 Effect on other projects. 9 Time and cost to develop. **C** *Marketing* 1 Potential market size. 2 Potential market share. 3 Pricing policy and customer acceptance. 4 Estimated product life. 5 Effect on existing product lines. 6 Compatibility with existing channels of distribution, promotion and advertising. 7 Difficulty to copy. 8 Export potential. 9 Stability during economic depression. 10 Seasonality and the counter-cyclic effect of other products. 11 Possibility of captive market: effect of long-term contracts. 12 Useful by-products. 13 Scope for further development. 14 Competitive reaction. 15 Proximity to markets. 16 Probability of commercial success. 17 Marketing costs. **D** *Legal* 1 Patentability. 2 Chance of patent infringement. 3 Licence position. 4 Territorial franchise. 5 Marketing agreements. 6 Product liability problems.	**E** *Production* 1 Utilization of spare capacity. 2 Better utilization of machinery. 3 Familiarity of machines, plants and processes. 4 Familiarity with techniques and materials. 5 New plant or process needed, and time to institute these. 6 Availability of skills. 7 Size, type and nature of product. 8 Safety implications of production. 9 Waste and scrap disposal. 10 Environmental and noise pollution. 11 Probability of production success. 12 Production costs. **F** *Design* 1 Appearance of product. 2 Standards of measurement and tolerances. 3 Component rationalization. 4 Quality, reliability and maintainability. 5 Safety aspects of using product. 6 Climatic effects on product performance. 7 Cost of design and life-cycle costs of ownership. **G** *Supply* 1 Security and diversity of supply. 2 Internal availability of components. 3 Stock-handling problems. 4 Transport access. 5 Proximity to supply. **H** *Financial* 1 Fixed capital requirements. 2 Working capital requirements. 3 Availability and method of finance. 4 Effects on other projects. 5 Potential cash flow. 6 Adequate return on investment. 7 Tax implications. 8 Time to break even. 9 Probability of success. 10 Other risks involved. 11 Dividend implications.

from that required for the everyday control of a firm. Business research shows that firms should develop and show more interest and method in their searching for technological opportunities and they should treat with respect ideas which appear to be generated outside so-called rational sources, especially those ideas which are generated by people who may have little in the way of conventional technical credibility, because the productivity of one excellent idea can be huge relative to that of a good idea. Knowing how to stimulate human inventiveness is a specialist subject which is properly covered by the writings of De Bono (1967) and Gordon (1961).

Their publications are recommended to all those seeking better ways of developing new product and process opportunities.

Invariably the first statement of a new idea is primitive, and needs refining into a specific statement of the opportunity or threat facing the firm before alternative means for its resolution can be assessed and compared. In the initial phases of a project, it is quite likely that a crude screening study using the following broad-based criteria would be sufficient to expose the intrinsic strengths and weaknesses of each alternative:

(i) Is the concept illogical? Does it violate common sense or the principles of scientific and technological logic?

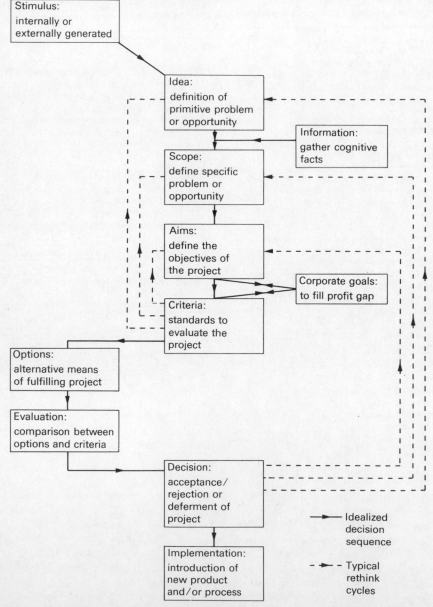

Figure 4.4.1 *A schematic representation of the phases of an idea for a new project.*

(ii) Is the solution inferior to other solutions or to some other method which has already been tried?

(iii) Does the idea involve too great an extension beyond known scientific and/or technical knowledge and the firm's existing capability?

(iv) Is the suggestion safe, legal and ethical?

Numerous ideas for new products and processes will fail to pass these preliminary tests, but those which survive then have to be submitted to a much more exacting analysis using some, if not all, of the criteria listed in Table 4.4.1.

It will be noticed that several of these criteria are qualitative in nature, some involve points of strategy, whereas others suggest the need for quantitative analysis using known techniques for the economic appraisal of alternatives and the comparison of their economic value against specific and unambiguous standards. Pressures of space, coupled with the need to develop the major thrust of this book, have prevented us from dealing thoroughly with the former criteria, but we hope we have dealt with them in sufficient depth for the reader to appreciate the complexity of the decision-making process, and interpret the remainder of this book in a realistic way. Our aim now is to develop economic methods for evaluating new products and/or process opportunities in depth, mindful of the fact that such criteria and evaluation schemes are not an end in themselves, but only links in the inevitable chain between the creation of a good idea and its realization of adequate and timely profits. Figure 4.4.1 is only one way of illustrating the phases of an idea for a new corporate project from its inception to its ultimate implementation.

4.5 SUMMARY

Our reason for incorporating this descriptive chapter here is to demonstrate that decisions of economic choice, especially those involved with manufacturing, cannot be taken in isolation of a firm's overall strategy if its objectives are to be realized and the firm's security is to be enduring. Instead, each economic decision should ideally take cognizance of the firm's overall strategy since it is only by these means that a firm can reinforce that distinctiveness which clearly differentiates its performance and its products from those of its competitors. Uppermost amongst these strategic considerations must be concern for the firm's product and R & D strategies since they often dictate its competitiveness. However, grandiose strategies are of little avail if a firm does not possess the capability for their realization, so a thorough self-appraisal of the firm's strengths and weaknesses is critical to the formulation of any reasonable strategy.

Once sensible product and R & D strategies have been devised, a major task confronting management is to develop a catalogue of projects which have the potential to fill the firm's profit gap requirements. This requires a creative but purposeful search for new manufacturing opportunities which then have to be appraised using a variety of criteria, which include the criteria developed in the next two chapters.

4.6 BIBLIOGRAPHY

General texts

Ansoff, H. I., *Corporate Strategy*, McGraw-Hill, 1965. This author is the father figure of the formalized approach to corporate and strategic planning and his views are most relevant to this chapter.

Bright, J. R. (Ed.), *Technological Forecasting for Industry and Government*, Prentice-Hall, 1968. This book is recognized as one of the more fundamental texts in the area of technological forecasting and product planning.

Wills, G., Hayhurst, R. and Midgley, D., *Creating and Marketing New Products*, Crosby Lockwood, 1973. This is an excellent introductory book to the problems involved with developing a new product strategy and new product planning.

Specific texts

Ansoff, H. I. and Stewart, J. M., 'Strategies for technology-based business', *Harvard Business Review*, November/December 1967.

Cooper, A. C., 'Small companies can pioneer new products', *Harvard Business Review*, September/October 1966.

de Bono, E., *The Use of Lateral Thinking*, Jonathan Cape, 1967.

Gordon, W. J. J., *Synectics*, Harper & Row, 1961.

Jewkes, J., Sawers, D. and Stillerman, R., *The Sources of Invention*, St Martin's Press, 1958.

Mueller, W. F., 'Origins of du Pont's major innovations 1930–50', in *Research Development and Technological Innovation* (ed.) J. R. Bright, Irwin, 1964.

Tiles, S., *Making Strategy Explicit–A Special Commentary*, Boston Consulting Group, 1966.

5. The Choice of Investment Appraisal Criterion

'To this day many of our comrades still do not understand that they must attend to the quantitative aspects of things – the basic statistics. They have no figures in their heads, and, as a result, cannot help making mistakes.'

Mao Tse Tung, *The Little Red Book*, 1950

From the argument of the previous chapters we realize that eventually most companies need to invest in new, more productive assets if they wish to survive and prosper. The vital question which we address in this chapter therefore is: How does one evaluate the value of investment opportunities available to a firm? Such a question is at the very heart of the management discipline known as capital budgeting. This basic field of decision making is one of the most difficult, most recurrent, and most controversial of management areas. It is also an area where there is tremendous scope for basic improvements in company operations and policies. Its difficulty lies in the fact that all investment decisions are made on the basis of future benefits which need predicting, sometimes for many years ahead, thereby involving uncertainty and risk. Investment in substantial fixed assets, therefore, carries the risk that they may not realize the benefits for which they are intended, that their capital may not be recoverable on their premature liquidation, and the company's long-term strategy may, as a result, be inadequate to meet its profit needs. The recurrence of the capital budgeting problem is, of course, in the very nature of company business – new products, processes and plants have to be invented, appraised and selected *continually* to maintain the economic health of a firm.

The kernel of good investment management is the measure of the investment worth of a project, but to achieve this we need some standard – preferably some cardinal standard – to help us decide which investment proposals to select and reject. This is sometimes called a yardstick, others call it a criterion. Much of the reason for the controversy surrounding capital budgeting results from the fact that several different ways exist for measuring the economic worth of an investment proposal and these can lead to contradictory decisions. Such a controversy will unfold in this and subsequent chapters but will not be fully resolved because fundamental management research has yet to understand properly the total implications of the investment decision. Nevertheless, we shall formulate some rules and principles which can be followed for most practical purposes.

The basic requirement of any capital appraisal criterion is that it should help to

(i) *predict* the economic consequences of alternative projects or courses of action,
(ii) *evaluate* and compare the desirability of the outcomes predicted for each alternative, and
(iii) *select* the preferred course of action.

71

Furthermore, to be readily acceptable to managers such a criterion should:

(i) summarize all the estimates relating to a project to give a single figure which measures its desirability,
(ii) be versatile and capable of application to all types of project,
(iii) be simple to calculate,
(iv) be easily adapted to show the effect of uncertainties in the estimates involved, and
(v) be easy to understand and interpret.

Several different criteria have been developed to achieve these ends and the main ones are surveyed below where the measures of desirability are given in units of either money, time or as a percentage rate of return.

5.1 THE PRINCIPLES OF COMPOUND INTEREST

In the following sections we need to understand the basics of compound interest. To help in this matter, we use a convention which assumes that sums of money (cash flows) occur at discrete end-of-year moments. According to this convention, a future cash flow occurring 't' years hence, is represented by the symbol F_t and an initial cash flow – it could be money invested in a project – is denoted P_0. Here the suffix '0' suggests that the sum of money is realized at the end of Year '0', which is identical to 'the beginning of Year 1'. Although such a convention might at first appear somewhat strange, it will help unravel some of the complexities associated with capital budgeting problems.

It is well known and understood that 100 munits invested for one year at an interest rate of 10 per cent per annum yield 10 munits of interest after one year, thereby increasing the original capital sum to 110 munits. Furthermore, if the 110 munits are reinvested for a further year then an extra 11 munits of interest are earned providing a final total cash sum of 121 munits. Such is the principle of compound interest. This relationship can be represented algebraically as follows.

Let P_0 = the initial value of a sum of money, F_t = the future value of P_0, $100r$ = the investment interest rate (per cent per annum), I_t = the interest accruing during some year 't', t = the end of a particular year such that $t = 0, 1, 2, 3 \ldots$ For interest gained during the first year of an investment we therefore have

$$I_1 = P_0 r$$

and

$$F_1 = P_0 + I_1 = P_0 + P_0 r = P_0(1+r)$$

For interest gained during the second year of an investment we therefore have

$$I_2 = F_1 r = P_0(1+r)r$$

and

$$F_2 = F_1 + I_2 = P_0(1+r) + P_0(1+r)r = P_0(1+r)^2$$

If we were to continue this exercise we would find that

$$F_3 = P_0(1+r)^3$$

$$F_4 = P_0(1+r)^4$$

and the general equation for such an investment would be given by

$$F_t = P_0(1+r)^t \tag{5.1.1}$$

Any reader unacquainted with this formula is recommended to use the following values

$$P_0 = 100 \quad \text{and} \quad r = 0.10$$

to check the validity of this equation against the commonsense results expounded at the outset of this section. We shall need to discuss the implications of the time convention underlying this formula later, but for the while we shall use it for mortgage and discount problems in the next two sections.

5.2   INVESTMENT ON A MORTGAGE BASIS

Most adults are well aware of the details involved with buying a house using a mortgage. These involve borrowing money from a financial institution, such as a bank, an insurance company, a friendly association or a building society, and repaying the loan and the interest on a prescribed basis. Normally the lending company requires some collateral, such as the title deeds of the property, in case the borrower defaults on the repayments. In times of steady interest rates, the annual repayments are constant, and are known as annuities.

The following example highlights the principles involved in this technique. If we borrow 1000 munits to finance a project which offers an end-of-year income of 615 munits for two years, we can afford to pay interest at the rate of 15 per cent per annum on the outstanding debt, and repay the interest and loan on the basis shown by Table 5.2.1. Here we see that interest charges amounting to 150 munits arise at the end of the first year, making the total debt 1150 munits. With our income, we can repay 615 munits leaving a debt of 535 munits to be settled during the next year. However, during the second year, this debt accumulates further interest of approximately 80 munits thereby requiring a total debt of 615 munits to be paid off by our second year's income, at the end of the second year.

According to this example, an interest rate of 15 per cent per annum would be the *maximum possible* rate of interest we could afford to pay to redeem the loan by the end of the project's life. In other words this interest rate would just allow the project to break even financially by the end of the second year, providing neither a surplus nor a deficit. This notion of an interest rate which just permits a break even on a project is central to a capital budgeting concept which we shall develop later. Had we *not* known the value of this break even interest rate in advance of our sums, then we could have calculated it by a process of trial and error. For example, had we guessed interest rates of 10 and 20 per cent per annum then the former would have resulted in a surplus, a profit of 81.5 munits, whereas the latter would have created a deficit, a loss of 87 munits, by the end of the second year. The interested reader might like to confirm these two results by reworking the sums of Table 5.2.1, but at interest rates of 10 and 20 per cent per annum instead. Consequently, our best estimate of the true break even interest rate would have fallen half way between 10 and 20 per cent at 15 per cent coinciding with the true break even rate. Unfortunately, this procedure is somewhat cumbersome: it involves too many calculations

Table 5.2.1   *Repaying a debt on a mortgage basis*

Year	Debt outstanding at beginning of year	Interest at 15 per cent per annum	Total end of year debt	End of year repayment
1	1000	150	1150	615
2	535	80	615	615

for each estimate of the break even interest rate, and although this causes few problems with our simple example, nevertheless it could create a substantial problem if we had to employ this technique for a project of long duration. To overcome this computational problem we employ another technique known as 'discounting'.

5.3   THE DISCOUNTING TECHNIQUE

Equation 5.1.1 can be rewritten in the following form

$$P_0 = \frac{F_t}{(1+r)^t}$$

or as

$$P_0 = F_t(1+r)^{-t} \tag{5.3.1}$$

where the factor $(1+r)^{-t}$ is known as the 'discount factor' for which comprehensive tables of values are provided in Appendix G. If we experiment with this equation for a while, we note that a cash flow of 110 munits, realized one year hence when the annual interest rate is 10 per cent per annum provides a value P_0 equal to 100 munits, that is

$$P_0 = \frac{110}{(1+0.1)} = \frac{110}{1.1} = 100$$

or alternatively

$$P_0 = 110(1+0.1)^{-1} = 110 \times 0.9091 = 100$$

Expressed verbally, these two relationships mean that a future cash flow of 110 munits received one year hence is equivalent to 100 munits *now*, at the beginning of the investment project, if the going interest rate is 10 per cent per annum. It will be realized that this equivalence concept makes no allowance for uncertainty and its attendant risk, it being assumed that the future cash flows of a project will definitely occur. Quite obviously we shall have to devise a means for dealing with problems of risk, and this is discussed in Chapter 9. However, equation 5.3.1 allows us to commute any *future* cash flow into its *present* equivalent value.

The second point to notice is that the discount factor $(1+0.1)^{-1}$ equals 0.9091. This means that a cash flow of 1 munit realized one year hence, when the interest rate is 10 per cent per annum, is equivalent to 0.9091 munits at the beginning of the investment project. If we assume that the beginning of such a project is the present moment, then it would seem reasonable to address the discount factor $(1+r)^{-t}$ as 'The Present Value of 1', as suggested by the alternative title given to its values in Appendix G. Discount factors are also symbolized by the following relationship:

$$P/F_{r,t}$$

where P denotes the present value of a future cash flow F of 1 munit realized t years hence when the appropriate discount interest rate is $100r$ per cent per annum. It therefore follows that

$$P/F_{r,t} = 0.9091, \quad \text{when } r = 0.1 \text{ and } t = 1.$$

This symbolic notation also appears in the heading given to the discount factors of Appendix G.

Using the relationship provided by equation 5.3.1 we can now reformulate our

Table 5.3.1 *Table 5.2.1 reworked using discount factors*

Year	A Actual cash flow (F_t)	B Discount factor @ 15% pa	C Present values (P_0) or discounted cash flows (DCF)
0	−1000	×1.000	=−1000
1	615	0.8696	535
2	615	0.7561	465
Net cumulative discounted cash flow or net present value (NPV)			= 0

previous example given by Table 5.2.1. The results are shown in Table 5.3.1 which incorporates several special features. First, it should be noted that the sum of 1000 munits invested in our hypothetical project is considered a cash outflow and, according to the convention which we adopt, it is allocated a negative sign. Similarly, the earnings from our project are considered cash inflows and allocated positive signs. Next, it must be realized that the multiplication of the numbers in columns A and B provide the results of column C. (Note: the multiplication sign (×) and the equals sign (=) will *not* feature in subsequent tables of results.) Column C is provided with two alternative headings. The former 'present values' results from the equivalence concept previously mentioned, whereas the latter, 'discounted cash flows', results from discounting the future cash flows by multiplying them by their appropriate discount factors. This second title is abbreviated to DCF in everyday management jargon, giving rise to the name DCF techniques which describes the methods employed here and elsewhere throughout this book. The net effect of the sums of column C is shown at the base of Table 5.3.1 with two alternative titles, the the net present value (NPV) being the title preferred in business jargon. The fact that the resultant NPV equals zero means that, measured in present value terms, the project breaks even, producing neither a surplus nor a deficit, confirming that the interest rate of 15 per cent per annum is the maximum rate of interest one could afford to pay on the borrowed capital. In essence, therefore, the calculations shown in Table 5.3.1 achieve the same result as Table 5.2.1 but with less computation, thereby making this discounting technique computationally more efficient. It is primarily for this reason that we employ the discounting technique throughout the remainder of this book as a means for understanding the life-cycle economics of physical assets.

If we rework the results of Table 5.3.1 at interest rates of 10 and 20 per cent per annum we discover that the corresponding NPVs are (plus) 67.33 and (minus) 60.46 munits respectively. How do these statistics relate to their previous mortgage-based counterparts? This interrelationship is shown in Table 5.3.2 where it can be seen that the two NPVs are the present equivalent values of the corresponding mortgage-based cash surplus and deficit. Net present values are therefore nothing

Table 5.3.2 *Relationship between the future cash surplus and deficit and their corresponding NPVs, for our example*

Interest rate 100r (% pa)	NPV (munits)	Compound interest factor $(1+r)^2$	Future cash surplus/deficit (as per Section 5.2)
10	+67.33	×1.21	= +81.5
20	−60.46	×1.44	= −87

more than the net wealth-creating abilities of a project but translated through time back to some arbitrary moment which we call the present. Hence if we predict the likely future cash flows of some new project then its corresponding NPV, at some prescribed interest rate, is a measure of that project's wealth (cash) generating ability.

5.4 THE DISCOUNTED CASH FLOW RATE OF RETURN INVESTMENT (DCFRR)

For a moment let us forget our previous mortgage sums and concentrate on using the discounting technique, which we now know to be nothing more than the principles of compound interest in disguise! Let us imagine some hypothetical investment project has the following end of year cash flows, which are wholly and exclusively attributable to that project:

Year	0	1	2	3	4
Cash flow	5000	2000	4000	1223	0

The NPVs for this project at various interest rates are shown in Table 5.4.1 which exhibits the following features:

(i) when the discount interest rate is zero, each discount factor is unity irrespective of the timing of the cash flow because:

$$(1+0)^{-t} = 1^{-t} = 1.000$$

(ii) as the discount interest rate increases so the corresponding discount factors decrease,

(iii) the further away in time that a cash flow arises, the less valuable it becomes because the discount factor, at a given interest rate, diminishes rapidly with time thereby demonstrating the effect of the time value of money.

(iv) irrespective of the discount interest rate, the discount factor at the end of Year 0 is always unity because $(1+r)^{-0} = 1.000$ by mathematical definition,

(v) as the discount interest rate increases, so the NPVs of our hypothetical project diminish, becoming negative and ultimately approaching the value of the project's initial cash flow.

The NPV results of Table 5.4.1 are plotted in Figure 5.4.1, where it can be seen that the curve intersects the abscissor at an interest rate of 22 per cent per annum. Again the reader is recommended to confirm this point by reworking the NPV calculations of Table 5.4.1 using a discount interest rate of 22 per cent per annum, when it will be found that the NPV is approximately zero. What interpretation can we place on this 22 per cent interest rate other than the fact that it makes the NPV equal zero? From our previous analysis we know that it is the maximum rate of interest one could afford to pay on the 5000 munits borrowed to finance the project so that it would break even. In other words if we *had* to pay an interest rate of 22 per cent per annum we would be no better nor worse off as a result of implementing this project. This interest rate is known by a variety of names. In academic circles it is called the internal rate of return (IRR). In financial circles it is known as the yield, while in most manufacturing business circles it is known as the discounted cash flow rate of return on investment (DCFRR). (This is sometimes abbreviated to DCF but we shall not do so since DCF is used to denote 'discounted cash flow' in this book.) Another way of interpreting the significance of the DCFRR is illustrated in Table 5.4.2 where we notice that the quotient of the interest payment

Table 5.4.1 *Net present values (NPV) at various interest rates for example 5.4*

| | | Interest rate (% pa) | | | | | | | | | | | | | | |
| | | 0 | | 5 | | 10 | | 15 | | 20 | | 25 | | 30 | | ∞ | |
Year	End of year cash flow	Discount factor	DCF	Discount factor	DCF	Discount factor	DCF	Discount factor	DCF	Discount factor	DCF	Discount factor	DCF	Discount factor	DCF	Discount factor	DCF
0	-5000	1.000	-5000	1.000	-5000	1.000	-5000	1.000	-5000	1.000	-5000	1.000	-5000	1.000	-5000	1.000	-5000
1	2000	1.000	2000	0.9524	1905	0.9091	1818	0.8696	1739	0.8333	1667	0.8000	1600	0.7692	1538	0	0
2	4000	1.000	4000	0.9070	3628	0.8264	3306	0.7561	3024	0.6944	2778	0.6400	2560	0.5917	2367	0	0
3	1223	1.000	1223	0.8638	1056	0.7513	919	0.6575	804	0.5787	708	0.5120	626	0.4552	557	0	0
NPV			2223		1589		1043		567		153		-214		-538		-5000

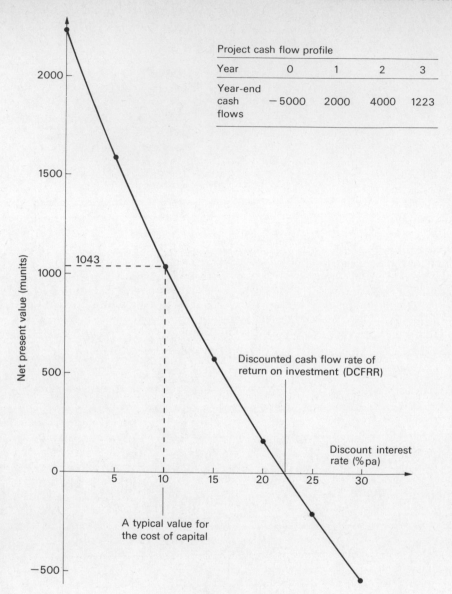

Project cash flow profile				
Year	0	1	2	3
Year-end cash flows	−5000	2000	4000	1223

Figure 5.4.1 *The relationship between the net present value and the discount interest rate.*

Table 5.4.2 *An alternative interpretation of the DCFRR*

Year	Year end cash inflow	Year end payments to reduce the outstanding investment	as interest (A)	Capital outstanding at the beginning of each year (B)	DCFRR = (A)/(B)×100%
1	2000	900	1100	5000	22
2	4000	3098	902	4100	22
3	1223	1002	221	1002	22
4	0	0	0	0	

Table 5.4.3 *Alternative investment in a bank at an interest rate of 22 per cent per annum*

Year	Investment capital	Interest @ 22%	Capital plus interest	End of year withdrawals
0	5000	1100	6100	2000
1	4100	902	5002	4000
2	1002	221	1223	1223
3	0	0	0	0

and the capital outstanding at the beginning of each year constantly equates to 22 per cent per annum showing how the DCFRR is really the rate of interest on the capital *outstanding* in a project at any given moment in time. We can enlarge our understanding of the DCFRR if we consider investment of the initial 5000 munits of capital in a bank, for example, instead of in some hypothetical manufacturing project. Table 5.4.3 demonstrates that if the corresponding deposit interest rate was 22 per cent per annum then end of year withdrawals of 2000, 4000 and 1223 munits could be released from such a deposit account in just the same way as from our hypothetical manufacturing project. This realization is hardly surprising however since it must be remembered that the mortgage principle with its compound interest implications is at the root of all our calculations. In many, but not all* circumstances, the DCFRR is therefore analogous to the interest rate one could obtain from normal investment in a bank or, for that matter, any other investment opportunity.

5.5 APPRAISING THE ECONOMIC MERITS OF PROJECTS USING NPV AND DCFRR CRITERIA

We now have a means of measuring the investment worth of a capital project. If we assume that the cost of capital (that is the interest rate we are obliged to pay on the money invested in our project) is 10 per cent per annum and the cash flows of 2000, 4000 and 1223 will definitely occur according to the schedule postulated by Table 5.4.1, then our hypothetical project could be *said* to generate an equivalent surplus of 1043 munits now, at the outset of our decision to finance such a venture. It would therefore appear worthwhile to finance this project on the basis of its having a positive NPV. Similarly, since the DCFRR for this project is greater than the cost of capital, its DCFRR also suggests that investment in such a project is worthwhile. In effect therefore we have developed two decision criteria, the NPV and the DCFRR and, for the moment at least, it appears that both provide consistent decision rules. In some cases, however, these criteria can give conflicting solutions as we shall discover later. Of course, several other factors would influence the decision to accept or reject such a project. Uppermost amongst these considerations would be one's attitude to risk, the availability of investment funds and, of course, competition for those funds by other worthwhile projects. In the course of the next few chapters we shall deal with all these matters. For the moment however we can formulate two equivalent decision rules:

(i) We should seriously consider funding an investment project if it promises to provide a sufficiently positive NPV at its cost of capital, to warrant the risks involved,

---

* The reason for this qualification will be explained in detail later. One qualification which should be made here is that the DCFRR does not assume that the proceeds from a project are necessarily reinvested at any particular interest rate.

(ii) We should likewise consider such a funding exercise if the project yields a DCFRR sufficiently greater than its cost of capital.

From the calculations given in Table 5.4.1 it will be realized that the NPV of a project is computed according to the relationship

$$\text{NPV}_T = C_0 + \frac{C_1}{(1+r)} + \frac{C_2}{(1+r)^2} + \frac{C_t}{(1+r)^t} + \frac{C_T}{(1+r)^T}$$

which can be rewritten in the following form

$$\text{NPV}_T = \sum_{t=0}^{T} \frac{C_t}{(1+r)^t} \qquad (5.5.1)$$

where NPV_T = net present value of a project over some expected economic life cycle time of T years; C_t = the net cash flow (either positive or negative) at the end of some year t, where $t = 0, 1, 2 \ldots T$; $\sum$ = 'the sum of', and $100r$ = discount interest rate (per cent per annum). It naturally follows that the DCFRR is that interest rate which applied to equation 5.5.1 makes the NPV equal to zero.

The economic appraisal of a prospective investment project using DCF techniques requires two types of information: forecast cash flows, and an assessment of the firm's cost of capital. We shall study the sources of this information in subsequent chapters. However it might be instructive here to consider what constitutes a cash flow. Most people have heard of costs, profits and revenues, but many will be unacquainted with the term cash flow. To understand this better it is appropriate to imagine a project having a wall built around its perimeter with a gateway. During the construction phase, the company would have to pay cash for the plant and machinery needed by the project so that anyone standing by the gate would see these flows of cash as outflows. Likewise, when the project is built and commissioned, he would register payments to suppliers, the tax authorities and employees as being cash outflows, because such payments would physically flow from the project, through that gateway. By contrast, payments by customers for goods and/or services received from the company would be registered as cash inflows. In effect, therefore, our use of the term cash flow suggests that we can *physically* measure the wealth-creating ability of a project, during its lifetime. Such a measure is not governed by any arbitrary accounting practice* but instead is based entirely on physics – the measurement of money. It is realized, of course, that not all modern-day transactions are conducted in cash. Some take the form of cheques, whilst others involve direct debiting and crediting by way of computer information services. Nevertheless, all these methods involve physical entities which can be directly related to the physical counting of the amount of money flowing into and away from an investment project at various moments in time.

The above ideas concerning the cash flows of a project are true if and only if the operations of that project are completely independent of the operations of other projects contained within a company. If, however, there should be some physical dependence between the operations of a prospective project and any other prospective or existing projects then our definition of what constitutes the cash flows of a new prospective project has to be modified as follows: 'The cash flows which are solely attributable to any investment proposal are the incremental changes to the firm's cash flow profile for which that project alone is responsible.'

---

* It is important to realize that accounting profits are not cash flows. Accounting measures the historical creation of wealth according to certain concepts and conventions which have evolved with time and experience. These matters are briefly dealt with in Appendix B.

For example, if a prospective project were to use a feedstock which was currently being sold as a company product earning a positive cash flow, then quite obviously the cash flow profile of the new project would have to take account of the fact that the sales of that product would diminish if the new project were built and operated. Unfortunately, one of the most common errors in investment decision making revolves around the wrong interpretation of this definition. To calculate the incremental changes to the firm's cash flow profile resulting exclusively from a project necessitates the prediction of the firm's cash flow profile as far into the future as the prospective project will last first *without* the new project (this is known as the base case) and then *with* the prospective project, the differences between these two projected cash flow profiles being that which is solely attributable to the new project. We shall have occasion to study this matter in greater detail later, by way of a case study.

Most capital investment projects of the type normally witnessed by the manufacturing industry have cash flow profiles similar to that shown in Figure 5.5.1 where:

(i) Curve 1 relates to the undiscounted net cash flows,
(ii) Curve 2 relates to the net cash flows but discounted at the project's cost of capital, and
(iii) Curve 3 relates to the net cash flows but discounted at the project's DCFRR.

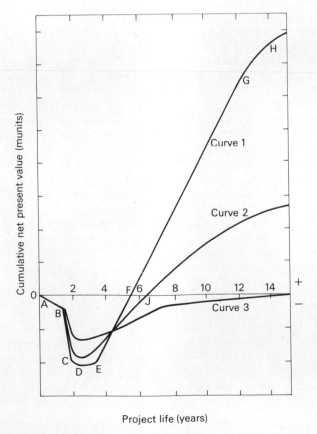

Figure 5.5.1 *Typical cash flow profiles for capital investment in manufacturing projects. AB = Preliminary expenditure; BC = capital investment; CDE = commissioning period; EFGH = profitable production.*

According to this diagram it will be noticed that:

(iv) point F denotes the time it takes the project to recoup its initial investment (this time is known as the payback time), and
(v) point J denotes the time it takes the discounted positive cash flows to equal the discounted negative cash flows; thereby deriving a position of break even, where the time is known as the discounted payback time.

Moreover it will be noticed that the cash flow profiles comprise initial negative cash flows followed *only* by positive cash flows. For any project adhering to these conditions the following definition of the DCFRR applies: The DCFRR is that interest rate which a project could just afford to pay on the debt outstanding in that project so that subsequent positive net cash flows would be just sufficient to pay the interest and the debt outstanding, permitting the project to finally break even.

The condition of break even described by this definition is illustrated by Curve 3 of Figure 5.5.1. Some projects possess cash flow profiles which differ from those shown above. Instead of a single DCFRR, they give rise to multiple DCF returns thereby violating our previous definition of the DCFRR. Because such cases are mathematically more complicated than the normal subject content of this book, they are confined to Appendix F. In these situations the more general definition of the DCFRR is 'the interest rate(s) which make(s) a project's NPV zero'. By contrast the definition of the NPV remains unaffected by such complexities and can be defined as follows: 'The NPV is the value of a project, yet unrealized. It is that value for which we would, under conditions of certainty, be willing to sell the project because, under such conditions, we would be indifferent between the NPV and the project's future cash flows. Because life is by no means certain, it follows that under conditions of uncertainty the NPV is that value for which we would *consider* selling the project. Lastly, of course, and more mechanically, the NPV is the net value of the project's discounted cash flows'.

The trial-and-error method for calculating the DCFRR has already been described. In the majority of real-life situations, this method involves discounting no more than 15 or 16 predicted cash flows taking perhaps 10–15 minutes to accomplish the exact value of the DCFRR. This task can be expedited using a computer specially programmed for this task, and it should be mentioned that electronic hand calculators are readily available for this purpose. If a trial-and-error method is necessary then it should be noted that several methods for quickly converging on the exact DCFRR solution are available in the literature. Two notable examples of such methods are by Wild (1978) and Holland (1974), and are given in the bibliography to this chapter.

5.6 DISCOUNTING ANNUITIES

It is conceivable that some investment projects *might* realize net cash inflows which are actually annuities. In other cases, however, especially during the embryonic stages of a project when there is a dearth of cost and marketing information, it might be necessary to assume that the subsequent cash flows to be realized by the prospective project approximate annuities. Under such conditions the net present value of a project realizing year end cash annuities of 'A' munits per year is given by the expression

$$NPV = \frac{A}{(1+r)} + \frac{A}{(1+r)^2} + \cdots \frac{A}{(1+r)^T} \tag{5.6.1}$$

Table 5.6.1 *NPV calculations for the example of Section 5.6*

Year	Year end cash flows	Conventional annual discounting technique		Alternative technique using the annuity method	
		Discount factor at 10% pa	DCF	Discount factor or present value of an annuity factor, at 10% pa	DCF
0	−5000	1.0000	−5000	−5000×1.000=	−5000
1	1000	0.9091	909.1		
2	1000	0.8264	826.4		
3	1000	0.7513	751.3		
4	1000	0.6830	683.0		
5	1000	0.6209	620.9	1000×6.1446 =	6144.6
6	1000	0.5645	564.5		
7	1000	0.5132	513.2		
8	1000	0.4665	466.5		
9	1000	0.4241	424.1		
10	1000	0.3856	385.6		
	NPV using the conventional discounting technique		1144.6	NPV using the annuity method	1144.6

Multiplying both sides of equation 5.6.1 by $(1+r)$ we get

$$NPV(1+r) = A + \frac{A}{(1+r)} + \cdots \frac{A}{(1+r)^{T-1}} \qquad (5.6.2)$$

and subtracting equation 5.6.1 from 5.6.2 we get

$$NPV = A\left[\frac{1-(1+r)^T}{r}\right] \qquad (5.6.3)$$

where the factor $\left[\dfrac{1-(1+r)^{-T}}{r}\right]$ is known as the 'present value of an annuity of 1' for which tables are provided in Appendix G. The significance of this factor is that it helps expedite discounting calculations when the cash flows are annuities, as the following example demonstrates.

Suppose a project costing 5000 munits realizes end of year net cash inflows of 1000 munits a year for 10 successive years commencing one year after the project is built. If we assume that the project can be built instantaneously, then the NPV calculations for this project are as shown in Table 5.6.1. This table shows how laborious is the conventional discounting technique when compared with its annuity counterpart, which simply involves looking up the present value of an annuity for 1 munit over a period of ten years at an interest rate of 10 per cent (which the reader should verify to be 6.1446), multiplying this factor by the actual annuity cash flow (which is 1000 munits per annum) and then subtracting from this value the present value of the discounted initial cash flows.

Later in this book, we shall discover that our ability to convert annuities into NPVs, and vice versa, will prove to be very useful, especially when we consider asset replacement problems in Part IV.

5.7 TWO SPECIAL CASES INVOLVING ANNUITIES

To interpret correctly some of the comments which are made later in Section 5.8 we need to investigate the economic merits of two special types of projects: those involving perpetual annuities and those whereby the project can be sold for its original purchase price.

Combining equations 5.6.3 and 5.5.1 we obtain the expression

$$NPV_T = -C_0 + A\left[\frac{1-(1+r)^{-T}}{r}\right]$$

where $C_0 =$ the initial investment in a project, and $A =$ its year end annuity cash flows over an anticipated economic life-time of T years. For the case of perpetual annuities, the value of the factor $[1-(1+r)^{-T}]/r$ becomes $1/r$, and the NPV equation becomes $NPV_T = -C_0 + A/r$. So the DCFRR is given by the following identity:

$$DCFRR = \frac{A}{C_0} \times 100\% \text{ pa.}$$

The same result is realized if a project initially costing C_0 munits, realizes year end annuity cash flows of A munits per annum throughout its economic life and is then sold for the same initial cost. In these circumstances the NPV will be given by

$$NPV_T = -C_0 + A\left[\frac{1-(1+r)^{-T}}{r}\right] + C_0(1+r)^{-T}$$

or

$$NPV_T = -C_0[1-(1+r)^{-T}] + \frac{A}{r}[1-(1+r)^{-T}]$$

At an interest rate equal to the project's DCFRR, when its NPV is zero, we would therefore discover that the DCFRR is again given by expression

$$DCFRR = \frac{A}{C_0} \times 100\% \text{ pa.}$$

It must be stressed however that these cases represent very unusual investment opportunities.

5.8 ALTERNATIVE MEANS OF MEASURING THE ECONOMIC WORTH OF PROSPECTIVE INVESTMENT PROJECTS

One might think that in this day of electronic computers and complex information retrieval systems the philosophy and techniques for measuring the economic worth of investment projects would have been developed, proven, universally accepted and formalized as standard procedures in most firms. Unfortunately, this is not so, as successive business reports, which are listed in the references to this chapter, have shown. The methods in use today are legion but seldom do any two, other than the DCFRR and NPV, yield consistent and meaningful results. Two methods in common use involve the payback time and the traditional accounting rate of return on capital (ROC) criteria.

The payback method

Although there is no universally approved definition of the payback time criterion, in its most plausible and scientific form it measures the time required to recoup the

Table 5.8.1 *An example of payback time calculations*

Year	Project cash flows A	B
0	−1000	−1000
1	200	500
2	300	300
3	500	200
4	0	200
Payback time	3 years	3 years
DCFRR (% pa)	0	9

cash invested in a project. In essence, therefore, it determines how long a project takes to achieve a cash break even and is thus a measure of liquidity* rather than economic efficiency. According to such a criterion, therefore, the two projects listed in Table 5.8.1 are equivalent. If a payback time of three years is acceptable, we would find ourselves indifferent in our choice between these two projects on the basis of their payback times. Looking at them on the basis of their *economic merits*, however, we find that Project B is preferable to Project A on three counts:

(i) it generates greater cash flows earlier during its life,
(ii) it provides a cash surplus, a profit, of 200 munits, and
(iii) the DCFRR for Project B approximates 9 per cent per annum, whereas that of Project A is zero.

From this trivial example we see that the payback time criterion does not measure up to the attributes of the ideal investment criterion, outlined at the beginning of this chapter, in that it suffers several major deficiencies:

(i) it is incapable of measuring the economic merits of a project and, as such, cannot differentiate between the economic merits of competing projects;
(ii) it does not cater for the time value of money; and
(iii) it completely ignores the economic value of the cash flows of a project which mature after the payback time.

Proponents who support the use of the payback time criterion as an investment decision making tool, argue that forecasting, by its very nature, is imprecise and the longer into the future one attempts to forecast, the less reliable forecasting becomes. Such a claim is undeniably true, but the payback criterion is too crude a tool to deal with problems of risk, especially as it completely ignores the existence of risk up to the payback time. They also advocate the use of this tool on the basis that many companies find that their liquidity is often a major constraint to their ability to finance lucrative projects and, as such, they claim that matters of liquidity predominate. Unfortunately they are very misguided in this claim. Although no firm can ignore problems of liquidity, there exist much more direct and less costly ways of resolving liquidity problems other than sacrificing profitable projects by allowing the payback time criterion to govern the selection of capital projects. It should also be realized that some projects incur substantial capital investments later in their lives and can exhibit more than one payback time, thereby confusing the use of this criterion as a decision-making tool.

To some extent (ii) can be countered if one uses the discounted cash flow payback

* In accounting jargon the term liquidity denotes the ability of a firm to keep sufficient of its assets either as cash or in a form readily convertible into cash, to meet any business eventuality, at short notice.

time instead of the more traditional payback time, as illustrated by points J and F in Figure 5.5.1. However, this still does not overcome the other major criticisms of this technique.

Finally, it should be noted that when the cash outflows all occur at the outset of a project and the subsequent cash inflows are forecasted as perpetual annuities, then the traditional payback time criterion becomes the mathematical reciprocal of the DCFRR under the very special conditions which were highlighted at the end of Section 5.7. In these circumstances the payback time is given by the following expression:

$$PBT = \frac{C_0}{A} = \frac{1}{DCFRR}$$

where PBT = payback time. However, it cannot be overemphasized that the conditions which make this relationship possible are rare.

The rate of return on capital method

One obstacle to the acceptance of sound, objective, decision-making criteria is the desire by many executives to evaluate investment projects in terms which are directly comparable to the accountant's way of evaluating the current performance of a company. To this end they employ what has become known and widely accepted as the accounting rate of return on capital (ROC) method which measures the profit of a project as a percentage of its capital cost, according to the relationship

$$ROC = \frac{annual\ profit}{capital\ cost} \times 100\%$$

Unfortunately protagonists of this method remain inconsistent in the way they define profit and capital cost. Some use the profit after tax, interest charges and depreciation, whereas others use different combinations of tax, interest charges and depreciation*. Furthermore, some advocate that only the first year's profit should be used, whereas others feel that it is fairer to judge a project by its average annual profit. Of course none is correct because each is quite arbitrary and there is little virtue in propounding a precise definition to maintain consistency if, in so doing, the resultant business decision is consistently *wrong*. If we rework the example given in Section 5.2 according to the sums of Table 5.8.2, we can get some idea of just how misleading this criterion can be. If for the moment we assume that the denominator in our sums should be 1000 munits and straight line depreciation is appropriate, then the resultant ROC works out at 11.5 per cent per annum. But we know the DCFRR for this project is 15 per cent per annum, and we also know that we can relate this 15 per cent rate to interest rates available in the financial market. So what does an ROC of 11.5 per cent mean?

The answer is 'Nothing, other than the fact that it is an arbitrary quotient'!† Any change to the numerator of this quotient, such as a change in depreciation policy, would alter the value of the resultant ROC statistic, as would any change to its denominator. For example, if we assumed a negligible scrap value for our hypothetical project we could reasonably argue that its average capital cost was 500 munits. Such a denominator would double our ROC statistic, demonstrating only too clearly that we were doing nothing other than 'playing with numbers'.

---

* The reader is also reminded that there exist many ways of depreciating an asset, each way being as valid as the next and each equally arbitrary. This point is dealt with in detail in Appendix B.

† Despite this criticism, ROC statistics are used in financial ratio analysis, as described in Appendix B.

Table 5.8.2 *An example of the return on capital (ROC) calculation*

Year	(A) Year end cash flow	(B) Depreciation (straight-line basis)	(C) = (A) − (B) Profit	$ROC = \dfrac{\text{annual profit} \times 100\% \text{ pa}}{\text{capital cost}}$ $= \dfrac{(C) \times 100\% \text{ pa}}{1000}$
1	615	500	115	11.5%
2	615	500	115	11.5%
		Initial capital cost = 1000 munits		

Several researchers have endeavoured to discover a direct relationship between the DCFRR attributes of new capital ventures and the resultant ROC statistics of a dynamic company, but have failed. One of the most comprehensive of these studies is that reported by Hutchinson (1971). Only when the highly improbable conditions highlighted at the end of Section 5.7 prevail is it possible to find a direct relationship between a project's DCFRR and its ROC.

In real-life situations, two other ways exist for justifying investment in new capital assets. These are qualitative not quantitative in nature, and belong to the must invest and high strategy syndromes of management. The former of these belongs to replacement problems which are discussed in Part IV. The rationale that one must invest is based on the premise that the failure of some machine, for example a pump, vehicle or lathe, can place the economic viability of an entire plant or factory in jeopardy, and that the return on investment in the replacement machine is obviously so high as not to warrant calculation. Undoubtedly, these situations do arise. The unfortunate deficiency with such a philosophy however is that it implies that top management has no alternative which, of course, is not so. Several alternative ways of overcoming such a breakdown might exist which are economically more efficient. These alternatives need to be appraised objectively, albeit quickly, when the predicament facing the firm demands haste. The other major weakness with the must replace philosophy is that, unwittingly, less senior managers can prolong the life of existing assets which no longer form a major part of the company's long-term strategy. The blind acceptance of such a philosophy therefore has more sinister undertones; it can result in starving the company of funds which would be better employed protecting its long-term strategic future. This brings us to the other fallacy concerning high strategy projects. Some managers believe that certain projects are so pivotal to the long-term welfare of their firm that they require no formalized and quantitative economic appraisal. Quite obviously, strategic implications are vital to the survival of a company but it would be nonsense to invest in capital projects on such a basis without first evaluating their economic merits because, in real life, several alternative ways of achieving the same strategic end will always exist.

5.9 THE SUPERIORITY OF THE DISCOUNTING TECHNIQUE

Unlike the alternative means of assessing investment projects which we have just examined and, for that matter, those methods which do not feature in this book because they are so inappropriate, the NPV and DCFRR criteria do not rely on arbitrary accounting conventions, nor on any qualitative expression of judgement. Instead, they rely plainly and simply on the prediction of the incremental cash flows to be realized by a project. Some managers, unaccustomed to the principles of these two criteria, criticize them for not incorporating any direct means for depreciating the value of assets. Such a criticism is, however, unfounded. Although the point was not highlighted at the time, the DCFRR example used in Section 5.4 demonstrates that the capital invested in that hypothetical asset is depreciated over its economic life but at a rate which is governed by the arithmetic of DCF calculations. Evidence of this is shown in column B of Table 5.4.2. However, it must be stressed that such a depreciation policy is implied by the calculations and *must not* be catered for explicitly in DCF sums because depreciation expense does *not* constitute a cash flow. To allow for some arbitrary method of depreciating in such sums would be tantamount to allowing for depreciation twice! Under no circumstances therefore should arbitrary means of depreciating be used in DCF calculations.

Although we have to postpone a detailed discussion of the taxation implications of a project until Chapter 7.11, nevertheless it is appropriate to state here that the DCF technique is the only way of properly accommodating the complexities of taxation in capital project evaluations. Furthermore, the DCF technique allows for the fact that money has a time value in that the sooner a cash sum is realized, the quicker it can be reinvested to gain interest. None of the other techniques has this facility.

Finally, it should be noted that the DCF technique lends itself to a study of the risk implications of investment in a more meaningful way than any alternative technique. (A discussion of uncertainty and risk is given in Chapter 9.)

5.10   AN ECONOMIC LIFE CYCLE MODEL

Without considering all the complexities of the capital budgeting decision which follow in subsequent chapters, it would appear that the best means available for evaluating the economic implications of a capital project across its projected life-cycle is offered by the simple relationship given in equation 5.5.1, that

$$\text{NPV}_T = \sum_{t=0}^{T} \frac{C_t}{(1+r)^t}$$

where NPV = the project's net present value, T = the expected economic life of the proposed assets, C_t = the end-of-year incremental cash flows to be realized by the project, $100r$ = the interest rate at which the cash flows are discounted, and $\sum$ = the sum of. Reformulated, this equation can be rewritten as

$$\text{NPV}_T = \sum_{0}^{T} \frac{\text{cash inflows}}{(1+r)^t} - \sum_{0}^{T} \frac{\text{cash outflows}}{(1+r)^t}$$

or more simply as

$$\text{NPV}_T = \text{life-cycle benefits} - \text{life-cycle costs} \qquad (5.10.1)$$
$$\qquad\qquad\quad (\text{LCB}) \qquad\qquad\qquad (\text{LCC})$$

Since these costs and benefits result from the *ownership* and *operation* of the project's fixed assets, this equation can be considered as a model of their life-cycle economics. It is the keystone to the philosophy of this book, and provides the skeleton upon which we shall develop a broader understanding of the life-cycle costs and benefits involved in physical assets. It must be realized, however, that like all models, it is an imperfect representation of the real world situation it attempts to resemble, and is only as good as the assumptions which form its basic logic. One of the assumptions which needs to be challenged concerns the convention that cash flows are realized at the ends of years. For the interested reader the controversies which surround this assumption are dealt with in Appendix F.

5.11   COST–BENEFIT ANALYSIS

In many industrial and public administration situations it is often extremely difficult to place a sensible value on the service provided by an asset which does not realize a cash income either because it forms part of a large complex of assets, or because it provides some 'free' public service. Typical examples include the provision of a workshop stores and a works canteen, or the building of a non-toll paying bridge or tunnel. In these circumstances it is not possible to evaluate the merits of the project strictly in commercial terms. Instead, the problem becomes one of providing the service at optimum cost. This necessitates a proper specification of the required service, a search for all conceivable means of meeting that service, and the selection of the preferred alternative exhibiting the best combination of life-cycle cost and risk characteristics*. Providing its risks are acceptable, and the project can be afforded, then our previous calculus suggests that the alternative providing the specified service at the least net present value of costs constitutes the optimal alternative. In effect, therefore, such a decision rule invokes just one part, the life-cycle cost (LCC) part, of our life-cycle economic equation 5.10.1. In these circumstances the computation of the life-cycle costs attributable to each alternative becomes a study of engineering designs and costs, whereas the appraisal of the benefit to be realized from the service can often become a political issue. Whether or not the benefits of such a project sufficiently justify the costs to warrant its implementation remains, of course, a matter of judgement; that very illusive characteristic which is so difficult to appraise except with hindsight.

The difficulty with cost–benefit studies is that cash limits invariably preclude the financing of all those projects whose costs seem justified. In these circumstances the vagueness of their economic merits makes objective cash rationing difficult. To circumvent this problem public authorities involved with substantial capital projects often attempt to evaluate their benefits in economic terms by placing monetary values on the benefits of health, safety, convenience and leisure. Two excellent references showing how this can be done are Feldstein (1964) and Prest and Turvey (1965).

5.12   SUMMARY

Although several different methods exist for assessing the economic merits of capital investment projects, this chapter demonstrates that the DCF technique, which is nothing more than the principle of compound interest in disguise, provides the best investment criteria currently available. Based on the assumption that it is possible to forecast the cash flows to be realized throughout the economic life of a project, this chapter shows how the net present value (NPV) and the discounted cash flow rate of return (DCFRR) of a project can be calculated using the tables of discount factors given in Appendix G. Although the NPV and the DCFRR criteria lead to consistent decisions where most manufacturing projects are concerned, nevertheless the inference of this chapter is that the NPV criterion is the superior criterion partly for the reasons given in Appendix F. It should however be noted that no account of uncertainty and its attendant risks, limitations on the availability of funds, or the prospect of competing projects have been allowed for in this chapter. We shall need to study the implications of these matters in detail before we finally accept or reject these criteria.

---

* A full discussion of the cash flow and risk implications of a project follows in Chapters 6 and 9.

5.13 BIBLIOGRAPHY

General texts

Grant, E. L., Ireson, W. G. and Leavenworth, R. S., *Principles of Engineering Economy*, John Wiley & Sons, 1976. This is one of the most successful of text books concerning engineering economics. It provides a wealth of examples and tables concerning the details of DCF type calculations.

Imperial Chemical Industries Limited, *A Programme for Learning*, Methuen, 1972. This set of six booklets comprises a programmed learning approach to DCF techniques. It employs a fictitious project which requires economic evaluation from its inception through to its replacement.

Merrett, A. J. and Sykes, A., *Capital Budgeting and Company Finance*, Longman, 1974. This book has become a standard text for students of management economics. It contains a wealth of material drawn from the authors' business experiences, is easy to read and yet profound.

Specific texts

Feldstein, M. A., 'Cost–benefit analysis and investment in the public sector,' *Public Administration*, **42,** Winter 1964, pp. 351–372.

Holland, F. A., Watson, F. A. and Wilkinson, J. K., *A Critical Examination of Methods for Assessing Profit and Profitability*, Paper C10, Third International Cost Engineering Symposium, London, 6–9 October 1974.

Hutchinson, A. C., 'Annual profitability expressed in terms of DCF', *Management Decision*, **9** (3), Winter 1971, pp. 252–259.

Istvan, D. F., 'Capital expenditure decisions – how they are made in large corporations', *Indiana Business Report*, No. 33, 1961.

Klammer, T., 'Empirical evidence of the adoption of sophisticated capital budgeting techniques', *Journal of Business*, **45** (3), July 1972.

Prest, A. R. and Turvey, R., 'Cost–benefit analysis: a survey'. *Economic Journal*, **75,** December 1965, pp. 683–735.

Rockley, L. E., *Investment for Profitability*, Business Books, 1973. This book is based on the author's research into the principles and practice adopted by companies when evaluating their investment decisions.

Wild, N. H., 'Logical calculation of DCF rate of return on investment projects', *The Chemical Engineer*, July 1978, pp. 575–579.

5.14 QUESTIONS

5.14.1 Compute the DCFRR for a project with the following profile of cash flows:

Year	0	1	2	3	4	5	6	7 to 11
Cash flow	−6273	600	1000	1500	1800	1600	1400	1000 per annum

5.14.2 Compare and contrast the traditional accounting rate of return method with the discounted cash flow rate of return method as a means of testing the economic viability of a new capital project. Be rigorous and concise in your answer.

5.14.3   A firm has the option of investing in one of four projects, A, B, C or D, all of which have capital costs of 50 000 munits with the end of year cash flow profiles listed below. Show that the ROC criterion based on straight-line depreciation and the average profit per year is unable to differentiate between such projects, whereas the DCFRR criterion can.

Year	Year-end cash flows ('000 munits) project			
	A	B	C	D
0	−50	−50	−50	−50
1	20	8	32	0
2	20	14	26	0
3	20	20	20	40
4	20	26	14	20
5	20	32	8	40

5.14.4   'The decision as to which projects a company should finance depends upon many other factors besides their DCF attributes.' Comment on the validity of this statement and incorporate in your answer those aspects which you believe to be important to capital project selection.

5.14.5   In many property deals, the proprietor purchases a property for £K and sells it n years later for the same amount (in real terms). During the interim period, he leases the property for a net after tax annuity income of £A per annum, which he receives at end of year instants, from Year 1 up to and including Year n. Show that the DCFRR for such a project is given by:

$$DCFRR = \frac{A}{K} \times 100\% \text{ pa.}$$

Using this relationship for such investment projects, select the most economical project from the mutually exclusive alternative projects listed below. The marginal cost of capital is 12 per cent per annum after tax. Justify your preferred choice of project. What additional factors might influence your selection?

Project

	I	II	III	IV
K	65 000	76 000	92 000	110 000
A	8 150	10 950	12 950	14 600

5.14.6   Write an essay on the reasons why economic criteria based upon the discounted cash flow principle are superior to criteria based upon traditional accounting rates of return methods.

5.14.7   A company is considering building a new capital project which will take two years to complete. It is estimated that this project will have an expected economic life of ten years. Compute the NPVs for this project at discount rates of 10 and 20 per cent pa, on the assumption that the project cash flows are realized at the beginning of their respective years, for the following conditions:

Estimated sales volumes (thousands tonnes pa)

Year	3	4	5	6	7	8	9	10	11	12
Sales	2.8	5.5	8.7	11.7	14.3	16.3	17.7	18.8	19.5	20

Variable production costs = £142/tonne, Net selling price = £250/tonne, Plant capital cost (£1.16 million) divided equally between Years 1 and 2. Overhead capital cost = 15 per cent of plant capital cost, also divided equally between Years 1 and 2. Capital related fixed costs = 10 per cent of plant capital cost per annum (Years 3–12 only). Operating labour costs = £60 000 pa (Years 3–12). Other annual fixed costs = £50 000 pa (Years 3–12). Commissioning expenditure = £100 000 (Year 3 only).

5.14.8 An investment project receives end of year cash payments of £c per year, from Year M through to and including Year N. The net present value (P) of this series of cash flows is computed by discounting the cash flows back to the beginning of Year 1. Prove, from first principles, that the following relationship is true:

$$P = \frac{c}{r(1+r)^{M-1}} \left[1 - \frac{1}{(1+r)^{N-M+1}} \right]$$

where r is the appropriate discount interest rate.

5.14.9 Prove, from first principles, that the following relationship could be used to calculate the minimum economic price for a product:

$$P = C + \frac{K(1+r)}{V} \left[\frac{1-X^n}{1-X} \right]$$

where P = minimum economic price per unit of product sold, C = cost per unit of product sold, K = installed capital cost of the plant, V = end of Year 1 sales volume, $X = \frac{1+g}{1+r}$, g = annual growth in sales (fraction pa), r = cost of capital (fraction pa), and n = economic life of the project. What factors would have to be taken into consideration before using such a relationship to fix real market prices?

5.14.10 The repayment of a capital loan, subject to interest charges, can be accomplished by two methods:
(A) The straight-line redemption method, which involves annual year end repayments of equal amounts of the borrowed capital sum and, in addition, year end interest payments on the outstanding capital; and
(B) The annuity method, which involves equal annual year end payments which cover both capital *and* interest charges.

Prove, from first principles, that the total repayments of capital with interest for these two methods are given respectively by

$$SA = \frac{Kr}{2}[n+1] + K$$

$$SB = Krn[1-(1+r)^{-n}]^{-1}$$

where SA = total repayments by Method (A), SB = total repayments by Method (B), K = initial capital debt (£S), r = annual interest rate (fraction per annum), and n = total project life (years). For the conditions $K = £5000$, $r = 6$ per cent per annum, and $n = 5$ years.

Demonstrate that $SB > SA$.

Under what set of business conditions would you be indifferent between your choice of repayment method? The sum (S) of an arithmetic progression given by

$$S = a + [a+d] + [a+2d] + \ldots [a+(n-1)d]$$

is

$$S = \frac{n}{2}[2a + (n-1)d]$$

and the sum (S) of a geometric progression given by

$$S = a + ar + ar^2 + \ldots ar^{n-1}$$

is

$$S = a\left[\frac{1-r^n}{1-r}\right]$$

6. *Choosing Between Competing Projects*

In this chapter we re-examine the validity of the two decision rules formulated in Chapter 5, recognizing that people have a time preference for money which was not allowed for in our previous analysis. Furthermore, we accommodate the fact that investment projects are often competitive in that some are mutually exclusive while others vie for the same company resources. It will be shown that, in certain respects, both the NPV and the DCFRR criteria are insufficient tests of the wider economic and financial implications of a project and that, generally speaking, the NPV criterion is the preferred economic yardstick. Throughout this chapter it should be noted that risk aversion still has not been allowed for, it being assumed that a project's predicted cash flows are risk free and deterministic.

6.1 THE TIME PREFERENCE FOR MONEY

It is conceivable that some people might prefer one project with a modest NPV but with cash flows realized quickly to another more lucrative project with a greater NPV but with its cash flows realized at a later date. Such a preference arises for reasons other than risk aversion and primarily because people have financial obligations to meet. The timing of these cash flows can therefore be critical. For example, an old age pensioner, using some of his savings to supplement his pension, might be reluctant to invest in a long-term but high-yield scheme for fear of not being able to meet his consumption requirements. By the same token, a firm might feel obliged to postpone investment in some profitable project in order to maintain its dividend payments. It would therefore appear that the timing of the cash flows associated with a project involves yet another dimension which we have so far neglected. This dimension is known as the 'time preference for money'.

To proceed with our analysis we need to reconsider two features of Chapter 2. The first concerns the assumption that the firm is owned and operated by an entrepreneur, rather than by a remote group of shareholders. This assumption will help us develop some notional ideas about the ways in which a company might be expected to behave in the face of a time preference for money. The second point is the assumption that this entrepreneur has a utility-indifference map as shown by Figure 6.1.1, but whereas Figure 2.3.1 was associated with 'apples and oranges', here we assume there exist certain combinations of money which he can spend in the present (Year 0) and one year in the future (Year 1) which give him the same overall degree of satisfaction–utility. His problem, therefore, is to select that portfolio of investment projects which gives the greatest satisfaction. A most elegant graphical means of resolving this problem, first developed by Hirshleifer (1958), is presented below but unfortunately, being graphical, it is limited to a two-dimensional presentation and therefore also limited to projects of one year's duration. Nevertheless, the lessons to be learnt from this analysis can be used in a general sense and will allow us to re-interpret the usefulness of our DCF techniques.

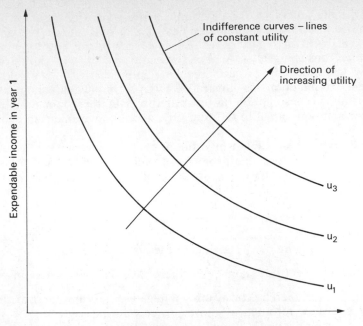

Figure 6.1.1 *A two-time period indifference map for a hypothetical entrepreneur.*

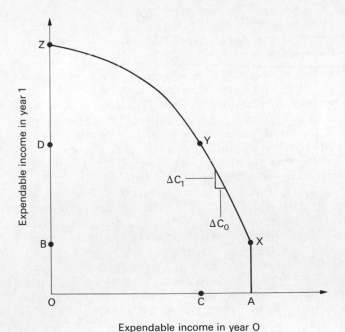

Figure 6.1.2 *Project opportunity curve for a hypothetical entrepreneur. OA = expendable income in year 0 without capital investment; OB = expendable income in year 1 without capital investment; XYZ = capital investment opportunity curve.*

To commence our analysis we shall assume that the sums of money which can be released from his firm for his spending in Year 0 and Year 1 are represented by the distances OA and OB in Figure 6.1.2. During Year 0, the entrepreneur has the option of either consuming all OA or investing a part of it in capital investment projects. Any investment in projects realizing future cash flows would therefore reduce present consumption, as illustrated by AC, but would make possible an increase in his future consumption, as illustrated by BD, thereby making his present and future consumptions equal to OC and OD, and the investment in extra projects equal to AC.

The profitability of these capital investment projects is represented by the curve XYZ. If it were possible to divide projects into infinitesimally small parts and then rank those parts as though they constituted separate and independent investment opportunities, according to the diminishing future cash flows they generate per munit of present investment, then a curve such as XYZ would result. In effect, curve XYZ is the locus of points representing the diminishing returns of these small, incremental projects and the instantaneous slope of this curve is a measure of their diminishing return. Reference to Figure 6.1.2 shows that the instantaneous slope of such a curve is approximated by the expression $\dfrac{\Delta C_1}{\Delta C_0}$ where $\Delta C_0 =$ a very small investment in projects during Year 0, thereby constituting a negative cash flow, and $\Delta C_1 =$ the very small positive cash flow returned by those projects during Year 1.

According to our previous DCF analyses, the NPV of such a small (incremental, marginal) investment would be given by

$$NPV = -\Delta C_0 + \frac{\Delta C_1}{(1+r)}$$

and its DCFRR by

$$DCFRR = \frac{\Delta C_1}{\Delta C_0} - 1$$

The diminishing slope of the capital investment opportunity curve XYZ therefore implies that these infinitesimally small projects have been ranked, from the original position given by point X, according to their DCFRR + 1. Such a representation is therefore equivalent to ranking these one year projects according to the DCFRR on their *incremental investment**. If it were possible to construct such a schedule of capital investment opportunities, then presumably one would only consider infinitesimally small projects with returns greater than zero since projects with negative returns would have to be subsidized by the investor. As such, curve XYZ should not extend beyond a point at which its instantaneous slope becomes negligible.

If we combine the last two graphs, we get the relationship shown in Figure 6.1.3. According to this the entrepreneur should forego current consumption and invest in projects which would provide him with a greater future income thereby allowing him to increase his future consumption. Starting at point X, with a utility level of u_1, the entrepreneur would discover that investment in production opportunities would increase his utility until it reached a maximum level of u_2, as dictated by his capital investment opportunities curve, at point P. Any increase or decrease in investment beyond point P would lead to a reduction to his welfare (satisfaction, utility).

Although this analysis is correct, it takes no account of the fact that money has a time value, as dictated by market interest rates. If we assume that market borrowing

---

* By contrast the slope of the line joining the two points X and Z would measure the DCFRR + 1 for the *entire* portfolio of projects represented by the capital investment opportunity curve XYZ.

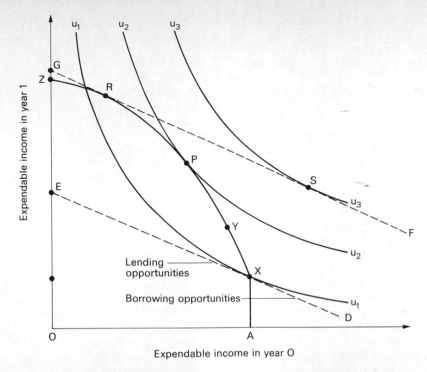

Figure 6.1.3 *The optimum investment strategy for a hypothetical entrepreneur.*

and lending rates are equal, we discover that the optimal investment plan no longer coincides with point P but moves to point S instead.

Borrowing and lending opportunities can be represented by a host of parallel lines of equal slope*. For presentation purposes, only two such lines are shown in Figure 6.1.3, namely DE and FG. If we now re-examine the best strategy open to our entrepreneur we find that at the outset, point X, he would be confronted with three options:

(i) do nothing other than consume his existing income of OA munits,
(ii) borrow or lend money according to the relationship shown by line DE, or
(iii) invest in capital projects according to the capital investment opportunity profile XYZ.

If we assume that all three options are risk free and if, for the moment, we confine our analysis to Figure 6.1.3, then we find that the entrepreneur would not wish to lend or borrow money on the financial market because, according to Figure 6.1.3, both would reduce his utility. This results from the particular geometry of Figure 6.1.3 and depends on the slopes of the interest rate lines and the indifference curves. If drawn differently it is possible that his utility could increase *initially* from borrowing or lending but ultimately both would decrease his utility. Instead he would prefer to finance projects according to his investment opportunity curve XYZ and would continue to do so until his utility was maximized at point P. However, at point P he would find that the slope of his project investment opportunity curve is still greater than the slope of the line FG, meaning that the return on incremental investment is still greater than the interest rate which he would have to pay if he

---

* The slope of these lines is equal to $r+1$, where $100r$ denotes the market interest rate defined as an annual percentage.

borrowed money. He would therefore finance projects up to point R and, on the security of these projects, *would borrow money up to point S*. Such a strategy would maximize his subjective welfare according to two restrictions: the profitability of his capital projects and his ability to borrow and lend money in the financial market. By these means he *could* end up with more money than he started, and he *could* increase his income one year hence. The actual outcome would depend on the precise shapes of his indifference and capital investment opportunity curves, and the slope of the market interest rate lines. Generally speaking, the net effect of such a strategy would be tantamount to borrowing money to finance projects and either subsidizing such investments with current income or, alternatively, subsidizing current income with borrowed money. If no subsidies were required then, quite obviously, his investment in projects would be financed entirely by borrowed money.

Although the lines DE and FG are ostensibly lines of constant interest rate and originally intended to represent borrowing and lending opportunities, nevertheless they also represent the locus of points of equal NPV. The line FG therefore represents combinations of current and future income having a greater NPV than combinations on the line DE. As our entrepreneur invests in projects and moves up the curve XYZ so he increases the total NPV of his project portfolio. Beyond point R however this NPV would decline. This strategy of financing projects up to point R is therefore consistent with the NPV rule which we formulated in Chapter 5 but it will be realized that our previous rule was quiet about the subsequent borrowing strategy which allows our entrepreneur to maximize his welfare at point S.

Since the slope of the project investment opportunity curve is a measure of the DCFRR on incremental investment, Figure 6.1.3 also suggests that the entrepreneur should continue to finance projects provided their incremental DCFRRs* are greater than their incremental cost of capital. Graphically, this means that he should continue to invest in projects provided the slope of the curve XYZ is greater than the slope of the lines DE and FG. At point R, when both curve and line are of equal slope, he should terminate investment in projects. This result is similar to but not identical with our DCFRR decision rule of Chapter 5 which suggested that we should accept a project if its DCFRR is greater than the cost of capital. The basic difference between these decision rules results from our use of the word 'incremental'. According to the rule defined by Chapter 5, our entrepreneur should continue to invest in projects if any straight line drawn from point X to the curve XYZ is of greater slope than the line DE. Regarding Figure 6.1.3, therefore, our entrepreneur would be advised to invest all of his present money in capital projects. Clearly such a decision is wrong because it does not recognize the fact that beyond point R the DCFRR on incremental investment is less than the cost of capital, and additional investment would reduce both his wealth and welfare. In other words, to finance a project simply on the basis that its total DCFRR is greater than the cost of capital is not, strictly speaking, correct. Instead, one should examine the economics of a project from an incremental viewpoint to ensure that each increment of investment is justified. We shall return to this point later in Chapter 11.

We shall now change our assumptions about the capital market and, instead of assuming that borrowing and lending rates of interest are equal, we shall assume that the borrowing rate is greater than the lending rate, which is generally true for most investors. Such a phenomenon does, of course, suggest that the financial market has a means of accommodating risk. In the subsequent analysis, however, we shall continue to assume that the cash flows realized by our hypothetical entrepreneur are risk-free.

---

* Instead of writing discounted cash flow rates of return we have used the abbreviation DCFRRs which unfortunately is not grammatically correct.

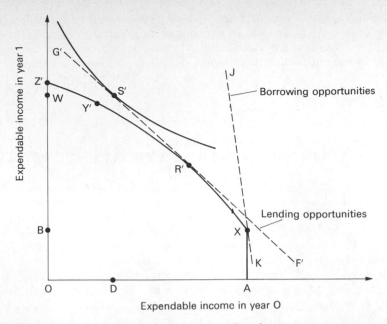

Figure 6.1.4 *Maximization of utility in an imperfect capital market.*

Under these new assumptions the analysis previously given by Figure 6.1.3 can be taken to represent the case where capital investment opportunities exist which have incremental DCFRRs greater than the *cost of borrowing* money and there is no reason to consider such a case any further. However, it could transpire that the projects available to our entrepreneur might be far less lucrative than our previous example suggests. They could provide returns on incremental investment which are less than the cost of borrowing money but greater than the interest rate obtained by lending money. Such a case is represented by Figure 6.1.4 where the slope of the project investment opportunity curve XY^1Z^1 is less than the borrowing opportunity line JK. However the slope of XY^1Z^1 is greater than the lending opportunity line F^1G^1 up to point R^1, where the NPV of his project portfolio would be maximized but now evaluated at the cost of *lending money* instead. As with the previous analysis however such an outcome, as represented by position R^1, is only the first of a two-part strategy because, in this case, the entrepreneur would now maximize his welfare by lending money until he reached point S^1. By these means he would therefore reduce his current consumption from OA to OD, but by the same token he would be able to increase his consumption one year hence from OB to OW.

Had none of his projects yielded a return greater than the lending rate then, of course, he would have lent as much money as was consistent with his utility maximization preference. At this juncture we can therefore formulate two funda-mental principles. When a company can obtain funds to finance its independent capital investment projects, it should observe the following decision rules:

(i) It should invest in projects which provide positive NPVs on their incremental capital, when assessed at the cost of borrowing money (the borrowing rate). This decision rule is equivalent to financing projects which have DCFRRs, on incremental capital, greater than the incremental borrowing rate. In addition however it *must* borrow money to realize its optimum utility.
(ii) If a firm does not possess such projects as those defined by (i) above but has funds of its own, then it should invest in projects which provide positive NPVs

on their incremental capital when assessed at the cost of lending money (the lending rate). This decision is equivalent to financing projects which have DCFRRs on incremental capital greater than the incremental lending rate. In addition, however, it *must* lend money to realize its optimum utility.

We now need to test these two principles in light of the fact that projects are often mutually exclusive.

6.2 THE ECONOMICS OF MUTUALLY EXCLUSIVE PROJECTS

New projects are the life-line in the survival of any firm so it behoves management to search for and invent lucrative projects. However, it must never be forgotten that Nature, either through her perversity or generosity, makes possible the attainment of any given objective by numerous means. The task facing all firms therefore is to appraise and select between such alternative means. Competition between projects therefore results from the fact that there are often several, if not many, ways to accomplish a given end, making such projects *mutually exclusive*. Table 6.2.1 provides us with but a few examples of the ways in which mutually exclusive projects might differ from one another.

Our first category of mutually exclusive projects involves those which have the same first cost but different NPVs and DCFRRs. We shall restrict our attention here to projects lasting one year only, so that we can readily accommodate our comparison between such projects within the framework of our utility theory analysis. Let us imagine that Project A can be represented by the curve XYZ in Figure 6.2.1, and another more lucrative Project B can be represented by XY^1Z^1. For the same investment in both projects (i.e., the same first cost) it will be noted that the DCFRR of Project B is always better than that of Project A. This point is demonstrated by the fact that any straight line drawn from point X to the curve XY^1Z^1 is always steeper than that drawn to the curve XYZ, for the same investment in Year 0. Likewise for the same interest rate, the NPV of Project B is always greater than Project A, as illustrated by the two lines F^1G^1 and FG. In the same vein as our analysis in Section 6.1, it therefore follows that by borrowing or lending (whichever is

Table 6.2.1 *Categories in which mutually exclusive projects might differ*

No.	Category	Description
1	Raw material	Different raw materials can be used to produce the same final product.
2	Plant	Different combinations of plant can produce the same product at different costs.
3	Plant layout	Different layouts can alter the project's capital and operating costs as well as its safety.
4	Process	Completely different physical and chemical processes can produce the same product.
5	Plant location	Different plant locations can alter the raw materials and product distribution costs.
6	Product	Different forms and types of products can compete for the same market.
7	Distribution outlets	Different distribution outlets alter the cost and effectiveness of marketing.
8	Markets	Different markets exist for the purchase of the same product.
9	Project life	The project life can be affected by the durability of the product and its plant.

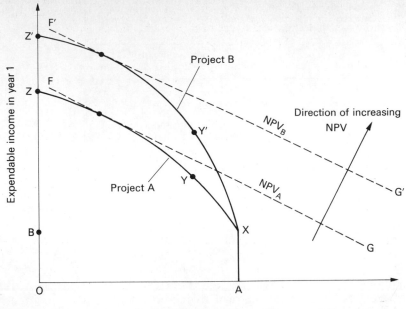

Figure 6.2.1 *Economic comparison between two mutually exclusive projects.*

appropriate) our entrepreneur could attain a greater utility by investing in Project B. Under conditions of certainty it would therefore appear that, for mutually exclusive projects with the same first costs and equal one year lives, the NPV and DCFRR criteria lead to the same decision. A numerical example which illustrates this point is provided in Table 6.2.2.

A more realistic example of mutually exclusive projects having the same first cost but different DCF attributes is given in Table 6.2.3. Comparing these three projects it will soon be realized that Project A_2 is always superior to Project B_2, providing the discount rate is not zero (in which case all three projects would have the same NPV of 500). This conclusion results from the fact that Projects A_2 and B_2 both possess the same cash inflows but reversed time-wise, so that Project A_2 has monies arriving at a faster initial rate, which results in its superior DCFRR. One cannot decide the relative merits of Projects A_2 and C_2 without first computing their NPVs, at various interest rates, as shown in Table 6.2.3 and Figure 6.2.2.

The diagram shows that, for any arbitrary but no-zero interest rate, the NPV of Project A_2 is always superior to that of Project C_2 which likewise is always superior to Project B_2. In these circumstances we would prefer to invest in Project A_2 and,

Table 6.2.2 *An example of mutually exclusive projects having the same first cost and equal lives of one year*

| Year | Forecasted cash flows | |
	Project A_1	Project B_1
0	−1000	−1000
1	+1200	+1300
NPV @ 10% pa	91	182
DCFRR (% pa)	20%	30%

Table 6.2.3 *The relative economic merits of mutually exclusive projects with the same first cost, same lives and the same cumulative undiscounted cash flows*

| Year | Forecasted cash flows | | |
	Project A2	Project B2	Project C2
0	−1000	−1000	−1000
1	500	100	300
2	400	200	300
3	300	300	300
4	200	400	300
5	100	500	300
Cumulative undiscounted cash flow (NPV @ 0% pa)	500	500	500
DCFRR (% pa)	20	12	15
NPV @ 10% pa	209	65	137

under conditions of certainty, would do so if it possessed a positive incremental NPV at the firm's relevant cost of capital, or if its incremental DCFRR was greater than its cost of capital.

This example could also be analysed using our indifference–utility theory technique if we assumed that our hypothetical entrepreneur could borrow money in Year 1 on the security of subsequent cash flows. By these means these five-year projects would *effectively* become one-year projects, and it would be found that the project

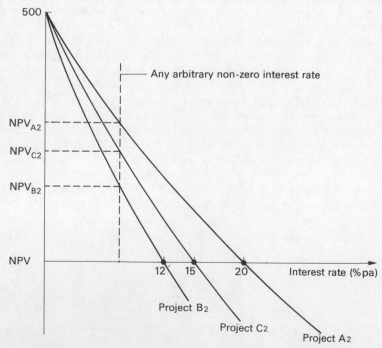

Figure 6.2.2 *A comparison of projects with the same first costs, same lives and equal cumulative undiscounted cash flows.*

Table 6.2.4 *The relative economic merits of mutually exclusive projects with the same first costs and unequal cumulative undiscounted cash flows*

Project	Year end cash flows			NPV@ 0% pa	NPV@ 5% pa	DCFRR % pa
	Year 0	Year 1	Year 2			
A₃	−10 000	–	12 100	2100	975	10
B₃	−10 000	11 400	–	1400	857	14

with the highest NPV, at the *relevant* cost of capital, would also be the preferred choice from a utility viewpoint.

The relevance of a firm being able to borrow on the security of future earnings is illustrated by Table 6.2.4. Here we see that both projects have the same first cost of 10 000 munits, but one project possesses the greater NPV (at a 5 per cent cost of capital) but the poorer DCFRR. Reference to Figure 6.2.3 shows that the NPV profiles of these two projects intersect at an interest rate of 6.14 per cent per annum, when both have the same NPV of 741 munits. The interest rate at which we discount the future cash flows of a project is now seen to be very important since, to the left of this 'intersection rate', Project A₃ has the better NPV but the poorer DCFRR whereas; to its right, Project B₃ has the better NPV and the better DCFRR. In this case, the DCFRR values of 10 and 14 per cent completely ignore the existence of this intersection rate.

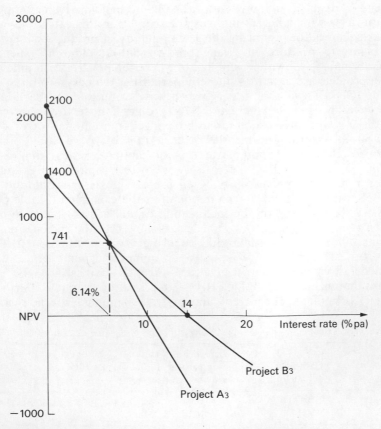

Figure 6.2.3 *A comparison of projects with the same first costs but different cumulative undiscounted cash flows.*

Table 6.2.5 *A reformulation of Table 6.2.4 on the assumption that extra money can be borrowed at 5 per cent pa*

Project	Year end cash flows Year 0	Year 1	Year 2	NPV @ 0% pa	NPV @ 5% pa
A₃	−10 000	11 400	130	2100	975
B₃	−10 000	11 400	–	1400	857

If extra funds could be borrowed at 5 per cent per annum, the 12 000 munits realized by Project A₃ in Year 2 could be used to raise 11 400 munits in Year 1, repay this debt and its interest of 570 munits in Year 2, and *still* realize a positive cash flow of 130 munits at the end of Year 2. In other words, the effective cash flow profiles of the two projects compared would now be as shown by Table 6.2.5. In this case the natural superiority of Project A₃ over Project B₃ is now made manifest by its having the same Year 1 cash flow as Project B₃ but, in addition, a second year cash flow too. Quite clearly however the superiority of Project A₃ over Project B₃ depends on the cost of borrowing money. If money could only be borrowed at an interest rate in excess of 6.14 per cent per annum, then Project B₃ would be the preferred choice. Unlike other examples which we have studied so far, this example demonstrates just how sensitive the decision outcome can be to small changes in the assumed cost of capital!

A special variant of the previous example occurs when comparing mutually exclusive projects with different first costs. Examples in this category could involve alternative machines for producing the same quantity of product or indeed different sizes of plants to produce the same product but at different rates. A simple numerical example is shown in Table 6.2.6, where the positive cash inflows accruing to the two projects are annuities, thereby permitting the easy computation of their NPVs and DCFRRs using the theory which was promulgated in Section 5.6. Here again we have an example where the NPV profiles intersect, as shown by Figure 6.2.4. In this case the intersection rate is 8.6 per cent per annum, corresponding with a NPV of 3018. According to the NPV criterion therefore we would prefer Project A₄ to Project B₄, if the appropriate cost of capital was less than 8.6 per cent, whereas the reverse would be the case if the cost of capital was greater than the intersection rate. For comparison between projects possessing different first costs, the DCFRR criterion is not quite so impotent as the example of Table 6.2.4 would suggest, since the DCFRR on the incremental capital at risk is able to discern this intersection rate. The statistics of Table 6.2.6 show that the incremental capital of 2500 munits put at risk by embarking on Project A₄, as opposed to Project B₄, provides extra cash inflows of 383 munits per annum over ten years. If we consider this additional investment, another project, Project (A₄–B₄) as shown by Table 6.2.6, it transpires that its incremental DCFRR is 8.6 per cent per annum. Furthermore, its incremental NPV (at 7 per cent per annum) is 190 munits, which is equal to the

Table 6.2.6 *An example of projects possessing different first costs and different DCF attributes*

Project	Cash flow Year 0	Year end cash flows during each of the subsequent ten years	DCFRR (% pa)	NPV at 7% pa
A₄	−10 000	1993	15%	3998
B₄	−7500	1610	17%	3808
(A₄–B₄)	−2500	383	8.6%	190

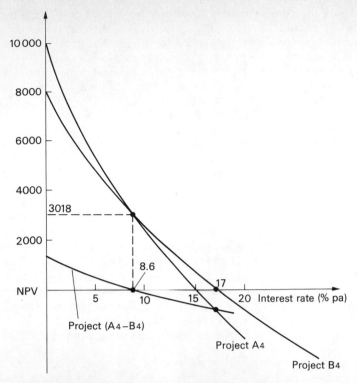

Figure 6.2.4 *A comparison of projects with unequal first costs.*

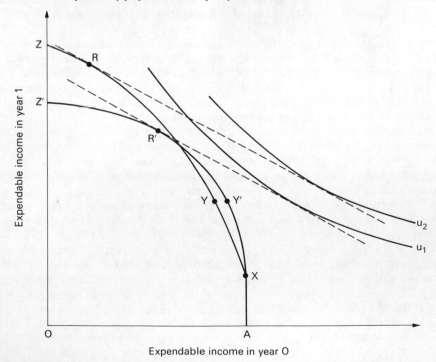

Figure 6.2.5 *Comparison between mutually exclusive projects with opposing NPV–DCFRR attributes. XYZ = capital investment in Project A; XY'Z' = capital investment in Project B.*

difference between the NPVs of the two projects. In this case, therefore, the NPV and the DCFRR on the incremental capital at risk provide a consistent decision, namely, invest in Project A₄ in preference to Project B₄, providing the incremental cost of capital is less than 8.6 per cent per annum.

Our utility theory analysis is quite capable of selecting between projects with opposing NPV–DCFRR attributes. In the example shown by Figure 6.2.5, we see that the capital investment opportunity profile XYZ for Project A results in a higher NPV than does the profile XY^1Z^1 for Project B, although straight lines drawn from point X to points R and R^1 show that the DCFRR for Project B is greater than that for Project A. In this case, however, the utility theory shows that the project with the greater NPV is the preferred choice.

It will be realized, however, that the decision to invest in the more expensive project implies two basic assumptions. First, it assumes that cash rationing does not exist otherwise a firm might prefer to invest the incremental capital in some other project. For example, if it were possible to invest the differential capital of 2500 munits in some other project (Project C₄) with a NPV in excess of 190, when evaluated at 7 per cent per annum, then the preferred choice of projects would be Project B₄ and Project C₄ instead of Project A₄. Secondly, the analysis assumes that the cost of capital remains the same irrespective of the quantity of money borrowed. Should this not be so then, of course, a different decision could result. If the cost of the incremental 2500 munits was greater than 8.6 per cent per annum then one would naturally prefer Project B₄ to Project A₄. Hirshleifer (1958) has demonstrated how utility decision theory can also accommodate an increasing cost of capital.

6.3 THE CHOICE OF PROJECTS WHEN CAPITAL IS RATIONED

Projects are also competitive in the sense that they vie for the scarce resources of a company. In this section we consider the effects of competition arising from a cash shortage precluding investment in all of those lucrative projects available to a firm. We refer to such a situation as one of cash rationing. Of course other constraints, such as the shortage of managerial talent, skilled labour, space and raw materials could also result in different forms of rationing.

A shortage of funds to finance projects results from several causes. Young companies wishing to expand rapidly under the dynamic leadership of an entre-preneur invariably find their growth stunted by a shortage of funds. This results from their having limited access to the various institutional forms of finance because of their unestablished position in the financial market and the paucity of their assets against which to secure loans as collateral. It also arises from their inability to gain the confidence of moneylenders because of the limited evidence of their business competence.

By contrast, fully developed companies have access to various forms of finance such as commercial banks, mortgage companies, debenture loans and new shares floatations, with the possibility of funds being raised locally, nationally or interna-tionally. Of course, any company attempting to borrow substantial sums of money quickly is likely to find most moneylenders unreceptive because they also need time to assess properly the merits of such projects. Borrowing large sums of money, therefore, requires professionalism, with proper planning according to a budget, and a pre-determined financial strategy. Having access to lucrative projects is not in itself a sufficient guarantee that loans will be forthcoming. Moneylenders still need to assess the firm's ability to repay such loans according to some prescribed schedule, and need to assess the firm's competence to execute such projects properly. To a large extent such appraisals are influenced by the firm's past performance, as monitored by its accounting statements. A poor past performance could therefore impede a company's economic improvement/recovery by limiting its access to reasonably priced money.

The ability of a firm to borrow money is also determined by its financial structure, as measured by certain of its balance sheet ratios, especially its long-term debt to tangible net worth ratio. These ratios are dealt with in Appendix B. At this juncture however it is important to realize that a firm's depreciation policy, its borrowing limits (as laid down in its Articles of Incorporation) and its policy for revaluing assets (because of inflation) can all act either separately or in concert to limit its borrowing powers, severely, thereby restricting its economic growth and its ability to survive and prosper.

Restrictions on the borrowing capacity of a firm are also internally generated by its management's reluctance to borrow. Some companies severely restrict their growth rate by limiting all investment to that made possible by retained earnings. Such a condition would be understandable if the firm's investment proposals were expected to give returns less than the borrowing rate. However this is not usually the case, and companies often forego projects with apparently high expected returns because they are either unwilling to take the risk of the company defaulting on its loan obligations, or else they are reluctant to lose control of the firm by issuing additional equity. This is often true of family-owned companies.

Other firms restrict their borrowing to their ability to manage capital investment projects properly, their problem being one of human resource limitation rather than one of funding, but it has the same effect. As such, it is not uncommon for firms to use such yardsticks as 'Each of our project managers can just about control expenditures up to 10 million munits per annum, but no more', being used to regulate their capital investment programmes at any one time. Their investment portfolios are therefore constrained by their inability or indeed reluctance to engage extra human resources.

To understand the cash rationing problem better, we need to return to the simple example given in Table 6.2.4. It will be realized that we can no longer compare these two projects according to the analysis of Table 6.2.5 if we *now* assume that the firm is unable to borrow in Year 1 on the security of the second year cash flows accruing to Project A^3. How then can we make a valid comparison between these two projects? If money is so limited, then it follows that Project B^3 could finance some hitherto undefined project with its first year cash inflow, whereas Project A^3 could not. Cash rationing therefore forces one to consider the reinvestment implications of a project. As with the previous analysis shown by Figure 6.2.3, the outcome of such a consideration rests on whether Project B^3 could reinvest money at an interest rate in excess of 6.14 per cent per annum. If it could, then quite obviously Project B^3 plus its reinvestment opportunity would be the preferred choice. For example, if the first year cash inflow of 11 400 munits could be reinvested at 10 per cent per annum, its effective second year cash inflow would be 12 540 munits, or 440 munits in excess of that realized by Project A^3, as shown by Table 6.3.1. In cash rationing situations, therefore, the NPV criterion is unable to distinguish the correct decision *unless the full implications of reinvestment are also taken into account.*

A considerable controversy ensues over what constitutes the appropriate reinvestment rate. Some writers contend that the firm's cost of capital should be used. Such a suggestion however is preposterous because no firm in its right mind would intentionally finance a project designed to maintain an economic status quo. Other writers suggest that the DCFRR of each project should be used as the reinvestment rate. If we return to the trivial example shown by Table 6.2.2, it will be realized that

Table 6.3.1 *The economic merits of example 6.2.4, but incorporating the effects of reinvestment at 10 per cent per annum*

Project	Year end cash flows			
	Year 0	Year 1	Year 2	NPV @ 5%
A₃	−10 000	–	12 100	975
B₃ plus re-investment at 10% pa	−10 000	–	12 540	1375

such a suggestion is tantamount to the 1200 munits realized by Project A₁ being reinvested at 20 per cent per annum, and the 1300 munits realized by Project B₁ being reinvested at 30 per cent per annum. But such an idea is unreasonable if the cash flows from either project could be reinvested in the same independent third project. Under such conditions the DCFRR of that third independent project would be the logical reinvestment rate. Only under conditions of physical dependence would it be proper to consider the reinvestment opportunities of different projects at different reinvestment rates and such rates would have to be specified in advance if the optimal economic strategy were to be followed.

Under conditions of cash rationing, it would therefore appear that the problem of selecting between mutually exclusive projects has grown: the analysis is no longer confined to the projects themselves but their successors too! We can resolve this problem but only if we are willing to predict our subsequent reinvestment policy and future reinvestment rates of return.

Researchers have devised various ways of allocating funds between competing projects under cash rationing conditions. These methods fall into two broad categories. The first uses simple rule-of-thumb techniques, whereas the second involves mathematical programming techniques. Although neither of these methods properly resolve this allocation problem, they do shed some light on the more sensitive areas of capital budgeting.

6.4   RULE-OF-THUMB TECHNIQUES

One suggestion is that projects should be ranked according to the descending order of their NPVs until the cash rationing budget is completely absorbed. Such an idea has much merit in that it is extremely simple to use and it employs the NPV which *appears* to be the better of the two DCF criteria. Unfortunately, this method cannot cope with the problem that most projects involve discrete 'lumps' of investment, and need reappraising if their divisibility into smaller discrete lumps is required. To illustrate this point, suppose a firm has a capital ration of 1000 munits and the choice of two mutually exclusive projects, one costing 600 munits with an NPV of 1000, the other costing 500 munits with an NPV of 600. According to this rule-of-thumb method, the firm should finance the former of these alternatives. But such a decision would under-utilize its cash budget so, ideally, it should finance two of the smaller projects, if that were possible, because they would completely utilize its cash budget and collectively yield the greater NPV.

To overcome this problem, other researchers have suggested ranking projects according to the descending order of their profitability index, which is defined as the NPV per unit of scarce capital employed. For example, faced with the prospect of financing the three projects listed in Table 6.4.1, a firm should allocate funds to

Table 6.4.1 *The ranking of capital investment projects by their profitability indices*

Project	NPV	Present value of initial capital expenditure (c)	Profit-ability index $\rho = \dfrac{NPV}{c}$	Rank order
1	30	6	5.00	1st
2	25	20	1.25	3rd
3	20	5	4.00	2nd

Project 1 first, Project 3 second, and Project 2 last, because such a strategy would maximize its NPV according to this method.

This technique works well for projects involving a single period cash constraint providing they are divisible† and completely independent. However, it often fails to differentiate between projects when more than one cash rationing constraint exists, as the example in Table 6.4.2 demonstrates. In this example, Project 1 is the preferred project according to the profitability index, based on its capital require-ment in Year 1, whereas Project 2 becomes the preferred choice according to the profitability index and its capital requirement in Year 2. If, however, we sum the present values of each projects' capital requirements for both years, we discover that Project 3 becomes the preferred choice based on the profitability index and its combined capital requirements. In effect, therefore, this trivial example shows how such a simple yardstick as the profitability index can lead to inconsistent results, especially when multi-period cash rationing prevails, so its use cannot be considered seriously for anything but the most simple of capital budgeting problems.

Table 6.4.2 *The multi-period ranking of capital investment projects by their profitability indices*

Project	NPV	Present value of capital expenditure in Year 1 (c_1)	Present value of capital expenditure in Year 2 (c_2)	Profitability index $\rho_1 = \dfrac{NPV}{c_1}$	$\rho_2 = \dfrac{NPV}{c_2}$	$\hat{\rho} = \dfrac{NPV}{c_1 + c_2}$
1	30	6	20	5.0[a]	1.5	1.15
2	25	20	5	1.25	5.0[a]	1.00
3	20	5	5	4.00	4.00	2.00[a]

[a] Denotes the preferred choice of project.

6.5 CASH RATIONING BETWEEN PROJECTS USING MATHEMATICAL PROGRAMMING TECHNIQUES

The profitability index (ρ), which we have just used, suggests that any number of projects (n) should be ranked so that some number (k) are selected and ($n-k$) are rejected according to the following relationships

$$\text{(i)} \quad \frac{NPV_{k+1}}{c_{k+1}} < \rho^* \leqslant \frac{NPV_k}{c_k} \qquad (6.5.1)$$

$$\text{(ii)} \quad C - \sum_{i=1}^{k} c_i \geqslant 0 \qquad (6.5.2)$$

---

† The profitability index implies that projects are divisible and they exhibit 'constant returns to scale'. However such an assumption may be invalid for the reasons previously given in Chapter 2.6.

where NPV_k = the NPV of the worst accepted project 'k', NPV_{k+1} = the NPV of the best rejected project '$k+1$', ρ^* = the limiting value of the profitability index which meets the needs of equation 6.5.2, C = the cash constraint for a single period, c_i = the present value of the single period capital cost of the ith accepted project, where $i = (1, 2 \ldots k)$.

Recognizing the basic inclusiveness of this simple-minded method, and the problems caused by the assumption of divisibility, Lorie and Savage (1955) suggested a modification to overcome the multi-period cash rationing problem, and recommended that projects should be selected only if the two following conditions were satisfied:

$$\text{(i)} \quad NPV_i - \sum_{t=1}^{T} \rho_t c_{t,i} \geq 0 \qquad (6.5.3)$$

and

$$\text{(ii)} \quad C_t - \sum_{i=1}^{k} c_{t,i} \geq 0 \qquad (6.5.4)$$

where C_t = the present value of the cash constraint for year t, and $t = (1, 2 \ldots T)$, $c_{t,i}$ = the present value of the capital cost of the ith project expended in year t, ρ_t = the cut off criterion during time 't', and k relates to the projects which are selected according to the criterion set by equation 6.5.3.

They illustrated the usefulness of their technique employing the example which is shown in Table 6.5.1, where Trial A shows that selecting values for ρ_t, which are too high, results in an under-utilization of the cash budgets and a small NPV for the portfolio of selected projects. By contrast, Trial B indicates that the values of ρ_t have been set too low, causing budget deficits. For this particular problem, the optimal values of ρ_t coincide with Trial C, which results in the complete absorption of the second year's budget and the maximization of the NPV of the selected portfolio consistent with using whole non-divisible projects. So what do these values of ρ_1 and ρ_2 mean? In effect, they are a *crude evaluation* of the benefit which each unit of scarce cash resource contributes to the NPV of the selected project portfolio. (This idea is developed below.) They have the property that an increase in the value of one, combined with a compensating decrease in the value of the other, will not allow the inclusion or substitution of projects which increase the NPV of the selected portfolio without violating one or both of the constraints†.

Although the technique by Lorie and Savage does overcome the problems experienced by the ordinary profitability index, its trial-and-error method of computing the optimal values of ρ is extremely tedious and inefficient. A better way of resolving such problems involves using the technique of linear programming, which is briefly described below and is dealt with in detail in Chapter 17. To demonstrate the application of this technique to capital budgeting problems under cash rationing conditions, let us consider the following example. Suppose that a firm is considering investment in two independent projects, A and B, according to the economic and financial data listed in Table 6.5.2. (Exactly how such data were derived, does not concern us here, since such matters are properly dealt with in Chapter 7.) What is important is to decide the optimal capacities of these two projects such that the greatest economic benefit, as measured by the NPV criterion, is achieved from their use, consistent with meeting their cash budget constraints.

An unstructured and piecemeal approach to this problem could involve much wasted time and effort. For example, noting that Project A is more valuable per

---

† In effect, therefore, they are a kind of opportunity cost similar to but not identical with the Lagrange Multipliers, discussed in Appendix A.

Table 6.5.1 *An application of the Lorie and Savage technique to multi-period cash rationing problems*

Project (i) $i = 1, 9$	NPV_i	Present values of capital expenditures Year 1 ($c_{1,i}$)	Year 2 ($c_{1,i}$)	Trial A $\rho_1 = 1.00, \rho_2 = 3.00$ $NPV_i \geqslant \sum_{t=1}^{2} \rho_t \cdot c_{t,i}$	Trial B $\rho_1 = 0.10, \rho_2 = 0.50$ $NPV_i \geqslant \sum_{t=1}^{2} \rho_t \cdot c_{t,i}$	Trial C $\rho_1 = 0.33, \rho_2 = 1.00$ $NPV_i \geqslant \sum_{t=1}^{2} \rho_t \cdot c_{t,i}$
1	14	12	3	×	✓	✓
2	17	54	7	×	✓	×
3	17	6	6	×	✓	✓
4	15	6	2	✓	✓	✓
5	40	30	35	×	✓	×
6	12	6	6	×	✓	✓
7	14	48	4	×	✓	×
8	10	36	3	×	✓	×
9	12	18	3	×	✓	✓

Present value of cash rationing constraints		$C_1 = 50$ $\quad$ $C_2 = 20$		Budget surplus Year 1 = 44 Budget surplus Year 2 = 18	Budget deficit Year 1 = 168 Budget deficit Year 2 = 46	Budget surplus Year 1 = 2 Budget surplus Year 2 = 0

Net present value of the preferred solution (Trial C) = 70 munits

✓ = a selected project; × = a rejected project.

tonne of capacity than Project B, we might suggest investment in 36 tonnes of capacity in Project A, since such an investment would completely absorb the first year's cash budget (i.e., $36 \times 5 = 180$) only to find that such a decision would not absorb the second year's budget, leaving a surplus of 27 munits (i.e., $135 - 36 \times 3 = 27$). A better approach results from formulating the problem algebraically, and then (if possible) solving the algebra either by graphical or numerical means. If we denote the undetermined optimal capacities of Projects A and B by the symbols x_A and x_B, the following relationships hold:

$$NPV = 3x_A + 2x_B \tag{6.5.5}$$

$$5x_A + 2x_B \leqslant 180 \tag{6.5.6}$$

$$3x_A + 3x_B \leqslant 135 \tag{6.5.7}$$

The first means that the total NPV to be realized from both projects is the sum of their individual net present values, obtained by multiplying each of their NPV contributions per tonne of capacity by their undetermined capacities. In mathematical parlance this relationship is known as the objective function, whose value we wish to maximize. The other two mathematical equations are known as constraint

Table 6.5.2 *The economic and financial specifications of two independent capital proposals*

Detail	Project A	Project B
NPV per tonne of plant capacity (munits)	3	2
Present value of first year capital costs per tonne of capacity (munits)	5	2
Constraints Present value of second year capital costs per tonne of capacity (munits)	3	3

(i) Present value of first year's cash budget = 180 munits
(ii) Present value of second year's cash budget = 135 munits

equations. They denote that the amount of cash needed per tonne of capacity, multiplied by the individual capacity of each project, collectively must be less than or equal to, but not greater than, the stated budget constraint. Since there are only two variables to determine in this problem, x_A and x_B, we can represent these three equations graphically.

Let us consider equation 6.5.6 first.

$$5x_A + 2x_B \leqslant 180$$

If we postpone the problem of the '$\leqslant$' (inequality) sign, we discover that when $x_A = 0$, then $x_B = 90$, and when $x_B = 0$, then $x_A = 36$, so that the geometrical co-ordinates of this relationship are given by $(36, 0)$ and $(0, 90)$, where convention suggests that the values of x_A are written before those of x_B. By similar reckoning, the corresponding co-ordinates for equation 6.5.7 are $(45, 0)$ and $(0, 45)$ respectively. Both are shown by the straight sloping lines of Figure 6.5.1. The values which x_A and x_B assume cannot exist above and to the right of these two sloping lines without violating the budget cash constraints. Instead they can assume values

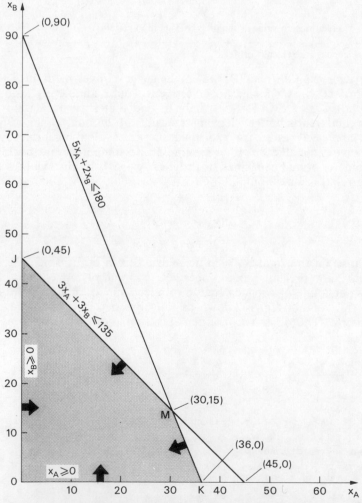

Figure 6.5.1 *A graphical representation of the firm's budget constraints. Hatched area OJMK is the area of feasible solutions.*

touching and below these lines, as indicated by the arrows in Figure 6.5.1. To complete the rationale of this diagram, it will also be appreciated that negative values of x_A and x_B cannot be tolerated in a problem of this kind because 'negative projects just don't exist'! As a result the values which x_A and x_B assume must be greater than or equal to zero, as shown by the diagram.

All feasible solutions to this problem are therefore contained within the hatched polygon OJMK, which is known as the area of feasible solutions. It will be appreciated that countless feasible solutions exist in such an area so we need a method to discover the optimal solution. Two such methods exist for a two-dimensional problem of this kind. The first states that the optimal solution is contained by the extreme points of the area of feasible solutions, providing the variables can assume fractional values. In our case this means that the optimal solution is located at one or more of the points O, J, M and K, which are known as vertex points, providing the solution variables are not restricted to integer values. If we compute the net present values for each of these four points, using their co-ordinate values and the identity given by equation 6.5.5, we obtain the following results:

| Point | Co-ordinates | | NPV $= 3x_A + 2x_B$ |
| | x_A | x_B | |
	(tonnes)		(munits)
O	0	0	0
J	0	45	90
M*	30	15	120
K	36	0	108

showing that the optimal solution is contained by point M. The second method is a graphical construction which highlights how the optimal solution is discovered and validates the hypothesis of the previous method. Figure 6.5.2 illustrates this graphical solution. It shows the same polygon OJMK and an array of straight lines of equal slope and diminishing NPV approaching the polygon from the right. Each of these lines is the locus of points of equal NPV so the line containing the two points R and S, with co-ordinates (10, 60) and (30, 30) respectively, is the locus of all combinations of x_A and x_B with an aggregate NPV of 150 munits. Furthermore, all of these lines are of equal slope and in this problem their slope is -1.5†.

This diagram shows how a line with a NPV of 120 passes through point M. Since no other line with a greater NPV passes through the area of feasible solutions, point M represents the optimal combination of Projects A and B. For this example therefore the firm should consider building both Projects A and B with the following installed capacities:

Project A: 30 tonnes per unit time

Project B: 15 tonnes per unit time

---

† If we set the value of the NPV to zero then we get the following relationship:

$$3x_A + 2x_B = 0$$

so that the slope of these lines is given by:

$$\frac{x_B}{x_A} = -\frac{3}{2} = -1.5$$

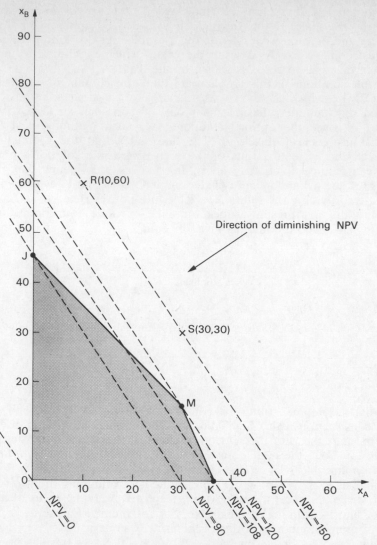

Figure 6.5.2 *Graphical optimization of the cash rationing problem.*

It follows that this method* contains the means of resolving the complexities of the cash rationing problem when more than one cash budget constraint exists. In this respect it overcomes the difficulties encountered by the crude rule-of-thumb methods, and the Lorie and Savage technique. It also contains a means of evaluating the opportunity costs incurred by the firm as a consequence of its cash rationing. It will be remembered that we discussed opportunity costs in Chapter 2.10, and developed a generalized technique for their evaluation in Appendix A. In the

---

* This method is known as linear programming (LP) when both its objective function and its constraint equations can be written as linear combinations of the solution variables. A graphical means of solving LP problems is not available for problems involving more than three variables, but a mathematical method, pioneered by Dantzig (1963), does, and is discussed in greater detail in Chapter 17. Nowadays proprietary computer programs exist to solve the most complicated LP problems. Two excellent texts describing the application of linear programming to capital budgeting problems are in Weingartner (1963) and Baumol and Quandt (1965).

context of Chapter 2, we defined these opportunity costs as the profit foregone as a consequence of some active constraint restricting the realization of extra profit. In other words, opportunity costs were shown to represent the extra profit to be gained by the relaxation of the active constraint by *one incremental unit*. This definition is especially useful in the context of our current problem because, being linear, its opportunity costs stay constant, permitting an even broader definition of their meaning, namely 'an opportunity cost for a linear programming problem is the contribution* made by each unit of the actively constraining resource towards the objective function'.

To demonstrate this point we shall use the following notation, let $\rho_1 =$ the opportunity cost due the cash constraint of 180 munits in Year 1, and $\rho_2 =$ the opportunity cost due to the corresponding cash constraint of 135 munits in Year 2. Returning to the optimal solution represented by point M in Figure 6.5.2, it will be realized that Project A contributes 90 munits (30×3) to the aggregate maximum NPV and, in so doing, consumes 150 munits (30×5) of the first year's cash ration, and 90 munits (30×3) of the second year's cash budget. According to our definition of what constitutes an opportunity cost it therefore follows that:

$$150\rho_1 + 90\rho_2 = 90 \qquad (6.5.8)$$

Likewise, Project B contributes 30 munits (15×2) to the aggregate maximum NPV, using 30 munits (15×2) of the first year's constraining cash ration, and 45 munits (15×3) of the second year's budget, thereby giving rise to the following relationship:

$$30\rho_1 + 45\rho_2 = 30 \qquad (6.5.9)$$

Solving equations 6.5.8 and 6.5.9 we find that

$$\left.\begin{array}{l} \rho_1 = 1/3 \\ \text{and } \rho_2 = 4/9 \end{array}\right\} \text{munits per munit of active scarce resource}$$

These values need to be interpreted carefully. They mean that keeping all but one of the constraints fixed, successive unit relaxations in this constraint would increase the objective function by successive amounts (equal to the corresponding opportunity cost) *until some other constraint became active*. For example, if we relaxed the first year's constraint by 45 munits (from 180 to 225), the NPV would increase by 15 munits ($45 \times 1/3$) to a new value of 135 munits, at which point the new solution variables would become:

$$x_A = 45$$
$$x_B = 0$$

This solution would therefore indicate that the previously *inactive* constraint $x_B \geqslant 0$ was now *active*, preventing further increases in aggregate NPV through additional relaxations in the first year's budget constraint. Likewise, if we relaxed the second year's constraint by 135 munits (from 135 to 270) the NPV would increase by 60 munits ($135 \times 4/9$) to a new value of 180 munits, at which point the new solution variables would become:

$$x_A = 0$$
$$x_B = 90$$

Such a solution would indicate that the previously *inactive* constraint $x_A \geqslant 0$ was now *active*, preventing further increases in the aggregate NPV through additional relaxations in the second year's budget.

---

* In the context of capital investment problems we are more concerned with NPVs rather than profits.

In the context of this particular problem, the two values for the opportunity costs*
$\rho_1 = 1/3$ and $\rho_2 = 4/9$ have three major capital budgeting implications:

(i) They show that the firm should be willing to pay up to, but no more than,
one-third of a munit per munit borrowed to relax the cash rationing budget in
Year 1. Since all these money units are present values, this conclusion can be
reinterpreted to mean that the firm should be willing to pay up to
33.33 per cent on borrowed money in order to relax this constraint because, in
so doing, it would earn 33.33 per cent on the borrowed money. If it could
borrow money at a lower interest rate then quite obviously it would profit from
so doing.

(ii) In the same vein, they show that the firm should be prepared to pay up to
four-ninths of a munit per munit borrowed to relax the budget constraint in
Year 2, in other words an interest rate of 44 per cent.

(iii) They challenge the validity of the discount rates which were used to derive the
NPVs of these projects initially.

Quite naturally the two former points are of considerable interest, in that they
place values on the relaxation of the cash constraints. They emphasize the relative
merits of relaxing the second year's constraint first, either through external borrowing, or through a redistribution of cash from Year 1 to Year 2. The real purpose of
developing this problem in the depth presented here however rests with the last of
the three implications. Since the objective of this hypothetical problem is to
maximize the wealth (and hence the utility) of the firm by maximizing its NPV, it
follows that the unit NPV contributions of each project are crucial to the resultant
optimal solution as is the discount rate used in their initial evaluation. So far,
however, we have remained silent on the method of evaluating these individual unit
net present values. Normal convention would suggest that the projected cash flows
for each project should be discounted at the firm's cost of capital and then divided
by the project's capacity†. But our trivial problem contained in Table 6.3.1 proved
that such a discount rate would probably lead to incorrect decisions when cash
rationing conditions prevail, and it was suggested that we really need to know the
reinvestment rate if we are to choose correctly between projects. In these circumstances, the opportunity costs contained in the solution to our linear programming problem give *some indication* as to how this problem should be resolved. They
measure this reinvestment rate, but only so long as each constraint remains dominant. It therefore follows that a progressive relaxation in the constraint possessing the
greatest opportunity cost will invariably result in other constraints becoming dominant, resulting in lower opportunity costs in different time periods, thereby frustrating
our understanding of what properly constitutes the reinvestment rate. It might also
be realized that these opportunity costs in themselves are affected by the discount
rate(s) used to derive the NPVs for each project in the first place, so their direct use
as discount rates results in a complicated reiterative problem, of the chicken and egg
variety!

It will now be appreciated that capital budgeting, under cash rationing conditions,
is an extremely complicated subject and the problem of what constitutes the correct
discount rate remains unresolved. Furthermore, little seems to be known about the
effects of using the wrong discount rates. The only point where there does seem to be
agreement in the literature is that the appropriate discount rate should be higher than
the firm's cost of capital but how much higher is not known. Such a result is hardly

---

* In linear programming parlance they are also known as shadow prices and dual values.
† Dividing the project's NPV by its capacity tacitly assumes that constant returns to scale prevail. Such an
assumption in itself is highly unrealistic for many real world applications.

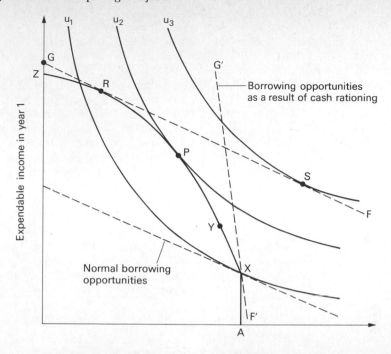

Figure 6.5.3 *Maximization of subjective utility under conditions of cash rationing.*

surprising, however, because Hirshleifer's utility analysis points to the same conclusion for a single period project. This point is partly demonstrated by Figure 6.5.3, which is virtually a replica of Figure 6.1.3 but for one subtle difference arising out of different borrowing opportunities. Starting at point X, Figure 6.5.3 shows us how our hypothetical entrepreneur would normally invest in capital projects up to point R and then borrow money up to point S, in order to maximize his utility. Under conditions of cash rationing, however, his ability to borrow money is severely restricted. This can be represented graphically by the borrowing opportunity lines becoming very steep*, indicating an extremely high interest rate, such that line GF becomes line G^1F^1 instead. In these circumstances, the best option open to our entrepreneur would involve investing in capital projects so as to maximize his utility subject to his cash constraints. It is conceivable that this process of optimization could occur at any point between X and P depending on the shape of his utility curves, the amount of cash internally available in Year 0, the shape of his capital project opportunity curve, and the severity of his borrowing limitations. All that we can predict from the geometry of such a picture is that the optimal solution would normally correspond to an interest rate greater than the firm's usual borrowing rates. A similar situation arises if the capital investment opportunities available to a firm yield returns poorer than the borrowing rate, but better than the lending rate. Under such conditions the firm might conceivably exhaust all of its available cash before attaining the position R^1, previously shown in Figure 6.1.4. In such circumstances the optimal solution would normally correspond to an interest rate in excess of the firm's usual lending rate.

---

*Theoretically, the interest rate would become infinite, resulting in vertical lines of infinite slope.

6.6 CONCLUSIONS

Much of the material in this chapter has been developed assuming that a hypothetical entrepreneur has a utility-indifference map, which we could use for capital budgeting decision-making purposes. However, such information does not normally exist and even if it could be made available, there is evidence to suggest that executives would be reluctant to use it. If one relaxes the assumption about the firm being owned and operated by an entrepreneur, and instead considers the firm as a coalition of various interest groups as suggested in Chapter 3, then the problem of what constitutes the relevant indifference-utility map for such a decision analysis becomes even more complicated. Furthermore, most investments in physical assets are made with a view to realizing benefits for many years ahead, not one, as our previous analysis suggests. Although our utility analysis can deal with projects of long duration on a conceptual basis simply by considering them as a sequence of successive one year projects, nevertheless it cannot deal with them numerically. The last significant criticism of this analysis is the fact that it requires capital investment opportunities to be plotted as a continuous smooth curve. Such a curve is plotted on the assumption that projects are infinitesimally divisible. In practice, however, projects occur as discrete 'lumps' of investment, and generally speaking the cost of refining their analyses so that they can be represented by a smooth curve is not warranted.

Despite these major criticisms of our somewhat esoteric analysis, it does provide us with six fundamental decision rules:

(i) A firm should finance all risk-free and independent capital projects possessing positive NPVs on their *incremental* investment when discounted at the relevant *borrowing* rate, providing cash rationing does not pertain. Such a policy is equivalent to maximizing the NPV of the firm's project portfolio and is identical to accepting projects each with a DCFRR on incremental capital greater than the incremental borrowing rate. In addition, the rule stipulates that money must be borrowed if an optimal decision is to be achieved but remains quite silent on exactly how much money should be borrowed.

(ii) A firm should finance all risk-free and independent capital projects which do not satisfy (i) above, but *do* possess positive NPVs on their incremental investment when discounted at the relevant *lending* rate, providing cash rationing does not pertain. Such a policy is equivalent to maximizing the NPV of the firm's project portfolio but now at the lending rate and is equivalent to accepting projects providing their DCFRR on incremental investment is greater than the incremental lending rate. In addition, the rule suggests that the firm should lend money but is silent on exactly how much money should be lent.

(iii) If a firm does not possess any risk-free and independent capital projects satisfying (i) and (ii) above, then it should maximize its satisfaction-utility by lending some of its current cash surplus. Here again the rule remains silent on the magnitude of such lending.

(iv) If investment in new capital projects is constrained by the availability of cash so that cash has to be rationed between projects, then a firm should finance that project portfolio which provides the greatest overall degree of satisfaction-utility consistent with its cash budget constraints. Such a solution is tantamount to maximizing the NPV of that project portfolio. In such circumstances, however, neither the borrowing nor the lending rates are likely to be appropriate for discounting purposes.

(v) If two or more of a firm's capital investment projects are physically interdependent, they should be amalgamated and considered as one integral project, subject to (i)–(iv) above.

(vi) If some of a firm's capital investment proposals are physically mutually exclusive then it should select those alternatives which provide the greatest NPV consistent with (i)–(v) above.

It will now be appreciated that the DCFRR on the *total* investment involved with a project is rather a poor criterion for selecting between projects and, considering the fact that some projects possess multiple DCFRRs (discussed in Appendix F), its use cannot be recommended but for the most simple of decision making problems. Likewise the overall NPV of a project conceals the fact that the NPV on *incremental* investment might be unsatisfactory. Where possible it behoves the decision maker to question the economic merits of a project on an incremental basis (see Chapter 11). It will also be realized that the contents of the two preceding chapters glibly refer to the cost of capital, which we now recognize as a principal element in determining the economic merits of a new capital project and a complete project portfolio. This matter will be resolved in Chapter 8. Lastly, it will be realized that everything which has been propounded to date completely ignores the problem of uncertainty and its attendant risk. Such matters obviously have a considerable bearing on the appropriateness of these six decision rules as we shall discover in subsequent chapters.

6.7 BIBLIOGRAPHY

General texts

Bierman, H. and Smidt, S., *The Capital Budgeting Decision*, MacMillan, 1975. The capital budgeting problem receives a very full and complete treatment in this book along with a coverage of some of those controversies which appear in this chapter.

Bromwich, M., *The Economics of Capital Budgeting*, Penguin, 1978. This book provides excellent reading of the problems and controversies which pervade the arena of management/engineering economics.

Thuesen, H. G., Fabrycky, W. J. and Thuesen, G. J., *Engineering Economy*, Prentice-Hall, 1977. This book provides ideal background reading to the subject matter of this chapter since it employs many fine examples to illustrate the problems of capital budgeting when alternatives solutions to an engineering problem exist.

Specific texts

Baumol, W. J. and Quandt, R. E., 'Investment and discount rates under capital rationing: a programming approach', *Economic Journal*, **75** (298), June 1965, pp. 317–329.

Dantzig, G. B., *Linear Programming and Extensions*, Princeton University Press, 1963.

Hirshleifer, J., 'On the theory of optimal investment decision', *Journal of Political Economy*, **66** (4), 1958, pp. 329–352.

Lorie, J. H. and Savage, L. J., 'Three problems in capital budgeting', *Journal of Business*, **28** (4), October 1955, pp. 229–239.

Weingartner, H. M., *Mathematical Programming and the Analysis of Capital Budgeting Problems*, Prentice-Hall, 1963 (reprinted, Markham Publishing Company, 1966).

6.8 QUESTIONS

6.8.1 The managing director of a medium-sized, mediocre profit-making company is faced with a dilemma: to assure the perpetuity of his company, he must diversify his product line. The manager of the corporate planning department has screened all possible projects and has recommended two new projects. Unfortunately, it is felt that the company can only afford one of these projects. The economics for the two projects are as follows:

Project	Capital cost £ (Year 0)	Net annual cash flows after tax (£ per annum) Years 1–5	Years 6–10	Economic life (yrs)	Scrap Value
A	£500 000	100 000	150 000	10	0
B	£782 000	150 000	200 000	10	0

To finance these projects the company would have to borrow money. It has been ascertained that the cost of the first £500,000 would be 10 per cent per annum after tax. However, if the company were to finance the more expensive project then the cost of the *incremental* capital could range from 10–15 per cent per annum after tax.

Which project would you recommend? At what incremental cost of capital would you be indifferent between these two projects?

6.8.2 The directors of a firm are considering which of two alternative processes, X and Y, to install in order to manufacture 6400 tonnes per annum of a product, which is expected to have a selling price of $1000/tonne. The capital costs of the plants would be 4×10^6 for X and 1.6×10^6 for Y, and the total annual operating costs when the plants are in production are estimated as 2.16×10^6 for X and 2.72×10^6 for Y. Whichever of the processes is installed, half the capital costs will be incurred in the present year (year 0) and half in the following year (year 1). The design rate of production and sales should be achieved at the start of the following year (year 2), and should continue throughout the lifetime of the process, which is assumed to be seven years of production for either process.

The cost to the firm of the investment funds raised to finance the chosen process is uncertain at present, but should be known shortly. It will certainly be in the range 10–20 per cent per annum.

Following a discounted cash flow analysis of the investment decision, based on the estimates quoted, give advice to the board concerning the choice of process. (Taxation, scrap values, commissioning, any other charges and inflation effects may be ignored.)

6.8.3 The managers of a firm are considering investment in one of the following projects. If the cost of capital to the firm is expected to be within the range 12–17 per cent per annum, give reasoned advice which, if any, of the projects should be chosen.

| End of | | Project | | |
year	A	B	C	D
Initial cash investment (£k) — 0	220	200	200	200
Net cash inflows (£k) — 1	0	48	0	90
2	50	48	0	70
3	50	48	0	60
4	50	48	0	50
5	50	48	0	40
6	50	48	0	30
7	50	48	0	20
8	50	48	800	20
9	50	–	–	–
10	50	–	–	–

6.8.4 A firm has the option of repairing a machine or replacing it by a new machine according to the following year end cost data:

| | | | (munits per annum) | | |
Year	0	1	2	3	4
Repair	900	2450	3200	3700	3950
Replace	6000	1250	1500	2000	1500

If the service provided by each option is the same, which option would you select? Would your answer remain the same if you delayed the replacement?

6.8.5 The management of a firm, for which the cost of capital is expected to be in the range 10–15 per cent, is considering investment in one of the following projects. Give fully reasoned advice, which should include a discounted cash flow analysis, concerning which, if any, of the projects should be selected.

| End of | | Project | | |
year	A	B	C	D
Capital investment (£k) — 0	1700	1640	1960	1600
Annual net cash inflows (£k) — 1	350	0	0	600
2	350	0	0	600
3	350	560	0	400
4	350	560	0	300
5	350	560	0	200
6	350	560	0	200
7	350	560	0	150
8	350	560	5000	100

6.8.6 'In comparing the relative economic merits of alternative projects with different first costs, it is the return on their differential capital at risk which matters.' Comment on the validity of this statement and describe the business conditions which necessarily support it.

6.8.7 A company's management is considering the following projects:

	End of year	A	B	C	D	E	F
Initial cash outlay	0	110 000	100 000	210 000	180 000	50 000	200 000
Net cash inflows	1	0	20 000	70 000	0	20 000	15 000
	2	20 000	20 000	70 000	0	20 000	15 000
	3	20 000	20 000	70 000	0	20 000	15 000
	4	20 000	20 000	70 000	0	20 000	50 000
	5	20 000	20 000	70 000	0	20 000	50 000
	6	20 000	20 000		0		50 000
	7	20 000	20 000		0		50 000
	8	20 000	20 000		0		50 000
	9	20 000	20 000		0		50 000
	10	20 000	20 000		900 000		50 000
	11	20 000					
	12	20 000					
	13	20 000					
	14	20 000					
	15	20 000					

Calculate the following in respect of each of the six projects: the payback period, the accounting return (based on initial investment), the net present value (at a cost of capital 16 per cent), and the DCFRR.

6.8.8 The capital projects committee of a large company are considering new investment proposals from the operating divisions. Resources are limited and funds will only be allocated to projects promising the best return with the least risk.

Investment proposals

	End of year	A £	B £	C £
Initial cash outlay	0	150 000	70 000	110 000
Net cash inflows	1	–	16 000	–
	2	–	16 000	–
	3	40 000	16 000	–
	4	40 000	16 000	–
	5	40 000	16 000	–
	6	40 000	16 000	–
	7	40 000	16 000	
	8	40 000	16 000	–
	9	40 000	16 000	–
	10	40 000	16 000	500 000

The cost of capital is estimated to be 15 per cent per annum. Calculate the following for each project: the accounting return, the net present value, and the DCFRR. Comment on the results. Recommend one project, giving your reasons.

7. On the Systematic Search for Relevant Information

'We can no longer afford to approach the longer-range future haphazardly. As the pace of change accelerates, the process of change becomes more complex . . . Our need now is to seize on the future as the key dimension in our decisions, and to chart the future as consciously as we are accustomed to charting the past.'

President Richard Nixon, 12 July 1969

This quotation is most appropriate in the context of capital budgeting. No firm can afford to invest in expensive plant and machinery without first attempting to chart the future which might hold forth all sorts of threats and opportunities for a capital investment project. To make our life-cycle economic equation operable, therefore, we are obliged to forecast all those exogenous and endogenous factors (such as prices, sales volumes, and capital and operating costs which form an integral part of that equation), whose interdependence is illustrated by the schema shown in Figure 7.1 below. Limitations of space preclude a full treatment of each of these factors here, because they constitute whole specialized books. However, our treatment of these factors, both singularly and collectively, will be sufficient for the reader to appreciate the full economic implications of the capital budgeting decision. Furthermore, in studying these matters to the degree offered here, we should gain a better appreciation of the uncertainties involved with forecasting each of these factors, and a fuller understanding of the risks involved with capital investment. In this respect the chapter is a prelude to Chapter 9 which deals with matters of risk and uncertainty in detail.

To reinforce our brief but comprehensive treatment of each factor involved with the NPV equation, detailed references are provided at the end of each section of this chapter. As a last introductory point it should be mentioned that mathematical forecasting models permeate the entire structure of this chapter. Our reasons for their liberal use is to ensure consistency in the assumptions used, consistency in the logic framework of forecasting and consistency in the detailed manipulation of data. Mathematics also enables the implied assumptions of decision analysis and its results to be tested against a background of accumulated business experience. Despite their use, however, we must concede the point that mathematical models, applied to human purchasing behaviour in particular, are far less profound than those applied to the physical sciences. It often becomes a matter of intuitive judgement whether or to what extent the conditions are, or will be, met which make the model applicable to the forecasting problem at hand. Faced with this predicament, unsatisfactory as it may seem, one often has to rely on the intuitive judgement of experts specialized in those areas which are relevant to the desired forecast, and to combine their opinions as effectively as possible to resolve the forecasting problem.

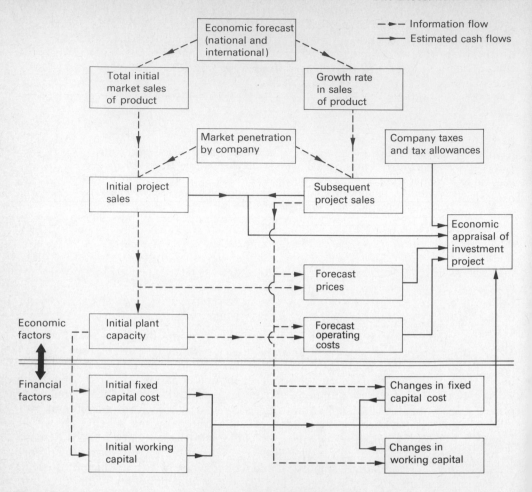

Figure 7.1 *Schema showing the information needs of a prospective capital project.*

7.1 AN EVALUATION OF THE BUSINESS AND ECONOMIC ENVIRONMENT

Planning the future operations, investments and acquisitions of a firm so that it can respond to threats and take advantage of opportunities in a timely and efficient manner is one of the major duties of management. To do this properly requires an assessment of the changing nature of the business environment in which the firm operates or intends to operate. By implication, however, all planning must be based on forecasts, the purpose of which is to identify areas of uncertainty in the firm's likely future operations so that their risks can be assessed and they can be planned for accordingly.

The accepted truism about forecasting is that forecasts are inevitably *wrong*, but this does not imply that forecasting is too hazardous to be useful because we really have no other alternative except our own intuitive feelings about the future. The real purpose of forecasting therefore is to map out what we believe the future might bring and attempt to assess the likelihood of particular events happening by specified dates.

The problems of forecasting differ from one firm to the next. As we shall see in Section 7.2, it is often appropriate to forecast the demand for commodity products on the basis of some functional relationship, which depends on secular changes in the economy at large. In these circumstances a prediction of the aggregate growth rate of the economy in the future is required. For many manufacturing companies, however, it is difficult to trace a direct relationship between the company's performance and the secular growth of the economy containing it.

Perhaps the most conspicuous causal relationship, which exists between the performance of the economy and that of any individual firm comes from the cyclic pattern of behaviour of the former and its pronounced effect on corporate profits. Indeed, an analysis of the profits accruing to many different types of firms in different economies typically shows that the peaks and troughs in their profits correspond with a 3–5-year periodic, which resembles the fluctuations in the overall performance of the economy at large.

Economists distinguish four phases in these cycles, each phase moving into the next in a wheel-like sequence involving (i) an up-turn or revival from the trough of the cycle, moving into (ii) an expansion, followed by (iii) a recession as the turning point or peak is passed, followed by (iv) a contraction until the lower turning point is passed. When the peaks and troughs are pronounced they are known respectively as booms and depressions. Business cycles, such as these, are a natural manifestation of the business psychology which exists in unregulated free-market economies. Their existence can be explained by two principles known as the accelerator and multiplier effects.

According to proponents of the accelerator principle, a change in customer demand can bring about a greater than proportionate change in business investment. The effect of this principle is most apparent in the capital goods market, where customers often show a reluctance to increase their capacity until the gap between their production capacity and sales is quite small. By stark contrast, faced with a diminution in the rate of *increase* of demand for their products, they tend to reduce their orders for new capital plant and machinery quite drastically, often to the point of driving down the absolute demand for capital goods.

The multiplier effect is quite a different phenomenon which deals with the magnifying effect of independent changes in spending – especially investment spending – on the total income and consumption of an economy. The basic idea of this principle is that the first effect of money spent is to increase the incomes of the recipients in like amount. Some of this income is absorbed in taxes (also to be spent), some is spent on consumable goods, and the remainder is saved and invested to provide more income for the saver, business for the investment recipient, and of course business for downstream borrowers of funds too; and so the cascade ripple effect percolates throughout an economy but at a diminishing rate governed largely by the propensity to save. By these means one unit of money saved can lead to four or five units of money invested in capital assets through this process of multiplication. By contrast, however, a decrease in investment spending has the reverse effect.

Both the accelerator and the multiplier principles can interact to have a reinforcing effect, which is a measure of the total business confidence held by the economy at large and the influence which international trade might have on that economy too. The interesting thing is that people tend to expect a continuation of what is currently happening. If unemployment is rising many feel that they too might soon be made redundant so they spend less which, of course, aggravates unemployment by driving down prices which, in turn, cause businessmen to defer purchases – and so the spiral continues.

Left alone, the momentum of booms and depressions becomes exhausted, but not before economic, financial and social havoc have been wreaked on the way. It is for this reason that government control of an economy is essential to prevent the recurrence of the economic plight witnessed during the Great Depression of the 1930s. To that end, governments apply various fiscal and monetary policies to counter cyclic swings. These measures include (i) progressive taxation, which means that people retain proportionately less of their total increasing incomes but proportionately more of their decreasing incomes, (ii) the use of government budget surpluses to regulate business booms and budget deficits to minimize business recessions, and (iii) various instruments of trade credit control, including changes to the interest rates operating throughout an economy and the international rate of exchange of its currency.

Governments possess another dimension to the way they can regulate an economy when a part of the production capacity of a nation is nationally owned, as is the case in mixed economies*. This means that they can retain employment in national enterprises, albeit at an economic loss, in the face of a business recession, thereby enhancing what would otherwise be a declining national income. Unfortunately, evidence suggests that, operated in this way, national enterprises become highly inefficient in economic terms, and an excuse for job 'featherbedding'.

Faced with the fact that business cycles occur and are likely to continue, the task facing the corporate forecaster is to identify the cyclic relationships of importance to the particular firm. This can only be done through a rigorous examination of the historical performance of the firm to determine the particular cyclic pattern in its economic and trading behaviour, and the correlation of these cycles with the appropriate cycles in the economy at large. The next step involves finding some *economic indicator(s)* which forewarn(s) the changing direction of the business cycle and its likely affect on the firm. A variety of business leading indicators exist including: spot market prices, stock prices, new capital appropriations, housing starts, building permits, construction contract awards, manufacturers' new orders, and many more. An example of the way in which the number of housing starts affects the sales of the chemical product Phenol, which is used extensively in the manufacture of furniture, household fixtures and fitments, is shown in Figure 7.1.1.

Data on these macroeconomic indicators are regularly published by the statistical offices of most governments†. Of course all this study is to little avail unless the firm can exercise authority over a sufficient number of factors to control its own destiny, if not in whole at least in part. This is where a properly formulated corporate strategy is essential. Each company must muster its resources to take advantage of any business upturn and mitigate the affect of business downturns, and it is in this respect that corporate distinctiveness, which clearly differentiates one firm and its products from the next, is all-important. It should never be forgotten that all firms are in competition to win a limited degree of spending power. For this reason alone, companies need to study the environment in its widest sense, recognizing that their forecasting effort must be made cost-effective, so they need to concentrate on those aspects of forecasting which are of greatest concern to the firm. To this end considerable attention should be paid to movements in costs and prices, including international rates of exchange, as well as changes in volume and quantities. This is yet another reason why attention must be given to the performance of the economy at large, and government efforts to control aggregate supply and demand, international indebtedness, inflation and unemployment. In this respect, each firm must

* Technically speaking aggregate business cycles should not occur in planned economies, as for example in some of the socialist states, providing (i) the planners anticipate aggregate demand and the prices people are willing to pay for goods and services, and (ii) that planned production is realized. These conditions are seldom met in practice.
† An excellent account of business cycles and the usefulness of economic indicators is provided by McKinley, Lee and Duffy (1965).

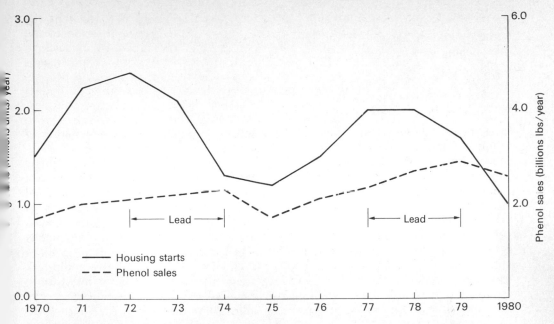

Figure 7.1.1 *An example of a leading economic indicator.*

assess the likely pattern of taxation and interest rates which could seriously affect its overall performance and its investment strategy in particular. Furthermore, it must assess the influence of likely changes in the political nature of the economies in which it operates, or intends to operate, and design its corporate strategy accordingly.

So far we have tended to concentrate our attention on the short-term cyclic performance of the economy because short-term changes can have a dramatic effect on large sections of business. Long-term secular changes in an economy are much more gradual, and more readily forecasted with a fair degree of confidence*. For this reason, it is thought that a most appropriate form of environmental forecasting might be the frequent reappraisal of a company's plans in light of expected short-term changes where the launching of a new product, the borrowing of money and investment of capital projects is concerned but such forecasts as these must mesh with long-term forecasts especially those involved with political and technological forecasts (dealt with in Chapter 10.4).

7.1.1 Bibliography

McKinley, D. H., Lee, M. G. and Duffy, H., *Forecasting Business Conditions*, American Banking Association, 1965.

Samuelson, P. A., *Economics*, McGraw-Hill, 10th edition, 1976.

7.2 DETERMINING MARKET SIZE

From an overall corporate viewpoint, forecasting the size of the market into which a company plans selling its products and/or services is important as an aid to making

---

* An excellent introductory account of secular movements in an economy is given by Samuelson (1976).

the following types of decisions:

  (i) the optimal sizing, timing and location of new capital assets,
 (ii) launching new products,
(iii) plans for diversification,
 (iv) breaking into new markets,
  (v) mergers and takeovers and, of course,
 (vi) the selection of R & D projects.

Depending on the life-cycle characteristics of the product or service, and the flexibility of the manufacturing assets involved, it is conceivable that some firms might only need to forecast a year or so ahead. However, other companies planning substantial R & D and capital expenditure might need to forecast ten or more years ahead. Irrespective of the type of products or assets involved, however, the need to forecast the likely future comprehensively for any marketing endeavour is *proven*. Three out of every ten new products fail in some important respect to come up to expectation, and one out of these three invariably has to be withdrawn from the market because of its poor performance. Such is the experience of companies which participate in business opinion and experience reviews which regularly feature in marketing journals. Furthermore it is usually found that the principal factors which cause product failures are *within a firm's own control*.

The major reasons given for new product failures, in descending order of importance, are:

(i)	inadequate market analysis	(35%)
(ii)	product defects	(25%)
(iii)	higher costs than expected	(15%)
(iv)	poor timing	(7%)
(v)	competitive pricing policies	(5%)
(vi)	insufficient marketing effort	(5%)
(vii)	an inappropriate sales force	(3%)
(viii)	inadequate distribution	(3%)
(ix)	others	(2%)

Insufficient knowledge and understanding of the market and misjudging its receptiveness is the single most important reason for the disappointing performance of many new products; most troublesome of all is gauging the *size* of the market and understanding customers' *buying habits* and their *needs*.

7.2.1 The need for market research

Quite clearly the scenario we have just outlined calls for market research to help resolve these deficiencies but like all other forms of research it must be made cost-effective, and the risks involved with its results and recommendations must be carefully weighed before executive action is taken*. This is especially relevant where research based on consumer opinions of future purchasing behaviour is involved because it is human nature to give encouraging and pleasant replies to interviews so long as it does not cost money to do so. In other words the results of market research can sometimes be fickle and misleading unless the research is conducted professionally.

The type of information which market researchers regularly seek is of the

---

* In this respect market research is very similar to technical research and amenable to the same kind of economic analysis given in Chapter 10.3.

following kind:

(i) the size of the market for a particular product,
(ii) trends in the volume of demand,
(iii) the share of the market which the firm can expect,
(iv) the structure of the market – analysis of actual and potential customers by type and location,
(v) channels of distribution and sales – relative importance of different outlets as the means of reaching the customer,
(vi) competitors' activities,
(vii) customer information – identification and continuing study of key customers whose buying habits can be indicators of overall market tendencies, and
(viii) studies of the acceptability of a product or service to determine both what customers buy and why they buy it, plus technical and commercial considerations such as product design, application, appearance, price, packaging, advertising support and the frequency of service.

Of course the scope and depth of a market research study must fit the particular need – it must be problem orientated. To that end it has to be planned for and controlled like any other corporate activity. Market research is conducted in two ways: by desk research and by field research. The first involves a continuous monitoring of the firm's and known competitors' performances, involving such considerations as:

(i) invoiced sales: analysis by products, customer type, region, outlet, cyclical or seasonal fluctuations and rates of growth or decline,
(ii) orders received: analyses as in (i) above,
(iii) enquiries received: analyses as in (i) above,
(iv) customer information to identify key customers,
(v) competitor information to identify key competitors: from lost orders, salesmen's, agents' and distributors' reports and the monitoring of competitors' activities through advertising, pricing and market analyses,
(vi) product acceptability: analysis of complaints, returns, enquiries and the general trend in orders.

Besides reviewing the firm's performance and the performance of competitors, desk research also relies on the study of published statistics of which the most important are those published by government departments, trade associations, banks and information derived from published surveys in articles and books. Indeed, good desk research requires a wide knowledge and experience of published statistics, of their method of collection and the reliability of such data.

Field research is undertaken to provide answers to specific and important questions which cannot be answered by any other means. This form of research is more expensive than desk research so it has to be thoroughly planned and executed. It is used to:

(i) establish the size of markets too specific to be isolated by published data,
(ii) establish trends in consumption in such markets,
(iii) establish competitors' share of the market,
(iv) assess the relative importance to buyers of different sources of supply,
(v) determine customers' requirements, such as design, price, terms of trade, etc., and
(vi) assess the acceptability of current and proposed products or services and the reasons for customers' brand preferences.

Field research involves asking questions of informed respondents, who are usually selected on the basis of a some representative sample, which might conceivably be determined by statistical means. Quite clearly, however, there is a considerable distinction between market research studies conducted for mass-produced consumer goods and industrial capital goods, and these distinctions have to be considered carefully when designing market research surveys, questionnaires and experiments.

7.2.2 The techniques of market forecasting

A whole armoury of techniques has evolved to meet the challenge of forecasting the likely extent of future sales for a particular product. These techniques can be classified by three *models*, known as holistic, disaggregated and atomistic forecasts, and four *types* known as opinion analysis, time-trend analysis, historical analogy and econometric forecasting techniques, as illustrated by the matrix shown in Figure 7.2.2.1.

Holistic models involve forecasting the demand for the markets as a whole; in other words no attempt is made to differentiate and understand the different end uses which the product might serve.

Disaggregated models involve a greater level of understanding by dividing the total market into segments such as:

(i) different industries which use the product,
(ii) different regions,
(iii) different end-use applications,
(iv) different demographic, social and income groupings of customers, and
(v) subtle differences in the sales of different products competing in the same market.

Disaggregation is probably normal practice in forecasting most products. A fully-worked example of this technique is given in the NIESR (National Institute of Economic and Social Research) (1965) study of UK paper and cardboard sales. In this study the following segments were identified, and a functional relationship was developed to forecast their independent segmental requirements using the determinants shown below:

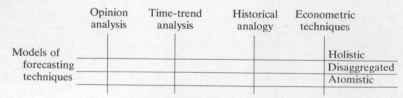

Types of forecasting techniques

Figure 7.2.2.1 *A matrix of sales forecasting techniques.*

Segment	Determinant
Newsprint	Population
Printing	Consumer expenditure
Food wrapping	Consumer food expenditure
Household toilet and tissue	Consumer expenditure on non-durable goods
Industrial	Gross industrial output
Packing	Gross industrial output
Building board	Gross output of the construction industry

Atomistic models constitute the final step in disaggregation. In this case the atoms are the individual customers who might comprise large corporations. In its simplest form this involves salesmen's opinions after consulting customers. Alternatively, it could involve forecasting the particular needs of that customer well into the future, with or without his co-operation.

According to Fisher (1969) the variables most affecting forecasts of industrial goods sales, in declining order of importance, are:

(i) the overall growth rate of the economy,
(ii) the growth/decline rate of the customer's industry,
(iii) expected business with specific customers,
(iv) government intervention in the market-place by a variety of fiscal, monetary, statutory and other means,
(v) pricing policies,
(vi) technological change in the customer's business,
(vii) technological change in one's own business.

It is not our intention to deal with technological issues here since this matter receives full attention in Chapters 10 and 19. However, based on Fisher's results and those of the NIESR study, it would appear that the performance of the economy containing a firm *can* have a significant affect on its sales. The type of forecasting technique which can best deal with this situation is econometric forecasting.

7.2.3 Econometric forecasting

This involves the regression of the historical demand data for a product against other independent macroeconomic variables such as population size, gross national or domestic product, the index of industrial production, and national earnings and savings, which can be forecast more easily. This method is most appropriate when the particular product is diverse in its end-use, so that its growth rate is similar to that of the economy at large. To use this technique implies there exist some rational grounds for believing that the product demand must vary with aggregate business activity. This technique involves linear, curvilinear and mixed regression analysis using equations of the following form:

$$Y = a_0 + a_1 \cdot X_1 + a_2 \cdot X_2 + \ldots a_n \cdot X_n$$

and

$$Y = a_0 + a_1 \cdot X_1^{b_1} + a_2 \cdot X_2^{b_2} + \ldots a_n \cdot X_n^{b_n}$$

where Y = the historical consumption per unit of time of the particular product (the dependent variable), X = the historical performance of a particular macroeconomic indicator (the independent variable), and a_i, b_i = regression coefficients where $(i = 0, n)$.

Statistical computer programs are available to determine the best fits for these relationships, and by these means the most appropriate independent variables can be found. A very concise introductory paper on the use of these models with a most useful selective bibliography of the extensive literature on this subject is provided by Wagle (1966). Econometric models vary in the numbers of independent variables they require to explain the variation in the demand level of the product of interest. For example, an analysis of the demand for petroleum products in the UK during the period 1946–64 showed that the relationship:

$$\log_{10} D_t = -147 + 20 \log_{10} P_t$$

Table 7.2.4.1a *Properties of common time-trend analysis models*

Model	Type	Equation $S_t =$	Instantaneous growth rate $\dfrac{dS_t}{dt} =$	Instantaneous % Growth Rate^a $100\dfrac{d\ln S_t}{dt} =$	Comments
1	Linear	$S_0 + rt$	r	$r/(S_0 + rt)$	This is unlikely to occur during the initial growth phase. However it often represents the full-scale development phase of the market.
2	Exponential	$S_0 e^{rt}$	$rS_0 e^{rt}$	r	This is often written in the form $S_t = a(1+r)^t$. It implies a constant annual percentage growth. This is often experienced by mature products which become an important part of the economy and grow at a rate similar to that of the economy.
3	Negative exponential	$S^*(1 - e^{-rt})$	$r(S^* - S_t)$	$\dfrac{re^{-rt}}{(1 - e^{-rt})}$	This is often written in the form $S_t = a - br^t$. The major objection to its use is the very high initial growth rate. It has been used to represent the approach to saturation, however.
4	Negative exponential growth rate	$S_0 \exp[r_\infty t + A(1 - e^{-kt})]$	$r_\infty - (r_0 - r_\infty)e^{-kt}$	$\dfrac{r_\infty - (r_0 - r_\infty)e^{-kt}}{S_0 \exp[r_\infty t + A(1 - e^{-kt})]}$	Here $A = (r_0 - r_\infty)/k$. This model well represents those cases where the annual growth rate declines at a constant percentage each year until saturation is approached. In this respect it is very like the Gompertz curve.

	Model				Description
5	Parabola	$S_0 + bt + ct^2$	$b + 2ct$	$\dfrac{b+2ct}{(S_0+bt+ct^2)}$	Both this and the log parabola ($\log S_t = S_0 + bt + ct^2$) give concave upwards curves if coefficients b and c are positive. Both have been used to represent the high growth phase of a market. With the coefficients b and c of opposite sign, both parabolas have a turning point and in this respect can represent market decline.
6	Simple logistic	$S^*(1-e^{a-bt})^{-1}$	$\propto S_t(S^*-S_t)$	$\propto (S^*-S_t)$	Here $a = \ln[(S^*-S_0)/S_0]$ and $b = \propto S^*$. This model permits the inclusion of psychological mass pressure on the individual to buy. However its shortcoming is that it assumes a homogeneous market. This model invariably underestimates the saturation level and is symmetrical, an unlikely real world quality.
7	Gompertz	e^{a-bc^t}	$-\ln cS_t[\ln S^*-\ln S_t]$	$-bc^t \ln a$	This is probably the most popular of models. Its instantaneous growth rate r_t the log transform of the logistic model. This model is asymmetrical with inflection point coordinates: $t = -\ln b/\ln c$; $S_t = e^{a-1}$. This function is often written as: $S_t = ab^{c^t}$.

$\ln$ = logarithm; [a] For an annual % growth rate r_t the increase in market sales over a time interval dt is given by

$$dS_t = S_t r_t\, dt \qquad \therefore r_t = \frac{1}{S_t}\frac{dS_t}{dt} \qquad r_t = \frac{d\ln S_t}{dt}$$

From de la Mare (1978), with kind permission of the Editor of *Engineering and Process Economics*.

where D_t = demand for all petroleum products per annum (tens of millions of tonnes), P_t = UK *de facto* population (millions), and t = the year of interest could explain 98 per cent of the variation in petroleum product demand. By contrast, it was found that UK sales of domestic refrigerators, up to 1963, were best modelled using the equation

$$\log_{10} R = 6.46 + (8.6 \log_{10} Y - 24.1)(0.64 + 0.009T)^x$$

where R = the numbers of refrigerators sold each year (thousands), Y = UK personal disposable income adjusted by the retail price index, T = the sales tax on refrigerators, and x = the number of years from 1950. Since forecasting the expected sales of a product using econometric forecasting transfers the forecasting problem from the dependent variable to the independent variable, it will be appreciated that the former of these examples lead to a much easier forecasting problem than the latter, especially as population growth rates can be forecast with greater accuracy than other macroeconomic variables.

Another kind of econometric forecasting technique uses the principle of input-output analysis, first developed by Leontief (1966). This method is concerned with the interindustrial flow of goods and services. It is based on the technical factors which relate the inputs of a firm or industry to its outputs, and it relies on forecasts of the changes in these technical factors and the output of an industry to make its use effective.

7.2.4 Time-trend analysis and projection

This technique is similar to the preceding technique, except that it requires the extrapolation of historical sales data on the basis of some mathematical functional relationship which varies with time. This technique is most useful for fast growing products such as electronic components and certain petrochemical products. In these circumstances, the more traditional market research technique of opinion analysis (which is normally based on statistical sampling) is often inappropriate because of the smallness and unhomogeneity of the market (which of course for electronics and petrochemicals is a market of derived demand, unlike the markets for final demand as featured by consumer goods). Moreover, for rapidly growing markets, it may be more fruitful to heed the views of the innovative few who make the market grow, rather than the complacent majority who are often satisfied to maintain the status quo. Furthermore, fast growing products do not normally lend themselves to accurate prediction using econometric models because of their immaturity, although it has to be admitted that there exist some excellent exceptions to this generality; Phenol is a notable example.

Seven of the better known time-trend models feature in Table 7.2.4.1a, where the following notations have been used: S_t = the sales level at some time t, such that $(t = 0, \infty)$, S^* = the saturation sales level, r = a constant rate of sales growth, r_t = the rate of sales growth at time 't' such that $(t = 0, \infty)$, and all the other symbols denote regression parameters.

With the exception of the negative exponential and logistic models, which represent special forms of buying behaviour and can be developed from reasoned hypotheses, the remainder of these models are simply empirical, and the underlying assumption to justify their use is that market forces which affected past sales will join in a like manner to affect future sales. Although this assumption might be somewhat naive, Harrison and Pearce (1971) in particular show that these models have been used quite successfully. With the exception of the exponential model, which is best applied to products which have already gained widespread acceptance in an economy and tend to grow at a rate which is similar to that of the economy, the remaining models attempt to emulate all or part of the classical S-shaped curve, which is a common feature of the product life-cycle. Many statistical distributions, such as the normal, log-normal and gamma distributions can be used for this purpose, but each has its own serious limitations. Amongst existing models, the Gompertz function (which was devised to model human mortality) is probably the most successfully used model to date, but the computation of its regression parameters is somewhat involved. Research by de la Mare (1978) has shown that most of these models can be outperformed by the model:

$$S_t = S^* \left\{ 1 - \exp\left[-\left(\frac{t}{A}\right)^\beta \right] \right\}$$

which can be supported by reasoned hypotheses of buying behaviour. An example of this model, applied to the sales of the optical whitener Titanium Dioxide, is shown in Table 7.2.4.1b and a graph depicting the best regression using this equation is shown in Figure 7.2.4.1. This graph incorporates several interesting features. First, it exhibits a pronounced S-shape. Secondly it shows how the sales are tending towards a saturation level. Thirdly, it illustrates how the fitted curve represents a weighted moving average around which the actual sales fluctuate in a cyclic and random fashion. In this case the cyclic tendency can be ascribed to fluctuations in the economy at large. These oscillations could be damped using some microeconomic index, such as the index of industrial production, as a deflator to normalize the actual sales. However, one really needs to include these short-term cyclic variations in any forecast of future sales by extrapolating them into the future on the basis of the best regressed long-term equation and short-term variations modelled either by the moving average, exponential moving average or the Box–Jenkins (1970) techniques, which are described by Chambers et al. (1971).

Table 7.2.4.1b *A comparison of the actual US consumption of titanium dioxide (KG per capita) per annum and the consumption predicted by the best regressed model*[a]

Year	Actual consumption	Best regressed model	Year	Actual consumption	Best regressed model	Year	Actual consumption	Best regressed model
1925	0.02	0.0009	1940	0.68	0.546	1955	2.10	1.939
1926	0.02	0.0047	1941	0.82	0.621	1956	2.20	2.036
1927	0.02	0.0121	1942	0.72	0.700	1957	1.91	2.132
1928	0.03	0.023	1943	0.69	0.784	1958	2.20	2.226
1929	0.04	0.039	1944	0.82	0.870	1959	2.31	2.317
1930	0.04	0.060	1945	1.10	0.960	1960	2.30	2.406
1931	0.06	0.085	1946	1.10	1.052	1961	2.34	2.493
1932	0.09	0.116	1947	1.30	1.147	1962	2.49	2.576
1933	0.09	0.152	1948	1.56	1.243	1963	2.60	2.656
1934	0.16	0.193	1949	1.37	1.341	1964	2.70	2.733
1935	0.27	0.239	1950	1.65	1.441	1965	2.82	2.807
1936	0.36	0.291	1951	1.60	1.541	1966	2.91	2.877
1937	0.42	0.347	1952	1.67	1.641	1967	2.80	2.944
1938	0.38	0.409	1953	1.72	1.741	1968	3.01	3.007
1939	0.55	0.475	1954	1.81	1.840	1969	3.07	3.067

[a] Where the equation for the best regressed model is:

$$S(t) = 3.70 \left[1 - \exp\left\{ -\left(\frac{t}{35.24}\right)^{2.324} \right\} \right]$$

From de la Mare (1978), with kind permission of the Editor of *Engineering and Process Economics*.

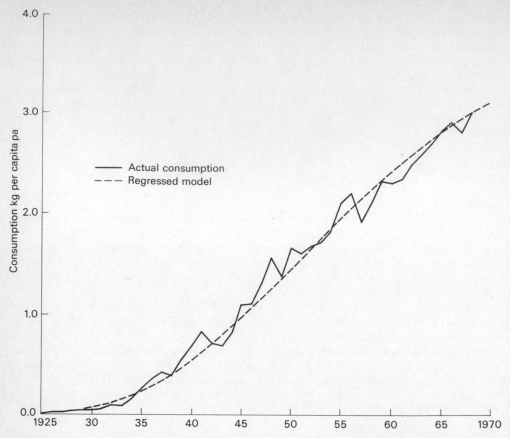

Figure 7.2.4.1 *Comparison between actual consumption of titanium dioxide and best regressed model. Reproduced with kind permission of the Editor of* Engineering and Process Economics.

7.2.5 Forecasting using historical analogy

Historical analogy is sometimes a convenient way of predicting the future sales of a relatively new product. This technique, which basically involves relating the growth of the new product to that of a similar, known product at a comparable stage in its development, is a risky way to forecast, and has many pitfalls. However, in spite of the high degree of subjectivity involved, it is a useful tool when used with other methods. Van Arnum (1964) illustrated the use of this technique in forecasting the market for polyester fibres by analogy with the known previous growth of nylon fibres in the same market. In a similar fashion, Mumford (1963) suggested that in making a projection for a particular product or class of product, it is often fruitful to consider what has already happened in other countries where the market is more advanced. He showed how per capita sales of aerosol cans in the USA preceded sales in the UK by approximately seven years, so the former could be used as a precursor to predict the latter.

7.2.6 Opinion sample analysis

This technique is often employed in conjunction with the previous numerical methods to qualify their results. Alternatively, if these numerical methods are inappropriate because of the unique nature of the product and/or the lack of historical data, then this method might comprise the last resort in forecasting future product demand.

Several techniques can be used. *Market Research*, as a generalized technique, comprises a systematic procedure for evaluating and testing hypotheses about real markets using questionnaires interviews, and market testing, possibly using product samples. *Panel Consensus* is sometimes used when the options of several experts are thought to be better than a 'visionary forecast' by a single executive, whereas the *Delphi Technique*, which is described in Chapter 10.4.1, is often used to overcome the band-wagon deficiency resulting from the panel consensus approach. Whichever approach is used, however, the essential feature of opinion sample analysis is to identify the particular market segment within which the company wants to operate. The results of opinion sample analysis should reveal the needs of potential customers and evaluate the utility of the product being offered. By these means a firm should identify and evaluate the existing and potential *end-uses* of its product offering.

It will be realized that market research based on industrial capital goods differs markedly from that involved with consumer goods in the nature of the analysis conducted. In the latter, the size of the potential market often justifies opinion analysis on the basis of a statistical sampling procedure. For many industrial capital goods, however, this approach is often inappropriate because of the paucity of customer-firms involved. In these circumstances it is often far better to identify those firms which are the pacemakers in technological innovation and change and heed their views when attempting to forecast demand for such a product.

7.2.7 Some objections to market sales forecasting techniques

So far we have only described the rudiments of the forecasting techniques which are available, but quite clearly there exist certain objections to their use. After all, relying on people's opinions concerning imminent purchases might be quite a satisfactory way of predicting short-term forecasts, but the results of such opinions would have to be gauged against a background of changing social attitudes, technological innovation and the possibility of political strife in the longer term, making the accuracy of such forecasts questionable. Up until now, short-term market research findings based on attitude surveys, personal attributes and social (environmental) influences have played only a small part in long-term forecasts, but the evidence suggests that this is likely to change as market researchers develop a better understanding of these sociological/psychological factors using such techniques as cluster analysis.

When econometric forecasting is used, the indicative variables in the resulting correlations must be measurable and consistent. Not only must the correlation be mathematically significant, in a statistical sense, but it must also be logically explained, otherwise it is useless. Some correlations are obviously correct – for example, only people with deep-freezers buy deep-frozen food – but other correlations are far from obvious. For example, there appears to be a strong correlation between the educational level which people attain and their propensity to drink wine. The reason for this is not properly understood although various conflicting hypotheses, which remain untested, have been suggested. The point which we wish to make therefore is that a prediction is likely to be *wrong* unless the psychology of the market-place is understood.

Similarly the other two techniques – time-trend analysis and historical analogy – can be criticized. It is inviting to think that by getting hold of a past time series of sales, analysing them to extract secular and cycle trends, and making some kind of projection, one can estimate future sales without going through the tiresome process of actually trying to understand the determinants of demand. Up to a point purely statistical methods are useful, but the fact remains that they are naïve since they neither give the reasons why sales changed in the past nor why they are likely to change in the future. If sales varied in the past, there must have been reasons for this. In principle, these causes are discoverable and it is surely only right to attempt to isolate these factors and what their effects have been. Unless one can do this, there are serious risks that changes in these underlying factors will go unnoticed and this will jeopardize the forecasts. Indeed several of the mathematical relationships given in Table 7.2.4.1 can be criticized for their assumption that an absolute market saturation level of sales will be reached. When applied to the sales of television sets, Mathur and Padley (1974) showed how the saturation levels themselves are also likely to be moving targets. Moreover, from a more profound viewpoint, Welkes (1979) suggests that there exist certain statistical weaknesses in the use of growth curves which should be understood before they are used.

7.2.8   The accuracy of sales forecasting techniques

Our purpose in briefly describing the techniques involved with sales forecasting is to expose the fundamental reasons for their inaccuracy, because the uncertainty in their prediction places investment decisions at risk. Evidence of their inaccuracy is mixed. On the one hand Van Arnum (1964) and Stobaugh (1965) show how these

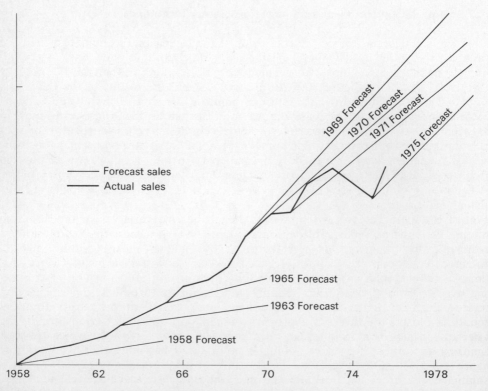

Figure 7.2.8.1 (*a*) *Errors in the sales forecasts for ethylene. Sources of Forecasts*: Oil and Gas Journal; Chemical Engineering Progress; Chemical Engineering; Chemical and Engineering News.

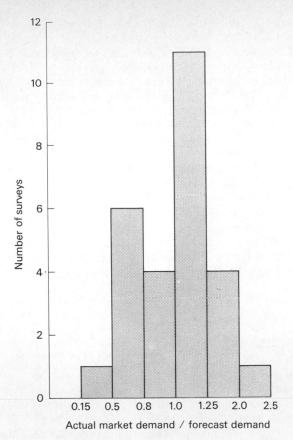

Figure 7.2.8.1 (b) *Frequency of over- and under-estimates in end-use market surveys. From Caudle (1972), with kind permission of the Institution of Chemical Engineers.*

techniques were able to predict market demands 1–6 years ahead, with errors as low as ±10 per cent for the petrochemical products Phenol and Polypropylene, whereas Stobaugh also shows how forecasts for other petrochemical products during the early 1960s tended to err on the low side, and underestimated the market by as much as 60 per cent. This point is borne out by Figure 7.2.8.1a which shows how early sales projections for the petrochemical Ethylene were over-pessimistic when its rate of sales growth approximated 13 per cent per annum, whereas they were over-optimistic when its rate of sales growth had declined to approximately 5 per cent per annum. This example demonstrates how forecasters are conditioned by their most recent experiences and how they endeavour to avoid repeating past errors by a process of over compensation. If anything, this example bears out the belief that if demand moves steadily and slowly, then extrapolation will give reasonably satisfactory results for products which are widely used, but that such results will become increasingly sensitive to the rate of development of a market if that market is immature and fast growing.

Perhaps one of the most useful single pieces of information which is available regarding the accuracy of sales forecasts is that provided by Caudle (1972), shown in Figure 7.2.8.1b. Although this evidence suggests that the accuracy of forecasts is usually good on average, nevertheless it highlights the point that single market forecasts can be almost 100 per cent out in their long-term predictions. This evidence reinforces the need to use ranges of forecasts in capital investment appraisals, so that the risks involved with their inaccuracies can be fully exposed and appreciated.

Besides the deficiencies in the forecasting techniques outlined above, another reason for such errors is due to technological innovation. For a variety of good reasons we must postpone a full discussion of this subject until Chapters 10 and 19. In the meanwhile however, it is sufficient for us to realize that different products compete for a share of limited spending power. To extrapolate the sales of one product without considering its natural alternatives is not only naïve but ludicrous. Classical cases of the substitution of one product and/or process by others abound in all walks of industry. For example, synthetic fibres displaced wool and cotton as the premier clothing fibres, detergents displaced soap, and robots and microprocessors in manufacturing are now replacing man. Rates of substitution can just as readily be modelled as rates of growth. For example, Martino (1971) showed how the initial rate of substitution of soap by detergent could be modelled using a simple exponential model and it has been found that, as the numbers of active substitutes increase, so there exist mathematical means for dealing with them. Research by Menon and Bowonder (1979) shows how the substitution of cotton and other natural fibers by synthetic fibres could be modelled by the following set of equations:

$$Y_s = 0.0397 + 0.9603[1 - e^{-\alpha_s t}(1 - \alpha_s t)]$$
$$Y_c = 0.8459[e^{-\alpha_c t}(1 - \alpha_c t)]$$
$$Y_o = 0.1144\left[e^{-\alpha_o t}\left(1 + \alpha_o t + \frac{\alpha_o^2 t^2}{2!} + \frac{\alpha_o^3 t^3)}{3!}\right)\right]$$

where Y_s = market share due to synthetic fibres, Y_c = market share due to cotton, and Y_o = market share due to other fibers, and they demonstrated that the best regressed equations corresponded with the parametric values 0.035, 0.032 and 0.116 for α_s, α_c and α_o respectively.

In effect, therefore, an arsenal of techniques for predicting future sales demand and substitution effects is available, but what we really need to understand is why people buy certain products and what products are likely to be required in the future, which will provide opportunities for some firms and threats for others.

7.2.9 Bibliography

Box, G. E. and Jenkins, G., *Time Series Analysis, Forecasting and Control*, Holden-Day, 1970.

Caudle, P. G., 'New projects definition', Paper 4, proceedings of the conference *The Financing and Control of Large Projects*, Institution of Chemical Engineers, 22–26 April 1972.

Chambers, J. C., Mullick, S. K. and Smith, D. D., 'How to choose the right forecasting technique', *Harvard Business Review*, July–August 1971, pp. 45–74.

de la Mare, R. F., 'Long-term forecasting: a novel time-trend analysis technique', *Engineering and Process Economics*, **3**, 1978, pp. 129–140.

Fisher, L., 'The methodology of long-term forecasting of demand for industrial products', *Journal and Proceedings of the Institute of Marketing Research*, **5** (1), February 1969.

Harrison, P. J. and Pearce, S. F., *The Use of Trend Curves as an Aid to Market Forecasting*, Paper presented to the European Association of Industrial Marketing, London, 10 May 1971.

Leontief, W., *Input-Output Economics*, Oxford University Press, 1966.

Martino, J. P., 'Technological forecasting for the chemical process industries', *Chemical Engineering*, 27 December 1971, pp. 54–62.

Mathur, S. S. and Padley, H., 'Forecasting first owner sales of consumer durables', *Industrial Marketing Management* **3,** 1974, pp. 137–152.

Menon, K. A. P. and Bowonder, B., *A Generalised Substitution Model*, Centre of Science Policy and Management of Research, Administrative Staff College, Hyderabad, India, 1979.

Mumford, L. S., 'The loneliness of the long-range forecaster', *Chemistry and Industry*, 9 November 1963, pp. 1788–1796.

National Institute Economic Review, *Paper and Board: Trends and Prospects*, May 1965.

Stobaugh, R. B., 'Chemical marketing research', *Chemical Engineering*, 22 November 1965, pp. 153–160.

Van Arnum, K. J., 'Measuring and forecasting markets', *Chemical Engineering Progress*, **60** (12), December 1964, pp. 18–22.

Wagle, B., *Journal of the Institute of Petroleum*, **52** (509), May 1966, pp. 161–171.

Wilkes, R. E., 'Statistical considerations in the fallacy of growth curves', *Technological Forecasting and Social Change*, **15** (2), October 1979, p. 107.

7.3   DETERMINING PRODUCT PRICE

The price of a product is usually the most critical factor in the economic evaluation of any new capital project so a realistic projection of the prices which the firm can expect to receive throughout its life-cycle is essential. To achieve this, the firm must not only appraise the price which the market will bear at one set moment in time, but it must also predict the affect which competitive pressures and technological changes might have on the future stability of its product prices. Furthermore, it has to develop a pricing strategy which best suits the firm's needs and allows for the particular characteristics of the product and its intended market, so that the firm can enjoy the most favourable economic benefit from that product which is consistent with its overall corporate objectives.

7.3.1   The microeconomic aspects of pricing

It is an axiom of economic theory that for perfectly competitive markets the price paid for a good or service is that which equates supply and demand, so that prices are fixed by what the market will bear rather than by cost considerations. Undoubtedly near perfectly competitive markets of this kind do exist, mainly for staple commodities such as natural fibres (wool, cotton and jute), grain (wheat, barley, oats and maize), and base metals (copper, lead, zinc and tin), and open markets, such as the London Metal Exchange, exist for the purpose of auctioning such products. However, the special characteristics of these markets are their large numbers of buyers and sellers and the *undifferentiated* nature of the products offered. These characteristics are not usually met in markets selling manufactured goods where producers endeavour to create a partial monopoly through product differentiation. Faced with this situation the microeconomic theory, which we previously developed in Chapter 2, suggests that the price of a product should be determined so that it maximizes the profit accruing to the firm, in which case the firm's cost structure and the price elasticity of demand for the product would have to be taken into account. In these circumstances it is quite a simple matter to prove that the most economic price of a product is given by the expression

$$P_{\text{opt}} = \left(\frac{\varepsilon}{\varepsilon - 1}\right)v \qquad\qquad (7.3.1.1)$$

where P_{opt} = the optimal price, ε = the price elasticity of demand which must initially be elastic, and v = its unit variable production cost, which is assumed to be constant.

The problem with this equation is that it assumes that the price elasticity of demand is known or can be found by market experimentation. The main problem in analysing historical market data to deduce a product's demand elasticity is that of differentiating price changes from other effects, such as changing incomes, tastes and preferences. The usual way of accomplishing this is to use multiple regression analysis, which has yielded some interesting and indeed consistent results when applied to macroeconomic planning. For example, Robinson (1971) has shown that the price elasticity of demand for butter approximates 0.4. By contrast, however, ten estimates of the price elasticity of demand for automobiles, reported to the Senate Sub-Committee on Antitrust and Monopoly (1958), showed that the estimates ranged from 0.6–1.4. These two extremes would have suggested quite different pricing policies. The basic problem with market experimentation is that customers often buy ahead to take advantage of short-term experimental price reductions, which competitors will tolerate only if they believe them to be temporary, but which they will react to if they believe them to be permanent. The difficulties of obtaining meaningful estimates of the price elasticity of demand for a manufactured product are therefore obvious.

The other problem with equation 7.3.1.1 is the assumption that firms endeavour to maximize profits by equating marginal cost with marginal revenue. It will be remembered that we previously examined this matter in Chapter 2. Although one has to admit that many gaps in economists' knowledge of how firms actually do price their products still exists, what evidence there is seems to refute the profit maximization hypothesis. The better known studies which provide this evidence are:

 (i) the Oxford Study of price theory and business behaviour by Hall and Hitch (1939),
 (ii) a study of 110 *excellently* managed firms by Earley (1956),
(iii) the Brookings Study of pricing in big businesses by Kaplan, Dirlam and Lanzilotti (1958),
(iv) a study of price decisions in small businesses by Haynes (1962) at the University of Kentucky.

It is not our intention to delve into the details of these studies here since the necessary references are provided for the interested reader. However, we should take note of their most important findings:

 (i) many firms *attempt* to establish their prices on the basis of full absorption costs plus a target return on investment*,
 (ii) usually only firms which enjoy relatively protected and stable markets for their products achieve (i) above,
(iii) most firms have to adapt their pricing policy to accommodate vacillating market pressures,
(iv) many firms endeavour to fit their costs to their perceptions of what the market will bear,

---

* It was on the basis of this evidence, plus rational argument, that the business objectives, previously enunciated in Chapter 3, were developed.

(v) firms use price to gain and/or retain market share as a long-term strategic objective; and
(vi) many firms feel obliged to follow the leader, when they compete in an oligopolistic market, which is dictated by one company with a large market share and considerable financial resources.

The evidence made available by Pearce (1956) on the ways in which firms react to real or anticipated market pressures by altering their profit mark-up is most revealing. For one particular firm he showed that the average mark-up was 8 per cent, but the range varied from 0–44 per cent. Such a large range as this can be explained by various good reasons.

(i) promotional considerations,
(ii) the degree of price awareness or lack thereof by customers,
(iii) the relative importance of price in the total context of the life-cycle costs of owning the product,
(iv) the extent and the means of product differentiation,
(v) the nature of the firm's product-line and its overall pricing policy,
(vi) the firm's policy towards wholesale, retail and volume discounting,
(vii) geographical factors including demographic, ethnic, social and freight considerations and any tax/exchange rate implications involved with international trade,
(viii) legal constraints on pricing decisions,
(ix) the prestige of the product and the firm's market image, and
(x) product life-cycle considerations.

An excellent and most comprehensive account of all these matters is given by Livesey (1976).

7.3.2 Product life-cycle pricing strategies

Firms whose catalogue only contains products which have already reached saturation can only expect growth from secular trends in the economy at large. Growing firms must either imitate products already on the market, in which case their prices will be dictated by the prices of established brands, or they have to innovate by successfully pioneering and marketing new products which are substantially different from existing products. In this latter case the firm has a greater degree of freedom in the selection of its pricing policy, and it has to decide what pattern of profit margins and risks best serves its purpose. It must, however, recognize that the distinctiveness which differentiates its product (which could comprise a manufacturing process or technique as well as an artefact) from others will eventually erode in time due to life-cycle reasons which we have already studied in Chapter 3. The basic choice of strategies proposed by Dean (1969) is between 'skimming' and 'penetration', or some other pricing strategy which is a mixture of these two extremes.

A skimming price strategy involves setting a high initial price for the product and subsequently lowering the price throughout its life-cycle in order to expand sales and ultimately to match competitors' prices. By contrast a penetration price policy involves entering the market with a low price to develop market sales quickly. In choosing between these two several major factors have to be considered:

(i) the likely rate of growth of the market as a whole and the influence of varying pricing policies,
(ii) the impact which advertising might have on (i) above and its cost-effectiveness,

(iii) the price consciousness of various demographic and social groups and the impact this might have on their purchasing behaviour,

(iv) the likely lead-time which the new product and/or process is likely to enjoy, as dictated by patent protection and the rate of technological and marketing innovation and diffusion,

(v) the need to recoup monies spent on R & D,

(vi) the innovating firm's capacity to manufacture and sell the product, as governed by the extent of its financial and manufacturing resources, in addition to its management capacity,

(vii) the firm's cost structure and the influence of economies of scale, technological improvements and learning, the price implications of which are discussed in the next section.

7.3.3   The influence of experience on product prices and costs

The concept of experience curves was first introduced by the Boston Consulting Group (1968) as a result of its studies of extremely fast growing sectors of the petrochemical and electronics industries. These studies showed how the costs and subsequently the prices of these products declined with experience in their production for three quite different reasons:

(i) *productivity gains* resulting from repetitive, standardized production; this is known as the learning effect which is well illustrated by the work of Wright (1968) and is discussed later in Section 7.5,

(ii) *technological improvements* in manufacturing involving different production techniques and processes, such as modular fabrication, group technology, different materials and improved catalysts,

(iii) *large-scale manufacturing plants* exhibiting economies of scale, which we have already discussed in Chapter 2, and which we develop further in Section 7.5 of this chapter.

According to the study by the Boston Consulting Group, the characteristic decline in the prices and costs (both measured in constant purchasing power or real terms) for fast growing products was consistently between 20 and 30 per cent each time accumulated production doubled. This phenomenon can be modelled by the exponential relationship:

$$D_t = a\left(\sum P_t\right)^{-b} \tag{7.3.3.1}$$

where D_t = the value of the dependent variable (either cost or price) at time t, $\sum P_t$ = the cumulative production of that product up to time t, and a and b are regression parameters which best suit the particular product.

The log transformation of equation 7.3.3.1 is given by

$$\log_{10} D_t = \log_{10} a - b \log_{10}\left(\sum P_t\right)$$

This equation plots as a straight line on log-log paper and results in what is known as the experience curve. An example of such a log-log plot is given by Figure 7.3.3.1a showing the response in the price of Styrene to its cumulative production experience and further examples of experience curves are provided by Taylor and Craven (1979).

The value of the constant b in equation 7.3.3.1 depends on the rate of decline of the

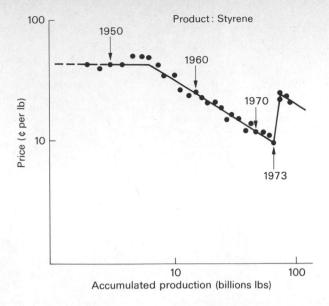

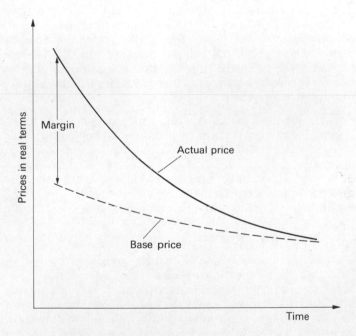

Figure 7.3.3.1 (a) *An example of a price experience curve. Source:* Chemical Marketing Reporter. (b) *The price response of fast growing products.*

cost or price with experience, its values being 0.322 and 0.515 for experience factors of 20 per cent and 30 per cent respectively. On the basis of such a model as this, it is quite a straightforward matter to deduce the erosion in product prices resulting from predicted percentage increases in the overall sales rate of a product and typical erosion rates are shown in Table 7.3.3.1.

The benefit of these experience curves is that they provide a formalized framework in which one can consider the likely future price response of a product as it

Table 7.3.3.1 *The erosion in product prices and costs resulting from experience*

% annual growth rate in sales of product	Approximate number of years to double annual production	Approximate % annual decline in costs and prices	
		20% experience factor	30% experience factor
2	35	0.6	1.0
5	14	1.6	2.5
7	10	2.2	3.4
10	7	3.0	4.8
15	5	4.4	6.9

penetrates a market, throughout the various stages of its life-cycle. However, it must be emphasized that these results pertain to commodity-type products.

A more profound understanding of price erosion comes from reading the work of Malloy (1971) and the empirical research evidence of de la Mare (1977). Both these works confirm that the prices in real terms of many products erode approximately exponentially with the passage of time, but at a rate which is governed by a base-price, which also erodes but more slowly. They define this base-price as the price which would provide the most efficient manufacturer, using the largest scale of plant employing the most cost-effective technology, a minimum acceptable return on investment. Below this price manufacturers would not normally be expected to build production capacity. The evidence suggests that actual prices approach this base-price as shown by Figure 7.3.3.1b, and that the margin between these two prices depends on the following factors:

(i) the rate of development of the market, which depends on the product's technological superiority over traditional products as well as on its price,
(ii) the nature and extent of the retaliation by manufacturers whose products are being superseded,
(iii) the speed with which manufacturers are induced to build new plants embodying the advantages of scale and technological innovation,
(iv) the extent of the production over-capacity available in a market at set moments in time, and
(v) the rate at which innovators attempt to recoup their R & D expenses.

Unlike the experience curve model, which suggests that *real* prices decline indefinitely, de la Mare's work suggests that base prices eventually stop declining when the product reaches maturity and that subsequently a product's *actual* prices inflate at a similar rate to that of the economy at large. Although a declining price margin might seem unimportant in itself, Malloy shows how under estimating the rate of decline in the price margin can seriously affect the economic viability of a project turning what is ostensibly an economically viable capital project into an economic disaster.

Both the previous models underline the importance and the significance of a strategy which leads to price erosion and both could be used for predictive purposes, by way of extrapolation. However, it should be noted that neither of these models can properly accommodate abnormal price perturbations or the effect of a declining market. The former is illustrated in Figure 7.3.3.1a which shows how the price response of Styrene went through four distinct phases. Up to 1950 its real market price was fairly constant as it held-up, under cover of patents, to recoup R & D expenses and, as the market developed, to take advantage of subsequent large-scale plant sizes and technical innovations. During the period 1954–73 the price fell for the reasons already outlined, but then rose dramatically as a result of the OECD oil embargo in the wake of the Yom Kippur War. After this period the price continued its inexorable decline, but then became disturbed by other real price increases reflecting the massive escalation in petroleum prices throughout the 1970s. Quite obviously such models as these are incapable of forecasting these unusual, politically motivated price increases. Regarding the problem of pricing in a declining market, there is a paucity of pricing evidence to help us model these conditions. In these circumstances the best strategy depends on the price elasticity of demand for the product, which, as we have already noted, is difficult to determine. For some declining products it might be advisable to drop prices in the face of severe competition whereas, in other circumstances, the opposite tactic might be more appropriate. The object is simple: to maintain a satisfactory positive cash flow into the company's coffers. The means of accomplishing this objective however is quite another matter, which is often best left to informed and imaginative judgement.

7.3.4 Bibliography

Boston Consulting Group, *Perspectives on Experience*, 1968.

Dean, J., 'The pricing of pioneering products', *Journal of Industrial Economics*, **17,** 1969, pp. 165–179.

de la Mare, R. F., 'Chemical commodity price erosion', *Engineering and Process Economics*, **2,** 1977, pp. 295–304.

Earley, F., 'Marginal policies of excellently managed companies', *American Economic Review*, **46,** Part 1, 1956.

Hall, R. L. and Hitch, C. J., 'Price theory and business behaviour', *Oxford Economic Papers*, **11,** 1939, pp. 12–45.

Haynes, W. W., *Pricing Decisions in Small Businesses*, University of Kentucky, 1962.

Kaplan, A. D. H., Dirlam, J. B. and Lanzilotti, R. F., *Pricing in Big Business*, The Brookings Institute, 1958.

Livesey, F., *Pricing*, MacMillan, 1976.

Malloy, J. B., Planning criteria for return on investment in the 1970s', *Chemistry and Industry*, 30 October 1971, pp. 1242–1250.

Pearce, I. F., 'A study of price policy', *Econometrica*, **23,** 1956, pp. 114–127.

Report to the Senate Sub-Committee on Antitrust and Monopoly, Washington, DC, 1958.

Robinson, C., *Business Forecasting*, Nelson, 1971.

Taylor, J. H. and Craven, P. J., 'Experience curves for chemicals', *Process Economics International*, **1** (1), Autum 1979, pp. 13–19.

Wright, T. P., 'Factors affecting the cost of airplanes', *Journal of Aerospace Science*, February 1968, pp. 122–128.

7.4 DETERMINING MARKET SHARE

Having forecast the magnitude and growth rate of the market in which a firm wishes to compete, the next step in the economic evaluation of any project is to appraise the market penetration rate which the firm believes it can achieve. To determine the extent and the timing of the market share it *must* achieve in order to yield a satisfactory return on investment is quite a straightforward matter of reverse-economics*. To demonstrate that a firm is able to maintain or indeed increase market share a priori, however, is quite another matter. It is usually at this stage of market research that many firms abandon attempts to make explicit forecasts in which their assumptions and their logic are made clear; instead, they prefer to rely on the judgement of their marketing staff. Such an attitude is quite understandable since the marketers obviously possess a detailed knowledge and understanding of the complexities and dynamics of the market-place and it might reasonably be supposed that they are the only people within the firm who are really in a position to assess future market share. There can be no doubt that a forecast of market share has to be made with the co-operation of these people. This said, however, a strong case also exists for making explicit the reasons why they feel confident that such a market share will be realized. After all, market share is one of the main indications of a firm's competitiveness, so it must somehow reflect the competitive strengths and weaknesses of a firm's product and service relative to its competitors'. The problem of forecasting on the basis of judgement alone is that management is not in a position to understand the reasons for such forecasts, so it cannot really assess whether that judgement is soundly based or not, even though the marketing staff might have a good track record of judgematical successes. The real danger with such forecasts is the tendency to confuse what can reasonably be expected to happen with what one *wants to happen.*

To some extent these problems can be overcome if the forecast of market share is made within a logical framework which minimizes the chances of people being carried away by their own aspirations. The best way of doing this is to decompose the considerable problem of market share prediction into its constituent parts which people can understand and discuss, such as the relative functional merits of the firm's present and prospective products, the effectiveness of its advertising, the selectivity of its retail coverage, the competitiveness of its pricing policy, the commitment of its agents, and many more considerations besides. Of course, the discerning reader will recognize these ideas as nothing more than an extension to the capability analysis concept which we discussed in Chapter 4.3. On the basis of such analyses, formed on the basis of market research and best expert opinion (sometimes using the Delphi technique), some firms have devised ordinal scoring schemes, using measured check-lists (which are described in Chapter 10.2), to assess their competitive strengths and weaknesses relative to those of known and expected competitors. This provides one means of assessing a firm's market share capability. Of course the numbers coming from such a study must always be treated with caution. At best they may confirm intuitive feelings; at worst they may be an irritant if they do not. Their real benefit is that they provide a logical framework in which executive attention can be applied to those factors which matter in the competitive contest for market share. On the basis of such ordinal scoring schemes it is known that some firms have devised their overall corporate strategy to increase market share using competitive gaming techniques which are similar to war games.

A search of the literature shows there is a dearth of published information concerning the prediction of market share. Amongst those which are available however the results of a market survey in the USA, reported by Hodge (1971), are most interesting. These are shown in Figure 7.4.1 which plots the *most likely* split of a definitive market for different numbers of competitors. The findings of this study suggest that to be the market leader in Position 1 usually means that there has been

---

* Reverse economics is a branch of economic decision making which requires the evaluation of the price, volume, cost, market share or any other economic factor which yield a prescribed DCFRR or NPV result. In other words it involves DCF sums in reverse.

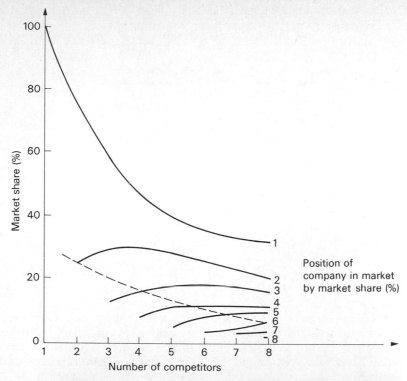

Figure 7.4.1 *The most likely split of the market for different numbers of competitors. From Hodge (1971).*

a long, sustained and costly programme to ensure that the firm uses up-to-date technology, intensive after-sales service, above average marketing and distribution and extensive advertising too. It would therefore appear that the position cannot be bought but, instead, requires a dedicated commitment and strategy to realize and maintain this position. Even so, the evidence of Figure 7.4.1 suggests that the market leader might be lucky to secure one-third of the market if there are six or more competitors. Lower market shares can obviously be secured with less demanding market development, technical effort and expense but the evidence suggests that those positions falling beneath the dotted line are likely to be unprofitable.

7.4.1 Bibliography

Hodge, H. P., 'Market research and investment decisions', *Chemistry in Britain*, **7** (5), 1971, p. 199.

7.5 CAPITAL COST ESTIMATING

The economic viability of any project is under question from its inception. It is, therefore, important that realistic and sufficiently accurate estimates of its fixed capital cost should be available at an early stage in its development. Such an estimate not only has economic but financial implications in that it determines the

Table 7.5.1 *Categories of plant capital cost estimates*

Type of estimate	Other names	Basis	Usual range of error
Order of magnitude	Ratio estimate	Variable accuracy, usually based on previous similar cost information	$>\pm30\%$
Study	Factored estimate	Estimate usually based on knowledge of flow-sheet and major equipment items: better than order of magnitude estimate	$\pm30\%$
Preliminary	Budget authorization estimate, scope estimate	Sufficient data for budget preparation	$\pm20\%$
Definitive	Project control estimate	Detailed data, but incomplete drawings and specifications	$\pm10\%$
Detailed	Firm estimate contractor's estimate	Complete engineering drawings and specifications	$\pm5\%$

funds which a firm has to raise to support such a capital project. Because projects compete for the scarce cash resources of a company, regular up-dating of these capital needs is required to sanction the continued study of a project and provide a justification for the resources employed by that study; help compare and select between the various options of the same project as well as between quite different projects; and help optimize the design of the preferred choice(s) of project(s).

Capital cost estimates are usually made at the initial stage of a project, during development, and for the plant layout, engineering design and construction phases. Although the terminology used in cost engineering has yet to be standardized, efforts have been made towards that end, and the American Association of Cost Engineers (AACE) has published five different classifications of cost estimates, as shown by Table 7.5.1. Not all of these stages have to be followed for all projects. Sometimes, for example, a firm might contemplate building a duplicate of a recently completed project so that its initial estimate could actually be the budget estimate. Moreover, under special circumstances, a firm might be willing to accept a greater latitude in the accuracy of its budget estimate in order to capitalize quickly on a lucrative marketing opportunity.

One very important point about cost estimating is the fact that the cost of preparing an estimate rapidly increases with its accuracy, as discovered by several researchers and especially by Perry and Chilton (1973). A firm therefore has to balance the desired accuracy of the estimate with the cost of producing it, to avoid wasting money, time and precious talent in preparing an estimate of a greater accuracy than is really justified.

To meet the need for rapid, cheap, yet fairly accurate cost estimates, cost engineers have devised a comprehensive range of estimating techniques. Only the more conventional of these are surveyed here, although their sophisticated counterparts are listed in the references. In passing, it should be mentioned that some major companies have computerized their use of these techniques to improve the accuracy of their cost estimating, and at the same time increase the productivity of their estimators. A noteworthy example of such computerization is the 'Factest' program developed by Imperial Chemical Industries Limited, reported by Kay (1974).

7.5.1 Analogy costing

When a project is first mooted there is usually insufficient data available to determine the dimensions of the machinery and equipment, or to draw the flow-sheet needed by the production process. The first estimate of the capital cost of the project, therefore, has to be made using relatively simple and somewhat crude costing techniques, which come under the general heading of analogy costing, so named because the capital cost estimate is based on analogy with existing production plants, the capital costs of which are known. The particular approach depends on the closeness of the analogy. The closest possible analogy concerns equipment which is identical to that previously installed on the same site. Here differences in cost result from cost inflation and productivity improvements – two factors which are discussed further in Sections 7.5.6 and 7.5.7 respectively.

To some extent these two influences tend to counteract one another so that, providing only a few years separate the building of the two projects and the existing plant is not grossly under- or over-designed, the estimated cost of new plant should be quite close to that which exists. If it is intended to erect the same plant but at a different location, then other factors have to be taken into account, such as extra delivery charges, the need for different site preparation to accommodate the new machines, and differences in the cost of ancillary equipment and facilities to support their operation. When a production capacity different from that currently installed in the existing plant is contemplated, then the estimating technique must accommodate for such a change. A most useful method for this purpose is known as exponential costing.

7.5.2 Exponential costing

The principle of exponential costing states that 'for many real-world production systems proportionate increases in production capacity can be achieved by *less than* proportionate increases in capital cost'! This principle is a special manifestation of the law of increasing returns to scale, and is known as 'the law of increasing technical returns to scale'. The basis of this principle is as follows: if a production system can be likened to a cube/or sphere with its side (or radius) of size r units, then the following relationships hold:

(i) the ratio of the surface areas (S) of two plants A and B is given by:

$$\frac{S_A}{S_B} = \left(\frac{r_A}{r_B}\right)^2$$

(ii) likewise, the ratio of their volumetric capacities (V) is given by:

$$\frac{V_A}{V_B} = \left(\frac{r_A}{r_B}\right)^3$$

(iii) from the two previous relationships we get:

$$\frac{S_A}{S_B} = \left(\frac{V_A}{V_B}\right)^{2/3}$$

(iv) if we further assume that the capital cost (C) of a machine is proportional to its surface area (S) and that its production capacity (Q) is proportional to its cubic capacity (*V*) then we get the relationship:

$$\frac{C_A}{C_B} = \left(\frac{Q_A}{Q_B}\right)^{2/3}$$

This relationship is extremely well known in cost engineering circles as the 'two-thirds power rule'. Quite obviously the assumptions postulated in (iv) above need scrutinizing. On the one hand, the amount of fabrication effort needed to build a machine or piece of plant could well be proportional to its surface area, especially if welding, surface treatment, painting and lagging are involved. On the other hand, the thickness of the material of construction receives no mention in the above simple-minded derivation. Likewise, for some production processes it is conceivable that production capacities (through-puts) are governed by their internal voidage (volumetric capacity), but for other machines it is difficult to imagine any direct relationship of this kind. Resulting from the imperfections of these assumptions it is generally recognized that the following relationship applies for most homologous equipment, especially for equipment employed by the process industries:

$$\frac{C_A}{C_B} = \left(\frac{Q_A}{Q_B}\right)^{\alpha} \tag{7.5.2.1}$$

where the exponent factor α can range in value from 0.4 to more than 1.00, but often approximates 0.5–0.8. Table 7.5.2.1a lists such factors for various categories of machinery and plant. It should be emphasized, however, that these values are approximate, and that much more accurate exponent cost factors can be obtained from the references to this section.

The effects of this principle can be quite startling. For example, a machine with an exponent of 0.5 can be doubled in size for a 41.5 per cent increase in its capital cost. Put another way, this means that such a plant would be 41.5 per cent more productive per munit invested than its smaller version. The relationship between the relative capital costs of plants of different design capacities and exponential cost factors is shown in Figure 7.5.2.1a.

It follows from equation 7.5.2.1 that the relationship between the capital cost of a plant and its design capacity is given by the relationship:

$$C = kQ^{\alpha}$$

where C = the capital cost of the plant, k = a cost/capacity constant, Q = the production capacity of the machine, and α = the exponential cost factor.

Taking logarithms of this equation we get:

$$\log C = \log k + \alpha \log Q$$

which plots as a straight line relationship with a slope of α on log-log paper, as shown by Figure 7.5.2.1b. It should, however, be realized that such a straight-line relationship only applies over a limited range of production capacities for most types of equipment. As machines become very large, they get more difficult to fabricate and handle so the exponent cost factor tends to increase, and above certain sizes it can actually exceed unity, thereby exhibiting decreasing technical returns to scale.

It stands to reason that if such exponent factors can be applied to single pieces of equipment, then they can likewise be applied to complex production systems comprising several, indeed many, pieces of equipment. Overall process exponent factors can be derived by synthesis, using the exponents and capital costs of all the pieces of equipment comprising a process or, alternatively, they can be derived by plotting the capital cost–capacity relationships of homologous processes on log-log paper. Exponent cost factors are available for many processes costing up to several

Table 7.5.2.1a *Typical cost exponent factors*

Process industrial equipment		Material handling equipment		Comminution equipment		General industrial equipment	
Agitators	0.3–0.5	Bagging machines	0.8	Crushers	0.8–1.2	Air compressors	0.4
Centrifuges	0.7–1.3	Blending plant	0.5	Dust	0.8	Air driers	0.6
Ejectors (steam)	0.5–0.7	Conveyors	0.7	collectors		Cranes	0.6
Evaporators	0.5–0.7	Conveyors (bucket)	0.6–0.8	Mills	0.6–0.8	Driers (product)	0.4–0.5
Filters	0.6	Conveyors (roller)	0.9	Screens	0.6	Electric motors	0.8
Flakers	0.6	Conveyors (screw)	0.7–0.9	Scrubbers	0.3–0.8	Elevators (passengers)	0.95
Heat exchangers	0.7–0.9	Conveyors (vibrating)	0.8–0.9			Steam boilers	0.5
Piping	0.7–0.9	Elevators	0.4			Building (single storey)	0.8
Pumps	0.5–0.9	Hoppers	0.7–0.9			(two storey)	0.7–0.8
Tanks (rectangular)	0.5						
(spherical)	0.7						
Towers (constant length)	1.0						
(constant diameter)	0.7						

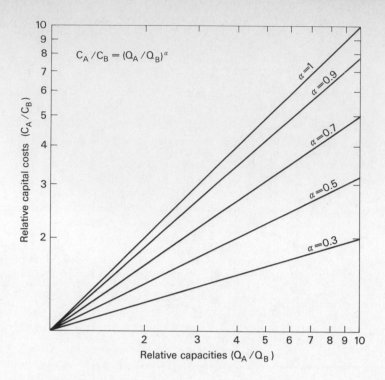

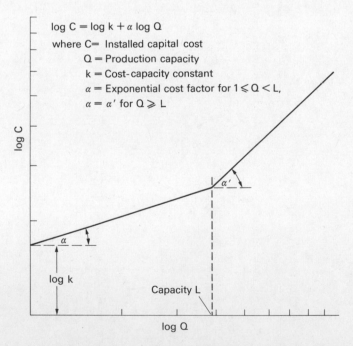

Figure 7.5.2.1 (*a*) *Relationship between the relative capital costs of two similar plants and their relative production capacities.* (*b*) *The relationship between the installed capital cost and the capacity of a manufacturing process.*

Table 7.5.2.1b *Typical exponential cost factors for complete processes*

Type of plant	Factor
Acetylene	0.75
Ammonium nitrate	0.54
Ammonia (steam-reformed synthesis gas)	0.74
Benzene	0.61
Butadiene	0.59
Butyl alcohol	0.55
Caustic	0.85
Chlorine (electrolytic)	0.85
Delayed coking	0.58
Ethanol (synthetic)	0.60
Ethylene	0.58
Ethylene oxide	0.79
Formaldehyde	0.55
Hydrogen cyanide	0.71
Isopropyl alcohol	0.60
Methanol	0.83
Nitric acid	0.56
Oxygen	0.64
Phosphoric acid	0.58
Polyethylene (high pressure)	0.90
Polyethylene (low pressure)	0.67
Sulphuric acid (contact)	0.62
Styrene	0.68
Urea	0.59

hundreds of millions of US dollars; some examples are given in Table 7.5.2.1b. Here again, it must be stressed that these values are only approximate and apply over limited ranges of plant capacity. Far more detailed information concerning their exact values and ranges is available in the references. As with individual machines, it is usually found that such exponent cost factors tend to increase once a process exceeds a definite capacity. This results from the difficulty of making and transporting very large equipment, the need to duplicate or proliferate machines in order to achieve that capacity, and the human organizational problems involved with building giant complexes.

It follows that an estimate of the capital cost of a single machine or a complex process can be derived from the following relationship:

$$C_A = C_B \left(\frac{Q_A}{Q_B}\right)^{\alpha} \cdot I_I \cdot I_P$$

where C_A = capital cost of proposed plant, C_B = known capital cost of an existing plant, Q_A = production capacity of the proposed plant, Q_B = production capacity of the existing plant, α = appropriate cost exponent factor, I_I = index of cost inflation, and I_P = index of productivity improvement.

This relationship assumes that both plants are constructed from the same materials. Quite obviously the accuracy of this technique depends on the closeness of the analogy, the accuracy and the appropriateness of the exponent cost factor and a proper evaluation of the capacities of the two plants. The error involved with this technique is usually in the range ±10 per cent to ±30 per cent of the actual final cost.

To obtain very quick capital cost estimates, some estimators use capital cost–capacity ratios such as £ per tonne or $ per item produced per year. The use of these quick cost estimates either implies that the exponential cost factors are sufficiently close to unity that makes no difference or, alternatively, that the errors involved with their use are acceptable. It will be realized, however, that the joint effect of small exponent cost factors and a substantial range of equipment capacities can result in substantial errors in this cost estimating technique. For example, since the capital cost–capacity ratio of a machine costing 10 000 munits with a production capacity of 1000 tonnes a year is 10 munits per tonne per annum then, according to the use of this technique, the comparable cost of a 2000 tonne per annum machine would be:

$$2000 \times 10 = 20\ 000 \text{ munits}$$

However, if the true cost exponential factor were 0.5 then the best estimate of the capital cost would be:

$$10\ 000 \times \left(\frac{2000}{1000}\right)^{0.5} = 14\ 140 \text{ munits}$$

and the resultant error defined as:

$$\frac{\text{quick estimate} - \text{true estimate}}{\text{true estimate}} \times 100\%$$

would be 41.4 per cent. This trivial example demonstrates that such capital cost–capacity ratio techniques have to be employed with caution, since they can produce very misleading results.

7.5.3 Analogy costing using historical data from different plants producing different products

This method, which is often known as the module method or functional unit method is much used by the petroleum, petrochemical and chemical industries. Essentially, it relates the capital cost of a plant to the conditions affecting its capacity, complexity, severity of operations and the number of distinct steps in its production process. In general functional form it can be represented by the expression:

$$C = f\{N \cdot Q \cdot T \cdot P \cdot M\}$$

where C = the total capital cost of the project, f = the functional relationship, N = the number of distinct process steps, Q = the capacity of the process, T = some temperature relationship, P = some pressure relationship and M = some relationship which allows for various materials of construction.

Several ingenious ways of using this costing concept have been devised and feature in the references. Allen and Page (1974) demonstrated that some of these methods are able to provide estimates with errors in the range ±15 per cent. Such a technique is therefore most useful at the initial stages of a project when detailed flow-sheets and machine designs are not available.

7.5.4 Factorial costing

This technique, which is attributed to Lang (1947), requires much more information than the previous techniques in that it relies on detailed cost estimates of the main plant items (MPI), which constitute the production process, and a good idea of the type and nature of the ancillary equipment needed for their proper operation. Lang's original method, which has been considerably up-dated and extended, recommends that the total installed cost of a plant be obtained by multiplying the delivered cost of the main plant items by a factor, which has become known as the Lang factor, according to the following relationship:

$$TCC = \bar{F}_L \cdot (CMPI)$$

where TCC = the total installed capital cost of the plant, $\bar{F}_L$ = the overall average Lanf factor, and CMPI = the delivered total capital cost of the main plant items.

To meet the needs of this relationship, Lang factors have been derived empirically, but of course require up-dating as equipment costs change. Typical values for these factors for relatively small projects are 3.9 for plants using solids only, 4.1 for plants using solid-fluid processes, and 4.8 for plants using fluid processes only. These factors allow for the civil and structural engineering works required to support plant and machinery, supply of electrical, gas, fuel, water, air and refrigeration services, the interconnection of the main plant items by ducting and piping and for their instrumentation and insulation.

The accuracy of this technique is improved using cost curves which relate the average cost per main plant item to the appropriate values of the Lang factors. Such a relationship is represented graphically by Figure 7.5.4.1a. In this case, the estimate of the total installed capital cost is obtained from:

$$TCC = N \cdot F_{LA} \cdot (ACMPI)$$

where N = the number of main plant items, F_{LA} = the Lang factor for the average cost of the main plant items, and ACMPI = the average cost of the main plant items.

A large improvement in the accuracy of this technique comes from using Lang factors specifically determined to satisfy the needs and complexity involved with each main plant item. Again these factors are derived empirically and require regular updating. Table 7.5.4.1a lists some of the Lang factors which are currently published for use in the chemical and petrochemical industries and relate to equipment costs in the UK during December 1976. An example of the way in which this information should be used is provided in Table 7.5.4.1b which refers to the process flow-sheet given in Figure 7.5.4.1b. In this particular case the following relationship holds:

$$TCC = \sum_{i=1}^{n} CMPI_i \times F_{Li}$$

where $CMPI_i$ = the cost of the ith main plant item, F_{Li} = the Lang factor pertaining to the ith main plant item (where $i = 1, 2, 3 \ldots n$), and n denotes the total number of main plant items.

Kay (1974) has tested the accuracy of this refined Lang factor estimating technique and, on the basis of several hundred projects undertaken by Imperial Chemical Industries Ltd (ICI), has found that the errors involved are usually quite low and in the range of ± 10 per cent for as many as 95 per cent of all estimates.

Two important points relating to the use of this technique need emphasizing. In the first place, the factors invariably relate to equipment fabricated from mild steel. To use them for main plant items fabricated from more expensive and exotic materials would lead to an excessive over-estimation of the total installed capital cost unless some correction factors were used, examples of which are given in Table 7.5.4.1c. It should also be realized that these cost estimates only include the cost of the equipment within a plant's battery limits. This is a hypothetical limit or boundary around the plant but nonetheless is a concept which is deeply ingrained in process and cost engineering terminology. It is defined as, the production area enclosing all of the production machines and plant and their related facilities which are *directly* involved with the conversion of raw materials to finished products. It includes

Table 7.5.4.1a *Lang factors for main plant items*[a]

	Ref.	Over £150 000	50 000–150 000	20 000–50 000	10 000–20 000	3000–10 000	1500–3000	under 1500
Main plant items — Value of individual main plant item revised to carbon steel basis, (vessels, furnaces, machines and drives, materials handling equipment)		1.00	1.00	1.00	1.00	1.00	1.00	1.00
Much of site erection included in purchase cost of equipment, e.g., large tanks	1	0.01	0.02	0.03	0.05	0.06	0.07	0.20
Erection of MPI — Average erection	2	0.04	0.06	0.08	0.09	0.10	0.12	0.30
Equipment involving some site fabrication, e.g., large pumps requiring lining up, serpentine coolers	3	0.06	0.08	0.10	0.12	0.14	0.16	0.38
Equipment involving much site fabrication or fitting, e.g., large distillation columns, furnaces	4	0.24	0.30	0.36	0.45	0.54	0.62	0.90
At discretion of estimator, interpolation may be made.								
Piping, ducting and chutes, including erection — Ducting and chutes	5	0.02	0.04	0.08	0.14	0.22	0.34	0.46
Small bore piping or service piping only	6	0.05	0.10	0.20	0.34	0.55	0.83	1.12
Average bore piping and service piping, e.g., predominantly liquid piping.	7	0.13	0.21	0.32	0.53	0.78	1.12	1.41
Large bore piping and service piping, e.g., predominantly gas and vapour piping, or	8	0.16	0.26	0.39	0.62	0.89	1.26	1.55
Average bore piping with complex system, e.g., much manifolding, recirculation, etc.	9	0.20	0.33	0.49	0.77	1.10	1.57	1.94
Large bore piping complex system, e.g., much manifolding, recirculation, etc. Multiply piping factors by 1.3 for special pipe materials or steam tracing	10							
Instruments — Local instruments only	11	0.02	0.03	0.05	0.10	0.19	0.34	0.60
1 controller and instruments	12	0.07	0.10	0.18	0.27	0.39	0.52	0.80
2 controllers and instruments	13	0.10	0.16	0.26	0.36	0.48	0.63	0.91
3 or more controllers and instruments	14	0.15	0.26	0.35	0.48	0.62	0.77	1.10

Category		No.							
Electrical	Lighting only	15	0.02	0.02	0.03	0.05	0.08	0.10	0.15
	Lighting and power for ancillary drives, e.g., conveyors, stirred vessels, air coolers, etc.	16	0.08	0.11	0.16	0.21	0.27	0.33	0.48
	Lighting and power excluding transformers and switchgear, i.e., this equipment off-site, for machine main drives, e.g., pumps, compressors, crushers, etc.	17	0.10	0.14	0.20	0.26	0.34	0.41	0.50
	Lighting and power including transformers and switchgear for machine main drives, e.g., pumps, compressors, crushers, etc.	18	0.15	0.20	0.27	0.37	0.48	0.59	0.80
Civil	Average civil work, including plant and structure foundations, floor and services	19	0.06	0.08	0.11	0.14	0.18	0.22	0.28
	Above average civil work, complicated machine blocks, special floor protection, elevator pits in floors, considerable services	20	0.12	0.17	0.25	0.32	0.40	0.48	0.68
	Multiply civil factor by 1.3 to allow for piling plant and structure foundations	21							
Structures and buildings	Negligible structural work and buildings	22	0.01	0.02	0.02	0.03	0.04	0.05	0.06
	Open air plant at ground level with some pipebridges and minor buildings	23	0.05	0.06	0.08	0.11	0.14	0.17	0.21
	Open air plant within a structure	24	0.11	0.19	0.25	0.33	0.40	0.47	0.59
	Plant in a simple covered building	25	0.15	0.23	0.31	0.39	0.46	0.55	0.88
	Plant in an elaborate building on a major structure within a building	26	0.25	0.39	0.50	0.61	0.72	0.85	1.10
Lagging	Lagging for service pipes only	27	0.01	0.02	0.03	0.05	0.08	0.12	0.18
	Average amount of hot lagging on pipes and vessels	28	0.02	0.03	0.06	0.11	0.17	0.25	0.30
	Above average amount of hot lagging on pipes and vessels	29	0.03	0.05	0.08	0.14	0.21	0.28	0.35
	Cold lagging on pipes and vessels	30	0.05	0.08	0.12	0.20	0.25	0.33	0.45

[a] This table is to be used taking single item costs.
Reproduced with kind permission of Institution of Chemical Engineers.

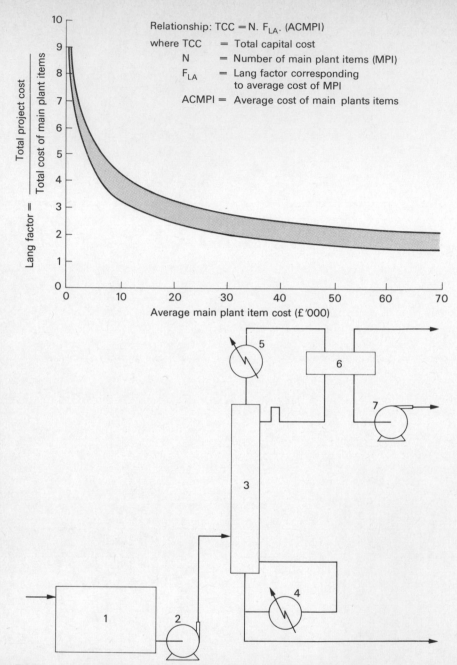

Relationship: TCC = N. F_{LA}. (ACMPI)

where TCC   = Total capital cost
      N   = Number of main plant items (MPI)
      F_{LA} = Lang factor corresponding
                to average cost of MPI
      ACMPI = Average cost of main plants items

Figure 7.5.4.1 (*a*) *Approximate relationship of Lang factor to average main plant item cost.* (*b*) *A simple plant flow-sheet. Reproduced with kind permission of Institution of Chemical Engineers.*

building, machinery, equipment, piping and instruments that specifically involve the manufacturing process and that proportion of compressed air, electrical, refrigeration, steam, water, air conditioning and waste disposal facilities which *are inside the process area*. However, it *excludes* major storage and handling facilities, such as warehouses and storage tanks for raw materials and final products. It also excludes loading facilities for land, sea and air transport, steam boiler houses, air compressor

Table 7.5.4.1b *An example of the use of the data of Table 7.5.4.1a applied to the flow-sheet shown in Fig. 7.5.4.1b*

Item number		1	2	3	4	5
Description		Storage tank	Still feed pump	Refining column	Reboiler	Dephlegmator
Number off		1 Wkg	1 Wkg	1 Wkg	1 Wkg	1 Wkg
Dimensions				2m dia. 30 plates	75 m^2	75 m^2
Material of construction		CS	CS/13 Cr	CS	CS with 316 tubes	CS shell alumbro tubes
Rate or capacity		3000 m^3	60 m^3/h max	48 t/h	12.5 MJ/h	12.5 MJ/h
Working temperature		Atmos.	Atmos.	75° C	75° C	65° C
Working pressure		Atmos.	415 kN/m^2	125 kN/m^2	350 kN/m^2	125 kN/m^2
Steam					6 t/h	
Power			10 kW		3 bar	
Cooling water						100 m^3/h
Main plant item est. cost		39000	1800	32600	6700	9150
Main plant Item cost Carbon Steel basis	Vessels	39000	–	32600	4900	7300
	Machines[a]	–	1500	–	–	–
	Handling[a]	–	–	–	–	–
Erection of MPI	Ref.	1	2	4	[b]	[b]
	Factor	0.03	0.12	0.36		
	Cost	1170	180			
Piping	Ref.	7	7	8		
	Factor	0.32	1.12	0.39		
	Cost	12480	1680			
Instruments	Ref.	11	11	13		
	Factor	0.05	0.34	0.26		
	Cost	1950	510			
Electrical (ex. motors)	Ref.	15	17	15		
	Factor	0.03	0.41	0.03		
	Cost	1170	615			
Civil	Ref.	19 & 21	19	19 & 21		
	Factor	0.14	0.22	0.14		
	Cost	5460	330			
Structures and buildings	Ref.	22	22	2		
	Factor	0.02	0.05	0.25		
	Cost	780	75			
Lagging	Ref.	–	–	28		
	Factor	–	–	0.06		
	Cost	–	–			
CS basis	Total Factor	1.59	3.26	2.49		
	Exp'd Cost	62010	4890	81170		
Estimated installed cost		62010	5190	81170		

[a] Machines and material handling equipment costs include motor costs.
[b] The reader might like to complete these columns.
Reproduced with kind permission of Institution of Chemical Engineers

Table 7.5.4.1c *Typical multiplying factors for converting alloy and other fabricating costs to a carbon steel equivalent cost*

Materials		Pumps, etc.	Other equipment
All carbon steel		1.0	1.0
Stainless steel type	410	0.7	0.5
	304	0.55	0.4
	316	0.5	0.35
	310	0.5	0.3
Rubber-lined steel		0.7	0.8
Bronze		0.65	
Monel		0.3	
		Heat Exchangers	
Carbon steel shell and tubes		1.0	
Al tubes		0.8	
Monel tubes		0.48	
304 stainless steel tubes		0.6	
304 stainless steel shell and tubes		0.35	

Reproduced with kind permission of Institution of Chemical Engineers.

Table 7.5.5.1 *A broad outlined check-list for determining the installed capital cost of a project*

Site

Complete site land and soil survey
Land purchase plus all associated legal costs
New roads, road improvements and diversions
New rail tracks and facilities
Pipe and cable trenches
Dock and wharfage requirements
Water supply and distribution
Sewage disposal works

Plant and machines

All plant machinery and equipment from detailed design schedules
Special erection costs, e.g., clean conditions, etc.
Costs of special materials
Costs due to special manufacturing techniques or a limitation on manufacturing capacity
Inspection and testing
Delivery, particularly large and heavy lifts
Initial catalyst charge
Safety equipment
Containment of hazardous operations
Ventilation, with particular reference to hot conditions, toxic gases and vapours, dusts and fire risks
Fire protection equipment, including fire engines
Equipment to meet requirements of regulatory authorities
Effluent treatment plants, including developments costs
Instrumentation and control
Development of instrumentation
Pipework and valves
Insulation and painting
Costs of process development and prototype testing
Allowance for modification after erection
Stand-by plant
Mechanical handling facilities such as lifts and conveyers

Service plant and equipment

Steam-raising plant and water treatment facilities
Electricity connection charges
Transformers, switchgear and electrical substations

Cabling
Starters
Stand-by power supplies
Plant and pipework for storage and handling of water for process, cooling, fire fighting and portable supplies
Internal transport, conveying and storage of raw materials, intermediate, and finished products and fuel
Heating and lighting
Cranes, jigs, maintenance equipment and machinery
Test equipment
Lightning protection
Compressed air services
Refrigeration, local or centralized
Inert or special gas supplies
Operating and maintenance manuals, drawings, etc.
Spares, in so far as chargeable to capital account
Telephones and communications

Civil works

Foundations
Main plant buildings
Plant structural steelwork
Chimneys
Buildings for service plant
Stores, storage buildings, warehousing, laboratories, workshops, offices
Medical and first aid centres, fire station
Canteen, changing rooms, lavatories
Site security, fencing, gatehouses
Garages, car parks, cycle sheds
Customs and excise offices, weighbridge
Drainage – surface, chemical and soil water
Pipe and cable ducts
Land reinstatement, landscaping, etc.

Overhead costs

Engineering costs
Detailed drawing office design, procurement and inspection
Use of consultants or specialists
Departmental overheads
Construction of models
Insurance inspection and certification
Travel
Engineering involvement testing and commissioning
Special licences

Temporary facilities required for construction
Site engineer's office and furniture
Temporary power and water supplies
Temporary access and storage areas, fencing, site security
Construction workshops
Site fabrication facilities
Labour camp canteen

Direct construction costs
Contractor's fee (overheads and profit)
Direct labour or contract labour
Subsidies to labour – travelling, canteen, etc.
Specialists
Transport costs
Overtime working, abnormal weather conditions, local customs and regulations

Contingency allowance
Allowance for unexpected inflation, unplanned occurrences and miscellaneous items

and refrigeration services including water cooling towers and effluent treatment plant, site offices, gatehouses and laboratories, canteens, roads and railway lines, unless, of course, these are listed as main plant items which would be unusual. To allow for the outside battery limit costs it is common practice to increase the total installed battery limit capital cost by up to 40 per cent, for initial estimation purposes.

7.5.5 Detailed costing

This is the most thorough method of all but, as it requires the most information, it is also very time consuming and expensive. It is only used for sanction and control estimates. It requires detailed equipment specifications, so that proper budget quotations can be obtained from equipment manufacturers and sufficiently detailed drawings of civil and structural work to permit a materials take off (that is an estimation of the volume and weight of concrete and steel) to be made for costing purposes. Without a detailed check-list it is doubtful if the accuracy of such estimates would satisfy the standard expected for sanctioning purposes. Such a check-list is given in broad outline in Table 7.5.5.1, where it will be noticed that several new cost factors appear. Conspicuous in this respect is an allowance for the contractor's fee, drawing office costs, special testing and commissioning expenses, and a contingency allowance which is discussed in Section 7.5.6.

7.5.6 Allowing for uncertainty and risk

The only true test of the capital cost of a project is the sum of all the invoices which have to be paid once it is built. Even the most detailed of estimates can fall short of this ultimate cost because of time factors, which of themselves create uncertainty. Two major time factors are involved, the time delay between the completion of the estimate and the commencement of the project and the duration of the project building programme and its schedule of contractual payments up to the point of commissioning the project. It is not uncommon for this whole process to take between two and five years, during which time the actual capital cost could escalate considerably. To allow for this, cost estimators attempt to forecast the likely extent of cost inflation. This is by no means an easy matter because inflation can be affected by many diverse causes. For example, international pressure on the price of petroleum can affect the prices of fabricating materials and the delivered cost of plant and machinery. National price and wage policies can have a profound affect on construction costs, especially when such policies terminate. As a last example, local trade union bargaining can have a considerable impact on the construction cost of a new factory, especially during the later stages of its development, when the management's bargaining power is often quite weak. A detailed account of the methods which companies employ in an attempt to forecast inflation is beyond the scope of this book, excepting the details of Chapter 8.6. A simple-minded approach would involve the extrapolation of cost indices relating to the type of project being undertaken into the future, according to their most recent trends. Many indices exist for this purpose, some prepared by government statistical offices, others by professional and trade journals.

7.5.7 Allowing for productivity improvements

Besides inflation and the phenomenon of technical returns to scale, the estimation of a capital cost should also allow for productivity improvements during the design, fabrication and erection stages of a project as well as during its subsequent operation. In management jargon this phenomenon is known as learning. One of the first quantifications of learning involved the production of aero-frames, when it was discovered that the man-hours needed to complete a frame diminished with the number of frames completed. The same phenomenon has been witnessed in the building of complex factories and their subsequent operation, whereby operators have realized substantial capacity improvements, at modest cost, by discovering and removing the production limitations, or bottlenecks as they are known.

Research has discovered that improvements to the production capacities of plants and machines can be quite adequately modelled by the following equation, which is attributed to Hirschmann (1964):

$$Q_t = Q_0 + (Q_\infty - Q_0)(1 - e^{-kt})$$

where Q_t = the plant capacity at some time t, Q_0 = the plant capacity as designed, Q_∞ = some upper limit in the capacity of that plant after debottlenecking, e = the exponent 2.71828 which is the base to the Napierian or natural logarithms, k = an empirical learning coefficient, and t = the time interval since the plant was first built.

Quite obviously, allowance has to be made for learning in any capital cost estimating exercise otherwise the estimate will be overstated, possibly by as much as 3 per cent per annum. It is important, therefore, to regularly up-date any cost data file, forming the basis of capital cost estimates, to allow for this affect.

Having recognized all means for uncertainty in a final cost estimate and having attempted to remove much of this uncertainty, nevertheless it is a truism that uncertainty will still remain with the consequential risk that the capital cost of the project could over-run its estimate unless some contingency allowance is made. To hedge against running out of money most capital cost estimates incorporate a contingency allowance of magnitude equal to the level of error anticipated at each phase of the project, as defined by Table 7.5.1.

Although we have only been able to devote a few pages to this subject, which constitutes great books by other authors as listed in the references, it is nevertheless to be hoped that the reader will appreciate that much ingenuity and diligence on the part of cost engineers, has been deployed in making cost engineering the profession which it is. Nevertheless, errors still persist in cost estimates as Miller (1965) demonstrated by his analysis of 53 projects, costing between $10 000 and $9 millions (in 1965 terms). He showed that (i) 38 per cent of these projects over-ran their control estimate by an average 19 per cent (ii) 6 per cent broke even with their control estimate, and (iii) 56 per cent under-ran their cost estimate by an average of 14 per cent. On average the overall error for these 56 projects was a mere 1 per cent and, as might be expected, cost estimating has improved considerably since 1965. However, this case demonstrates that it might be unreasonable to expect the final cost of any *one* particular project to be within ±10 per cent or even ±15 per cent of its control estimate.

7.5.8 Bibliography

General texts

Guthrie, K. M., *Process Plant Estimating, Evaluation, and Control*, Craftsman Book Company, 1974. This is a massive book containing a huge quantity of cost data relating to the process industries.

Institution of Chemical Engineers, *A New Guide to Capital Cost Estimating*, 1977. This book contains an excellent introduction to capital cost estimating and a considerable volume of cost data.

Kay, S. R., *Factorial Estimating System* – 'Factest' Paper A3, ibid.

Lang, H. J., 'Engineering approach to preliminary cost estimates', *Chemical Engineering*, **54,** 10 (1947), pp. 130–133.

Miller, C. A., 'New cost factors give quick accurate estimates', *Chemical Engineering*, **72,** 19 (1965), pp. 226–236.

Perry, R. H. and Chilton, C. H. (Eds.) *The Chemical Engineer's Handbook* (5th edn) McGraw-Hill, New York, 1973.

Popper, H. (Ed.), *Modern Cost Engineering Techniques*, McGraw-Hill, 1970. This book constitutes a collection of some 99 technical articles published by the US journal *Chemical Engineering* during the period 1960–70. It covers most of the subject content of this entire book as well as relating to capital cost estimating.

Wilson, R. M. S., *Cost Control Handbook*, Gower Press, 1975. This book shows readers how to develop a cost estimate in detail.

Specific texts

Allen, D. H. and Page, R. C., *The Pre-design Estimation of Capital Investment for Chemical Plant*, Paper A1, Third Cost Engineering Symposium, London, 1974.

Bridgewater, A. V., *Rapid Cost Estimating in the Chemical Process Industry*, Paper A6, ibid.

Hirschmann, W. B., 'Profit from the learning curve', *Harvard Business Review*, January/February 1964.

Miller, C. A., 'New cost factors give quick accurate estimates', *Chemical Engineering*, **72** (19), p. 226, 1965.

7.6 ESTIMATING WORKING CAPITAL REQUIREMENTS

Working capital is the money which has to be spent on a new capital project in addition to that spent on fixed assets, such as equipment, machinery and buildings, to transform a project into an operating entity. The accounting definition of working capital* is 'the excess of current assets over current liabilities which has to be financed by the firm's long-term sources of funds'.

Table 7.6.1 *A skeleton balance sheet for a hypothetical company*

Assets	(munits)	Liabilities and Owner's Equity	
Current Assets		Current Liabilities	
Cash	100 000	Accounts payable	800 000
Inventories	3 500 000	Short-term debt	700 000
Accounts receivable	2 400 000	Taxes payable	600 000
		Dividends payable	400 000
Fixed Assets		Long-term debt	4 000 000
Plant, machinery	10 000 000	Owner's capital	
and buildings		and retained earnings	9 500 000
	16 000 000		16 000 000

According to the skeleton balance sheet given in Table 7.6.1, the working capital requirement of this hypothetical example is 3.5 million munits, determined by the relationship:

$$\text{working capital} = \text{current assets} - \text{current liabilities}$$
$$= 6.0 \times 10^6 \qquad -2.5 \times 10^6 \qquad = 3.5 \times 10^6$$

---

* A brief summary of accounting definitions, concepts and conventions is given in Appendix B.

Table 7.6.2 *The deployment of assets according to Table 7.6.1*

Fixed Assets		10 000 000
Current Assets		
Cash	100 000	
Inventory	3 500 000	
Accounts		
receivable	2 400 000	
	6 000 000	
Current Liabilities		
Accounts payable	800 000	
Short-term debt	700 000	
Taxes payable	600 000	
Dividends payable	400 000	
	2 500 000	
Working capital		3 500 000
Assets employed		13 500 000

We can get a better idea of the contribution which working capital makes to the total assets employed by this hypothetical company if we rearrange the balance sheet, as shown by Table 7.6.2.

Although working capital funds are continuously liquidated and regenerated (according to the definition of the word current, as used in accounting theory), this money is unavailable for other purposes so it must be regarded as an investment. However, the accounting definition of working capital has to be modified before it can be applied to the economic appraisal of capital projects. DCF sums fully allow for all taxation considerations in a project, as demonstrated by Section 7.11, so it would obviously be wrong to include taxation effects in the computation of working capital, since this would be tantamount to double-counting. Similarly, DCF sums allow for all the cash flows into and out of a project, but do not specify how the net cash inflows should be used, that being decided by the firm's dividend policy as formulated by its board of directors. As a result, the working capital needs of a prospective investment project must *not* include any allowance for dividends payable either. Resulting from these differences, the working capital investment in our hypothetical example would be 4.5 million munits funded by long-term sources of finance or, alternatively, 5.2 million munits funded by *long*-term sources of finance using debt and equity capital.

Traditionally, the working capital needs of a prospective capital project have either been completely overlooked or, in the case of more professional companies, they have been allowed for as a percentage of its fixed capital cost, with typical values varying between 10 and 20 per cent. Due to the ravages of inflation, however, such a yardstick as this is now inappropriate and research has shown that working capital computations based on percentages of annual sales revenue are more appropriate. For example, Scott (1978) showed that companies typically invest between 15 and 60 per cent of their annual sales revenue as working capital. Quite obviously each individual project has its own unique working capital requirements, which depend on such things as the nature of its production process (whether batch, campaign or continuous), the sources and destinations of its raw materials and products, and the level of credit used in its line of business. Typical values of the working capital requirements to meet most business conditions are given in Table 7.6.3, where the extent of the working capital is expressed in weeks of sales revenue. According to this table the minimum working capital requirement of a project approximates 7–12 weeks (13–23 per cent) and the maximum approximates 32–57 weeks (62–110 per cent) of annual sales revenue and it is these sums of money which have to be jointly financed by long- and short-term sources of finance.

Table 7.6.3 *Typical working capital needs of a firm expressed in weeks of sales revenue*

Category	Examples	Weeks of sales revenue (typical values)
Raw material stocks:		
daily delivery and use	Pipeline delivery of petroleum	1–3
intermittent delivery by truck or train	Steel sheet and rod deliveries to fabricators	2–4
large batch deliveries by barge or ship	Petroleum or mineral ore especially from abroad	4–8
Work in progress stocks:		
continuous process or assembly line production	Chemical products, consumer capital goods and motor vehicles	1–3
campaign production on a continuous process or assembly line	Different consumer goods on the same production line	4–5
batch production	Pharmaceutical products, machine-shop assembled products	6–8
Final goods stocks at factory:		
daily delivery	Pipeline delivery of naphtha, cement deliveries to wholesalers	1–3
intermediate delivery	Train loads of coke to steelworks	2–4
large batch deliveries	Product export consignments	4–8
Final goods stocks in warehouse:		
daily delivery	Distribution of petrol	1–3
product repacked in crates or drums	Distribution of domestic appliances	2–4
products blended and repacked in boxes or cartons	Distribution of food products	4–8
Finished products for export stocks:		
short distance	Germany to France	1–2
medium distance	USA to EEC	4–6
long distance	Australasia to Scandinavia	10–20
Accountants receivable (debtors):		
local		4–8
overseas		10–15
Accounts payable (creditors):		
local		2–6
overseas		6–10
Typical working capital	Minimum	7–12
requirements	Maximum	32–57

On the basis that working capital is computed as a percentage of sales revenue, it is obvious that the working capital needs of a project rise and fall with its sales activity. In this respect, therefore, working capital is analogous to the head of water in a tank, the greater the head (level) the faster the flow out through a hole in the bottom of that tank, where such a flow is analogous to the sales revenue of a project. In DCF calculations, therefore, the initial working capital needs of a project must feature in that project's cash flow profile from the moment that raw material purchases are envisaged, and *additions* to or *subtractions* from that initial working capital sum must be incorporated in such a way as to reflect the actual working capital needs of the project throughout its economic life, including an allowance for liquidating any terminal working capital. The example given later in Table 7.11.2 illustrates this.

Only that working capital which has to be financed by long-term sources of finance should normally feature in the DCF economics of a project. By contrast, working capital financed by short-term sources of finance, such as bank overdrafts, should be excluded from such sums. However the interest charges arising from short-term borrowing should feature in DCF appraisals as deductible expenses. Such a stipulation ensures that only those cash flows which are relevant are discounted by the firm's long-term cost of capital, which is discussed in the next chapter. As a last point we should emphasize that most investment projects are moderately sensitive to errors in the prediction of their working capital needs, typical errors being in the range shown below in Table 7.6.4.

Table 7.6.4 *Economic sensitivity of a capital project to errors and changes in the computation of its working capital*

Basis for working capital computation	Type of project	
	average profitability	high profitability
Not allowed for	15	33
Computed at 15 per cent of fixed capital	13	29
Computed at 30 per cent of annual sales revenue	11	26

Units: DCF return after tax (per cent per annum)

7.6.1 Bibliography

Scott, R., 'Working capital and its estimation for project evaluation', *Engineering and Process Economics*, Vol. 3, **2,** March 1978.

7.7 OPERATING COST ESTIMATING

There are probably as many ways to estimate the operating costs associated with a new capital venture as there are companies engaged in the task. This arises from the fact that, unlike capital cost estimating, there exist no prescribed guidelines as to how operating cost estimates should be prepared. One way to derive a composite operating cost could involve the aggregation of individual cost components along the lines suggested by Figure 7.7.1, but it should be noted that these broad cost category headlines are seldom consistent in their employ even between companies engaged in the same industry let alone between companies engaged in different industries. The other point which must be stressed is that the expense of cost estimating must also be borne in mind when preparing an operating cost estimate and the accuracy of the estimate should fit the need. This latter point is most relevant during the formative stages of a new capital project because there would be little merit developing an operating cost estimate to a tolerance of ±20 per cent when the market sales forecast might be in error by ±50 per cent or more. In other words, management should remain selective in its apportionment of estimating and forecasting effort throughout the various stages of a capital investment appraisal.

The estimation of operating costs for a new manufacturing process during its early stages of planning has received much less attention than capital cost estimating. Much of the work which has been done is reviewed by Bridgewater (1973) and an excellent case study, based on the methods which are available, is due to Wilson

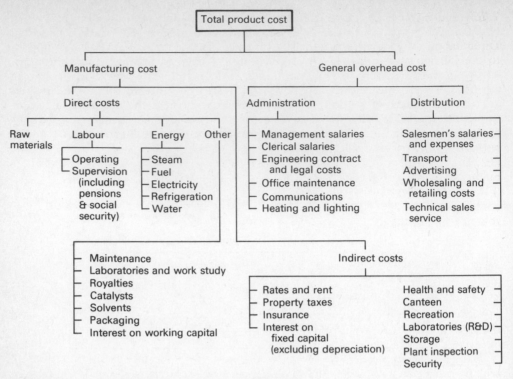

Figure 7.7.1 *The disaggregation of product operating costs.*

(1978). As with capital cost estimation, however, most of the methods used in operating cost estimation rely either on ratio analysis or empirical equations resulting from statistical regression analysis. The more important categories of costs and approximate means for their evaluation are surveyed below.

7.7.1 Direct materials costs

Evidence by the Centre of Interfirm Comparison (CIC) (1978) suggests that direct materials costs of manufacturing, measured as a percentage of the free on board (fob) sales price of a product, vary according to the following statistics:

	%
Upper decile	62.3
Median	42.0
Lower decile	21.8

for a large variety of manufactured products and the research evidence of Grumer (1967) would tend to confirm these findings. In effect, therefore, raw materials costs comprise a major element in the estimation of overall operating costs and it behoves the estimator to forecast this category of cost with caution. This requires the estimation of the purchase prices of raw materials (already outlined in Section 7.3) and an estimation of the material yields which can be expected in the manufacturing process. In the case of chemicals and some commodity products, materials yields depend on the physical efficiency of the conversion process. For manufactured artefacts, however, material yields depend on the shape and size of the artefact and its means of fabrication.

7.7.2 Labour costs

Direct labour costs vary as a percentage of the fob sales price of a product according to the following statistics:

	%
Upper decile	18.8
Median	10.8
Lower decile	4.1

for a variety of manufactured products. These cost statistics are in close agreement with those involved with the manufacture of cement as reported by Bridgewater (1973), but they are considerably higher than those incurred with the exclusive manufacture of chemical products as reported by Fidgett (1972).

A most interesting means of calculating the labour costs involved with machined components is given by Mahmoud (1981) according to the following statistically regressed equation:

$$C_L = \frac{RN_d}{60} \left[\frac{K_c L D_m}{4.77} + \frac{S_t}{XQ} \right]$$

where C_L = the labour cost per component, R = the labour rate + factory overheads, $K_c = K_1 \times K_2 \times K_{mat}$, K_1 = a machining factor, K_2 = a machine type factor, K_{mat} = a material factor, L = the machined length of the product, D_m = the mean diameter of the product, S_t = the time to 'set' the machine, X = the relative capacity of the machine tool, Q = the size of the batch produced.

Using this equation and the parametric values provided in his paper, Mahmoud reckons that it is possible to derive a study estimate of the labour costs of producing an artefact with an error in the range ±10 per cent, 90 per cent of the time!

In a similar vein, it has been shown that the research results of Wessel (1953) still apply and his correlation, given below, can be used to forecast direct labour requirements in the manufacture of chemical products:

$$L = KNQ^{-0.76}$$

where L = operating labour (man hours per ton of product), N = number of distinct process (functional) steps, and Q = plant capacity (tons per day); and the values of the parameter K are 23 for batch processes, 17 for operations with average labour requirements, and 10 for well-instrumented continuous processes.

To translate these labour requirements into costs requires an estimate of the direct labour rate and an allowance for social security taxes, pensions and supervision costs too.

According to CIC data, *indirect labour costs* involved with manufactured products vary according to the following percentages of a product's price.

	%
Upper decile	15.6
Median	3.8
Lower decile	0.7

7.7.3 Energy costs

Energy costs comprising power and fuel are another significant cost area according to CIC data and in this case the three relevant statistics are: 8.3 per cent, 3.4 per cent and 1.4 per cent. These results are in accord with many of those reported by Fidgett (1972) for chemical manufacture.

7.7.4 Overhead costs

This category of costs comprises all those other costs listed in Figure 7.7.1, so it is little wonder why the CIC data show the enormous range given below.

	% sales price
Upper decile	24.9
Median	8.0
Lower decile	4.1

However, these results are also in accord with those provided by Bridgewater (1973).

7.7.5 The accuracy of operating cost estimates

Quite clearly, from the foregoing material, we have not endeavoured to show how to derive accurate operating cost estimates, since these would require detailed engineering data involving proper product design drawings and plant flow-sheets, coupled with product yield, power requirement, and time and motion study results. Instead, what we have attempted to do is to give some idea of the magnitude of these costs, and to show how they can be *roughly* estimated using ratio analysis data, which is readily available for companies and products alike, and/or statistically regressed equations based on empirical evidence.

It is important to note, however, that, since these data are required for DCF analyses they must comprise *cash flows only*. By definition, therefore, they *must not* include an allowance for *any* arbitrary depreciation expenses.

7.7.6 Bibliography

Bridgewater, A. V., 'How to control costs', *The Chemical Engineer*, November 1973, pp. 538–544.

Centre of Interfirm Comparison, *Maintenance Aspects of Terotechnology; 2, Management by Maintenance Ratios*, Dept of Industry, Committee of Terotechnology, 1978.

Fidgett, M., M.Sc. Thesis, The University of Aston, Birmingham, 1972.

Grumer, E. L., 'Selling price versus raw material cost', *Chemical Engineering*, **74** (24), April 1967, pp. 190–192.

Mahmoud, M. A. M., 'Turned component costs', *Engineering*, **2** (21), January 1981, p. 35.

Wessel, H. E., *Chemical Engineering*, **60,** January 1953, p. 168.

Wilson, D. C., 'The economics of resource recovery from solid waste', *Engineering and Process Economics*, **3,** 1978, pp. 35–59.

7.8 A SPECIAL COSTING PROBLEM INVOLVING THE USE OF EXISTING FACILITIES

Most academic examples of DCF calculations assume that the intended project is *self-contained*. In many circumstances, however, this is not so. Instead new projects often require either the direct or the indirect use of existing service facilities such as steam, water, compressed air and refrigeration. When *existing* facilities are used by *one* prospective project, the opportunity for their use by some other project is foregone. This means that the future cash flows from the alternative use of these facilities will be lost, and an opportunity cost will be incurred, as a result of their pre-emptive use by the proposed project. Rather than forgo the alternative use of the facilities, it might be economically justifiable to pursue *both* projects by expanding the existing facilities to accommodate both. In these circumstances, because the expansion is made necessary by the pre-emption of the proposed venture, it should pay for expanding those facilities to the extent that it uses them but *at such a time when they are needed.* This will depend on the annual rate at which their spare capacity is being absorbed.

By these means projects are treated on a comparable basis and this method ensures that operating cost estimates only incorporate actual cash flows without the need for any arbitrary accounting depreciation allowances or any irrational arguments about sunk costs (which are discussed in detail in Chapter 19.4).

7.9 TEROTECHNOLOGY AND THE LIFE-CYCLE COSTS OF ASSET OWNERSHIP

The proportion of manufacturing costs spent on the maintenance of productive assets is normally relatively small compared with direct materials and labour costs of production. Nevertheless, in recent years the maintenance function has increasingly become the focus of management attention. Hitherto, this function was often considered the Cinderella of all business functions and maintenance costs, like taxes, were considered inevitable. Evidence* suggests that, arising from this attitude, the maintenance departments of *many* firms are managed by default, with managers and staff reacting to whatever situation besets them without proper means of planning, or adequate sources of information to make management control effective. As a result, the scope for economy in maintenance is considerable and many manufacturing firms could increase their maintenance labour productivity by 30 per cent or more if only they could break away from restrictive working practices and manage their maintenance resources properly.

Besides concern for the relative inefficiency with which many maintenance departments operate, it is also recognized that an efficient maintenance function can be a strategic source of corporate strength in a competitive environment, especially when production capacity limits sales. Furthermore, it is now recognized, more than ever before, that pressure to minimize the first costs of owning an asset can be misguided. Instead, the accent of current management thinking is that the aggregate costs of owning and maintaining an asset should be considered over its complete life-cycle; from its purchase to its ultimate retirement and a cradle-to-the-grave philosophy should apply to the *design* and the *procurement* of physical assets, whether they are consumer goods or industrial capital goods. Although this life-cycle approach is certainly not new to many industries, especially the more capital intensive process industries, nevertheless, it is not well known in manufacturing, and it is certainly not universally applied. To counter this deficiency the concept of terotechnology was developed, and it has been promoted throughout most industrial countries during the past decade. The term is derived from a Greek word, the latinized version of which is *terein*, meaning 'to care for', 'to watch over', 'to maintain; the official

---

* A most comprehensive form of this evidence is the *Study of Engineering Maintenance in the Manufacturing Industry*, reported to the Ministry of Technology (UK), 1969.

definition of terotechnology is:

> a combination of management, financial, engineering and other practices
> applied to physical assets in pursuit of economic life-cycle costs. Its practice is
> concerned with the specification and design for reliability and maintainability
> of plant, machinery, equipment, buildings and structures, with their installa-
> tion, commissioning maintenance, modification and replacement, and with
> feedback of information on design, performance and costs.

In other words, terotechnology is a total systems *design concept*, the economic
significance of which epitomizes the philosophy which is germane to this entire book.

7.9.1   The design implications of terotechnology

Customers only reward those firms whose goods and services offer a useful rendering
of economic service. As such the pursuit of economic life-cycle costs *starts* with a
proper market appraisal of what the customer wants/needs, can afford, and *will* buy.
It is the job of corporate management, working through *all* the functions of the
business, including design and marketing, to translate those wants into artefacts and
services which will successfully compete for limited spending power in an ever-
increasingly competitive environment. The task facing the design function, therefore,
is to satisfy a variety of interrelated needs which require the fulfilment of some
functional performance, but also include requirements for reliability, maintainability,
durability, adaptability, safety, ease of use and environmental suitability, and offer a
product of a quality and style which is aesthetically pleasing. This is the stage when
the designer needs to establish *specifications* for the performance and feature
requirements of the product, because it is only through using specifications that a
designer can make that inevitable trade-off between conflicting product characteristics which permits the optimization of the design. Typically, trade-offs have to be
made between first cost (capital cost), operating cost and maintenance costs, durability and weight, corrosion resistance and cost, reliability and complexity, reliability
and the cost of spare parts, and many more considerations besides. Parameters
dealing with the type of environment in which the product will be used, its intensity
of use and the reliability required are usually some of the most important design
features of a product, especially from a cost viewpoint.

   Design as a corporate function cannot be permitted to degenerate into a back-
room activity staffed with boffins who have little vested interest in the ultimate use of
the product other than fulfilling their own artistic, scientific and engineering interests. Instead, design must be a function which receives top management attention
and, of necessity, it has to be involved with other corporate functions, especially
marketing, production and cost estimating. Absolutely essential to an effective
design function is the feedback of previous experience gained by the customer use
and company manufacture of a product. This information must be precise, comprehensive, timely and, above all else, cost-effective. It should comprise the costs of
the product as made, the difficulties in its manufacture and it should record such
details as warrantee claims, product returns, service engineering reports, spare parts
sales and salesmen's experience of customer satisfaction as well as dissatisfaction, so
that past design successes can be reinforced wherever possible, and design errors can
be rectified. Such an information system should also report the company's own
experience in developing the product so that future generations of designers do not
reinvent the wheel, so to speak, by repeating past errors and mistakes. An information system such as this is essential to good design, because design is an evolutionary
process forever adapting to changes, treats and opportunities. It must be stressed,

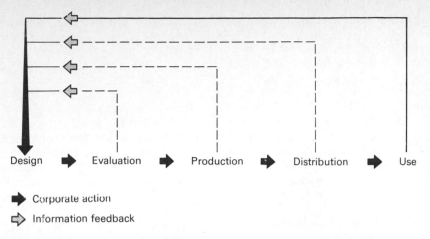

Design ➡ Evaluation ➡ Production ➡ Distribution ➡ Use

➡ Corporate action

⇨ Information feedback

Figure 7.9.1.1 *Information feedback to design.*

however, that it is not sufficient to make such information available, instead designers must be fired with the passion to design products which will sell well, and to do this they must *act* on the information received. Since the design of a product or service affects and is affected by other corporate functions, it follows that information feedback to design, as illustrated in Figure 7.9.1.1, from the other corporate functions is extremely important.

7.9.2 The reliability and maintainability implications of design

Unreliability is the major cause for the extension in the costs of owning an asset beyond its first cost, because the loss of the functional performance of an asset, due to its failure, necessitates either its replacement or repair if that functional performance is still required.

In certain markets, especially consumer goods markets, where fashion is often the prime factor in determining the rate of product obsolescence, it is often necessary to design products to low first costs and minimum acceptable standards of reliability-maintainability because of the competitive force of market price. In these circumstances little or no attention might be paid to subsequent problems of maintenance and repair. Such products as these typify the throw-away products of society – paper and plastic products are excellent examples. However, where assets have high capital cost and are intended to be in continuous use for long periods, it is possible that an increase in first cost designed for long term fault-free operation will be more than compensated by a reduction in subsequent costs of overhaul and repair during the planned life-cycle of the product. More often than not, however, the life-cycle of complex equipment or installations is interrupted, sometimes with disastrous effects, by the failure of a part which was not designed to match the life cycle of the system as a whole, either as an initial installation, or as a replaceable item with reliability high enough to permit economic and effective periodic overhaul, repair or replacement.

Evidence suggests that, faced with the tripartite problem of (i) dwindling world-wide reserves of raw materials, (ii) an ever-increasing awareness of the seriousness of environmental contamination, and (iii) the need on the part of the developed nations to retain their standards of living in the face of ever-increasing market competition from developing nations, customer preference is changing to products with greater reliability and ease of maintenance. Moreover, it appears that customers are often willing to pay a premium price to avoid subsequent service and repair problems. Some evidence to this effect is the threefold reduction during the past decade in the frequency with which automobiles require routine maintenance, and the fact that the more expensive Japanese television sets sell so well because of their perceived high standards of reliability. Furthermore, where subsequent service and repair is justified, product designers have demonstrated their ingenuity by making parts more accessible for speed and economy in repair or replacement, and nowadays they often design into a product a quick means of monitoring its 'health' so that incipient or actual failures can be diagnosed and speedily rectified.

Although limitations of space preclude a proper treatment of the fundamentals of reliability engineering matters here*, it is important to realize that the quest for greater technological capability and greater reliability are often conflicting requirements. Greater technological capability, as might arise from the development of some multi-purpose computerized machine tool, possibly serviced by a mechanical robot, necessitates the use of many component parts in series with the result that the failure of any one part can put the operation of the complete system in jeopardy. This effect is analogous to the idea that a chain is only as strong as its weakest link. In reliability engineering terms it can be shown that the overall reliability of a system designed on the basis of 'n' independent component parts in series can be represented by the equation:

$$R_s = \prod_{i=1}^{n} R_i$$

where R_s = the reliability of the overall system, R_i = the reliability of the ith component, π = the product of the n terms $R_1 \cdot R_2 \ldots R_i \ldots R_n$, and the reliability of a component, device or system is defined as 'the probability that it will sustain its specified duty, when operated under prescribed conditions, for a specified duration'.

According to this equation, a system comprising two independent series components, each with a reliability of 90 per cent, would have an overall reliability of only 81 per cent $(0.9 \times 0.9 = 0.81)$ and Figure 7.9.2.1a shows how the reliability of a system would diminish rapidly with increasing numbers of components despite their having excellent individual reliabilities.

Perhaps one of the best examples which demonstrates the extent of the conflict which exists between the need to achieve greater technological capability and greater reliability comes from the conventional generation of electricity. Faced with the need to increase thermal efficiency, to contain the inexorable advance in fuel costs, power station designers have increased the operating temperatures and pressures of steam drums and turbogenerators. Furthermore, motivated by technical economies of scale, they have also designed increasingly larger generating units. Unfortunately, the evidence reported by the Edison Electric Institute (1977) shows that these changes brought about a serious decline in the on-stream availabilities of these larger units as demonstrated by Figure 7.9.2.1b.

The reasons for this decline are:

(i) *Size:* To some degree there is a direct inverse relationship between the size of a generating unit and its availability. This results from the fact that the boiler of a large set (say a 500 MW set) contains approximately the same amount of tubing as the boilers of small sets with the same aggregate capacity (say ten 50 MW sets), but whereas one tube failure on the large set might lose 500 MW for three days,

---

* The interested reader is referred to the texts by Jardine (1973) and Kelly and Harris (1978) for a better understanding of these matters and how they relate to the maintenance problem in general.

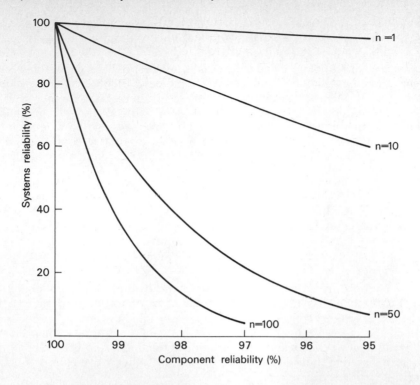

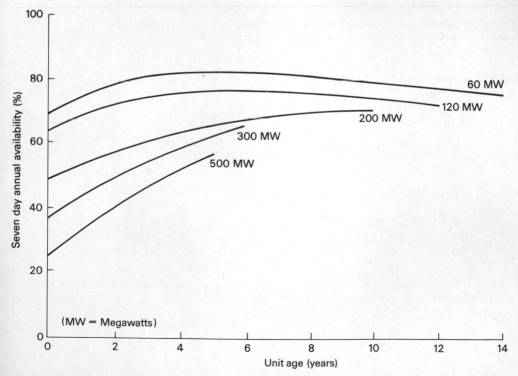

Figure 7.9.2.1 (a) *The relationship between the reliability of a system and the reliability of its series components.* (b) *Relationship between the availability and the capacity of electricity turbogenerating sets.*

the same failure on the smaller sets would only lose 50 MW for approximately three days. In other words a tenfold increase in quality control would be necessary to compensate the affects of scale.

(ii) *Complexity:* Technological advances have made possible generating sets with larger capacity without a corresponding increase in physical dimensions, but whereas a 30 MW alternator would only need simple air cooling, a 500 MW alternator requires a hydrogen cooling system with all the paraphernalia that entails. Furthermore, to contain the higher pressures of more modern power stations it has been necessary to use more safety orientated control systems with the 'knock-on' unreliability effect which comes from having more equipment in series.

It will of course be realized that having units operate in parallel is one way of increasing reliability. In these circumstances the reliability of a system comprising '*n*' independent components operating in parallel is given by the expression:

$$R_s = 1 - \prod_{i=1}^{n} (1 - R_i)$$

where the symbols are as before. In this case the overall system reliability of two components, each with a reliability of 90 per cent, operating in parallel is 99 per cent.

In effect, therefore, designing systems so that they incorporate some element of parallel redundancy is one way of enhancing the reliability and the availability* of a manufacturing system; but redundancy costs money. Alternative means of enhancing the availability of a system comprise:

  (i) increasing the reliability of individual components,
 (ii) increasing their maintainability†, and
(iii) devising maintenance strategies to provide the most effective maintenance possible;

but these alternatives also cost money.

The task facing the designer, therefore, is to select that combination of reliability–maintainability attributes which, combined with rigorous standards of quality control and a judicious application of parts standardization, provides the most effective design consistent with meeting other design criteria such as material efficiency and ease and flexibility of operations.

7.9.3 The life-cycle cost of ownership

We are now at the stage where we can appreciate what is meant by the term the life-cycle costs (LCC) of ownership. Given that some artefacts only involve their initial purchase plus subsequent maintenance, their LCC is given by the following

---

* Availability in this context is the proportion of time that a system actually accomplishes its specified duty when operated under prescribed conditions so that:

$$\text{Mean availability} = \frac{\text{Mean time to failure}}{\text{Mean time to failure} + \text{mean time to repair}}$$

$$= \frac{\text{MTTF}}{\text{MTTF} + \text{MTTR}}$$

† Maintainability is the probability that a failed device will be repaired in a given time when maintained under specified conditions.

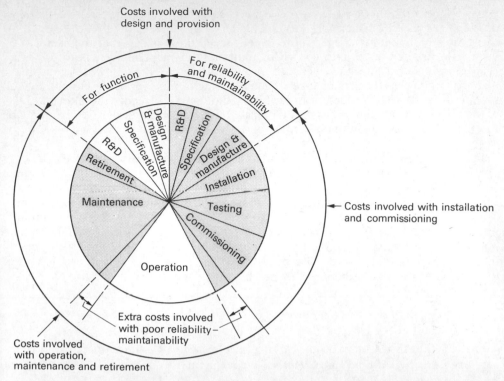

Figure 7.9.3.1 *The relationship between the life-cycle cost of ownership (shaded) and the total life-cycle costs involved in purchasing and operating an asset.*

NPV relationship:

$$\text{LCC} = \sum_{i=0}^{n} \left(K + \frac{\text{MC}_i}{(1+r)^i} - \frac{S_n}{(1+r)^n} \right)$$

where K = installed capital cost, MC_i = maintenance cost in year $i = (0, n)$, S_n = scrap value at the end of year n, n = optimal life (see Chapter 19.2) of the asset, and $100 \cdot r$ = appropriate discount rate (per cent per annum).

Research by the Centre of Interfirm Comparison (1978) has shown that the annual maintenance costs of manufacturing assets, measured as a percentage of their valuation, vary according to the following statistics:

	%
Upper decile	26.7
Median	13.8
Lower decile	5.3

On the basis of this evidence the maintenance work incurred by owning an asset over a period of ten years, assuming a 10 per cent per annum cost of capital, contributes 25–62 per cent of its overall life-cycle costs.* This in itself demonstrates

---

* Using the discount tables for the present value of an annuity (given in Appendix G), we find that $P/A_{10,10} = 6.1446$. Neglecting any allowance for scrap value therefore, the maintenance contribution to LCC would be:

(i) upper decile: $\dfrac{6.1446 \times 0.267}{6.1446 \times 0.267 + 1} = 0.62$

(ii) median: $\dfrac{6.1446 \times 0.138}{6.1446 \times 0.138 + 1} = 0.46$

(iii) lower decile: $\dfrac{6.1446 \times 0.053}{6.1446 \times 0.053 + 1} = 0.25$

why designers should be concerned for the costs of ownership beyond the first cost of buying an asset. Furthermore, arguments as to why they should be concerned for these later costs are made even more cogent when one realizes that the user can do very little to alter these later costs. All that subsequent maintainers can do, other than modify an asset, is to select that mix of preventive, breakdown, opportunistic and condition-based maintenance schemes which provides the optimal overall maintenance strategy. Indeed, it is a salutary thought that freedom to alter the LCC of owning an asset diminishes throughout the stages of its design, so it might be foolhardy to select between alternative design options until their LCCs can be properly assessed.

From the material in Section 7.9.2 it will, of course, be realized that the LCC of owning an asset, which also incurs operating costs, can be substantially more than just its first cost plus maintenance costs. Reliability and maintainability difficulties can affect its initial commissioning and subsequent operations thereby involving all sorts of extra operating costs such as contractual penalties, the need to purchase products which should have been made, the hire of additional equipment, and possibly the loss of sales too. In these circumstances the life-cycle cost of ownership might be represented by the shaded area of Figure 7.9.3.1 where we have endeavoured to distinguish between ownership costs and operating costs.

7.9.4   Bibliography

Centre of Interfirm Comparison, *Maintenance Aspects of Terotechnology and Management by Maintenance Ratio*, Department of Industry, Committee of Terotechnology, 1978.

Edison Electric Institute, *A Report of the Equipment Availability Task Force of the Prime Movers Committee of EEI for the Ten-year period 1968–1977*, New York, 1977.

Jardine, A. K. S., *Maintenance, Replacement and Reliability*, Pitman, 1973.

Kelly, A. and Harris, M. J., *The Management of Industrial Maintenance*, Newnes-Butterworth, 1978.

P. A. Management Consultants Ltd, *Study of Engineering Maintenance in the Manufacturing Industry*, Ministry of Technology, April 1969.

7.10   THE DURATION OF A PROJECT'S BUILDING PROGRAMME AND ITS ECONOMIC LIFE

Two time estimates are crucial to the proper economic evaluation of a prospective capital project: the length of that project's building programme and its economic life. The second of these considerations usually depends on the rate of obsolescence of its products and/or its manufacturing process. Either one or both of these effects will eventually cause the replacement and ultimately the retirement of a manufacturing asset. It is in this respect that a cradle-to-the-grave philosophy is so important for the thorough economic appraisal of a prospective project. Matters pertaining to the evaluation of a project's economic life receive proper consideration in Chapter 19.2, so it will not be repeated here. However, one thing must be mentioned. Details concerning the survival lives of a large variety of assets are given by Russo and Cowles (1980) thereby permitting the physical lives of assets to be forecast on a probabilistic basis. However, the point which we must stress is that the physical live of most assets are usually considerably greater than their economic lives, as most industrial museums testify, so that NPV sums based on physical life forecasts or engineering predictions will invariably be wrong.

The duration of a project's building programme obviously depends on its size, complexity and location, the extent of the labour skills involved, the professionalism of the project management team, the fairness of the project contract, the degree of harmony which exists between the unions and the project management and, possibly above all else, the urgency of the project and the financial incentives which are available to reinforce that urgency. Using statistical regression analysis, Gates and Scarpa (1980) show that the durations of building programmes for projects built in the USA costing between $10 000 and $100 million in 1979 terms can be modelled by the relationship:

$$T = 1.92C^{0.334}$$

where T = project building programme (days), and C = construction cost ($ USA), and they suggest that such a model could be used within limits to forecast the durations of future projects. Although such an idea has a definite appeal, it should however be noted that large differences exist between the times required to build similar installations in different countries, and the evidence reported by the National Economic Development Office (NEDO) (1977) would suggest that British performance in this direction is often exceedingly poor. This suggests that certain national as well as local considerations, possibly of a political as well as a cultural nature, have to be considered when attempting to predict the duration of a building programme. From the details of our life-cycle economic equation, first developed in Chapter 5.10, it will be realized that an unplanned extension to the length of a building programme can seriously mar the economic merits of a project. The objective facing project management therefore is to build the capital project within budget time and cost, according to specification. It should also be mentioned that, in certain circumstances, the end of year convention for discounting capital expenditures is most inappropriate, as the work of de la Mare (1979) shows. In effect therefore not only is a reasonable estimate of the total duration of the building programme needed, but the timing of that capital expenditure is also important to the proper economic appraisal of a project.

7.10.1 Bibliography

de la Mare, R. F., 'Modelling capital expenditure', *Engineering and Process Economics*, **4** 1979, pp. 467–477.
Gates, M. and Scarpa, A., 'Preliminary time and overhead estimates by the one-third rule', *Cost Engineering*, **22** (6), December 1980, p. 331.
NEDO, *Engineering Construction Performance*, 1977.
Russo, J. G. and Cowles, H. A., 'Revaluation of the Iowa-type survivor curves', *Engineering Economist*, **26** (1) Fall 1980, p. 1.

7.11 COMPANY TAXATION

Many managers, engineers and economists ignore taxation effects in their appraisal of a project's economic worth on the pretext that such factors are outside a firm's control. They are most definitely wrong in this assumption, because tax payments and allowances constitute legitimate cash flows which are uniquely determined by a project's economic performance. In many (indeed most) countries taxation has two identifiable effects. The first and best known is payment of taxes to the national exchequer to finance the government's budget (for defence, education, health and other purposes). The second involves encouraging firms to build factories and invest in productive machinery with the dual purpose of creating wealth and jobs and, to this end, various taxation inducements are offered which vary in form from tax offsetting allowances to direct capital grants. The variety and scope of such inducements is too great to study in detail here since they depend on the country of concern, the magnitude of its unemployment both nationally and regionally, the physical nature of the equipment involved, and its anticipated longevity. Precise details of the rate of company tax and the nature of tax allowances are published by most governments in their Finance Acts every year.

The tax rate which a company has to pay depends on its legal status. Those registered as partnerships pay taxes according to formulae prescribed for private individuals, with low rates for those of modest income and escalating rates for those of higher income. By contrast, firms registered as limited liability companies or corporations usually pay taxes at a fixed rate which approximates 50 per cent of their taxable income in most industrialized countries. The timing of tax payments varies from country to country. Some involve payments according to a plan agreed with the tax authorities, balancing adjustments being accomplished at the end of the fiscal year. Others however allow taxes to be paid sometimes as much as one to two years in arrears.

Tax offsetting allowances are devised to help a company keep its capital intact throughout the life of an asset. Effectively, they permit a company to reduce its tax liability by an amount equal to the project's installed capital cost. In this respect, such allowances serve the same purpose as accounting depreciation (see Appendix B) but, unlike a firm's depreciation policy which can be quite arbitrary, such allowances are precisely formulated, being legally binding. The precise rate at which a company can claim this partial tax exemption depends on the details of the government's allowance formula. For example, some governments permit a company

Table 7.11.1 *Taxation allowances, for an asset costing 100 munits, computed on a declining balance basis*

Beginning of year	Written down value (WDV) at beginning of year	End of year annual allowance @ 20% of WDV
1	100.00	20.00
2	80.00	16.00
3	64.00	12.80
4	51.20	10.24
5	40.96	8.19
6	32.77	6.55
7	26.21	5.24
8	20.97	4.19
9	16.78	3.36
10	13.42	2.68
11	10.74	2.15
12	8.59	1.72
13	6.87	1.37
14	5.50	1.10
15	4.40	4.40[a]

[a] Since this computation continues indefinitely, it is common practice in DCF sums to terminate the computation when the expected economic life duration of the asset is reached.

Table 7.11.2 Allowing for corporation taxes and taxation allowances in DCF computations

Year	A	B	C	D	E	$F = D + E$	$G = 0.5F$	H	$I = A+B+C$ $+H-G$	J	K
	Capital expenditure	Investment grant	Actual cash inflow before tax	Cash inflow one year in arrears	Tax allowances	Taxable income after allowances	Taxes @50%	Working capital	Net after tax cash flows	DCF @ 10% pa	DCF @ 22% pa
1	-100 000	0	0	0	0	-100 000	0	0	-100 000	-100 000	-100 000
2		20 000	23 000	0	100 000	23 000	-50 000	-30 000	63 000	57 273	51 639
3			44 000	23 000		44 000	11 500	-10 000	22 500	18 595	15 117
4			38 000	44 000		38 000	22 000	-4 000	12 000	9 016	6 608
5			34 400	38 000		34 400	19 000	+800	16 200	11 065	7 313
6			30 800	34 400		30 800	17 200	+800	14 400	8 941	5 328
7			27 200	30 800		27 200	15 400	+800	12 600	7 112	3 821
8			23 600	27 200		23 600	13 600	+800	10 800	5 542	2 685
9			20 000	23 600		20 000	11 800	+800	9 000	4 199	1 834
10			11 000	20 000		11 000	10 000	+2 000	3 000	1 272	501
11			2 000	11 000			5 500	+38 000	34 500	13 301	723
12	+10 000		0	2 000	-10 000	12 000	6 000	0	4 000	1 402	449
Totals	-90 000	20 000	254 000	254 000	90 000	164 000	82 000	0	102 000	37 718	0

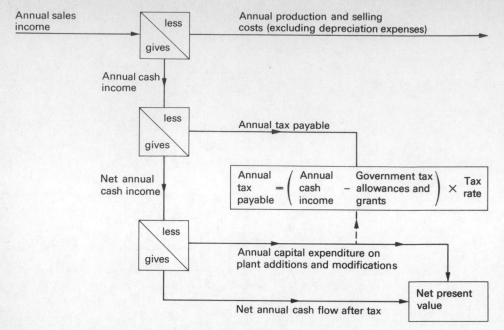

Figure 7.11.1 *A schematic presentation of the method of cash flow calculation. Note: this diagram applies to the capital budgeting decision prior to fixed capital expenditure but post-R & D expenditure.*

to freely depreciate an asset in a way which best suits that company's purpose. It naturally follows therefore that such a company would claim the 100 per cent allowance immediately or as quickly as possible if it could absorb all of that allowance to reduce its tax liability. The example given in Table 7.11.2 incorporates such an allowance.

Other methods allow a company to recoup its capital at a constant fixed rate. For example, an annual allowance of 4 per cent per annum on a straight-line basis would signify that the company could reduce its taxable income by 4 per cent of the fixed capital cost of that plant each and every year for 25 years. Such allowances are commonly used for industrial buildings. By contrast an annual allowance computed on the basis of 20 per cent of an asset's written down value* would mean that the allowances would diminish annually in absolute terms according to the schedule laid down in Table 7.11.1. Such allowances are known as declining balance allowances and are typically used for plant and machinery.

Governments employ special investment allowances or capital grants as extra incentives to induce companies to build factories in areas of high unemployment. The first permit a company to depreciate its assets by more than 100 per cent of their capital cost. Where capital grants apply, they can usually be claimed once a machine is installed or a plant built, and usually require evidence that investment has been incurred and that adequate provision for extra employment has been made. The magnitude of such grants depends on (i) the rate applying at the time of grant application, (ii) the categories of assets attracting such grants, and (iii) the fixed capital expenditure involved.

As a numerical example, Table 7.11.2 incorporates the following features (i) a 20 per cent cash grant payable at the end of the first year of operations, (ii) free

---

* Accounting jargon, meaning the 'book' value of an asset having reduced its initial capital cost by allowances for depreciation. Such a value must not be confused with the asset's real value, which can be quite different.

Table 7.11.3 Example 7.11.2 with delayed absorption of tax allowances

Year	A Capital expenditure	B Investment grant	C Actual cash inflow before tax	D Cash inflow one year in arrears	E Tax allowances	F=D+E Taxable income after allowances	G=0.5F Taxes @50%	H Working capital	I=A+B+C+H-G Net after tax cash flows	J DCF@ 17.3% pa
1	-100 000	20 000	0	0	—	—	0	0	-100 000	-100 000
2			23 000	0	—	—	0	-30 000	13 000	11 083
3			44 000	23 000	23 000	0	0	-10 000	34 000	24 711
4			38 000	44 000	44 000	0	0	-4 000	34 000	21 066
5			34 400	38 000	33 000	5 000	2 500	+800	32 700	17 273
6			30 800	34 400	—	34 400	17 200	+800	14 400	6 484
7			27 200	30 800	—	30 800	15 400	+800	12 600	4 837
8			23 600	27 200	—	27 200	13 600	+800	10 800	3 535
9			20 000	23 600	—	23 600	11 800	+800	9 000	2 511
10			11 000	20 000	—	20 000	10 000	+2 000	3 000	714
11			2 000	11 000	—	11 000	5 500	+38 000	34 500	6 996
12	+10 000		0	2 000	-10 000	12 000	6 000	0	4 000	691
Totals	-90 000	20 000	254 000	254 000	90 000	164 000	82 000	0	102 000	0

depreciation allowances available as soon as the project can take advantage of them, and, (iii) corporation taxes payable one year in arrears at a rate of 50 per cent of taxable income.

In an attempt to make this example a little more realistic it also incorporates working capital, which increases and decreases throughout the project's life, and an allowance for the scrap value of the project at 10 per cent of its original capital cost. A diagrammatic representation of the way in which the taxes and the cash flows of this example have been calculated is presented in Figure 7.11.1. According to the calculations, the DCFRR for this project is 22 per cent per annum after tax. This example presumes that such a company could take advantage of the project's initially large tax allowance of 100 000 munits before tax (50 000 munits after tax) by offsetting this allowance against other taxable profits occurring elsewhere in the firm. If this were not the case, as might transpire if this project was the firm's only project, then these allowances would not be absorbed until Year 5, as shown by Table 7.11.3, and the project's DCFRR would fall to 17.3 per cent per annum after tax as a consequence. In effect, therefore, these two tables demonstrate just how important is the timing of the tax allowances absorbed by a project.

As a complete contrast, Table 7.11.4 shows the economics of the same project, but this time reworked without allowing for any taxation considerations. What might surprise many readers is the fact that the DCFRR of the project *before tax* is now shown to be less, not more, than that *after tax*. How does one explain this phenomenon? The reason lies in column I of Table 7.11.2 and column D of Table 7.11.4. We see that the total cumulative cash flows of the former are smaller than the latter but column I incorporates larger positive cash flows in its formative years, resulting from its having an investment grant and a taxation shield provided by its taxation allowances. In effect, therefore, the taxation system has caused the economics to provide a more favourable return after taxation because of its timing effect: a most crucial aspect in DCF calculations.

Because of the influence which taxes have on the economic merits of a project, especially during its formative years, it behoves the management of a firm contemplating the building of a capital intensive project to forecast any likely tax changes which could develop during the time it takes to bring such a project to fruition. Normally this is not an easy matter, but the redeeming virtue is that most governments usually modify their tax structures only slightly each year. Despite such a

Table 7.11.4 *Example 7.11.2 but without any taxation considerations*

Year	A	B	C	D = A + B + C	E	F
	Capital expenditure	Working capital	Cash inflow	Net cash flow	DCF @ 10% pa	DCF @ 19.6% pa
1	−100 000	0	0	−100 000	−100 000	−100 000
2		−30 000	23 000	−7 000	−6 364	−5 853
3		−10 000	44 000	34 000	+28 099	+23 769
4		−4 000	38 000	34 000	+25 545	+19 874
5		+800	34 400	35 200	+24 042	+17 204
6		+800	30 800	31 600	+19 621	+12 913
7		+800	27 200	28 000	+15 805	+9 567
8		+800	23 600	24 400	+12 521	+6 971
9		+800	20 000	20 800	9 703	+4 968
10		+2 000	11 000	13 000	5 513	+2 596
11		+38 000	2 000	40 000	15 422	+6 680
12	+10 000	0	0	10 000	3 505	+1 396
Totals	−90 000	0	254 000	164 000	53 412	0

small rate of change, however, the cumulative effect throughout the duration of a project could be substantial.

7.12 PROJECT OPTIMIZATION

At this stage, one must realize that the life-cycle economic equation, previously developed on the basis of net annual cash flows, can be expanded to include all those factors appearing in earlier sections of this chapter, so that the life-cycle economic equation becomes:

$$\text{NPV}_T = \sum_{i=0}^{T} [\{-\text{RD}_i - \text{DE}_i - \Delta K_i - \text{CE}_i - \Delta \text{WC}_i + (p_i v_i \eta_i - \text{VC}_i - \text{FC}_i)\} f_i(\text{tax}).(1 + r_i)^{-i}]$$
$$+ [\Delta \text{WC}_T + S_T f_T(\text{tax})](1 + r_T)^{-T}$$

These symbols imply that their respective cash flows are attributable only to the capital project under review and they have the following meaning:

RD_i	Research and development expenditure in Year i
DE_i	Design engineering expenditure in Year i
ΔK_i	Incremental capital expenditure in Year i
CE_i	Commissioning expenditure in Year i
ΔWC_i	Incremental working capital expenditure in Year i
p_i	Product/service price realized in Year i
v_i	Material/service input in Year i
η_i	Material/service yield in Year i
VC_i	Variable costs of manufacture in Year i
FC_i	Fixed costs of manufacture in Year i
$f_i(\text{tax})$	Net effect of corporation taxes, tax grants and allowances realized in Year i
$(1 + r_i)^{-i}$	Discount factor pertaining to Year i
$100 \cdot r_i$	Cost of capital pertaining to Year i
ΔWC_T	Incremental working capital released at the termination of the project
S_T	Salvage value realized by the retirement of the project's assets
$f_T(\text{tax})$	Terminal tax consideration
$(1 + r_T)^{-T}$	Discount factor pertaining to Year T
$100 \cdot r_T$	Cost of capital pertaining to Year T
T	The economic life of a project
i	The particular year of interest such that $(i = 0, T)$.

Above all else it should be realized that these factors are *estimates*, and being estimates they induce *uncertainty* into the calculation of the NPV. Furthermore, this uncertainty implies there are certain *risks* involved with capital investment which must be fully evaluated. We shall delay a full treatment of the risk implications of a project until Chapter 9, but in the meanwhile it is instructive to consider that the factors in the expanded version of our life-cycle economic equation are, to some extent, *interrelated*. Prices depend on costs, which in turn depend on the scale of plant, which likewise depends on the size of the market which, of course, depends on the price of the product. In other words we have a complete tautology. Only when the price of a product is completely decided by market forces, as might transpire for commodity products, is the size of the capital investment then decided by such

Table 7.12.1   *Some of the implications of different scale of plant*

Plant size	Production implication	Marketing implication	Financial implication
(a) Plant capacity designed to meet maximum demand	Fluctuating production rate. Ability to satisfy promptly all anticipated customer demands.	No delivery delays due to manufacturing limitations	High investment in plant capacity. Lay-off and re-training cost of labour to meet fluctuating production rate. High overhead costs
(b) Plant capacity adequate to meet average demand	Steady production rate. Large inventories or, otherwise, delivery backlogs during periods of peak demand	Lost orders and possibly the loss of customer goodwill	Inventory financing costs
(c) Plant capacity larger than (b) but smaller than (a)	Fairly stable production rate with some labour-free adjustment	Few delays	Some inventory costs, but lower than (b). Higher investment than (b)

considerations as:

  (i) the economic merits of different size investments,
 (ii) the rate of market penetration which the company believes it can achieve and the market share it can maintain,
(iii) the size of the capital investment which the company can afford and, of course,
(iv) the risk implications of investment.

When the intended product is sufficiently differentiated from others in the marketplace, the firm has to decide an optimal product pricing strategy which set limits to the scale and timing of the capital investment, consistent with meeting those considerations given by items (i)–(iv) above. The implications of different sizes of capital investment are considerable. First, different production capacities have the effects shown in Table 7.12.1. In addition, however, one must decide how best to meet a growing sales commitment, bearing in mind that technical economies of scale and time value of money considerations have opposing effects.

Without working through an actual case in detail we are unable to consider all these matters here, although it should be noted that the economic decision making game, in Chapter 12, does allow these matters to be explored in greater depth. Ultimately, however, the firm must decide that production capacity which *optimizes* its investment decision. To achieve this end it must consider the *incremental* benefits derived from succesive *increments* of investment, and it should then choose between those projects which possess positive NPVs on *incremental* investment. This is important because ultimately most capital projects exhibit diminishing returns to scale yielding negative incremental NPV benefits.

7.13   SUMMARY

In this chapter we have given a brief account of all the mundane details which are needed in the proper economic evaluation of a prospective capital project using DCF techniques. Despite our initial elaborate development of these techniques, it will now be appreciated how the work involved with DCF sums in themselves is merely the tip of the computational iceberg involved with the evaluation procedure in general. Our real purpose in developing the detail of this chapter however was to expose the reader to the reality that each and every number which appears in our life-cycle economic equation is nothing more than an *estimate*, the *uncertainty* about which puts the decision to invest in a project *at risk*. These matters are important in themselves because their existence questions the validity of our using these techniques as decision analysis tools. We shall address these matters more fully in Chapters 9, 10 and 11.

8. The Cost of Capital

'What we want is a basis for measuring a company's cost of capital (r) under realistic conditions of economic and political uncertainty. A realistic measure of r must take into account the general uncertainty of future returns on present capital investment and the fact that different uses of funds within the same company may involve different degrees of uncertainty. It must also reflect changing conditions in the capital market.'

E. Solomon, *The Theory of Financial Management*,
Columbia University Press, 1964

To make the decision rules of Chapter 6 operable we need to specify the magnitude of a company's cost of capital because this figure forms the basis of all NPV calculations and the yardstick against which to measure a project's incremental DCFRR. Despite the apparent simplicity of the discount factor $(1+r)^{-t}$, the evaluation of r is by no means easy and it cannot be plucked from the air in the hope that any figure is good enough. Instead, a firm's cost of capital is closely linked with its past economic performance, and its financial structure. National and international monetary and fiscal policies, and expectations of the firm's future performance compared with other financial securities, also affect the magnitude of this cost. This figure must also take account of uncertainty and risk. It is perhaps more appropriate to refer to the cost of capital as the minimum required return on capital but the term cost of capital is so entrenched in financial literature that there seems little point calling it by any other name.

It should be noted that several major problems relating to a proper evaluation of a company's overall cost of capital remain unresolved despite abundant research in this area. As a result this chapter endeavours to expose the reader to a simple understanding of these problems and related issues. A fuller appreciation of these matters comes from reading the references contained herein.

8.1 THE COST OF SHORT-TERM SOURCES OF FINANCE

Short-term sources of finance involve loans which are redeemable within a period of one year. They include trade credit, bank loans, deferred tax payments and bills of exchange.

8.1.1 Trade credit

Unlike the retail trade where customers normally settle their accounts immediately it is commonplace for manufacturing companies to be given a period of grace to pay for raw materials, goods and services received from other companies. The sum o this credit is known as accounts payable. The duration of the period of grace depends on the general custom and practice of the industry involved, the extent of the business transacted, the method of product delivery, and any special geographical considerations. Usually no direct charge is made for this credit but it could be *implied* in the product's price. Prompt payment is sometimes encouraged by offering price discounts if bills are settled quickly.

It is not unusual for trade credit to constitute 10–20 per cent of all the forms of finance available to a company, but companies normally extend similar credit to *their* customers. Since most companies trade on the basis of value added, generally they have to finance their trade credit deficit by longer-term sources of finance. This aspect is covered in greater detail in Sections 7.6 and 8.5.

8.1.2 Bank loans

In several countries firms maintain a line-of-credit with their banks so they may borrow money up to an agreed limit *on a regular basis*, by running their current bank accounts in deficit. In the UK, this facility is known as an overdraft, which the customer can redeem at any time, being liable for interest payments only to the extent of the debt outstanding and the agreed interest rate. Normally the interest charges are compounded daily (see Appendix F). In some countries, bankers require the firm to deposit (without interest) a modest sum of money with the bank as security against the possibility of the firm defaulting on its interest payments; these deposits are often known as compensating balances. The preferred method of bank loans in the USA is via promissory notes which comprise fixed interest loans over a period of 30 days or more, with the interest deducted from the principal at the outset. In both cases a key factor limiting these funds is the firm's current asset/liability ratio (see Appendix B), which is known as the current ratio. Bank loans are usually of relatively low risk, to the banker, because they can be withdrawn at short notice. Normally, interest on these loans is tax deductible, which means that their *after tax* rate of interest is approximately one-half their nominal rate, making them relatively cheap compared with equity forms of finance. The full implications of taxation are covered in Section 7.11.

8.1.3 Bills of exchange

These comprise post-dated cheques which the vendor draws in his own favour to be signed by the customer when consummating a buismess transaction. These bills are usually payable up to three or six months *after* the goods have been exchanged, and they enable the vendor to receive cash payment for the goods by selling the bill at a discount, either to a bank, a discount house or a factor. In this case the extent of the discount determines the *effective* interest charge. For example a 2 per cent discount on a bill maturing three months hence would be equivalent to an interest rate of 8.4 per cent per annum*.

8.1.4 Deferred tax payments

Another source of short-term funds is automatically extended to companies by the interval of time which elapses between the earning of profit and the payment of

---

* The effective quarterly interest rate would be $\dfrac{2 \times 100}{98} = 2.04\%$ and the corresponding effective annual interest rate would be $(1.0204^4 - 1)\ 100 = 8.4$ per cent.

taxes. Tax authorities do not levy any interest on this debt provided it is met by its due date. Despite the apparent desirability of this source of interest-free credit, however, it cannot be overstressed that in *no way* should it feature in the computation of a firm's weighted cost of capital. The reason for this is given in Chapter 7.6.

8.2 THE COST OF MEDIUM- AND LONG-TERM DEBT

Medium-term debt is usually redeemable within three to five years, whereas long-term debt may last 10 to 15 years or more. Both can comprise loans and bonds. Interest rates on the former usually vary with market rates. Interest rates on bonds, however, are often fixed and they are usually redeemable by prescribed dates. As such, they cannot be recalled providing their interest payments are maintained on schedule so that, coupled with infrequent interest repayments (perhaps once or twice a year), they represent a more risky form of debt to the lender. To reduce this risk, they are either secured against specific assets of the borrowing company, in which case they may be known as fixed charge debentures or simply mortgage bonds, or alternatively they may take a ranked precedence in their claim against the liquidated assets of the company. In the latter case they are often known as floating charge debentures. Both types of debentures are commonly controlled by a trust deed administered by a trustee (either a trust company, an insurance firm or a bank) to ensure the financial requirements of the deed are met, and the interests of the debenture holders safeguarded. Furthermore, both types are usually bought and sold as stocks in the financial market at prices decided by the market. The interest on this category of debt is tax deductible, making it relatively cheap compared with equity capital. However there exist limits to the proportion of this debt which a company can borrow. This matter is covered in Section 8.4.

To make bonds economically attractive to potential lenders it is sometimes necessary to sell them at a discount on their face value. This happens when their interest rates appear marginally unattractive compared with other investment opportunities of similar risk which are readily available in the financial market. Conversely, it is sometimes possible to sell them at a premium over and above their face-value. In both instances, the bond interest rate does *not* reflect the true cost to the borrower. To compute this cost we have to discount all the cash flows attributable to the sale of a bond according to equation 8.2.1 below*.

$$\text{NPV (of costs)} = \sum_{t=1}^{N} \frac{Q_t(1-x)}{(1+k_d)^t} + \frac{R}{(1+k_d)^N} - I \tag{8.2.1}$$

where Q_t = the total yearly fixed interest payments per bond, $100 \cdot x$ = the effective tax rate, R = the redemption value of the bond, I = the initial price of the bond, k_d = the effective annual interest rate of this form of debt, N = the duration of the loan, and t = end of year intervals such that $t = (1, N)$.

According to our previous DCF sums, the effective cost of this source of capital is given by the internal resolution of equation 8.2.1 when the net present value is nought, in which case we obtain the following expression:

$$I = \sum_{t=1}^{N} \frac{Q_t(1-x)}{(1+k_d)^t} + \frac{R}{(1+k_d)^N}$$

---

* For illustrative purposes, this equation ignores some real-world complexities such as the timing of the interest payments and the possibility of future tax changes.

For perpetual bonds, that is bonds which are never redeemable, the relationship above simplifies to the following form:

$$I = \frac{Q_t(1-x)}{k_d}$$

or alternatively:

$$k_d = \frac{Q_t(1-x)}{I}$$

On the basis of this simple model, and for the assumptions stated, it follows that a 10 per cent discount on the certificated value of a bond would effectively mean an 11 per cent increase in its annual cost to the borrower. Such a cost, computed by these means, should form an integral part in the computation of a firm's *overall* cost of capital.

As a last point it should be mentioned that the proportion of capital raised by these means could have a direct effect on the cost of other sources of capital available to a company. Traditionally, companies in the UK and USA raise 15–20 per cent of their funds through long-term debt, but in other countries the proportion is quite often higher.

8.3 THE COST OF EQUITY SOURCES OF FINANCE

Equity sources of capital comprise the funds invested in a firm by the initial owners, retained profits, and any further funds raised by the sale of new shares. Collectively these form the majority of the funds available to most firms and the basis for their securing alternative forms of finance. Unlike the previously mentioned sources of capital, however, equity funds normally bear no obligation to pay interest to shareholders, who participate in benefits only when all other financial obligations have been met. This means that ordinary dividends can only be paid when interest-bearing loans have been honoured. Thereafter, the amount of dividends paid to shareholders depends on the company's profitability and its dividend policy. When liquidating a firm, ordinary shareholders are only entitled to whatever residual monies remain (if any) after all other claims have been met. In effect, the shareholders accommodate the major risks of a firm and therefore expect a return higher than lenders to compensate for such risks. Essentially, investors require a return similar to that given by other securities of similar risk. This return comes in two forms: expected dividends, and expected capital appreciation in share prices. Although these benefits represent no cost to the firm in an accounting sense and they do *not* form tax deductible expenses, they do represent an opportunity (or imputed) cost (see Chapters 2.10 and 6.5, and Appendix A) which can be estimated, if the firm's shares are bought and sold in the financial market. Exactly how the market translates all publicly available information about a firm into the price for its shares is something which is not fully understood. As such, the models which are used for this purpose tend to be somewhat crude.

Our first model assumes that the market price of a company's shares equals the sum of its expected future dividends to perpetuity, according to the following relationship:

$$P_0 = \sum_{t=1}^{\infty} \frac{D_t}{(1+k_e)^t} \tag{8.3.1}$$

where P_0 = the currently transacted market price for a company's shares, D_t = the dividend payments, per share, which shareholders expect in the future, k_e = the cost of equity capital, and t = the end of year periods such that $t = 1, \infty$.

This model implies that the total capitalized market value of a company's shares, represented by $n \cdot P_0$ (where n = the number of issued shares) represents the NPV of the entire firm and its ongoing capital projects when evaluated at the firm's equity cost of capital. It is at this juncture, therefore, that we now interpret the meaning of the NPV in an entirely different light. Previously, the NPV represented some measure of the economic worth of a project. Now, however, we see that the NPV of each project contributes to the capitalized value of the company through the evaluation of its shares.

Based on the assumption of constant annual dividends in perpetuity this simple model can be rearranged in the following form:

$$k_e = \frac{D_t}{P_0} \tag{8.3.2}$$

where the quotient D_t/P_0 is known as the dividend yield, which we previously used in Chapter 3.4.

A second means of computing the effective cost of equity capital is based on the assumption that a share, initially costing P_0, will be sold in T years time at a price P_T having realized end-of-year dividend payments of D_t in the interim. According to this model, the cost of equity capital is determined by the internal resolution of equation 8.3.3 below:

$$P_0 = \sum_{t=1}^{T} \frac{D_t}{(1+k_e)^t} + \frac{P_T}{(1+k_e)^T} \tag{8.3.3}$$

A third means of computing the cost of equity capital is based on the assumption that dividends grow at a compound rate of 'g' per cent per annum, so a firm's share price could be modelled by:

$$P_0 = \frac{D}{(1+k_e)} + \frac{D(1+g)}{(1+k_e)^2} + \dots \frac{D(1+g)^{t-1}}{(1+k_e)^t} \tag{8.3.4}$$

where D = the dividend payment per share distributed one year hence, and g = the dividend growth rate per cent per annum.

This equation simplifies to the following form:

$$P_0 = \frac{D}{(k_e - g)} \cdot \left[1 - \frac{(1+g)^t}{(1+k_e)^t} \right] \tag{8.3.5}$$

which becomes

$$P_0 = \frac{D}{(k_e - g)} \tag{8.3.6}$$

if we assume that the dividends grow indefinitely. If we rearrange equation 8.3.6 we obtain the new identity:

$$k_e = \frac{D}{P_0} + g \tag{8.3.7}$$

which is identical to the model previously used in Chapter 3.4 to forecast the profit target for a firm.

Long-term dividend growth is made possible through retaining earnings which are then reinvested in further capital projects. On this basis other economic models, similar to those previously mentioned, can be developed using earnings per share as the important attribute instead of dividends. For example, the equivalent earnings model to equation 8.3.7 is:

$$k_e = \frac{E(1-b)}{P_0} + br \tag{8.3.8}$$

where E = the cash earnings per share realized one year hence, $(1-b)$ = the fraction of such earnings paid out as dividends, r = the return on capital in new investment opportunities, and E/P_0 is the price-earnings ratio.

In this particular case it should be noted that retained earnings, like equity shares, have no cost in the accounting sense but they have an opportunity cost, namely the benefit foregone from their investment elsewhere by the shareholder had such monies been distributed as dividends. This opportunity cost must be equal to the return which the shareholders obtain from their existing shares, otherwise they would no longer be willing to subscribe to such shares on the basis of their existing yield. For this reason alone no attempt has been made to differentiate between the cost of capital of existing shares and retained earnings. However, one would expect the cost of new equity capital to be more expensive than existing share capital to reflect the expense of their preparation, promotion, sale and distribution.

In effect therefore we have four basic models of the ways in which shareholders *might* translate publicly available information into the price of a firm's shares, providing four means of estimating a firm's cost of equity capital. Each of these models can be criticized for basic weaknesses in their underlying assumptions. For example, it is most unlikely that shareholders have access to sufficient information to enable them to predict future dividends or earnings per share with assuredness. Also, the danger with perpetual growth models is that high historical growth is not realized in perpetuity. Furthermore, the proportion of a firm's distributed dividends obviously varies with time as does the rate of return on its capital projects. Moreover the implied assumption in all of these models that the level of risk involved with future *unknown* projects will be similar to that involved with historical, existing or known future projects, is also suspect, especially as these models make no allowance for borrowed capital.

In effect, the assumptions of these models ignore most of the real world problems involved with estimating the cost of equity capital. Nevertheless they do provide a *framework* for estimating such costs, based on historical data. Notable examples of such studies are those by Merrett and Sykes (1966; 1974) and Fisher and Lorie (1970). Using the method involved in equation 8.3.3, Merrett and Sykes discovered that the cost of equity capital tends to fluctuate erratically for most single firms, even for so-called 'blue chip' companies. Furthermore, their evidence showed that the cost of equity capital for many firms, in aggregate, also tends to oscillate significantly over long periods. Nevertheless, their studies showed that over longer periods the *average* cost of equity capital incurred by publicly quoted companies approximated 7 per cent per annum after all taxes in *real* (constant purchasing power) terms. Such a statistic as this provides a starting-point for estimating the cost of equity capital for an individual firm. Alternatively, if its shares are quoted on a stock exchange then it could compute its own historical cost of equity capital by the same method. To provide shareholders with a 7 per cent return means that a firm has to earn at least 10 per cent per annum in real terms, after corporation tax. Depending on the rate of inflation, this could represent an actual cost of capital between 10 and 20 per cent per annum.

8.4 THE COMBINED COST OF LONG-TERM DEBT
AND EQUITY CAPITAL

We now have a means of calculating a firm's cost of long-term capital. We have already suggested that debt capital is normally cheaper than equity capital because the risks incurred by lenders are usually less than those accommodated by shareholders. This difference in cost is further increased by taxation because the former attracts tax allowances whereas the latter does not. In certain circumstances, therefore, it would seem reasonable for a firm to borrow as much money as possible. To explore the implications of this, let us consider a simple model based on the following symbolic notation:

$100r$ = the return on total capital,
$100k_e$ = the cost of equity capital,
$100k_d$ = the cost of long-term debt capital,
V_e = the value of the firm's equity capital,
V_d = the value of the firm's long-term debt capital, and
R = the firm's annual cash flows which are assumed constant in time.

At this stage these notation have not been rigorously defined for reasons which will become apparent. Simple but crude expressions of the returns on total capital and equity capital could therefore be calculated from the following equations:

$$r = \frac{R}{V_e + V_d}$$

and

$$k_e = \frac{R - k_d \cdot V_d}{V_e}$$

which provide the following identity:

$$k_e = r + (r - k_d)(V_d/V_e) \tag{8.4.1}$$

According to this simple equation, the return (cost) of equity capital *should* be enhanced as the relative amount of debt capital increases *provided* its cost is *less* than the return on total capital. In financial circles this effect is known as leverage or gearing due to certain similarities with the principle of mechanical advantage. It follows from equation 8.4.1 that, if a firm realizes a return on total capital of, say, 20 per cent per annum, with a cost of long-term debt capital of, say, 10 per cent per annum, then its return on equity capital *should* be levered upwards with increasing proportions of debt as follows:

Degree of leverage (V_d/V_e)	Cost of equity capital $100k_e$ (% per annum)
0	20
1	30
2	40

This simple example, therefore, suggests that the relative amount of debt capital can have a direct impact on the cost of equity capital because of leverage. It would seem reasonable to suppose that the financial uncertainty felt by shareholders and moneylenders would remain unchanged if a firm continued to raise capital on the basis of a *constant* leverage ratio. In these circumstances a reasonable estimate of a firm's overall cost of capital would be given by the following expression:

$$k_0 = k_e \cdot \frac{V_e}{V_0} + k_d \cdot \frac{V_d}{V_0} \qquad (8.4.2)$$

where

$$V_0 = V_e + V_d$$

and the additional symbols have the following definitions: $V_0 =$ the value of the firm's long term securities, and $k_0 =$ the firm's overall cost of long-term capital.

According to equation 8.4.2, the weighted overall cost of capital (k_0) to a firm, with equity and long-term debt costs of capital approximating 15 per cent and 5 per cent respectively and a leverage ratio (V_d/V_e) of $1:3$, would be 12.5 per cent.

Quite obviously, equation 8.4.2 can be used to compute the overall cost of capital on a before tax or an after tax basis provided the appropriate values for debt capital are used. Furthermore, this equation can be used for any arbitrary timescale (a year, month or day). However, the credibility of equation 8.4.2 rests on the so-called values ascribed to V_e and V_d.

Based on the arguments in Sections 8.2 and 8.3, we have suggested that these values *must* be the capitalized market values of a firm's securities, because only these values reflect the true cost of money to that firm. The implication here is that the debt and equity figures in the company's balance sheet represent historical values which cannot accommodate the effects of discounts or premiums, leverage and risk, and the future expectations of the shareholders, as previously mentioned. In effect, therefore, it is suggested that the computation of a firm's overall cost of capital based on balance sheet figures could seriously distort the magnitude of the resultant cost, and lead to erroneous decision making. Despite this warning, it has to be admitted that the way in which the financial market assesses risk is not fully understood. It is conceivable that the market's perception of risk *could be* based in part on balance sheet ratios. Furthermore, it must be realized that the capitalized values of a company's shares often fluctuate considerably, thereby frustrating the use of equation 8.4.2. It will also be appreciated that firms whose shares are not quoted on a stock exchange might have no option other than to use balance sheet figures in such a computation.

The preceding arguments are based on the assumption of a constant leverage ratio. Excepting the effects of taxation brought about by leverage, there exists no authoritative evidence to suggest exactly how a firm's overall cost of capital would change with increasing leverage. As things stand, two quite opposing theories exist on this matter and neither has been properly ratified or repudiated. A detailed account of the controversies is given by Solomon (1964).

The traditional approach suggests that as a firm increases its leverage three phases are experienced:

(i) *Phase I*: increasing leverage should increase the firm's market value. It is suggested that this would result from a declining overall cost of capital brought about by the dilution of the higher cost of equity capital by the lower cost of debt capital. During this phase the cost of equity capital might rise a little due to a slight increase in risk, but not at a rate which is fast enough to offset the affects of leverage. It is thought that the cost of debt capital would remain constant or rise only negligibly, reflecting creditors' satisfaction with the degree of leverage.

(ii) *Phase II*: it is thought that the overall cost of capital would remain constant, as would the total market value of the firm's securities, despite rising costs for both equity and debt capital, because increasing leverage would neutralize the effects of these rising costs.

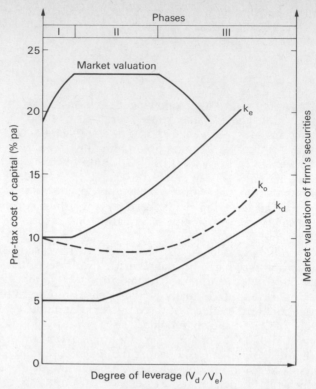

Figure 8.4.1 *The traditional view of the effect of leverage on a firm's costs of capital.*

(iii) *Phase III*: it is thought that the overall cost of capital now would increase as a result of increasing leverage and risk, thereby decreasing the capitalized value of the firm's securities.

All three phases are shown in Figure 8.4.1. Several researchers have challenged this traditional approach and its tenet that pre-tax leverage can alter the overall cost of capital and the market value of a firm's securities. The most vigorous challenge to this view comes from Modigliani and Miller (1958) who suggested that two identical companies comprising the same assets and earnings of the same quality should have the same price (market value) and the same overall cost of capital, *irrespective of their financial structure and their degrees of leverage.*

It is not our intention to dwell at length on this issue since it remains unresolved and it is examined in detail by many books on finance. Instead, our purpose in bringing this controversy to the reader's attention is to highlight the fact that the response of a firm's overall cost of capital to changing leverage is unknown. This suggests the need for caution and restraint if a firm seriously considers departing from its normal leverage in order to finance some seemingly lucrative project. Furthermore, if a firm should embark on such a venture then, consistent with our previous decision rules, it should appraise the marginal NPV of such a project at the firm's marginal overall cost of capital, after tax.

Besides the influence of leverage, variability in a firm's earnings, both in absolute terms and relative to the rest of the securities market, also induces uncertainty and risk into the computation of a firm's overall cost of capital. The effects of uncertainty on the economic attributes of a prospective capital project receive a formal treatment in Chapter 9. In the context of determining the overall cost of capital of a firm however it would be remiss of us not to mention that, based on the seminal work of Markowitz (1952), finance academics have developed what is known as the capital asset pricing model which is partly attributed to Sharpe (1963), and to Mossin (1973). This model offers a means of calculating a risk-adjusted equity cost of capital based on the way in which the firm's returns on equity capital statistically co-vary with the returns of an efficient portfolio of market securities. Unfortunately, a proper appreciation of this model requires a knowledge of statistics and finance which extends beyond the scope of this book. Furthermore, it is probably true to say that, as yet, it cannot readily be applied within the technical resources of most manufacturing firms. An introductory account of this model is given by Ryan (1979).

Besides the difficulties involved with estimating a firm's likely future cost of capital, Rubinstein (1973) suggests that the application of a single overall cost of capital to appraise the economic merits of capital projects, with different levels of risk, could lead to poor investment decisions. Of course, businessmen pragmatically allow for this by loading the cost of capital to reflect their own intuitive feelings about the risks involved with each capital project. We shall have occasion to review this matter again in Chapter 9.

8.5 THE INFLUENCE OF SHORT-TERM DEBT ON A FIRM'S OVERALL COST OF CAPITAL

The reader may have noticed that we commenced Section 8.1 by discussing the forms and cost of short-term capital normally used by firms, but no mention was made of these in the computation of a firm's overall cost of capital. To some extent the reasons for this are covered in Chapter 7.6, but a few words are appropriate here. Typically, the current assets of a firm will nearly always suffice to repay short-term creditors and lenders so it could be argued that the maximum total capital at risk in a capital project comprises the long-term capital only (equity and long-term debt). In these circumstances short-term loans should not be incorporated in the calculation of a firm's overall cost of capital. Instead, the interest charges attributable to such loans should feature in its DCF calculations as *negative cash flows*. However, if it is felt that the liquidation value of the current assets of a firm or capital project is likely to be low and insufficient to meet the needs of short-term creditors and lenders, then the computation of the overall cost of capital should reflect this situation by incorporating the weighted cost of short-term debt too. In these circumstances the DCF sums would *not* include the short-term interest payments as cash flows.

8.6 THE EFFECT OF INFLATION ON A FIRM'S OVERALL COST OF CAPITAL

Inflation is the phenomenon of too great a demand, backed by too much money, chasing too few resources, goods and services. It stems from the escalation of prices and the erosion in the purchasing power of money, leaving people with fixed incomes poorer. To invest in some security on the basis of its yielding a 10 per cent per annum return in money terms would therefore appear a dubious economic proposition, if the going rate of inflation was 20 per cent per annum, because the monies realized by such an investment would possess a lower purchasing power than their original principal. For this reason, it is *essential* for a firm to forecast the effects of inflation in the future cash flows of its investment projects and sensibly accommodate these effects in the computation of its appropriate discount rate (its overall cost of capital). This can be done in two ways:

(i) by discounting the cash flows which are forecast *in money terms*, by a cost of capital which incorporates an allowance for inflation, or
(ii) by discounting the forecast cash flows which have been adjusted to allow for the effects of inflation (that is, cash flows in *real terms*) by an inflation free cost of capital.

Both methods will, if correctly used, provide the same value for the NPV of a

Table 8.6.1 *The effects of inflation on the economic merits of a proposed capital investment project*

Project description (estimates)

Installed capital cost	= 20 000 munits
Sales Volume	= 10 000 units per annum
Project life	= 3 years
Product unit price	= 2.00 munits escalating by 5% pa
Total labour costs	= 4000 munits escalating by 10% pa
Total other costs	= 6000 munits escalating by 15% pa
Retail Price Index inflation rate	= 8% pa
Cost of capital (real terms)	= 7% pa

I DCF analysis in real terms

End of year	0	1	2	3
Capital cost	−20 000			
Sales revenue		20 000	21 000	22 050
Labour costs		4 000	4 400	4 840
Other costs		6 000	6 900	7 935
Net cash flows (money terms)	−20 000	10 000	9 700	9 275
Inflation deflator	1.000	0.926	0.857	0.794
Net cash flow (real terms)	−20 000	9 260	8 313	7 364
Discount factor (real terms)	1.000	0.935	0.873	0.816
DCFs (real terms)	−20 000	8 658	7 257	6 009

NPV = +1924

II DCF analysis in money terms

End of year	0	1	2	3
Net cash flow (money terms)	−20 000	10 000	9 700	9 275
Discount factors @ 15.56% pa	1.000	0.865	0.749	0.648
DCFs (money terms)	−20 000	8 650	7 265	6 010

NPV = +1925

III DCF analysis assuming no inflation

End of year	0	1	2	3
Capital cost	−20 000			
Sales revenue		20 000	20 000	20 000
Labour costs		4 000	4 000	4 000
Other costs		6 000	6 000	6 000
Net cash flows	−20 000	10 000	10 000	10 000
Discount factors @ 7% pa	1.000	0.935	0.873	0.816
DCFs	−20 000	9 350	8 730	8 160

NPV = +6240

project. To differentiate between actual money and money with constant purchasing power, economists refer to the latter as money in real terms. In effect, therefore, the real purchasing power of 100 munits received one year hence, when the appropriate rate of inflation is 10 per cent per annum, is only 90.91 munits. Put another way, this means that in one year's time the 100 munits would only buy 90.91 per cent of the goods which could originally have been bought. This is tantamount to another form of discounting which must be clearly differentiated from the time value of money effect. There exists no established way of accommodating the effects of inflation when discounting the cash flows of a capital investment, but a large body of opinion advocates the use of the Retail Price Index (RPI) as the appropriate deflator. The rationale for this approach rests on the premise that the cash flows realized by a new capital project will be paid ultimately to shareholders as dividends, to be spent on goods and services witnessing inflation at a rate registered by the RPI. The real value of a sum of money 'C_t' realized t years hence is therefore given by the expression $C_t/(1+\text{RPI})^{-t}$ where the relationship '$100\,\text{RPI}$' represents the percentage annual rate of inflation.

The example of Table 8.6.1 illustrates the application of both these methods, and shows how they provide identical NPVs. This example also shows how ignoring the effects of inflation can overstate the true economic merits of a proposed capital project. In this example, the discount rate (r) used in Part II is determined as the combined effect of the real cost of capital (k_0) and the overall rate of inflation, as measured by the RPI, using the relationship:

$$(1+r) = (1+k_0)(1+\text{RPI})$$
$$= 1.07 \times 1.08 = 1.1556$$

so that $r = 0.1556$, and $100r = 15.56$ per cent per annum.

To accommodate the effects of inflation properly therefore a firm has to forecast the likely rates of inflation for each individual cash flow involved with a prospective capital project. In addition, the future rates of inflation, as registered by the RPI, must also be forecast. This is no mean requirement* but, unless it is done, it is conceivable that a firm could adopt a project in the mistaken belief that it will enhance its wealth.

8.7 SUMMARY

In this chapter we have endeavoured to show that the computation of a firm's overall cost of capital, from first principles, is by no means a straightforward matter. It depends on the interdependent effects which different sources of finance have on each other's costs and, above all else, it depends on the ways in which people perceive and allow for risk. Since these matters are not fully understood, the best advice to any firm contemplating a change in its leverage is to make such changes slowly so that it can properly monitor the response in the costs of its various sources of finance. Since uncertainty exists in the valuation of a firm's overall cost of capital, it follows that this transmits uncertainty to the valuation of a project's NPV. Furthermore, this uncertainty is enhanced by the influence of inflation, though we are able to offer a means of combating this sort of uncertainty providing we are willing and able to predict inflationary effects in all the cash flows attributable to a project.

---

* Besides the problem of forecasting, it should also be noted that money interest rates in the financial market do not always reflect the ravages of inflation. For example, in recent times interest rates have been *less* than the corresponding rates of inflation indicating *negative* returns on investment in real terms.

8.8 BIBLIOGRAPHY

General texts

Merrett, A. J. and Sykes, A., *The Finance and Analysis of Capital Projects*, Longman, 1974. This book is most relevant background reading for this chapter because the authors have researched the problem of how to assess a firm's cost of capital and employ their results throughout this book.

Solomon, E., *The Theory of Financial Management*, Columbia University Press, 1964. This book has become one of the classics of financial management, and is both profound and easy to read.

Specific texts

Beranek, W., *Analysis for Financial Decisions*, Irwin, 1963. Especially Chapters 7–11.

Fisher, L. and Lorie, J. H., 'Some studies of variability of returns on investments in common stocks', *Journal of Business*, April 1970.

Markowitz, H., 'Portfolio selection', *Journal of Finance*, March 1952.

Merrett, A. J. and Sykes, A., 'Return on equities and fixed interest securities 1919–66', *District Bank Review*, No. 158, 1966, pp. 29–44.

Modigliani, F. and Miller, M. H., 'The cost of capital, corporation finance and the theory of investment', *American Economic Review*, **48,** 1958, pp. 261–297.

Mossin, J., *The Theory of Financial Markets*, Prentice-Hall International, 1973.

Rubinstein, M. G., 'A mean variance synthesis of corporate financial theory', *Journal of Finance*, March 1973.

Ryan, R. R., 'The discount rate problem in capital budgeting', *Terotechnica*, **1** (2), October 1979, p. 141.

Sharpe, W., 'A simplified model for portfolio analysis', *Management Science*, January 1963.

9. *Uncertainty and Risk*

> '*All the business of War and indeed all the business of life is to endeavour to find out what you don't know from what you do.*'
>
> Duke of Wellington

So far we have completely ignored one of the most crucial elements of decision making, namely the consideration of uncertainty and its attendant risks, it being assumed that the cash flows involved with a new capital project can be predicted accurately. Obviously this is not so. Forecasting future events is an occupation fraught with difficulties which are exacerbated when a project has longevity, as is often the case with investment in manufacturing assets. Despite the utmost care and diligence by forecasters and estimators, errors can develop between the forecasts of a project's anticipated performance and its actual results. Such errors thereby expose the investment decision to uncertainty which can ultimately result in its becoming economically unviable, possibly straining the company's resources, and even placing the financial security of the company in jeopardy. Each substantial capital investment project is therefore a venture which involves taking risks, and it is the uncertainty about the future which creates those risks. Risk means exposure to mischance or more specifically the consequences of mischance. In any project assessment therefore the problem of dealing with uncertainty and its consequences must be faced.

As a result, we are obliged to study the complicated subject of uncertainty and risk in detail to see if the decision rules which we previously formulated can accommodate such matters, or whether they need to be modified to retain their credibility under conditions of risk. To this end, we are obliged to study another branch of management science, known as decision theory, which involves utility and probability concepts and techniques. It must be stressed, however, that our reason for studying these somewhat sophisticated matters is not perverse and they are not considered ends in themselves. What they do provide is an analytical framework within which we can sensibly tackle the problems of risk and uncertainty in an organized manner.

The fact that the techniques contained within this chapter are currently unable to provide categoric and authoritative decision rules to resolve the problem of risk endorses the fact that such matters are extremely complex. However, these techniques do provide a means of reinforcing our understanding of what constitutes reasonable decision making under conditions of risk. Furthermore, they reinforce the notion that a firm must not only consider the risks involved with a single project but must devise a strategy to mitigate risk effects when it designs its portfolio of projects. Such a strategy involves diversification.

9.1 THE EXISTENCE OF UNCERTAINTY

So far in this book we have assessed the economic merits of a proposed new capital investment on the basis of a single set of estimates for its capital cost, annual sales

203

volumes, prices and operating costs, and have demonstrated the credibility of our DCF techniques under assumed conditions of certainty. However, the reader must have doubts about their veracity when applied to conditions of risk. Risk in capital budgeting occurs for several reasons and at various stages of decision making in the evolution of a project from its inception to its acceptance. It starts with prejudice and bias with the people involved with the project from the outset. It results from ill-conceived definitions of the scope of the project to be studied and difficulty in properly defining the competitive market environment for the project. It also results from the improper analysis of available data, the use of incorrect and inappropriate decision criteria and, ultimately, the selection of the wrong course of action. Quite obviously, some of these sources of risk involve human behavioural problems, which lie outside the scope of this book. Others, however, result from the inadequate prediction of the magnitude and direction of change, with time, of all of those parameters which effect the economic attributes of a real capital project. All these important parameters feature below in equation 9.1.1 which is an extension of our previous life-cycle economic equation and results from the considerations given in Chapters 7 and 8.

$$\text{NPV}_T = \sum_{t=0}^{t=T} \{[S_t(p_t - VC_t) - FC_t] - \Delta WC_t - \Delta K_t\} f_t(\text{tax}) \cdot (1+r)^{-t}$$
$$+ \{\Delta WC_t + S_t \cdot f_T(\text{tax})\}(1+r)^{-T} \tag{9.1.1}$$

where T = the predicted economic life of the capital project, t = end-of-year moments in time such that $t = (0, 1, 2, \ldots T)$, S_t = the annual sales volume, p_t = the unit sales price, VC_t = the unit variable costs of production, FC_t = the annual fixed costs, ΔWC_t = changes in working capital with time, ΔK_t = changes in fixed capital with time, $f_t(\text{tax})$ = the fact that company tax payments and incentives must be included in the economics, $(1+r)^{-t}$ = the discount factor at some appropriate cost of capital 'r' and allows for the fact that money has a 'time value', and S_t = any terminal scrap value accruing from the sale of the project's assets.

In Chapter 7, we gave a 'snap-shot' of the methods employed in forecasting all of the elements of this equation, and we illustrated the typical ranges of errors in their prediction. Although such errors obviously depend on many considerations, including the precise nature of the capital investment at risk, nevertheless it might be instructive to reflect on the magnitude of some of these errors. These are given in Table 9.1.1, which gives the impression, albeit imprecise, that collectively several of the factors involved with a capital project could ruin its chances of economic success.

From what has been said, any firm contemplating investment in fixed assets should isolate, carefully consider, and weigh the influences of all those factors which put its intended investment at risk, and it should devise a policy which ensures that risk is

Table 9.1.1 *Typical tolerances in the prediction of parameters affecting the economic merits of a capital project over a ten-year life*

Parameter	% error in the capital budget forecast estimate	
	Overestimate	Underestimate
Installed capital cost	10	25
Construction time	5	50
Start-up costs	10	100
Sales volume	50	50
Sales prices	50	20
Variable production costs	25	50
Working capital	20	50

reduced to a level which the firm can absorb without financial ruin. Such a policy must operate from the inception of a project, when the firm's ability to reduce risk is greatest and the cost of reducing risk is least, for it is true that as a project progresses through the stages of its capital appraisal, so decisions are made which are often *irreversible*. By these means initial options and alternative ways of accomplishing the desired end result are assessed, sifted and rejected so refining the scope of the project throughout the appraisal process. It is very important, therefore, that the risks attached to each option should be carefully appraised before decisions are made to ensure that the option with the best balance of profit and risk is accepted. Quite obviously as each stage of the feasibility study is frozen, to become the basis for further study, so the cost of resolving previous errors increases. This is especially true for projects involving capital intensive continuous process plants which are highly specific in their application. In their case the greatest risk is the prospect of losing the majority of their investment capital, if they have to be retired for want of an economically viable market for their produce. Quite obviously such plants constitute an extreme case of risk but they emphasize the point that risk assessment cannot be left to the final project sanctioning decision.

9.2 ALLOWING FOR RISK IN PRACTICE

Business managers often ignore a formalized treatment of risk and work with single estimates of sales volumes, annual cash flows and NPV statistics just as we have done so far. They allow for risk intuitively whenever a decision has to be taken. In this way, a new capital project promising a handsome profit could be rejected because it is thought to be too risky for the company to undertake. Of course there is nothing wrong with such an intuitive method if it yields the correct decision, and one must admit that many executives seem to have a keenly developed sixth sense to deal in such matters with facility. Just how they accommodate for risk in an intuitive sense is not understood. One can only surmise that experience of making and witnessing the outcomes of similar decisions helps develop this faculty. It would also seem plausible that certain personal qualities like a vivid imagination (which can conceive all those situations likely to place an investment at risk), coupled with an acute sense of perception (which enables seemingly diverse and scrambled data to be coherently appraised) are important. Of course, one must also remember that the ability to select and plan a lucrative project is one matter, the ability to execute the operations of the project to realize the fruits of that plan is quite another distinct quality. Quite often therefore the ability to accommodate for risk intuitively is a testimony of the executive's faith that he would be able/unable to develop the intended project plan against all odds. Many executives who possess this ability look contemptuously on the substance which follows in this chapter and regard its ideas and techniques as nothing more than crutches to decision making. Unfortunately, most of us do not possess their skills and, realizing that projects do often fail even in seemingly benign markets, we are forced to look beyond intuitive decision making as a means of accommodating risk.

One way of accommodating risks is to use *conservative* single figure estimates for the sales volumes, prices and all those other parameters which feature in equation 9.1.1. The main problem with this method is its arbitrariness coupled with its tendency to preclude lucrative projects by its undue pessimism.

Another well known and commonly used method of allowing for uncertainty and risk involves the payback method, which we so blatantly condemned in Chapter 5. This method recognizes that cash flows realized in the distant future are more difficult to predict accurately than more imminent ones, so it allows for uncertainty by concentrating attention on the short-term results of a project. With this approach, the time required to recoup the investment in a capital project is shortened for more risky projects. Essentially, this technique can only accommodate risk involved with a sudden cataclysm. In this respect its use is justified for such cases as a disruption to production due to civil strife in areas of political instability, the expropriation and nationalization of a firm's foreign assets without proper compensation, or the sudden development of a new product or process which completely revolutionizes business, making other firms' products and/or processes obsolete overnight. Obviously, cases such as these are extremely rare. It is important to understand, however, that this technique is quite inappropriate for reasonable business risks, such as those associated with a sales decline or a cost increase which result in a deterioration in the expected economic merits of a project. This unsuitability stems from the fact that this technique helps to select economically worthwhile projects only if their post-payback cash flows are economically satisfactory. In essence therefore, it involves a judgement that these further cash flows will mature. Furthermore, it requires an arbitrary stipulation of what constitutes a reasonable payback time and still needs an intuitive appraisal of the riskiness of the cash flows up to the payback time. It should also be noted that insistence on short payback periods does not necessarily reduce risks since the overall degree of risk facing a firm depends on how it employs the cash flows released from its projects. In effect therefore the payback criterion has little to offer in the way of risk measurement outside the sudden cataclysm effect and its obvious liquidity considerations, which were discussed in Chapter 5. It must also be remembered that it suffers the grave deficiency of not being an indicator of the economic merits of a project either.

The fourth intuitive method for dealing with risk and uncertainty involves adjusting the firm's cost of capital according to the risk classification of the project studied. In other words, an interest premium over and above the normal cost of capital is used. This premium is negligible for projects of extremely low risk but substantial for projects of high risk. Such an idea emanates from the financial market which requires firms to pay greater interest as their borrowing increases. It follows therefore that the minimum accepted rate of return on a project (the required cost of capital) comprises two components according to the relationship:

$$i_r = i_{rf} + p$$

where i_r = the required interest rate, i_{rf} = the required interest rate on a risk free basis, and p = the risk premium interest rate, which could range between 1 per cent for low-risk projects up to 20 per cent for high-risk project per annum.

Numerous ways of classifying the risk class of a project abound and it must be remembered that such categories that do exist are not necessarily mutually exclusive or indeed collectively exhaustive. In reality a project could embrace more than one risk category, which might be defined as follows:

9.2.1   Cost-saving investments

These can be considered in two classes – projects incorporated within the operation of existing assets, and those incremental projects incorporated within the framework of planned capital projects. The first type usually attracts the same degree of risk as the ongoing process. If the business of that process is well established and there appears to be no good reason to anticipate its deterioration or demise, then the risk of such cost savings schemes is usually low and revolves around such considerations as the errors in their capital cost and savings estimates and any risks due to the technologies involved. In these circumstances little, if any, premium above the firm's nominal cost of capital would normally be needed to cover such risks. However, if such a cost-saving scheme were intended as a means of resurrecting the economic viability of an existing and declining process then quite a different assessment would have to be made. In these circumstances one would need to assess the likelihood of these improvements being realized.

When the cost-saving scheme is only a part of some larger and planned capital project then, of course, it attracts the same degree of risk as the integral project, whose risk classification might best be described by Sections 9.2.3 or 9.2.4 below.

9.2.2 Capital replacement projects

Matters of plant replacement are covered in detail in Part IV, but a few observations are warranted here. No replacement investment should occur automatically just because some machine or piece of equipment has come to the end of its economic life. Instead, replacement projects must be judged by their future economic merits just like any other capital investment project. The risk to replacement investments depends on their capital scale and the technology involved with the replacement assets and their processes. For well tried and tested technology it is obvious that the risks increase with the scale of the plant involved because the costs, the disruption to existing business and the strains put upon the firm's project management all increase with the size and complexity of the replacement project. Replacement assets incorporating novel technologies obviously expose the firm to greater risk – the risk that such new assets might not work correctly, thereby jeopardizing the firm's existing business. As with cost saving-projects, it will be realized that the risk of replacement projects is also governed by the general level of risk to the business containing that project. Such matters are governed by product life-cycle, technological innovation and government regulation considerations.

9.2.3 Market expansion investments involving existing technology

Much more risky investment projects are those associated with entirely new ventures, which involve direct competition with well established firms possessing large resources. Examples in this category include the development of a new ore body to increase the sales of ferrous or non-ferrous metals, the expansion of the market for an existing product, or the production and marketing of a product which is new to the company involved. Because of their inherent uncertainties and their substantial degree of risk it is commonplace for such projects to carry a considerable premium over and above the firm's nominal cost of capital.

9.2.4 Market expansion investments necessitating new technology

This category involves the greatest risks because the firm not only has to assess the competitive element of risk but the likelihood of encountering technical trouble when scaling up its laboratory and/or pilot plant results to full-scale production.

Evidence of the use of this technique is readily available in the literature on project evaluation, one of the more notable treatments being that due to Malloy (1971). In common with the other pragmatic techniques which we have discussed so far, this technique has the advantage of being simple to understand and easy to apply. However, its arbitrariness means that potentially lucrative projects could be rejected.

9.3 SENSITIVITY ANALYSIS

The preceding methods deal with the problem of uncertainty and risk at the total-system level of a capital project, without investigating the fundamental causes for uncertainty. However, we have already noted that every parameter constituting equation 9.1.1 is subject to error in its forecast according to the ranges suggested by Table 9.1.1. It would seem reasonable and indeed prudent to investigate those parameters most likely to be forecast in error which could also place the project at greatest risk, because means for improving their accuracy could be considered with a view to reducing the overall risk to a tolerable level. One method for doing this is known as sensitivity analysis. In its most basic form, this technique involves varying the parameters of equation 9.1.1 *one at a time* to discover the sensitivity of the project's NPV and/or DCFRR to *reasonable* percentage variations within those single parameters. In effect, therefore, such a technique is equivalent to asking 'What if'? questions such as, '*What* would be the change to the project's DCF attributes *if* the capital cost of the project were to be in error by, *say*, ±10 per cent?' To be meaningful, such an analysis has to be applied to a particular project with its own particular cash flow forecasts, so the examples which follow are meant for illustrative purposes only. Table 9.3.1 contains the sensitivity analysis for the example previously studied in Table 7.11.1, which had a base case NPV and DCFRR of 37718 munits and 22 per cent per annum after tax respectively. This example shows how the overall economic merits of this project are especially sensitive to 10 per cent variations in the product price and a six months' change in the project's construction time, whereas it is fairly insensitive to 10 per cent variations in all the other parameters of Table 9.3.1. On the face of this evidence it would appear that the greatest risk to the economic viability of *this* project would come from a decay in the product price below that used in its single figure forecasts.

Several means of reducing this risk are open to management, including:

 (i) long-term price contracts for its products,
 (ii) a strategy of gradual product improvement to stay ahead of competition and possibly obviate a price decay, consistent with realizing economies to pay for such improvement, and
(iii) non-capital intensive productivity schemes designed to arrest a drift in net cash income.

Of course, it is conceivable that the first of these propositions might be inappropriate and the two later remedies might already be contained in the base case study anyway. Under such conditions the only reasonable options open to management would involve outright acceptance or rejection of the project on intuitive grounds, or

Table 9.3.1 *Sensitivity analysis applied to the example previously given in Table 7.11.2*

Item	Variation	Positive variation DCFRR (% pa)	NPV (munits)	Negative variation DCFRR (% pa)	NPV (munits)
Base case	–	22	37 718	22	37 718
Selling price	±10%	39.5	97 190	2.8	−21 754
Sales volume	±10%	27.9	58 358	15.7	17 078
Capital cost	±10%	20.2	34 082	24.1	41 354
Direct labour cost	±10%	19.2	28 668	24.8	46 768
Construction time	±6 months	16.7	23 669	38.8	62 264
Delayed tax allowance	Yes	17.3	29 566	–	–

the postponement of the project until the chances of a 10 per cent price decay could be evaluated on the basis of extra information, possibly from a market research study.

One of the greatest criticisms of sensitivity analysis is that the ranges of variation placed on the controlling parameters are often misconstrued to mean that such parameters are *likely to be* in error by ±10 per cent (or whatever other level of sensitivity is used). This is not the case: the sensitivity range is selected on an arbitrary basis to reflect what *might happen if* such parameters were so in error.

Another basic problem with the previous example is the fact that it only shows the effects of varying one parameter at a time. Quite obviously several of the parameters could be incorrectly forecast in concert. For example, a six months' over-run on the project's construction time would reduce the DCFRR by 5.3 per cent per annum, after tax. However, if this occurred a capital cost over-run would *also* be highly likely, perhaps by 10 per cent or more. Reference to Table 9.3.1 shows that such a cost increase would, of itself, reduce the project's DCFRR by 1.8 per cent. *In concert*, however, the joint effect of these two errors in prediction would reduce the DCFRR to 15.3 per cent per annum, after tax. It will be appreciated that this result is *not* the sum, product or indeed any simple mathematical relationship of the two independent effects, but has to be evaluated as a separate sensitivity analysis in its own right. Naturally, the joint effect of variation in other parameters could also be affected in the same way – the price-sales volume combination being the most obvious example to spring to mind. Of course, nowadays with fast, cheap and readily available computers, such an analysis as the one suggested here can easily explore the full range of all possible variations in the single statistic forecasts. One word of warning, however: such an analysis can result in so many numbers that the quality of the ultimate decision making can be confused rather than improved, unless middle

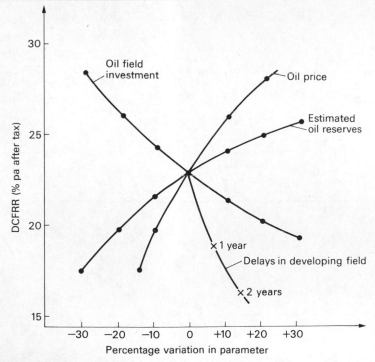

Figure 9.3.1 *The economic sensitivity of a typical North Sea oil field investment to variations in its important economic parameters.*

management select, for the scrutiny of senior management, those data which best illustrate the uncertainties and risks prevailing in a project. Such a selection obviously requires skill and good judgement.

To some extent graphical display can help alleviate the problem of interpreting the results of large sensitivity analyses. Perhaps of topical interest is the example given in Figure 9.3.1 which relates to a typical North Sea oil field, showing the variation in its return to possible errors in the forecasts of its oil reserves, oil price, the oil field development investment and delays in developing the field. This technique shows the relative sensitivity of the project's DCFRR to errors in the prediction of its major economic parameters according to the steepness of each line. It will be noticed that a delay in developing an oil field, possibly due to bad weather conditions and/or unusual technical problems, could have a most damaging effect on the economic merits of such a project.

The example given in Figure 9.3.2 is a two-dimensional method illustrating the risks inherent in a project, combining the joint effects of sensitivity analysis and payback considerations. This technique is often employed by companies to show the economic consequences of whatever critical risks senior management want investigating and usually covers the extreme conditions which the forecasters believe possible. The hypothetical example of Figure 9.3.2 incorporates the combined effects of high and low sales revenues and operating costs giving four combinations in all,

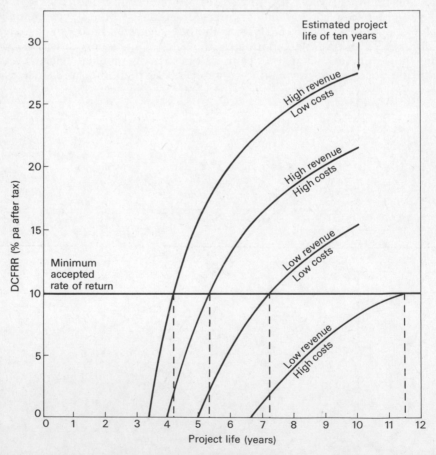

Figure 9.3.2   *A method of combining sensitivity analysis with payback-time analysis. Note: the dotted lines indicate the capital recovery periods at a 10 per cent pa cost of capital.*

showing how the low sales revenue–high operating cost extreme could not possibly be countenanced because it would not achieve a discounted break even (see Chapter 5) prior to the expected termination of such a project.

9.4 MAKING INVESTMENT DECISIONS UNDER CONDITIONS OF COMPLETE UNCERTAINTY

One of the major benefits of sensitivity analysis is that it highlights those situations which could benefit or threaten a firm. For example, it could show that investment in a new factory with the purpose of manufacturing a certain product could be economically disastrous *if* some competitor also entered the same market, whereas it could be very lucrative otherwise. In management science parlance these alternative conditions (whether or not a competitor enters the market) are known as the states of nature (they are also known as the states of the environment or chance events): they are the circumstances which could prevail.

In many circumstances, the management of the firm contemplating such an investment might be completely ignorant of their competitors' intentions, and might be quite unwilling to guess the chances or odds of a competitor entering the market. In other words they would insist their complete uncertainty of the state of nature which would prevail if their new plant were built. Such a situation is known as decision making in the face of complete uncertainty. As we shall see, it forms the neutral ground between the somewhat pragmatic decision methods which we have studied so far and the more esoteric methods discussed below. Five different techniques can be applied to such decision making.

  (i) the maximin method,
 (ii) the maximax technique,
(iii) the minimax regret method,
 (iv) the Laplace method,
  (v) the Hurwicz rule.

The relative strength and weaknesses of these five techniques are explored in the following sections of this chapter when applied to a hypothetical example which presupposes that a firm wishes to select the best strategy and choose the optimal capacity of its intended plant when faced with an uncertain demand for its products. The numbers in Table 9.4.1 refer to the NPVs which *would* materialize *if* the corresponding plant capacities were built, and *if* the stated market demands developed. In decision theory this table is known as a payoff matrix. In this particular

Table 9.4.1 *The NPV payoff matrix for a hypothetical example* (NPVs in *munits* $\times 10^6$)

Alternative strategies– plant capacities (tonnes per annum)	States of nature-market demand (tonnes per annum)				
	20 000 (B_1)	30 000 (B_2)	40 000 (B_3)	50 000 (B_4)	60 000 (B_5)
A_0 10 000	22	14	8	2	–
A_1 20 000	26	16	12	6	0
A_2 30 000	20	40	30	24	20
A_3 40 000	0	20	60	50	40
A_4 50 000	−20	0	40	80	60
A_5 60 000	−40	−20	20	40	100

Table 9.4.2 *The reduced payoff matrix after allowing for dominance (NPVs in munits $\times 10^6$)*

Option	State of nature				
	B_1	B_2	B_3	B_4	B_5
A_1	26	16	12	6	0
A_2	20	40	30	24	20
A_3	0	20	60	50	40
A_4	−20	0	40	80	60
A_5	−40	−20	20	40	100

example the NPVs reflect the influence of technological returns to scale and diminishing price with increasing demand for the product.

Before proceeding with our analysis, the payoff matrix should first be examined to see if any of the decision options are dominated by others, in which case the dominated options should be discarded. Reference to Table 9.4.1 shows that under all conceivable market demand conditions, as stipulated by the matrix, alternative A_1 is always better than option A_0. Within the context of this hypothetical example, therefore, we could not entertain the idea of building a plant of 10 000 tonnes per annum capacity and the payoff matrix would be reduced to the form shown in Table 9.4.2.

9.5 THE MAXIMIN AND THE MAXIMAX RULES

The maximin rule is based on a condition of extreme pessimism and constitutes a most conservative approach to decision making, suggesting a high aversion to risk. This rule recommends that the company should select that option which is likely to cause the least economic damage. In terms of the example given in Table 9.4.2, the worst that could happen if option A_1 were built would be a NPV payoff of zero. The corresponding worst values for all the options are:

Option	Minimum payoff (*munits* $\times 10^6$)
A_1	0
A_2	20 (optimal choice)
A_3	0
A_4	−20
A_5	−40

In these circumstances most conservative managers would choose option A_2, with an installed capacity of 20 000 tonnes per annum, because it represents the best of the worst possible outcomes. This decision would preclude the chances of the firm making high profits.

By stark contrast, the maximax rule is based on extreme optimism and constitutes a most speculative approach to decision making. In terms of our hypothetical example, the best possible outcome which could transpire from building option A_1 would be a NPV payoff of 26 million munits. The corresponding best values for all the options are:

Option	Maximum payoff (*munits* $\times 10^6$)
A_1	26
A_2	40
A_3	60
A_4	80
A_5	100 (optimal choice)

Such a rule would therefore advocate the building of a 60 000 tonnes per annum plant according to option A_5. It will of course be realized that such an outcome takes no account of the losses – the risks – which could result from such a choice.

9.6 THE MINIMAX REGRET RULE

Having made a decision, which Nature in her perversity then proves wrong, people often regret that decision and they measure the difference between the payoff which could have been achieved with perfect insight and the actual result. To understand the implications of this phenomenon we have to reformulate the data of Table 9.4.2. This is accomplished by identifying the greatest payoff for each state of nature and subtracting from that value the payoffs which would arise from alternative strategies. For example, the greatest possible gain in Table 9.4.2 results from B_5. If a plant of 20 000 tonnes per annum *were* built and the market *then* developed to 60 000 tonnes per year then an opportunity cost of 100 million munits would have been realized – with great regret!

The corresponding values of the lost opportunity, or regret, for each option are provided in Table 9.6.1. From this table we note that if option A_1 were chosen the

Table 9.6.1   *The lost opportunity or regret matrix corresponding to Table 9.4.2 (regret NPV in munits $\times 10^6$)*

Option	B_1	B_2	B_3	B_4	B_5
A_1	0	24	48	74	100
A_2	6	0	30	56	80
A_3	26	20	0	30	60
A_4	46	40	20	0	40
A_5	66	60	40	40	0

(State of nature heading spans B_1–B_5.)

greatest possible regret would be 100 million munits. The corresponding worst values for all the options are:

Option	Worst possible regret
A_1	100
A_2	80
A_3	60
A_4	46 (optimal choice)
A_5	66

People who worry over past wrong decisions and/or have a strong aversion to criticism might be tempted to select that option which minimizes their regret. In these circumstances they would select option A_4 and build a plant of 50 000 tonnes a year capacity. It will, of course, be realized that such a decision rule smacks of psychotic tendencies, and runs counter to the more rational approach which suggests that one should attempt to make the best of all future decisions. The only real benefit of hindsight is the knowledge and information it imparts. For these reasons, therefore, this decision-making method cannot be recommended, even though such behaviour is known to exist.

9.7 THE LAPLACE METHOD

This rule, named after the famous mathematician, suggests that in the face of complete uncertainty each of the conceivable states of nature is equally likely. In other words, it assumes that Nature is indifferent to the outcome of what is really a game of chance, and suggests that the average outcome to each possible option should be used to form the decision. Reformulating Table 9.4.2 therefore we get the average values shown in Table 9.7.1. This decision rule therefore suggests that we should select option A_3 with an installed capacity of 40 000 tonnes per year.

Table 9.7.1 *The average payoff matrix corresponding to Table 9.4.2 (NPVs in munits $\times 10^6$)*

Option	Average payoff
A_1	$(26+16+12+6+0) \div 5 = 12.0$
A_2	$(20+40+30+24+20) \div 5 = 26.8$
A_3	$(0+20+60+50+40) \div 5 = 34.0^a$
A_4	$(-20+0+40+80+60) \div 5 = 32.0$
A_5	$(-40-20+20+40+100) \div 5 = 20.0$

[a] Denotes optimal choice.

9.8 THE HURWICZ RULE

Most people possess a degree of optimism or pessimism which lies somewhere between the extremes previously assumed in Section 9.5, these extremes being somewhat alien to most managers. Evidence suggests that managers compromise between these two extremes using weighting factors which reflect their relative optimism or pessimism. To make such an idea operational, the Hurwicz rule uses an index of optimism α with values ranging between nought and unity, where nought reflects extreme pessimism, and unity reflects extreme optimism. Once the value for α is chosen, the rule suggests that the option possessing the greatest expected payoff according to the relationship:

$$\max_i \left\{ \alpha \left[\max_j P_{ij} \right] + (1-\alpha) \left[\min_j P_{ij} \right] \right\}$$

should be chosen, where P_{ij} denotes the payoff for the ith option and the jth state of nature.

The example given in Table 9.8.1 illustrates the use of this rule for $\alpha = 0.2$, and shows why option A_2 should be chosen. Figure 9.8.1 illustrates the use of this rule

Table 9.8.1 *Payoff matrix using the Hurwicz rule*

Option (i)	Option maximum payoff $\max_j P_{ij}$	Option minimum payoff $\min_j P_{ij}$	$\{\alpha[\max_j P_{ij}] + (1-\alpha)[\min_j P_{ij}]\}$ $\alpha = 0.2$
A_1	26	0	5.2
A_2	40	20	24.0^a
A_3	60	0	12.0
A_4	80	-20	0.0
A_5	100	-40	-12.0

[a] Denotes optimal choice.

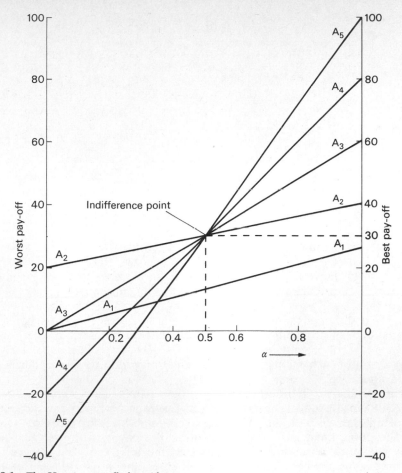

Figure 9.8.1 *The Hurwicz payoff alogorithm.*

for varying values of α. In these circumstances option A_1 is always inferior to options A_2 and A_3, except in the extreme case of pessimism when it is equivalent to option A_3. Furthermore, all four options, expecting A_1, are equivalent when $\alpha = 0.5$ because they all yield a payoff of 30 million munits. This graph also features the results of the maximin and the maximax rules, the former being measured by the lefthand ordinate, the latter by the righthand ordinate. The philosophy of this rule is that people tend to focus on the extreme outcomes or consequences of their actions when appraising their intended strategy, and weigh these outcomes in a way which reflects their propensity to risk taking.

9.9 SUMMARY OF THE ELEMENTARY RULES FOR DEALING WITH INVESTMENT UNDER CONDITIONS OF UNCERTAINTY

The results of the preceding five sections are listed in Table 9.9.1 where one immediately notes that they give inconsistent and conflicting recommendations. This illustrates two points: (i) the difficulty of dealing with such matters at a pragmatic level, and (ii) the need to develop a much more fundamental calculus to deal with risk. We shall now turn our attention to the latter of these considerations.

Table 9.9.1 *A summary of the results of the elementary decision rules applied to conditions of uncertainty*

Decision rule	Alternative selected
Maximin	A_2
Maximax	A_5
Minimax regret	A_4
Laplace	A_3
Hurwicz	A_2

9.10   SOME BASIC PROBABILITY CONCEPTS*

Both the Laplace and the Hurwicz rules have paved the way for a formal application of probability theory to investment decision making. Before we deal with such matters properly, however, it might be beneficial if we first consider some of the basic concepts of probability theory. Unfortunately, many people possess a blind spot when it comes to a mathematical treatment of the subject because they have not previously had the opportunity to study such matters, especially at school, where a formal treatment of probability theory has only been introduced in recent years. We live with the laws of probability on a daily basis, accepting the chance of getting run over by a motor vehicle and dying, getting married, having children, getting promoted and even the remote possibility of winning on the horses, or by some other game of chance. Furthermore we recognize that many companies earn their living from chance events. For example, life assurance companies analyse actuarial data and, on the basis of the information contained within those data, they are prepared to quote financial terms for life insurance cover, in the certain knowledge that they will profit from such transactions in the long run. The same philosophy applies for the insurance of motor vehicles, ships and property – and of course it applies to betting games too!

The literature on probability theory is vast, and limitations of space preclude a full treatment of the subject here, so any reader wanting more than a most basic treatment of the subject is recommended to read a further account elsewhere. An excellent introductory yet practical text is that by Maroney (1967).

Essentially probability theory involves putting numbers on the chance that some outcome will, or will not, occur. For example, given that something will definitely occur, we say that its probability of occurring is unity. Such a situation is called deterministic and many everyday occurrences comply with this situation. The best examples are those observed in Nature, like the setting of the sun, the coming of the seasons and the free-falling of a heavy object to the ground. In mathematics we express such a probability by the following notation:

$$p(A) = 1$$

where p = probability of event 'A' occurring, and where A could be the setting of the sun. Conversely, when we know that something will definitely *not* occur then we denote such a probability by the notation:

$$p(B) = 0$$

_____

* This section is meant for the reader who is unacquainted with probability calculus.

where B now stands for the event which we know cannot occur. Examples in this latter category include the fact that none of us get any younger – or at least medical science has yet to find a means of achieving this end! Likewise, heavy objects do not fly off into space on their own volition.

Many other occurrences in Nature possess probabilities which lie between these two extremes, the weather pattern of temperate climatic zones being one of the most common examples. Many people have lost their shirts, metaphorically speaking, betting on the outcome of the following day's weather which is often quite fickle and extremely difficult to forecast with assuredness, despite there being copious amounts of historical weather data to help in such predictions.

To put such matters into some reasonable perspective let us consider a few games of chance. For example, what is the probability that a true coin when fairly tossed will come down heads? The answer is one-half (1/2). The reason for this is that the probability of the coin coming down heads or tails is unity and, for a true coin, each of these alternative outcomes is equally likely (has the same chance). Since we are ruling out the chance of the coin staying on its edge, it follows that the event heads and the event tails comprise the totality of all possible events for the outcome. In other words, they comprise the collectively exhaustive set of all possibilities, and since the outcome heads precludes that of tails then such events are also said to be mutually exclusive. For any game of chance which meets these prescribed conditions, the probability of any unique event is given by the expression:

$$p(c) = \frac{1}{n} \qquad (9.10.1)$$

where $c =$ that event of interest, and $n =$ the number of mutually exclusive and collectively exhaustive events of equal likelihood. This equation suggests that under conditions of fair play we would *expect* the coin to come down heads and tails with equal frequency, *if we tossed the coin many times*. Of course, there is absolutely no reason why it should not come down heads for 20 occasions before a tail appears. In the event of such an outcome we might suspect the fairness of the coin, but we would also have to admit there exists a remote probability that such an outcome could happen by chance. What is this probability? If we confine our attention to tossing a coin twice only for the moment, then we could say that such a game is equivalent to tossing two coins together, once only (provided fair play prevails). The possible outcomes of this game are:

Event	Coin 1	Coin 2
1	H	H
2	H	T
3	T	H
4	T	T

In other words there are four equally likely outcomes. The total number of possible outcomes is given by the expression:

$$(\text{Number of sides})^x = 2^2 = 4$$

where x denotes the number of coins. The probability of *both* coins showing heads is therefore:

$$\frac{1 \text{ event}}{4 \text{ possible events}} = 1/4$$

In a similar fashion the probability of 20 heads occurring in 20 tosses of a coin is given by:

$$\frac{1}{2^{20}} = \frac{1}{1\,048\,676} \simeq 0.000001$$

The probability of such an outcome as this is therefore extremely remote, but nevertheless possible.

Returning to our original ideas of probability, it transpires that heads and tails will only prevail with equal overall frequency if we are willing to conduct the game *many, many times*. To accommodate this condition, the probability of an event occurring is defined as its *limiting relative frequency*. For our coin game this condition can be represented by the expression:

$$p_N(T) = \lim_{N \to \infty} \left[\frac{\text{number of events showing tails}}{\text{total number of tosses of the coin } (N)} \right] = 1/2$$

where $p_N(T) =$ the probability of the coin showing tails (T) for N tosses of the coin, as N tends to infinity.

Suppose we were offered the following bet: we would receive 2 munits for every occasion that the coin showed heads but we would have to pay 1 munit each time it showed tails. We would be willing to play the game in the knowledge of the coin being fair, because we would stand to profit from such a game. How much would we gain? If the coin came down heads and then tails in two successive tosses, we would win 1 munit overall, and if the game continued for a long time we would *expect* to win 1/2 munit per toss *on average*. This can be represented mathematically by the expression:

$$E(x) = x_1 \cdot p(x_1) + x_2 \cdot p(x_2)$$

where $E(x) =$ the expected value of the game, $x_1 =$ the value of winning a game, $x_2 =$ the value of losing a game, $p(x_1) =$ the probability of winning, and $p(x_2) =$ the probability of losing.

Substituting the previous values into this equation we get:

$$E(x) = 2 \times (1/2) + (-1) \times (1/2) = 1/2$$

confirming our original intuitive ideas. Of course, if the stakes were different, say 2000 munits for heads and 1000 munits for 'tails', then the *expected value* of the game would be 500 munits. In other words, a scale factor would be involved with such sums and our winnings would be enhanced accordingly if we played the game many, many times. However, it will be realized that we could lose on 20 successive tosses, as our previous example shows. Despite the fact that such a game appears lucrative on the evidence of its expected value* it will now be realized that it contains risks with a definite probability of losing money†. Such an understanding as this is pivotal to the entire philosophy of decision making under conditions of risk, which pervade the rest of this book.

So far we have illustrated three important principles:

(i) the sum of the probabilities of all independent and collectively exhaustive events equals unity. This is known as the addition rule of probability. In the context of our coin problem, the probability of the coin showing *either* heads or

---

* It will now be appreciated that the expected value is that value we would expect from the game on average, as the number of trials of the game approaches infinity.
† We shall return to this point later in a more practical sense, when it will be emphasized that a firm could go bankrupt investing in projects, subject to chance outcomes.

tails is unity. This can be formulated by the expression:

$$p(\text{heads OR tails}) = p(\text{head}) + p(\text{tails})$$
$$= 1/2 + 1/2$$
$$= 1$$

and in a more generalized sense it follows that, if two events A and B are independent of one another, the probability of *either* can be represented by:

$$p(A \text{ OR } B) = p(A) + p(B) \qquad (9.10.2)$$

(ii) the probability of two events occurring *jointly* is the multiple of their independent probabilities. This is known as the multiplication rule of probability. In the context of our coin problem it was shown that the probability of there being two heads in two tosses of a coin is given by:

$$p\left\{ \begin{array}{l} \text{heads for the first toss and} \\ \text{heads for the second toss} \end{array} \right\} = p(\text{heads}) \times p(\text{heads})$$
$$= 1/2 \times 1/2$$
$$= 1/4$$

In a more generalized form it, therefore, follows that the probability of the *sum* of two independent outcomes A and B is given by the relationship:

$$p(A \text{ AND } B) = p(A) \cdot p(B) \qquad (9.10.3)$$

(iii) the expected value of any given game of chance is the mean average value obtained by *weighting* each possible outcome by its respective probability according to the relationship:

$$E(x_i) = \bar{x} = \sum_{i=1}^{n} x_i \cdot p(x_i) \qquad (9.10.4)$$

where $\bar{x} =$ the mean average value, $x_i =$ the value of the ith possible outcome, and $p(x_i) =$ the probability of the ith possible outcome for $i = (1, n)$.

Given these three principles, let us examine a dice game, which is more complicated than its coin counterpart due to each die having six possible results. According to equation 9.10.1 each side has a probability of one-sixth of occurring, so, using equation 9.10.4, we find that the expected value from throwing a die is 3.5. But no side contains this number! This point demonstrates one special feature of the mean average (expected value) criterion, namely that such a value need not resemble any of the real-world values which the game of chance can actually assume, and again reinforces the idea that the expected value only results from taking the average value of many different throws of the die.

One of the interesting features of probability theory made possible by our dice-playing game is the variability of the results of each outcome about its expected value. This variability is illustrated by Figure 9.10.1, and it will be noticed that, for this example, the positive and negative variations (deviations) equate. A better way to regard this variability is to square each of the deviations thereby obviating their zero sum. By these means we obtain another statistical criterion known as the Variance which is 'the sum of the squares of the deviations of each possible result of a game of chance, about the mean average value, weighted by their respective probabilities'. In mathematical notation the Variance is represented by:

$$V(x_i) = \sum_{i=1}^{n} (x_i - \bar{x})^2 \cdot p(x_i) \qquad (9.10.5)$$

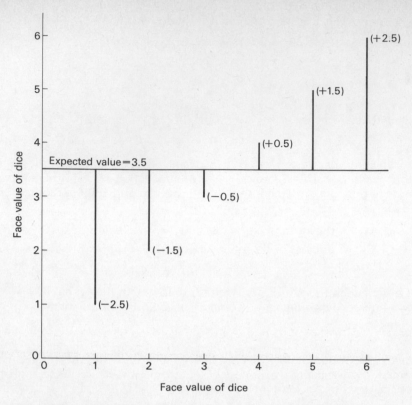

Figure 9.10.1   *The variability of the face values of a die about its expected value.*
( ) = *variation about the mean (expected) value.*

where $V(x_i)$ = the variance of some game of chance which assumes values x_i = $(x_1 \ldots x_n)$, $\bar{x}$ = the mean average (expected value) of that game, and $p(x_i)$ = the probability of occurrence of outcome x_i.

Another useful statistic is the standard deviation. This is the square root of the variance and is denoted as follows:

$$\sigma(x_i) = \sqrt{\text{Var}(x_i)} \qquad (9.10.6)$$

Table 9.10.1 shows that the variance and standard deviation for the single dice game are 2.92 and 1.71 respectively, and the total dispersion of possible results, from 1–6, lie within ±1.46 standard deviations of the mean*.

If we pursue this matter one step further, we can derive some principles which will help us resolve later problems associated with capital investment decision making under conditions of risk. To do this we need to consider throwing two dice together. The total scores derived from such a game are shown in Figure 9.10.2, demonstrating that 36 possible outcomes of equal probability exist. However a careful examination of this table shows that the probabilities of each combined score are far from being equal, there being six possible combinations giving a score of seven, and only one possible combination for a score of two. Why should this be so? If we consider the probability of a combined score of three for the moment then, according to

---

* The mean is the expected value which is the same as the *mean* average value.

Table 9.10.1 *The mean, variance and standard deviation of a single dice game of chance*

Face value (x_i)	Probability of face value $p(x_i)$	$x_i \cdot p(x_i)$	$(x_i - \bar{x})$	$(x_i - \bar{x})^2$	$(x_i - \bar{x})^2 \cdot p(x_i)$
1	1/6	1/6	−2.5	6.25	1.041667
2	1/6	2/6	−1.5	2.25	0.375000
3	1/6	3/6	−0.5	0.25	0.041667
4	1/6	4/6	0.5	0.25	0.041667
5	1/6	5/6	1.5	2.25	0.375000
6	1/6	6/6	2.5	6.25	1.041666

Totals	$\sum_1^6 p(x_i) = 1$	$\bar{x} = 3.5$			Var $(x_i) = 2.916667$
					$\sigma(x_i) = 1.707825$

equation 9.10.3, its probability should be:

$$p(1 \text{ and } 2) = p(1) \cdot p(2)$$
$$= 1/6 \cdot 1/6$$
$$= 1/36$$

In words, this says there should be '1 in 36 chance of a combined score of three'. But Figure 9.10.2 shows that this is wrong! The reason for this apparent discrepancy lies in the fact that two possible ways exist in which a score of three can be realized, namely:

$$p(3) = p(1 \text{ and } 2) + p(2 \text{ and } 1)$$
$$= 1/36 + 1/36$$
$$= 2/36$$

which of course agrees with Figure 9.10.2. The same reasoning holds true for all the other scores, each having several different combinations of individual dice scores to achieve their aggregate total. The corresponding values for the probabilities of these combined scores along with their mean, variance and standard deviation are given in Table 9.10.2.

Several interesting and indeed quite important results follow from this example. The first concerns the fact that the mean average value of this game is '7' which is exactly twice that of the single dice game proving that the expected value of the *sum*

Individual results for die 1 (x_i)

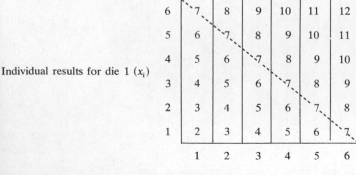

Individual results for die 2 (x_j)

Figure 9.10.2 *Combined score from throwing two independent dice.*

Table 9.10.2 *Values for the probabilities of the combined scores, their mean, variance and standard deviations from throwing two dice*

Combined score (x_k)	Probability of combined score $p(x_k) \times 36$	$x_k p(x_k)$	$(x_k - \bar{x})$	$(x_k - \bar{x})^2$	$(x_k - \bar{x})^2 p(x_k)$
2	1	2	−5	25	25
3	2	6	−4	16	32
4	3	12	−3	9	27
5	4	20	−2	4	16
6	5	30	−1	1	5
7	6	42	0	0	0
8	5	40	1	1	5
9	4	36	2	4	16
10	3	30	3	9	27
11	2	22	4	16	32
12	1	12	5	25	25

Totals $\quad \dfrac{\sum_1^{12} p(x_k)}{36} = 1 \qquad \bar{x} = \dfrac{252}{36} = 7 \qquad$ — $\qquad$ — $\qquad \text{Var}(x_k) = \dfrac{210}{36} = 5.833333$

$$\therefore \sigma(x_k) = 2.415229$$

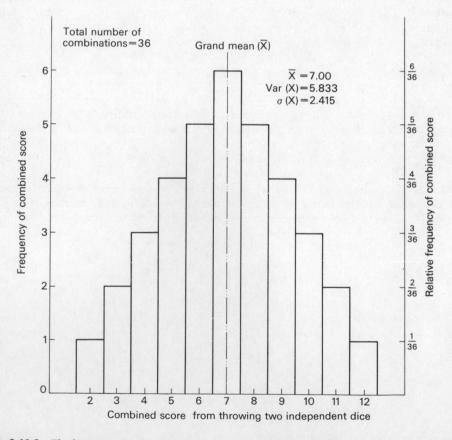

Total number of combinations = 36

Grand mean ($\bar{X}$)

$\bar{X} = 7.00$
Var (X) = 5.833
σ (X) = 2.415

Frequency of combined score

Relative frequency of combined score

Combined score from throwing two independent dice

Figure 9.10.3 *The histogram for the combined score from throwing two dice.*

of two independent games of chance is the sum of their individual expected values. This identity is given by equation 9.10.7:

$$E(x_i + x_j) = E(x_i) + E(x_j) \qquad (9.10.7)$$

or

$$\bar{X} = \bar{x}_i + \bar{x}_j$$

where x_i = all possible values for some variable $i = (1, n)$, x_j = all possible values for some variable $j = (1, m)$, $E(x_i) = \sum_{i=1}^{n} x_i \cdot p(x_i) = \bar{x}_i$, and $E(x_j) = \sum_{j=1}^{m} x_j \cdot p(x_j) = \bar{x}_j$. Likewise the variance of the two-dice game is 5.83, which is twice that of the single dice game, proving that the variance of the sum of two independent games of chance is the sum of their individual variances. This identity is given by equation 9.10.8:

$$\text{Var}\,(x_i + x_j) = \text{Var}\,(x_i) + \text{Var}\,(x_j) \qquad (9.10.8)$$

where $\text{Var}\,(x_i) = \sum_{i=1}^{n} (x_i - \bar{x}_i)^2 \cdot p(x_i)$, and $\text{Var}\,(x_j) = \sum_{i=1}^{m} (x_j - \bar{x}_j)^2 \cdot p(x_j)$. It will also be noticed that the standard deviation of the two-dice game is 2.415 so that all conceivable scores from this game are within approximately two standard deviations of the mean. The variability of this game has increased over and above that of the single dice game. This variability is shown by Figure 9.10.3, which plots the

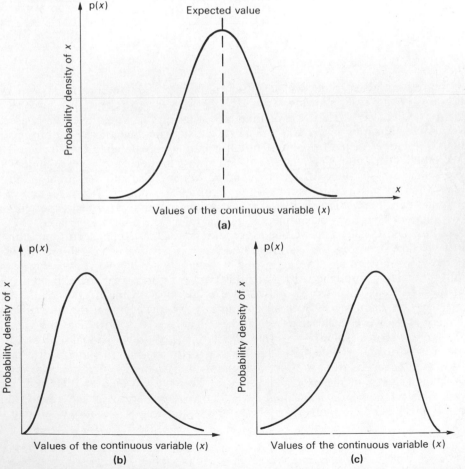

Figure 9.10.4 (a) A symmetrical bell-shaped probability density function (pdf). (b and c) Examples of asymmetrical probability density functions (pdfs).

Table 9.10.3 *The average scores, their mean, variance and standard deviation from throwing two dice*

Combined score x_k	Average score $\dfrac{x_k}{2}$	Probability of x_k $p(x_k)\times 36$	$x_k/2 \cdot p(x_k)$	$x_k/2-\bar{x}$	$(x_k/2-\bar{x})^2$	$(x_k/2-\bar{x})^2 p(x_k)$
2	1.0	1	1.0	−2.5	6.25	6.25
3	1.5	2	3.0	−2.0	4.00	8.00
4	2.0	3	6.0	−1.5	2.25	6.75
5	2.5	4	10.0	−1.0	1.00	4.00
6	3.0	5	15.0	−0.5	0.25	1.25
7	3.5	6	21.0	0.0	0.00	0.00
8	4.0	5	20.0	+0.5	0.25	1.25
9	4.5	4	18.0	+1.0	1.00	4.00
10	5.0	3	15.0	+1.5	2.25	6.75
11	5.5	2	11.0	+2.0	4.00	8.00
12	6.0	1	6.0	+2.5	6.25	6.25

$$\text{Totals} \qquad - \qquad \dfrac{\sum_{1}^{12} p(x_k)}{36}=1 \qquad \bar{x}=\dfrac{126}{36}=3.5 \qquad - \qquad - \qquad \mathrm{Var}(x_k)=\dfrac{525}{36}=1.458333$$

$$\sigma(x_k)=1.207615$$

probabilities (relative frequencies) of this game in a discrete form known as a histogram, in this case, showing symmetry. If we were to repeat this game, using many more dice, we would discover that such a histogram would eventually assume the structure shown by Fig. 9.10.4a. Several classical mathematical distributions are available to model such a bell shape, notably amongst them being the Normal, Beta and Weibull distributions. By contrast, other distributions are able to model the skewed shapes, illustrated in parts b and c, which arise out of other games of chance*. When histograms assume these continuous shapes they are known as probability density functions (pdfs), in statistical parlance, and they plot the outcome of the game of chance as a continuous, rather than as a discrete, variable.

As a last theoretical point, we need to understand what happens with our game of dice if we take averages. This is illustrated by Table 9.10.3 which shows the same total score arising from throwing two dice but now we take their average score simply by dividing throughout by 2. In this case we notice that the expected value from taking the average scores of two dice is identical to the average value from tossing one die, namely 3.5. Such an outcome is to be expected if the dice are truly independent. However a closer examination of Table 9.10.3 shows that the variance of the average scores (1.458) is less than the variance of the individual scores (2.917) as previously shown in Table 9.10.1, and it is actually one-half the latter! How do we explain this? It results from the fact that the average score of two dice is always as close, if not closer, to the expected value as the most extreme of their individual scores. This phenomenon leads to a well known law known as the central limit theorem which states 'whatever the shape and dispersion of the pdf containing the

---

* We shall not have need to study the mathematics of such classical distributions here or elsewhere in this book, since we only need to appreciate their graphical implications. However, the interested reader is advised to refer to some of the readings at the end of this chapter, for a more advanced understanding of such matters.

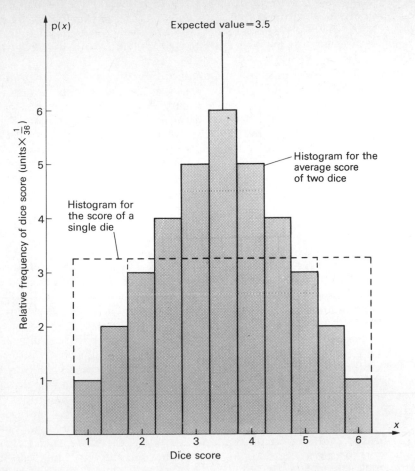

Figure 9.10.5 *A comparison of the histograms for the score of a single die with the average score of two dice.*

original outcome of a chance game, the shape of the pdf containing the averages of such chance games will become bell-shaped with a lower variance and standard deviation and when the number of results contained in the average becomes large, the distribution will become normal'. Such a law has a very special significance to problems of investment as we shall see later. Before we leave this point, however, it should be noted that the variance of an average obtained from independent games of chance is equal to the average of their individual variances* according to the following relationship:

$$\text{Var}(\bar{x}) = \frac{\text{Var}(x)}{n} \tag{9.10.9}$$

It follows from equation 9.10.9 that the standard deviation of the mean values of a game of chance is given by the expression:

$$\sigma(\bar{x}) = \frac{\sigma(x)}{\sqrt{n}} \tag{9.10.10}$$

---

* Some special conditions have to prevail for this to be true and such matters are dealt with in detail in the readings at the end of this chapter.

where $\sigma(\bar{x}) =$ the standard deviation of the means (average scores) of independent games of chance, $\sigma(x) =$ the standard deviation of the individual outcomes (scores) of the game of chance, and $n =$ the number of individual outcomes (scores) contained in each average score.

Equation 9.10.9 illustrates how the standard deviation of the mean values of a game of chance diminishes rapidly as the size of the sample, comprising the average, increases. It follows that the standard deviation of mean average values based on a sample of 4 is *half* that based on individual scores. Figure 9.10.5 is a physical manifestation of this principle. It shows how the highly dispersed individual scores of one die, represented by the rectangular distribution, become centralized (hence its name, the *central* limit theorem) and significantly bell-shaped when average scores are plotted, even when these averages are based on sample sizes as small as 2! It will, of course, be realized that the area under both the distributions of Figure 9.10.5 is unity.

9.11 A PRACTICAL APPROACH TO THE USE OF PROBABILITY THEORY IN CAPITAL BUDGETING

If we were both willing and able to predic⁺ the probabilities of the occurrences of future events which individually and/or collectively could place the economic merits of some prospect capital project in jeopardy, then the probability calculus of Section 9.10 could be put to good use. For example, it would allow us to choose between two projects either on the basis of one having the better average value for the same standard deviation, or on the basis of one having the smaller standard deviation for the same expected value*. Alternatively, confronted with results like those shown in Table 9.11.1, we might decide to reject Project A because of its higher chance of losing money, whereas others might prefer Project A because of its higher chance of making returns in excess of 5 million munits. In effect, therefore, such data as these would allow us to extend our decision analysis beyond the limits imposed by single aggregate DCF estimates. In business jargon the application of probability theory to this end is known as risk analysis.

Table 9.11.1 *The probabilities of the economic merits of two alternative projects*

| NPV (munits) | Chance of NPV falling within different ranges | | | | |
	Below −5 million	−5 million to 0	0 to 5 million	5–10 million	Above 10 million
Project A	15%	10%	30%	35%	10%
Project B	–	10%	70%	15%	5%

To develop these notions further into a practical decision-making tool requires a method for deriving these probability estimates. To some extent the roots of such data are contained within each company's information system. For example, the *track record* of the firm's capital cost estimators can readily be compiled by comparing their historical budget estimates with the actual invoiced costs of each completed project, and by this method one *could* develop a histogram (pdf) of the errors which they had made in their past forecasts. Depending on the similarity of these past projects, the experience of the estimators and their length of service with the company, the state of the capital project market and indeed many other

* This statement is only valid if the probability distributions are symmetrical.

considerations which are too numerous to elaborate here, we *just might* be willing to use this historical evidence to derive a histogram (pdf) of the capital costs of some *future* project, which is considered sufficiently similar to justify this approach. Alternatively, if we felt that such historical data were inappropriate, then we might seek better data elsewhere, possibly from the experience of other companies.

In the last resort one might be forced to develop such probability estimates on the basis of *subjective* expert opinion, either with or without the benefits of hindsight. Such an idea is not so ridiculous as it might first appear for there is a growing body of opinion which suggests that subjective probabilities have much merit, especially if the method employed in their evaluation is conducted in a scientific manner (see the Delphi technique, p. 258). Savage (1954) has shown that, for a given person, it is possible to treat these *subjective* probabilities in the same way as one would treat objective probabilities for they obey the same rules of transformation*.

This applies equally well to the projected prices, sales volumes, operating costs and all the other economic and physical factors which feature in our life-cycle economic equation. Given the *will* and some *care* it therefore transpires that the probabilities of the economic outcomes of a proposed capital project could be derived using the following generic method.

Let us imagine that the probability data of Table 9.11.2 are made available, and one can reasonably assume that the two sets of data are independent. Our problem,

Table 9.11.2 *The calculation of the probability of each sales revenue*

Sales volume (tonnes pa) V_i	Probability of sales volume $p(V_i)$	Sales price (munits/tonne) Z_i	Probability of sales price $p(Z_i)$
1000	0.1	3	0.4
2000	0.5	4	0.3
3000	0.4	5	0.3

Calculation of sales revenue R (munits pa) $V_i \times Z_i = R_i$	Calculation of the probability of sales revenue: $p(R)$ $p(V_i) \times p(Z_i) = p(R_i)$
$1000 \times 3 = 3\,000$	$0.1 \times 0.4 = 0.04$
$1000 \times 4 = 4\,000$	$0.1 \times 0.3 = 0.03$
$1000 \times 5 = 5\,000$	$0.1 \times 0.3 = 0.03$
$2000 \times 3 = 6\,000$	$0.5 \times 0.4 = 0.20$
$2000 \times 4 = 8\,000$	$0.5 \times 0.3 = 0.15$
$3000 \times 3 = 9\,000$	$0.4 \times 0.4 = 0.16$
$2000 \times 5 = 10\,000$	$0.5 \times 0.3 = 0.15$
$3000 \times 4 = 12\,000$	$0.4 \times 0.3 = 0.12$
$3000 \times 5 = 15\,000$	$0.4 \times 0.3 = 0.12$
	$\sum_{i=1}^{9} p(R_i) = 1.00$

therefore, is to calculate the probability distribution of the resulting sales revenues. This is quite a simple matter as Table 9.11.2 shows, and involves nothing more than the application of equation 9.10.3. For example, a sales revenue of 10 000 munits is made manifest by the sales volume being 2000 tonnes and the price being 5 munits

---

* An excellent introductory account of this is given by Schlaifer (1959).

per tonne, so it follows that the probability of this event is given by:

$$p(10\ 000\ \text{munits}) = p(2000\ \text{tonnes } and\ 5\ \text{munits per tonne})$$
$$= p(2000\ \text{tonnes}) \times p(5\ \text{munits per tonne})$$
$$= 0.5 \times 0.3$$
$$= 0.15$$

All the other calculations of Table 9.11.2 are executed in the same way and we see that, according to the addition law of probability, the summation of the probabilities of all possible sales revenues must equal unity. It will however be appreciated that a considerable number of calculations were necessary to derive the results of Table 9.11.2, and that many more would be required to obtain the distribution of the NPV of some real prospective project. Table 9.11.2 shows that for two factors, volume and price, each with three different values, the total number of combinations is nine. If, however, there were ten different factors in the assessment each with ten different prospective values (as could be the case for a real project) then the total number of combinations would be 10^{10} or 10 000 million! This is not just a lot of arithmetic, it is an *impossible* amount even with computers, so a different approach to combining the probabilities of joint events *has* to be found!

To deal with problems of this kind statisticians resort to statistical sampling. In essence, this means that no attempt is made to test all possibilities or calculate all combinations, but instead they settle for a limited number which is considered enough for all practicable purposes if it yields results which give the required degree of confidence*. To achieve this end, random samples are taken from each of the distributions of attributes contributing to the objective of the study (in our case the NPV) in such a way that the resultant distributions of the samples are not very different to the original distributions from whence they came. To accomplish such sampling requires the use of a random number generator (RNG) which could comprise:

  (i) picking numbers from a hat,
 (ii) tossing several coins,
(iii) rolling a few dice,
 (iv) picking cards from a pack,
  (v) spinning a roulette wheel,
 (vi) using a table of random numbers, or
(vii) using a computer specially programmed for the task of sampling by random number generation.

This is not meant to be an exhaustive list of the methods available for generating random numbers, but simply illustrates some of the better known techniques, the selection of the preferred technique depending on the time and resources available, and the nature and speed with which the task has to be accomplished. We shall now demonstrate the application of two of these methods using the dice game for which we already possess probability data, and the computerized approach based in the Monte Carlo simulation technique. To do this we need the probability forecasts of some future project, so let us assume that the sales executives of some hypothetical firm have forecast the following sales volume and price probabilities, which we shall continue to assume independent.

Sales (tonnes pa)	5000	6000	7000	8000	9000
Probability of sales	0.08	0.25	0.42	0.17	0.08
Price (munits/tonne)	40	45	50	55	
Probability of price	0.14	0.42	0.30	0.14	

---

* The concept of confidence is germane to statistical theory, but outside the scope of this book.

If we also assume that the actual outcome of the firm's sales revenue has all the features of a game of chance, then it follows that we can *model* the outcome of the firm's sales revenue on the basis of our previous two dice game. This is made possible by the fact that there exists a direct correspondence between the scores of our dice game and the probability forecasts of our hypothetical firm, as listed above. It will be remembered that the joint scores resulting from our two dice game gave rise to the following probability data:

Joint score:	2	3	4	5	6	7	8	9	10	11	12
absolute probability of joint score:	1/36	2/36	3/36	4/36	5/36	6/36	5/36	4/36	3/36	2/36	1/36
approximate probability of joint score:	0.03	0.06	0.08	0.11	0.14	0.16	0.14	0.11	0.08	0.06	0.03

It *could* therefore be said that joint scores of 5 or 9 or 12 represent the possibility of our hypothetical firm selling 6000 tonnes of product per annum because their combined probabilities are identical to the probability of such a sales level, viz:

$$p(5 \text{ or } 9 \text{ or } 12) = p(5) + p(9) + p(12)$$
$$= 0.11 + 0.11 + 0.03$$
$$= 0.25$$
$$= p(6000 \text{ tonnes per annum})$$

Similarly, it *could* be said that a joint score of 8 represents the possibility of the sales price being 40 munits per tonne because their probabilities of occurrence are identical, viz:

$$p(8) = 0.14 = p(40 \text{ munits per tonne})$$

By these means we could obtain the total correspondence between the anticipated results of our real-world investment decision and our dice game of chance, as shown by Table 9.11.3. By rolling two dice we therefore possess a means of simulating the outcome of the chance events which govern the sales volumes and prices of some future project, such that one joint score of, say, 6 would represent a sales volume of 7000 tonnes per annum and another score of 9 would represent a sales price of 50 munits per tonne. In concert, therefore, these two independent games of chance would represent the realization of a sales revenue of 350 000 munits per annum. If

Table 9.11.3 *The correspondence between the scores of a two-dice game of chance and the sales prices and volumes of our hypothetical project*

		Probability	Corresponding joint scores in a two-dice game with the same overall probability
Sales volumes (tonnes pa)	5000	0.08	10
	6000	0.25	5, 9, 12
	7000	0.42	2, 3, 6, 8, 11
	8000	0.17	7
	9000	0.08	4
Sales prices (munits/tonne)	40	0.14	8
	45	0.42	2, 6, 7, 11, 12
	50	0.30	4, 5, 9
	55	0.14	3, 10

Table 9.11.4 *Simulating the sales revenue of our hypothetical project using two-dice as a random number generator*

Throw No.	Joint score	Corresponding value of the sales volume (V_i)	Throw No.	Joint scoe	Corresponding value of the sales price (Z_i)	Combined value of the sales revenue $R_i = V_i \times Z_i$
1	9	6000	11	7	45	270 000
2	5	6000	12	5	50	300 000
3	9	6000	13	9	50	300 000
4	10	5000	14	11	45	225 000
5	8	7000	15	10	55	385 000
6	7	8000	16	5	50	400 000
7	12	6000	17	5	50	300 000
8	7	8000	18	6	45	360 000
9	6	7000	19	6	45	315 000
10	8	7000	20	5	50	350 000

Expected value of sales revenue (munits) = 320 500

Sales revenue R_i (munits $\times 10^4$)	Frequency of R_i	Probability of R_i $p(R_i)$
20–22.5	1	0.1
+22.5–25.0	–	0.0
+25.0–27.5	1	0.1
+27.5–30.0	111	0.3
+30.0–32.5	1	0.1
+32.5–35.0	1	0.1
+35.0–37.5	1	0.1
+37.5–40.0	11	0.2
+40.0–42.5	–	0.0
+42.5–45.0	–	0.0
+45.0–47.5	–	0.0
+47.5–50.0	–	0.0

we proceed in this fashion we can develop the complete histogram for the anticipated sales revenue from this hypothetical project. Such a simulation exercise is illustrated in Table 9.11.4 which represents the actual outcome from rolling two dice. In this case, the simulation game has been terminated after 20 rolls of the dice to demonstrate a few important features. In the first place we notice the complete absence of the joint dice scores 2, 3 and 4 demonstrating that there is absolutely no reason why these results should appear by right but, of course, we would expect them to feature if we repeated this game many times. The second point is that the average value of all 20 throws is 7.5 which is very close to the theoretical value of 7. When we compare the histogram of the simulated results of this game with their theoretical counterparts (derived in the same manner as described by Table 9.11.2), using the ranges of sales revenue indicated in Table 9.11.4 and Figure 9.11.1, we see that the simulation exercise is devoid of results in some frequency bands, but that its histogram is already fast approaching that of the theoretical distribution despite the paucity of the simulation trials. Furthermore, the expected (mean average) value of the sales revenue for the simulation exercise is extremely close to that of the theoretical distribution as is shown in Figure 9.11.1. In effect therefore we see that simulation is an excellent substitute for the more orthodox method of calculating the joint probabilities of the outcome of some project. It follows that the greater the number of simulation trials, the closer become the results of these alternative techniques. In the limit, when the number of simulation trials is extremely large, their histograms become identical. From a practical viewpoint it follows that we have to balance the marginal cost of conducting more simulation

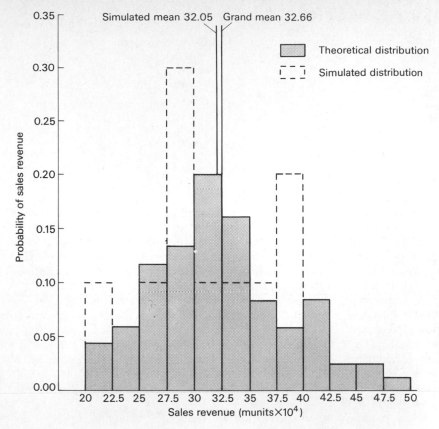

Figure 9.11.1 *A comparison of the theoretical and simulated distributions for a firm's sales revenue.*

trials against their added benefit. Since the marginal cost is usually small, using computerized simulation techniques, it is customary to repeat such trials 2000–3000 times.

The generic method which we have just studied is known as Monte Carlo simulation, deriving its name from the somewhat obvious gambling connections. Outside of its benefit as a classroom exercise, the multi-dice variant of this technique is not seriously recommended, especially for assessing the economic merits of a real capital project. Instead, its computerized version is advocated. To accommodate this version we need to expand our understanding of probability theory just one step further.

The two-dice game is constrained by the probabilities of its joint scores, each score possessing a probability which is some multiple of 1/36. As it stands, therefore, the game cannot accommodate some chance event having, say, a probability of 0.02 unless, of course, we make our simulation very approximate. To overcome this weakness we resort to a different form of probability distribution which we have not previously mentioned, namely the cumulative distribution function. A cumulative distribution function (cdf) is simply the summation of the probability density function for some chance attribute. Returning to our dice game, we know that the probability of a single throw of a dice yielding a 1 is 1/6, and similarly for a 2 or 3, et cetera. It therefore follows that the probability of the score of the single throw of a dice giving a result which is *less than* 1 is zero. Similarly, the probability that the score is *less than or equal to* 1 is 1/6, less than or equal to 2 is 2/6, and so on. In effect therefore the cdf of our single dice game is:

Score	Probability of score (cdf)
<1	0
≤1	1/6
≤2	2/6
≤3	3/6
≤4	4/6
≤5	5/6
≤6	6/6

where < = less than, and ≤ = less than or equal to whatever number follows.

If we plot such a cdf then we obtain the typical staircase distribution shown in Figure 9.11.2a for the single die, and Figure 9.11.2b for the two-dice games. Furthermore, if the variables of interest are continuous rather than discrete, then the corresponding cdf could assume a shape similar to one of the curves shown in Figure 9.11.2c, the exact shapes depending on the nature of their distribution equations.

It follows that each probability density function (pdf), whether of discrete or continuous form, can readily be converted into its corresponding cumulative density function (cdf) which in turn helps to expedite the Monte Carlo simulation on the basis of a random number generator as previously outlined. *In this case*, however, the outcome of the game of chance is that value, on the cumulative distribution function, corresponding to the value of the random number plotted as the cumulative probability*. For example, a random number (RN) of 5/12 would correspond with the random outcome of the number 3 if such a simulation were conducted on the basis of Figure 9.11.2a. Alternatively a random number (RN) of 20/36 would correspond with the value 7 on the basis of Figure 9.11.2b, and a similar outcome is shown in Figure 9.11.2c.

To develop the complete histogram of the NPV of some prospective project requires:

(i) the pdf for each of the variables of our life-cycle economic equation so that their corresponding cdfs can be used,
(ii) a computerized means of random number generation,
(iii) a computer program devised to sample each cdf independently using the results of (ii) above,
(iv) an extension to the program of (iii) above, which will permit the forecast cash flows resulting from each random sampling (each iteration) to be calculated,
(v) an extension to the program of (iv) above, which will permit the corresponding NPV to be calculated and stored,
(vi) a computerized means of repeating steps (iii)–(v) for many iterations (possibly as many as 2000–3000), and
(vii) an extension to the program of (v) above, which will permit the complete histogram (pdf) of the resulting NPVs to be displayed in a form which is useful for decision-making purposes.

A pictorial display of this complete procedure is given in Figure 9.11.3.

This technique forms part of the frontier in the practical application of decision analysis to capital budgeting problems, and has received wide publicity over the years due in part to the efforts of Hertz (1964). Exactly how management should use

---

* The rationale behind the use of a cdf and random numbers in this way is that each outcome of the game of chance (it could be the capital cost, operating costs or any other variable from our life-cycle economic equation) will be selected on this basis with the same frequency as such outcomes would appear in the real world.

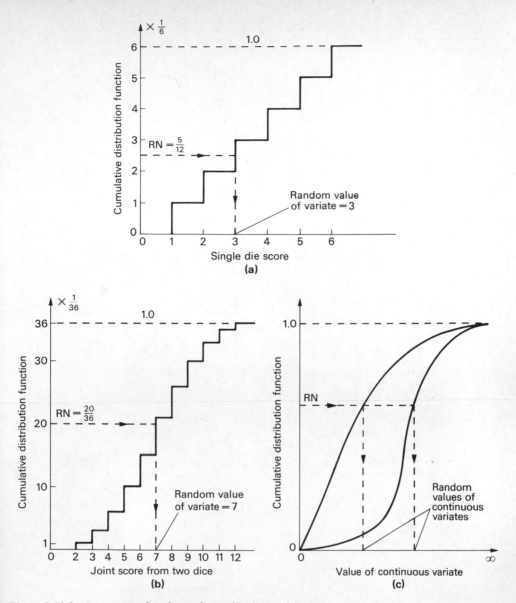

Figure 9.11.2 *Some examples of cumulative distribution functions.*

the results of such an analysis very much depends on their aversion to risk, or their propensity to gample – two factors which are determined by the characters of the decision makers. The nature of such a decision also depends on the probability of the project being economically unviable or extremely lucrative, the magnitude of its possible loss relative to the firm's resources and, of course, on the firm's ability to spread its risk by financing a portfolio of projects. There exists no right or wrong decision – except in hindsight! Nevertheless, from the content of this chapter it follows that we are especially interested in the expected value and the deviation of results derived from such an analysis. Of course, one must be careful not to be mesmerized by the apparent accuracy of this technique, always remembering that the adage 'rubbish in, rubbish out' applies to all decision analysis problems. With

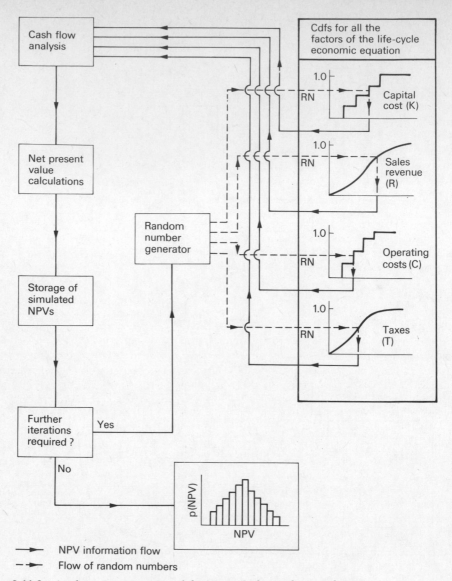

Figure 9.11.3   *A schematic presentation of the Monte Carlo simulation technique.*

this in mind, it is most relevant to note that our analogy between games of chance and real-world investment problems rests on the premise that the attributes forming an inherent part of the simulation exercise are *independent*. When this is not so, and the attributes possess some inter-dependence, the histogram (pdf) of their inter-related outcome should be used in their stead*. Despite our frequent use of the sales revenue examples, it transpires that the separate use of probability data for sales volumes and prices is *incorrect*, excepting the presence of pure and perfect competition, because under normal conditions of imperfect competition there exists a definite inverse relationship between these two parameters.

---

* Herein lies the roots of a problem in that many of the economic factors of our life cycle economic equation are interdependent, thereby necessitating the use of Conditional Probability Theory.

The greatest difficulty associated with this simulation technique involves the estimation of the probability data. Confronted with this problem, many analysts may point out that it is difficult enough to forecast the single figure estimates of the outcomes of future events let alone their complete probability distributions! Despite their protestations, however, evidence shows that most executives and engineers do think in terms of extreme limits and are quite prepared to give estimates of the best, worst and most likely outcomes of some future attribute. On the basis of such estimates, mathematical statisticians have devised ways of estimating the complete pdfs of such chance events. This involves using classical distribution functions such as the Normal and Beta distributions, one good practical account of their use being given by Malloy (1971a). Of course, any doubts over the accuracy of the data forming a part of such a simulation exercise could be investigated by a sensitivity analysis of the kind discussed in Section 9.3.

Although the publication of economic data on the post-mortems of capital projects is rare, the evidence which does exist suggests that single-figure estimates of the economic merits of capital projects are usually *over-optimistic,* and some studies have shown that this over-optimism could have been exposed by simulation exercises of the type promoted here. Based on historical data, Malloy (1971b) showed that only 26 per cent of the projects in his study lived up to their single-figure expectations. Furthermore, he proved conclusively that such a result could have been forecast by Monte Carlo simulation. It would therefore appear that much money could be made (or saved) by the application of this technique, which after all is nothing more than a formal approach to focus attention on the problems of uncertainty and risk.

A common criticism of the use of probability theory as a capital budgeting tool is that its whole philosophy rests on the tenet that the particular game of chance can be played many times. We demonstrated this earlier, pointing out that a true coin would only be expected to land heads or tails with equal frequency if it were tossed *many, many times.* Moreover, we demonstrated that the assumption of repeatability is central to a proper understanding of the expected value concept. By stark contrast the funding of a substantial capital project represents a special opportunity which, more often than not, cannot be repeated – at least under the same environmental conditions. How then are we justified in applying probability theory to such a problem? Our only justification rests in the assumption that over a long period a firm will need to finance *many* capital projects if it intends staying in business. Provided their economic outcomes are *independent,* such investments can be regarded as multiple trials of an economic game of chance, obeying the same rules of probability theory as those already propounded. In this vein, it follows that the expected value of a firm's long-term economic strategy is the sum of the expected values of its sanctioned projects, the NPV being the economic measure of these expected values. On this basis one accepts the fact that, due solely to chance events, the economic merits of individual investment projects will either be better than, equal to, or worse than their expected values, but in aggregate one would expect their net effect to be very close to the sum of their individual expected NPVs providing the probability forecasts are reasonably accurate and they are truly independent.

Unfortunately, the expected value criterion says nothing about the possibility of a firm investing in a series of failures, resulting in its ruin well before it can realize this long-term expected benefit. Such a possibility may be remote – like the chance of realizing 20 heads in 20 tosses of a coin – but it could happen. It is for this reason that firms pay particular attention to the element of risk inherent in new capital projects, both singularly and in aggregate, as well as in the context of the operations of the firm as a whole. (We shall return to the implications of managing risk in Chapter 11.) To reduce the probability of a run of loss-making projects, managers diversify their selection of projects so that the possibility of a business decline in one market area might be compensated by business improvement in another area. In some respects, therefore, diversification incorporates the principle that the variability of the average cash flows from several projects is smaller than the variability of their individual cash flows. A proper appreciation of the implications of diversification is given in the next section.

9.12   RISK ANALYSIS USING UTILITY THEORY

The inference of Section 9.11 is that, given accurate forecasts of the probabilities and the economic outcomes of future events, their expected value and variance are sufficient criteria for any economic decision under conditions of uncertainty, and this remains so irrespective of whether the probabilities are based on objective measurement or subjective estimation, providing the projects are independent. This view has been strongly challenged on two accounts. In the first place it is suggested that people make decisions influenced by their current financial status and their attitude towards the possibility of losing money, as well as on the basis of the two previous criteria. Secondly, the assumption that subjective probabilities can be manipulated in the same way as their objective counterparts has been questioned. We shall deal with both these issues in turn, and then examine what currently appears to be the only technical means of resolving them.

To illustrate the first issue, let us suppose that a hypothetical entrepreneur has the opportunity to invest in three mutually exclusive projects of the same first cost and one year lives, having the forecast attributes shown in Table 9.12.1.

Table 9.12.1   *The payoff matrix for three mutually exclusive projects available to a hypothetical entrepreneur*

State of nature	Probability	Project NPVs A	B	C
1	0.5	−10	−1000	−10 000
2	0.5	310	1400	10 500
NPVs (in money terms)		150	200	250

If his decision is based exclusively on the maximization of the expected NPV to be realized by a project, then Project C is the preferred choice. Whereas our entrepreneur might be able and willing to risk losing 10 munits on Project A with the even chance of gaining 310 munits, it is possible that he would feel uneasy about financing Project B for fear of losing 1000 munits, and he might be positively reluctant to finance Project C, despite its greater expected value, because the chance of losing 10 000 munits could lead to his financial ruin. Risk, then, is about losing money and it follows that an economic decision is much more complicated than our previous analysis would suggest. It follows, too, that people make decisions which they believe they can afford to make, recognizing that the odds could turn to their disadvantage. In the same vein we must recognize that monetary rewards or penalties can be valued differently, depending on the financial status of the decision maker, and his attitude towards risk and uncertainty.

Although a proper account of the similarities and differences between subjective and objective probabilities is beyond the scope of this book*, nevertheless it is important to realize that some researchers have challenged their similarity, and, on the basis of empirical evidence, have shown that their results can be quite different when reviewing the same game of chance. For example Edwards (1961) showed that one's subjective probabilities could change depending on the rewards of winning or losing in a betting game, and other empirical studies have suggested that one's subjective probabilities of all the outcomes of a game of chance do not necessarily sum to unity. This would suggest that the application of probability theory to decisions of economic choice cannot, nay must not, be used unquestionably – especially when probabilities are derived by subjective assessment, as is often the case!

To help resolve these matters we have to resort once more to using the concept of utility initially formulated in Chapter 2, and used quite extensively in Chapter 6. On this occasion however, our employment of this concept is slightly different in that we use the decision calculus attributed to von Neumann and Morgenstern (1944). Their technique, which is generally referred to as decision theory analysis, incorporates the same notions of welfare as does the classical economic concept, but also allows for the element of risk. To illustrate the application of this technique let us consider the following example. Suppose a person could win 10 000 or lose 6000 munits on the luck of a draw on the understanding that if he did not wish to play the game of chance he could buy his way out. On this basis it stands to reason that the gambler would be willing to accept 10 000 munits to be released from playing the game in the certain knowledge of winning because, under such conditions of certainty, he would be indifferent between being bought out and playing the game. In other words, the consequences would be identical. Similarly, in the certain knowledge of losing the game he would be willing to pay 6000 munits to be released from the game. The point of greater interest to us, however, is how much he would be willing to accept/pay to be released from playing the game if the odds of winning or losing made the outcome of the game less certain. The answer to this rests on the character of the gambler and his attitude towards winning or losing sums of money in this range. To proceed further, we shall assume that such receipts or payments and the corresponding known odds of winning or losing separate games of chance are:

Probability of winning ($\times 100\%$)	Sum paid/accepted to be released from playing the game	
0.125	5000	
0.250	4000	
0.375	3000	sums paid
0.500	2000	
0.615	1000	
0.700	0	
0.760	1000	
0.800	2000	
0.850	4000	sums accepted
0.900	6000	
0.950	8000	

On the basis of such evidence we could compile that person's utility–risk curve which would then permit us to overcome some of our previous conceptual difficulties. To accomplish this we have to accept the fact that utility, satisfaction, welfare – call it what you will – have no standards of measurement, so in the context of our

---

* An excellent collection of readings on this matter is provided by Kyburg and Smokler (1964).

hypothetical problem we have every right to assign a payment of 6000 munits (that is a gain of −6000) the arbitrary value of *zero utility* and the gain of 10 000 munits the arbitrary value of *unit utility*. The utility of the sum which would have the same value to the decision maker as the gamble giving a 12.5 per cent chance of unit utility and an 87.5 per cent chance of zero utility is calculated from the relationship:

$$0.125 \times 1 + 0.875 \times 0 = 0.125$$

This means that for our example the utility of −5000 is 0.125. In the same fashion the utility of −4000 is 0.25 with the utility values:

$$0.375, 0.5, 0.615, 0.7, 0.76, 0.8, 0.85, 0.9 \text{ and } 0.95$$

corresponding to the monetary values:

$$-3000, -2000, -1000, 0, 1000, 2000, 4000, 6000 \text{ and } 8000$$

respectively.

We can now draw the implied utility–risk map for such a person, and this is shown in Figure 9.12.1. In passing, it should be noted that the concavity of this map reflects a conservative attitude towards risk taking and an aversion to risking the loss of money. This point is emphasized by the fact that a monetary loss of 2000 munits results in a greater fall in utility than does its corresponding monetary gain. Put another way, this implies that such a person would require odds of better than a 50:50 chance of winning before he would be willing to play a game which involved the prospect of winning or losing 2000 munits. Also shown in Figure 9.12.1 is the straight line joining the origin (*w*) to point (*z*). This line forms the locus of points for the expected monetary values of all conceivable games of chance resulting from these data.

Once we possess such a utility–risk map, many different types of economic analysis become possible. For example, faced with the opportunity of placing a bet with a 20

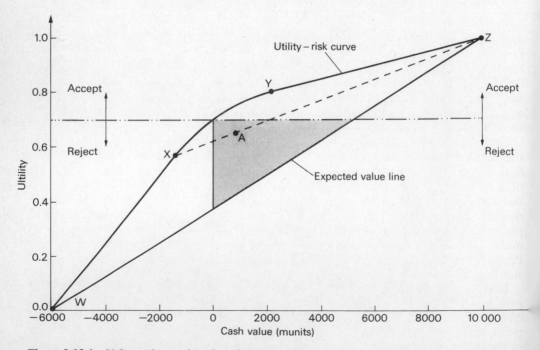

Figure 9.12.1 *Utility–risk map for a hypothetical example.*

per cent chance of winning 10 000 munits and an 80 per cent chance of losing 1500 munits we discover that such a bet can be represented by point A in Figure 9.12.1. Graphically, this results from joining together the two points Z and X, with the corresponding coordinates (10 000, 1.0) and (−1500, 0.56), by the straight dotted line, and measuring off the distance XA so that it represents 20 per cent of the length of that line. Alternatively, since the expected monetary value of this game of chance, at point A, is given by:

$$E_A(x) = 0.8 \times (-1500) + 0.2 \times 10\ 000$$
$$= 800$$

then it follows that point A is located at the confluence of a vertical line drawn through the abscissa at the value 800, and line ZX. Using the identity that the expected utility of a game of chance obeys the same mathematical rules of summation as any other expected value and can be derived from the relationship:

$$E(u) = \sum_{i=1}^{n} U_i p(x_i) \tag{9.12.1}$$

where $E(u)$ = the expected utility of the game, U_i = the utility of each ith outcome of that game, and $p(x_i)$ = the probability of each ith outcome, where $i = (1, n)$, then it follows that the expected utility of point A is given by the expression:

$$E_A(u) = 1 \times 0.2 + 0.56 \times 0.8$$
$$= 0.65$$

so that a horizontal line drawn through the ordinate (0.65) would also intersect the dotted line at point A, thereby permitting point A to be located by several, internally consistent means. Once having located point A, however, it is important to note that its expected utility is worse than the utility of the alternative of doing nothing, so a rational decision would be to reject the opportunity to play such a game *despite its having a positive expected monetary value.* For the same reason a rational decision maker would also reject all of those betting opportunities represented by the shaded area of Figure 9.12.1 and it goes without saying that opportunities with negative expected monetary values would be rejected for the same reason. In effect, therefore, Figure 9.12.1 can be divided in two representing accept/reject decisions, thereby demonstrating the theoretical power of this simple tool.

One interesting phenomenon, which can be illustrated quite readily on a map like this is the effect of reducing the scale of a bet, or any game of chance. For example, if both the possible losses and gains of our previous bet were scaled down by a factor of 1000, we would discover that the expected monetary value would *decrease* to 0.8, but the expected utility would *increase* to approximately 0.712. As such, the rational decision maker would *now* be willing to accept such a game or project. This phenomenon is well recognized in the insurance world and explains the motives for underwriting an insurance project. In the context of our hypothetical example, Project A is unacceptable to an individual, but to a consortium of 1000 people, each sharing the risks and the pay-offs equally, then Project A becomes acceptable!

Besides the obvious relevance and importance of scale, this map also permits us to gain insight into other important issues which previously we have been frustrated from evaluating for want of a proper methodology. It will be appreciated that any point, such as A, can be located by any number of straight lines joining remote parts of the utility–risk curve WXYZ. As such, any given point represents combinations of opportunities possessing the same expected utility and monetary values yet different

Table 9.12.2 *The economic attributes of fictitious capital investment projects subject to risk and uncertainty*

Project	NPV of chance outcome x_1	x_2	Probability of chance outcome $p(x_1)$	$p(x_2)$	Expected NPV $E(x)$	Standard deviation of NPV σ (NPV)	Expected utility value $E(u)$
A	1 600	0	0.5	0.5	800	800	0.74
B	2 000	−6 000	0.9	0.1	1 200	2 400	0.72
C	0	0	1.0	0.0	0	0	0.70
D	6 000	−2 000	0.5	0.5	2 000	4 000	0.70
F	4 000	−6 000	0.8	0.2	2 000	4 000	0.68
G	10 000	−1 500	0.2	0.8	800	4 600	0.65
D+F[a]					4 000	5 657	0.765
2×G[a]					1 600	6 505	0.6

[a] Some economic results for the joint probabilities of these composite projects lie outside the range of Figure 9.12.1, so their corresponding utilities have been derived by extrapolation.

monetary variances. This proves that choosing between projects with the same expected value on the basis of their variances is not advisable.

Having set the basis for our utility–risk analysis and destroyed a few decision-making myths in the process, it is now appropriate to demonstrate the use of this tool when applied to the capital budgeting decision, which is the whole reason for developing it here in the first place. In line with our conclusions of Chapters 5 and 6, let us substitute the NPV for the monetary value of a project and the fictitious examples of Table 9.12.2 to demonstrate some more interesting points*.

In the interests of economy, and to ensure that we concentrate on points of principle, the probability calculations of Table 9.12.2 are not given here. They can easily be derived using the methods of Section 9.11. Likewise, their expected utility values can be calculated using equation 9.12.1. These five individual projects have been ranked in descending order of expected utility using the data from our previous utility map, and on this basis we note that a rational decision maker would accept Projects A and B, would be quite indifferent to Project D, and would reject Projects F and G. On the basis of Projects A and B being mutually exclusive, it follows that Project A would be preferred *despite its smaller expected NPV*. To some extent this results from its having the smaller standard deviation, but such a choice also reflects the fact that, by accepting Project B, the decision maker could stand to lose money. Similarly, Project A is to be preferred to Project G, with the same expected NPV, because of its smaller standard deviation *and* the fact that it possesses no anticipated chance of losing money. A study of Projects D and F completes this one-for-one comparison, showing that the project with the smaller possible loss is the preferred choice, despite both projects having identical expected NPVs and standard deviations. As things stand, however, our capital budgeting decision analysis is not yet complete because it is conceivable that combinations of projects could collectively possess attributes which are superior to their constituents. In other words, it is conceivable that some projects might enhance one another through some sort of synergy. We have already noted that underwriting is one example of this phenomenon, but the point which we wish to expose here involves a different aspect which we previously called diversification. In a practical sense, this means that businessmen like to spread their risks between several projects in the belief that some will be

* Several special problems of interpretation ensue when the NPV is employed as the economic decision criterion instead of simple cash flows. A proper treatment of this complex matter is outside the scope of this book, but receives a full coverage by Hayes (1975).

lucrative, others mediocre and that some might be economic failures. Providing such projects are independent, however, the rationale of such a diversification policy is that the aggregate result will be satisfactory from the point of view of its magnitude, variation and the chance that an economic loss might be sustained. Reference to the lower part of Table 9.12.2 shows that such a diversification policy would prove most beneficial if Projects D and F were considered together as a portfolio. Previously we would have rejected Project F out of hand, and we would have been quite indifferent to Project D. In concert, however, they offer a combined project which is the preferred choice in this table.

We were in a position to calculate their joint expected value and standard deviation in Section 9.10 but only now with the benefits of our utility–risk map are we able to resolve the full economic implications of such a diversification policy. By stark contrast, however, a joint project comprising two of Project G would result in a portfolio possessing an overall poorer utility attribute than its constituents. This proves the point that the benefits/detriments of diversification are quite subtle. They are inextricably linked to the magnitude of the possible cash flows accruing to a project, their probability of occurrence *and* the extent of possible losses.

In effect, therefore, such a map as Figure 9.12.1 allows us to appreciate the much neglected trade-off which exists between the two quite separate and distinct desires to minimize the variability of some chance outcome and also minimize the financial loss which could transpire. It also leads us to the conclusion (which we realized intuitively anyway) that three factors have to be appraised *collectively*, if the optimal selection of capital projects is to be achieved, namely: the expected monetary value, its variance, *and* the loss. Of course, the objective of such a decision is to strike the correct balance between these opposing factors, but this cannot be done without such a utility–risk map.

Our treatment of this subject would not be complete without mentioning a few more points. It will be realized that the outcome of all the calculations contained in Table 9.12.1 depends in large measure on the precise shape of the utility–risk map. Conceivably quite different shaped maps could be obtained in practice, some showing a high propensity to gamble while others might exhibit unusual shapes*. In the main, however, it would appear that for most serious decision-making situations a concave map of the type illustrated by Figure 9.12.1 prevails. Evidence of the tendency for conservative decision making in industrial organizations is provided by Green (1959). Again on a technical matter, it should be stressed that the selection or rejection of projects contained in the same straight part of a utility–risk curve yields the same decisions of preference on an expected monetary basis as on a utility basis. Furthermore, it is important for the reader to realize that decision theory has developed to a point far in advance of the simple but practical contents of this chapter; a major thrust to such work was made by Markowitz (1959). Moreover probability calculus is able to deal with and resolve problems of interdependence. Although a practical use for these more complicated techniques does exist – their use being mainly confined to stock exchange evaluations – they cannot readily be applied to capital investment decisions due mainly to a lack of adequate data. This brings us to the focus of this chapter! Despite the obvious elegance of the utility–risk theory promulgated here, there is little evidence of its practical use in business. This results from the difficulty of developing the data for a single decision maker, and the virtual impossibility of developing it for a coalition of decision makers. Grayson (1960) endeavoured to pioneer the practical application of this decision tool only to find that the top decision makers of one company possessed quite different utility–risk

---

* For example Chernoff and Moses (1959) suggest that utility–risk maps tend to become sigmoid in shape if the range of payoffs is sufficiently large.

preferences, and Swalm (1966) reported a similar discovery. In effect, therefore, while this tool offers great potential, we seem unable to realize it.

9.13   CONCLUSIONS

We have spent considerable time here establishing an understanding of risk and uncertainty only to realize that, in the main, the techniques developed to help in such matters fall short of their initial promise. Currently no authoritative decision rules exist which permit the decision maker to deal properly with risk and uncertainty in a quantitative sense, despite the existence of libraries of books on the subject. Hopefully, however, this literature is to some avail, and offers decision makers and would-be decision makers the opportunity of gaining further insight into such problems. As things stand, several companies have used Monte Carlo simulation to good avail (or at least they believe so) for it has provided them with an easy to understand, yet fairly cheap vehicle to focus attention on the problems of risk and uncertainty. In the majority of cases their use of this tool has been pragmatic, without too much concern for the finer statistical points of interdependence and the problems which exist when employing subjective probabilities.

The major point to derive from our treatment of this subject, however, must be the fact that an optimal capital investment decision must incorporate knowledge of the possible variations in the cash flows anticipated for the project, their probabilities of occurrence *and* the likelihood of loss. This suggests that we must look beyond the limitations of the expected NPV of a project when making such decisions. Intuitively we knew this beforehand, so the contents of this chapter have really only confirmed our feelings, and then only in a qualitative sense.

9.14   BIBLIOGRAPHY

General texts

Imperial Chemical Industries Limited, *Assessing Projects, A Programme for Learning*, Book 5, *Risk Analysis*, Methuen, 1970. This booklet forms part of a collection of six, all designed to introduce the reader to specific aspects of the capital budgeting decision.

Kyburg, H. E. and Smokler, H. E. (Ed.), *Studies in Subjective Probability*, Wiley, 1964. This book contains a fine collection of readings concerning the similarities and differences of objective and subjective probabilities.

Savage, L. J., *The Foundation of Statistics*, Wiley, 1954. This book provides an excellent account of subjectivity probability and its similarity to objectivity probability.

Schlaifer, R., *Probability of Statistics for Business Decisions*, McGraw-Hill, 1959. This book provides a fine account of the use of subjective probability theory as a decision tool.

Specific texts

Chernoff, H. and Moses, L. E., *Elementary Decision Theory*. Wiley, 1959. (Especially Chapter 4.)

Edwards, W., 'Behavioural decision theory', *Annual Review of Psychology*, **12**, 1961, pp. 473–498.

Grayson, J. C., *Decisions under Uncertainty. Drilling Decisions by Oil and Gas Operators*, Division of Research, Harvard Business School, 1960.

Green, P. E., 'Risk attitudes and chemical plant decisions', *Chemical Engineering Progress*, **59** (35), 1959.

Hayes, R. H., 'Incorporating risk aversion into risk analysis', *Engineering Economist*, **20** (2), 1975, pp. 99–121.

Hertz, D., 'Risk analysis in capital investment', *Harvard Business Review*, January–February 1964, pp. 95–106.

Malloy, J. B., 'Planning criteria for return on investment in the 1970s', *Chemistry and Industry*, 30 October 1971, pp. 1242–1250.

Malloy, J. B., 'Risk analysis of chemical plants', *Chemical Engineering Progress*, **67**, (10), October 1971, pp. 67–77.

Markowitz, H. M., *Portfolio Selection*, Wiley, 1959.

Maroney, M. J., *Facts from Figures*, Penguin Books, 1976.

Swalm, R. O., 'Utility theory – insight into risk taking', *Harvard Business Review*, November–December, 1966, pp. 123–136.

von Neumann, J. and Morgenstern, O., *The Theory of Games and Economic Behaviour*, Princeton University Press, 1944.

9.15   QUESTIONS

9.15.1   A trucking company has been offered a bankruptcy stock of ten new 20 tonne trucks for the very low price of £10 000 each. At this price, the firm feels confident it could use them for three years, which is its normal replacement period, and then sell them for the same amount. In the interim, it reckons that each truck would convey 1000 tonnes per annum of product at a price and variable cost of £5 and £3 per tonne respectively. Ignoring taxation considerations, determine the DCFRR for this project, and the sensitivity of this return to reasonable changes in the parameters affecting the economic merits of this project.

9.15.2   Sensitivity analysis is a method for assessing the inherent risks in a new capital venture. Using numerical examples to reinforce your answer, describe what this technique accomplishes and discuss its strengths and weaknesses.

9.15.3   A company is considering investment in a steel-making plant having five different capacity options and the possibility of three different levels of demand. The NPV pay-off matrix is:

		Market demand		
		A	B	C
	1	−8000	2000	4 000
Capacity	2	2000	2000	8 000
Options	3	−4000	3000	12 000
	4	0	4000	10 000
	5	2000	6000	4 000

What plant capacity would you recommend according to the five elementary decision rules given in Sections 9.5–9.10? Assume a Hurwicz factor $\alpha = 0.2$, and plot the effect of different values of α.

9.15.4 A firm is contemplating three alternative plants for reducing atmospheric pollution but is uncertain of the severity of future statutory regulations. Three severities are being considered and the cost of meeting each using the three possible means are listed below:

		Regulation severity		
		A	B	C
Alternative	1	10 000	15 000	20 000
Plant	2	12 000	16 000	18 000
Options	3	14 000	17 000	18 000

Which plant option would you recommend using the five elementary decision rules given in Sections 9.5–9.10? Assume a Hurwicz factor $\alpha = 0.4$.

9.15.5 The board of directors of a company wishes to invest a certain sum in a new project. Two projects are being considered, each requiring identical investment. Project A, it believes, will yield net present values of −£3000, £0, £20 000, £40 000 with probabilities 0.1, 0.35, 0.5 and 0.05 respectively, whilst Project B will yield −£10 000, £0, £10 000, £30 000 with probabilities 0.05, 0.15, 0.5 and 0.3 respectively.

Using the expected criterion as your decision tool, decide which project you would recommend.

9.15.6 A plant is to be built to recover a valuable material A from a waste product. The amount of feed available to the plant is uncertain and may be anywhere from zero to 30 000 tonnes/year of material A. Assume a uniform distribution function for this uncertainty. The investment required for the plant will be £10 per tonne of A per year recovered, and the fixed charges associated with investment will amount to 35 per cent per annum of the total investment. The net sales income will be £11 per tonne of A recovered, and the operating costs £2 per tonne recovered.

Determine the expected plant capacity or throughput in terms of material A. And find the optimum overdesign factor, f, where $f = $ most optimistic throughput/expected throughput.

9.15.7 Market research and industrial engineering studies of a newly proposed project, which is thought to be of high risk, have yielded the following probability densities:

Price per item $P(i) \cdot$ (£s)	Probability of $P(i)$
100	0.3
200	0.5
300	0.2

Quantity sold per month $Q(i)$	Probability of $Q(i)$
1000	0.8
2000	0.2

Unit cost per item $C(i)$ (£s)	Probability of $C(i)$
50	0.2
100	0.3
150	0.3
200	0.2

Under what conditions and assumptions would you accept this project? Would you accept the project if the company laid down a rule that any single project exhibiting a greater than 15 per cent chance of making a loss should be rejected?

9.15.8 Discuss the strengths and weaknesses of the expected value criterion as an economic decision tool for investment analysis. In what way does it, or does it not, allow for risk?

9.15.9 Initial estimates of the *independent* probabilities of two series plants making profits R_1, R_2 and T_1, T_2 in two sequential years $i = 1, 2$ are given below:

Year (i)	Profit (R_i)	Probability of R_i	Profit T_i	Probability of T_i
1	40	0.4	20	0.5
	50	0.6	30	0.5
2	30	0.5	25	0.25
	50	0.5	45	0.75

Subsequent estimates however show that the probabilities of these plants making profits are *dependent* according to the following probability data:

	Year 1				Year 2		
R_1	T_1 20 30		Probability of R_1	R_2	T_2 25 45		Probability of R_2
40	0.4 0.0		0.4	30	0.25 0.25		0.50
50	0.1 0.5		0.6	50	0.00 0.50		0.50
Probability of T_1	0.5 0.5		1.00	Probability of T_2	0.25 0.75		1.00

Determine the expected total profits according to the independent and dependent probability estimates given above and show how their variances differ.

9.15.10 Simulate the effect of 9.15.9 by the Monte Carlo simulation technique using numbers drawn and replaced in a hat as the random number generator.

10. *The Economics of Research and Development*

> *'Evidence strongly suggests two things: that technological innovation is a major – most economists would argue the major – determinant of economic growth of rapidly growing economies and that the forces shaping technological change are, at least to a very large extent, economic and ... can be understood directly in terms of economic analysis.'*
>
> Nathan Rosenburg, *The Economics of Technological Change,*
> Penguin, 1971

From previous chapters we have come to realize that the economic merits of most manufactured products, plants and processes are governed by life-cycle considerations, which in turn reflect the changing rate of technological, as well as marketing, innovation. Indeed, the corporate ability to recognize and anticipate some latent market need or desire, and to prosecute such wants by developing new or improved products and systems, can be considered the engine of economic change. Technological innovation, therefore, is fundamental to corporate survival and a firm's ability to harness the fruits of R & D is one of the keys to corporate success.

Unlike expenditure on raw materials, services and utilities and expenses incurred with distributing and marketing, expenditure on R & D involves a sacrifice of current consumption to realize a future gain greater than would otherwise be forthcoming. In effect, therefore, expenditure on R & D involves *investment* – somewhat different from capital investment admittedly, but investment all the same, and amenable to the same types of economic analysis as suggested in earlier parts of this book.

In this chapter we study the sequential relationship between R & D and capital investment projects, and we show that one of the greatest difficulties involving the economic appraisal of R & D projects is our inability to predict their probability of technical (as well as commercial) success accurately. To remedy this we recommend that companies should attempt to forecast future technological change with a view to better understanding the forces of technological innovation and as a means of improving the success rate of a firm's R & D and capital investment projects.

10.1 THE COSTS AND BENEFITS OF R & D

Nowadays the major thrust of most corporate R & D work is directed towards the creation of new or improved products and processes. Admittedly, some firms undertake other forms of research such as supportive research, designed to improve their in-house analytical and computational abilities, whilst others maintain some pure or fundamental research which is completely unrelated to their current operations, and often designed to retain and attract high calibre scientific staff. This latter

246

type of research, however, is less common now than formerly and work so undertaken cannot be justified by formal economic analysis. As a result, analyses of the amounts of monies spent on R & D show that less than 10 per cent is spent on the 'R' and therefore more than 90 per cent is spent on the 'D' of R & D. So accentuated has the need for target orientated research become, that several previously held views concerning the nature and benefits of R & D have now been abandoned. For example, it was once thought that scientific research was, so to speak, a good thing in that knowledge push was the major source of new invention. This view has been refuted by many researchers, notably Schmookler (1966). According to him 'the historical record of important inventions in petroleum refining, papermaking, railroading, and farming revealed not a single unambiguous instance in which either discoveries or inventions typically provided the stimulus for [further] inventions'. Instead, he emphasized that the direction of invention and its subsequent innovation lay with the need to solve a properly defined and costly problem, or to exploit some well identified opportunity. His findings are supported by those of Project Hindsight, reported by Isenson (1968), showing how more than 95 per cent of the technological content of many recent innovations can be attributed to technology at least 40–50 years old. Furthermore, the creative ability of the individual researcher is now no longer considered the all important attribute for invention and innovation. Instead research, such as that pursued by Project SAPPHO in the UK, tends to emphasize the importance of the link between the entrepreneurial manager and the inventor. The factors favouring technological innovation are now clearly recognized as being:

 (i) the need for a clearly defined objective,
 (ii) the availability of the necessary resources,
(iii) the personal commitment of both the inventor and his manager, and
(iv) the need for a good data base and communications system.

Collectively these factors constitute a principle of how to succeed in technological innovation, and they represent a powerful strategic tool in the hands of those executives who can fulfil their requirements at the correct time and in the right market-place.

We have discussed the implications of the product life-cycle before, but one last example might be justified to underpin how important is a positive and realistic approach to technological innovation.

In the 1930s, cotton was the predominant tyre-cord but it was made obsolete by rayon during the mid-1950s. In its turn rayon was virtually displaced by nylon and then polyester during the mid-1970s. Likewise, these newer fibres are already being substituted by glass and steel fibres – and who knows? – the day might yet arrive when carbon fibres offer an economic alternative. Dewhurst (1970) shows how the average life-cycle of a tyre-cord fibre has approximated 35 years with an economically viable substitute being introduced on to the market every 10–15 years. This example shows how the appearance of a new product does not necessarily mean the immediate loss of the non-innovating firm's market. There may be plenty of time for the development of a competitive product (with which to retaliate), possessing advantages over the original innovative threat, especially if its introduction to the market-place is well timed. However such a gestation period should never be allowed to breed complacency because the penalty for failing to retaliate in ample time can be substantial, as several UK tyre-cord companies found to their cost when they proved themselves unable to meet the innovative threat in this market, and were forced to retrench their operations with the closure of large factories and the severance of many jobs. Technological innovation therefore costs money and has social consequences whether a company likes it or not.

Investigations of the direct costs and benefits of R & D show several interesting results. First, there appears to be a strong positive correlation between the growth rate of firms and the extent of their R & D expenditure, expressed as a percentage of their value added*. Typically, low growth firms, such as those involved with lumber and furniture, only spend about 0.2 per cent of their value added on R & D, whereas high growth firms, such as those associated with electronics and aviation, tend to spend more than 20–30 per cent (see Brichter and Sharp, 1970). Furthermore, there appears to exist a significant positive correlation between a firm's price earnings ratio (expressing the value of its equity capital) and the proportion of its sales revenue spent on R & D. Indeed, several researchers such as Gilman (1980) even suggest that companies should be able to optimize their R & D expenditure on the basis of such correlations.

Unfortunately there appears to be a dearth of published information on the *direct* profits arising from successful product and process innovations. That which does exist suggests that *successful* R & D can be very profitable, with returns in excess of 50 per cent and 100 per cent per annum reported by Enos (1962) and Griliches (1958). However, it must also be remembered that such studies say little about the economics of *unsuccessful* R & D, and the fact that the success rate of R & D work is generally low. For example, a study by the management consultants Booz, Allen and Hamilton (1960) showed that seven out of every eight hours devoted to technical product development are spent on products which fail at some stage in the evaluation process. Furthermore, for every ten products which eventually emerge from R & D, they showed that five fail in product and market testing, and only two become commercial successes.

In effect, therefore, expenditure on R & D exhibits all the features of an investment under conditions of risk and uncertainty, so it is perhaps not surprising to find that executives usually look for a payback time of three to five years on such investment. However, it must also be appreciated that a subtle difference normally exists between R & D and capital investment. Usually the greater proportion of R & D costs involve wages and salaries. This means that expenditure on a particular project can be terminated quickly and redirected to other projects with little financial risk other than the possibility of an opportunity foregone. Moreover, when R & D expenditure does embrace capital investment, the costs so incurred are usually small relative to the firm's subsequent full-scale capital involvement. By contrast, capital plant investment cannot be terminated so easily without incurring contractual penalties and the prospect of losing the majority of the asset value of the partly completed project. By definition, however, the uncertainty involved with R & D investment is greater than that facing its sequential capital investment because of the greater time-span involved. Perhaps the greatest uncertainty facing any prospective R & D investment is the extent of future technological innovation which might render the proposed R & D project stillborn and uneconomic.

10.2 THE APPRAISAL OF R & D PROJECTS

Since the odds of discovering economically fruitful R & D projects are stacked against a company, it follows that most dedicated firms purposefully and continually seek to develop a whole catalogue of new product and process ideas in the hope of garnering a few lucrative ones. Indeed, the evidence of Tietjen (1963) would suggest that small companies often review as many as 25 new product ideas every year, whereas the comparable figure for large companies is often in excess of 100

* Value added is the difference between net sales revenue and the cost of raw materials.

Such ideas have to be screened and appraised in a meaningful way, just like any prospective capital project, to ensure that the company's resources are put to best use. These ideas will involve both exploratory and developmental projects. Some will offer the opportunity for a quick return, possibly resulting from the modification of an existing product. Others might entail considerable R & D effort to create new products and processes, designed to give the firm a long-term competitive advantage. Each type has to be appraised against three important factors:

(i) the time, effort and resources needed to bring the latent project to fruition,
(ii) the probability of its technical success, and
(iii) the probability of its commercial success.

The first factor necessitates an estimate of the time needed to bring the idea to the market-place as a new product or process. This is quite different from the time needed to develop its technical success and involves a host of logistic considerations, involving not only the R & D function but many other corporate functions too. Quite obviously there is little virtue developing an idea if it cannot be translated into a useful product or process in time to take advantage of some marketing opportunity. By the same token, however, it must also be remembered that certain R & D projects possess a natural time-span, as would be the case in life testing a product to deduce its reliability or resistance to wear, or any other form of deterioration.

In assessing the probability of technical success, a firm has to be guided by expert opinion and it may require the advice of external consultants in addition to the

Table 10.2.1 *A qualitative means of assessing the merits of an R & D project*

	Unacceptable	Unfavourable	Adequate	Favourable	Most favourable		Unacceptable	Unfavourable	Adequate	Favourable	Most favourable
Economic merits						*Marketing implications*					
Estimated sales revenue						Product advantage					
Production costs						Market size					
R & D costs						Market variability					
Time to reach peak sales						Number of customers					
Capital investment						Number of competitors					
Return on capital						Growth rate					
Risk level						Compatibility with existing products					
R & D implications						Market organizational needs					
Probability of success						Market development requirements					
Degree of novelty						Promotional requirements					
Company's existing know-how						Technical service needs					
Time to develop product						Product adaptability					
Manpower requirements						Competitors ability to imitate					
Patent status						Export potential					
Production implications						Product hazards					
Process familiarity						*Corporate implications*					
Process flexibility						Relation to company objectives					
Compatibility with existing operations						Required corporate size					
Equipment availability						Public image					
Raw materials availability						Diversification requirements					
By-product outlets						Portfolio effect					
Waste disposal problems						Management enthusiasm					
Corrosion problems						Employee enthusiasm					
Production hazards											
Freight or transport problems											

Table 10.2.2 *An ordinal scoring method for ranking R & D projects*

		½	1	2	5	10	Aggregate score
1	Peak sales revenue	Value (millions) score	10	40	80	130	190	
2	Production costs (as % of 1 above)	%	20	30	40	50	60	
		Score	60	40	20	10	0	
3	Capital investment (as % of 1 above)	%	0	50	75	100	150	
		Score	50	40	30	20	10	
4	R & D costs	Value	10 000	50 000	100 000	300 000	500 000	
		Score	150	100	60	30	0	
5	Extent of competition	Degree	None	Slight	Moderate	Appreciable	Extensive	
		Score	100	70	50	20	0	
6	Synergy with existing products	Degree	Negative	None	Little	Appreciable	Extensive	
		Score	−20	0	5	10	50	

		Most inadequate	Needs training	Adequate	More than adequate	Most appropriate
7 Production know-how	Degree Score	−10	0	5	10	20
8 Probability of technical success	%	20	40	60	80	100
	Score	0	30	40	50	60
9 Market acceptance of product	Degree	Much resistance	Some resistance	Neutral	Willing acceptance	Ready acceptance
	Score	−50	0	10	20	50
Product life	Years	2	5	10	15	20 or more
10 R & D time *plus* time to establish production, *plus* time to gain market acceptance, *plus* time to build sales to 50% of peak	6 months	100	120	140	160	130
	1	20	100	120	140	160
	2	project unfeasible	80	100	120	140
	3	project unfeasible	60	80	100	120
	5	project unfeasible	project unfeasible	60	80	100
Standard ratings	more than 600 excellent	500–600 good	400–499 fair	less than 400 poor		

Total aggregate score =

opinions of its own staff. Any consideration of technical success must, of course, be related to the effort and resources which the company is able to apply within the limits of available time.

Similarly, a firm has to rely on expert opinion when endeavouring to assess the probability of a project's commercial success and to that end requires estimates of all those factors (such as market size, the likely rate of market penetration, prices, operating and capital costs) which contribute to a life-cycle economic evaluation of the project in hand. Initially, such estimates may be difficult to come by, but as the project proceeds so the accuracy of these estimates can be improved, enabling a proper economic assessment of the project to be made. The point to be stressed here is that the sooner a firm can undertake some sensible evaluation of the new idea the better. Indeed, so important do firms consider this early evaluation that the techniques devised for this purpose are literally legion. They are well covered by Ruberstein (1966), Pearson and Topaling (1969) and Baker (1964; 1967; 1970), so it is not our intention to review them in detail here. Basically they comprise the following generic methods:

(i) *Check-lists.* Sometimes these simply involve a qualitative assessment of the project using the criteria previously reviewed in Table 4.4.1. On other occasions, however, some qualitative type of scoring method, similar to that shown in Table 10.2.1, might be required to focus management's attention on the intrinsic benefits, sacrifices and risks inherent in a new R & D venture.

(ii) *Measured check-lists.* These are similar to (i) above but for the fact that they incorporate an ordinal scoring scheme agreed by the firm's executives. The product of these measured check-lists is an overall score which helps to concentrate management's attention on the aggregate attributes of the project and provides a crude means of ranking R & D projects. A typical example of such a scheme is shown in Table 10.2.2.

(iii) *Project ranking formulae.* This category comprises simple formulae of the payback time and accounting rate of return type which might be of sufficient merit to rank projects in their formative stages but, as the content of previous chapters suggests, cannot be defended when large-scale expenditure is contemplated.

(iv) *Discounted cash flow methods.* These normally employ the NPV criterion in one of two ways. When the estimators feel reluctant to provide more than single figure estimates of the prospective economic merits of a project, these estimates of the probabilities of technical and commercial success are often renamed credibilities* and they permit the ranking of projects according to a project selection index (I) of the following form:

$$I = P_T \cdot P_C \cdot \text{NPV}$$

where P_T = the credibility of the project's technical success, P_C = the credibility of the project's commercial success, and NPV = the anticipated NPV of the project. Alternatively, when more than single figure estimates are available, each project can be ranked according to the expected value and standard deviation of its NPV, coupled with the likelihood of its making a cash loss; as previously shown in Chapter 9.11.

(v) *Programming techniques.* The last catch-all category of R & D appraisal methods involves mathematical programming techniques, more usually referred to as operational research techniques, involving linear, non-linear and dynamic programming methods, which build upon the substance of the methods listed in (iv)

* The differences between probabilities and credibilities is reviewed by Allen (1968).

above. Such techniques are justified when substantial investment is envisaged and the economic implications of alternative courses of action are difficult to comprehend without the use of such computational tools, because of their interactive complexity. Practical examples of the application of these techniques are provided by Hess (1962), Collcutt and Reader (1967), Souder (1967) and Bell et al. (1970).

It will be appreciated that these methods are listed in ascending order of complexity, so that the information requirements of the first in order of magnitude is less than that of the last. Furthermore, all of these methods have their difficulties. Even a simple points-rating scheme is difficult to devise so that it meets with the agreement of all those who have to use it. As with all numerical rating schemes, the numbers coming from such analyses have to be used with care. Their purpose is to help focus management's attention on the selection problem at hand, but they should never be considered ends to the decision-making process in their own right. The major benefit which arises from a formal assessment of R & D projects along these lines is that, properly designed, such methods ensure that no important factors are overlooked. Furthermore it must always be remembered that quantification, even if it is uncertain, is at best a comfort if it supports intuitive feeling, and at worst an irritant if it does not. In the last resort it is entrepreneurial judgement (that most difficult of qualities to measure except in retrospect) which is the deciding factor as to which new product or process idea will be researched and developed further.

Using such techniques as these, a firm can select those R & D projects which appear to fulfil its economic and strategic objectives. However, it will be realized that the development of such projects implies an undertaking to make further *sequential* decisions, which might necessitate substantial capital investment. It is this sequential decision making aspect which we shall now explore in more detail.

10.3 SEQUENTIAL DECISION MAKING

In decision analysis it is often found that the outcome of some *current* decision affects and, in the same token, is affected by the outcome of some *future* decision. In a general context this applies to all projects exhibiting life-cycle costs and benefits. In particular, however, it applies to R & D projects which subsequently involve capital expenditure in manufacturing assets. A special technique for resolving sequential decision making problems of this kind is known as decision tree (or decision network) analysis. This is a graphical technique which embodies payoff matrices and the expected value criterion, both of which were described in Chapter 9.

To demonstrate the principles of this technique, let us consider the example shown in Table 10.3.1. Suppose a decision maker has the choice of investing in some R & D project which offers an overall profit of 1000 munits, if successful, but a loss of 500 munits if unsuccessful. Alternatively, the decision maker might decide to reject

Table 10.3.1 *The payoff matrix for a hypothetical R & D project*

State of nature	Probability	Option payoffs	
		Undertake R & D	Do nothing
R & D project successful	0.6 (A)	1000 (Y)	300 (Y)
R & D project unsuccessful	0.4 (B)	−500 (Z)	300 (Z)
Expected payoff = (AY)+(BZ)		400	300

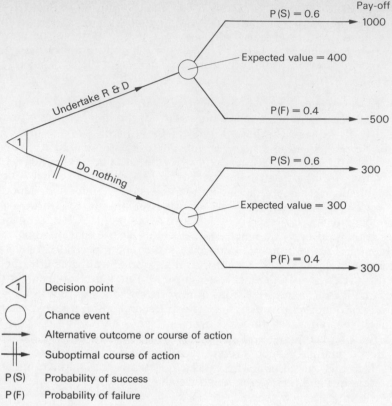

Figure 10.3.1   *The decision tree for Table 10.3.1.*

the R & D venture and continue to use existing products and/or facilities which offer a profit of 300 munits, providing he foregoes the R & D alternative. On the basis of this information and the explicit assumption that the expected payoff forms a realistic and legitimate decision criterion, one would select the R & D alternative if the chances of its success were 60 per cent because it would provide the greater expected payoff, as shown by Table 10.3.1.

Diagrammatically this payoff matrix can be represented by Figure 10.3.1, where we notice that the network starts at decision point 1 from which arrows, representing alternative actions, lead to chance events. The arrows leaving these chance events represent the alternative states of nature. In this case they represent whether or not the outcome of the R & D work is successful and are labelled according to the probability of success or failure. Lastly these arrows terminate at the forecast payoffs to be realized if the appropriate courses of action *and* the anticipated chance events occur. The analysis of this decision tree is made simple using what is known as the rollback technique. This involves commencing at the extreme right-hand tips of the branches of the decision tree and *working backwards* towards the initial decision point using two very simple decision rules in the process: (i) on locating a chance event, calculate the expected value of that event using the probabilities and the payoffs which emanate from that event, and (ii) on locating a decision point, select only the optimal course of action emanating from that decision point and cross out all suboptimal courses of action.

A careful examination of Figure 10.3.1 shows that the expected values of the chance events have been calculated and the suboptimal, do nothing alternative has

Table 10.3.2 *A sequential R & D and capital investment programme*

Research and development programme	R & D 1	R & D 2
R & D investment	10 000	5 000
Probability of success	0.8	0.2
Sequential capital investment	50 000	60 000
Sequential NPV of cash inflows	100 000	80 000

been crossed out. This outcome would prevail for the same pay-offs providing the probability of the R & D project being successful remained in excess of 53.4 per cent.

Let us now consider a slightly more complicated example. Suppose a firm has the option of investing in an initial research and development programme (R & D 1). If successful, R & D 1 could result in the capital expenditure programme shown in Table 10.3.2 with its own special payoff. Alternatively, if R & D 1 were unsuccessful, then programme R & D 2 could be financed, possibly leading to its own special capital investment opportunity, which is also shown in Table 10.3.2. It is also assumed that the firm would have the option of doing nothing whenever it chose but in these circumstances the payoff would be nought.

The corresponding decision tree for this example is shown in Figure 10.3.2. It

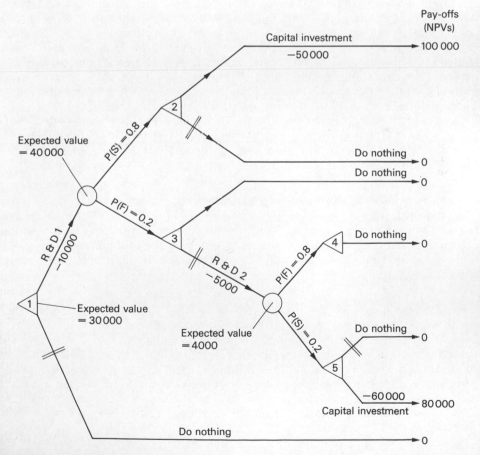

Figure 10.3.2 *The decision tree for Table 10.3.2.*

Table 10.3.3 *The economic analysis of the decision tree contained in Figure 10.3.2*

Decision point	Expected NPV of each course of action		Optimal NPV
5	(a) 80 000 − 60 000	= 20 000	20 000
	(b)	= 0	
4	(a)	= 0	0
	(b)		
3	(a)	= 0	0
	(b) 20 000 × 0.2 + 0 × 0.8 − 5 000	= −1000	
2	(a) 100 000 − 50 000	= 50 000	50 000
	(b)	= 0	
1	(a) 50 000 × 0.8 + 0 × 0.2 − 10 000	= 30 000	30 000
	(b)	= 0	

No allowance for conditional probabilities has been made in this example.

comprises five decision points (DP), and two chance events. If we assume that the legitimate business objective in these circumstances involves maximizing the expected NPV, then the results for this example are as shown in Table 10.3.3. At DP 5 the best of the available options is to invest in the capital plant because this provides the greater NPV of 20 000 (80 000 − 60 000). Since no alternative exists at DP 4, it follows that the expected NPV from pursuing R & D 2 is given by the expected NPV of its benefits *minus* the expected NPV of its costs. The calculation for DP 3, shows that this value is negative and worse than the alternative of doing nothing. Consequently, within the bounds of this trivial example, R & D 2 could not currently be justified in economic terms. By contrast, Table 10.3.3 shows that the NPV from pursuing R & D 1 is positive and greater than its only alternative of doing nothing.

Faced with such a situation, the firm would be advised to initiate R & D 1 in the expectation of making a profit of 30 000. The actual outcome would either be a profit of 40 000 (100 000–50 000–10 000) or a loss of 10 000 (0–10 000). Whether or not the firm would subsequently decide to build the initially envisaged capital project would depend on three considerations:

(i) the success of R & D 1, upon which depends the realization of the subsequent capital project,
(ii) the economic merits and risks involved with that sequential capital investment project when reappraised at that subsequent moment in time, and
(iii) the economic merits of alternative projects competing for the firm's scarce resources.

In a similar vein it follows that if the outcome of R & D 1 were unfavourable, then the firm would need to reappraise all those options available to it.

The basic strength of this technique derives from its methodology requiring the provision of data in a systematic way and if it serves no other purpose than to focus management's attention on the full implications of their R & D decisions then its use is justified. In addition to selecting between options on the basis of their expected values, this sequential decision-making technique also permits one to consider the risks inherent in alternative R & D strategies and it naturally lends itself to sensitivity analysis.

Our real purpose in providing these examples here, however, is to illustrate the nature of sequential decisions in a way which we have not done before. Furthermore, their analyses highlight just how important is a realistic assessment of a project's probability of success.

10.4 THE TECHNIQUES OF TECHNOLOGICAL FORECASTING

Most economics textbooks give little guidance as to how probability estimates are made and, more often than not, it is assumed that such probabilities (or credibilities) are developed intuitively, based on long experience of making similar decisions in the past. But is this reasonable when one considers that the time lag which exists between the initiation of an R & D programme and the realization of its commercial effect can often take ten years or more? During this time the executive responsible for making the original R & D investment decision will probably have moved on without reaping the benefits of feedback. Studies of these time delays are well covered in the literature. For example, Enos (1962) examined 35 significant innovations developed during the period 1911–50 and found that the mean time-lag was 14 years (with a standard deviation of 16 years) whilst for nine petroleum cracking processes, introduced during the period 1917–50, the mean time-lag was 13 years. Likewise, the spin-off from the US space programme was estimated by Wells (1963) to have a time-lag of 5–10 years. As a last example, Jantsch (1967) summarizes the time-lag as 3–4 years for major chemical industries, 4–7 years for industries producing complex electronics, 5–10 years for pharmaceutical products and ten years or more for complicated weapon systems. Despite the fact that research by Gillfillam (1952) and others has clearly shown a significant decline in this time-lag over the past century signifying the increasing rate of technological innovation, the evidence would suggest that the gestation period between the initiation of an R & D project and its commercialization is considerably longer than the time most executives remain with one company, let alone in the same job. To compensate for this learning deficiency, more and more companies are turning to technological forecasting (TF) as a means of improving their ability to forecast future technological threats and opportunities which could effect their future operations and corporate strategy, all with a view to improving the success rate of their new product and process ventures.

Despite its title, TF is not confined to considerations of technology *per se*, but is involved with the prediction of the level of technology which *might be* achieved or needed in a well defined market by a particular date. In effect, therefore, TF recognizes that the determinants of technological change are often economic, social and political and that such change is usually evolutionary but sometimes revolutionary. A variety of TF techniques exists; the main ones are reviewed below. As with all other methodologies, however, it must be realized that the greatest benefit from using these techniques comes from a careful examination of past experiences coupled with the insight of imaginative and competent people. Each of these techniques has its own data requirements, which often cannot be fully met, and each technique has its own limitations and sources for error. In these respects therefore TF is no better or worse than other forms of forecasting. However, in no way do these shortcomings denigrate the usefulness of TF because its purpose is not to forecast the *precise* form of technology embodied in some process, product or system by some future data, but rather to predict the *likelihood* and the *significance* of possible future developments, which could place the firm at risk, or provide some previously unforeseen opportunity.

The major techniques of technological forecasting are already well known and are amply covered by the detailed works of Bright (1968) and Wills et al. (1972) so only a brief review of these techniques is justified here. Essentially the major techniques comprise:

  (i) Expert opinion analysis (the Delphi technique),
 (ii) Time-trend analysis,
(iii) Analogy forecasting,
(iv) Morphological forecasting,
 (v) Conditional demand analysis, and
(vi) Scenario writing

A careful examination of this list shows that the first three are very similar to those mentioned in Chapter 7.2.

10.4.1 Expert opinion analyses and the Delphi technique

In this chapter and elsewhere it has been intimated that experts might reasonably be expected to provide probability forecasts of certain technological advances occurring by prescribed dates. The problem with single estimates, however, is that they are constrained by the knowledge, experience and foresight of the individual. Furthermore, conventional consensus forecasting, on the basis of panels of experts, suffers certain behavioural deficiencies such as the ability of one persuasive participant to sway others to his own view. To overcome these shortcomings, the Rand Corporation developed the Delphi technique, which has been widely publicized by Helmer (1966). Without allowing face-to-face contact and communication between the panel members, this technique involves questioning the experts for their best estimates of the time when certain well defined developments might be expected to reach fruition. These estimates are then analysed centrally by a co-ordinator who raises questions where divergent points of opinion exist. The processed results, supplementary questions, and any further evidence are then returned to the experts for their further consideration. This process is reiterated until a steady consistent pattern of results emerges possibly, but not necessarily, showing a consensus of opinion. On the basis of such results as these, subjective probability histograms can be developed for subsequent use in economic analyses.

10.4.2 Time-trend analysis

This exploratory technique involves plotting the historical performance of some interesting parameter against time, and extrapolating its underlying trend into the future with a view to predicting its future level of performance. Such a relationship can either be hand drawn or fitted mathematically by varying degrees of refinement. The strength of this technique resides in its simplicity. However, its weakness results from the underlying assumption that the forces which influenced the historical pattern of performance will combine in a like manner to influence the future performance. The inherent danger in extrapolating such parameters results from not fully understanding the cause and effect relationships which govern their behaviour. Despite these problems this technique is well tried and tested and has much merit. It is, of course, identical to the method discussed in Chapter 7.2.4 but for the fact that our interest here lies more with the impact which future market demand and needs have on the rate of technological innovation. Two types of analysis are used: demographic cum sociological analysis and technical parameter analysis. The former is used to predict the aggregate market demand for such things as food, water, electricity and energy and it is usually based on forecasts of population growth rates and per capita requirements. The objective here is to discern the demand gap which will develop between current and future needs. Such gap analysis allows one to measure the value of future opportunity which will provide some incentive for the creation of new products and processes, employing new technologies. The latter of these two is used to predict such parameters as the speed of aircraft, the efficiency of engines and the tensile strength of composite materials. In both cases it is quite common for the S-shaped sigmoid curve, which we have experienced so frequently throughout this book, to prevail. This is especially interesting where the rate of technological innovation is concerned because it implies that, at a certain stage in the development of a particular and precisely defined technology, diminishing returns to further improvement ensue, providing an ideal opportunity for some different, superior technology to develop in its stead. Of course this is precisely what happens in practice (as industrial museums will testify) to the point that products and processes employing the newer technology gradually increase their market share, especially in areas where higher performance and economy are important. Such a thesis as this is borne out by the example in Figure 10.4.2.1 which shows how the electrical efficiency of mercury vapour fluorescent lighting has outstripped the efficiency of incandescent lighting, permitting the former to displace the latter in certain applications. Of special interest is the shaded area of this diagram, illustrating the near exponential rate of technological innovation for electric lighting in general.

Of course natural limits exist to the advancement of all technologies, as governed by thermodynamic and quantum mechanic principles, so an exponential rate of growth could not be expected to continue indefinitely. Ultimately, one would expect such graphs to become S-shaped. The interesting point to come from this

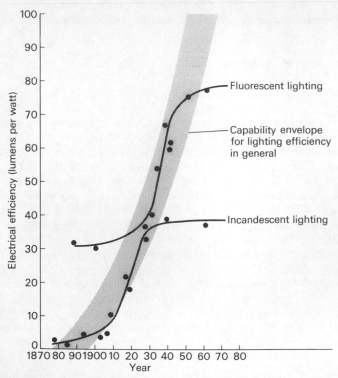

Figure 10.4.2.1 *Growth curves for electric lighting efficiency.*

example is the fact that, for most technologies, one can develop a capability envelope of the sort shown in Figure 10.4.2.1 and, on the basis of such an envelope, forecast the likely future performance of the parameter of interest without knowing the precise nature of the future technology involved. Ayres (1968) has shown that such 'envelope curve forecasting' can be usefully employed for a variety of different technologies.

However, it will be appreciated that parameters which appear to be of great importance today may become less important in the future. For example, one would expect the world's diminishing reserves of petroleum to affect fundamentally a whole variety of economic, social and political issues, so any would-be forecaster would be advised to look beyond the meagre confines of his numerical analysis before making any prognosis.

10.4.3   Predicting by analogy

We have demonstrated the use of this technique before, so only a few thoughts are justifiable here. In many fields of endeavour it is possible to predict some future trend by direct comparison with the trends of some precursor technology. Evidence in many technologies shows that what is done in the USA today follows in other countries several months or years later. Providing the nature of the time-lag can be predicted with reasonable accuracy it follows that such an exploratory technique can be useful. In a similar vein, it has been shown that time lags exist between the development and/or employment of a technology by one industry and its subsequent imitation by another. For example, Lentz (1962) showed that a ten-year gap exists between the air speeds of combat and commercial aircraft, and it is well known that the quench-cool technique employed in naphtha cracking was used many years later in the joint refining of zinc and lead by the Imperial Smelting Process.

10.4.4   Morphological* analysis

This method of forecasting involves structuring the form of the investigation in such a way that the full range of conceivable options can be developed and systematically appraised with a view to determining those factors which will be important to the realization of future developments. For example, faced with the future problem of what kind of nuclear reactor technology to employ, one would be forced to consider all the possible means of nuclear fission and fusion as a starting point. However the realization of these methods would depend upon such considerations as the means of controlling the nuclear reactions, the nature of the heat transfer media, the extent of uranium or other fuel enrichment, the likely temperatures and pressures involved, and hence the materials required in construction. Each of these secondary factors could be further broken down, and the entire problem could be represented by a multi-dimensional array of technological factors, some well known and understood, others requiring different degrees of technological improvement before they could possibly be realized. The elegance of this mind expanding technique is that it forces the assessors to consider all conceivable options, and prevents the premature rejection of possible alternatives by their initial exclusion from such an array. Nicholson (1968) cites the application of this technique to the selection of nuclear reactors both in the USA and the UK. In itself, the technique is incapable of

---

* The lantinized version of the Greek word for form is 'morphe'; hence the derivation of the word 'morphological'.

identifying the time required to develop a particular technology so it has to be employed in conjunction with other technological forecasting techniques.

10.4.5 Conditional demand analysis

In this technique the technological goal is first defined and the factors necessary for its realization are then explored with a view to appraising their economic potential. For example, if one were to investigate the prospects of man continually living under the sea, then the question of what types of equipment he would require to live in such a habitat would naturally follow. On the basis of brain storming sessions, it is conceivable that one could glean some idea of the nature of this equipment and its economic potential so that, coupled with the results of a Delphi appraisal, the results of such an analysis could be used to justify R & D expenditure.

10.4.6 Scenario writing

This technique involves the postulation of possible alternative futures and the appraisal of how those futures could be realized. Alternative futures could comprise a 20-hour working week, a per capita income twice as large as it is currently, or 50 per cent of gasoline made from coal. In essence, therefore, this technique involves escaping from the constraints of conventional thinking to postulate what might happen, and then to determine what sequence of collective events could bring about that particular future. Once developed, such scenarios then require further development using the Delphi method to forecast the probabilities of such futures occurring within prescribed time-scales. Scenario writing is best known through the writings of Kahn and Weiner (1967), but has also found favour with large companies as a backcloth to their long-range planning studies. The scenario *Britain 1984: Unilever's Forecast* (Brech, 1963) is a particularly notable example.

10.5 THE CORPORATE SIGNIFICANCE OF TECHNOLOGICAL INNOVATION

Space has precluded a full discussion of the details involved with TF. To overcome this deficiency, we have provided ample references in the hope that any reader convinced that the subject is as vague and woolly as the previous section might suggest, will be convinced otherwise by their reading. The essential point to be grasped however is that tomorrow's technology is governed by a host of complex and inter-related factors, which are technological, economic, sociological and political. Technological forecasters recognize this complexity and endeavour, within the limits of their capabilities and their arsenal of techniques, to map out the environment in which the company might find itself 5, 10 or 15 years from now with a view to formulating strategies, devising plans, and instigating actions to avert competitive threats, and place the company in a position where it can take advantage of future opportunity. After all, there would be little merit in a firm developing a novel means of producing non-ferrous metals by blast furnace coke reduction if society at large was prepared to accept nuclear power generation on a large scale, since its cheaper electricity could make an electrical reduction process economically more attractive. It will also be recognized that future technological innovation is much more complex than we have implied. Significant technological improvements usually necessitate the confluence of technical advances in several technical fields of endeavour, which often seem unrelated. Furthermore, the substitution of an older technology by a newer one is not a simple matter of graphical manipulation, but one about human will and the need to survive and prosper, so it is perhaps not surprising that firms, practising older technology retaliate by a variety of means, often giving the older technology a new lease of life. One of the better known examples of this phenomenon is the radical improvement in the efficiency of older coal-fired power stations to meet the challenge of nuclear power, something which was not considered when the proliferation of nuclear power was first envisaged.

Of course there always exists the possibility that some completely unforeseen occurrence might invalidate the integrity of any forecast – that is the occupational hazard of forecasting – but such occurrences are rare. More often than not the lead time before an R & D idea reaches commercial development is so prolonged that the origins of innovations to be realized many years hence are with us now – if only we could recognize them! In essence, therefore, technological forecasting endeavours to provide a firm with answers to three basic questions:

 (i) How will technological innovation influence the sales, revenues and profits of our existing products?
 (ii) How will technological innovation affect the demands for new or improved products and the processes for their manufacture?
(iii) What product and R & D strategies should the firm pursue which will allow it to prosper?

We have discussed questions of this kind in Chapter 4, but not with the accent so firmly focused on the effects of technological innovation, which we now recognize as being of fundamental importance to any life-cycle economic analysis and the major determinant in the analysis of product life-cycles.

10.6 SUMMARY

On the basis that R & D expenditure involves economic decision making under conditions of uncertainty often involving only modest chances of commercial success, this chapter has concentrated on the probability of success attributes of R & D ventures as well as on their alternative payoffs. Using the rollback technique as applied to decision trees (decision networks) we showed how the sequential effects of R & D and capital expenditure could be formally evaluated, but the product of these deliberations was to concentrate our attention on the validity of the probability forecasts used in those calculations. Recognizing that the benefits of experience are often of limited value where R & D projects involving long gestation periods are concerned, our attention turned to technological forecasting as a means of assessing the overall probability of success for a new product and/or process idea.

10.7 BIBLIOGRAPHY

General texts

Bright, J. R. (Ed.), *Technological Forecasting for Industry and Government*, Prentice-Hall, 1968. This book contains several detailed papers illustrating the practical application of the various techniques of TF.

Wills, G. et al, *Technological Forecasting*, Penguin Books, 1972. This easy to read book provides a fine introduction to all the techniques of TF.

Specific texts

Allen, D. H., 'Credibility forecasts and their application to the economic appraisal of R & D projects', *Operations Research Quarterly*, **19** (1), 1968, p. 25.

Ayres, R. U., 'Envelope curve forecasting', in J. R. Bright (Ed.), *op. cit.*

Baker, N. R. and Pound, W. H., *Project Selection: Where We Stand*. Institute of Electrical and Electronic Engineers. Transactions in Engineering Management, **E7–11** (4), pp. 124–134, 1964.

Baker, D. J., 'Control of research – possible aids', *Operations Research Quarterly*, **18** (1), 1967, pp. 5–12.

Baker, D. J., *An Approach to R & D Project Planning and Control with ICI Paints Division*, Conference on Practical Aids to Research Management, O. R. Society, London, February 1970.

Bell, D. C. et al, *Resource Allocation Modelling*, Conference in Practical Aids to Research Management, O. R. Society, London, February 1970.

Booz, Allen and Hamilton Inc; *The Management of New Products*, 1960.

Brech, R. *Britain 1984: Unilever's Forecast*. Darton, Longmans & Todd, 1963.

Brichter, A. M. and Sharp, E. M., *From Project to Production*, Pergamon Press, 1970.

Collcutt, R. H. and Reader, R. D., 'Choosing the operational research programme for BISRA', *Operations Research Quarterly*, **18** (3), 1967, pp. 219–242.

Dewhurst, H. A., *The long-range research that produced glass-reinforced tires*. *Research Management*, **XIII** (3), May 1970.

Enos, J. L., *Petroleum Progress and Profits: A History of Process Innovation*, M.I.T., 1962.

Gillfillam, S. C., 'The prediction of technical change', Review of Economics and Statistics, **XXXIV,** November 1952, pp. 368–385. Reprinted in J. R. Bright *op. cit.*

Gilman, J. J., 'You can calculate optimal spending for industrial R & D', *Industrial Research and Development*, **22** (8), 1980, p. 87.

Griliches, Z., 'Research costs and social returns: hybrid corn and related innovations, *Journal of Political Economy*, October 1958, pp. 419–431.

Helmer, O., *Social Technology*, Basic Books, 1966.

Hess, S. W., *A Dynamic Programming Approach to R & D Budgeting and Project Selection*, Institute of Electrical and Electronic Engineers, Transactions in Engineering Management, EM-9, 1962, pp. 170–179.

Isenson, R. S., 'Technological forecasting lessons from project hindsight', in J. R. Bright (Ed.) *op. cit.*

Jantsch, E., *Technological Forecasting in Perspective*, OECD, 1967.

Kahn, H. and Weiner, A. J., *The Year 2000 – A framework for Speculation on the Next Thirty-three Years*, Macmillan, 1967.

Lentz, R. C., *Technological Forecasting*, Report ASD-TDR-62–414, USAF, June 1962.

Nicholson, R. L. R., *Technical Forecasting as a Management Technique*. Programmes Analysis Unit, Report M, HMSO, 1968.

Pearson, A. W. and Topaling, A. S., 'Project evaluation in research and development, *Management Decision*, **3** (3), 1969, pp. 26–29.

Ruberstein, A. H., 'Economic evaluation of research and development. A brief survey of theory and practice', *Journal of Industrial Engineering*, **17**, 1966, pp. 615–620.

Schmookler, J., *Invention and Economic Growth*, Harvard University Press, 1966.

Souder, W. E., 'Selecting and staffing R & D projects via operations research', *Chemical and Engineering Progress*, **63** (11), 1967, pp. 27–37.

Tietjen, K. H., *Organizing the Product – Planning Function*, American Management Association, 1963.

Wells, J. R. et al., *The Commercial Application of Missile/Space Technology*, Denver Research Institute, 1963.

10.8   QUESTIONS

10.8.1   A computer manufacturer must decide whether or not to embark on an R & D programme with a view to developing a new and better computer memory bank circuit. The following conversation took place in the MD's office.

MD   Well, Joe (technical director), just how much will the R & D programme cost?

Joe   £10 000 I'd say, but you must remember that at this stage there's a possibility that the project might fail for two reasons. For a start, the project might prove to be technically impossible, at least within the constraints of £10 000 budget and ...

Harry   (marketing director) It could also fail from a marketing point of view!

MD   O.K., I accept that. But what are the chances of failure? And what do we do if at the end of the programme we have to scrap the project?

(Joe and Harry then discuss the technical and marketing details for a while and then ...)

Joe   We think there's a 60 per cent chance that the project will succeed, but if it does not we could mount a second R & D programme designed to finish the research for, say, another £10 000. With more research information we could possibly reduce the assembly line set-up costs. What do you think Bert?

Bert   (manufacturing director) Yes, I agree. From what you've told me and from the work which my cost estimators have done, I would think the assembly line would cost £50 000 to install based upon the first R & D programme, but only £40 000 if we went the whole R & D route.

MD   That's all very well, but what are the chances of the second R & D programme being successful, and what would be the respective payoffs?

Harry   Joe and I have been looking at this point. We feel that the chances of the second R & D programme failing are 20 per cent. Jim can give you the payoffs.

Jim   (corporate economist) I've done some sums which show that the NPV of future cash flows from sales would be £400 000 based upon the first R & D programme and slightly better than that if we went

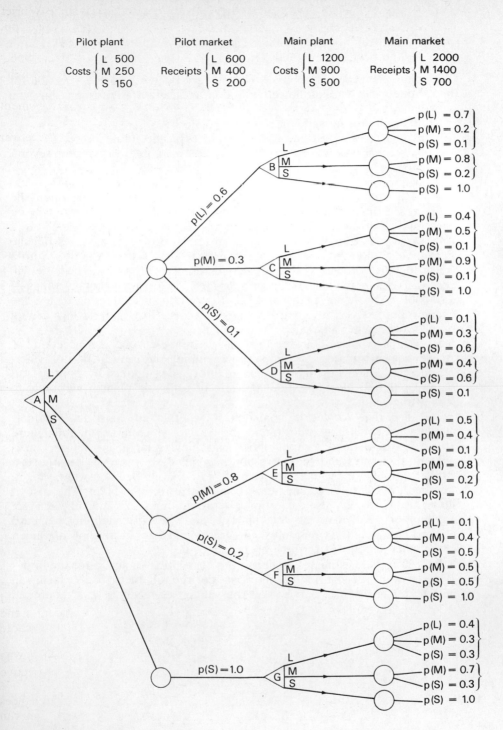

Figure 10.8.3.1 *L, M and S = the building of a large, medium or small plant and the realization of large, medium and small markets.*

the whole route, because of the slightly better product quality that
we could offer – say, £450 000.

MD   You fellows have bounded around so many figures, I really don't
know what we should do!

Formulate the problem for the MD, and recommend a course of action for
him. State your decision objective and criteria. State any assumptions you
may use.

Would your recommendations be the same if:
(a) this project was just one in a series of expected future projects?
(b) this project was unlikely to be followed by another project for several
years?

10.8.2   A firm is considering whether to undertake a R & D project which could
lead to an improved process capable of replacing an existing one. The
project is estimated to cost £25 000 and have a 0.75 probability of being
successful; if it is, it will cost £44 000 to install the new process and result in
total savings of £240 000. If the initial research project is unsuccessful, the
firm could undertake a secondary research project costing £15 000, with a
0.2 probability of success. If the second research project succeeds, it will
cost £30 000 to implement the new process and result in total savings of
£100 000. At any stage, the firm has the option of continuing to use the
existing process, with no extra savings or costs. Costs and savings are all
quoted at present values.

By means of a decision tree analysis, recommend a course of action.

10.8.3   A chemical manufacturing company is planning the introduction of a new
product and intends to market this on a pilot scale, supplied by a pilot plant,
before making a decision about the size of full-scale plant it will erect to
supply the main market.

The firm has to decide immediately whether to construct a large-,
medium- or small-scale pilot plant, the cost of which are shown in Figure
10.8.3.1. The estimated probabilities of achieving large, medium or small
pilot market sales and the corresponding net cash receipts from the test
market, are also indicated. Two years from now, the decision will be taken
whether to build a large, medium or small size of main plant. The cost of
these alternative plants, the estimated probabilities of capturing a large,
medium or small main product market, and the corresponding net cash
receipts complete the decision tree diagram. All costs and receipts are given
in £k units discounted to the present value.

Based on these estimates, calculate the best course of action for the firm.

10.8.4   'The decision tree algorithm cannot consider the full effects of risk facing an
investment decision'. Comment on the validity or falsity of this statement.

11. A Total Systems Approach to Investment in Manufacturing Assets

'Industry needs a sensible approach to investment analysis more than it needs a sophisticated one. As a matter of fact the crudest tool that gives the right answer is the one which should be used.'
L. C. Hackamack, *Making Equipment Replacement Decisions*, American Management Association, 1969

When one considers the sophistication of some of the previous chapters, especially Chapters 6 and 9, one will appreciate the sentiment in the quotation given above. Of course, our reason for presenting this complicated material is not perverse, nor is it intended to glorify academic niceties. Instead, it is meant to focus our attention on some of the controversial and indeed complex issues concerning the economic appraisal of capital projects.

In this chapter we try to coalesce the lessons of previous chapters, recognizing that real-life decision making is far more complicated than our theoretical treatment of the subject would suggest. We commence this chapter by recommending the adoption of NPV and DCFRR criteria conscious of their superiority over other criteria, but mindful of their weaknesses too. To interpret properly the economic impact which a single project has on a firm's intended portfolio of projects, we also recommend the adoption of computerized models, which allow the risk and cash rationing implications of an investment strategy to be fully explored from a pragmatic viewpoint. Lastly, we suggest that the economic appraisal of a prospective project is only a part – albeit an important part – in the total process of inventing, screening, evaluating, selecting, implementing and operating projects throughout their economic lives, and we suggest that knowledge of all these matters amounts to little if a firm's strategy is ill-conceived at the outset. In effect, therefore, this chapter returns our attention to the corporate strategic issues concerning investment in manufacturing assets.

11.1 A MISPLACED EMPHASIS ON CAPITAL BUDGETING

Before drawing any conclusions from the substance of previous chapters it is well to remember that the preceding material was developed on the basis that the most reasonable objective for any firm is to yield a satisfactory return on its shareholders' capital. Despite our allegiance to this principle, however, it must be recognized that many firms pursue a policy of growth for various reasons. From a strategic viewpoint, growth can often provide a firm with a larger market share and more control over its own destiny and the larger a firm becomes, the more able it is to marshal the resources necessary to enter new fields of endeavour. From an economic standpoint,

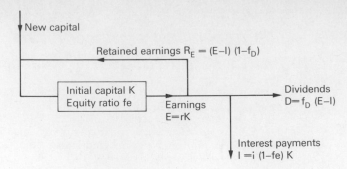

Figure 11.1.1 *A simplified cash flow model of the firm. From de la Mare (1975), with kind permission of the Editor of* Chemical Engineer.

the greater a firm's sales, the more able it is to exploit the advantages of scale. Furthermore, an expanding firm offers its employees good job prospects. These are but some of the advantages of growth, but growth cannot be sustained for long unless there exist profits to finance it: in effect growth and profitability are interdependent.

To gain some appreciation of this interdependence, we offer the following rather simple, but unfortunately imprecise model, which is shown in Figure 11.1.1. In this model* we assume that a firm's rate of return on capital (in real terms) is given by the following relationship:

$$r = E/K.$$

where $100\,r =$ the firm's return on total capital per cent, per annum after tax, $E =$ the firm's annual net cash earnings after tax, and $K =$ the firm's total capital.

To make the model as realistic as possible, we assume that a firm endeavours to maintain the same equity ratio, f_e, as it expands and has to pay an interest rate of $100\,i$ per cent per annum after tax on its debt. Furthermore, we also assume that the firm endeavours to maintain a consistent dividend policy which is made manifest by its dividend payout ratio, f_D. Using such a model we find that the algebraic expressions for the various cash flows of the firm are as shown in Figure 11.1.1. On this basis, it is quite a simple matter to develop the relationship between a firm's profitability, growth rate, capital structure and dividend payout ratio, as shown by Figures 11.1.2 and 11.1.3. These graphs demonstrate the following points:

 (i) For a given capital structure, as measured by the firm's equity ratio, f_e, the rate of return on capital needed to finance a given rate of capital growth *increases* as the firm's dividend payout ratio, f_D, *increases*.
 (ii) For a given capital structure, and a given return on capital, the growth rate *increases* as the dividend payout ratio *decreases*.
(iii) The rate of return needed to finance a given rate of capital growth *decreases* with an *increasing* proportion of debt capital when the rate of return is greater than the cost of debt capital, but *increases* with an *increasing* proportion of debt capital when the cost of debt financing is greater than the overall return on capital.
(iv) The rate of return needed to finance a given rate of capital growth *increases* as the cost of debt financing *increases* for a given capital structure and a consistent dividend policy.

---

* Our reservations concerning this model stem from the fact that it does not accommodate the time value of money concept, nor does it allow for the complexities of taxation.

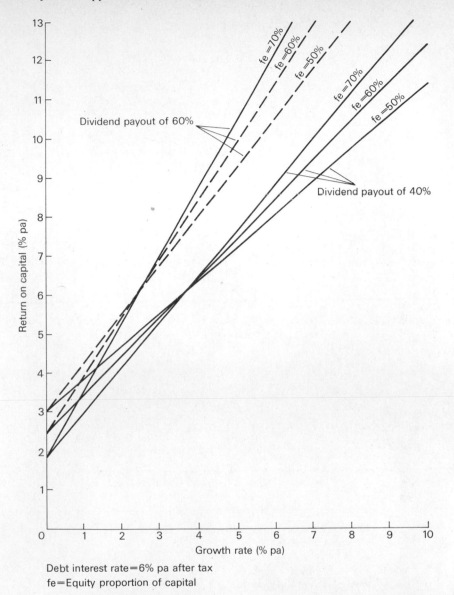

Debt interest rate=6% pa after tax
fe=Equity proportion of capital

Figure 11.1.2 *Relationship between growth in company's capital and rate of return on capital. From de la Mare (1975), with kind permission of the Editor of* Chemical Engineer.

(v) For a given return on capital, the rate of capital growth *decreases* as the cost of debt financing *increases* for a given capital structure and a consistent dividend policy.

These results confirm our intuitive expectations. Conclusions (i) and (ii) explain why managers prefer, whenever possible, to retain earnings within the firm to enhance its growth and profitability. Conclusion (iii) is nothing more than a confirmation of the principle of gearing or leverage shown in equation 8.4.3, whereas conclusions (iv) and (v) illustrate the negative effect on companies brought about by an increasing *real* cost of debt finance.

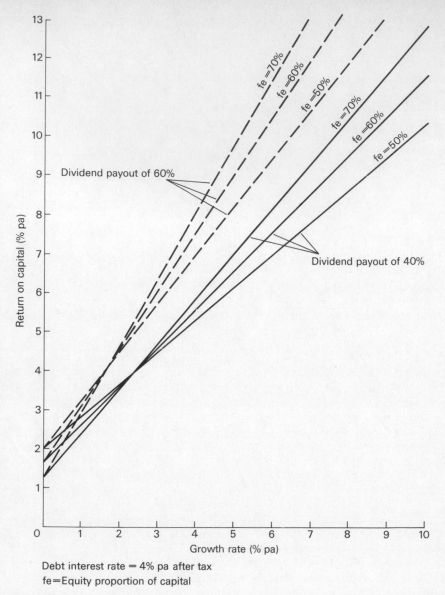

Figure 11.1.3 *Relationship between growth in company's capital and rate of return on capital. From de la Mare (1975), with kind permission of the Editor of* Chemical Engineer.

Despite the deficiencies of this model, our purpose in presenting it here is to demonstrate the fact that decisions concerning the choice between competing investment projects cannot be taken in isolation of the other major parameters affecting the operations and financial security of the firm. In addition to such matters as economic efficiency, uncertainty in the cash flows realized by future investment projects, and the collective risk which their investment implies, a firm also has to consider its capital investment strategy in the context of its *overall* corporate performance, which includes its dividend and capital gearing policies and the strategic implications of growth. To consider all these matters together over a period of five years or more, especially when many different combinations of capital investment projects can be employed, is beyond the mental capability of most people. What is required is a computerized mathematical 'number crunching' model which will help managers explore the economic, financial and growth implications of alternative investment policies quickly and comprehensively. This can be achieved using a heuristic model* of the firm which provides corporate management with answers to 'What if?' questions, such as '*What* would be the effect on the firm's capital structure *if* we financed projects X and Y and, in addition, we maintained the same dividend payout each year for the next five years?' Many of the larger manufacturing corporations of the world have developed such models to aid their top executive decision-making process. Indeed, some executives have immediate on-line access to such models because they offer the following distinct advantages:

(i) a reduction in the time needed to assess the effects of change,
(ii) a rapid total systems evaluation of alternative outcomes and courses of action, and
(iii) the opportunity to investigate the long-term effect of different strategies.

Such models as these allow executives to simulate the operations of the firm using various economic, financial and political scenarios, and they make investigations of the effects of different combinations of projects and different project timings a fairly straightforward matter†.

At this juncture the discerning reader may question our wisdom in presenting the sophisticated theoretical treatise of previous chapters. Indeed, it could be argued that our emphasis on the capital budgeting decision is *misplaced*. Hayes and Solomon (1962) forcibly criticize such an emphasis saying that 'the manager would be mistaken to devote much attention to the usual refinements of investment theory', and they point out that 'precise computations applied to the wrong information cannot result in correct measurements of investment worth'. With such criticisms in mind it is opportune to take stock of all our previous deliberations. There is little doubt that DCF techniques are superior to other methods in that they consider the time value of money implications of investment, whereas other techniques do not. However, it must be admitted that no comprehensive empirical studies of the increased profits resulting from DCF techniques have been published. One can only presume that their extra utility is proven by the increasing number of companies employing these techniques and, more importantly, the fact that they ensure a consistent approach to investment appraisal in which the need to consider *all* the various factors contributing to the cash flow profile of a project throughout its economic life-cycle is made explicit. In this they necessitate a forecast of all the economic consequences of implementing a project and logically this should place the project investment decision on as sound an economic footing as is possible. However, the difficulties of forecasting cannot be under-rated, they have been explicitly acknowledged throughout this book and to that end the tool of sensitivity analysis is

---

* A heuristic is the name of a branch of study belonging to logic and philosophy, the aim of which is to investigate the method of discovery and invention. In the context of this book, a heuristic is an aid to discovering the solution to an investment problem and it is essentially a device or procedure used to reduce problem-solving effort. It is not an optimization technique in the true sense, like linear programming, but simply a means of calculating the effects of different options quickly so that management can explore that option which best serves its overall purpose.

† Two interesting descriptions of corporate decision models are provided by Wierst (1966) and the Planning Executives Institute (1968) (see Bibliography). An excellent practical example of such a model is the Financial Management Program (FMP) used by Rio Tinto Zinc Corporation. This program is devised to forecast all the cash flow, profit and loss, balance sheet, tax, loan, dividend and capital structural effects which new investment projects have on the economic and financial performance of the firm as a whole, over a time horizon chosen by the executive. It calculates all the DCF attributes of each project, and permits a fast and thorough sensitivity analysis to be conducted with very little effort.

considered a sensible approach to decision making under conditions of risk, especially if the total systems implications of risk can be assessed using a corporate model of the type just described. Several companies reckon they have been successful applying Monte Carlo simulation to the risk appraisal of single capital projects, but such success that is reported is attributed more to using the technique to focus on the conditions which *cause* risk rather than the use of the numbers emanating from such a study.

From the foregoing arguments, therefore, it would appear that the justification for the *use* of these techniques is proven. Whether managers need to *understand* the weaknesses and limitations of these techniques is quite another matter. In Chapter 6 we demonstrated that the NPV criterion is theoretically superior to the DCFRR criterion, but we have to admit that the precise evaluation of the cost of capital, which is an integral part of the NPV computation, is difficult. Moreover, for conditions of cash rationing, which inevitably prevail in the majority of companies, we have shown that a proper objective appraisal of the appropriate discount rate is impossible. Faced with these imponderables it is understandable why so many managers prefer using the DCFRR criterion as a decision tool despite its theoretical inferiority and the problem caused by multiple roots. Providing these limitations are understood and accommodated it is thought that managers will make near optimal decisions in their selection of projects, especially if they employ a corporate model and sensitivity analysis, because they will apply, as an inherent part of their decision-making process, their own innate utility criteria, which form the key to the investment optimization process. Although our theoretical treatment of this subject is by no means conclusive, therefore, it should provide a framework of knowledge against which decision makers can evaluate their own intuitive decision-making ideas.

11.2   THE MANAGEMENT OF RISK

So far we have treated risk analysis in an abstract, numerical sense. But risks occur at all stages in the life-cycle of a project – from its inception to its eventual retirement – so it is incumbent on management to reduce risks both singularly and collectively to a level which can be tolerated as an on-going process, not as some academic numerical fancy. The optimization of a capital project can be defined as 'choosing that combination of risk and profitability which is in the best long-term interests of the firm'. To ensure that optimization does occur, however, requires carefully prescribed guidelines for the economic, financial, risk and policy implications of a prospective project to be properly formulated in advance.

The next problem facing management is to identify all those significant choices in the way the project can be accomplished and the likely economic, financial and risks implications of each alternative. By these means a proper dialogue concerning the risk implications of each capital investment alternative becomes an on-going part of every day corporate management.

Risks can be handled in three ways: by avoidance, insurance and control, and it is the prerogative of top management to decide that course of action and that blend of risk management, which best serve its purpose. A study of the total risk implications of a project should start at its inception when it must be realized that the perpetuation of a project involves a sequence of risks. Proper risk management necessitates a thorough feasibility study to be made of the total corporate implications of embarking on the proposed project. Such an overview must consider every conceivable facet of the project which could increase its risks, including technical, economic, marketing, financial, insurance, transport, labour, taxation, legal, political and environment aspects. Furthermore, such studies should not only identify risks but equally they should identify unforeseen opportunities. Since feasibility studies contribute 1–5 per cent of the overall cost of most investment projects, they cannot be dismissed as unimportant in themselves, so there must exist a prima facie case showing that the project can be turned into reality. This in itself suggests the need for a properly administered approach to capital investment projects which we shall deal with later. For the moment, however, it is important to realize that a feasibility study must, of necessity, attempt to unearth all conceivable events which individually or in concert could place the project in jeopardy. This requires a multi-disciplined team approach to investment feasibility analysis and the recognition that one vital area missed in the study can render its conclusions incorrect, even though all the other areas of the study might be excellently covered. Often the first thorough examination of an intended project shows that it should be postponed until certain key events take place which the firm can either patiently await or attempt to influence.

Risk options occur at every stage in a feasibility study. They are involved with the inevitable trade-offs which exist between the various alternative process routes and plant combinations for realizing the intended project objective. Typically these include terotechnological trade-offs such as: first cost versus subsequent life-cycle costs, reliability versus flexibility, excess capacity versus subsequent investment, and a long building programme versus a short one. Risk options even include different forms of building and labour contracts. There is no knowing in advance which factors of risk will predominate, because they will be uniquely determined by the nature of the project and the conditions affecting it. In some cases the geographical deployment of the intended capital project might be one of the decisive risk factors, as many firms have found to their cost. In other circumstances the economic or political environment might be all important, especially in times of high inflation or political unrest. From a purely manufacturing viewpoint, however, the greatest risks often derive from the high rate of technological innovation and the equally high rate of product and process obsolescence experienced by manufacturing industries.

Besides the need to minimize the risks involved with a particular project, it is incumbent on corporate management to maintain the risk of the firm's total portfolio of projects and products at a level which is tolerable. To this end it has to devise a risk strategy which considers the relative merits of project diversification and project concentration. The more of its resources a company commits to a particular strategy, the more pronounced are the consequences. If the strategy is successful, the pay-off will be considerable. If the strategy fails, then the consequences may be dire. What proportion of its available resources a firm should commit to a particular course of action is therefore one of the most crucial questions it faces. It will be remembered that we discussed this problem in Section 9.12, when it was shown how some projects enhance their mutual benefits (thereby exhibiting true synergy), whereas others show the reverse effect. The most fundamental issue of all, however, is whether or not a firm has devised its strategy correctly. We shall return to this matter later.

Although the management of risk receives little, in the way of practical treatment, by most academic texts, it should be noted that an excellent approach to the subject is provided by a series of ten essays promoted by OYEZ–IBC (1978). These relate the problems of and solutions to successfully accomplishing giant projects throughout the world.

11.3 THE ORGANIZATION OF CAPITAL BUDGETING

To minimize the risks involved with developing new products and capital projects, coupled with the need to harness the resources of a firm in the most effective way, it is essential for management to maintain control over its projects throughout all of their various stages. This requires a formalized approach to capital budgeting which incorporates the following sequential steps, from the inception of a product or project idea to its realization and ultimate termination.

The conception stage. This recognizes the benefits arising from a purposeful, continuous and creative search for new investment opportunities to fill that inevitable profit gap which we discussed in Chapter 4. Focus on the need for such a search is intensified if projects have to be submitted for the scrutiny of top management by prescribed dates.

The formalization stage. This is where the project is recognized as an on-going corporate activity, albeit with very limited resources.

Continuation of the project with a limited degree of authority. This stage calls for a preliminary review of the project. It is important to establish as early as possible whether the new venture has any real promise of meeting the requirements for return on capital, growth and other basic objectives. For this purpose the project must be reviewed using the best information and estimates at hand, preferably with the aid of detailed check lists. Such a study should endeavour to identify those factors which are critical to the success of the venture so that their likely effect can be properly appraised. In many cases the preliminary review will be a more or less continuous procedure from which the feasibility study will gradually emerge. The resources required for a proper feasibility study are usually substantial, so a formal justification for their use is normally required.

The feasibility study evaluation. Providing the preliminary reviews show good grounds for further detailed investigation, they should be able to justify a proper feasibility study which should determine the broad lines on which the project should be developed, and demonstrate its viability. Between the preliminary review stage and the feasibility study a number of intermediate reviews might often be necessary, each dealing with a particular aspect of the project such as marketing, transportation, financing, etc. Generally, for manufacturing projects, it is the marketing aspect about which there is the most uncertainty and this is the area which repays the most careful analysis which should be backed, wherever possible, by independent studies.

Providing the feasibility study shows that the project meets all criteria set for its evaluation and it competes successfully against other similar projects then it should be incorporated in the firm's formal capital budget and plans should be made for its funding at a time which is thought to be optimal. Only when this stage is reached, however, should authority be given to release resources for the next stage in the procedure which involves the optimization of the project.

The definitive (optimum) plan. Having decided that the project is economically viable and compatible with the firm's strategic needs, it should then be optimized in terms of profitability, selecting amongst other things the most economic level of production and the optimal size of plant. Experience has shown that coming to a conclusion too early about some of the project fundamentals, particularly the scale of plant, should be avoided if at all possible. The definitive plan should culminate in a thorough financial and economic appraisal dealing with all those aspects of previous chapters.

Capital appropriation request. Providing the results of the definitive (optimum) plan above still show that a project is economically viable then a proper capital appropriation request should be prepared and submitted to the firm's board of directors for authority to spend the funds planned for the project in the capital budget. Such a document should comprise a definitive statement concerning all the strategic, economic, financial, political and other resource implications of the project and it should explicitly deal with all aspects of risk which might arise from the project's acceptance. Furthermore, such a document should highlight the compatibility or incompatibility of the proposed project with any of the firm's other projects and any positive or negative synergistic effects arising therefrom. In order to take advantage of some recently discovered highly lucrative project, it is quite conceivable that this stage in the budget procedure might be reached by short-circuiting some of the preceding stages.

Capital expenditure authorization. Even when a project reaches the capital appropriation request stage, there is still no guarantee that it will be financed. The directors still have to assess the wisdom in committing possibly a large proportion of the firm's resources to a particular strategy.

Capital expenditure control. Providing there is no radical departure from the firm's original plans, the job of the project manager is to develop the project within the limits of time, quality and cost specified for the project in the capital appropriation request, once approval for the project's realization has been given. This calls for imaginative management control over substantial, sometimes vast, resources. This is a most sensitive stage for any project because a building programme or cost over-run usually has a deleterious effect on the project's economic return. Several matters concerning project management control are given in Chapter 14.

Subsequent stages in the execution of a project involve its optimization throughout its economic life; the post-auditing of its performance and the feeding back of information to ensure that the company learns by its experiences; and the abandonment of the project either by way of its replacement or retirement. All these considerations receive detailed coverage in Parts III and IV of this book.

11.4 THE STRATEGIC IMPLICATIONS OF CAPITAL INVESTMENT

No good military commander would undertake even a small-scale attack on a limited objective without a clear understanding of his overall strategy. In the business arena, however, it is not uncommon to find senior managers deploying resources on a large scale without a clear notion of what their strategy is. Undoubtedly this applies to many successful companies too, whose philosophy is to seek and exploit lucrative opportunities, but the moment arrives in the development of most firms when it becomes difficult to branch out into new ventures without a precise appreciation of their strategic significance. This is why many established firms often fail miserably when they attempt a programme of business expansion either through corporate acquisition or merger, or by way of product and market diversification.

The major purpose of any investment programme must be to enhance the performance of the total corporate entity and such investment should magnify that corporate distinctiveness which clearly distinguishes the firm and its products from other firms and their products. In effect, therefore, investment should comprise the most tangible expression of a firm's strategy because the essential feature of capital resources is that they represent the potential future performance of a firm. In aggregate they represent the firm's capacity to respond to threats and to take advantage of opportunity. In some respects, therefore, capital investment projects are like gaming chips which the firm has to play in the serious game of business.

For didactic reasons, our concentration on the economic aspects of the capital budgeting decision has focused on the project singular, although we have persistently emphasized the need to consider a particular project in the context of the firm as a *set* of investment projects, particularly from a risk and synergy standpoint. We cannot overstress the point, however, that it is essential for an investment project not to be considered as a separate self-contained entity since the introduction of a new project, possibly involving a new product, is not an end in itself, but merely an extension in a continuing competitive context. The major strategic implication of capital investment is whether the new project signals (i) a growing resource commitment to an existing product line or technology in order to stay in an existing competitive contest; (ii) a growing resource commitment to enter a new product line or technology in order to diversify away from an existing line of business; or (iii) a unique opportunity to realize high profits to finance future strategic projects. When one considers investment opportunities from these three different points of view one will understand why business executives set different threshold returns on investment for the acceptance of projects with different strategic as well as risk implications.

11.5 SUMMARY

In this chapter we have endeavoured to coalesce some of the lessons learned from previous chapters in a way which describes the strategic implications of capital investment and its affect on the corporation as a whole. In doing this we freely admit that the problem of capital investment is much more complex than our original mathematical treatment of the subject would suggest, especially as that original treatment did not properly consider the growth, strategic and corporate risk implications of a single project in the context of the firm as a total system. Despite these criticisms, however, we conclude that the DCF technique, which embodies the philosophy of life-cycle costs and benefits permeating this entire book, provides the best known means of appraising the economic merits of investment projects both singularly and collectively. To appreciate the total effect which investment projects have on the economic and financial performance of the company as a whole, we seriously recommend the adoption of a corporate financial model where its employment is justified. We also recommend that managers should be made aware of the shortcomings in existing investment analysis theory and they should endeavour to accommodate these deficiencies when making their investment decisions. Above all else, however, we wish to stress that corporate investment is much more than facts and figures. It represents the hopes and aspirations of the body corporate for the future. Such matters cannot be taken lightly or without a properly conceived strategy, which must recognize the corporate strengths and weaknesses as well as recognizing the required goals and objectives.

11.6 BIBLIOGRAPHY

de la Mare, R. F., 'Parameters affecting capital investment', *Chemical Engineer,* **296,** April 1975, pp. 227–247.

Hayes, W. W. and Solomon, M. B., 'A misplaced emphasis on capital budgeting', *Quarterly Review of Economics and Business*, February 1962.

OYEZ–IBC, *A Multi-Disciplined Study of Problems and Solutions to Successfully Accomplishing Giant Projects*, An edited version of ten essays given at an international conference in London, 17–18 May 1978.

Planning Executives Institute, Ohio, USA, *Development and Application of a Corporate Financial Model*, 1968.

Wierst, J. D., 'Heuristic programs for decision making', *Harvard Business Review*, September–October 1966, p. 129.

12. *A Capital Budgeting Game*

So far, we have assumed that the information concerning the physical and cash-flow attributes of a new capital venture would be readily available to permit a thorough economic appraisal to be made, based on discounted cash-flow techniques. At the initial stage of a new capital venture, however, it is more likely that many of the physical and cash-flow considerations will be very uncertain. All that might be known is the contemplated capacity of the plant, its capital cost estimate and some ideas regarding the raw material costs and selling price. Despite the paucity of information, decisions still have to be made to decide whether or not to continue with the project. For example, it might be decided that there is a need to build a pilot plant to overcome some technical problem, or to produce some product for market testing. This investment would have to be justified and so there would be a need for some type of appraisal, albeit approximate.

In addition to these considerations, there remains the need for the serious student of manufacturing economics to understand the ramifications of decision making beyond the narrow scope presented by the text, and the academically contrived numerical examples and questions. Ideally this need could be met using a computer programmed to analyse the economic merits of a complicated capital budgeting problem quickly. Such a method is ideal when teaching groups of people. However, this method is hardly justified for the individual reader, yet the need to understand the iterative nature of the capital budgeting process still remains.

To meet both these needs, a mathematical model has been developed and is described below*. It cannot be overstressed that the model is approximate, in that it does *not* incorporate any allowance for company taxes which can have a significant effect on the economic merits of a project. Because of their complexity, however, taxation considerations have been excluded. Anyone intending to use this model in real-life application is therefore advised to check its sensitivity to the particular taxation factors involved. Its use here is justified as a pedagogical technique. To that end a game, which progresses in a realistic manner, has been developed. Answers to each part of this game are provided in Appendix C. As with the case studies also provided, the greatest benefit to be derived from this game will be realized from role playing the game and resolving the problems at each stage, prior to reading their solutions.

12.1 THE DEVELOPMENT OF THE MODEL

The equation for the model is:

$$N = a[(S - bV) \cdot T \cdot U - L \cdot M - A] - cF$$

where N = net present value at the start of the project (£k), a = coefficient (a function of the time to build the plant, its productive life and the discount rate),

---

* This model and the accompanying game are reproduced by kind permission from Mr N. J. Le Page, formerly of Imperial Chemical Industries Ltd, Mond Division.

S = variable net selling price of the product (£ per tonne); b = coefficient of seasonality, V = variable cost of the product (£ per tonne), T = installed capacity of the plant (k tonnes per year), U = capacity utilization factor, L = labour cost (£k/shift team/year), M = number of shift teams needed, A = annual fixed costs other than capital-related or labour-related fixed costs (£k/y), c = coefficient (a function of coefficient a, maintenance intensity and the ratio of spent to unspent capital, F = fixed capital cost (£k), and k = a dividing factor (= 1000, in this game) and the abbreviation £k/y is used to denote £k per year.

The derivations of the coefficients used are given below, where the net present value is computed as the sum of five components relating to five different types of cash flow.

Variable cash flows

If we ignore the possibility of a time-lag between the purchase of raw materials and the sale of product, then the variable cash flows would be:

$$£ (S - V) \text{ per tonne}$$

where S = unit selling price, and V = unit variable cost of production. Because the raw materials are purchased and other variable costs are incurred before the product is sold, a discounting effect has to be allowed for, according to the expression:

$$(S - bV)$$

where b = a function of the discount rate and the time-lag, with values given in Table 12.1.1.

If it took Y_c years to build the plant which was then operated until Year Y_p at full capacity T, the net present value of the variable cash flows would be:

$$N_V = \sum_{t=Y_c}^{Y_p} \frac{(S-bV)T}{(1+r)^t} = (S-bV)T \sum_{t=Y_c}^{Y_p} \frac{1}{(1+r)^{-t}}$$

This can be simplified to $a(S - bV)T$ where:

$$a = \sum_{Y_c}^{Y_p} \frac{1}{(1+r)^{-t}}$$

Values of a are given in Table 12.1.1 for $Y_c = 2$ years, and $Y_p = 7$ or 12 years (corresponding to 5 or 10 years of production, respectively).

It is unlikely that a plant would start to produce at 100 per cent occupancy when construction is complete, because of start-up and marketing problems. Instead, if the actual production in Year t were P_t, we could define the capacity utilization factor U

Table 12.1.1

Discount rate (% pa)	Numerical value of coefficients			
	a		b	
	10-year life	5-year life	Non-seasonal	Seasonal
0	10.0	5.0	1.00	1.00
5	7.35	4.12	1.012	1.048
10	5.59	3.45	1.023	1.091
15	4.36	2.92	1.032	1.130
20	3.49	2.49	1.042	1.161

Table 12.1.2　*Capacity utilization patterns for ten-year productive lives*

| Pattern no. | Actual percentage occupancies | | | | | |
	I	II	III	IV	V	VI
Year						
3	100	55	82	7.3	14.0	31.6
4	100	60	84	10.3	27.7	63.7
5	100	65	86	14.4	43.5	84.0
6	100	70	88	19.9	58.6	93.5
7	100	75	90	27.0	71.4	97.4
8	100	80	92	36.0	81.4	99.0
9	100	85	94	47.5	88.7	99.6
10	100	90	96	61.7	93.9	99.9
11	100	95	98	79.1	97.5	100.0
12	100	100	100	100.0	100.0	100.0
Total	1000	775	910	403.2	676.7	868.7
Capacity utilization factor (at 15% pa discount rate)	1.00	0.72	0.89	0.30	0.56	0.79

Note: Years 1 and 2 are construction years.

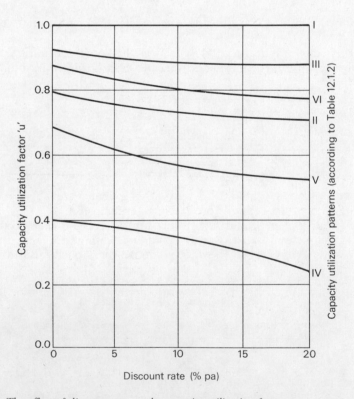

Figure 12.1.1　*The effect of discount rate on the capacity utilization factor.*

by the expression:

$$U = \frac{\sum\limits_{Y_c}^{Y_p} \dfrac{P_t}{(1+r)^t}}{\sum\limits_{Y_c}^{Y_p} \dfrac{T}{(1+r)^t}}$$

so the net present value of the variable cash flows would be:

$$N_v = a(S - bV)TU$$

Values of U for various sales patterns are shown in Table 12.1.2 and Figure 12.1.1, where Pattern I represents full occupancy.

Fixed (once and for all) expenditures

If a plant cost £F and takes two years to build, the net present value of capital expenditure is:

$$N_{FO} = -c_0 F$$

where c_0 is a discount factor for the particular construction pattern. However, there are usually other costs related to the fixed capital cost, such as overhead allocated capital for buildings accommodating the extra R & D effort involved with the new project. Furthermore, there is the large cost of commissioning the plant, so the net present value of the fixed expenditure becomes:

$$N_{FO} = -c_1 F$$

where c_1 replaces c_0 and allows for the effect of discounting and these other costs. Values for c_1 are shown in Table 12.1.3.

Table 12.1.3 *Values of factors c_1 and c_2 when operating labour is not capitalized*

Discount interest rate (% pa)		0	5	10	15	20
Ten years' production	c_1	1.18	1.12	1.07	1.03	0.98
	c_2	1.18	0.87	0.66	0.55	0.41
	c	2.36	1.99	1.73	1.58	1.39
Five years' production	c_1	1.18	1.12	1.07	1.03	0.98
	c_2	0.59	0.49	0.41	0.34	0.29
	c	1.77	1.61	1.48	1.37	1.27

c_1 undiscounted $= 1$ (for plant capital) $+ 0.1$ (for 10 per cent overhead allocated capital) $+ 0.08$ (for capitalized commissioning) $= 1.18$ (for the total fixed once and for all expenditure).

$$c_2 \text{ undiscounted} = \frac{d \times \text{number of production years}}{100} \times \begin{array}{l} \text{total fixed} \\ \text{once and for} \\ \text{all expenditures} \end{array}$$

where $d = \%$/year capital related costs.
(In the data provided, $d = 5$ per cent for OR & M, 3 per cent for overheads on OR & M labour, and 2 per cent for central services, giving a total of 10 per cent.)

Annual fixed costs related to capital

Each year a plant sustains annual fixed costs due to ordinary repairs and maintenance (OR & M) and other special costs associated with the maintenance of the plant. The net present value of these fixed capital related costs is:

$$N_{FR} = -c_2 F$$

Values of c_2 are shown in Table 12.1.3.

Process labour costs

If M shifts are needed to operate the plant and each team costs £L per production year, then the net present value of the labour costs (N_L) will be $-aLM$, where a is the same coefficient as previously used.

Other fixed annual costs

These include selling expenses, R & D running costs, etc. (unrelated to either process or capital costs). If these amount to £A per production year, then their net present value (N_A) will be $-aA$.

The total net present value of a project is therefore given by the sum of five values according to:

$$N = N_v + N_{FO} + N_{FR} + N_L + N_A$$
$$= a[(S - bV)T \cdot U - LM - A] - cF$$

where $c = c_1 + c_2$ with values also shown in Table 12.1.3.

12.2 PROJECT 'UNOWAT' – A CAPITAL BUDGETING GAME

Document 1

The senior executives of a manufacturing company are considering investment in Project 'UNOWAT'. They believe that product sales could fall between the pessimistic and optimistic forecasts given below and they are recommending building a plant of 20 000 tonnes per annum capacity at an estimated and installed capital cost of £1.16 millions. This plant would take two years to build, and would involve the following economic factors:

(i) Estimated sales volume (k tonnes per annum)

Year	3	4	5	6	7	8	9	10	11	12
Pessimistic	1.5	2.1	2.9	4.0	5.4	7.2	9.5	12.3	15.8	20
Expected	2.8	5.5	8.7	11.7	14.3	16.3	17.7	18.8	19.5	20
Optimistic	6.3	12.7	16.8	18.7	19.5	19.8	20	20	20	20

(ii) Variable production cost = £142/tonne,
(iii) Net selling price = £250/tonne,
(iv) Plant capital cost (£1.16 m) divided equally between Years 1 and 2,

(v) Overheads capital = 15 per cent of plant capital, also divided equally between Years 1 and 2.
(vi) Capital related fixed costs = 10 per cent of fixed plant capital per year (Years 3–12),
(vii) Operating labour costs = £60k/year (Years 3–12),
(viii) Other annual fixed costs = £50k/year (Years 3–12),
(ix) Commissioning expenditure = £100k (Year 3), and
(x) The firm's cost of capital is reckoned to approximate 10 per cent per annum.

Requirement

Compute the net present value of Project 'UNOWAT' for all three sales forecasts using the traditional NPV method and the discount factor tables of Appendix G. Do not use the mathematical model of Section 12.1 yet!

Document 2

This shows the use of the shortcut DCF method based on the mathematical model, to obviate the year-by-year calculations based on the particular sales predictions shown in Document 1.

Basic equation for net present value determination:

$$N = a[(S - bV)TU - LM - A] - cF$$

where

N = net present value (£k),
a = coefficient (function of number of construction and production years and discount rate),
S = net selling price (£/tonne),
b = coefficient (function of seasonality of product),
V = variable cost (£/tonne),
T = capacity or maximum production rate (k tonne/year),
U = capacity utilization factor,

$$= \frac{\Sigma \text{ (discounted actual production)}}{\Sigma \text{ (discounted maximum possible production)}},$$

L = labour rate (£k/shift team),
M = no. of shift teams needed,
A = annual fixed costs other than capital-related or labour-related (£k/year),
c = coefficient (function of coefficient a, maintenance intensity and ratio of spent to unspent capital),
F = fixed battery limits capital (£k).

Values at beginning of Project history
a = 5.6 (value for two years' construction and ten years' production, 10 per cent/year discount rate), see Table 12.1.1,
b = 1.02 (value for a non-seasonal product), see Table 12.1.1,
c = 1.73 (average value when there are no existing assets), see Table 12.1.3,
S = 250 (NSP = £250/tonne),
V = 142 (variable cost = £142/tonne),
LM = 60 (operating labour costs = £60 k/year),
A = 50 (other annual fixed costs = £50 k/year), ⎫
F = 1160 (fixed battery limits capital = £1.16 m), ⎬ See Document 1
T = 20 (capacity = 20k tonne/year), ⎪
U = ? ⎭

Requirement. Using the mathematical model and the details given above, calculate the NPV for this project at three different levels of capacity utilization given by:

$U = 0.3$ (for poor) capacity utilization,
$U = 0.6$ (for medium) capacity utilization,
$U = 0.9$ (for good) capacity utilization.

Draw a graph showing the relationship between the NPV and the capacity utilization factor, and deduce the minimum level of capacity utilization which would make this project profitable.

Document 3

MEMORANDUM

To: Head Corporate Planning Department   **Date:** 3 February 19X1

From: Head Technical Department   **Subject:** Project 'UNOWAT –
                                                          plant corrosion

The materials testing laboratory has just done an appraisal of the corrosion problems likely to be encountered by this new process. They reckon that the plant made from mild steel and costing £1.16 m would require an extra £30k/y to maintain in working order. Alternatively, special materials could be used in the corrosive zone adding an extra £340k to the capital cost. I felt you should know these facts as quickly as possible since they might have a significant effect on the economic merits of this project.

J. B. James

Requirement. Appraise the economic consequences of this news, but do *not* read the solution yet!

Document 4

MEMORANDUM

To: Head of Corporate Planning   **Date:** 10 February 19X1

From: Head of Technical Department   **Subject:** Project 'UNOWAT' –
                                                          materials of
                                                          construction problem

Our chemical engineers have just discovered that mild steel, as a material of construction, contaminates the product. To overcome this effect we would need to provide an extra process unit costing £130k installed and the raw materials costs would increase by £4.70 per tonne.

J. B. James

Requirement. Appraise the economic consequences of this news, but do *not* read the solution yet!

Document 5

MEMORANDUM

To: Head of Corporate Planning   **Date:** 22 February 19X1

From: Market Research Executive   **Subject:** Project 'UNOWAT' –
                                                           sales forecast

At last we have been able to assess the likely sales of the new product and
reckon that it will be of medium growth potential, with a capacity utilization
factor approaching 0.6.

W. A. Jenkins

Requirement. Using this new information reappraise the merits of the project and
check your answers against the solution in Appendix C.

Document 6

MEMORANDUM

To: Head of Corporate Planning   **Date:** 10 March 19X1

From: Export Executive   **Subject:** Project 'UNOWAT' –
                                                  exports to USA

In addition to the home market, we could sell 'UNOWAT' at £160/t in the USA.
The growth is likely to be fast at first, rising to $5k$ t/y in four to five years. After
that, we are likely to experience intense competition from two American firms
who are known to be researching in this field. The extra annual fixed cost would
be small (£20k/y).

A. P. Martins

Note: For this extra business, $a = 3.5$, $T' = 5$ and $U = 0.9$.

Requirement. Evaluate the economic merits of this export opportunity, but do not
refer to the solution yet!

Document 7

MEMORANDUM

To: Export Executive   **Date:** 19 March 19X1

From: Transport Department   **Subject:** Project 'UNOWAT' –
                                                                                    exports to USA

Freight charges, insurance premiums and import duty into the USA are likely to cost £20 per tonne for our new product.

P. D. Harris

Requirement. Re-evaluate this export opportunity and check your answer.

Document 8

MEMORANDUM

To: Head Corporate Planning Department   **Date:** 20 April 19X1

From: Head Technical Department   **Subject:** Project 'UNOWAT' –
                                                                                    R & D progress

---

We have been experimenting with the selectivity of the chemical reactions involved with 'UNOWAT' and have found that we could improve the raw material efficiency and also reduce the size of the plant. Our best estimates are that the plant of corrosion-resistant material would now cost £1.46 million and that the unit variable production cost would be £126/tonne.

J. B. James

Requirement. Reappraise the economics of the project in light of this news and check your answer.

Document 9

MEMORANDUM

To: Department Heads   **Date:** 23 April 19X1

From: Managing Director   **Subject:** 'UNOWAT' – competition

---

A news item in the technical press states that a company in West Germany is working on a product which resembles 'UNOWAT'. It would appear that their product will be superior. I have asked the Heads of the Marketing and Technical Departments to validate this claim.

I would like your views as to how we should accommodate the effect of this threat.

R. B. McAllen

Document 10

MEMORANDUM

To: Managing Director and   **Date:** 27 April 19X1
Corporate Planning Dept.

From: Marketing Director and Head   **Subject:** 'UNOWAT' – competition
Technical Dept.

We have confirmed the seriousness of the rivalry from West Germany and see three alternative ways of accommodating it:

(A) We believe that by spending more time developing 'UNOWAT' we could provide a better product than the Germans. This would require:
  (i) Three chemists, costing Project 'UNOWAT' £45 000 but no extra cost to the firm's existing R & D budget,
  (ii) a pilot plant costing £40 000,
  (iii) modifications to the full-scale plant costing an extra £100 000.
  We reckon that this work would raise the probability of overall technical and commercial success to 80–90 per cent.

(B) We are confident that a £30/tonne reduction in our price would hold off the German threat.

(C) We believe that we could license the German process for £50 000 with a royalty of £5/tonne. However, modifications to our existing plant design would cost a further £200 000 and the product variable cost would increase by £4/tonne.

S. T. Williams,
J. B. James

Requirement. Decide the best strategy now available to the firm, but do not refer to the solution yet!

Document 11

MEMORANDUM

To: Head of Corporate Planning   **Date:** 1 May 19X1

From: Managing Director   **Subject:** Project 'UNOWAT' –
                                                    risks involved

To better assess the risks involved with this project, I would like to know the
effects of having to abandon the project, say at the end of its fourth full year of
operation.

R. B. McAllen

Requirement. Evaluate this effect, and then check your results for Documents 9, 10
and 11.

Document 12

MEMORANDUM

To: Managing Director   **Date:** 21 May 19X1

From: Project Manager   **Subject:** Project 'UNOWAT' – progress

The R & D project was successful in improving the quality of product
'UNOWAT', and Marketing Dept. are confident that we shall hold our own
against the competition from West Germany.

We estimate that the modifications to the new capital plant required for
upgrading the product will now cost £150k instead of £100k as previously
estimated. We also reckon that the variable cost will increase (due to extra
services and handling losses) by £6/tonne to £132/tonne and that extra labour
costs, amounting to £10k/year, will be incurred. I think we should now press
ahead with this project.

A. B. Happel

Requirement. Develop the economics for this new base case, but do not confirm
your results yet!

Document 13

MEMORANDUM

To: Head of Corporate Planning   **Date:** 17 June 19X2

From: Project Manager   **Subject:** Project 'UNOWAT' –
                                            Progress report

We are now half way through the building programme which has gone completely
to plan. According to the marketing dept., and contrary to their initial findings,
they now believe that sales of 'UNOWAT' will be highly seasonal. This means
that we shall need to carry larger stocks of raw materials and finished product
and have to invest in more storage capacity at an estimated extra cost of £90 000.
In light of this new information, I would like your estimate of the economic
merits of Project 'UNOWAT' as from *now*. Furthermore I would like to know if
we really did make the right decision by not licensing the German process.

A. B. Happel

Requirement. Reappraise the economic merits of the project as from *now*. Factors a,
b and c will change, but how? Check your answers *after* your computations.

Document 14

MEMORANDUM

To: Head Corporate Planning   **Date:** 1 June 19X3

From: Marketing Director   **Subject:** New developments

I gather that the 'UNOWAT' plant will be commissioned next week and would
like to bring to your attention two new developments:

(1) now that we shall be entering the EEC within the next few months, we could
    improve the sales of 'UNOWAT' markedly even up to a plant utilization
    factor of 0.9, but this would require an increased sales force, costing another
    £100 000 per annum.
(2) International Intermediates Inc. (3 I's) are offering at £101 per tonne
    delivered the intermediate product C which we produce in Stage 1 of the
    'UNOWAT' plant. This would make the unit variable cost of product
    'UNOWAT' work out at £135 per tonne, which is more than we currently
    expect it to cost. However, this purchase would allow us to shut down Stage
    1, which cost £840k, sell off the plant as scrap for £20k and realize
    economies in maintenance.

What do you recommend?

S. T. Williams

Requirement. Evaluate these two new propositions and make your recommendations
accordingly. Check your answers before proceeding to Document 15.

Document 15

MEMORANDUM

To: Head Corporate Planning   **Date:**   10 June 19X3

From: Marketing Director   **Subject:**   Sale of Intermediate C

We approached 3 I's about a long-term contract, but they replied in rather evasive terms, so we made a quick survey of suppliers of Intermediate C and found several other firms selling the product on a job-lot basis. From what we know of the market, we are confident that we could sell as much Intermediate C as we can make in our spare capacity at £101/t without entering into long-term contracts. I understand that we have a 22kt/y Intermediate C plant (Stage 1 of the 20kt/y 'UNOWAT' plant) with spare capacity until 'UNOWAT' demand builds up, so we could consider entering the Intermediate C market selling job lots at £101/t for some time. The manager of our 'UNOWAT' plant tells me that 1.1 tonnes of C are required to make 1 tonne of 'UNOWAT', so that the cost breakdown for the manufacture of Intermediate C is given below:

Inputs per tonne of Int. C	t/t	$£/t$	$£/t$ Int. C
Raw material A	0.45	50	22.5
Raw material B	0.58	100	58.0
Catalyst	0.002	1000	2.0
Other variable costs			2.0
Services			6.4
Licence			5.0
			95.9

What would you recommend us to do?

S. T. Williams

Requirement. Make your recommendation, and check your answer.

Document 16

MEMORANDUM

To: Head Corporate Planning   **Date:** 12 December 19X3

From: Marketing Director   **Subject:** Health effects of
                                                                    product 'UNOWAT'

Recent adverse publicity arising from reports of harmful side effects caused by
'UNOWAT', and the probability that legislation will be introduced to prohibit its
sale, have made us revise our market forecasts drastically. We now believe that a
capacity utilization factor approaching 0.1 would be more appropriate. From a
discussion with R & D department, we understand that they have traced the
harmful effect to an impurity introduced in raw material D which is used in Stage
2 of the process. This did not show up in the early screening tests when
predistilled D was used, but it appears that raw D supplied to the plant is
undistilled. R & D are confident that 'UNOWAT' made from pre-distilled D
would pass any government test, but the harm has now been done and public
confidence lost. Even if 'UNOWAT' is made safe, its sales are unlikely to give
us a capacity utilization factor better than 0.4.
  We are discussing the problem with a marketing consultancy firm.

S. T. Williams

PART III

The Optimal Employment of Existing Assets

In earlier chapters we explained why every manufacturing company should formulate its corporate objective in terms of a required rate of return on capital, recognizing that profits from the sale of existing products and services eventually erode due to the effects of technological change. We also suggested that two of the prime responsibilities of management are to market aggressively and innovate its products to ensure that the firm survives and prospers in the long term. To this end, the accent of Part II was on the corporate need to seek and generate new business opportunities actively and to appraise their economic merits using proper evaluation procedures, the implication being that all firms inevitably have to invest in new capital assets if they want to stay in business. In effect, therefore, Part II deals with the *future* business needs of the firm in general, and the capital budgeting problem in particular.

In Part III, the emphasis changes, and we now concentrate on how the firm should make the best possible use of its existing resources. This does not imply that the material of Parts II and III deal with unrelated business problems. On the contrary, their contents are inextricably linked by virtue of the fact that approval to spend money on new plant and machinery, with a view to exploiting new marketing and technical opportunities, bears an implicit *promise* by management that the forecast benefits of that investment will be realized. This means that corporate management is morally obligated to do all in its power to attain the targets established in its capital appropriation requests, and it is incumbent on management to control these assets throughout their economic life to ensure that they are used in the most effective way possible.

The principal functions of corporate management are to plan, co-ordinate, motivate and control the seemingly disparate activities of the firm to attain a common goal, recognizing that the needs and aspirations of many people form an integral part of that goal. Co-ordination and motivation are two aspects of management which lie outside the scope of this book, but this does not mean that we underrate their importance. Indeed, organizational and human behavioural matters are all important to the realization of corporate objectives for there is no substitute to an enlightened

293

and perceptive management working in harmony with a co-operative and diligent workforce. Instead, Part III concentrates on the planning and control functions of management in as much detail as space permits, recognizing that our primary aim is to understand the economic implications of alternative manufacturing strategies and tactics.

Chapter 13 deals with the conventional methods used by many companies to control their operations, including responsibility costing, budgetary control, standard cost and variance analysis and marginal costing. However, its emphasis concerns the need to understand the *economic significance* of accounting information properly and to have available a comprehensive information system to help management implement effective control.

Initially, Chapter 14 might seem singularly misplaced, because it dwells at considerable length on the mechanics of network analysis. The main reason for its inclusion here, however, lies in the fact that network analysis is an important means of helping project management exercise effective and timely control over capital, R & D and resource intensive projects, whose delay can often damage a firm economically.

In Chapter 15 we recognize that capital investment in inventories is second only to that in fixed assets for most manufacturing firms, and that modest economies in stockholding could provide a firm with much needed funds for capital expansion and new product development. In effect, therefore, Chapter 15 deals with methods of stock control.

Chapter 16 deals with the problem of the inevitable queues which form throughout any manufacturing organization, and it shows how management must strike an economic balance between the need to minimize idle resources standing in-line and the concomitant need to maximize the utilization of service facilities.

Chapter 17 provides a variety of management science techniques for the optimization of existing resources. In particular, it deals with linear programming which has proved an invaluable tool for reducing costs and increasing profits, especially in the process industries.

To conclude Part III, we offer readers the opportunity to exercise their knowledge and skills in a case study which highlights the practical significance and some of the limitations of the material contained herein. For pedagogical reasons, we have treated the substance of each of the following chapters separately, but we realize that it would be most inadvisable to do this in practice. To some extent, therefore, we hope that the case study will reduce this deficiency and readers will appreciate that the objective of a firm is to realize a satisfactory return for the company as a whole.

13. *The Control of Existing Resources Using Accounting Information*

Approval to fund the development of a new product or the building of a new factory is a difficult decision in itself, but the outcome of that decision only provides a firm with the *potential* to perform well. To realize that potential, management has to exercise effective control over its projects throughout their life-cycle. This requires several important ingredients. Above all else it requires a dedication of purpose to achieve the stated objects of each project. However, experience has shown that such a professional management ethic is not enough. Instead three other prerequisites are needed for effective project control, namely:

(i) the availability of a comprehensive and cost-effective information system which permits corporate activity to be monitored and controlled through timely and instrumental action;
(ii) the use of relevant management control techniques such as responsibility costing, budgetary control, standard cost and variance analysis, and marginal costing, which facilitate corporate control; and
(iii) a proper understanding of the significance and the limitations of the cost and accounting information used in (i) and (ii) above. These three form the basis for this chapter.

13.1 THE BASIC NEED FOR COST CONTROL

From the material of Chapters 3 and 7 we have come to realize that in a free market economy customers only reward those firms whose products and services are judged to offer value for money. The precise meaning of this term defies definition but, in the context of this book, we suggest that the decision to buy or not to buy a product is governed by (i) its known first cost (price), (ii) its expected future costs, (iii) its functional capability, and (iv) its aesthetic appeal, as assessed by each individual's judgement, which is tempered by their particular preferences, experiences and, of course, their income. The net effect is that a company does not have absolute control over its level of sales and profitability. It can influence the customer by a variety of legitimate means, but the only sales decision over which a firm has absolute sovereignty concerns the nature of its product.

It has been argued earlier that a firm can often justify selling its products at a premium price relative to its competitors' products if they are sufficiently differentiated by higher technological capability and/or quality. In these circumstances their better performance and/or quality must be cost-effective to warrant their premium price. By contrast, the prices of commodity products are decided by market forces over which a firm may have little control. The point which we wish to emphasize is that firms usually exercise more control over their profits by way of *cost control* than via *price control*. Effective cost control within a firm is therefore an essential prerequisite to corporate long-term survival.

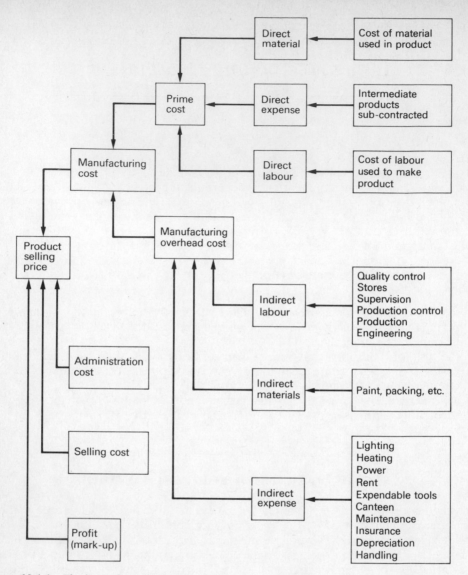

Figure 13.1.1   *The basic elements of costing.*

Costs are incurred at every stage of the manufacturing conversion process, from the procurement of supplies to the ultimate delivery of the finished product, and effective cost control can only be exercised by *linking* and *informing* the distinctive areas of responsibility in the chain of events which lead to the manufacture and distribution of a product. A schema showing these different costs and their overall relationship with a product's selling price is shown by Figure 13.1.1.

Effective cost control requires:

(i) the analysis of *past* performance to isolate those factors of production which might influence future performance,

(ii) the anticipation of conditions which might affect future performance,

(iii) adequate planning of future operations to optimize the return on assets based on sales forecasts, budgets and a firm's pricing policy,

(iv) a regular review of actual and planned performance coupled with timely executive action to exploit advantages and avert threats to the firm's actual level of performance, and

(v) the use of comprehensive cost analyses which can make cost control an objective exercise such that poor performance can be corrected, good performance perpetuated, and planning can constantly be improved.

From these it can be deduced that there are three phases to effective cost control:

(i) planning before the action (this is the most effective phase),
(ii) supervision during the action, and
(iii) analysis of the cost difference between actual and planned performance after the action.

Although phase (iii) is the least effective, it is often the basis on which stages (i) and (ii) are formulated.

13.2 THE ELEMENTS OF CORPORATE CONTROL

Before we proceed with the details of responsibility costing and budgetary control, it is important to gain a proper perspective of the control systems which are exercised by most progressive firms, especially those with diverse business interests. These firms usually institute a mandatory form of budgeting and reporting according to well established procedures which are formulated and regularly updated in the form of a profit and financial planning manual. Their justification for using a manual is that it imposes on management the discipline of thinking through the financial implications of business plans and, at the same time, it ensures some degree of consistency in the way financial, production and marketing information is disseminated within a firm. The basic elements of corporate control usually comprise:

(i) an annual operating plan,
(ii) a longer-term (2–5 years') forecast,
(iii) a review of the main factors affecting profitability,
(iv) a strategic planning review,
(v) capital expenditure controls and the post-auditing of capital projects, and
(vi) periodic performance-variance reports comparing actual and planned performance.

Annual operating plans. These are known as budgets which we examine in more detail in Sections 13.4 and 13.5. They deal with the cash and resource activities of the firm for the coming year in detail. They include the forecast profit and loss account, the balance sheet and the funds flow statement along with projected changes to inventories, manpower, R & D expenditure, external funding, etc. Such plans as these are needed by a firm's head office by a prescribed date to enable consolidated plans to be developed, and quite often they include sensitivity analyses based on those parameters most likely to put the plans at risk.

Longer-term forecasts. These normally give a broad-brush forecast of profits, balance sheets and fund-flow statements over a time horizon which is considered reasonable. Essentially, these forecasts represent a dynamic activity, being submitted whenever changing circumstances warrant their updating. Unlike budgets, which ideally constitute an achievable objective, these forecasts are normally conservative but realistic.

Review of the main factors affecting profitability. Each year a firm should also consider:

 (i) the major problems affecting profitability which have to be overcome if profitability is to be maximized in the long run,
 (ii) alternative solutions to the problems envisaged in (i) above,
(iii) the action programme to implement the selected solution,
(iv) the estimated financial results of the proposed action programme, and
 (v) opportunities both in the short and long term for increasing profits through new business and/or products.

Strategic planning reviews. These concentrate on the broader aspects of corporate planning being directed more towards the long-term growth philosophy of the firm, dealing with such matters as:

 (i) the possibility of entering into new fields of business,
 (ii) the possibility of raising more finance,
(iii) the possible effect on the business of likely technological, political, economic, fiscal and legislative developments, and
(iv) possible changes to dividend and share control policy.

Capital expenditure controls including post-audits. These serve three purposes:

 (i) to ensure that necessary expenditure *is* undertaken,
 (ii) to ensure that whenever capital expenditure is undertaken it is justified and yields optimal results, and
(iii) it prevents capital expenditure which cannot be justified.

   At this juncture we note that the ongoing activities of some corporate control are involved with capital budgeting not *infrequently*, as some people might think, but *continually*. It might also seem odd to advocate that a firm must spend money to survive, but evidence suggests that this is necessary, especially for those industries witnessing a considerable rate of technological advancement.

   Post-audits are an essential element in the professional management control of capital projects. In the short term they simply involve the scrutiny of any project whose capital cost deviates substantially from its control estimate. In the medium term, however, such post-audits involve the reappraisal of a project in retrospect to determine what lessons it offers. For example, if such reappraisals show that the company's forecasters are consistently conservative or speculative in their forecasts then this knowledge can be used to improve subsequent investment appraisals. However, these post-audits should not be the means of recrimination, nor a method to discourage initiative; their sole purpose is to learn ways to improve subsequent decisions via information feedback.

Periodic performance reports comparing actual and planned performance. These comprise very short-term post-audits, which are designed to help management exercise control over the company's operations on a regular short-term basis. They usually apply to companies using responsibility costing and budgetary control techniques, which are the objects of the next two sections.

13.3 RESPONSIBILITY COSTING

The traditional approach to cost control by many companies involves a comparison of the successive monthly costs incurred by a particular operation. Unfortunately, this type of costing, which is sometimes known as activity or absorption costing, is now recognized by many companies to be quite ineffective in the control of day-to-day costs, and more especially, quite misleading as a basis for decision making. This ineffectiveness results from the fact that absorption costing is not able to hold any one person responsible for a particular cost, and it does not allow one to identify the reasons for cost variations between successive months readily. Furthermore, absorption costing can mask the real effect of indirect expense and it can result in allocating to activities expenses which would not be directly affected by changes to those activities.

Under responsibility costing each item of cost is charged to a particular manager so his department becomes a recognizable cost centre* and he is then held responsible for controlling those costs which are prescribed for his department.

Responsibility costing is normally, but not necessarily, used in conjunction with budgetary control, which involves the preparation of budgets and a comparison of their target estimates with actual performance. The effectiveness of these techniques is improved if the manager responsible for such costs plays a major role in formulating his budget and readily accepts it as a target against which his performance may, in part, be judged. In management parlance such a scheme is known as management by objective (MBO). However, it must be recognized that each cost centre can affect the costs of the next by its performance so a sensible management overview of responsibility costing must be exercised to prevent any disagreements which may ensue.

The major advantage of responsibility costing is that it greatly increases cost-consciousness and encourages cost rivalry as each cost centre vies with the next to improve its performance through an evolutionary process of standardization and innovation.

13.4 BUDGETARY CONTROL

A budget is a financial or quantitative statement, prepared prior to a defined period, of the policy to be pursued during that period for the purpose of attaining a given objective.

A long-term budget is normally prepared in general broad-brush terms to give the overall plan for a number of years ahead. The long term is then broken down into annual budget periods for more detailed budgeting. Detailed budgets are prepared for each area of business activity prior to being combined into a master budget to reveal the co-ordinated business plan for the budget period. Since each budget interacts with every other budget, budgeting must start by isolating the *limiting factor*. Every other budget should then follow in a logical sequence. The limiting factor is that activity of a business which constrains the operations of the business at a particular point in time. Normally the forecast sales volume is the limiting factor so that the logical sequence of short-term budgets is as follows:

(i) *Sales budget* The sales budget should be prepared in terms of both quantity and value. Factors to which attention should be given include: market conditions, the introduction of new products, the present level of sales and the market potential, selling prices, publicity campaigns, special conditions such as national programmes, and the extent of the current order book.

---

* In companies where products pass from one department to the next, it is also possible to organize profit centres on the basis of an intermediate product transfer pricing system.

  (ii) *Production budget.* The production budget forecasts what is to be produced if the sales budget is to be met and it takes into account management's policy on the holding of stocks. The production budget would normally assume a stable rate of production, creating a budgeted buffer stock to meet any fluctuations in demand presented by the seasonal nature of the sales budget.

 (iii) *Labour requirements budget.* This would show potential recruitments or redundancies, or the need for shift or overtime working.

 (iv) *Materials requirements budget.* This budget forecasts the materials required to meet the production budget.

  (v) *Purchasing budget.* The purchasing budget should recognize management's stock policy and reflect bulk purchase and other buying policies.

 (vi) *Plant budget.* New plant, retirements and major overhauls should all be taken into account in the plant budget and, of course, new plant and other fixed assets should be planned on a long-term basis in the capital budget.

(vii) *Departmental overhead cost budget.* This would embrace the whole spectrum of overhead costs – for example, production, administration, selling and distribution overhead expenses.

As already inferred in Section 13.3, budgetary control is the establishment of budgets relating the responsibility of executives to the requirements of a policy and the continuous comparison of actual with budgeted results either to secure by action the objectives of that policy or to provide a basis for revision. However, budgetary control does not stop at mere comparison of costs, but studies the causes of differences between budget and actual performance. This gives rise to the term management by exception which means that:

  (i) responsibility for each item of expense is fixed and control is exercised over results,

 (ii) managerial attention is directed towards exceptions where action can be taken quickly to rectify the situation, and

 (iii) the process acts as a discipline, stimulating departmental efficiency and more effective utilization of resources.

To be effective, a system of budgetary control should observe the following principles:

  (i) a budget should be prepared in conjunction with the person on whom the control is to be exercised, and he should agree the budget before it is finally accepted as the basis for control of future operations. Furthermore, the budget figures should represent attainable goals not so high as to be frustrating, yet not too low as to encourage complacency;

 (ii) the budget centre structure must ensure that no item is included in any budget unless it is primarily within the control of the person responsible for that budget centre;

 (iii) control must recognize changed conditions.

A budget is normally developed on the basis of a given volume of sales. Should the actual volume differ from that budgeted then it would be unrealistic to draw comparisons between actual results and the original budget. Flexible budgetary control recognizes this by preparing a range of budgets appropriate to a range of volumes and selecting that budget which is most appropriate for comparative purposes. If, however, there is a radical change in conditions, quite apart from fluctuations in volume, it may be necessary to revise the budget completely.

13.5 THE RUDIMENTS OF SHORT-TERM BUDGETING

In planning the activities of a firm, it is quite conceivable that a forecast of a year's operations based exclusively on the final balance sheet could suggest an overall satisfactory state of affairs and yet the firm could be depleted of some resource, such as cash or inventory, during the interim period. Short-term budgeting is therefore essential to ensure that the demands on resources can be met and transitional problems can be avoided, by proper planning. To illustrate this point let us follow the step-wise construction of the quarterly budget (by monthly intervals) for a fictitious company assuming the following data:

13.5.1 Opening balance sheet

Oil Traders Incorporated

Balance Sheet as at 1 January 1960

Fixed assets	630 000		Share capital		800 000
Less accumulated			Revenue reserves		
depreciation	160 000	470 000	retained profit		520 000
Current assets			Current liabilities		
Stock	750 000		Creditors	520 000	
Debtors	600 000				
Cash	200 000	1 550 000	Tax	180 000	700 000
		2 020 000			2 020 000

To trace the trading activities through the next three months in order to draw up an estimated closing balance sheet for 31 March, we have to answer the following questions:

(i) Are any of the fixed assets to be disposed of or will new assets be acquired?
(ii) Will stock levels be held or varied?
(iii) Will debtors increase or decrease?
(vi) Will payments to creditors be more prompt or delayed?
(v) Are there proposed changes in the capital structure?
(vi) What is the estimated value for this period of cost of goods sold, appropriations for tax and dividends, and hence retained profits accruing in the period?
(vii) Are there any changes likely in liabilities for tax and creditors?

13.5.2 Sales budget

The most important limiting factor is usually the sales budget, but occasionally production capacity or finance may be the limiting factor in times of peak demand. Information from customer profiles, government statistics, competitor intelligence, and many other sources are used by the marketing department to estimate the most probable demand for the products over the budget period.

Let us assume that the following forecasts for the period 1 January–31 March 1960 are reasonable:

	Barrels (bls)	Value (£)
January	450 000	600 000
February	450 000	600 000
March	600 000	800 000
	1 500 000	£2 000 000

13.5.3 Stock budget

The level of stock held by a company is an important element in the amount of working capital tied up in the firm. Conflicting interests are involved in setting inventory levels. For example the sales manager might advocate high stocks of finished goods for prompt customer delivery, whereas the buyer might advocate the purchase of large lot sizes to get the best discounts available. Quite obviously excessive bias towards these policies would reduce the firm's rate of return on capital and impair its liquidity.

For our trivial budgeting problem we shall assume that the management policy is to maintain an average stock level equal to $6\frac{1}{2}$ weeks' sales, or 50 per cent of the quarter's requirements. Since stock is held in anticipation of sales, we need to extend the sales forecast through April, May and June. Let us assume that the sales forecast for the second quarter is 1 900 000 barrels, so that the planned stock for 31 March is 950 000 barrels. If the purchase price of oil is £1 per barrel then the opening and closing stocks are as follows:

	(bls)	Value (£)
1 January	750 000	750 000
31 March	950 000	950 000

13.5.4 Purchasing budget

	(bls)	Cost (£)
Sales January–March	1 500 000	1 500 000
Stock at 31 March	950 000	950 000
	2 450 000	2 450 000
Less opening stock 1 January	750 000	750 000
Purchases required	1 700 000	£1 700 000

13.5.5 Budgeted gross profit (1 January–31 March 1960)

Budgeted sales revenue		£2 000 000
Budget purchases	£1 700 000	
Plus opening stock 1 January	750 000	
	2 450 000	
Less budgeted stock 31 March	950 000	
Cost of goods sold	1 500 000	
Budgeted gross profit c/d	£ 500 000	

13.5.6 Departmental expense budgets

We shall assume that only two departments are involved: (i) Marketing, involving advertising, selling and distribution, and (ii) Administration, involving buying, stock control, personnel and accounting; and that they incur the following expenses: Marketing, £100 000 (including £10 000 depreciation) and administration, £300 000 (including £20 000 depreciation).

13.5.6 Budgeted net profit (1 January–31 March 1960)

Budgeted gross profit b/d		£500 000
Less departmental expenses		
marketing	100 000	
administration	300 000	400 000
Budgeted net profit		100 000
Less tax (@ 40%)		40 000
Budgeted net profit after tax		60 000
Cumulative retained profit at		
1 January		520 000
		580 000
Less dividends		20 000
Cumulative retained profit at		
31 March		£560 000

13.5.7 Debtors' budget

To add some semblance of realism we shall assume the following profile for accounts receivable (debtors):

10 per cent of invoices are paid during the current month of invoicing, 70 per cent of invoices are paid one month later, and 20 per cent of invoices are paid two months later.

We also need to know the sales revenue for months preceding 1 January which we shall assume to be November, £300 000 and December, £600 000.

Budgeted cash receipts

Invoices dated (£)	January	Cash receipts February	March	Totals (£)
November (300 000)	60 000 (20%)			60 000
December (600 000)	420 000 (70%)	120 000 (20%)		540 000
January (600 000)	60 000 (10%)	420 000 (70%)	120 000 (20%)	600 000
February (600 000)		60 000 (10%)	420 000 (70%)	480 000
March (800 000)			80 000 10%	80 000
	540 000	600 000	620 000	1 760 000

Total estimated cash receipts for the quarter are therefore £1 760 000.

Debtors at 1 January	600 000
Invoices to customers 1 January–31 March	2 000 000
	2 600 000
Less budgeted cash receipts	1 760 000
Budgeted debtors 31 March	£840 000

13.5.8   Creditors' budget

We shall assume the policy stated below for payments to creditors:

No payments to suppliers in the month of receipt of invoice.
70 per cent of suppliers invoices discharged one month after receipt of invoice.
30 per cent of suppliers invoices discharged two months after receipt of invoice.

Suppliers invoices dated:

November	400 000	From purchasing records
December	400 000	
January	400 000	
February	600 000	Assumed phasing of purchasing budget
March	700 000	

Budgeted cash payments to suppliers

Invoices dated (£)	January	February	March	Totals (£)
November (400 000)	120 000 (30%)			120 000
December (400 000)	280 000 (70%)	120 000 (30%)		400 000
January (400 000)	– (0%)	280 000 (70%)	120 000 (30%)	400 000
February (600 000)		– (0%)	420 000 (70%)	420 000
March (700 000)			– (0%)	–
	400 000	400 000	540 000	£1 340 000

Creditors at 1 January	520 000
Suppliers invoices 1 January–31 March	1 700 000
	2 220 000
Less budgeted payments to suppliers 1 January–31 March	1 340 000
Budgeted creditors at 31 March	£880 000

13.5.9   Cash Budget

If we further assume that the company is to acquire and pay for additional fixed assets valued at £50 000 during January, and the £180 000 tax liability is discharged during January, we get the following cash balance:

Cash balance as at 1 January		200 000
Budgeted cash receipts from customers during 1 January–31 March		1 760 000
		1 960 000
Less budgeted payments to suppliers during 1 January–31 March	1 340 000	
	620 000	
Less payment for additional fixed assets	50 000	
Less tax	180 000	
Less marketing expense (excluding depreciation)	90 000	
Less administration expense (excluding depreciation)	280 000	600 000
Budgeted cash balance as at 31 March		20 000

This example shows that the cash balance will be reduced from £200 000 on 1 January to £20 000 by 31 March despite the realization of a £60 000 profit. With such a small surplus remaining, the firm might suffer a cash deficit at some point during the first quarter. It is most important to forecast such an occurrence in advance, as bank managers will normally grant overdraft or loan facilities if given adequate notice, and will be made aware of the company's attention to money management. Should an overdraft or loan not be available, then replanning of activity levels, delaying payments to suppliers, expediting payment by debtors, or deferring capital expenditure would enable the company to avoid the need for overdraft facilities, but such actions might reduce the company's profitability.

We shall now analyse the cash movements over the intervening months to determine if in fact there are any temporary cash deficiencies.

Monthly cash budget	January	February	March
Opening Balance–surplus or (deficit)	200 000		70 000
		(10 000)	
Budgeted cash receipts from customers	540 000	600 000	620 000
	740 000	590 000	690 000
Budgeted cash payments to suppliers	400 000	400 000	540 000
Additional fixed assets	50 000	–	–
Tax	180 000	–	–
Marketing expenses	30 000	30 000	30 000
Administration expenses	90 000	90 000	100 000
	750 000	520 000	670 000
Closing Balance–surplus		70 000	20 000
or (deficit)	(10 000)		

13.5.10

We now have all the information necessary to draw up a final balance sheet for 31 March 1960.

Oil Traders Incorporated
Budgeted balance sheet as of 31 March 1960

Fixed assets	680 000		Share capital	800 000
Less depreciation	190 000	490 000	Budgeted revenue reserves	560 000
Current assets			Current liabilities	
Budgeted stock	950 000		Budgeted creditors 880 000	
Budgeted debtors	840 000		Budgeted tax 40 000	
Budgeted cash	20 000	1 810 000	Budgeted dividends 20 000	940 000
		2 300 000		2 300 000

This simple example demonstrates how crucial it is to budget carefully, because this final balance sheet does not emphasize the point highlighted in 13.5.9 that the company is going to run out of money unless it takes necessary precautionary measures. Moreover, this example demonstrates how planning expenditure on capital assets (capital budgeting) is an inherent part of the overall budgeting activity of the firm.

13.6 STANDARD COSTING AND VARIANCE ANALYSIS

Responsibility costing and budgetary control is made even more effective when standards of business performance based on industrial engineering studies, including method, time and measurement (MTM) analyses are available.

Standard cost control

Where the performance of a process remains similar from one month to the next as, for example, in a chemical process or a car assembly line, it is possible to establish costs for the expected level of performance for that process. In other words, it is possible to establish standards. A typical example might involve a sulphuric acid plant working at a designed sulphur efficiency of 98.5 per cent, and a planned plant utilization of 95 per cent producing 600 tons of 96 per cent acid a day. For such an example it is possible to develop standards along the following lines:

  (i) total cost/tonne,
 (ii) labour cost/tonne,
(iii) labour time/tonne,
 (iv) power/tonne, and
  (v) sulphur burnt/tonne,

and a host of other such standards. Similar standards could be developed for a wide range of mass production processes. The prime benefit of standard costing when it is combined with budgetary control is that it helps focus management's attention on the reasons for the ultimate difference between actual and standard budgeted costs using cost variance analysis*.

Variance analysis

To illustrate the principles of variance analysis, let us use the following notation for a simple example based only on the price and the usage of some resource:

	Standard performance	Actual performance
Overall cost:	C	$C+\Delta C$
Item price:	P	$P+\Delta P$
Item usage:	U	$U+\Delta U$

where Δ = a small change to the symbol following it. According to these symbols, the actual cost incurred using the resource is given by the relationship:

$$C+\Delta C=(P+\Delta P)(U+\Delta U)$$

and the standard cost is given by:

$$C=P\cdot U$$

The difference (variance) between the actual and the standard cost is therefore given by:

$$\Delta C=P\cdot\Delta U+U\cdot\Delta P+\Delta P\cdot\Delta U$$

According to accounting convention, and here again we must note the arbitrariness of this convention, the term $P\cdot\Delta U$ is known as the usage variance, whereas the term $(U\Delta P+\Delta P\cdot\Delta U)$ or $(U+\Delta U)\cdot\Delta P$ is known as the price variance.

  Clearly $\Delta P\cdot\Delta U$ could be allocated with equal logic to either the price or the usage variance or, if extremely small, could be left unallocated.

Example. Suppose a job should take 2 man-hours to complete at a rate of £1 per hour. If the job actually took 3 hours and cost £1.50 per hour then we would

---

* This term has nothing to do with statistical variance, but simply means the difference between an actual and standard cost.

have:

	Standard performance	Actual performance
Overall cost (£):	$C = 2$	$C + \Delta C = 4.5$
Item price (£/hr):	$P = 1$	$P + \Delta P = 1.5$
Item usage (hrs):	$U = 2$	$U + \Delta U = 3$

In this case we find that:

(i) the total cost variance $\Delta C = £2.50$
(ii) the usage variance $P \cdot \Delta U = £1.00$
(iii) the price variance $(U + \Delta U) \cdot \Delta P = £1.00 + £0.50 = £1.50$

In this particular case we cannot overlook $\Delta P \cdot \Delta U$ because it contributes 20 per cent of the overall cost variance, but we cannot help noticing how the arbitrary allocation of this term to the price variance makes the price change *appear* the more important cause for the cost increase. Of course, this is not so because the price and usage changes affect the overall cost change equally. Although this trivial example only deals with two variables–price and usage–it will be appreciated that the technique can deal with as many variables as necessary. For example, the introduction of a third variable would allow one to consider efficiency variances.

To demonstrate a more meaningful application of standard cost and variance analysis, let us prepare an income statement and a variance analysis for the following example:

Bon Appetit is a one-product firm making high quality cheese. One kg packs of cheese contain materials normally costing 5F. The normal wage rate is 25F per hour, and one hour is the standard time to produce a one kg pack of cheese. During the month of January it is anticipated that 2000 kg packs will be sold at 40F each. Overhead costs (all fixed in relation to output) are budgeted to be 10 000F per month. The actual performance for January was as follows:

(a) Materials purchased during the month = 1000 kg at 5F and 700 kg at $7\frac{1}{2}$F.
(b) It took 1650 hours to produce 1600 one kg packs of cheese, all of which were sold at $42\frac{1}{2}$F per pack.
(c) Overheads incurred equalled 8000F.
(d) Premiums for overtime working amounted to 4125F, which represented an increase of 10 per cent ($2\frac{1}{2}$F in the hourly rate).

Profit and loss account

Revenue: 1600×42.5			$= 68\,000F$
Cost of goods sold: 1000×5.0	$= 5\,000F$		
700×7.5	$= 5\,250F$		
Labour	$1650 \times 27.5 = 45\,375F$		
Overheads:	8000	$= 8\,000F$	$63\,625F$
		Profit $=$	$4\,375F$

The standard cost of a 1 kg pack is computed as follows:

Materials: 1 kg @5F	5F
Labour: 1 hour @25F	25F
Overhead: 10 000F/2000	5F
Standard cost $= 35F/kg$	

The Sales variances are as follows:

Budgeted sales revenue $= 2000 @ 40$ $=$ 80 000F
Sales price variance $= (42.5 - 40.0) \cdot 1600$ $=$ 4 000F
Sales volume variance $= (1600 - 2000) \cdot 40$ $= -16$ 000F

                     Actual sales revenue $=$ 68 000F

Less standard cost of sales $= 1600 @ 35F$ $=$ 56 000F

The Production variances are as follows:
(i)	Material price variance: $(7.5 - 5.0) \cdot 700$	$=$	1 750F
(ii)	Material usage variance: $(1700 - 1600) \cdot 5$	$=$	500F
(iii)	Labour rate variance: $(27.5 - 25) \cdot 1650$	$=$	4 125F
(iv)	Labour usage variance: $(1650 - 1600) \cdot 25$	$=$	1 250F
(v)	Overhead spending variance: $(8000 - 10\,000)$	$= -$	2 000F
(vi)	Overhead volume variance: $(10\,000 - 1600 \times 5)$	$=$	2 000F

                     Total production variance $=$ 7 625F

A check that all these variances are correct is provided by the following calculation:

Surplus prior to production variances $= 12\,000F$
Production variance $= \underline{\;\;7\,625F}$
                 Profit $= \;\;4\,375F$

    A listing of the reasons why the company's profits were not as high as budgeted shows the following priority of adverse variances:

	Amount (F)
(i) Sales volume variance	16 000
(ii) Labour rate variance	4 125
(iii) Materials price variance	1 750
(iv) Materials usage variance	500

To some extent the effect of these adverse variances was reduced by the firm increasing its price by 2.5F, but (within the confines of this academic example) the real questions which the management of this firm must attempt to answer are:

(i) Do these adverse variances reflect a deterioration in corporate performance, or do they simply register the fact that budget planning is inadequate?
If the former is the case then the following supplementary questions also need answering.
(ii) Why did the sales deteriorate? Was this due to the price increase?
(iii) How do we increase productivity so as to avoid overtime working at a premium rate?
(iv) Can we purchase our basic materials cheaper?
(v) Can we improve our material usage efficiency?

In effect, therefore, we see that the product of a standard costing and variance analysis study is the search for physical and financial reasons why variances occur. In cases where the functional operation of an entire process can be mathematically modelled by an equation, it is possible to trace cost variances back to their root source quite readily. For example, Walsh (1972) has shown how to apply such a model to explain cost variances experienced by a sugar refinery.

    A moment's reflection shows that standard costing and variance analysis can only be as accurate as the data used. Moreover the fact that we have used standard costs for labour, materials and other resources suggests that those standard costs must, by definition, be variable costs and, for the example quoted, all fixed costs must be accommodated within the category overhead costs. We have dealt with fixed and variable costs in Chapter 2, but we now need to consider how accountants report and allocate costs if we are to make sensible economic decisions based on accounting data.

13.7 THE ELEMENTS OF JOB COSTING

It is not our intention to deal with the many concepts and conventions of accounting practice here since they are partly dealt with by Appendix B, however it is important for us to understand how accountants report the costs associated with a manufacturing process, since such an understanding is fundamental to making sensible economic (as opposed to accounting) decisions. These might involve the expansion or cessation of an existing line of business and changes in product-mix or projects involving cost economies. To do this we need to understand the convention of double-entry book-keeping which is central to the rationale of accounting.

On the basis that a balance sheet reports assets on its left-hand side and liabilities on its right-hand side (the convention used in Appendix B), we discover that each and every transaction of a firm can be reported by a system of debiting and crediting. Neither of these terms connotes goodness or badness. Instead, debiting simply means place on the left-hand side, and crediting means place on the right-hand side. To illustrate this convention, let us consider the following transactions: A firm buys 10 tonnes of steel for £5000 cash and sells half of it for £3000 cash. Using the abreviation Dr for debit and Cr for credit, these transactions would be entered into a firm's daily record of transactions (its journal) in the following way:

		Dr	Cr
(i) Purchase of metal:			
Inventory		5000	
	Cash		5000
(ii) Sale of metal			
Cash		3000	
	Sales revenue		3000
Cost of goods sold		2500	
	Inventory		2500

According to this double-entry book-keeping method, every transaction involves at least one debit and credit entry of equal magnitude, so that they balance, thereby providing the basis for the balance sheet.

In addition to journal entries, which comprise the accountants' equivalent to a shipmaster's log-book, accountants also register the details of each and every transaction in appropriate trading accounts (T accounts), using the same left/right-hand convention. For example, the two transactions listed above would appear in the firm's T accounts in the following manner:

Cash account		Inventory account	
	5000 (i)	(i) 5000	
(ii) 3000			2500 (ii)

Sales revenue account		Cost of goods sold account	
	3000 (ii)	(ii) 2500	

Using this convention, all the business details involved with the transactions of a firm can be traced through its accounts, their ending balances providing the end of period balance sheet and, by the same process, the income statement (profit and loss account) would also be generated*. To demonstrate this point, let us consider a slightly more detailed example which demonstrates how the costs of manufacturing a product are developed.

Chemsol (Inc) uses two raw materials, Benzene and Toluene, to make two solvent products Solv-X and Solv-Y. Opening balances plus all the company's transactions for the last quarter of 1982 are given below. During this period four job orders were issued, of which two were completed and two remain unfinished by the end of the period. A single estimated overhead cost recovery rate is used to apportion indirect manufacturing expense among the jobs in proportion to the direct labour cost of each job. This recovery rate is estimated at 1.5 times.

History of transactions: 1 October–31 December 1982

	A Opening balances	Dr ($)	Cr
	Cash	18 000	
	Debtors	12 000	
	Plant & machinery	90 000	
	Accumulated depreciation		18 400
	Accounts payable		6 000
	Capital		60 000
	Earned surplus		35 600
		120 000	120 000

B Purchased on credit 20 000 lb of Benzene @ 42¢/lb = $8400, and 5000 lb of Toluene @ 90¢/lb = $4500.

C ⎫
D ⎪   4000 lb of Benzene to Job 107
E ⎪   4000 lb of Benzene to Job 108
F ⎬ Material issued 6000 lb of Benzene to Job 109
G ⎪   2100 lb of Benzene to Job 110
H ⎭   2400 lb of Toluene to Job 108
        1300 lb of Toluene to Job 110

C   4000 lb of Benzene to Job 107
D   4000 lb of Benzene to Job 108
E   6000 lb of Benzene to Job 109
F Material issued 2100 lb of Benzene to Job 110
G   2400 lb of Toluene to Job 108
H   1300 lb of Toluene to Job 110

I Direct labour payroll for the period $5680

J ⎫
K ⎪ Analysis of $1880 to Job 107
L ⎬ direct labour payroll $1760 to Job 108
M ⎭ $1400 to Job 109
            $ 640 to Job 110

J $1880 to Job 107
K Analysis of $1760 to Job 108
L direct labour payroll $1400 to Job 109
M $ 640 to Job 110

N Accounts payable is credited a total of $11 400 in respect of the following expenses:

Heat, light & power $2200
Maintenance repairs $1800
Indirect labour $3400
Selling expense $2600
General office expenses $1400

O Overhead is debited to the work in progress job accounts and credited to the manufacturing overhead account at the estimated recovery rate of 1.5 times direct labour cost.

---

* Nowadays, all these calculations would be computerized, but the same accounting convention would apply to the financial analysis programs.

P   Job 107 is completed, producing 10 drums of Solv-X.
Q   Job 108 is completed, producing 40 drums of Solv-Y.
R   7 drums of Solv-X are sold on credit @ $1000 each = $7000.
S   20 drums of Solv-Y are sold on credit @ $300 each = $6000.
T   Cash receipts from debtors, $15 000.
U   Cash payments on accounts payable, $26 000.
V   Estimated depreciation on plant & machinery, $800.
W   Close all indirect manufacturing expenses into the overhead account.
X   Close manufacturing overhead account into the profit & loss account.
Y   Close all income and expense accounts into the profit & loss account.
Z   Close profit & loss into the earned surplus account.

The appropriate T account entries for all of these transactions and an explanation for each entry follows:

Ledger records

Cash				Plant & machinery				Accounts payable		
A	18 000	26 000	U	A	90 000			U	26 000	6 000	A
T	15 000									12 900	B
										5 680	I
										11 400	N

Debtors				Sales				Cost of goods sold		
A	12 000	15 000	T	Y	13 000	7000	R	R	4466	8586	Y
R	7 000					6000	S	S	4120		
S	6 000										

Accumulated depreciation				Selling expenses				Office expenses		
		18 400	A	N	2600	2600	Y	N	1400	1400	Y
		800	V								

Capital				Depreciation expense				Direct labour		
		60 000	A	V	800	800	W	I	5680	1880	J
										1760	K
										1400	L
										640	M

Manufacturing overhead				Heat, light & power				Maintenance repairs		
W	2200	8520	O	N	2200	2200	W	N	1800	1800	W
W	1800										
W	3400										
W	800										
X	320										

Indirect labour				Job 107 (10 drums Solv-X)				Job 108 (40 drums Solv-Y)		
N	3400	3400	W	C	1680	6380	P	D	1680	8240	Q
				J	1880			G	2160		
				O	2820			K	1760		
								O	2640		

Job 109 (15 drums Solv-X)		Job 110 (20 drums Solv-Y)	
E	2520	F	882
L	1400	H	1170
O	2100	M	640
		O	960

Raw material – Benzene

B 20 000 lb @ 42¢ = 8400	4000 lb @ 42¢ = 1680	C
	4000 lb @ 42¢ = 1680	D
	6000 lb @ 42¢ = 2520	E
	2100 lb @ 42¢ = 882	F

Raw material – Toluene

B 5000 lb @ 90¢ = 4500	2400 lb @ 90c = 2160	G
	1300 lb @ 90c = 1170	H

Finished goods – Solv-X

P 10 drums @ $638 = 6380	7 drums @ $638 = 4466	R

Finished goods – Solv-Y

Q 40 drums $206 = 8240	20 drums $206 = 4120	S

Profit & loss				Earned surplus	
Y	8586	320	X	35 600	A
Y	2600	13 000	Y	734	Z
Y	1400				
Z	734				

Trial balance at 31 December 1982

Account	Dr	Cr
Cash	7 000	
Debtors	10 000	
Benzene	1 638	
Toluene	1 170	
Job 109	6 020	
Job 110	3 652	
Product X	1 914	
Product Y	4 120	
Plant & machinery	90 000	
Accumulated depreciation		19 200
Accounts payable		9 980
Capital		60 000
Earned surplus		36 334
	125 514	125 514

Profit & loss statement for quarter ending 31 December 1982

Cost of goods sold	8 586	Sales	13 000
Gross profit c/d	4 414		
	13 000		13 000
Selling expenses	2 600	Gross profit b/d	4 414
Office expenses	1 400	Add back overhead variance	320
Net profit c/d	734		
	4 734		4 734

Balance sheet as of 31 December 1982

Current assets			Current liabilities		
Cash	7 000		Accounts payable		9 980
Debtors	10 000		Shareholders' funds		
Inventories			Capital	60 000	
Raw material	2 808		Earned surplus	36 334	96 334
Work in progress	9 672				
Finished goods	6 034	35 514			
Fixed assets					
Plant & machinery	90 000				
Less accumulated					
depreciation	19 200	70 800			
		106 314			106 314

Explanation of transactions. The transactions (A–Z) for the period 1 October–31 December 1982 are used to update the accounting records. The following explanations for each transaction should be read in conjunction with the preceding accounting records:

A   These are the opening balances already nominated as Dr and Cr, and they are entered into the appropriate T accounts. *Note:* to simplify the working, nil opening balances of materials, work in progress, and finished goods have been assumed.

B   Create separate accounts for raw materials – Benzene and Toluene – and debit each account with the amount purchased. As these materials must be paid for enter the money owing (12 900) on the credit side of the accounts payable.

C
D
E   } Materials issued from stores. Credit the accounts for Benzene, and debit the work in progress accounts for Jobs 107, 108, 109 and 110.
F

G
H   } Materials issued from stores. Credit the account for Toluene and debit the work in progress accounts for Jobs 108 and 110.

I   Wages paid to direct labour (5680) is credited to accounts payable and debited to direct labour account.

J
K
L   } Wage payments are allocated and debited to jobs in accordance with the time booked against each job number. At the same time the direct labour account is credited.
M

N   The Manufacturing expense accounts and the selling & general office expense accounts are debited with the amounts listed. The total expense (11 400) is credited to accounts payable.

O   Overhead recovery is levied on each job. The method adopted is simply a multiplying factor based on direct labour content. The multiplying factor is predetermined based on anticipated overhead expenses and the level of activity, in this case the factor is estimated to be 150 per cent. The amount recovered is compared with actual expense when the period accounts are finalized, and the figures adjusted to accommodate any variance. Note the entries on the debit side of each of the work-in-progress job accounts:

$$\begin{aligned} \text{Job 107,} \quad & 1880 \times 1.5 = 2820 \\ \text{Job 108,} \quad & 1760 \times 1.5 = 2640 \\ \text{Job 109,} \quad & 1400 \times 1.5 = 2100 \\ \text{Job 110,} \quad & 640 \times 1.5 = 960 \end{aligned}$$

P⎫ Jobs 107 and 108 are completed in the period. The work in progress job
Q⎭ accounts are credited with the total recorded costs, and the appropriate
finished goods accounts are debited.

(*Note:* Job 107 produced 10 drums of Solv-X at a total cost of 6380, or 638 per drum. Job 108 produced 40 drums of Solv-Y at a total cost of 8240 or 206 per drum.)

R⎫ Sales made during the accounting period. Credit the finished goods accounts
S⎭ with the amounts sold (4466 and 4120). Debit the cost of goods sold account with the numbers sold at manufacturing cost (4466 and 4120). Credit the sales account with the amount sold at selling price (7000 and 6000). Debit the debtors account (7000 and 6000).

T   Debit the cash account with cash received from debtors during the accounting period (15 000) and credit the debtors account.

U   Debit accounts payable 26 000 for cash paid out during the accounting period, and credit the cash account.

V   Debit the depreciation expense account 800 and credit the accumulated depreciation account.

W   Close the four manufacturing expense accounts into the manufacturing overhead account.

X   Close the manufacturing overhead account into the profit & loss account.

Y   Close all income and expense accounts into the profit & loss account.

Z   Close the profit & loss account into the earned surplus account.

According to this example we see that:

(i) everything balances, as it should,
(ii) the actual recorded costs of Jobs 107 and 108 include a levy for indirect manufacturing expenses,
(iii) the manufacturing overhead expense allows for depreciation expenses and is over-compensated by the existing method of absorption costing,
(iv) several of the transactions involve promises to pay cash which have yet to be honoured.

Point (i) demonstrates that a strict application of the convention of double-entry book-keeping works well. Point (ii) however gives us grounds for concern in that the costs appearing in Jobs 107 and 108, ostensibly as variable costs, actually incorporate the *planned* total manufacturing overhead cost which has *quite arbitrarily* been allocated between the products on a direct labour cost basis. Numerous ways of allocating overhead costs exist, each as arbitrary and as reasonable as the next so there is no right or wrong way to accomplish this method of absorption costing. However the point is made that the unit costs of $638 and $206 per drum for the finished products Solv-X and Solv-Y are not true variable costs, but incorporate an element of fixed cost which would still be incurred, at least in the short term if no products were made. Point (iii) confirms the arbitrariness previously mentioned, and focuses our attention on the fact that *arbitrary* depreciation expenses are also involved with the computation of profits and losses. Depreciation expenses do not represent cash flows, they only represent an accounting convention which has virtually no economic effect (see Chapter 19.5). Lastly, point (iv) lends even more weight to our understanding that accounting involves conceptual as well as physical entities.

With these fundamental points in mind it is to be hoped that the reader will now be in a position to query and substantiate the relevance of cost information used throughout this book.

13.8 MARGINAL COSTING: A COST-ACCOUNTING TECHNIQUE

Marginal costing is a sub-system technique which is useful in determining the effect on profits of changes to the volume of sales, product mix, buying and pricing decisions.

It is basic to a consideration of marginal costing that costs are classified into two main groups: (i) fixed costs which remain unaffected by the level of sales, and (ii) variable costs which vary directly with the level of output. In this respect the fundamentals of marginal costing are similar to those of microeconomic theory, discussed in Chapter 2. The difference between the two approaches arises out of the fact that marginal costing assumes that the variable cost per unit of product sold *remains constant* over the range of output, whereas we previously made no such assumption in our microeconomic treatment of costs. In practice, assumptions of linearity do not apply over wide ranges of output, but within the deviations from budget normally found in a well managed company the inherent errors are not significant*.

The quality of the analysis flowing from the marginal costing technique can be affected by a loose classification of fixed and variable costs. The most difficult area is that of semi-variable costs; that is, costs which comprise both fixed and variable costs. For example, the cost of electric power can be represented by a fixed cost component relating to the connection and standing charges, and a variable cost component per kilowatt consumed. In Chapter 15, we shall reconfirm how important it is to classify manufacturing costs properly to make economic sense of inventory problems.

A basic concept of marginal costing is that fixed costs are *not apportioned* between products or cost centres. Instead, the difference between sales revenue and total variable costs is termed a contribution to the recovery of fixed costs and profit, so that contribution is used as a measure of relative profitability between products or courses of action. By these means, we overcome the arbitrariness involved with absorption costing and the economic distortion which it creates. A simple example of the way in which the contributions of individual products and their overall profits are calculated is shown below:

Product	A	B	C	Total
Sales revenue	150 000	200 000	100 000	450 000
Total variable costs	100 000	160 000	60 000	320 000
Contributions	50 000	40 000	40 000	130 000
Total fixed costs				80 000
Total profit				50 000

13.8.1 Marginal costing applied to break-even analysis

Just as microeconomic theory applies to break-even analysis, so does marginal costing. To illustrate this point let us consider the following example. A one product firm manufactures and sells a product according to the following data and we are required to compute the break-even point above which it would need to operate in order to remain profitable.

---

* At this juncture it should be apparent that marginal costing is the name of a technique which involves *incremental* or *marginal* changes on the assumption that average variable costs and marginal costs remain constant.

Manufacturing cost (munits per item):
Direct materials cost   40
Direct labour cost   40
Variable indirect cost   20
Total variable costs   100

Total fixed cost per annum = 1.5 million
Production capacity = 20 000–100 000 items per annum
Product price = 140 munits each

Plant occupancy		20%	40%	60%	80%	100%
Sales (items)		20 000	40 000	60 000	80 000	100 000
	per item			(munits × 1000)		
Sales revenue	140	2 800	5 600	8 400	11 200	14 000
Variable costs						
Direct materials	40	800	1 600	2 400	3 200	4 000
Direct labour	40	800	1 600	2 400	3 200	4 000
Indirect	20	400	800	1 200	1 600	2 000
	100	2 000	4 000	6 000	8 000	10 000
Contribution	40	800	1 600	2 400	3 200	4 000
Fixed costs		1 500	1 500	1 500	1 500	1 500
Profit			100	900	1 700	2 500
Loss		(700)				

$$\text{The break-even point} = \frac{\text{Total fixed cost}}{\text{Contribution per unit}} = \frac{1\,500\,000}{40} = 37\,500 \text{ items per annum}$$

Sales revenue at break-even = 5 250 000 munits per annum.

According to this analysis, the firm would need to sell 37 500 items per annum before it made a profit. The question which follows, of course, is 'Should the firm cease production if it fails to maintain this level of sales'? To answer this properly we need the answer to another question, namely: 'What would happen to the existing total fixed costs of 1.5 million munits per annum if production were to cease?' If these fixed costs were truly fixed then, of course, the firm would be advised to continue production because each item sold would make a contribution to recovering fixed costs. If, on the other hand, these fixed costs could be completely avoided then it *might* be justifiable to cease production. However, the whole issue of whether the firm should continue or cease manufacturing a product is much more complicated than this trivial analysis suggests. So-called fixed costs usually include depreciation expenses which are not costs at all in the true sense – they do not incur cash outflows from the firm, but only represent a sunk cost and a depreciation policy (see Chapter 19.4). From a cash management viewpoint, therefore, the real issue involving the continuation or cessation of a product rests not on accounting notions of profit, contribution or loss, but rather on the cash flow merits or demerits of the proposition. For example, faced with an acute shortage of talented managers and a portfolio of good product ideas, management might decide to cease production of one product to make way for another, even though the product might be making substantial cash inflows and a profit, according to the accounting definition of the word. On the other hand, a firm might be advised to continue subsidizing the sale of a product which is losing money and making an accounting loss if it shows promise of making handsome profits later on or, alternatively, if it enhances the sales of other products which in aggregate make satisfactory profits and positive cash flows. In other words, the decision analysis must incorporate a full understanding of the implications of the decision, which extend beyond the meaning of accounting data, albeit that such meaning is very important*.

In a similar vein, it follows that a firm should consider displacing one product by another of a different sales or production potential if the total contribution is enhanced by that decision, and the same logic holds forth for make-or-buy and incremental pricing and costing decisions too. (What we have in mind here are cases where it is economically profitable to sell incremental production at less than fully absorbed costs.)

13.9 THE NEED FOR A COMPREHENSIVE MANAGEMENT INFORMATION SYSTEM (MIS)

From the earlier sections of this chapter we have come to realize that the effectiveness of management control over its deployment of resources is governed by the rate at which management responds to data, and their perception of the meaning of that data. It also depends on the speed with which the data report historical events and the accuracy of those data. Too slow a response rate between the initiating business disturbance and any subsequent attempt to correct it can magnify the effect of that disturbance. Similarly, too fast a response rate to random perturbations in the information fed back to management can exacerbate business disturbances. What management needs, therefore, is a continuous, ongoing management information system (MIS) which permits the making of sound and timely decisions without the need for expensive and time-consuming studies. Such systems are now made possible by the proliferation of cheap, fast and flexible microprocessor computers which offer management the means for totally integrated information systems. Such systems are operating in several companies. Provided they are properly designed and used, they offer yet another means of gaining a competitive advantage. Of course, on a longer-term basis, the ultimate control of a firm's activities comes from comparing its performance with that of its competitors' by way of their financial statements and any other information which obtains. Here again the suitability of the resultant decisions rests on a proper understanding of the economic meaning of those data.

13.10 SUMMARY

In this chapter we have studied several of the management techniques which are used to control the activities of existing business resources in the pursuit of some prescribed corporate objective. We have done this mindful of the fact that unless a firm utilizes the resources at its disposal properly then it will invariably enter into a downward spiral in its fortunes. Of special interest is the fact that an uncritical use of accounting data can lead to incorrect decisions. This point is important and should be borne in mind through the remaining reading of this book.

13.11 BIBLIOGRAPHY

Edey, H. C., *Business Budgets and Accounts*, Hutchinson, 1960.
Edey, H. C., *Introduction to Accounting*, Hutchinson, 1963.
Walsh, M. J., 'Functional cost analysis for management', *British Chemical Engineering and Process Technology*, **17** (4), April 1972, pp. 315–317.

---

* It goes without saying that political and social issues also influence a decision, but such matters are outside the scope of this book.

13.12 QUESTIONS

13.12.1 Prepare a cash budget for the six months of company operations described below. At the beginning of January a company has a bank balance of £3000. The budgeted operating statements for each of the next six months show:

	Jan. £	Feb. £	Mar. £	April £	May £	June £
Sales revenue	42 000	48 000	50 000	54 000	54 000	60 000
Manufacturing expenses:						
Materials	17 000	19 000	20 000	21 000	21 000	23 000
Labour	9 000	10 500	10 500	11 000	11 000	11 500
Overhead	6 000	7 500	7 500	8 000	8 000	8 500
	32 000	37 000	38 000	40 000	40 000	43 000
Increase/ (decrease) in finished goods	1 000	1 000	1 000	–	–	(2 000)
	31 000	36 000	37 000	40 000	40 000	45 000
Administration	4 000	4 000	4 000	4 500	4 500	4 500
Selling and distribution	3 000	3 000	3 000	3 500	3 500	3 500
Total expense	38 000	43 000	44 000	48 000	48 000	53 000
Profit	4 000	5 000	6 000	6 000	6 000	7 000

The Materials expense is derived as follows:

	Jan. £	Feb. £	Mar. £	April £	May £	June £
Opening stock	2 000	3 000	4 000	4 000	5 000	4 000
Purchases	18 000	20 000	20 000	22 000	20 000	23 000
	20 000	23 000	24 000	26 000	25 000	27 000
Closing stock	3 000	4 000	4 000	5 000	4 000	4 000
	17 000	19 000	20 000	21 000	21 000	23 000

Materials purchased are paid for in the months following delivery. The materials purchased during December were £16 000.

On average 50 per cent of debtors pay the month after being invoiced, and 50 per cent in the following month. Sales for the previous November and December were £44 000 and £40 000 respectively.

The manufacturing overhead expenses include £1000 per month of depreciation.

Some of the overheads are paid other than monthly, but have been averaged on a monthly basis as follows:

	Monthly amount (£)	Actually payable in:			
		Jan.	April	July	Oct.
Manufacturing	300	900	900	900	900
Administration	200	—	1200	—	1200

Corporation tax of £5000 is payable in January.

The capital budget requires payments of £5000 and £8000 in March and June respectively.

13.12.2 From the following forecasts of income and expenditure and the information given below, prepare a cash budget for the three months 1 January–31 March 1980, showing the monthly balance.

1979	Sales (£k)	Purchases (£k)	Wages (£)
Nov.	90	41	5200
Dec.	76	40.5	5500
1980			
Jan.	78	38.5	5400
Feb.	95	37	5100
Mar.	36	34	5400

Note: (i) the bank balance of the firm on 1 January was £75 000,
(ii) customers all take a credit of one month on sales,
(iii) the company receives two months' credit from suppliers,
(iv) wages are paid in cash,
(v) a dividend of £50 000 will be paid in January 1980.

13.12.3 *Meteng Ltd*
Balance sheet as at 1 January 1977

Fixed assets		£	Share capital	£
Land and buildings	92 000		Authorized £100 000	
Less depreciation	11 000		issued	72 000
		81 000	Retained profit	22 750
Plant & equipment	14 900			
Less depreciation	2 000		Long-term liability	
		12 900	Loan secured on	
			property of 8%	20 000
Current assets			Current liabilities	
Stock	10 000			
Debtors	14 400		Creditors	8 800
Cash in hand	250			
Cash in bank	5 000			
		29 650		
		123 550		123 550

The transactions listed below occurred during the financial year ending 31 December 1977. Describe the application of these transactions, using T accounts where appropriate, and construct a profit and loss account for the financial year 1 January 1977–31 December 1977, and a balance sheet as at 31 December 1977.

Transactions 1977
1 £2000 of equipment was purchased from Ferrous Metal Processors Ltd. The life of this equipment is estimated at five years with no realizable scrap value.
2 Depreciation charges for the other assets during 1977 were £1500 for plant and equipment, and £4000 for property.
3 Payments received from debtors amounted to £64 000 by cheque and £1000 by cash.
4 1977 sales were £70 000.
5 A £1600 interest charge was paid in respect of the £20 000 loan.
6 Advertising expenses were £4000.
7 Miscellaneous office expenses were £900.

8 Creditors were paid £12 000 by cheque and £800 by cash.
9 Raw material purchases were £18 000.
10 Closing stocks of materials were £14 000 as of 31 December 1977.
11 Labour costs in respect of factory operations were £8000 for wages and £13 000 for salaries.
12 Building maintenance and repair costs were £1000.

13.12.4 Examine the following income statement and balance sheet of Diecasters & Co. Ltd to get a general view of the company's financial position; then answer the questions which follow.

Income Statement for Year Ending 31 December 1976
(£000's)

	£	1976 £	1975 £	£
Sales		650	620	
Works cost of sales		520	495	
Gross Profit		130	125	
Depreciation	28			26
Directors' fees	22			22
Debenture interest	5			5
Audit fees	2			2
		57	55	
Net profit before tax		73	70	
Corporation tax		18	37	
Net profit		55	33	
Ordinary dividend	18			16
Preference dividend	2			2
Transfer to general reserve	12			8
Current retained profit after appropriations		32	26	
Balance brought forward		23	7	
Retained profit		7	–	
		£30	£7	

Balance Sheet as of 31 December 1976:
(£000's)

Fixed assets	£ (at cost)	1976 £ (CD)[a]	£	1975 £
Land & buildings	55	–	55	55
Plant	350	230	120	105
Vehicles	18	6	12	8
	423	236	187	168
Current assets				
Stock and WIP[b]			115	95
Debtors and prepayments			40	36
Investments			22	15
Cash at bank			8	10
			185	156

Less current liabilities			
Creditors and accruals	20		17
Dividends	8		6
Taxation (payable 1 April 1977)	30		27
	58	127	50
Net assets		£314	£274
10% preference shares		20	20
Ordinary shares (144 000 @ £1)	144		143
Capital reserve	42		38
General reserve	16		4
Retained profit	30		7
Ordinary shareholders' funds		232	192
8% Debentures		62	62
Capital employed		£314	£274

[a] CD = cumulative depreciation; [b] WIP = work in progress.

Answer the following questions, commenting briefly on each.
(i) What was the total rate of ordinary dividend for the year?
(ii) Had an interim dividend been paid? How can the answer be obtained?
(iii) How many times was the preference dividend covered? Is this satisfactory from the point of view of the preference shareholders?
(iv) How many times was the ordinary dividend covered? Do you consider this satisfactory from an ordinary shareholder's point of view?
(v) Why would it have been unwise to have paid as much dividend as possible?
(vi) According to the latest balance sheet, what is the net assets value of each ordinary share?
(vii) Additional ordinary shares have been issued during the year. On what terms does this issue appear to have taken place?
(viii) For what main purpose(s) were the proceeds of the new issue used?
(ix) What can you say about the capital gearing of this company, and the accompanying advantages and disadvantages?
(x) Give a brief summary regarding the performance and financial position of the company?

13.12.5 Prepare the monthly profit and loss account along with a standard cost and variance analysis for the following case:

A sugar wholesaler buys granular sugar in bulk and distributes it to retailers in 1 lb bags which normally contain sugar costing 10p per pound. The normal wage rate for the wholesaler's employees is £1 per man hour where one man hour is the standard time required to produce 20 1 lb bags of sugar. During the month of February, it is anticipated that 5000 1 lb bags of sugar will be sold at 80p each. Overhead costs (which do not vary with the level of production) are budgeted to be £1000 for the month. The actual outcome of February is given below:

(a) Sugar purchased during the month:
     4000 lb @ 9p per pound
     800 lb @ 11p per pound
(b) It took 250 man hours to produce 4700 1 lb bags which sold for 70p each.

(c) The actual overhead cost incurred was £800.

(d) The premium paid for overtime working was 10 per cent.

13.12.6   A firm makes a product to the following standards:

   selling price: £50 per unit

   cost of materials: £3 per kg

   usage of materials: 5 kg per unit

   direct labour cost: 10 hours @ £2 per hour

Estimated factory overhead costs are £15 000 per year, and the standard yearly output is taken to be 3000 product units. At the end of the year to which the estimates refer, the actual output was 2900 units, there being no opening or closing stocks. Actual costs for the year were:

   materials: 14 000 kg: £44 500

   direct wages: 32 000 hours: £77 000

   factory overheads: £16 000

   sales: 2900 units: £165 000

Prepare a standard costing statement showing the standard cost and actual cost of output, and then analyse the variances.

13.12.7   The monthly standards and the actual performance statistics for the month of January for a milk bottle manufacturer are given in the table below. Prepare a profit and loss statement for January detailing the variances which must have occurred.

	Monthly standard	Performance in January
Production–sales rate	1000 batches	1100 batches
Price	£7.50 per batch	£7.35 per batch
Labour requirement	1 hour per batch	0.982 hours per batch
Wage rate	£1.20 per hour	£1.50 per hour
Material requirement	3 kg per batch	2.91 kg per batch
Fixed overhead cost	£300	£330
Material cost	£1.50 per kg	£1.62 per kg

13.12.8   Accountants calculate profits according to the accrual concept. Briefly, describe what this means. How would you use such profits in the computation of the DCFRR for a new project?

14. *Economic Appraisal Using Network Analysis*

Nowadays there seems to be a need to develop large, complex projects which require vast human, material and capital resources and take a considerable time to complete. To a considerable extent the emphasis on size results from the economic benefits of scale; something we studied in depth in Chapters 2 and 7, whereas complexity results from man's technological quest for ever-increasing efficiency and greater capability. As a result, power stations nowadays are much larger and more complicated than their predecessors and the same holds true for steelworks, refineries, petrochemical plants and motor vehicle assembly lines, to mention just a few examples.

Another factor affecting the size of projects is the ever-increasing demand placed on exhaustible natural resources such as petroleum, coal and mineral deposits, coupled with their declining rate of discovery. This has forced companies to exploit resources which hitherto have been uneconomic because of poor accessibility and/or poor quality and such ventures are only now made economically viable because of the sheer magnitude of such undertakings.

Typical examples of projects which were both large and complex include the US space programme, the Churchill Falls-Labrador project, the Alaskan pipeline, North Sea oil installations, the Concorde project and the construction of the Polaris submarine fleet.

The last example gave rise to the project management planning technique known as network analysis, which has now become a standard procedure in the planning of large and complex projects by many firms. Previously bar-charts of the Gantt variety were used to plan and control projects, but their inability to cope adequately with the interdependent activities of large projects forced project managers to devise alternative techniques. In 1958, PERT (program evaluation and review technique) was developed by the US Navy and quickly applied to the planning of the Polaris submarine fleet, where it is said to have saved two years during the engineering and development phases of that project. At about the same time, CPM (critical path method) was devised by E. I. du Pont de Nemours Co., and was quickly applied to the building of a chemical plant. In 1959, CPM was used for planning the maintenance turnaround at du Pont's Louisville works, where it is said to have reduced the plant planned down-time by 40 per cent, and during its first full year it is reckoned to have saved du Pont about $1 million.

Both techniques involve networks of arrow diagrams to represent the relationships between the various activities of a complex project, but whereas CPM deals with single estimates of the time durations of activities, PERT is able to deal with probabilistic estimates. Despite these subtle differences, their basic algorithm is essentially the same. In the wake of ever-increasing computer power, several similar methods, each with its own special mnemonic, have been devised by computer and consulting companies offering a service in this field. Since our purpose here is to understand the economic implications of using such tools, we shall refrain from getting too involved with the mnemonic maze of all the techniques which have

323

developed over the years and, at the risk of incurring the specialist's chagrin, we shall refer to these methods by their generic title network analysis.

In the context of manufacturing problems, network analysis can be profitably used for three quite different types of projects, namely:

(i) the planning, organizing and construction/destruction of capital projects,
(ii) the planning of new product development, and
(iii) the maintenance of capital assets.

14.1 THE BASIC LOGIC OF NETWORK DIAGRAMS

Any real world project involving multivarious activities and taking a considerable time to complete can be represented by a network diagram, comprising arrows and nodes. To maintain consistent logic, network analysis uses the following conventions:

(i) an activity, involving a time-consuming task such as the lagging of a pipeline, is represented by an arrow the length of which is unrelated to the duration of that task, and
(ii) an event involving the commencement or completion of some task is represented by a node or circle, which is given a unique number to distinguish it from all other events.

As such, any particular task can be coded by its initial and terminal event nodes, as shown by Figure 14.1.1, where the numbers in parentheses represent the duration of each task.

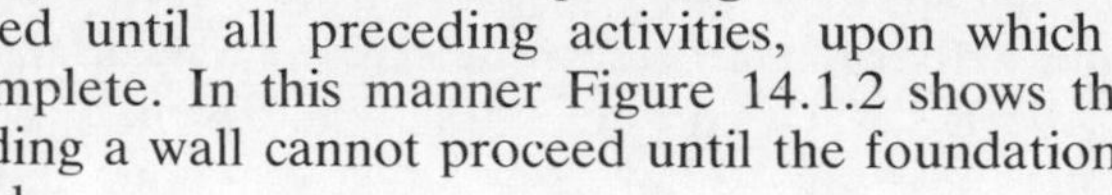

Event   Event   Event
$\textcircled{1}$ Activity A (10 days) $\rightarrow$ $\textcircled{2}$ Activity B (15 days) $\rightarrow$ $\textcircled{3}$

Figure 14.1.1

A network comprises arrows and nodes drawn in such a way that they represent the logical time sequence of their corresponding activities and events so that no activity can proceed until all preceding activities, upon which it is functionally dependent, are complete. In this manner Figure 14.1.2 shows that the bricklaying involved with building a wall cannot proceed until the foundations are laid and the bricks are delivered.

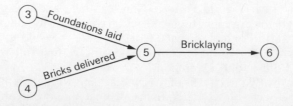

Figure 14.1.2

A continuous uninterrupted sequence of nodes, as shown by Figure 14.1.1, is called a path. The normal convention adopted by network analysis involves numbering the nodes of a path from left to right such that the diagram represents an increase in real time as it proceeds to the right.

To maintain a consistent logic which is orientated to time only, network analysis requires that the arrows of such a diagram must be unidirectional, so that a recycle or loop, such as that shown in Figure 14.1.3, is not permitted.

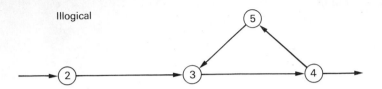

Figure 14.1.3

Furthermore, the logic also requires that a complete project should have only one initial and one terminal node so that 'dangles', such as those shown in Figure 14.1.4 below, are not permitted.

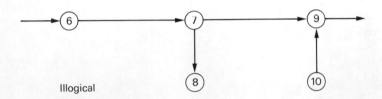

Figure 14.1.4

To overcome some of the limitations imposed by the previous logic, dummy activities are introduced into networks. These are quite fictitious activities which consume no time; they are of zero duration and are used solely for convenience in network analysis. Represented by dotted arrows they are used to overcome the following problems:

(i) *To overcome the problem of 'dangles'.* Figure 14.1.5 shows how the problem of 'dangles' can be overcome by introducing dummy activities into both networks.

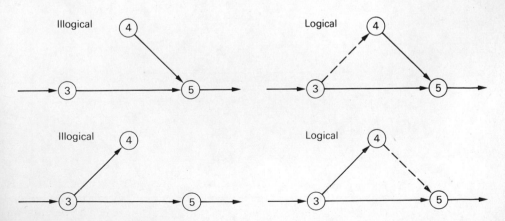

Figure 14.1.5   *The use of dummy activities to improve network logic.*

(ii) *To permit activity independence.* Figure 14.1.6a implies that the completion of both activities C and D is necessary before activities E and F may commence. In practice, however, it is quite conceivable that activity F might be quite independent of activity C. This independence is guaranteed using the dummy variable shown in Figure 14.1.6b, intimating that activity E is dependent on the completion of activity D.

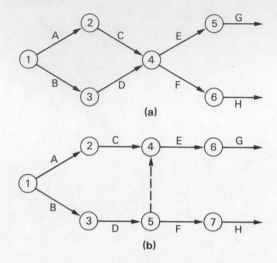

(a)

(b)

Figure 14.1.6

(iii) *To avoid having more than one activity represented by the same initial and terminal nodes.* Such a situation is shown in Figure 14.1.7a. Of course this completely violates the systems logic which we previously formulated. To overcome such a problem the corresponding admissible network can either be Figure 14.1.7b or c.

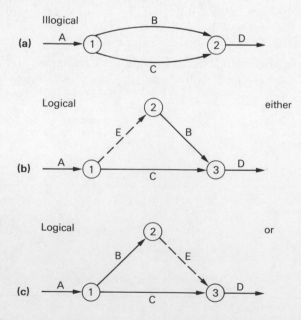

Figure 14.1.7

(iv) *For convenience in drawing.* Some network drawings can become quite complex and unmanageable without the introduction of dummy variables. To this end the two networks illustrated in Figure 14.1.8 are equivalent.

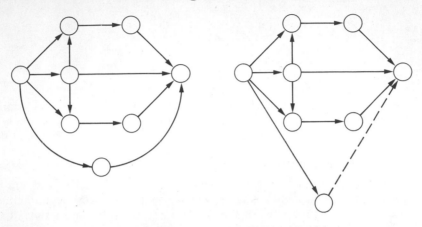

Figure 14.1.8

14.2   NETWORK ANALYSIS

The objective of any network analysis is to calculate the overall duration of a project with a view to assessing whether it is satisfactory or not, and how best it could be advanced or delayed. This requires two different types of information:

(i) a proper understanding of the precedence of the different tasks involved with the real world project, such that a network diagram can be drawn to properly represent the logic of the project, and

(ii) estimates of the durations of each individual task represented by an arrow in such a logic diagram.

The first obviously requires an intimate knowledge and understanding of the planning details involved with a project and a perception of the likely problems to be encountered with its execution. Several different ways exist to satisfy the latter requirement. The first of these involves the direct use of historical data derived from similar projects, where such data are considered to be appropriate. Secondly, such historical data could be modified to reflect the different conditions which are expected with the proposed new project. Thirdly, such estimates could be derived from generic data, based on fundamental industrial engineering and human behavioural considerations. Lastly, one might be forced to accept the best expert opinion available to the company in such matters. In so far as the data used to develop such networks are estimates, it goes without saying that the results of network analysis are subject to risk and uncertainty, two aspects which we have already discussed at length in this book. We shall return to this matter in a moment, meanwhile we shall continue to develop our understanding of network analysis assuming such estimates are deterministic.

Reference to Figure 14.2.1 shows that this fictitious project would take three days to complete as governed by the duration of the two sequential activities A and B. As such, the path described by the three nodes 1, 2 and 4 is called the critical path since it alone dictates the overall duration of the entire project. By contrast the alternative path, described by the nodes 1, 3 and 4 representing the activities C and D, only

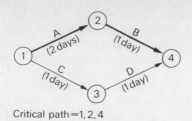

Critical path = 1, 2, 4

Figure 14.2.1   The critical path through a network diagram.

requires two days to complete so this path is not critical. With this trivial example in mind, our purpose now is to discover the critical path through more complex networks. To accomplish this we need to follow the time it takes to proceed through the activities of a real project on the basis of elapsed time and we need to employ two further definitions which are:

(i) the earliest starting time (ES) of any given activity is equal to the sum of the times of its preceding activities upon which it is functionally dependent, and
(ii) the latest finishing time (LF) of any given activity is the latest time it can be finished <i>without delaying the completion of the project.</i>

To demonstrate these ideas graphically let us consider the network shown in Figure 14.2.2.

This shows that the critical path (marked by a sequence of thick arrows) takes ten days, whereas the alternative path only takes eight days. If we assume that the project could start instantaneously at some date which we arbitrarily denote as time zero, then the earliest starting (ES) time of activities A and B would be zero. This is shown in the lower left-hand quadrant of Node 1. The earliest starting times of all the other activities <i>excepting G</i> simply involve the addition of the ES times of each preceding activity and the duration of the intervening activity. By these means it is shown that the earliest starting time of G is ten days. According to the non-critical path to Node 6, one might be led to believe that the earliest starting time of G is eight, not ten days. This is not so because the earliest starting time of activity G is governed by the critical path. As a rule, therefore, we must observe that when calculating the ES time of an activity from the <i>beginning</i> of a network, we have to use the <i>largest</i> ES time at <i>junctions</i> in that network.

The latest finishing (LF) date of any activity is calculated by working <i>backwards</i> through the network from its terminal node. These times are shown in the bottom

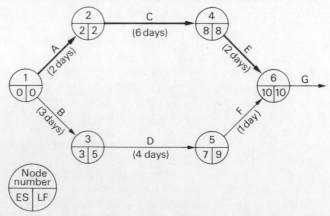

Figure 14.2.2   Following the earliest starting (ES) and latest finishing (LF) dates through a network diagram.

right-hand segments of each node. Accordingly, if we ignore activity G in our previous example, the LF time at Node 6 must be ten days otherwise the whole project would be extended in time, and it cannot be less than ten days otherwise the time duration of the critical path would be violated. In this manner we note that the ES and LF times at each node on the critical path are identical. This is not so, however, for the non-critical path, because its total time duration is less. Working backwards from Node 6, we see that activity F need not proceed until nine days after the project has started providing, of course, it only takes one day to accomplish and the same sort of consideration holds forth for activities B and D too. At Node 1, however, we have some conflict between activity A needing to start at time zero if the entire project is not to be delayed, whereas activity B need not start until two days later. In this event the rule stands that when calculating the LF dates working from the *end* of a network, the *smallest* LF date must be used at *junctions* in the network.

It is of interest to note that the non-critical path, denoted by the sequence of Nodes 1, 3, 5, 6, could take two days longer than anticipated without affecting the critical path scheduled time for this fictitious project. In project management jargon this particular contingency is known as total float.

Although networks involving 100–200 activities can be manipulated in the way just described, it is commonplace nowadays for more complex networks to be solved using an electronic computer and some proprietary computer program specially devised for the task, particularly if regular updating of the network is required for project control purposes. It is not our intention to delve into the computer aspects of network analysis, especially as such matters are better dealt with by some of the authors whose names appear in the bibliography to this chapter. However, it is instructive to consider the matrix method for analysing networks since this allows us to gain a better understanding of network analysis. Furthermore, the logic used by the matrix method is fundamental to such computer programs. To develop this method in detail let us consider the following example given in Table 14.2.1.

The network diagram corresponding with this data is shown in Figure 14.2.3 and its information matrix is shown in Table 14.2.2. According to this matrix, the nodes of the network are shown across the top of the matrix and down the left-hand side and the duration of each activity is shown in one particular cell such that its beginning node corresponds with the value i and its ending node corresponds with the value j. For example, the duration for the lead time for this problem is eight days. Since the lead time is bounded by Node 1 and Node 2 then the value 8 must enter the matrix in the cell corresponding with $(i = 1)$ and $(j = 2)$. Because the

Table 14.2.1 *The activity durations and the precedence order for some fictitious project*

Activity	Immediate preceding activities	Activity duration (days)
Lead time (LT)	–	8
A	LT	2
B	LT	10
C	B	16
D	A, C	8
E	A, C	12
F	B	4
G	B	7
H	D, F	3
I	E, G	8
J	H, I	2

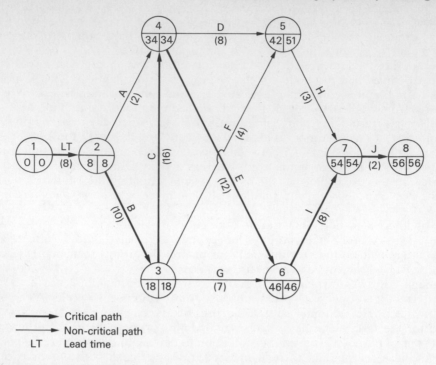

━━━━━▶ Critical path
─────▶ Non-critical path
LT   Lead time

Figure 14.2.3   *The critical path network corresponding with the data of Table 14.2.1.*

network shown in Figure 14.2.3 has been numbered sequentially, it follows that all of the activity durations appear above the diagonal of this matrix. This would not be the case, however, if some activity proceeded from a higher numbered node to one with a lower number, as could well happen. The earliest starting time (T_i) for each of the i nodes is calculated as follows. By convention, for convenience and unless stated otherwise the starting time of the first activity of any matrix is taken as zero in which case $(T_{i=1}) = 0$. To calculate subsequent values of (T_i) we simply apply the following basic algorithm:

(a) For successive values of i, follow each row until the diagonal is intercepted and add the values in the column above that point of intersection to their corresponding values of T_i.

(b) Determine the largest resultant value from (a) above and enter this value in the right-hand column of Table 14.2.2 against the corresponding value of i.

It naturally follows that for $(i = 2)$ the only value above its point of intersection (that is in column $j = 2$) is 8. Adding this to the preceding value $(T_{i=1}) = 0$ we get $(T_{i=2}) = 8$. When we arrive at $(i = 4)$, however, we find that there exist two values above its corresponding point of intersection on the diagonal such that:

$$(T_{i=4}) = \text{maximum } [(T_{i=3}) + 16, \text{ or } (T_{i=2}) + 2]$$
$$= \text{maximum } [18 + 16, \text{ or } 8 + 2]$$
$$= \text{maximum } [34, \text{ or } 10]$$
$$= 34$$

An interesting result occurs when we get to $(i = 6)$ in which case the cell immediately

Table 14.2.2 *The matrix equivalent to Figure 14.2.3.*

Ending node number

Beginning node number i= \ j=	1	2	3	4	5	6	7	8	Earliest starting time (T_i)
1		8							0
2			10	2					8
3				16	4	7			18
4					8	12			34
5							3		42
6							8		46
7								2	54
8									56
Latest finishing time (T_j)	0	8	18	34	51	46	54	56	

above the diagonal has no value. In this case we find that:

$$\begin{aligned}(T_{i=6}) &= \text{maximum } [(T_{i=4})+12, \text{ or } (T_{i=3})+7]\\ &= \text{maximum } [34+12, \text{ or } 18+7]\\ &= \text{maximum } [46, \text{ or } 25]\\ &= 46\end{aligned}$$

The latest finishing time (T_j) for each of the j nodes is calculated as follows. In the first place the finishing time of the last activity (in our case J) must be 56 by definition so that the value $(T_{j=8})=56$ is entered into the last row of the matrix. To calculate preceding values of (T_j) we simply apply the following basic algorithm:

(a) For preceding values of j, follow each column to the diagonal and subtract the values in the row to the right of the point of intersection from their corresponding values of T_j.
(b) Determine the smallest resultant value from (a) above and enter this value in the bottom row of Table 14.2.2 against its corresponding value of j.

It naturally follows that for $(j=7)$ the only value to the right of the point of intersection is 2. Subtracting this from the sequential value $(T_{j=8})=56$ we get $(T_{j=7})=54$. When we arrive at $(j=4)$ however we find that two possible results exist such that:

$$(T_{j=4}) = \text{minimum } [(T_{j=5}) - 8, \text{ or } (T_{j=6}) - 12]$$
$$= \text{minimum } [51 - 8, \text{ or } 46 - 12]$$
$$= \text{minimum } [43, \text{ or } 34]$$
$$= 34$$

When the earliest starting times and latest finishing times equate for $(i = j)$ this means that the particular node is located on the critical path. With this knowledge we discover that Node 5 is the only one not located on the critical path, as shown below:

Node	T_i	T_j	Critical path?
1	0	0	√
2	8	8	√
3	18	18	√
4	34	34	√
5	42	51	×
6	46	46	√
7	54	54	√
8	56	56	√

As one would expect, all the preceding results from the matrix method confirm those derived by inspection of Figure 14.2.3. However, the simple algorithms involved with the matrix method allow any sized problem to be readily tackled. A few other interesting results, which are not readily discernible by way of the network diagram, can be obtained if we develop the matrix calculations just one step further. These results are given in Table 14.2.3 and are illustrated by Figure 14.2.4. As previously mentioned, activities located on the non-critical paths of a network diagram can be extended in duration or delayed without affecting the critical path scheduled time of the entire project. This phenomenon is known as total float which is defined by the expression:

$$\text{Total float} = \begin{cases} \text{Latest starting time} - \text{Earliest starting time} \\ \qquad\qquad\qquad \text{or} \\ \text{Latest finishing time} - \text{Earliest finishing time} \end{cases}$$

Table 14.2.3 *The calculation of the total float and free float for Figure 14.2.3*

Activity	Nodes i	j	Duration D_{ij}	Earliest Start T_i	Earliest Finish $T_i + D_{ij}$	Latest Start $T_j - D_{ij}$	Latest Finish T_j	Total float $T_j - (T_i + D_{ij})$	Free float $T_{j=i} - (T_i + D_{ij})$
LT	1	2	8	0	8	0	8	0	0^a
B	2	3	10	8	18	8	18	0	0^a
A	2	4	2	8	┌---10	32	34	24	24
C	3	4	16	18	34	18	34	0	0^a
F	3	5	4	18	┌-22	47	51	29	20
G	3	6	7	18	25	39	46	21	21
D	4	5	8	34	42	43	51	9	0
E	4	6	12	34--┘ 46	34	46	0	0^a
H	5	7	3	42----┘ 45	51	54	9	9
I	6	7	8	46	54	46	54	0	0^a
J	7	8	2	54	56	54	56	0	0^a

^{a} = that the activity is located on the critical path; ---- = the means of calculating the free float.

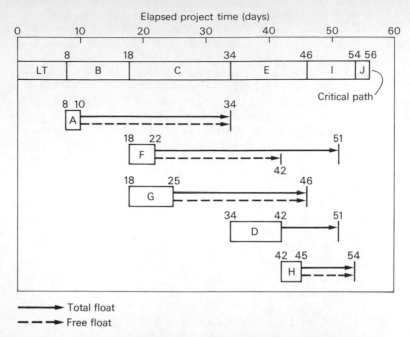

Figure 14.2.4 *A bar-chart showing the elapsed time, total float and the free float for Figure 14.2.3.*

Referring to Table 14.2.3 we see that all five activities not located on the critical path could be extended or delayed considerably without affecting the overall time of the entire project because they possess total float.

Free float is quite a different concept from total float. It is the difference between the time required by an activity and the time available for that activity if both its preceding and succeeding activities occur either as early (free float early) or as late (free float late) as possible. In cases where a non-critical activity is bounded by nodes which are located on the critical path we see that free float early, free float late and total float all equate, but not otherwise.

In project management jargon a third type of float time exists. This involves independent float which is defined as the difference between the time required by an activity and the time available for that activity without affecting any of its preceding or succeeding activities. In other words, it is the spare time which is available for an activity if preceding activities occur as late as possible and succeeding activities occur as early as possible. An inspection of Table 14.2.3 shows that activities A, F and G incur independent float of 24, 20 and 21 days respectively.

14.3   ALLOWING FOR UNCERTAINTY IN NETWORK ANALYSIS

In our presentation of this project management technique so far we have conveniently assumed that the duration of each activity can be forecast accurately. In practice, however, one has to allow for the possibility that an unexpected labour dispute, a late delivery of some vital piece of machinery, some hazardous event or a delay in some experiment might severely alter the duration of an activity, disrupting the work pattern for much of the project and possibly causing an extension to its critical path scheduled time to completion. As such, one would expect the actual time taken by some activity to fall within a forecast range. Quite clearly, sensitivity analysis (see Chapter 9.3) can be profitably used in conjunction with network analysis to focus management's attention on the possibilities and consequences of some prolonged activity. If, however, one is willing to predict optimistic, pessimistic, and most likely times for each activity, then the probabilistic approach used by the PERT network algorithm can be usefully employed.

It is not our intention to deal with the details of the PERT algorithm here since they are well covered by MacCrimmon (1964) and should be read by anyone planning to use the technique. Essentially, however, the PERT algorithm reduces these three time estimates to an expected value and a variance on the assumption that the classical Beta Probability Distribution* is appropriate for such time estimates. The expected value and the variance of the critical path scheduled time are then found by summing the expected values and variances of each activity contained within the critical path, according to the probability calculus presented in Chapter 9.10. By these means one can predict the probability of completing or partially completing the project by set dates. Unfortunately, however, criticisms of the PERT technique have raised some fundamental questions. For example, Fulkerson (1962) has shown that the expected critical path duration according to the PERT algorithm is always optimistic, whereas Grubbs (1962) challenges the rationale of the probability calculus used by PERT.

14.4 THE ECONOMIC IMPLICATIONS OF NETWORK ANALYSIS

Although the central theme of network analysis involves the calculation of the time required to complete some complex project, it is fairly obvious that its major thrust concerns the economic implications of alternative courses of action available to project management. Most of these considerations have already been dealt with in detail elsewhere in this book but a few examples are needed to underpin such ideas here.

In Chapter 9.3 it was shown how an extension to the time required to construct a capital project can have a deleterious effect on its economic viability. As such, it is incumbent on project management to explore and appraise ways of controlling the cost and duration of a project programme so that its life-cycle economic merits are optimized. Such an exercise as this is no easy matter: it involves a lot of hard work, but above all it requires a means of calculating the time required to complete the entire building programme for different project management strategies. Once these times are available then their results can be analysed using the life-cycle economic model which we promulgated in Chapter 6. Of course, different times to completion can involve different resource requirements and it stands to reason that a crash programme to build a project quickly is likely to cost more than another programme which takes longer. Such matters however cannot be considered in isolation of the full economic impact they might have on the project throughout its economic life.

A similar situation prevails when considering the time and resources needed to develop a new product so that it makes its market début ahead of competition. In

---

* According to the Beta Probability Distribution, the expected value ($\bar{x}$) and the variance (V) are given by the expressions:

$$\bar{X} = (a + 4b + c)/6$$

and

$$V = (c - a)^2/6$$

where a = most optimistic forecast, b = most likely forecast (the modal value), and c = most pessimistic forecast.

these circumstances the logistics involved with its multifunctional development, manufacture and marketing can be very complex and all the effort involved to little avail if the product offering is late. Here again management has to make a balanced judgement concerning the resources committed to the project at its various stages of development.

Besides strategic issues, such as those discussed above, network analysis also provides project management with a tool for investigating the economic merits of alternative tactics within the framework of an overall project strategy. In this respect the float times are most relevant. They expose the non-critical activities of a project thereby pinpointing the possibility of realizing economies, either by reallocating resources, using less resources for longer, or by delaying the commitment of resources, pending the discovery of cheaper and/or more efficient substitutes. A typical example in this category would involve the decision not to employ contract tradesmen during a refinery maintenance turnaround having realized that they would be employed on activities with free float. In such circumstances it is conceivable that their tasks could be delayed and fulfilled later by the company's own tradesmen, thereby giving a better overall use of resources.

To illustrate the economic implications of network analysis let us consider the case involving the complete rebuilding of a high speed centrifugal compressor used in ammonia production. Since there exists no standby compressor the opportunity cost for each day's lost production arising directly from the repair of the compressor is estimated at 20 000 munits. A complete listing of the tasks and the times involved with its dismantling and rebuilding along with the costs of accelerating the project programme are given in Table 14.4.1 and the corresponding network diagram is

Table 14.4.1 *The duration of the tasks and the costs of alternative crash programmes involving the ammonia compressor project*

Task	Task description	Normal duration (days)	Crash programme Total cost incurred with each activity	Total days saved
A	Remove faulty over-speed control system	3	16 000	1
B	Remove lagging and dismantle compressor	4	15 000	1
C	Fit new over-speed control system	5	14 000 18 000 25 000	1 2 3
D	Fit new compressor shaft, turbine blades bearing, etc.	2	–	–
E	Relag complete compressor plant	6	19 000 23 000	1 2
F	Test-run and recommission compressor	3	–	–

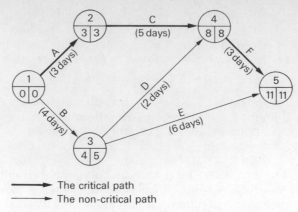

➤ The critical path
➤ The non-critical path

Figure 14.4.1 *The normal critical path schedule for the compressor project.*

shown in Figure 14.4.1. According to these data the so-called normal critical path schedule for this project is 11 days. To discover the economic merits of alternative crash programmes we simply apply the following commonsense procedure:

(i) reduce the duration of a critical path activity by successive time increments according to the most economic means available,
(ii) if as a result of (i) above the critical path shifts then continue the procedure on the new critical path,
(iii) if several critical paths coexist then reduce their durations by equal increments, and
(iv) stop this procedure when no further time reduction can be made and/or no further economic savings can be realized.

An inspection of Table 14.4.1 shows that some of the activities of this project can be

Table 14.4.2 *The economic implications of alternative crash programmes for the ammonia compressor project*

Critical path Duration (days)	Activities	Reduction in duration of activity	Increase in activity cost	Opportunity cost reduction	Total savings
11	A, C, F	–	–	–	0
10	A, C′, F B, E	C	14 000	20 000	6000
9	A, C″, F B′, E	C B	18 000 + 15 000	40 000	7000
8	A′, C″, F B′, E′ B′, D, F	A, C B, E B	16 000 + 18 000 + 15 000 + 19 000	60 000	−8000

☐ = optimal solution.
C′ = that activity C has been reduced by one day.
C″ = that activity C has been reduced by two days.

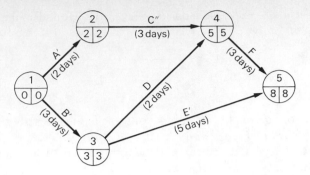

Figure 14.4.2 *The shortest crash programme for the compressor project.*

accelerated, but it also follows that the combined cost of accelerating several tasks simultaneously could outweigh their economic benefit. The overall times and the economic merits involving different crash programmes are shown in Table 14.4.2 where we see that a programme duration of eight days is feasible (as shown by Figure 14.4.2) but a nine-day schedule proves to be the most economic alternative, according to the data provided.

14.5 SUMMARY

Although this chapter devotes many pages to the mechanics of network analysis, its inclusion is justified by the fact that it is an invaluable tool in the timely and cost-effective execution of any substantial capital project and any other infrequent project employing substantial resources.

Like so many other management techniques, the application of critical path analysis is only worthwhile if proper attention is given to the details which form the bed-rock for its use. These details require a total-systems understanding of the project and its constituent tasks, in addition to proper estimates of its resource requirements involving people, machines and equipment, materials, cash and *time*. These details also require thorough planning, scheduling and control over the deployment of these resources throughout the duration of the project. In effect therefore the elegant method of network analysis is no more than an adjunct to project management, albeit a useful appendage when it comes to planning and controlling a complex project.

In the context of manufacturing systems economics, the major thrust of network analysis comes from controlling the building of a complete project within budget time and cost. Under most normal circumstances this is the primary objective of project management and it is something at which many companies are adept and yet others quite inept. The importance of this stage of a project cannot be overstressed; indeed the life-cycle economic merits of a capital project can be made or broken at this crucial stage.

14.6 BIBLIOGRAPHY

General texts

Lockyer, K. G., *An Introduction to Critical Path Analysis*, Pitman, 1967. This is a fine introductory book on network analysis.

Wild, R., *The Techniques of Production Management*, Holt, Rinehart and Winston, 1971. Chapter 9 gives a fine description of the use of computers in network analysis.

Specific texts

Clark, C. E., 'The optimum allocation of resources among the activities of a network', *Journal of Industrial Engineering*, January–February, 1961.

Fulkerson, D. R., 'Expected critical path lengths in PERT networks', *Operations Research*, **10** (6), November–December, 1962, pp. 808–817.

Grubbs, F. E., 'Attempts to validate certain PERT statistics or "picking on Pert"', *Operations Research*, **10** (6), November–December 1962, pp. 912–915.

Levy, F. K., Thompson, G. L. and Weist, J. D., 'The ABCs of the critical path method', *Harvard Business Review*, September–October 1963, pp. 98–108.

MacCrimmon, K. R. and Ryavec, C. A., 'An analytical study of the PERT assumptions', *Operations Research*, **12,** January–February 1964.

15. *Inventory Cost Control*

Investment in stocks* of raw materials, work-in-progress, finished goods, consumable supplies and spare parts constitutes a major part of the working capital needs of most manufacturing firms, and an investment second only to that involved with fixed assets, such as plant, machinery and buildings. Frequently surveys of manufacturing companies show that investment in stocks represents 20–30 per cent of their entire capital, and 30–60 per cent of their annual sales revenues. However, stocks are not an end in themselves, but only a means to an end in the context of a firm. They make possible the smooth operations of the firm by decoupling the otherwise mutually dependent and sequential functions of supply, manufacture and distribution.

We have emphasized the working capital requirements of inventory in Chapter 7.6 in connection with the capital budgeting decision when we laid great stress on the need to optimize stock levels without showing how to accomplish such an objective. In this chapter we study this problem in as much detail as is possible in a book of this kind, recognizing that even a modest reduction in stocks can have an appreciable effect on the profitability of a firm, releasing capital much needed for product process and plant development.

15.1 THE PURPOSE OF STOCKS

The various types of stocks and the impact which they have on the total systems operations of a firm are depicted by Figure 15.1.1. Stocks of materials delivered to a firm normally involve three essential categories:

(i) raw materials, such as steel plate and rod, ores, petroleum or synthetic plastics,
(ii) consumable supplies, such as coke, fuel oil, chemicals and catalysts, and
(iii) fabricated products, such as component parts, spare machinery and maintenance supplies.

Their benefit is that they permit the firm to:

 (i) continue operations, at least temporarily, when faced with a cessation of supply brought about by labour disputes, man-made or natural hazards, the termination of a contract, or through a scarcity of some material resulting from too great a demand chasing too small a supply,
 (ii) overcome such problems as lateness in delivery or the delivery of the wrong materials,
(iii) take advantage of some unusually lucrative but often short-term marketing opportunity, by depleting its total stocks to the minimum level made possible by its supply situation, and
(iv) take advantage of short-term price discounts and longer-term quantity discounts to an extent governed by the capacity of its storage space.

---

* Throughout this chapter the words stocks and inventories are synonymous.

339

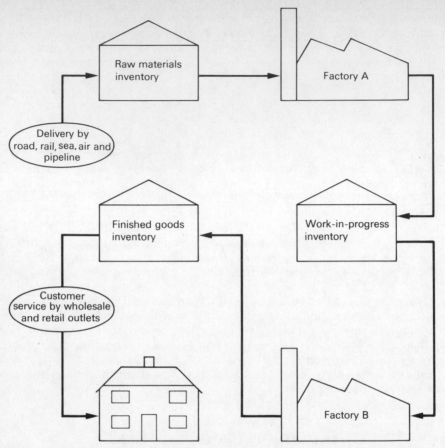

Figure 15.1.1 *A schema showing the relationships between a firm's stocks and its operations.*

Work-in-progress stocks permit the temporary continued operations of contiguous plant and machinery during machine stoppages, breakdowns, preventive maintenance overhauls and during statutory inspections. In this respect they serve to stabilize the production process as a whole, offering a basis for better job planning and an effective means of improving employee job satisfaction.

Stocks of finished goods provide a firm with the following benefits:

 (i) they provide a means of supplying goods to customers at rates which differ from the firm's production rate, acting as a buffer against fluctuations in demand as well as supply,

 (ii) they permit the firm to honour its marketing obligations when faced with a temporary production stoppage,

(iii) they represent a very effective means of providing customers with quick service which, in times of severe competition, can constitute a competitive advantage, and

(iv) they provide the only cost effective means of stabilizing operations and employment when product demand is highly seasonal.

15.2 THE VARIOUS CATEGORIES OF INVENTORY COSTS

Quite obviously the advantages cited above cost money. The use of storage space either entails capital investment or hire charges. Similarly, stocks represent a working capital investment and an investment opportunity forgone (an opportunity cost) and the handling of inventories involves labour, services and utilities costs too – costs which are incurred over and above those of the other functions of the firm. To be economically justified, it follows that any system set up to hold and retain stocks must be cost-effective, that is the cost benefits must outweigh the cost disadvantages, so it is incumbent upon management to identify clearly all the *relevant* costs and benefits involved with such schemes. On occasions this is not an easy matter as the dearth of its discussion, by books which should otherwise demonstrate, testifies. The first point to be stressed here, and we shall return to this matter again in a while, is that the costs involved with the control of any inventory scheme should *only* incorporate the incremental costs which are wholly and exclusively attributable to that scheme. These costs must represent either real out-of-pocket costs which have a recognizable cash flow, or else they must represent opportunity costs which can also be measured directly. No arbitrary costs, such as those involved with accounting depreciation expenses, the allocation of overhead costs*, or sunk costs, should enter into the economic appraisal of an inventory system.

With regard to the purchase of goods and supplies from outside the firm, the so-called relevant costs include:

(i) *Quantity discounts.* These cost benefits comprise a *reduction* in the unit price a firm has to pay for its purchases. They can result directly from its storage capacity making possible the bulk buying of supplies, without which such price discounts might not be possible. In the case of seasonally variable supply products, a firm with a large storage capacity could also take advantage of seasonal variations in price, thereby realizing effective seasonal discounts.

(ii) *Freight discounts.* These derive from the use of more cost effective methods of delivery made possible by economies of scale and the requisitioning of larger reorder quantities. Such benefits are again made manifest by a *reduction* in the unit cost a firm has to pay for its freight-in costs.

(iii) *Procurement costs.* Each time a purchase of supply materials is made, irrespective of the quantity requisitioned, a reorder cost is incurred, involving the preparation of requisition orders and their checking, the placing of orders, the receipt, checking and returning of goods, the payment of invoices and all the other necessary paper and/or computer work involved. Altogether, these costs can be substantial. Certain conceptual difficulties arise when one attempts to calculate the incremental costs of a single reorder. For example, it is quite conceivable that a fairly high proportion of these costs is fixed regardless of the numbers of orders issued. In such circumstances only the variable component of these costs reflects the true incremental element of cost arising from the requisitioning of different reorder quantities and these variable costs alone should feature in the economic analysis. It would be incorrect for the total costs involved with all this work to be apportioned between the numbers of reorders made per unit of time.

With regard to work-in-progress and final goods inventories the following costs are relevant:

(iv) *Set-up costs.* These comprise the costs involved with re-setting machinery or equipment for the production of different products, possibly involving their modification with new tools and jigs, their rearrangement or relocation. Furthermore, set-up costs can also involve labour redeployment and overtime working. As with the costs incurred under (iii) above, however, only those

---

* Although this statement is valid, at times it is extremely difficult to circumvent the problem of the arbitrary allocation of overhead costs. This matter is briefly discussed in Chapter 13.

incremental costs which result from changes to the numbers of set-ups required per unit of time are really relevant to the cost control of an inventory scheme.

(v) *Learning effects.* The resetting of machinery has two discernible learning effects. In the first place a transition period is necessary to restabilize the production process after a set-up and during this period the wastage rate of materials is likely to be higher than during normal operations. Secondly, the longer operatives maintain a given operation the more adept they become and their productivity often increases. Quite obviously frequent interruptions to the production process, made necessary by the reordering of different products, can incur the penalty of more off-grade product and poorer productivity. Although such penalty costs are often difficult to calculate nevertheless due allowance should be made for their effect when assessing the economic merits of alternative inventory policies.

In addition to these particular costs, certain general costs are also involved with an inventory scheme, namely:

(vi) *Storage costs.* These involve the cost of storage space, its heating, lighting, fire protection, insurance, security, air conditioning and whatever other amenities and services are required. In cases where the storage space is hired and especially when the hire charges are based on a unit capacity measurement, the cost of space (ullage) is easily discernible. However, when a firm possesses its own storage facilities then certain computational difficulties can arise. Some firms apportion the original capital cost of a storage facility between the numbers of years the facility is expected to last and its capacity, either on a discounted or undiscounted basis. Quite clearly such a calculation is economically misleading in that it incorporates the sunk cost* of the facility and the results of a previous economic decision which could have been wrong. The relevant cost is either the rate for which it could be rented or, if this is difficult to come by, the cost of hiring space in its stead. In other words the principle of opportunity costs should be invoked.

(vii) *Working capital costs.* Even if the average level of a particular stock remains fairly steady over a period of time so that no net change in working capital occurs, an investment cost is most definitely incurred. Such a cost is often the most significant of all the incremental costs involved with holding inventory, especially during times of high interest rates. Furthermore, when a firm has to forgo lucrative investments with DCF rates of return higher than the cost of borrowing money, because of a cash shortage, the appropriate interest rate to use is not the external cost of borrowing money but the opportunity rate forgone. In these circumstances, the holding cost is the product of the inventory value and the appropriate opportunity interest rate per unit of time.

(viii) *Deterioration and obsolescence costs.* Most goods deteriorate with age either in their appearance and/or in their functional capability. Furthermore, due to marketing and technological innovation, products also become obsolete. Both factors have a direct bearing on the quantities of product held by a firm and the reorder times which are best suited to guard against such risks.

(ix) *Stock-out costs.* Stock-out costs associated with finished goods inventories are the most difficult of all the inventory costs to assess. Because these costs are *thought* to be high, stock-outs are often deliberately avoided. In the most extreme cases, a firm's inability to provide a particular customer with stock can lead to a loss of goodwill, with the loss of profit from the sales of existing and future products, which *otherwise* would have been sold. By contrast, the cost ⊂

---

* A full discussion of the controversies arising from the use of sunk costs is given in Chapter 19.4.

a stock-out of raw materials or work-in-progress is often easier to measure because it can often be rectified by purchasing stock from other suppliers or by working overtime.

From the foregoing discussion, it is fairly obvious that there exist several conflicting issues in the storage of stock. It is clear that marketing departments would normally prefer fairly large stocks of finished goods to guard against the possibility of stock-outs and to ensure quick customer service. One would expect the production department to prefer large stocks of raw materials and moderate stocks of work-in-progress to retain operating flexibility. By contrast, however, a firm's accounting department would be concerned with the high level of working capital resulting from such preferences and the interest charges needed to service such capital. To some extent, therefore, one would expect the inventory preferences of the functional disciplines of a firm to be in conflict. The objective of a proper inventory regulatory system, therefore, is to balance these seemingly conflicting preferences in a way which best suits the needs of the company as a whole. Excepting the possibility of a finished product stockout, it should be noted that none of the other eight different categories of costs allows for the full cost of raw materials received into an inventory system or the price paid for final product delivered from such a system. Instead, our entire focus of attention has rested on the *incremental effects* which such an inventory system has on the operations of the rest of the firm and the *incremental costs and cost benefits* accruing *only* to that inventory system. Such an analysis as this is known as incremental cost analysis. It will be appreciated that our intended incremental analysis is only valid providing the full effects of different inventory strategies can be translated into these nine different categories of incremental costs.

15.3 THE PHYSICAL IMPLICATIONS OF STOCK CONTROL

Two kinds of stock control are often practised, the constant reorder quantity method and the constant reorder period method. Both methods are shown in Figure 15.3.1. The former entails ordering the same quantity Q to replenish the inventory from a prescribed level Q_1 to a level Q_2 but since the depletion rates can vary this means that the reorder periods can also vary. The classical application of this method is known as the two bin or two container method, frequently used for trading high volumes of inexpensive products, such as nuts and bolts. Starting with two full bins, this method entails placing an order once one bin becomes empty or nearly empty. In this particular case, it offers a cheap method of stock control involving the minimum of records, clerical effort and administration. In cases where the products are no longer cheap and need to be fully accounted for, the two bin system is not necessarily employed since the maintenance of records, to some extent at least, make its administrative simplicity redundant. By contrast the second method involves reordering variable quantities of stock at fixed time periods, to replenish the stock level to Q_2. This method is very efficient administratively because of its fixed reorder timing, but suffers the disadvantage of non-standardized reorder quantities which can often result in expensive purchasing. Of the two methods, it would appear that the former is the more popular.

Before we develop some cost models to explore the implications of various inventory policies, two more points need to be made. The first concerns the fact that managerial time and talent are extremely valuable to a firm and should not be wasted on problems of little account. This is especially relevant in the context of inventory costs, because evidence suggests that it is not uncommon for 20 per cent of a firm's

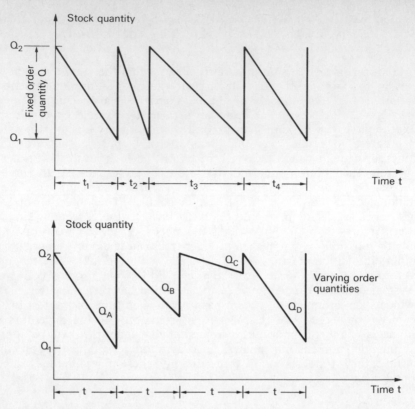

Figure 15.3.1 (*a*) *The constant reorder quantity method of stock control.* (*b*) *The constant reorder period method of stock control.*

products to incur up to 80 per cent of its inventory costs. This phenomenon is known in business circles as the Pareto effect, so named after the work of the famous economist; it emphasizes why management must be particularly selective in their choice of cost saving projects. The second point is that inventory cost models abound as a result of the imagination and diligence of operational researchers. Because our objective in studying such matters is to understand the *economic principles* underpinning the consequences of differing inventory policies, coupled with a limitation on space, we can only study a few of those models here. However, several references are provided for the reader wishing to study such matters in greater depth and breadth.

15.4   THE CLASSICAL INVENTORY MODEL

This model is the most simple of all the analytical inventory models. Upon close scrutiny, its assumptions might appear somewhat trivial and unrealistic but nevertheless its methodology forms the basis on which more complex models rely for their development. A graph of this model is given in Figure 15.4.1 showing the following very special features. First it assumes that a quantity of Q items* of inventory are

---

* Throughout the rest of this chapter an item may be thought of as a steel shaft, some electronic component, an engine or machine tool, some domestic appliance or any other manufactured artefact which springs to mind.

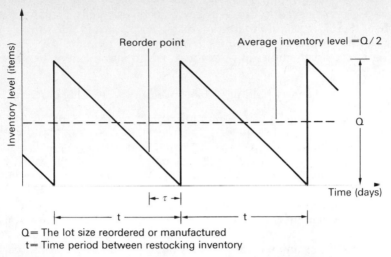

Q= The lot size reordered or manufactured
t= Time period between restocking inventory

Figure 15.4.1 *A graphical presentation of the classic inventory control model.*

ordered at some procurement lead time τ such that this quantity arrives in storage at the instantaneous moment when the inventory would otherwise be exhausted. Secondly, it assumes that the demand rate is time invariable so that the depletion of inventory is steady and constant and can therefore be represented by a straight sloping line. Thirdly, the model assumes that the whole process is repetitive, giving a graphical saw-tooth appearance.

To assist our understanding of this and subsequent models, we shall adopt the following notation:

C_H = the inventory *holding* cost (munits per item per annum),
C_R = the inventory *restocking* cost (munits per reorder or set-up),
C_S = the inventory *stock*-out cost (munits per item per annum),
N = the number of reorders or production runs each year,
N_0 = the optimal value of N which minimizes the total incremental cost of the inventory system,
p = the production rate of the product (items per day),
Q = the lot size (items per reorder or set-up),
Q_0 = the optimal value of Q which minimizes the total incremental cost of the inventory system,
D = the demand rate for the product (items per annum),
r = the usage rate of the product (items per day),
t = the time between restocking product (years),
t_0 = the optimal value of t which minimizes the total incremental cost of the inventory system,
TIC = the annual total incremental cost attributable to the inventory system (munits), and
TIC_0 = the minimum value of TIC made possible by the optimal inventory policy.

We shall also assume that the time between restocking t is relatively short, otherwise we would have to employ a discount factor to allow for the time value of money. Furthermore, we have to assume that all the cost factors listed above take into account the full implications of taxation.

Since stock-outs are not permitted by this model, it follows that any sales revenue realized by a hypothetical firm, using such an inventory scheme, would be completely unaffected by its inventory policy. The *maximization* of that firm's cash flow would therefore be achieved by the *minimization* of its total incremental inventory cost. In effect, therefore, the minimization of the costs attributable to such a scheme would seem a logical and indeed laudable objective.

According to the assumptions of our model, the total incremental costs are given by the relationship:

$$TIC = \text{inventory holding costs} + \text{inventory restocking costs}$$

where the holding costs include: storage, interest on working capital, deterioration and obsolescence costs (as listed under categories vi, vii and viii), and the restocking costs include either procurement costs (as listed under category iii in the case of ordering stocks from external suppliers) or set-up costs and their learning effects (as listed under categories iv and v in the case of a company manufacturing its own stocks).

Resulting from the linearity of the inventory model shown in Figure 15.4.1, it follows that the average inventory over any one cycle is $(Q/2)$ so the corresponding holding cost is given by the expression $(C_H \cdot Q/2)$. If the inventory holding costs were 0.1 munits per item per annum, the corresponding holding cost would be $(0.05Q)$, which plots as a straight line graph, as shown in Figure 15.4.2.

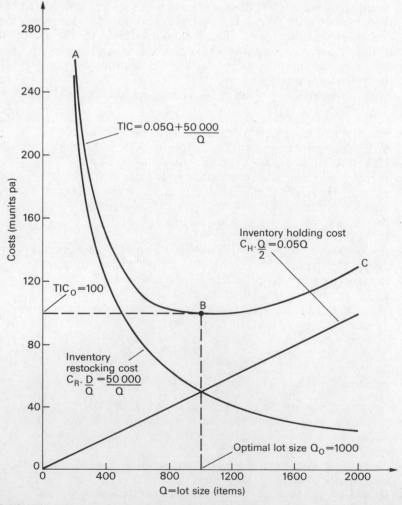

Figure 15.4.2 *The costs included in the classic inventory model.*

Similarly, a restocking cost C_R is incurred each time a reorder or set-up is involved. Since the annual demand rate is D and the reorder or set-up quantity is Q, it follows that the total number of restocking occasions each year is given by (D/Q) so the corresponding restocking costs on a yearly basis is represented by $(C_R \cdot D/Q)$. If the values of C_R and D were 20 and 2500 respectively, the corresponding value of the inventory restocking cost would be $(50\,000/Q)$. This does not plot as a straight line, but rather as the lower curve of Figure 15.4.2. The interesting feature of Figure 15.4.2 is the fact that, for increasing values of Q, these two graphs go in opposite directions. This is a graphical manifestation of the conflicting preferences which we mentioned in the preceding section and is typical of the trade-off which one regularly finds in problems of economic choice. In this case the holding costs increase as the restocking cost decreases, and vice versa. This conflict is resolved, by the total incremental cost curve which represents the sum (the addition) of the other two cost curves.

It will be noticed that the total incremental cost first decreases and then increases with increasing lot size Q, yielding a global minimum cost of 100 munits at a corresponding lot size of 1000 items. The reorder quantity of 1000 items is known as the economic order quantity (EOQ) and since no cheaper inventory policy prevails, such a policy, as depicted by point B, is said to be optimal. In other words such a policy resolves the conflict arising out of the two opposing forces of the holding and restocking costs in a way which best serves the interests of the company as a whole. For this particular model we see that the optimal condition coincides with the intersection of the two opposing graphs, but it should be noted that this phenomenon is not generally observed for other inventory models.

A general solution to this model can be derived algebraically from the identity:

$$\text{TIC} = C_H \cdot \frac{Q}{2} + C_R \cdot \frac{D}{Q} \tag{15.4.1}$$

If we differentiate equation 15.4.1 with respect to its single independent variable Q, we discover that the first derivative is given by the expression:

$$\frac{d\text{TIC}}{dQ} = \frac{C_H}{2} - \frac{C_R \cdot D}{Q^2} \tag{15.4.2}$$

Table 15.4.1 *The computation of the costs incurred with inventory model 15.4*

(1) Lot size Q	(2) Inventory holding costs $C_H \frac{Q}{2} = 0.05Q$	(3) Inventory restocking costs $C_R \frac{D}{Q} = \frac{50\,000}{Q}$	(4) = (2) + (3) Total incremental costs $\text{TIC} = C_H \frac{Q}{2} + C_R \frac{D}{Q}$ $= 0.05Q + \frac{50\,000}{Q}$
200	10	250	260
400	20	125	145
600	30	83	113
800	40	63	103
1000[b]	50	50	100[a]
1200	60	42	102
1400	70	36	106
1600	80	31	111
1800	90	28	118
2000	100	25	125

[a] = the minimum TIC; [b] = the optimal value Q_0.

and the second derivative is given by the expression:

$$\frac{d^2 TIC}{dQ^2} = \frac{2C_R \cdot D}{Q^3} \qquad (15.4.3)$$

The latter equation shows that the second derivative is always positive for all feasible values of Q so the necessary and sufficient conditions for a global optimal reorder quantity prevail when the first derivative equals zero. When this occurs, we find that the EOQ is given by the following relationship:

$$Q_0 = \sqrt{\frac{2C_R \cdot D}{C_H}} \qquad (15.4.4)$$

and the corresponding minimum total incremental cost is given by the equation:

$$TIC_0 = \sqrt{2C_R C_H D} \qquad (15.4.5)$$

Substituting the values from our previous numerical example into these two equations, we discover that:

$$Q_0 = \sqrt{\frac{2 \times 20 \times 2500}{0.1}} = 1000 \text{ items}$$

and

$$TIC_0 = \sqrt{2 \times 20 \times 0.1 \times 2500} = 100 \text{ munits per year}$$

These results verify the tabulated and graphical results previously given. In this case the optimal number of restocking occasions each year N_0 is given by (D/Q_0) and the optimal cycle time between restocking t_0 is given by (Q_0/D), with the following values:

$$N_0 = \frac{2500}{1000} = 2\tfrac{1}{2} \text{ occasions per year}$$

and

$$t_0 = \frac{1000}{2500} = 0.4 \text{ year between restocking.}$$

Such a simple model as this permits one to derive an optimal inventory policy with little difficulty. But how meaningful is it? From a didactic viewpoint, its relevance is threefold:

(i) it forms the starting point and uses a methodology upon which more complex models can readily be built,
(ii) its underlying philosophy demands that the decision maker explores the economic relationships, which exist between the operations of the firm as a whole and any subsequent inventory policy, in depth, and
(iii) its simplicity allows one readily to explore the sensitivity (see Chapter 9.3) of such an optimal inventory policy to changes and errors in the three parameters: D, C_H and C_R – the major cause for concern being the possibility of acute convexity in the TIC graph (depicted by ABC in Figure 15.4.2) about point B.

From a practical viewpoint, it is conceivable that such a simple model as this could have some limited application, possibly to map out an approximate inventory policy for a firm studying such matters for the first time. However, it would have to be used with caution if the real-world conditions departed significantly from its innate assumptions because under such conditions its recommendations could be misleading and economically damaging. To guard against the eventuality of the sales demand rate being different from that used in the optimality calculation, one could add on to the optimal quantity Q_0 some level of inventory to act as a buffer or safety stock, but such a decision would definitely be quite arbitrary. Better means of overcoming fluctuating sales rates are available, as we shall see in a while, providing their information needs can be met.

In subsequent models we relax the assumptions of this model in a systematic way, to explore the economic and policy implications of these assumptions in greater depth.

15.5 AN INVENTORY MODEL WITH STOCK-OUT COSTS

This model is a natural extension to its predecessor and the assumptions of constant, known and time invariable demand still stand. In this model, however, we assume that the inventory level becomes exhausted before the demand can be met in full. Such a condition results in what is known as a stock-out, in other words the firm runs out of stock. This is illustrated by Figure 15.5.1 which shows how the demand can be met for a time period of t_1 only, whereas a shortage prevails for a time period t_2 in each restocking cycle. The shaded areas below the abscissa represent the demand which would otherwise have been met had sufficient inventory been on hand. In this case, it is important that the new cost component C_S, representing the stock-out costs, should include the *full* economic implications of the firm not being able to meet its demand requirements. In this model, the quantity of inventory restocked

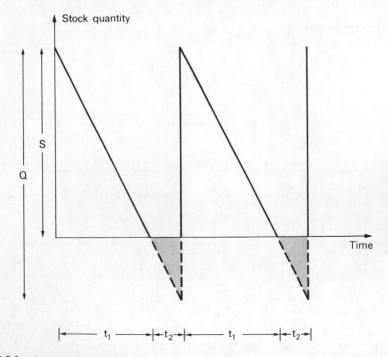

Figure 15.5.1 *An inventory model allowing for stock-outs.*

during each cycle is S, whereas the quantity Q is the hypothetical quantity which would have been required to avoid stock-outs*.

For such a model as this, the total incremental inventory cost is given by the following relationship:

$$\text{TIC} = \text{inventory holding costs} + \text{inventory stock-out costs}$$
$$+ \text{inventory restocking costs.}$$

Developing algebraic expressions for each of these costs we find that:
(a) The inventory holding costs *per unit of time* are given by the expression:

$$\frac{S}{2}\left(\frac{t_1}{t_1 + t_2}\right)C_H$$

From the similar triangular geometry of Figure 15.5.1 this expression simplifies to:

$$\frac{S}{2}\left(\frac{S}{Q}\right)C_H = \frac{C_H S^2}{2Q}$$

(b) The inventory stock-out costs *per unit of time* are given by the expression:

$$\frac{(Q-S)}{2}\left(\frac{t_2}{t_1 + t_2}\right)C_S$$

And again, using the geometry of Figure 15.5.1, we find that this simplifies to:

$$\frac{Q-S}{2}\left(\frac{Q-S}{Q}\right)C_S = \frac{C_S(Q-S)^2}{2Q}$$

(c) The inventory restocking costs *per unit of time* are given by:

$$C_R\frac{D}{Q}.$$

We, therefore, find that the total annual incremental cost attributable to such an inventory scheme is given by:

$$\text{TIC} = \frac{C_H \cdot S^2}{2Q} + \frac{C_S(Q-S)^2}{2Q} + C_R\frac{D}{Q} \tag{15.5.1}$$

If we partially differentiate this equation, first with respect to S and then to Q, we find that the following optimal relationships hold:

$$S_0 = \sqrt{\frac{2C_R D}{C_H}}\sqrt{\frac{C_S}{C_H + C_S}} \tag{15.5.2}$$

$$Q_0 = \sqrt{\frac{2C_R D}{C_H}}\sqrt{\frac{C_H + C_S}{C_S}} \tag{15.5.3}$$

$$\text{TIC}_0 = \sqrt{2C_R C_H D}\sqrt{\frac{C_S}{C_H + C_S}} \tag{15.5.4}$$

A comparison of equations 15.5.3 and 15.5.4 with their two counterparts for the previous model, equations 15.4.4 and 15.4.5, shows that the new optimal quantity

---

* This model also allows for back-orders, that is the ability of a firm to meet its previously unsatisfied demand requirements retrospectively. For this adaptation the quantity $(Q-S)$ is assumed to meet the back-orders instantaneously.

Q_0 is larger by a factor $\sqrt{(C_H + C_S)/C_S}$, but the corresponding cost TIC_0 is smaller by a factor $\sqrt{(C_S/(C_H + C_S)}$. The influence of a stock-out therefore depends on the relative magnitudes of the two cost factors C_H and C_S. If C_H is relatively large compared with C_S then the overall effect involves a substantial increase in the quantity Q_0, a substantial reduction in the actual quantity stocked S_0 and a considerable decrease in the overall cost. On the other hand, if C_S is substantially greater than C_H, only minor changes to Q_0 and TIC_0 result. In the limit when the costs of a stock-out become infinite, we notice that equations 15.5.3 and 15.5.4 become identical with their counterparts from the previous model. Under such conditions it also transpires that the actual quantity stocked S_0 equals Q_0.

Although this model still involves many assumptions, nevertheless the lesson which it offers is important, as it suggests that it might *not* be in the best economic interests of the firm to avoid stock-outs*.

15.6 AN INVENTORY MODEL INVOLVING PRODUCTION RUNS

In many manufacturing processes the accumulation of inventory occurs gradually over a period of time. This is especially true of batch production where the manufacture of a particular component or product is realized by the part-time use of some machine or plant which is put to a different use once a prescribed inventory requirement is met. A typical example might involve the use of a lathe to manufacture special shafts for gearboxes. These shafts could be produced during, say, a three-day production run, and during the rest of the week the lathe could be used to produce different products. During the production of shafts, their inventory level would increase to some predetermined level, only to decline once production ceased. Figure 15.6.1 illustrates the changing stock pattern for such a scheme on the assumption that the daily rates of production and demand are constant. It shows how an accumulation of inventory would occur if the daily production rate p were greater than the daily demand rate r, and a predetermined inventory level X would be attained during a production cycle time of t_p. Despite the significant difference between the graphical shape of this and our first inventory model, it will be noticed that a fictitious quantity Q, stocked at the outset of each production cycle, would sustain the same market needs but at a different cost. In this case the average level of the inventory is $(X/2)$. Using the relationships:

$$X = (p - r)t_p$$

and

$$Q = pt_p$$

we find that the average inventory is represented by the expression:

$$\left(1 - \frac{r}{p}\right)\frac{Q}{2}$$

and the corresponding annual inventory holding costs are given by:

$$C_H\left(1 - \frac{r}{p}\right)\frac{Q}{2}$$

---

* In fact, this model suggests that such a policy would definitely be wrong but it must also be remembered that, in the extreme case, a loss of goodwill resulting from persistent stock-outs could ultimately destroy a company's business. The point which needs emphasizing, therefore, is that a firm must look beyond its inventory policies and consider their effects on the company as a whole.

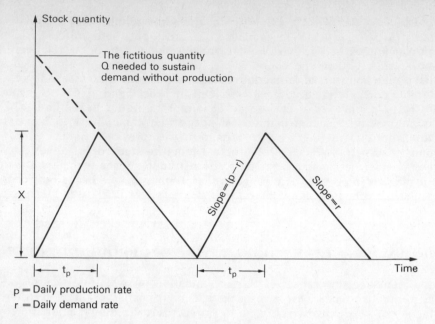

p = Daily production rate
r = Daily demand rate

Figure 15.6.1   *A stock control model allowing for production-runs.*

As with our two previous models, the annual cost of restocking the product now involving a true set-up cost, is given by the expression $C_R D/Q$. The total incremental cost of such a scheme on an annual basis is therefore given by:

$$\text{TIC} = C_H\left(1 - \frac{r}{p}\right)\frac{Q}{2} + C_R\frac{D}{Q} \tag{15.6.1}$$

If we differentiate this equation with respect to its only independent variable Q, we get the following relationships:

$$Q_0 = \sqrt{\frac{2C_R D}{C_H}}\ \sqrt{\frac{1}{(1 - r/p)}} \tag{15.6.2}$$

$$\text{TIC}_0 = \sqrt{2C_R C_H D(1 - r/p)} \tag{15.6.3}$$

and from the interrelationship between X and Q we find that

$$X_0 = \sqrt{\frac{2C_R D}{C_H}}\ \sqrt{(1 - r/p)} \tag{15.6.4}$$

Again, we find a striking resemblance between these equations and those of our first model. In this case, however, we notice that the total inventory cost and the optimal lot quantity of stock are both less than the results of the first model by a factor $\sqrt{(1 - r/p)}$. It follows therefore that if the production rate p were twice that of the demand rate r, TIC_0 for this model would be 29 per cent *less* than the corresponding statistic for our first model. However, such savings would only be realized if the cost factor C_R for the internal production of stock was equal to the equivalent cost factor involving external procurement from outside suppliers.

15.7 A MULTIPLE PRODUCT BATCH SEQUENCE MODEL

The previous model was ideal in that it showed how savings from the gradual accumulation of inventory would be made. In reality, however, it is conceivable that unequal production runs of different products on the same machine or process plant could create significant scheduling problems. In conditions of limited production capacity, it might be physically impossible to operate a system on the basis of our previous model, because it does not consider the interactive effects of scheduling. To overcome this problem, it is usual for a production process to be campaigned so the manufacture of each product follows in sequence, the entire process being repeated as many times as is necessary to meet the market requirements. For example, if three products A, B and C were required, one conceivable means of meeting their joint requirements could involve a campaigned production run comprising ten days of A, followed by six days of B, then by four days of C. In other words, they would be produced jointly during a 20-day campaign, the number of campaigns or cycles a year being governed by the annual demand for each product. For such a scheme, the variable of greatest interest is the optimal number of campaigns or cycles since, once determined, all other scheduling requirements and the cost of such a scheme can readily be determined.

With these points in mind, let us repeat the calculations of our previous model, but this time allowing for the possibility of there being m different products requiring sequential production *on the same machine*.

As before, the maximum inventory level realized by each ith product is X_i, so the average inventory is $X_i/2$. According to our previous model this is equal to:

$$\left(1 - \frac{r_i}{p_i}\right)\frac{Q_i}{2}$$

For this model, however, we note that the total quantity Q_i consumed in each production campaign is equal to the total demand for the ith product divided by the number of campaigns or cycles each year, that is:

$$Q_i = \frac{D_i}{N}$$

where N is now fixed for all products so the corresponding average inventory level for the ith product is given by:

$$\left(1 - \frac{r_i}{p_i}\right)\frac{D_i}{2N}$$

To be valid, however, this expression requires that the daily rate of demand should be based on the same numbers of days as there is available machine capacity. This is important because machine down-time, for servicing and inspection, could mean a loss of 50 days or more of production capacity each year. It therefore follows that the annual holding costs for the ith product are given by:

$$\frac{C_{H_i}D_i}{2N}\left(1 - \frac{r_i}{p_i}\right)$$

so that the total holding costs for all m products are:

$$\frac{1}{2N}\sum_{i=1}^{m}C_{H_i}D_i\left(1 - \frac{r_i}{p_i}\right)$$

Since the set-up cost for the production of each ith product is C_{R_i}, and N such set-ups are required each year, it follows that the total annual set-up costs for all m products is given by:

$$N \sum_{i=1}^{m} C_{R_i}$$

The corresponding total incremental cost for such a scheme on an annual basis is therefore given by the equation:

$$\text{TIC} = \frac{1}{2N} \sum_{i=1}^{m} C_{H_i} D_i \left(1 - \frac{r_i}{p_i}\right) + N \sum_{i=1}^{m} C_{R_i} \qquad (15.7.1)$$

Differentiating equation 15.7.1 with respect to the single independent variable N, we find that:

$$N_0 = \sqrt{\frac{\sum_{i=1}^{m} C_{H_i} D_i (1 - r_i/p_i)}{2 \sum_{i=1}^{m} C_{R_i}}} \qquad (15.7.2)$$

and

$$\text{TIC}_0 = \sqrt{2 \sum_{i=1}^{m} C_{R_i} \sum_{i=1}^{m} C_{H_i} D_i \left(1 - \frac{r_i}{p_i}\right)} \qquad (15.7.3)$$

where N_0 now represents the optimal number of production scheduling campaigns or cycles needed each year to minimize the total cost of such an inventory scheme, *on the basis of all the products being manufactured sequentially during each campaign.*

To demonstrate the significance of this model, let us determine the characteristics of the example given in Table 15.7.1, where it is assumed that the machine could operate for 250 days a year. Table 15.7.2 gives the calculation of the optimal numbers of campaigns required each year using equation 15.7.2 and it shows that 5.3 are needed, each lasting 43.36 days, with a total machine capacity requirement of 230 days and slack capacity of 20 days. It also shows that the minimum TIC on a campaign basis is 1167 munits per annum.

It is instructive to compare the results above with their counterparts based on the assumption of optimal stocking and completely independent scheduling, as shown in Table 15.7.3. Here we find that the combined total cost is 1135 munits per annum which is 32 munits cheaper than the campaigned alternative. Whether or not such savings could be realized would really depend on the precise nature of the scheduling problem. In a general context, such savings would be illusory if there were little

Table 15.7.1 *Sales, production and cost data for the manufacture of three different products on the same equipment*

(1)	(2)	(3)	(4)	(5)	(6)	(7)
		Sales per production day			Annual	
	Annual sales	(250 days	Daily production	Production days	inventory holding	Inventory set-up
Product number	(items) D_i	per year) r_i	rate p_i	required D_i/p_i	cost C_{H_i}	cost C_{R_i}
1	50 000	200	1000	50	0.025	40
2	60 000	240	750	80	0.050	30
3	70 000	280	700	100	0.075	40
				230		110

Slack capacity = 20 days

Table 15.7.2 *Calculation of the optimal number of campaigned production runs and the corresponding total incremental cost for three products produced sequentially*

(1)	(2)	(3)	(4)	(5)	(6)
Product number	Ratio r_i/p_i Col (3)/Col (4) of Table 15.7.1	$(1-r_i/p_i)$	$C_{H_i}D_i =$ Col (2)$\times$Col (6) from Table 15.7.1	$C_{H_i}D_i(1-r_i/p_i)$ Col (3)$\times$Col (4)	C_{R_i} Col (7) from Table 15.7.1
1	0.20	0.80	1250	1000	40
2	0.32	0.68	3000	2040	30
3	0.40	0.60	5250	3150	40
				6190	110

$$\therefore N_0 = \sqrt{\frac{6190}{2\times 110}} = \sqrt{28.14} = 5.304$$

$$\mathrm{TIC}_0 = \sqrt{2\times 110\times 6190} = \sqrt{1\,361\,800} = 1167 \text{ munits per annum}$$

Table 15.7.3 *Numbers of runs and the total incremental inventory cost if the three products are manufactured independently*

(1)	(2)	(3)	(4)	(5)	(6)
Product number	$C_{H_i}D_i(1-r_i/p_i)$ Col (5) of Table 15.7.2	C_{R_i} Col (7) of Table 15.7.1	$\dfrac{\text{Col (2)}}{2\times \text{Col (3)}}$	$N_i = \sqrt{\text{Col (4)}}$	$\mathrm{TIC}_0 = \sqrt{\dfrac{2\times \text{Col (2)}}{\times \text{Col (3)}}}$
1	1000	40	12.500	3.54	282.84
2	2040	30	34.000	5.83	349.86
3	3150	40	39.375	6.27	502.00
					1134.70

surplus production capacity, because independent scheduling would lead to congestion and stock-outs. On the other hand, with low machine utilization it is quite conceivable that independent scheduling would be perfectly feasible.

15.8 A CONSTRAINED INVENTORY MODEL

Each of the models we have studied so far assumes that the optimal storage requirements of that model could be met. In many real situations however this might not be so and a firm might have to continue operations on a less than optimal basis, at least in the short term. Nevertheless, the firm would still need to know how best to use its existing storage facilities and might require an economic model for that purpose. Such a model is devised in this section, but the reader should note the methodology of the model rather than its precise detail because literally hundreds of different models could be given here. To demonstrate the strength of a technique which was first used in Chapter 2 and then developed in Appendix A, we shall employ a model which is a hybrid of our classic inventory model.

Let us assume that a warehouse stores two bulk products which must be kept apart to avoid contamination. Both products sustain holding and reorder costs similar to those involved in our first model, but in this case we also assume that the cost of warehouse space required by each product is proportional to its reorder lot size, rather than to its average inventory level as we previously assumed. For such a model, the total incremental inventory cost due to the ith product is given by:

$$\text{TIC}_i = C_{H_i}\frac{Q_i}{2} + C_{R_i}\frac{D_i}{Q_i} + C_{W_i}Q_i$$

where C_{W_i} = the warehouse cost attributable to product i (munits per item per year). The aggregate total cost incurred by both products is given by:

$$\text{TIC} = \sum_{i=1}^{2}\left\{ C_{H_i}\frac{Q_i}{2} + C_{R_i}\frac{D_i}{Q_i} + C_{W_i}Q_i \right\} \tag{15.8.1}$$

Providing sufficient warehouse space could be made available to satisfy all the storage needs of these products, we would discover that a simple differentiation of equation 15.8.1 would determine the optimal lot quantities. But how would we apportion this space if insufficient room were available to accommodate the optimal storage requirements of both products, which must be kept segregated anyway? Two methods are available to solve this problem: the very tedious method of trial and error, and the optimization method offered by the Lagrange multiplier, which we use here.

To proceed with the development of this model, we require two more pieces of information; the storage capacity of the warehouse and the space requirements for each item (or unit) of product. To this end, let us use the additional notation K = storage capacity of the warehouse (cubic metres), and ρ_i = space requirements per product item (cubic metres).

The following expression obtains if the warehouse capacity constraint is not violated:

$$\sum_{i=1}^{2}\rho_i Q_i \leq K \tag{15.8.2}$$

Put into words, this means that the sum of the space requirements of both products together must be less than or equal to, but definitely not more than, the amount of space available.

As with our previous uses of this technique, we denote the opportunity cost arising from the storage space constraint by λ such that:

$$\lambda = 0 \quad \text{if} \quad \sum_{i=1}^{2}\rho_i Q_i < K$$

and

$$\lambda > 0 \quad \text{if} \quad \sum_{i=1}^{2}\rho_i Q_i = K$$

And we note that the product of the terms

$$\lambda \cdot \left\{ \sum_{i=1}^{2}\rho_i Q_i - K \right\} \tag{15.8.3}$$

is nought for all conditions. If we add equation 15.8.3 to both sides of equation 15.8.1 we get the following equation:

$$\text{TIC} + \lambda\left[\sum_{i=1}^{2}\rho_i Q_i - K\right] = \sum_{i=1}^{2}\left[C_{H_i}\frac{Q_i}{2} + C_{R_i}\frac{D_i}{Q_i} + C_{W_i}Q_i + \lambda(\rho_i Q_i - K) \right] \tag{15.8.4}$$

The left-hand side of this equation can be redefined by the notation $L[Q_i, \lambda]$, where L stands for the fact that we have a *Lagrange* function of two variables, Q_i and λ.

Differentiating this equation partially with respect to Q_i we get:

$$\frac{\partial L[Q_i, \lambda]}{\partial Q_i} = \sum_{i=1}^{2} \left\{ \frac{C_{H_i}}{2} - C_{R_i} \frac{D_i}{Q_i^2} + C_{W_i} + \lambda \rho_i \right\} \tag{15.8.5}$$

When the total incremental inventory cost is minimized subject to the constraint, we find that equation 15.8.4 equals zero and the following identity holds:

$$Q_i = \sqrt{\frac{2 C_{R_i} D_i}{C_{H_i} + 2(C_{W_i} + \lambda \rho_i)}} \tag{15.8.6}$$

But for the factor $\lambda \rho_i$, and the slight complication brought about by the warehouse rental cost, it will be noted that equation 15.8.6 is not very different from equation 15.4.4, belonging to our first model.

To demonstrate the utility of this equation, let us assume that our two hypothetical products have the attributes listed in Table 15.8.1, in which case Table 15.8.2 shows how to calculate the EOQs for these two products by varying the values of λ.

Table 15.8.1 *Data for the storage of two products subject to a warehouse space constraint*

Value	Product 1	Product 2
D_i (items per annum)	1300	4000
C_{R_i} (munits per restocking)	80	80
C_{H_i} (munits per item per annum)	8	4
C_{W_i} (munits per item per annum)	0.8	1.6
ρ_i (cubic metres per item)	4	8
K (cubic metres)	2400	

If we formulated the hypothesis that the total combined space requirement of our two products was less than the capacity of the warehouse, this would be equivalent to suggesting that no opportunity was forgone as a result of the warehouse size being constrained to 2400 units. In other words, such a hypothesis would assume that $\lambda = 0$ and we would discover that $Q_1 = 147$ and $Q_2 = 298$. These values constitute the global optimum (unconstrained) values for the lot sizes of the two products but collectively they *violate* the available space constraint, thereby repudiating our original hypothesis. According to Table 15.8.2, a value of $\lambda = 0.28$ just makes the space constraint active, so that the constrained EOQs are 132 and 234 for Products 1 and 2 respectively.

Table 15.8.2 *The calculation of the EOQs for two products using the data of Table 15.8.1 and equation 15.8.5*

Value for λ	Q_1	Q_2	Value of $\sum_{i=1}^{2} \rho_i Q_i - K$	Constraint active?
0	147	298	+572	Yes
1	109	166	−636	No
0.5	124	205	−264	No
0.25	134	239	+48	Yes
0.28	132[a]	234[a]	0	Just

[a] = optimal (constrained) lot sizes.

The virtue of this solution is that it provides a measure of the opportunity forgone by not being able to use more space, and it shows that the marginal opportunity cost of space is 0.28 munits per year per cubic metre of warehouse capacity.

As a last point, it should be noted that the technique used here is general in its application and can be used for much more complicated problems.

15.9 INVENTORY PROBLEMS UNDER CONDITIONS OF RISK AND UNCERTAINTY

All the previous inventory models assume that the product rate of demand is deterministic. Although they are all amenable to sensitivity analysis, nevertheless they are unable to deal with problems of risk and uncertainty in a fundamental way. To demonstrate the effect which risk and uncertainty have on any inventory policy, we need to apply the principles of probability theory, previously studied in Chapter 9.10, to such problems.

By way of an example, let us suppose that a retailer sells items which deteriorate with age. His historical records show that he has sold 1–10 items per month with equal frequency in the past, and he sees no reason to suppose that conditions will alter in the foreseeable future. Since he is obliged to purchase all his monthly requirements at the beginning of a month, his problem is to decide how many items to order. His accounts show that he makes 6 munits profit on each item sold, but unsold items result in a loss of 2 munits because they have to be returned to the manufacturer for servicing. From this simple scenario, it follows that the real problem facing the retailer is to decide the optimal order quantity (EOQ) which yields the best economic advantage, subject to the risks involved. The payoff matrix (see Chapter 9.4) for each of his procurement options is given in Table 15.9.1.

The last row of Table 15.9.1 shows that the strategy with the greatest expected pay-off involves ordering eight items per month. This means that, if our hypothetical

Table 15.9.1   *The pay-off matrix for a hypothetical retailer*

Number of items sold per month	Number of items ordered per month									
	1	2	3	4	5	6	7	8	9	10
	Profit or loss corresponding to a given purchasing strategy									
1	6	4	2	0	−2	−4	−6	−8	−10	−12
2	6	12	10	8	6	4	2	0	−2	−4
3	6	12	18	16	14	12	10	8	6	4
4	6	12	18	24	22	20	18	16	14	12
5	6	12	18	24	30	28	26	24	22	20
6	6	12	18	24	30	36	34	32	30	28
7	6	12	18	24	30	36	42	40	38	36
8	6	12	18	24	30	36	42	48	46	44
9	6	12	18	24	30	36	42	48	54	52
10	6	12	18	24	30	36	42	48	54	60
Total profit	60	112	156	192	220	240	252	256	252	240
Expected profit	6	11.2	15.6	19.2	22.0	24.0	25.2	25.6[a]	25.2	24.6

[a] = maximum expected profit (munits per month).

retailer consistently purchased eight items over a long period of time, he could
expect to realize a profit of 25.6 munits per month on average. There is absolutely
no reason why he should not witness the sale of only one item a month for the next
few months, with a loss of 8 munits per month, so he would need sufficient resources
to sustain such an eventuality. By the same token, of course, it is conceivable that he
could sell all of his stock in hand for the next few months, thereby realizing profits of
48 munits per month. After all, such possibilities are the consequences of uncertainty, and they constitute the risks which one takes under conditions of uncertainty.
Providing the probability forecasts and the sales data are accurate, such a pay-off
matrix as this tells us all we need to know to make an optimal decision. It provides
the expected values, the means of calculating the standard deviations, and the losses
involved with each strategy. A decision maker could therefore select that option
which best suits his risk–utility preference (see Chapter 9.12). Unlike our previous
discussion of this subject, when we considered investment in singular capital projects, the nature of the inventory reordering problem is sufficiently similar to a game
of chance for one to accept the expected value criterion as a logical long-term,
decision-making tool provided of course one can tolerate a reasonable number of
losses in the process. In effect, therefore, we are really suggesting that our would-be
retailer should order eight items per month because such a strategy would maximize
his long-term profits†.

This problem can be solved analytically by a variety of means but one method,
involving some complex integral calculus, is noteworthy in that it provides a
series of elegant and extremely simple formulae for solving a whole catalogue of
inventory problems under conditions of risk and uncertainty. We shall not develop
their calculus here, but it is covered by Bowman and Fetter (1961). However, we
shall use one of their formulae once we have developed some further notation.

Let a = the profit accruing from the sale of one item of product, b = the loss from
servicing an item which is ordered but not sold, v = the variable demand for the
product, q^* = the optimal reorder lot size to be determined by the retailer, and
$F_v(q^*)$ = the cumulative probability of v which optimizes the inventory problem at
a value q^*. For such a problem as this, the EOQ is given by the following relationship:

$$F_v(q^*) = \frac{a}{a+b} \qquad (15.9.1)$$

irrespective of the nature of the sales distribution function or the values of a and b.
Using our previous values ($a = 6$) and ($b = 2$) it follows that:

$$F_v(q^*) = \frac{6}{6+2} = 0.75$$

If we plot this value against the cumulative distribution function for our retailer
example, as shown by Figure 15.9.1, we discover that the optimal reorder quantity is
eight as before. Furthermore, if the values of a and b were different, we could
determine the corresponding EOQ immediately from Figure 15.9.1. Likewise, if the
probability density function were not rectangular but some different shape, the
redrawing of that distribution as a cumulative probability distribution would allow
one to discern quickly the appropriate optimal reorder quantity for any values of a
and b.

The kind of variability which we have just dealt with involves random fluctuations
in demand, that is fluctuations for which there appears to be no discernible cause.
We cannot predict this random effect, but we can devise a strategy for making the

† In the context of our previous inventory models, such an objective is equivalent to minimizing the total
incremental inventory costs.

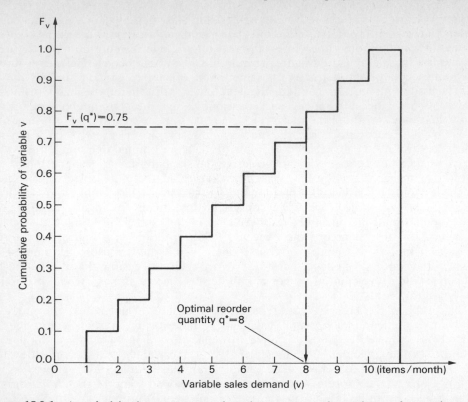

Figure 15.9.1   *A method for determining optimal reorder quantities under conditions of uncertainty.*

best of it, as the previous example demonstrates. Besides random effects, however, two other forms of variability exist involving seasonal (cyclic) and secular changes in demand. Ideally, we should be able to predict both these effects using a statistical forecasting technique which can separate the random effect from the truly time-dependent effects. On this basis we should be able to forecast different estimates of the average and standard deviations of demand with time, and devise optimal inventory policies accordingly. Unfortunately, human nature does not often work this way, and what often happens is that manufacturers try to out-guess shifts in requirements – often with disastrous consequences. To illustrate this point, let us assume that the average demand for a particular product over the past three months is 500 items per month. If the demand increases to 600 items during the following month, the inventory will decline. Registering this change as a seasonal or secular increase in demand, that is attempting to out-guess fate, the manufacturer might order 700 devices to cover such an expectation for the following month. But if during the following month the sales reduce to 400 units then, of course, he is left with a stock-holding surplus of 300 units. In this fashion it is possible for truly random fluctuations in demand to be misinterpreted as time-dependent changes.

   Forrester (1961) studied such problems as these using a dynamic simulation technique and he demonstrated that even modest changes in demand can cause significant changes to production rates, especially if there exists large time delays in the information system registering these changes. Our point in mentioning this here is that our previous models cannot accommodate ad hoc changes in procurement policies like these.

   As a last point it should be mentioned that inventory models do exist for inter-process stock situations in which there exists variability in supply as well as in demand. Unfortunately, their mathematics is beyond the scope of this book, and readers interested in such matters are advised to refer to operational research journals. When such problems defy mathematical analysis because of their complexity, one has to employ simulation techniques, such as the Monte Carlo method. An excellent account of a general purpose inventory control simulator is given by Brown (1957).

15.10 SUMMARY

The analytical models of this chapter illustrate the economic issues which are central to inventory investment and control. They are presented here to demonstrate the effects which different inventory policies have on the profitability of a firm, and on the life-cycle economics of any capital asset necessitating inventory investment. It is quite conceivable that several of these models could be profitably employed in certain practical applications, but in other circumstances they might have to be modified considerably. Our purpose in presenting them here is to focus attention on the principal economic issues which relate to inventory control in general, and to show how economic trade-offs are invariably encountered.

15.11 BIBLIOGRAPHY

General texts

All three books cited are extremely well known and develop the problem of
   inventory investment and control further than we have done in this chapter.
Brown, R. G., *Decision Rules for Inventory Management*, Holt, Rinehart and Winston,
   1967.
Buffa, E. S. and Taubert, W. H., *Production–Inventory Systems: Planning and
   Control*, Richard D. Irwin (rev. ed.), 1972.
Magee, J. F. and Boodman, D. M., *Production Planning and Inventory Control*,
   McGraw-Hill (2nd ed.), 1967.

Specific texts

Bowman, E. H. and Fetter, R. B., *Analysis for Production Management*, Richard D.
   Irwin, 1961.
Brown, R. G., in *Report of Systems Simulation Symposium*, co-sponsored by AIIE,
   ORSA and TIMS., New York, May 1957.
Forrester, J., *Industrial Dynamics*, MIT Press, 1961.

15.12 QUESTIONS

15.12.1   An oil well owner has one oil well which is situated several miles from his
   distribution tank, which is located next to a railway siding for prompt
   customer delivery. The oil is pumped from the underground reservoir to

this tank. The pump has to be started manually, but can be stopped by a remote control system, activated by the level of oil in the tank. The pump can deliver oil at twice the current, evenly distributed sales rate of 100 000 tonnes per year. To guard against the possibility of running out of oil in the tank, the owner has laid down a policy that a buffer stock of 25 per cent of the normally used quantity in the tank should be maintained.

It is reckoned that each return trip to the pump costs $2, and the opportunity cost of holding and storing oil is $20 per tonne per year.

What should the capacity of the tank be? How much should it cost to operate this system? How often would the tank have to be filled?

15.12.2 The manager of a warehouse remains unconvinced of the economic merits which result from the use of operations research techniques as applied to inventory control. If the inventory holding and reorder model is the one which best resembles his particular warehouse, *prove from first principles* that if he consistently reorders a quantity which is *proportionately* more than the EOQ by a factor b, the total annual inventory cost will be given by:

$$[1+b^2/2(1+b)] \cdot \sqrt{(2C_1C_2R}$$

where R = the annual sales of the stocked item, C_1 = the cost per reorder, and C_2 = the cost of holding one unit of inventory for one year. *Assume* that the rate of depletion of inventory is *constant* with time.

Using the above mathematical model, calculate by how much the total annual inventory cost will differ from the minimum total annual inventory cost if $b = 1$. By how much would the total annual inventory cost exceed the minimum total annual inventory cost if he consistently reorders 50 per cent less than the EOQ? What recommendations would you give the warehouse manager based on your answers?

15.12.3 A North Sea oil rig can pump oil ashore at the rate of 40 000 barrels per annum. The inclusive cost of starting and stopping the pump is £200. The oil is delivered into tankage hired at £4 per annum per barrel of tank capacity. The delivery of oil from this tankage is at an even and persistent rate of 20 000 barrels per annum into a trans-UK pipeline.

The oil well operator has just been informed that he will be limited to only 500 barrels of tank capacity next year at the current price, but that additional tankage can be made available at a premium price if he so wishes.

Should he consider hiring extra tankage? If you consider that he should, what price should he be willing to pay for it?

15.12.4 Discuss the considerable difficulties involved with estimating the various cost factors needed by inventory cost control analysis.

15.12.5 Sodium phosphate and sodium sulphite, both used in boiler-feed water quality control, are stored in a concrete bunker. In order to ensure proper quality control, the two products must be segregated and under no condition can space which is allocated to one be used for storage of the other. This is achieved by using timber partitions which can be adjusted in any required position. Both products are fed to the boiler-feed system by way of an overhead grab. Demand by the boiler house for these products can be assumed constant with time. The demand rates are: sodium phosphate, 1000 tonnes per year, and sodium sulphite, 325 tonnes per year. Under no account should the boiler-feed system run out of either product. Fortunately both these products can be obtained within a few hours from a local storage depot.

The costs of ordering, holding in storage and accommodating these products are given below:

	Sodium phosphate	Sodium sulphite
Cost per order (£)	20	20
Average inventory holding cost (£ per tonne per annum)	1.0	2.0
Warehouse costs (£ per tonne per annum)	0.4	0.2

The maximum total capacity of the storage bunker is 300 cubic metres. The bulk densities of the products are sodium sulphite, 1 tonne per cubic metre, and sodium phosphate, 0.5 tonne per cubic metre.

What reorder quantities would you recommend for these two products? (Use the Lagrange multiplier technique.)

15.12.6 Using a trial-and-error method other than the Lagrange multiplier method, rework 15.12.5 to demonstrate how difficult it is to obtain an optimal solution.

15.12.7 A discount warehouse sells 150 deep-freezers per week. Current warehousing policy is to replenish the stock as soon as it becomes depleted. Fortunately, the warehouse is located close to the manufacturer's factory thereby facilitating easy and rapid restocking. The estimated cost of reordering a deep-freezer is £3, whereas the warehousing costs approximate £1 per deep-freezer per week, whilst it is in stock. The current maximum storage space allocated to deep-freezers is 150 cubic metres. Each deep-freezer occupies an effective storage space of 10 cubic metres.

Develop a mathematical model which will permit the computation of the maximum rental charges which the warehouse management should be willing to pay in order to secure extra storage space, and compute this rental charge for the conditions currently prevailing in the warehouse.

15.12.8 A chemical reactor produces two different products on a separate batch basis. Current policy is to produce each product for the *same* duration. These products must be stored separately to avoid contamination. The costs, market requirements and the production and sales depletion rates, both of which are approximately constant with time, are given below:

Product	Annual sales (tonnes)	Sales per production day (tonnes)	Daily production (tonnes)	Annual holding cost (£/tonne)	Reactor set-up cost (£ per set-up)
1	10 000	40	250	0.05	20
2	20 000	80	500	0.10	15

The set-up time may be neglected. What would be (a) the optimal production cycle duration? and (b) the minimal total inventory cost for this production system? What would be the optimal production cycle durations and the minimal total inventory costs if the two products could be produced by *different* reactors?

Why are the total inventory costs different from one another in (a) both products produced by the *same* reactor? (b) both products produced by *different* reactors?

15.12.9 A pharmaceutical drug company manufactures a perishable medicine on a batch basis. Historical records have been kept of past sales and the results are shown below:

Empirical (continuous) cumulative probability distribution of demand $P(X \leq a)$

Probability	a(kg/week)	Probability	a(kg/week)
1.0	220	0.5	110
0.9	200	0.47	100
0.85	190	0.4	90
0.7	180	0.25	80
0.6	160	0.08	60
0.55	140	0.02	40
0.52	120	0.00	20

The company realizes a profit of £150/kg for each kg sold during a week. However, because of the perishable nature of the drug, any quantity left unsold during a week results in a loss of £50/kg. Furthermore, it has been discovered that customers who are turned away because of a shortage of medicine seldom return, and the goodwill loss is estimated to cost the company £80/kg. Using the identity $F_X(Y) = (P + G)/(P + G + L)$, where $F_X(Y)$ = the cumulative probability of X at the optimum stocking quantity Y, P = the profit per kg sold, G = the cost of goodwill per kg not available, and L = the spoilage loss per kg unsold, find the optimal quantity of medicine which should be available at the beginning of any week.

15.12.10 Repeat 15.12.9 using the Monte Carlo simulation technique and a pair of dice as a random number generator.

16. *Minimizing the Costs of Queueing*

Queues of people, vehicles and equipment awaiting a service are a common phenomenon. Mundane examples involve people waiting means of transport, ships queueing to enter a docks, and aeroplanes stacked above an airport awaiting landing instructions. In manufacturing, typical examples of queues involve transport ladles awaiting the tapping of pig iron from a blast furnace, the hold-up of machine-tools awaiting the production of intermediate components, and tradesmen awaiting the service of a storekeeper at a workshop stores. Indeed, examples of queues – or waiting-lines as they are sometimes called – abound in every walk of private and corporate life.

In economic terms, queues of idle people or things represent an opportunity cost – the opportunity forgone by not being able to put such resources to productive use. As such, it behoves management to consider the impact of queues not as a separate entity but within the framework of a total systems approach to decision making, because queues appear everywhere in the corporate functions of a firm, sometimes exhibiting a cascade effect. Ideally, therefore, one should consider the interaction of factory location and layout, different plant capacities and reliabilities and different inventory policies when considering alternative service options. Because of the inherent complexity of such interactions however we normally have to partition such a problem into its constituent parts in the hope that if we can understand the parts, then there is a chance that we can make wise corporate decisions too. In this chapter we shall consider the problems of queueing in isolation of most other corporate activities and we endeavour to highlight the economic implications of alternative servicing policies forever conscious of the dangers of sub-optimizing.

16.1 THE FUNDAMENTAL REASONS FOR QUEUES

Queues of people, vehicles, machines and equipment awaiting a service are commonplace in manufacturing and very evident whenever movement of stocks or the maintenance of equipment is involved. Some idea of the scope of queueing problems can be gleaned from the variety of different examples given in Table 16.1.1. Despite the obvious diversity of these examples, the feature which they share is that the resources awaiting a service, the so-called customers, seldom arrive at the service facility in an orderly manner or at a regular rate. Instead, they tend to cluster and scatter in a fashion which varies with time. Such an arrival pattern has a significant effect on investment decisions concerning the number and type of service facilities to provide because, once chosen, they in turn then influence the number of queueing customers. Furthermore, the dynamic behaviour of the ensuing queue(s) can also be affected by variability in the time required to provide the service. As a result, queueing (or waiting-line) problems involve the classic economic trade-off situation depicted by Figure 16.1.1, showing that as investment in the number of service facilities increases, so the opportunity cost of idle queueing resources diminishes, and

Table 16.1.1 *Some examples of manufacturing systems queues*

Example	Unit arriving	Service or processing facility	Service or process being performed
Vessels docking at a port	Ships and barges	Docks berth	Unloading and/or loading cargo
Vehicular deliveries	Trucks and trains	Delivery bays and marshalling yards	Delivery of raw materials and/or shipment of product
Maintenance and repair of plant, machines and transport facilities	Broken units	Maintenance crews, machines and tools	Repair and/or replacement of broken and worn parts
Batch-processing of a product	Raw materials or components	Production facilities	Manufacture of finished products
Materials or equipment testing	Material or devices	Laboratory testing facilities	Laboratory experiments to test suitability of products

vice versa. A major task of management, therefore, is to strike a balance between these opposing economic forces in a way which optimizes the use of the company's resources, always remembering that the ripple effect of these decisions also affects many other corporate activities besides the immediate servicing problem.

In an attempt to understand the economic implications of waiting-lines better, operational researchers have studied the physical behaviour of queues. This field of research started in 1905 with the pioneering work of the Danish telephone engineer, A. K. Erlang, whose particular interest lay with queueing problems found in the design of automatic dialling equipment. Since then, others have developed his work into a generalized system of queueing models which can deal with a wide variety of seemingly diverse queueing problems.

It is not our intention to develop these mathematical models from basic principles here because, unlike the models of the previous chapter, their derivation tends to be rather complicated and best dealt with by specialist books. An excellent introductory account of such models is given by Buffa (1972), whereas a much more comprehensive understanding comes from reading Churchman, Ackoff and Arnoff (1957),

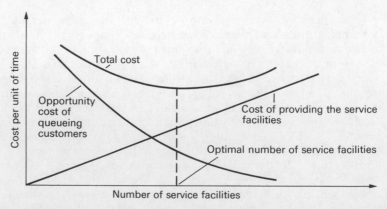

Figure 16.1.1 *The trade-off of costs involving queueing problems.*

Morse (1958) and Sasieni, Jaspan and Friedman (1959). Instead, our intention is to use some of the conventional equations, relating to such queueing models, to discover the economic implications of different servicing policies.

16.2 THE PHYSICAL BEHAVIOUR OF QUEUES

Figure 16.2.1 illustrates the four most basic forms of queueing problems. The most simple situation shown by Figure 16.2.1a concerns arrivals forming a single queue awaiting the attention of a single service facility. An everyday example of such a queue involves tradesmen waiting for spare machine parts at a workshop stores manned by a single storekeeper. With several independent storekeepers, however, one would obtain the simple alternative shown by Figure 16.2.1b.

In more complicated situations however it is conceivable that the overall service might entail several sequential servicing actions, each involving variability in their service time. A practical example of this situation might involve the repair of an

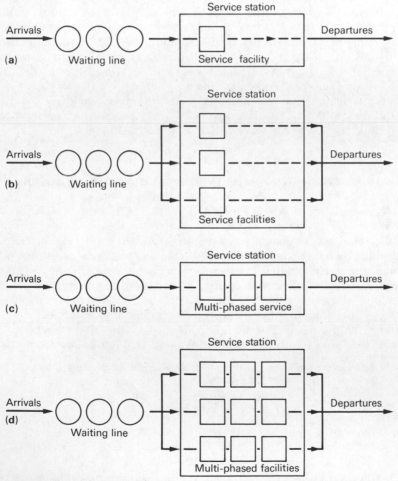

Figure 16.2.1 *Four basic waiting line models. (a) Single channel, single phase service. (b) Multiple channel, single phase service. (c) Single channel, multi-phased service. (d) Multiple channel, multi-phased service.*

engine requiring the use of several machine tools. This situation is depicted by Figure 16.2.1c and an even more complicated multi-channel variant is illustrated by Fig. 16.2.1d.

With these trivial cases in mind one will appreciate that the behaviour of a queue depends on several important factors, namely:

(i) the rate and arrival pattern of customers,
(ii) the queueing discipline,
(iii) the number of service stations,
(iv) the rate and variability of the service provided, and
(v) the servicing policy.

Research has shown that in many practical situations the arrival pattern of customers is often completely random, the number of arrivals per unit of time being quite unpredictable and independent of the numbers of arrivals in preceding time intervals. Such a situation can often be adequately modelled using the classical Poisson distribution* which is completely defined by the mean average arrival rate of customers per unit of time. Typically in queueing theory, this rate is denoted by the term λ. A special property of this distribution is the fact that the time between successive arrivals is given by the negative exponential distribution† with a mean inter-arrival time of $(1/\lambda)$.

In a reasonable proportion of practical situations, it is also possible to describe the servicing of customers by these two distributions using the term μ as the mean average number of customers serviced per unit of time, given that there are customers awaiting service. To stabilize the size of a queue, the service rate must be greater than the customer arrival rate, otherwise the queue would get completely out of hand and either its size would grow indefinitely or customers would leave the queue and look elsewhere for service, if that were possible.

16.3 THE ECONOMIC IMPLICATIONS OF QUEUES INVOLVING A SINGLE CHANNEL, SINGLE PHASE SERVICE

Where real queueing situations possess the structure shown by Figure 16.2.1a, with service provided on a first come first served basis and the assumptions of exponentiality apply, it is found that the queue possesses the characteristics shown in Table 16.3.1. These formulae apply when the queueing situation has stabilized so that the probability of a given number of customers being in the system stays constant. The model also assumes that an infinite number of customers seek service.

The striking feature of all these equations is the fact that they depend only on the utilization factor (λ/μ) for their complete evaluation. Herein lies the mathematical

* According to the Poisson distribution, the probability of n arrivals occurring in t units of time with an average arrival rate of λ, is given by the expression:

$$p(n, t, \lambda) = \frac{(\lambda t^n) \cdot \exp[-\lambda t]}{n!}$$

† According to the negative exponential distribution, the probability of an arrival occurring during an inter-arrival time of t units is given by the expression.

$$F(t) = 1 - \exp[-\lambda t]$$

where $\exp[-\lambda t]$ = the exponential value of $-\lambda t$ and the exponent is the base of the natural or Napieria logarithm such that $(\exp = 2.71828)$. Furthermore $n!$ is the factorial value of n such that:

$$n! = n \cdot (n-1) \cdot (n-2) \ldots 3.2.1$$

Table 16.3.1 *The characteristics of a single channel, single phase service station with Poisson arrival and servicing rates and service on a first come first served basis*

Characteristic number	Basis	Formula
1	The probability (P_0) of there being no customers in the queue and the service station. This is the probability of the service station being idle	$P_0 = 1 - \lambda/\mu$
2	The probability $(\bar{P}_0)$ that there are customers in the queue and service station. This is the probability of the service station being busy and the same as the probability that a customer will have to wait	$\bar{P}_0 = \lambda/\mu$ The utilization factor
3	The probability (P_n) of there being n customers in the queue and service station	$P_n = \left(\dfrac{\lambda}{\mu}\right)^n \left(1 - \dfrac{\lambda}{\mu}\right)$
4	The average number (L) of customers in the queue and service station	$L = \dfrac{\lambda}{\mu - \lambda}$
5	The average number (L_q) of customers in the queue only	$L_q = \dfrac{\lambda^2}{\mu(\mu - \lambda)}$
6	The average waiting time (W) of customers in the queue and the service station	$W = \dfrac{1}{\mu - \lambda}$
7	The average waiting time (W_q) of customers in the queue only	$W_q = \dfrac{\lambda}{\mu(\mu - \lambda)}$

elegance of this modelling technique, but it must be remembered that it is only as good as its basic assumptions.

Intuitively one might feel that it is most desirable for a service station to be fully employed; in other words, one might wish for the utilization factor to approach unity. However, a thorough inspection of the formulae of Table 16.3.1 shows that as the utilization factor increases, so the number of customers awaiting service rapidly increases and their average waiting time becomes very long. Quite obviously such a situation as this could be quite intolerable and such a policy could be quite wrong. Instead, one has to strike a balance between a reasonable utilization factor and a modest-sized queue so that, overall, the most economic situation prevails.

Providing we can estimate values for λ and μ and the costs of providing service and sustaining waiting time, we can appraise the economic merits of alternative queueing strategies using these formulae. To illustrate this point, let us consider the following queueing problem: The managers of a large chemical works are contemplating investment in a centralized workshop specially equipped to refurbish broken centrifugal pumps with an estimated average arrival rate (λ) of five every 24 hours. It is reckoned that working a full four-shift system, maintenance fitters could refurbish these pumps at the rate (μ) of six per man day. To maintain factory output during a pump failure necessitates a stock of duplicate pumps and an expensive system for their storage and retrieval. In all, it is reckoned that each idle pump represents an opportunity cost of 20 000 munits per annum. Furthermore, the estimated cost of such a workshop with around-the-clock maintenance cover by one fitter is 50 000 munits per annum. Alternatively, instead of providing a single, central workshop, the company could employ several local workshops strategically positioned around the factory, in which case it is assumed that each workshop would cost the same, and they would share the workload equally. Using these data and the formulae of Table

Table 16.3.2 *The physical and economic implications of different numbers of singly manned, local workshops*

Number of workshops (n)	Average pump arrival rate at each workshop (λ/n)	Average pump repair rate (μ)	Utilization factor (λ/μn)	Average number of idle pumps nL = nλ/(μ − λ)	Annual opportunity cost of idle pumps 20 000 nL	Annual cost of workshops 50 000n	Total cost of service provision 20 000nL + 50 000n
1	5	6	83.33%	5	100 000	50 000	150 000
2	2.5	6	41.67%	1.43	28 600	100 000	128 600
3	1.67	6	27.83%	1.16	23 140	150 000	173 141
4	1.25	6	20.83%	1.05	21 053	200 000	221 053

☐ = least cost alternative.

16.3.1 we discover that the physical and economic implications of providing alternative service schemes are described by the results shown in Table 16.3.2 where we note that the provision of two local workshops represents the cheapest alternative.

16.4   THE ECONOMIC IMPLICATIONS OF QUEUES INVOLVING A MULTI-CHANNELLED SINGLE PHASE SERVICE

In the preceding example we assumed that a maintenance organization similar to that shown by Figure 16.2.1a applied. However, we could equally employ the system shown by Figure 16.2.1b using a multi-channelled service system comprising more than one fitter in a single, centralized workshop. The formulae for such a system are slightly more complicated than those of our previous model and are shown in Table 16.4.1 where the same assumptions apply as before, but we now allow for there being s service channels.

A careful inspection of the characteristics of Table 16.4.1 shows that they are identical to those of Table 16.3.1 when only one service channel exists such that $(s = 1)$. If we now rework our previous calculations on the basis of the organizational structure given by Figure 16.2.1b we obtain the results shown by Table 16.4.2. In this case we discover that the costs involved with a centralized workshop employing two or more fitters are *less* than the costs involved with separate local workshops employing the same aggregate number of tradesmen. The reason for this difference is fairly obvious. If a tradesman in a centralized workshop is busy, a newly arrived pump can be serviced by one of his idle colleagues, whereas such a capability is impossible with a single manned workshop. In these circumstances, two or more tradesmen working in the same service station possess a form of synergy, providing of course there exist no extenuating circumstances which could neutralize this effect*. In effect, therefore, we would recommend that a centralized workshop employing two tradesmen working in parallel should be employed because such a scheme provides the least cost alternative. (In reality, of course, many other factors would need to be taken into account including the cost, time and means of conveying the pumps from site to the workshops, the effect of size on the cost of workshops, the influence of different plant layout policies, the effects of greater machine reliability, and different inventory policies, not to mention human organizational as well as behavioural problems.)

---

* The essential tenet is that the tradesmen continue to repair pumps at the rate ($\mu = 6$) pumps per man day.

Table 16.4.1 *The characteristics of a multi-channelled, single phased service station with Poisson arrival and servicing rates and service on a first-come-first-served basis*

Characteristic number	Basis	Formula
1	The probability (P_0) of there being no customers in the queue and service station. This is the probability of each service facility being simultaneously idle	$P_0 = \dfrac{1}{\left[\sum\limits_{n=0}^{s-1} \dfrac{(\lambda/\mu)^n}{n!}\right] + \left[\dfrac{(\lambda/\mu)^s}{S!\,(1-\lambda/\mu s)}\right]}$
2	The probability (P_w) that a customer will have to wait for service	$P_w = \dfrac{(\lambda/\mu)^s}{(S-1)!\,(S-\lambda/\mu)} \cdot P_0$
3	The probability (P_n) of there being n customers in the queue and the service station	$P_n = \dfrac{1}{S!}\left(\dfrac{\lambda}{\mu}\right)^n \cdot P_0$
4	The average number (L) in the queue and the service station	$L = L_q + \left(\dfrac{\lambda}{\mu}\right)$
5	The average number (L_q) in the queue only	$L_q = \dfrac{\left(\dfrac{\lambda}{\mu}\right)^{s+1}}{(S-1)!\,(S-\lambda/\mu)^2} \cdot P_0$
6	The average waiting time (W) of customers in the queue and the service station	$W = W_q + \dfrac{1}{\mu}$
7	The average waiting time (W_q) of customers in the queue only	$W_q = \dfrac{\left(\dfrac{\lambda}{\mu}\right)^{s+1}}{\lambda(S-1)!\,(S-\lambda/\mu)^2} \cdot P_0$

Table 16.4.2 *The physical and economic effects of different numbers of tradesmen working together in a single, centralized workshop*

Number of tradesmen S	The probability of the tradesmen being simultaneously idle (P_0)	The average number of pumps in the queue (L_q)	The average number of pumps in the queue and the service station (L)	Annual opportunity cost of idle pumps 20 000L	Annual cost of workshop 50 000S	Total cost of service provision 20 000L + 50 000S
1	16.67%	4.17	5	100 000	50 000	150 000
2	41.18%	0.175	1.01	20 200	100 000	120 200
3	43.21%	0.022	0.86	17 200	150 000	167 200

⬜ = least cost alternative.

16.5 DEALING WITH MORE COMPLEX QUEUEING SITUATIONS

Most real-world queueing situations are usually more complicated than the trivial problem we have chosen as a numerical example. For instance, in many situations the assumption that there exists a very large number of customers requiring a service is invalid, and the mathematical equations and their calculations become quite difficult as a result*. Such a situation would prevail if one was considering the arrival of a finite number of ships at a docks or jetty. In some situations, an organizational structure similar to that shown by Figure 16.2.1c might prevail. Here again mathematicians have devised a theoretical means for solving such problems, but only on the basis of limiting assumptions which are comprehensively described by Saaty (1961). When one considers an organizational problem such as that shown by Figure 16.2.1d, however, quite a different order of complexity is involved and only a few very limited algorithms such as those provided by Disney (1962), Disney and Solberg (1968) and Krishnamoorthi (1963), exist.

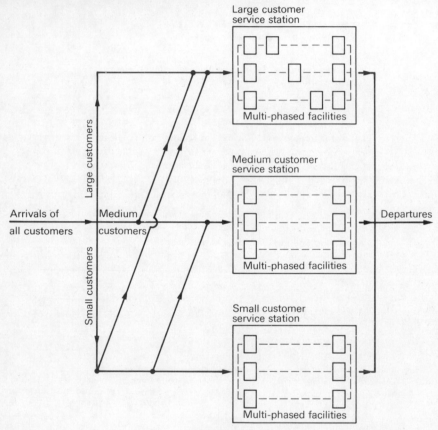

Figure 16.5.1 *A schematic representation of multiple channel, multi-phased queueing involving queue switching and facility–job priorities.*

Generally speaking, theoretical models are unable to represent practical queueing situations of the kind whereby multiple queues, queue switching and different servicing priorities are involved, or where the customer arrival rate is neither completely periodic nor random, but a mixture of both effects. Such a situation as this can often be represented by the organization structure shown in Figure 16.5.1 where a mixture of so-called customers seek a variety of different services which limit some but not others to using particular servicing facilities. A classic example of this problem is the arrival of different sized ships at an oil terminal where coastal

*Fortunately Peck and Hazelwood (1958) have devised finite queueing tables to circumvent this problem.

freighters might well be able to dock at all berths, including the largest, but the ocean-going vessels would be limited to using the largest berths at which they would normally obtain priority. In a similar fashion it is conceivable that most engineering jobs entering a comprehensive workshop could all be done on the most advanced and expensive lathes, but these would normally be used for the more complicated metal working jobs. In these circumstances one has to resort to simulation as a means of modelling queueing problems. This is not the proper place to deal with simulation techniques*, especially as we have already dealt with the subject in Chapter 9. However the reader will appreciate that, irrespective of the complexity of the queueing problem, simulation can provide the means of assessing the economic merit of alternative servicing strategies just as we have done throughout this chapter. Furthermore, such a simulation exercise can permit the uncertainties, risks and the total corporate implications of alternative servicing policies to be explored in depth.

16.6 SUMMARY

Limitations of space have prevented us from giving a detailed analysis of queueing problems here, but the reader should now appreciate that management has to strike a balance between the cost of providing service facilities and the opportunities foregone by having idle resources waiting in line. Of paramount importance is the realization that a service facility cannot be fully utilized if exorbitant queueing costs are to be avoided. Instead, management has to make a trade off between the opposing economic forces involved with waiting lines in a manner devised to serve the company's overall interests. Equally important is the realization that queueing problems affect, and are affected by, a host of other decisions especially those involving inventory and maintenance problems.

For pedagogical reasons we have chosen to use some of the classic analytical models of queueing theory to help the reader understand both the physical and economic complications of queueing. In most practical situations, especially those involving manufacture, these modelling techniques are often unsatisfactory: instead one has to use Monte Carlo simulation to gain an appreciation of the complex interactions of queueing problems.

16.7 BIBLIOGRAPHY

General texts

Morse, P. M., *Queues, Inventories and Maintenance*, John Wiley & Sons, 1958. This is a well rounded book dealing with the general and particular problems of queues, and it forms an especially good reference book for this chapter in that it also deals with the interaction between queueing, inventory and maintenance policies.

Buffa, E. S., *Operations Management*, John Wiley & Sons, 1972. This book incorporates a very readable chapter on waiting lines and also has the advantage that it deals with the problem of large-scale simulation.

---

* A fairly comprehensive treatment of this subject is provided by Tocher (1963) and Naylor et al. (1966).

Specific texts

Churchman, C. W. R., Ackoff, R. L. and Arnoff, E. L., *Introduction to Operations Research*, John Wiley & Sons, 1957.

Disney, R. L., 'Some multi-channel queueing problems with ordered entry', *Journal of Industrial Engineering*, **13,** 1962, pp. 46–48.

Disney, R. L. and Solberg, J. J., 'The effect of three switching rules on queueing networks', *Journal of Industrial Engineering*, **19,** 1968, pp. 584–590.

Krishnamoorthi, B., 'On Poisson queues with two heterogeneous services', *Operations Research*, **11,** 1963, pp. 321–330.

Naylor, T. H., Balintfky, J. L., Burdick, D. S. and Chu, K., *Computer Simulation Techniques*, John Wiley & Sons, 1966.

Peck, L. G. and Hazelwood, R. N., *Finite Queueing Tables*, John Wiley & Sons, 1958.

Sasieni, M., Jaspan, A. and Friedman, L., *Operations Research*, John Wiley & Sons, 1959.

Saaty, T. L., *Elements of Queueing Theory*, McGraw-Hill, 1961.

Tocher, K. D., *The Art of Simulation*, English Universities Press, 1963.

17. *Optimizing the Use of Existing Resources Using Mathematical Programming Techniques*

In many practical situations it is possible to construct mathematical models of complex manufacturing processes which are amenable to solutions using a variety of programming techniques, and by these means to optimize the operations of such processes. In this chapter we focus our attention on problems involving the allocation of scarce resources between competing needs subject to certain rules or constraints. Typical examples in this category include:

(i) deciding which feedstocks to use in an existing manufacturing process,
(ii) deciding the production rates of different manufacturing plants and machines,
(iii) deciding how best to employ skilled manpower and other scarce productive resources,
(iv) deciding how best to incorporate intermediate products in final products,
(v) deciding which products to manufacture with existing production resources,
(vi) deciding how best to distribute products between factories, warehouses, wholesalers and retailers,
(vii) deciding how to allocate an existing advertising budget between the various alternative forms of advertising,
(viii) deciding how best to spend an R & D budget,
(ix) deciding where to allocate new production and distribution facilities, and
(x) deciding which new projects to finance. (See Chapter 6.)

All these examples imply that scarce resources need to be *rationed* between competing needs in the most effective way possible by the restrictions on their use and availability.

In a mathematical sense, these problems can either be defined by sets of linear or non-linear equations. The first can be solved using linear programming (LP) techniques, which tend to be general in their application when applied to linear problems. By contrast, non-linear programming techniques tend to be specific in their application to non-linear programming problems, so that a variety of non-linear programming techniques exists. Because of the tremendous economic impact which LP techniques have made in the process industry, coupled with the fact that non-linear programming methods are still in the process of development, most of this chapter will describe LP algorithms, although one generic method for solving non-linear problems is also covered.

17.1 THE ALGEBRAIC METHOD OF SOLVING LINEAR PROGRAMMING PROBLEMS

To illustrate the methodology of the linear programming technique, let us consider a simple allocation problem. Suppose a firm sells two products, A and B, which are

Table 17.1.1   *The profitability and performance data for a linear programming problem*

Detail	Product A	B
Profit (munits per item of product)	3	2
Number of hours of Machine 1 required to produce one item of product	5	2
Number of hours of Machine 2 required to produce one item of product	3	3

Maximum availability of Machine 1 = 180 hours/month
Maximum availability of Machine 2 = 135 hours/month

manufactured by a process comprising two machines in series. The performance and economic data for this process are shown in Table 17.1.1.

Within the limitations of these data, it would seem reasonable to manufacture these two products in a way which maximizes profit (see Chapter 13). If we denote the optimal production rates of products A and B by the symbols x_A and x_B, and the monthly profit by the symbol P, then the following equations would apply:

$$P = 3x_A + 2x_B \tag{17.1.1}$$

$$5x_A + 2x_B \leqslant 180 \tag{17.1.2}$$

$$3x_A + 3x_B \leqslant 135 \tag{17.1.3}$$

The first of these relationships means that the total monthly profit P is the sum of the individual profits for each product obtained by multiplying their unit profitabilities by their independent production rates, which we need to determine. It will be remembered from the discussion in Chapter 6.5 that we refer to this equation as the objective function whose value we wish to maximize. By contrast, the other two equations are known as constraint equations. They mean that the aggregate amount of processing time needed to manufacture both products cannot exceed the availability of each individual machine. A careful inspection of all three equations shows that they are linear combinations of the undetermined variables x_A and x_B, in other words, they do not include any power terms such as x^2 or $x^{1/2}$ excepting powers of unity.

Reference to Chapter 6.5 shows that we previously solved this set of equations graphically, when we found that the maximum profit of 120 munits per month coincided with optimal production rates of 30 and 15 items per month for products A and B respectively. Our intention here is first to solve this problem by algebraic means, and then according to the linear programming simplex algorithm using Figure 6.5.1 to illustrate each step of the calculations.

To use ordinary algebra to solve the previous set of equations, we first have to remove the inequality signs from equations 17.1.2 and 17.1.3. This can be done using *positive* slack variables S_1 and S_2 such that:

$$5x_A + 2x_B + S_1 = 180$$

and

$$3x_A + 3x_B + S_2 = 135$$

In other words, these two equations show that if the production of both products A and B does not absorb the full capacities of Machines 1 and 2, then the individual and possibly different slack capacities of these two machines can be represented by the variables S_1 and S_2. Since slack capacity means that a certain amount of machine capacity remains unused, it follows that the economic worth of each unit of slack capacity is zero. With these points in mind, coupled with the fact that negative production rates and negative slack variables are infeasible, we find that this problem can be formulated using the following set of algebraic equations:

$$3x_A + 2x_B + 0S_1 + 0S_2 = P \tag{17.1.4}$$

$$5x_A + 2x_B + 1S_1 + 0S_2 = 180 \tag{17.1.5}$$

$$3x_A + 3x_B + 0S_1 + 1S_2 - 135 \tag{17.1.6}$$

$$x_A, \ x_B, \ S_1, \ S_2 \geqslant 0 \tag{17.1.7}$$

Since there are only two equations, 17.1.5 and 17.1.6, to solve four unknowns, x_A, x_B, S_1 and S_2, it follows that an infinite number of feasible solutions exist for this particular problem. This point is illustrated by the area of feasible solution OJMK shown in Figure 6.5.1. However, providing the values of these variables are not restricted to integer values it can be shown that two of these four variables will assume zero values at the optimal solution.

Selecting an initial solution

To start solving this problem we first develop an initial feasible solution which we may then improve by a stepwise procedure which takes us to the optimal solution. It is quite immaterial as to which initial solution we adopt, so let us adopt the worst possible solution, which is equivalent to letting both x_A and x_B equal zero. Transposing equations 17.1.5 and 17.1.6 we find that:

$$S_1 = 180 - 5x_A - 2x_B \tag{17.1.8}$$

and

$$S_2 = 135 - 3x_A - 3x_B \tag{17.1.9}$$

so that S_1 and S_2 are equal to 180 and 135 respectively when x_A and x_B are set equal to zero. Accordingly, the value of the objective function is given by equation 17.1.4 such that:

$$P = 5x_A + 2x_B + 0S_1 + 0S_2$$
$$= 5(0) + 2(0) + 0(180) + 0(135)$$
$$= 0$$

which is the profit expected when nothing is produced. Note that this initial solution is equivalent to point 0 in Figure 6.5.1.

Improving an initial solution

To improve the initial solution we obviously have to increase the values of x_A and/or x_B because these are the only variables which possess positive profitability coefficients in the objective function. The question is, Which variable, x_A or x_B, should we choose first? Since our purpose is to maximize the profit accruing from the sale of these products, the obvious answer to this question is to increase the production rate of that product which increases the profit by the greater amount, namely Product A. This is equivalent to increasing the value of x_A from zero to some positive value which we have to determine.

According to equation 17.1.9, x_A can be increased by 45 items per month before variable S_2 becomes negative. However, according to equation 17.1.8, variable S_1 would become negative if x_A were to assume such a value. Since negative values for these slack variables are infeasible it follows that equation 17.1.8 is the dominant constraint on the value which x_A can assume and it follows that its maximum value is 36 items per month. This can be demonstrated by transposing equation 17.1.8 into the following form:

$$x_A = 36 - 2/5x_B - 1/5S_1 \qquad (17.1.10)$$

where we see that the maximum possible value for x_A is 36 when both x_B and S_1 are zero. Substituting this expression for x_A into equation 17.1.9, we find that the following identity prevails:

$$S_2 = 27 + 3/5S_1 - 9/5x_B \qquad (17.1.11)$$

If both S_1 and x_B are set equal to zero it follows that the value of S_2 would be 27. Substituting this value and the expression for x_A above into our objective function we find that:

$$P = 108 + 4/5x_B - 3/5S_1 \qquad (17.1.12)$$

Since x_B is initially zero, it follows from equation 17.1.12 that the greatest improvement in the profit comes from making S_1 equal to zero, which of course is equivalent to making x_A equal to 36, when a profit of 108 munits per month is realized. This situation corresponds with point K in Figure 6.5.1. However, equation 17.1.12 also shows that we can improve the profit further by increasing the value of variable x_B. Transposing equation 17.1.11 we find that:

$$x_B = 15 + 1/3S_1 - 5/9S_2 \qquad (17.1.13)$$

This means that x_B can assume a value equal to 15 if both S_1 and S_2 are set equal to zero. Substituting this expression for x_B into equation 17.1.10 we find that:

$$x_A = 30 - 1/3S_1 + 2/9S_2 \qquad (17.1.14)$$

so that x_A is equal to 30 when S_1 and S_2 are zero. Furthermore, we find that substituting the expression for x_B into equation 17.1.12 we get the following new identity for the objective function:

$$P = 120 - 1/3S_1 - 4/9S_2 \qquad (17.1.15)$$

in which case we see that the expression for the profit no longer contains variables x_A and x_B. In effect, therefore, equation 17.1.15 shows that the maximum conceivable profit for this particular problem is 120 munits per month when the production rates of A and B are 30 and 15 items per month respectively. This situation corresponds to point M in Figure 6.5.1.

In conclusion therefore we have shown that the optimal solution to this problem is given by:

$$P_{max} = 120, \qquad x_A = 30, \qquad S_1 = 0$$
$$x_B = 15, \qquad S_2 = 0$$

and we have proved that the optimal number of variables in the solution is equal to the number of positive constraints, providing the solution variables are not restricted to integer values.

Equation 17.1.15 is especially interesting in that it shows how the overall profit would diminish if the availabilities of each machine were not fully used. The profit would decline by 1/3 munits per month for a drop in Machine 1 utilization by one hour per month, whereas the corresponding effect for Machine 2 would be a reduction of 4/9 munits per month. In linear programming jargon these values are known as shadow prices and are a real-world manifestation of opportunity costs. In effect, therefore, if S_1 and S_2 were set equal to their corresponding machine production availabilities of 180 and 135 hours per month respectively, we would expect the profit to vanish. This is borne out by equation 17.1.15 since:

$$P = 120 - 1/3 \times 180 - 4/9 \times 135$$
$$= 120 - 60 - 60$$
$$= 0$$

Conversely, we could say that each unit of Machine 1 availability contributes 1/3 munits per month to the firm's profit, whereas the corresponding value for Machine 2 is 4/9 munits per month. This means that, at the optimal solution, the following identity prevails:

$$F = \sum_{i=1}^{N} \rho_i K_i \qquad (17.1.16)$$

where F = the optimal value of the objective function, ρ_i = the shadow price for the ith constraint, K_i = the magnitude of the ith constraint when $i = (1, N)$, and N = the number of constraints.

This identity means that for a *real variable* linear programming problem*, the sum of the products obtained by multiplying each shadow price by its corresponding constraint is equal to the optimal value of the objective function.

In practice, these shadow prices serve a useful purpose in that they help the appraisal of the economic worth of additional resources. In the context of our trivial problem it follows that the monthly profit would increase if additional hourly increments of Machine 1 capacity could be secured for less than 1/3 munits per month, whereas the corresponding maximum cost which one would be willing to pay to secure additional hours of Machine 2 capacity would be 4/9 munits per month. Of course, there exist limits to these shadow prices benefits, as we previously demonstrated in Chapter 6.5.

Although the procedure we have just adopted is profound, the algebraic method is too slow and arduous to solve substantial linear programming problems. What is required is some general purpose algorithm which can be computerized so that the ensuing calculations can be rapidly executed. A very special, and indeed extremely efficient, algorithm for this purpose is the simplex algorithm which is described in the next section. Before dealing with its detail however, it is important to realize that it is nothing more than a mechanical means of duplicating our algebraic procedure, incorporating the following very elementary steps:

(i) formulate the problem by a set of linear equations,
(ii) remove the inequality signs using positive, zero-profit, slack variables,
(iii) set the initial solution so that the slack variables absorb all the available resources,
(iv) identify the solution variable which offers the greatest unit contribution to the objective function,

---

* Equation 17.1.16 does not necessarily apply to problems where the variables are constrained to integer values.

(v) determine the maximum amount of the variable identified by step (iv) above which can be introduced into the solution without violating the problem constraints,

(vi) introduce that variable into the solution and transpose the appropriate solution equation so that the value of that variable is readily discernible,

(vii) substitute the expression for the newly introduced variable into the equations for the other variables remaining in the solution,

(viii) substitute the expression for the newly introduced variable into the objective function and evaluate its magnitude,

(ix) isolate the solution variable in the modified objective function which *now* offers the greatest unit contribution to the objective, and

(x) repeat steps (vi)–(ix) until no further improvement to the problem objective is forthcoming.

17.2 A DESCRIPTION OF THE SIMPLEX ALGORITHM

To proceed further, we need to use a particular type of mathematical notation which may be unfamiliar to some readers*. To overcome any misunderstanding, we shall endeavour to explain the meaning and purpose of each symbol and step in the following algorithm, and shall demonstrate how similar it is to our previous algebraic method.

Excepting equation 17.1.7, which merely ensures that all solution variables are non-negative, the other three primary equations of our previous maximization problem – equations 17.1.4–17.1.6 – are incorporated in the initial solution shown in Table 17.2.1, albeit in a somewhat disguised form.

In this particular case the row and column numbers have been included for descriptive purposes only. Dealing with this tableau from the top, we see that Row 1 includes the coefficients[†] of our original objective function. These coefficients are referred to as the Y_j values and in this particular case they represent the unit profit contributions of the jth column variables (x_A, x_B, S_1 and S_2). Beneath these coefficients we find their corresponding variable identities in Row 2. In effect, therefore, Row 1 together with Row 2 tell us that:

$$3x_A + 2x_B + 0S_1 + 0S_2 = P_0$$

which is identical with our objective function, previously given by equation 17.1.4, but for the fact that the suffix o tells us that this is the *original* profit function prior to any equation transpositions and/or substitutions. Similarly we find that the two constraint equations can be read directly from the tableau. From Row 3 coupled with Row 2 we obtain:

$$5x_A + 2x_B + 1S_1 + 0S_2 = 180$$

and similarly from Row 4 coupled with Row 2 we get:

$$3x_A + 3x_B + 0S_1 + 0S_2 = 135$$

Column 3 informs us that each element in that column belongs to a separate equation, and that each element is effectively multiplied by x_A. By the same token, Column 4 deals only with variable x_B, Column 5 with variable S_1 and Column 6 with variable S_2.

---

* The procedure of the simplex algorithm is best explained using matrix algebra which has only become an integral part of school mathematics syllabuses in recent years.

† All positive coefficients in this tableau effectively follow an imaginary plus (+) sign.

Table 17.2.1 *The initial, zero-profit, solution tableau of our LP maximization problem*

	P_i	Y_j Basis	3 x_A	2 x_B	0 S_1	0 S_2	P_o K	Row 1 2
key → row	0	S_1	⑤	2	1	0	180	3
	0	S_2	3	3	0	1	135	4
		Z_j	0	0	0	0	0	5
		$P' = Y_j - Z_j$	3	2	0	0		6
Column	1	2	3	4	5	6	7	

□ = key number.

↑
key
column

Column 7 currently includes the right-hand side coefficients (K) of the original constraining equations 17.1.5 and 17.1.6.

The so-called basis is nothing more than a log, just like a captain's log. It registers which two of the four solution variables are currently positive. Since we have chosen to select the worst possible initial solution with x_A and x_B both equal to zero, only the slack variables S_1 and S_2 feature in the basis, absorbing the full availabilities of Machines 1 and 2. In effect, therefore, Row 3 (Columns 3–7) in combination with Row 2 can be read as follows:

$$5(0) + 2(0) + 1S_1 + 0S_2 = 180$$

showing that S_1 is currently equal to 180. Likewise Row 4 (Columns 3–7) in conjunction with Row 2 can be read as follows:

$$3(0) + 3(0) + 0S_1 + 1S_2 = 135$$

showing that S_2 is currently equal to 135.

Column 1 shows the unit profit contributions (P_i) of the ith row variables currently in the basis. Since the slack variables have zero profit contributions, as shown by Row 1, it follows that both the values of P_i are currently zero.

Row 5 provides the Z_j values. Each Z_j *column* value is obtained by multiplying the corresponding coefficients in that *column* (located along Rows 3 and 4) by their corresponding P_i *row* values and summing their products. The current Z_j values are calculated as follows:

Column (j)	Z_j
3	$5(0) + 3(0) = 0$
4	$2(0) + 3(0) = 0$
5	$1(0) + 0(0) = 0$
6	$0(0) + 1(0) = 0$
7	$180(0) + 135(0) = 0$

The last of these Z_j values is especially interesting since it gives the current value of the profit belonging to the initial feasible solution.

Row 6 simply involves the subtraction of Row 5 from Row 1, but for Column 7 where the current value of the profit also features. In effect Row 6 registers the profit (P') as it changes with successive iterations and, as it currently stands, Row 6 can be read as follows:

$$P' = 3x_A + 2x_B + 0S_1 + 0S_2 + 0$$

The coefficients of Row 6, excepting Column 7, are known as solution indicators. For a maximization problem it follows that further iterations (calculations) are needed to discover the optimal solution if an indicator in any column is positive and there exists a positive coefficient belonging to a constraining equation (Row 3 or 4) in the same column.

Excepting the details of Row 1, the other data of this tableau change with successive iterations until an optimal solution is found. At each stage in the transformation, however, one should be able to read the same equation identities which previously featured in our algebraic method.

As things stand, Table 17.2.1 effectively covers steps (i)–(iii) of our algebraic procedure. Step (iv) involves finding the most positive solution indicator. This is located in Column 3, which we now call the key column. This means that x_A should enter the solution because it makes the greatest unit contribution to the firm's profit.

For step (v), we now have to decide which of the variables, S_1 or S_2, in the basis should be replaced by x_A. We know from our previous algebra that the answer is S_1, but we now require a simple mechanical procedure which will help. The technique employed is to remove from the basis that variable which has the *least positive quotient* resulting from the division of the right-hand side coefficients (K) by their corresponding *positive* coefficients in the key column. This simple procedure is equivalent to finding the greatest value which the incoming variable (x_A) can assume without violating the problem constraints. For our problem, these quotients are;

For Row 3, $180/5 = 36$ (minimum)

For Row 4, $135/3 = 45$

We refer to the row with the least quotient as the key row and the coefficient at the conjunction of the key row and key column as the key number, as shown in Table 17.2.1.

Step (vi) involves replacing the key row variable, currently in the basis, and its P_i value by the key column variable and its appropriate P_i value. One way of accomplishing this involves partially changing the elements of Row 3 as follows:

$$3 \quad x_A \mid 5 \quad 2 \quad 1 \quad 0 \mid 180$$

As these coefficients stand, in relation to the variables now incorporated in the basis, they mean that:

$$5x_A = 180$$

Although such a relationship as this is quite correct, it would be more straightforward if the equation could be modified to show:

$$x_A = 36$$

This can readily be accomplished by dividing the elements of the constraint equation contained in Row 3 by the value of the key number (5), in which case we get the following values for the *new* Row 3 coefficients, which are also shown in Table 17.2.2:

$$3 \quad x_A \mid 1 \quad 2/5 \quad 1/5 \quad 0 \mid 36$$

In conjunction with Row 2, these new coefficients represent the equation:

$$x_A + 2/5x_B + 1/5S_1 = 36$$

which is the same as equation 17.1.10, and read in conjunction with the basis it means that $x_A = 36$.

Step (vii) involves the direct substitution of the equation for the newly introduced variable x_A into the other constraint equations. The procedure for this is to substract some multiple of the coefficients in the newly formed key row from the coefficients in each other row so that the values of their *existing key column coefficients become zero*. Since the value of the element currently in Row 4 and the existing key column is 3, this means that we have to subtract three times the value of the coefficients of the newly formed key from the corresponding elements in Row 4, as follows:

Existing Row 4 coefficients		Multiple		Coefficients of newly formed key row		New Row 4 coefficients
3	−	3	×	1	=	0
3	−	3	×	2/5	=	9/5
0	−	3	×	1/5	=	− 3/5
1	−	3	×	0	=	1
135	−	3	×	36	=	27

The newly formed Row 4 therefore appears in Table 17.3.2 as:

$$0 \quad S_2 \mid 0 \quad 9/5 \quad -3/5 \quad 1 \mid 27$$

so that, in conjunction with Row 2, it can be read as follows:

$$9/5x_B - 3/5S_1 + S_2 = 27$$

This equation is the same as equation 17.1.11 and read in conjunction with the basis it means that $S_2 = 27$.

So far we have changed the coefficients of Rows 3 and 4. Now we need to recalculate the values of Z_j according to our previous method, using these new coefficients. The new Z_j values are calculated as follows:

Column j	Z_j
3	$1(3) + 0(0) = 3$
4	$2/5(3) + 9/5(0) = 6/5$
5	$1/5(3) - 3/5(0) = 3/5$
6	$0(3) + 1(0) = 0$
7	$36(3) + 27(0) = 108$

The new value for Column 7 means that the profit is now 108 munits per month. Subtracting these Z_j values from the Y_j values of Row 1 we obtain the new values for Row 6 shown in Table 17.2.2. Read in conjunction with Row 2, these new coefficients in Row 6 mean that:

$$P' = 4/5x_B - 3/5S_1 + 108$$

This equation is the same as equation 17.1.12 and means that we have just completed step (viii) of our previous algebraic procedure.

At this stage we have completed one iteration of the algorithm. A careful examination of Table 17.2.2 however shows that Column 4 still possesses a positive indicator with positive constraining equation coefficients. This means that variable x_B should now enter the solution to replace either x_A or S_2. If we follow the algorithm as before we end up with the results given in Table 17.2.3. This tableau does not possess any positive solution indicators so its results are optimal. Read in conjunction with Row 2, the coefficients of this tableau give the following information:

(i) Row 3 can be interpreted as follows:

$$x_A + 1/3S_1 - 2/9S_2 = 30$$

Table 17.2.2 *The second tableau for our LP maximization problem*

P_i	Y_j Basis	3 x_A	2 x_B	0 S_1	0 S_2	P_0 K
3	x_A	1	2/5	1/5	0	36
0	S_2	0	9/5	−3/5	1	27
	Z_j	3	6/5	3/5	0	108
	$P' = Y_j - Z_j$	0	4/5	−3/5	0	

This is the same as equation 17.1.14 and read in conjunction with the basis it tells us that the optimal value of x_A is 30.

(ii) Row 4 can be interpreted as follows:

$$x_B - 1/3S_1 + 5/9S_2 = 15$$

This is the same as equation 17.1.13 and read in conjunction with the basis it tells us that the optimal value of x_B is 15.

(iii) Row 6 can be read as follows:

$$P' = -1/3S_1 - 4/9S_2 + 120$$

This is the same as equation 17.1.15 and read in conjunction with the basis it tells us that the maximum profit is 120 munits per month.

In effect, therefore, this algorithm has achieved the same results as the algebraic method, but without the need for equation transformations and substitutions. Instead, this algorithm simply relies on a numerical procedure which can readily be computerized.

A careful examination of the results of Table 17.2.3 also provides the following information:

(i) It shows that irrespective of the number of variables in the problem as formulated, the number of variables appearing in the solution must, by definition, be equal to the number of constraints. Four variables x_A, x_B, S_1 and S_2 appear in our formulated problem but only two appear in its solution.

(ii) Only those variables which appear in the basis are in the solution. This point emphasizes the importance of the information contained in the basis, without which the meaning of the tableau coefficients cannot be properly interpreted.

(iii) The values of the shadow prices on the active constraints appear as Z_j values in the columns of those active constraints. Since both S_1 and S_2 do not appear in the basis, this means that both their values are zero and that both their respective constraints are active. It therefore follows that the Z_j values of 1/3 and 4/9 are the shadow prices for Machines 1 and 2 respectively.

Table 17.2.3 *The third and final tableau for our LP maximization problem*

P_i	Y_j Basis	3 x_A	2 x_B	0 S_1	0 S_2	P_0 K
3	x_A	1	0	1/3	−2/9	30
2	x_B	0	1	−1/3	5/9	15
	Z_j	3	2	1/3	4/9	120
	$P' = Y_j - Z_j$	0	0	−1/3	−4/9	

(iv) The ultimate matrix of numbers appearing under those variables which appear in the solution assumes a very special form comprising values which are either unity or zero*. Indeed, the entire strategy of the algorithm is *to try* to accomplish this end.

17.3 SOLVING MINIMIZATION PROBLEMS USING THE SIMPLEX ALGORITHM

In problems of economic choice it is often more appropriate to minimize rather than maximize some objective. For example, given that a firm's sales revenue remains unaffected by its raw materials purchasing strategy, it would seem reasonable to minimize the cost of raw material purchases in the short term and the net present value of raw material costs in the long term, since both objectives are equivalent to maximizing the NPV of the firm, although such an objective as this is only valid if the resulting cash flow is sufficient to warrant continued operations.

The simplex algorithm of the preceding section can readily solve minimization problems providing the meaning of the solution indicators is properly interpreted. Starting with the worst possible initial solution which might, for example, comprise the most costly allocation of raw materials, one would introduce into the solution that variable with the most *negative* solution indicator, since it would lead to the minimization, rather than maximization, of the objective.

To demonstrate the application of the LP simplex algorithm to minimization problems, let us consider the following example which incorporates two *further* types of constraints. A firm needs to manufacture a pipeline to a particular specification. Each standard length of pipe must weigh exactly 120 tonnes so that the delivery costs to the pipeline site can be minimized. Because of the corrosive nature of the fluids to be conveyed in the pipeline, a strict metallurgical specification has to be met such that *no more than* 12 cubic metres of Material *A* and *at least* 16 cubic metres of Material *B* must be contained in each standard length of pipeline. Materials *A* and *B* weigh 4 and 6 tonnes per cubic metre, and cost 3 and 8 munits per cubic metre, respectively.

If we *assume* that the cost of fabricating each pipelength is unaffected by any feasible alterations to its metallurgical content, it follows that a reasonable objective would entail the minimization of the raw materials costs *C* associated with the manufacture of the pipeline. If we represent the quantities (measured in cubic metres) of Materials *A* and *B* in each standard length of pipeline by the symbols x_A and x_B, it follows that the objective function to be minimized is given by the relationship:

$$C = 3x_A + 8x_B$$

The specification requiring each standard length of pipeline to contain no more than 12 cubic metres of Material *A* involves a less than or equal to type of constraint, similar to those previously encountered in this chapter. In algebraic form, this specification can be represented by the following equation:

$$x_A \leq 12$$

---

* In the jargon of matrix algebra, this results from the fact that we have inverted the initial solution tableau and, in this particular problem, we have ended up with an identity matrix of the form $\begin{vmatrix} 1 & 0 \\ 0 & 1 \end{vmatrix}$.

which is equivalent to:

$$x_A + S_1 = 12$$

where $S_1 =$ a *positive* slack variable registering the fact that it is quite feasible for each length of pipeline to contain less than 12 cubic metres of Material A. Of course, no pipelength can contain less than zero units of any substance, so it follows that both x_A and x_B must be greater than or equal to zero, that is:

$$x_A, x_B \geqslant 0$$

The specification requiring each standard length of pipeline to contain at least 16 cubic metres of substance B involves a situation which we have not previously encountered. In algebraic form this specification can be represented by the following equation:

$$x_B \geqslant 16$$

or

$$x_B - S_2 = 16$$

where S_2 represents a *positive* slack variable registering the fact that it is quite feasible for each length of pipeline to contain more than 16 units of Material B. It will be realized that we have not dealt with *negative* coefficients in LP problems before. Unfortunately, they cause certain difficulties because they yield negative quotients in the search for the variable about to leave the LP solution. To overcome such problems we introduce artificial variables into the LP tableau so that the previous equation can be represented in the following form:

$$x_B + A_2 - S_2 = 16$$

where A_2 represents a positive artificial variable associated with this second constraint. Of course, being fictitious, artificial variables *cannot* feature in the *optimal* solution of any LP problem. To ensure such an outcome, a punitive economic value is attached to each artificial variable to expel them from the LP solution.

The specification requiring each standard length of pipeline to weigh exactly 120 tonnes also involves a situation which we have not encountered before in our linear programming problems. In this particular case we are confronted with an equal to identity such that:

$$4x_A + 6x_B = 120$$

As things stand, this equation requires no positive slack variables but this means that we cannot compute the Z_j values, so we have no means of determining the LP solution indicators. To resolve this problem we introduce an artificial variable into the equation so it becomes:

$$4x_A + 6x_B + A_3 = 120$$

where $A_3 =$ the positive artificial variable associated with this third constraint.

In effect, therefore, this problem can be formulated by the following set of linear equations:

$$3x_A + 8x_B + 0S_1 + 0S_2 + MA_2 + MA_3 = C$$
$$x_A + S_1 \qquad\qquad\qquad = 12$$
$$x_B - S_2 + A_2 \qquad\qquad = 16$$
$$4x_A + 6x_B + A_3 \qquad\qquad = 120$$

where the coefficients $+M$ in the objective function assume a very high punitive value* to ensure that such variables do not feature in the optimal solution.

Having formulated the problem, it can now be solved using the same simplex procedure as before, but for the fact that further iterations are now needed if any solution indicator is *negative* and there exist *positive* coefficients in the same column as that negative solution indicator.

The initial tableau, comprising the greatest cost for this problem, is given in Table 17.3.1, where the symbol C registers the fact that we are now dealing with costs instead of profits. In this particular case we note that there are three negative solution indicators. However, the most negative one is that belonging to variable x_B, namely $(8-7M)$, so we mark this column with an arrow and call it the key column as before. To discover which of the variables S_1, A_2 or A_3 must leave the basis to be replaced by x_B, we simply divide the values of the K column by the corresponding coefficients in the key column and that variable with the *least* quotient leaves the solution. For this particular problem we have chosen to show these quotients at the right-hand side of the matrix and we also depict the variable leaving the solution by an arrow.

Table 17.3.1 *The initial highest cost solution tableau for the LP minimization problem*

C_i	Y_j. Basis	3 x_A	8 x_B	0 S_1	0 S_2	$+M$ A_2	$+M$ A_3	C_0 K	Value of quotient
0	S_1	1	0	1	0	0	0	12	$\dfrac{12}{0}=\infty$
$\leftarrow +M$	A_2	0	1	0	-1	1	0	16	$\dfrac{16}{1}=16$
$+M$	A_3	4	6	0	0	0	1	120	$\dfrac{120}{6}=20$
	Z_j	$4M$	$7M$	0	$-M$	M	M	$136M$	
	$C'=Y_j-Z_j$	$3-4M$	$8-7M$	0	M	$-M$	0		

$\uparrow$

Adopting the same procedure as before, we discover that this problem requires three iterations to determine the optimal solution. Each of the intermediate steps is shown in Table 17.3.2 and the optimal solution tableau is shown in Table 17.3.3.

A careful examination of Table 17.3.3 shows that the optimal solution is given by:

$$C_{\min}=146, \qquad x_A=6, \qquad S_1=6,$$
$$x_B=16, \qquad S_2=0, \qquad A_2=0$$
$$A_3=0$$

so that the cheapest way to manufacture such pipelengths is to blend 6 cubic metres of Material A with 16 of Material B. Since the slack variable S_1 appears in the basis, this means that the constraint:

$$x_A \leq 12$$

is inactive, so no opportunity cost results from this constraint. This conclusion is endorsed by the fact that the Z_j value for S_1 is zero. However, the other two

---

* For mental calculations we do not need to specify the value of M. For computer calculations, however, one needs to select a value for M which guarantees that no artificial variables remain in the final optimal solution. For maximization problems the corresponding value for artificial variables is $-M$.

The Optimal Employment of Existing Assets

Table 17.3.2 *Tableau showing the intermediate iterations for the LP minimization problem*

C_i	Y_j Basis	3 x_A	8 x_B	0 S_1	0 S_2	+M A_2	+M A_3	C_0 K	Value of quotient
0	S_1	1	0	1	0	0	0	12	$\dfrac{12}{0}=\infty$
8	x_B	0	1	0	-1	1	0	16	not allowed
←+M	A_3	4	0	0	6	-6	1	24	$\dfrac{24}{6}=4$
	Z_j	4M	8	0	6M-8	8-6M	M	24M+128	
	$C'=Y_j-Z_j$	3-4M	0	0	8-6M	6M-8	-M		

↑

C_i	Y_j Basis	3 x_A	8 x_B	0 S_1	0 S_2	+M A_2	+M A_3	C_0 K	Value of quotient
0	S_1	1	0	1	0	0	0	12	$\dfrac{12}{1}=12$
8	x_B	4/6	1	0	0	0	1/6	20	$\dfrac{20\times6}{4}=30$
←0	S_2	4/6	0	0	1	-1	1/6	4	$\dfrac{4\times6}{4}=6$
	Z_j	16/3	8	0	0	0	8/6	160	
	$C'=Y_j-Z_j$	-7/3	0	0	0	+M	M-8/6		

↑

constraints are active and we find that the sum of their products obtained by multiplying their original K values by their corresponding shadow prices gives the minimum cost for the manufacture of this pipeline as follows:

$$7/2\times16+3/4\times120=146$$

This result confirms the fact that the identity given by equation 7.1.16 applies to maximization and minimization problems alike.

Table 17.3.3 *The final tableau showing the optimal solution for the LP minimization problem*

C_i	Y_j Basis	3 x_A	8 x_B	0 S_1	0 S_2	+M A_2	+M A_3	C_0 K
0	S_1	0	0	1	-6/4	6/4	-4	6
8	x_B	0	1	0	-1	1	0	16
3	x_A	1	0	0	6/4	-6/4	1/4	6
	Z_j	3	8	0	-7/2	7/2	3/4	146
	$C'=Y_j-Z_j$	0	0	0	7/2	M-7/2	M-3/4	

17.4 FORMULATING LINEAR PROGRAMMING MODELS

Most practical problems which are sufficiently complex to warrant using linear programming techniques usually involve too much calculation to be done manually.

Instead they need to be solved by computer using programs specially designed for the task. Fortunately, comprehensive computer software is readily available for this purpose so a full understanding of the methodology of linear programming techniques by the potential user, is not essential. However, three conditions have to be met for these techniques to be profitably employed. These are

  (i) the user must be able to recognize when a particular problem is amenable to solution by linear programming techniques,
 (ii) he must be able to transform his particular problem into a form which is suitable for LP solutions, and
(iii) he must be able to interpret the computer data in a way which relates to the original practical problem.

So far in this chapter we have concentrated our attention on the methodology of the linear programming simplex algorithm with a view to teaching fundamental points of principle. In this respect we hope to meet the needs of items (i) and (iii) above. However, item (ii) needs special mention. The transformation of a practical problem into a form of equations which can be solved is known as formulating a model of the real-world problem. To accomplish this requires a special knowledge of the interrelationships which exist between the various factors affecting the behaviour of a particular industrial system. Furthermore, for the results of the model to be meaningful in a practical sense, the model must be able to simulate real-world conditions sufficiently closely to satisfy the decision maker. The point which we wish to stress here is that the formulation stage of an industrial problem is usually the most difficult of the three steps, and usually involves many more equations than our trivial examples have shown. Furthermore, an incorrectly formulated model can lead to considerable computational difficulties.

To demonstrate this point let us consider the somewhat more complex example concerning the petroleum refining industry, shown in Figure 17.4.1. In this example we see that crude petroleum is fractionated in a primary distillation unit into its constituent products according to the yield data provided in Table 17.4.1. Some of the middle distillate, known as cat-feed, is fed to the Catalytic Cracker whose products are then blended with other intermediate products to produce motor

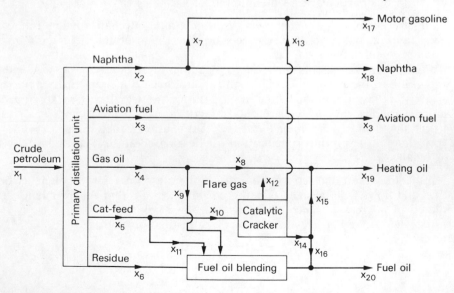

Figure 17.4.1 *A flow-chart showing the intermediate and final product flow rates for a simple refinery.*

Table 17.4.1 *Yield and throughput data for a simple petroleum refinery*

Unit	Product		Product flow rate (tonnes/day)	Yield or proportion (% by weight)
Crude distillation unit	Naphtha		x_2	10
	Aviation fuel		x_3	15
	Gas oil		x_4	25
	Cat-feed		x_5	20
	Residue		x_6	30
Catalytic Cracker	Flare gas		x_{12}	5
	Gasoline blendstock		x_{13}	40
	Oil blendstock		x_{14}	55
Product specifications	Motor gasoline	Naphtha		50
		Gasoline blendstock		50
	Heating oil	Gas oil		60
		Oil blendstock		40
	Fuel oil	Residue, cat-feed and oil blendstock		in any proportion
Maximum throughput rates governed by physical limitations	x_1		20 000	To the primary distillation unit
	x_{10}		4 000	To the Catalytic Cracker
	x_{17}		3 000	Motor gasoline
	x_{18}		2 000	Naphtha
	x_3		2 500	Aviation fuel
	x_{19}		1 500	Heating oil
	x_{20}		10 000	Fuel oil

gasoline and fuel oil, according to the information contained in Figure 17.4.1 and the data given in Table 17.4.1.

The minimum number of variables needed to define this system completely is important. In this particular case the number of variables is *three* because:

(i) *fixing the feed rate x_1 to the primary distillation unit* automatically determines the flow rates x_2, x_3, x_4, x_5 and x_6 according to the product yield data for the primary distillation unit,

(ii) *fixing the gasoline blendstock rate x_{13}* automatically determines x_7 and x_{17} according to the product specification for motor gasoline, and it fixes variables x_{10}, x_{12} and x_{14} according to the yield data for the Catalytic Cracker. Furthermore, variables x_{11} and x_{18} are determined by mass balance, and

(iii) *fixing the heating oil product rate x_{19}* automatically determines x_8 and x_{15} according to the product specification for heating oil and x_9, x_{16} and x_{20} by way of balances.

Adopting the traditional convention which denotes flows into a plant as being *negative*, and flows from a plant as being *positive*, we find that this problem can be formulated by 17 mass balance equations, as shown below:

(i) Fixed yield mass balances for the primary distillation unit:

$$-0.10x_1 + x_2 = 0$$
$$-0.15x_1 + x_3 = 0$$
$$-0.25x_1 + x_4 = 0$$
$$-0.20x_1 + x_5 = 0$$
$$-0.30x_1 + x_6 = 0$$

(ii) Fixed yield mass balances for the Catalytic Cracker:

$$-0.05x_{10}+x_{12}=0$$
$$-0.40x_{10}+x_{13}=0$$
$$-0.55x_{10}+x_{14}=0$$

(iii) Product specification mass balances for the blending of motor gasoline and heating oil:

$$0.5x_{17}-x_7=0$$
$$0.5x_{17}-x_{13}=0$$
$$0.6x_{19}-x_8=0$$
$$0.4x_{19}-x_{15}=0$$

(iv) Unrestricted mass balances for:

Naphtha:	$-x_2 +x_{18}+x_7 =0$
Gas oil:	$-x_4 +x_8 +x_9 =0$
Cat-feed:	$-x_5 +x_{10}+x_{11}=0$
Oil blendstock:	$-x_{14}+x_{15}+x_{16}=0$
Fuel oil:	$-x_6-x_9-x_{11}-x_{16}+x_{20}=0$

To define the mass balance for this particular problem properly we find that:

(i) the *minimum* number of variables	$= 3$
(ii) the *minimum* number of mass balance equations	$= 17$
(iii) the actual number of variables	$= 20$

Table 17.4.2   *The LP matrix for the refinery example*

Variable	Row	x_1	x_2	x_3	x_4	x_5	x_6	x_7	x_8	x_9	x_{10}	x_{11}	x_{12}	x_{13}	x_{14}	x_{15}	x_{16}	x_{17}	x_{18}	x_{19}	x_{20}		
Plant restrictions	1	1																				≤	20 000
	2							1														≤	4 000
	3																1					≤	3 000
	4																	1				≤	2 000
	5		1																			≤	2 500
	6																		1			≤	1 500
	7																			1		≤	10 000
Mass balances	8	−0.10	1																			=	0
	9	−0.15		1																		=	0
	10	−0.25			1																	=	0
	11	−0.20				1																=	0
	12	−0.30					1															=	0
	13										−0.05		1									=	0
	14										−0.40			1								=	0
	15										−0.55				1							=	0
	16							−1										0.5				=	0
	17													−1				0.5				=	0
	18								−1											0.6		=	0
	19															−1				0.4		=	0
	20		−1					1											1			=	0
	21				−1				1	1												=	0
	22					−1					1	1										=	0
	23														−1	1	1					=	0
	24						−1			−1		−1					−1				1	=	0
Check	Σ=	−1	0	1	0	0	0	0	0	0	0	0	1	0	0	0	1	1	1	1	1		

Formulating the mass balance with more equations than are needed by this simple identity can result in computational problems caused by degeneracy*. To minimize this possibility a simple check is conducted on the LP matrix, excluding slack and artificial variables, as shown in Table 17.4.2. For the mass balance section only, the vertical sum of coefficients representing inputs into the process system *must* equal minus unity (-1), whereas for outputs it *must* equal plus unity (1). Furthermore, it *must* equal zero (0) for variables representing internal streams.

17.5   AN INTRODUCTION TO TRANSPORTATION LINEAR PROGRAMMING (TLP)

In many industrial situations we find that the set of linear equations of the form:

$$a_{i1}x_1 + a_{i2}x_2 + \ldots a_{iN}x_N = K$$

representing the inputs and outputs of a manufacturing problem can be simplified to the form:

$$x_1 + x_2 + \ldots x_N = K$$

This happens when the product or service involved is homogeneous and there exists a one-for-one substitution between the various inputs and outputs so that:

$$a_{i1} = a_{i2} = \ldots = a_{in}$$

Such problems can be solved using a special, indeed simple, type of linear programming technique called transportation linear programming (TLP). This does not mean that this procedure is constrained in its use to transportation problems – far from it – but it so happens that this method was first demonstrated for a transportation problem by F. L. Hitchcock in 1941. Although the simplex algorithm of Section 17.3 is quite capable of solving such problems as these, the TLP approach is simpler and easier to understand; it is also computationally faster.

To demonstrate the application of the TLP technique, let us consider an example where there exist S sources of supply and D sources of demand for a given product. Let factories F_1, F_2 and F_3, with respective capacities of 75, 50 and 30 tonnes per week of product, constitute the sources of supply, and let the corresponding sources of demand comprise three warehouses, W_1, W_2 and W_3, requiring 40, 55 and 60 tonnes of product per week, respectively. These data are shown in the TLP matrix in Table 17.5.1, in which the availabilities and requirements for the product are known as rim constraints. In this particular example we note that the aggregate demand equals the aggregate supply potential, although this need not be the case as we shall see later. Also shown in the top left-hand sectors of this matrix are the transportation costs, measured in munits per tonne, for delivering product from each factory to each warehouse, it being assumed, at this stage that the unit production costs at each factory are identical.

Given these data and assumptions, it follows that our basic problem is to allocate product between factories and warehouses in such a way that the overall distribution cost is minimized. Several alternative variants of the TLP technique exist for solving such a problem. The main ones are (i) the stepping-stone method, (ii) Vogel's

---

* Degeneracy results when one row of the LP tableau is a partial sum of other rows. In these circumstances two or more variables need to leave the solution *simultaneously* thereby bringing the algorithm to an abrupt halt. To overcome this problem it is essential to avoid degeneracy wherever possible, and LP software must include means of circumventing this difficulty whenever such a possibility is unavoidable.

Table 17.5.1 *The transportation linear programme matrix showing the product availabilities and requirements and the distribution costs for each route*

Factory ＼ Warehouse	W_1	W_2	W_3	Factory capacities (tonnes per week)
F_1	30	30	30	75
F_2	10	30	30	50
F_3	30	20	20	30
Warehouse demands (tonnes per week)	40	55	60	155

approximation method, and (iii) the modified distribution method, and are surveyed below.

17.6 TRANSPORTATION LINEAR PROGRAMMING – THE STEPPING-STONE METHOD

The procedure adopted here involves finding an initial feasible allocation of product so that the rim constraints are met and then, through successive modifications, to seek the optimal solution such that the minimum distribution cost is obtained. One method of starting such an algorithm involves allocating product according to the Northwest Corner Rule*. This means starting at the top left-hand corner of the matrix shown in Table 17.6.1 and assigning the capacity of the first factory (F_1) as far as it will go, meeting the warehouse requirements in order. The first warehouse not completely supplied by the first factory is then assigned as much as needed by the second factory whose output is then used to supply succeeding warehouses. In this fashion all rim requirements are met.

By these means we obtain the initial feasible solution which is shown in Table 17.6.1. In this particular case we note that although Factory F_1 can supply 75 tonnes per week, Warehouse W_1 requires only 40 tonnes per week. To meet the rim constraints, therefore, only 40 tonnes per week are assigned to position F_1W_1, shown by the circled number in that position. According to this technique we find that only five assigned routes are required to meet the rim constraints so that four routes remain without any product allocation. This result is no accident since it agrees with a linear programming rule which states that for problems of this kind we require:

$$S + D - 1$$

assigned routes if the optimal solution is to be found. In our particular case of course ($S = 3$), and ($D = 3$) so that:

$$S + D - 1 = 3 + 3 - 1 = 5$$

This initial feasible solution results in a total distribution cost of 4350 munits per week. What we now need is a means of reducing this cost, if this is possible.

To discover if we can reduce this cost we must explore the possibility of using some of the unassigned routes and determine the incremental (marginal) cost of

---

* There are many other ways to start from which one can obtain an optimal solution more rapidly, but this is a well tried way which always works. Alternative methods involve allocating product to the cheapest routes consistent with meeting the rim constraints.

Table 17.6.1 *The initial feasible solution to the TLP problem according to the Northwest Corner Rule and the stepping-stone method*

Factory	Warehouse W_1	W_2	W_3	Factory capacities (tonnes per week)
F_1	30 (40)	30 (35)	30	75
F_2	10 (?)	30 (20)	30 (30)	50
F_3	30	20	20 (30)	30
Warehouse demands (tonnes per week)	40	55	60	155

Total distribution cost $= 4350$ munits per week.

transferring one unit of product from an assigned route to an unassigned route consistent with meeting the rim constraints. If the overall effective cost of using each unassigned route is zero or positive then this means that we have an optimal solution. If, however, this cost is negative then this means that we can reduce the overall transportation cost and further iterations to the TLP algorithm are necessary.

First, let us evaluate the effect of assigning 1 tonne per week of product to route $F_2 W_1$. One means of accomplishing this entails reducing the product allocation to route $F_1 W_1$, but, in so doing, we would violate the rim constraint of 75 tonnes per week for Factory F_1. To overcome this problem we need to move 1 tonne per week out of route $F_2 W_2$ into route $F_1 W_2$, and likewise out of route $F_1 W_1$ into route $F_2 W_1$; by these means all the rim constraints are met. Such a change is illustrated by the dotted lines in Table 17.6.1 and it will be noticed that this procedure is similar to crossing a river using stepping-stones – hence the name of this technique.

Let I be the indicator which represents the *overall cost effect* of allocating one unit of product to route $F_2 W_1$, and let c_{ij} denote the transportation or distribution cost for one unit of product for route $F_i W_j$, where $(i = 1, 2, 3)$ and $(j = 1, 2, 3)$. In our particular case therefore we find that:

$$I_{21} = c_{21} - c_{11} + c_{12} - c_{22}$$
$$= 10 - 30 + 30 - 30$$
$$= -20$$

In effect, therefore, indicator I_{21} shows that we could reduce the overall cost of the initial feasible solution by 20 munits for each tonne of product allocated to route $F_2 W_1$. Before we decide to use this route, however, we must first check if any of the other three unassigned routes offer more cost-effective alternatives. In a similar vein we find that:

$$I_{13} = c_{13} - c_{23} + c_{22} - c_{12}$$
$$= 30 - 30 + 30 - 30$$
$$= 0$$

$$I_{32} = c_{32} - c_{22} + c_{23} - c_{33}$$
$$= 20 - 30 + 30 - 20$$
$$= 0$$

It will be noticed that route F_3W_1 cannot be evaluated by the rectangular pattern used to evaluate the three previous unassigned routes. Instead, its evaluation involves six steps, namely:

$$I_{31} = c_{31} - c_{11} + c_{12} - c_{22} + c_{23} - c_{33}$$
$$= 30 - 30 + 30 - 30 + 30 - 20$$
$$= +10$$

The results of our analysis therefore show that allocating product to the currently unassigned route F_2W_1 is the most cost-effective change we can make since none of the other unassigned routes would reduce the overall transportation cost. According to the rim constraints we can allocate 20 tonnes per week to this route, limited by the current allocation of product to route F_2A_2, giving the second feasible solution shown by Table 17.6.2 with an overall distribution cost of 3950 munits per month.

Table 17.6.2 *The second feasible solution to the TLP problem*

Factory \ Warehouse	W_1	W_2	W_3	Factory capacities (tonnes per week)
F_1	30 / (20)	30 / (55)	30 /	75
F_2	10 / (20)	30 /	30 / (30)	50
F_3	30 /	20 /	20 / (30)	30
Warehouse demands (tonnes per week)	40	55	60	155

Total distribution cost = 3950 munits per week.

The result of our first iteration, therefore, is a cost saving on the initial feasible solution of 400 munits per week, but having made this change we must now check if further savings are possible. Using the same procedure as before we find that the *optimal* values of the cost indicators for the four unassigned routes are:

$$I_{13} = 30 - 30 + 10 - 30 = -20$$
$$I_{22} = 30 - 30 + 30 - 30 = 0$$
$$I_{31} = 30 - 30 + 30 - 20 = +10$$
$$I_{32} = 20 - 30 + 30 - 20 = 0$$

so that further cost savings can be realized by transferring 20 tonnes per week of product to route F_1W_3. In this case we obtain the third feasible solution shown in Table 17.6.3.

The result of the second iteration, therefore, is a cost saving on the second feasible solution of another 400 munits per month giving an overall distribution cost of 3550 munits per week.

A revaluation of the cost indices for the unassigned routes of Table 17.6.3 shows that:

$$I_{11} = 30 - 30 + 30 - 10 = +20$$
$$I_{22} = 30 - 30 + 30 - 30 = 0$$
$$I_{31} = 30 - 10 + 30 - 20 = +30$$
$$I_{32} = 20 - 30 + 30 - 20 = 0$$

Table 17.6.3 *An optimal solution to the TLP problem*

Factory \ Warehouse	W_1	W_2	W_3	Factory capacities (tonnes per week)
F_1	30	30 (55)	30 (20)	75
F_2	10 (40)	30	30 (10)	50
F_3	30	20	20 (30)	30
Warehouse demands (tonnes per week)	40	55	60	155

Total distribution cost = 3550 munits per week.

Since none of these unassigned routes possesses a negative, overall cost index, this means that the results of Table 17.6.3 represent an optimal solution to our distribution problem. The fact that some of the unassigned routes possess zero cost indices means that alternative optimal solutions exist with the same minimum total distribution cost of 3550 munits per week. On the basis that both I_{22} and I_{32} are zero, we obtain the two alternative optimal solutions given in Tables 17.6.4 and 17.6.5 below.

Table 17.6.4 *An alternative optimal solution to the TLP problem*

From \ To	W_1	W_2	W_3	Total
F_1	30	30 (45)	30 (30)	75
F_2	10 (40)	30 (10)	30	50
F_3	30	20	20 (30)	30
Total	40	55	60	155

Total distribution cost = 3550 munits per week.

Table 17.6.5 *An alternative optimal solution to the TLP problem*

From \ To	W_1	W_2	W_3	Total
F_1	30	30 (25)	30 (50)	75
F_2	10 (40)	30	30 (10)	50
F_3	30	20 (30)	20	30
Total	40	55	60	155

Total distribution cost = 3550 munits per week.

396 *The Optimal Employment of Existing Assets*

Table 17.6.6 *An alternative optimal solution using fractional allocations*

From \ To	W_1	W_2	W_3	Total
F_1	30	30 $(54\frac{1}{2})$	30 $(20\frac{1}{2})$	75
F_2	10 (40)	30 $(\frac{1}{2})$	30 $(9\frac{1}{2})$	50
F_3	30	20	20 (30)	30
Total	40	55	60	155

Total distribution cost = 3550 munits per week.

When fractional allocations are permitted we can generate an infinite number of alternative optimal solutions on the basis of a cost index being zero. A single example is shown in Table 17.6.6. Such solutions often make it possible to satisfy non-quantitative factors in the problem area, yet retain the same minimum distribution costs. In such cases as these, however, it will be noticed that more than $(S+D-1)$ product allocations are possible.

17.7 TRANSPORTATION LINEAR PROGRAMMING – VOGEL'S APPROXIMATION METHOD

This technique makes possible the discovery of an efficient initial feasible solution which significantly reduces the number of successive iterations needed to find an optimal solution. Indeed, in many instances, the VAM technique provides an optimal initial feasible solution. As an example of the procedure involved with this technique we shall use the same problem as before. The algorithm involved with Vogel's approximation method (VAM) is as follows:

(i) *Determine the difference between the two lowest distribution costs for each row and column of the TLP matrix.* This is shown in Table 17.7.1, and the figures at the heads of the columns and to the right of the matrix represent these differences,

Table 17.7.1 *The TLP matrix with the initial VAM row and column differences shown*

From \ To	W_1 ↓ 20	W_2 10	W_3 10	Total	
F_1	30	30	30	75	0
F_2	10	30	30	50	20←
F_3	30	20	20	30	0
Total	40	55	60	155	

(ii) *Select the row or column with the greatest difference.* For our example this involves either Column W_1 or Row F_2 as indicated by the arrows alongside Table 17.7.1.

(iii) *Allocate the maximum possible product to the route, conforming to (ii) above, which possesses the lowest distribution cost.* Irrespective of whether we use Column W_1 or Row F_2, we find that both lead to the allocation of 40 tonnes per week of product to route F_2W_1 as shown in Table 17.7.2.

Table 17.7.2 *The first VAM assignment and the second calculation of the row and column cost differentials*

From \ To	W_1	W_2	W_3	Total	
	↓ 10	↓ 10			
F_1	30 / X	30 /	30 /	75	0
F_2	10 / (40)	30 /	30 /	50	0
F_3	30 / X	20 /	20 /	30	0
Total	40	55	60	155	

(iv) *Cross out the row or column completely satisfied by the allocation according to (iii) above, and repeat the whole procedure from (i)–(iv) excepting those rows and/or columns which have previously been crossed out, until all assignments have been made.*

In this fashion Table 17.7.2 shows the second iteration using this technique, based on the fact that Column W_1 is no longer involved with the calculations concerning the cost differentials. In this particular case we note that Columns W_2 and W_3 now possess the greatest differential costs, so if we arbitrarily chose to allocate product to Column W_2 instead of Column W_3 then, according to rule (iii), 30 tonnes per week of product should be allocated to route F_3W_2 as shown in Table 17.7.3.

The third iteration using this technique now based on the fact that both Column W_1 and Row F_3 are crossed out involves allocating product to routes F_1W_2, F_1W_3, F_2W_2 and F_3W_3 on the basis that all four routes possess zero cost

Table 17.7.3 *One of the infinite variety of optimal solutions for our problem using the VAM technique*

From \ To	W_1	W_2	W_3	Total
F_1	30 / X	30 / ($24\frac{1}{2}$)	30 / ($50\frac{1}{2}$)	75
F_2	10 / (40)	30 / ($\frac{1}{2}$)	30 / ($9\frac{1}{2}$)	50
F_3	30 / X	20 / (30)	20 / X	30
Total	40	55	60	155

differentials. It therefore follows that we *could* allocate product to these routes according to the optimal solution previously shown by Table 17.6.5. Alternatively, if fractional allocations are permitted, we *could* obtain an infinite variety of optimal solutions, one of which is shown in Table 17.7.3.

17.8 TRANSPORTATION LINEAR PROGRAMMING – THE MODIFIED DISTRIBUTION METHOD

Although the stepping-stone method is an excellent means of teaching the rudiments of transportation linear programming, it cannot cope with large industrial allocation problems. Furthermore, a computer program based on its search technique would be most inefficient. The modified distribution (MODI) method has been devised to overcome both these shortcomings, and uses the opportunity cost–shadow price concept which we have previously discussed. In this particular case, these costs are broken down into two component parts, say a dispatch cost (Q_i) and a reception cost (R_i), where the suffixes i and j refer to the TLP matrix rows and columns respectively. To discover the optimal solution by this technique we employ two basic rules:

(i) For assigned routes $F_i W_j$ only, the values of the shadow prices are calculated according to the relationship:

$$Q_i - R_j - c_{ij} = 0$$

(ii) If any unassigned route $F_i W_j$ possesses the relationship:

$$Q_i + R_j - c_{ij} > 0$$

allocating product to that route will reduce the overall transportation cost.

To demonstrate the use of this technique, let us reconsider the initial feasible solution of our previous problem as exhibited by Table 17.6.1. According to rule (i) above we get the following relationships:

Assigned route $F_i W_j$	$Q_i + R_j = c_{ij}$
$F_1 W_1$	$Q_1 + R_1 = 30$
$F_1 W_2$	$Q_1 + R_2 = 30$
$F_2 W_2$	$Q_2 + R_2 = 30$
$F_2 W_3$	$Q_2 + R_3 = 30$
$F_3 W_3$	$Q_3 + R_3 = 20$

Since we have six unknowns but only five equations we cannot uniquely solve these relationships. One way round this dilemma is to set the value of one variable to zero arbitrarily. In our particular case this is quite legitimate because changes to one component part of each opportunity cost are compensated by equal changes to the other part. Setting Q_1 equal to zero we find that the values of the six variables are:

$Q_1 = 0$	$R_1 = 30$
$Q_2 = 0$	$R_2 = 30$
$Q_3 = -10$	$R_3 = 30$

These values are shown in their proper and corresponding positions in the new form of the TLP matrix shown in Table 17.8.1.

Table 17.8.1 *The initial Northwest Corner Ruler solution to the TLP problem using the MODI technique*

From \ To	W_1	W_2	W_3	Total	Q_i
F_1	30 / (40)	30 / (35)	30 / 0	75	0
F_2	10 / +20	30 / (20)	30 / (30)	50	0
F_3	30 / −10	20 / 0	20 / (30)	30	−10
Totals	40	55	60	155	
R_j	30	30	30		

Using rule (ii) for the unassigned routes we find that for:

Unassigned route $F_i W_j$	$Q_i + R_j - c_{ij}$
$F_1 W_3$	$Q_1 + R_3 - c_{13} = \quad 0 + 30 - 30 = 0$
$F_2 W_1$	$Q_2 + R_1 - c_{21} = \quad 0 + 30 - 10 = 20$
$F_3 W_1$	$Q_3 + R_1 - c_{31} = -10 + 30 - 30 = -10$
$F_3 W_2$	$Q_3 + R_2 - c_{32} = -10 + 30 - 20 = 0$

These differential opportunity costs are shown in the bottom left-hand corner of the unassigned routes of Table 17.8.1. In this particular case we discover that we are currently forgoing the opportunity to reduce the overall transportation cost by 20 munits per tonne per week by not allocating product to route $F_2 W_1$, so we are advised to allocate as much product as possible to that route, as shown in Table 17.8.2.

If we now rework the new values of Q_i and R_j using the extra row and column of our modified TLP matrix to help us with our calculations, so that we do not have to rewrite many tedious equations, we obtain the differential opportunity costs incorporated in Table 17.8.2. This shows that a further cost reduction, amounting to 20 munits per tonne per week, can be realized by allocating as much product as possible to route $F_1 W_3$, thereby yielding the results shown in Table 17.8.3.

Table 17.8.2 *The second feasible solution using the MODI technique*

From \ To	W_1	W_2	W_3	Total	Q_i
F_1	30 / (20)	30 / (55)	30 / +20	75	0
F_2	10 / (20)	30 / −20	30 / (30)	50	−20
F_3	30 / −30	20 / −20	20 / (30)	30	−30
Totals	40	55	60	155	
R_j	30	30	50		

Table 17.8.3 *An optimal solution to the TLP problem using the MODI technique*

From \ To	W_1	W_2	W_3	Total	Q_i
F_1	30 / −20	30 / (55)	30 / (20)	75	0
F_2	10 / (40)	30 / 0	30 / (10)	50	0
F_3	30 / −30	20 / 0	20 / (30)	30	−10
Totals	40	55	60	155	
R_j	10	30	30		

Reworking the values of the shadow prices for the last time we see that no further cost savings are possible, though routes F_2W_2 and F_3W_2 offer alternative optimal solutions by virtue of the fact that their differential opportunity costs are zero.

In effect, therefore, commencing with an initial feasible solution derived by using the Northwest Corner Rule, the MODI method provides the same solution obtained using the stepping-stone method. However, the MODI method uses a numerical technique which can readily be incorporated within a computer program, whereas the stepping-stone method involves a visual scanning technique for each successive iteration.

17.9 DEALING WITH DEGENERACY IN TLP PROBLEMS

Degeneracy exists in TLP problems when *less than* $(S+D-1)$ assigned routes appear in a TLP matrix. This occurs when some partial sum of the row totals is equal to some partial sum of the column totals. In such circumstances, it is impossible to evaluate the cost effect of transferring product to each of the unassigned routes. In practice, this phenomenon can occur at any stage of the calculations, so a means of overcoming such a problem has to be incorporated in the algorithm to prevent the calculations from coming to an abrupt halt before the optimal solution has been found and tested. Fortunately, a very simple means of overcoming this problem exists which involves altering the row and column totals by infinitesimally small amounts so that their partial sums can no longer be equal. To demonstrate this method, let us consider the slightly different problem shown in Table 17.9.1 where we observe that degeneracy has arisen because only four, instead of five, assigned routes exist.

To overcome this problem we merely assign some fictitious tonnage, ε, to any one of the unassigned routes, and then continue our step-wise calculations as before putting ε to equal zero after each iteration. For example, if we allocate ε units to position F_3W_3 then we get the following optimal values for the cost indices using the stepping-stone method:

$$I_{12} = 30 - 40 + 20 - 20 = -10$$
$$I_{21} = 30 - 30 + 40 - 10 = +30$$
$$I_{22} = 30 - 30 + 20 - 20 = 0$$
$$I_{31} = 30 - 10 + 30 - 20 = +30$$

Table 17.9.1 *The means of solving a degenerate TLP problem using a fictitious allocation ε*

From \ To	W_1	W_2	W_3	Total
F_1	10 (40)	30	40 (30)	70
F_2	30	30	30 (30)	30
F_3	30	20 (55)	20 (ε)	55
Total	40	55	60	155

Hence the best means of reducing the overall cost of this particular distribution problem involves allocating 30 units of product to route $F_1 W_2$ as shown in Table 17.9.2, in which case we see that the matrix is no longer degenerate.

Table 17.9.2 *The solution to the problem of Table 17.8.1 when ε is made equal to zero*

From \ To	W_1	W_2	W_3	Total
F_1	10 (40)	30 (30)	40	70
F_2	30	30	30 (30)	30
F_3	30	20 (25)	20 (30)	55
Total	40	55	60	155

17.10 UNEQUAL SUPPLY AND DEMAND IN TLP PROBLEMS

So far we have only dealt with TLP problems where the supply and demand for a product or service are equal. In reality this need not be the case, and it is quite conceivable that a firm's production potential could exceed the demand for its product. This is shown in Table 17.10.1, in which a potential supply of product exceeds the demand by 10 tonnes per week. To cater for this problem we devise a dummy variable – in this case a fictitious warehouse Y – to absorb the slack capacity and, since no actual movement of product to such a warehouse would happen in reality, the distribution costs to such a warehouse are zero. It should be noted however that the dummy warehouse features as one of the destinations in the allocation of product to the $(S + D - 1)$ assigned routes.

In cases where the demand exceeds the supply, a dummy factory would be incorporated in the TLP matrix, again with zero distribution costs, and the algorithm would proceed in the same manner as previously described.

Table 17.10.1 *A TLP problem involving unequal supply and demand and a dummy variable*

From \ To	W_1	W_2	W_3	Dummy warehouse Y	Factory capacities (tonnes per week)
F_1	30 / (40)	30 / (45)	30 /	0 /	85
F_2	10 /	30 / (10)	30 / (40)	0 /	50
F_3	30 /	20 /	20 / (20)	0 / (10)	30
Warehouse demands (tonnes per week)	40	55	60	10	165

Note: The dummy variable *must* be included in the $(S+D-1)$ assigned routes.

17.11 THE PRACTICAL APPLICATION OF TRANSPORTATION LINEAR PROGRAMMING

Now that we have covered the basic methodology of this form of linear programming, it is important to consider its underlying assumptions and the limitations of its use. As with all other forms of mathematical modelling, the TLP algorithm is only able to optimize a set of business conditions within the context of the problem *as formulated.* In this respect therefore the solution to a TLP problem might be *sub-optimal* if it fails to consider and make due allowance for other important business issues. By way of an example, it will be remembered that to facilitate our understanding of the mechanics of the TLP algorithm we conveniently assumed that the unit production costs for each source of product were equal. In effect, therefore, we confined our attention to distribution problems only, assuming the principle of *ceteris paribus.* In reality it is conceivable that the unit production costs at each factory and source of supply could be significantly different so that the pursuit of minimum distribution costs could be against the best overall interests of the firm.

In many practical applications the TLP problem can be formulated in such a way as to overcome some of these problems. As a matter of fact, this technique can just as readily be applied to problems concerning production planning and inventory control as it can to distribution problems. Furthermore, situations involving increasing marginal costs can easily be accommodated using multiple product sources with different cost structures. In addition, this technique can just as readily solve maximization problems. Common sense suggests that the decision rules of the stepping-stone, VAM and MODI methods have to be reversed to accommodate maximization problems.

By contrast, however, the TLP technique has to be applied with caution when situations involving increasing returns to scale are involved. Generally speaking, these cannot be directly incorporated with a linear programming model and due allowance for such effects can only be made using recursive techniques.

17.12 DEALING WITH NON-LINEARITY

So far in this chapter we have assumed that both the objective function and the constraint equations of an allocation problem exhibit linearity. In some practical situations however this is not so. Instead power terms, such as x^2 or $\sqrt{x}$, appear in the objective function and the constraint equations giving rise to non-linearity which prevails in circumstances where:

(i)   the price of a product varies with the quantity sold,
(ii) the unit variable cost of production varies with the quantity produced,
(iii) material efficiencies (yields) and labour productivity vary with the level of production, and
(iv) the mixing of products produces blends with characteristics different from the mean average characteristics of the blendstocks.

(i) and (ii) above are classic examples of the elasticity of demand and returns to scale concepts which we discussed in detail in Chapter 2. However, items (iii) and (iv) may need some clarification. In many practical situations the relationship between the quantity of material fed into a plant or machine and the amount of *desired* product manufactured need not be linear. This is certainly the case for many chemical reaction processes where the product yield* often increases with increasing residence time in the reactor. Put another way, this means that the product yield varies inversely with the reactor throughput. In a similar fashion the yield of on-specification components manufactured on a machine often deteriorates as the feed rate increases because of the greater stresses involved, not only by the machine tools and the component parts but also by the operatives. Typical examples of the phenomenon noted in item (iv) above include the viscosity blending of fuel and lubricating oils and the research octane number (RON) blending of motor gasolines to prevent pre-ignition (pinking).

Several alternative ways exist for solving non-linear allocation problems. Because of the popularity of the simplex procedure, coupled with the fact that computer software is readily available for this technique, there is every incentive to modify non-linear problems so that they can be solved using linear programming techniques. This is possible in the case of viscosity and RON blending because linear transforms of these blending properties exist. Secondly, the use of linear programming is often justified on the grounds that some curvilinear relationships can be approximated by a series of linear relationships. Indeed, there is plenty of evidence of the practical use of this approach which involves serial LP calculations using a recursive technique which is repeated until the required degree of accuracy and convergence is obtained. An example showing how a curvilinear problem can be structured to comply with the rationale of the simplex algorithm is given by Allen (1971).

In cases where the solution variables are not allowed to assume fractional or decimal values but are forced to take integer values†, a special hybrid of the linear programming technique known as integer programming must be used (see Bibliography). Here again the simplex algorithm can be profitably employed to map out the approximate solution which is then refined using the appropriate integer programming modifications.

---

* Product yield = $\dfrac{\text{total quantity of desired product manufactured per unit time} \times 100\%}{\text{total quantity of feedstock used per unit of time}}$.

† The capital budgeting decision involving the selection of a few projects from several mutually exclusive projects is a typical example in this category. In such circumstances the solution variables must either assume the value of unity or zero, meaning that a particular project is either accepted or rejected.

In cases where the use of linear programming cannot be justified because of the extreme non-linear nature of the particular problem, curvilinear programming techniques have to be employed. Unfortunately, these do not share the computational efficiency of LP and dynamic programming techniques (see Chapter 19) and in many instances they fail to converge on the optimal solution. The number of these techniques is legion and anyone requiring a better understanding of their methods is referred to the Bibliography. In their stead, however, a generic technique which can solve many different types of curvilinear problems is offered. This involves the Lagrange multiplier technique; the basic principles of this technique are described in Appendix A.

To demonstrate the application of the Lagrange multiplier technique to non-linear programming problems let us consider the following production problem. A manufacturer needs to produce 800 kg of a pharmaceutical product each month using two parallel reactors whose physical performance characteristics are given in Table 17.12.1. Because of the high cost of the feedstock to these two reactors, the firm's objective is to minimize the use of such feedstock consistent with meeting the monthly product requirements.

Table 17.12.1 *The physical performance characteristics of two pharmaceutical reactors*

Reactor (i)	Product rate (p_i) (kg/month)		Yield = product rate/feed rate $y_i = p_i/f_i$ Relationship
	Minimum	Maximum	
1	200	750	$y_i = 0.92 - 0.0001p_1$
2	50	400	$y_2 = 0.85 - 0.0001p_2$

Since the yield of the larger reactor is consistently greater than that of the smaller reactor, one might intuitively expect the optimal production policy to entail running the larger reactor to capacity, making up the production deficiency with the smaller reactor. However, a careful examination of the following calculations proves that this is not the case.

Using the nomenclature given in Table 17.12.1 it follows that the objective function of this problem is to minimize the total feed f to the reactors such that:

$$f_{min} = f_1 + f_2 \qquad (17.12.1)$$

subject to:

$$800 - p_1 - p_2 \geqslant 0 \qquad (17.12.2)$$

Rearranging equations 17.12.1 and 17.12.2 according to the conventional form used by the Lagrange multiplier technique we get equation 17.12.3:

$$L[f_1, f_2, \lambda] = f_1 + f_2 + \lambda[800 - p_1 - p_2] \qquad (17.12.3)$$

and substituting the relationships for the various yields we get:

$$L[f_1, f_2, \lambda] = \frac{p_1}{0.92 - 0.0001p_1} + \frac{p_2}{0.85 - 0.0001p_2} + \lambda[800 - p_1 - p_2] \qquad (17.12.4)$$

Differentiating equation 17.12.4 with respect to the three variables p_1, p_2 and λ, where λ = the Lagrange multiplier applicable to the production constraint of 800 kg per month, we get:

$$\frac{\partial L[f_1, f_2, \lambda]}{\partial p_1} = \frac{0.92}{(0.92 - 0.0001p_1)^2} - \lambda \qquad (17.12.5)$$

$$\frac{\partial L[f_1, f_2, \lambda]}{\partial p_2} = \frac{0.85}{(0.85 - 0.0001p_2)^2} - \lambda \qquad (17.12.6)$$

$$\frac{\partial L[f_1, f_2, \lambda]}{\partial \lambda} = 800 - p_1 - p_2 \qquad (17.12.7)$$

At the minimum consumption of feedstock, all three equations equal zero, in which case it follows that the optimal solution prevails* when:

$$p_1 = 583$$
$$p_2 = 217$$
$$\lambda = 1.24$$

In this particular case, therefore, we see that neither reactor should operate at maximum or minimum capacity since more feedstock would be consumed. A comparison of these alternate policies with the optimal policy is given in Table 17.12.2, which shows how the optimal policy is appreciably more efficient than the alternative policies. Of course, to translate these findings into economic terms we would also require all the details concerning the costs and prices involved with the manufacture of this pharmaceutical product.

Table 17.12.2 *A comparison of alternative production policies with the optimal policy*

Policy	Product rate p_1	p_2	Yields y_1	y_2	Feed rates $f_1 = p_1/y_1$	$f_2 = p_2/y_2$	Combined feed rate to both reactors	Increase in feed consumption over optimal policy kg/month
Optimal	583	217	0.862	0.828	676.6	262	938.6	–
Fill Reactor 1	750	50	0.845	0.845	887.6	59.2	946.8	8
Fill Reactor 2	400	400	0.880	0.810	454.6	493.8	948.4	10

It will be appreciated that, irrespective of the numbers of parallel reactors or the complexity of appropriate yield equations, this technique provides the same number of differential equations as there are variables, so theoretically speaking such problems can always be resolved using the Lagrange multiplier technique. In practice, however, it sometimes happens that the resulting equations are analytically intractable so they have to be solved numerically using optimum search techniques (see Bibliography).

17.13   THE HUNGARIAN ASSIGNMENT TECHNIQUE

In many industrial situations we find that different resources can accomplish the same tasks but with differing degrees of efficiency. For example, within a complex machine shop different types of machines can manufacture the same product but at different speeds, and the same holds true for the time taken to do set tasks by different tradesmen. As an illustration of such a problem, let us suppose that five

---

* It should be noted that certain second order derivative requirements must also be met for an optimal solution to exist, but these require a mathematical appreciation beyond the scope of this book.

Table 17.13.1 *The time taken by various machines to produce five different products (hours/item)*

	Product				
	P_1	P_2	P_3	P_4	P_5
Machine					
M_1	10	5	9	18	11
M_2	18	9	12	17	15
M_3	13	19	6	12	14
M_4	3	2	4	4	5
M_5	11	6	14	19	10

different products can be made on five different machines according to the durations shown in Table 17.13.1. If the firm can sell as much as it produces, a reasonable objective could involve the minimization of the time taken to produce all five products, since this could be equivalent to maximizing the firm's profitability.

Despite its apparent simplicity a moment's consideration shows that the optimal solution to this allocation problem is not obvious, and that some kind of optimization algorithm is needed. Such problems as these are a special, highly degenerate integer form of transportation linear programming problem, but a far better means of solving such problems involves the Hungarian technique. This technique utilizes the fact that one can add or subtract a constant amount to each element in a row or column of Table 17.13.1 above, without altering the optimal assignment. The steps involved with this algorithm are as follows:

(i) *Subtract the smallest element in each row from every other element of that row and find the smallest number of lines which will cover all the resulting zeros. If there are as many lines as there are tasks, then an optimal solution has been found, if not continue to step (ii).*

The results of this first iteration are shown in Table 17.13.2 where we see that only two lines are involved, so that further iterations are required.

Table 17.13.2 *The first iteration of the Hungarian method*

	Product				
	P_1	P_2	P_3	P_4	P_5
Machine					
M_1	5	0	4	13	6
M_2	9	0	3	8	6
M_3	7	13	0	6	8
M_4	1	0	2	2	3
M_5	5	0	8	13	4

(ii) *Repeat the same procedure on the results of step (i) above but this time using the columns. If an optimal solution is not found continue to step (iii).*

According to Table 17.13.3 (p. 408) we discover that three lines are required to cover the zeros, so that further iterations are required.

(iii) *Find the smallest element not covered by the lines of step (ii) above. Subtract this element from all elements not covered by lines and add it to elements at the conjunctions of lines, leaving all other elements unaltered. If the minimum number of lines needed to cover the zeros does not equal the number of tasks, repeat this procedure until it does.*

Table 17.13.3 *The second iteration of the Hungarian method*

Machine	P_1	P_2	Product P_3	P_4	P_5
M_1	4	0	4	11	3
M_2	8	0	3	6	3
M_3	6	13	0	4	5
M_4	0	0	2	0	0
M_5	4	0	8	11	1

Table 17.13.4 shows that four lines result from the first application of step (iii), but repeating this step once more we find that five lines result in the optimal solution, as

Table 17.13.4 *The third iteration of the Hungarian method*

Machine	P_1	P_2	Product P_3	P_4	P_5
M_1	3	0	3	10	2
M_2	7	0	2	5	2
M_3	6	14	0	4	5
M_4	0	1	2	0	0
M_5	3	0	7	10	0

shown in Table 17.13.5, in which case the zero elements, marked by each asterisk, denote the optimal allocation of the machines between the tasks. In effect, therefore, the minimum aggregate machine time needed to produce all five products is 39 machine hours, if all five machines are used to capacity.

Table 17.13.5 *The optimal solution to the machine allocation problem using the Hungarian method*

Machine	P_1	P_2	Product P_3	P_4	P_5
M_1	0*	0	3	7	2
M_2	4	0*	2	2	2
M_3	3	14	0*	1	5
M_4	0	4	5	0*	3
M_5	0	0	7	7	0*

Note: Each asterisk (*) denotes the optimal allocation of each machine to each product

17.14 SUMMARY

This chapter is concerned with the ways in which existing resources involving manpower, money, plant, machinery and buildings can be put to the best possible use. To that end, several mathematical programming techniques, including linear programming, transportation linear programming, the Lagrange multiplier technique and the Hungarian assignment method were described and discussed in the context of optimization procedures. Experience, especially of the two first methods, by the process industry has shown that they can be profitably employed to discover production economies, for evaluating the effects of new capital investments, and for optimizing distribution networks. These techniques are especially useful where complex interactions between the various decision variables of a problem can obscure the total systems effect of changes to those variables either singly or in concert.

The success of linear programming techniques lies in the ease with which they can be applied to a large variety of industrial problems including those which are ostensibly non-linear, coupled with the fact that comprehensive computer software is readily available and does not require the services of a mathematician or programming specialist. Literature on these techniques is abundant, ranging from the pioneering work by Dantzig (1963) and the original work on petroleum refinery optimization by Symonds (1955), to more modern treatment of the subject by Zionts (1974) and Cooper (1974).

By contrast, however, non-linear programming techniques have not been as successful because non-linear programming problems are computationally more difficult, although the number of techniques available both for the analytical and numerical optimization of such problems is legion, ranging from the initial work by Hooke and Jeeves (1961) to quadratic programming algorithms. Because of the large variety of these techniques, coupled with their mathematical complexity, only one non-linear programming technique is described here – the method of Lagrange undetermined multipliers. Although considerable economies can be realized through the skilful use of these techniques, one of their greatest benefits derives from the fact that their inherent discipline forces the decision maker to formulate his problem explicitly and, in so doing, permits him to gain a better insight into the total systems economic ramifications of his particular problem.

17.15 BIBLIOGRAPHY

General texts

Danø, S., *Linear Programming in Industry*, Prentice-Hall, 1974. This book contains several chapters which deal exclusively with the problems encountered with formulating models of real industrial problems.

Dantzig, G. B., *Linear Programming and Extensions*, Princeton University Press, 1963. This book provides excellent reading for anyone wishing to gain a profound understanding of linear programming in general, and the simplex algorithm in particular.

Moore, P. G. and Hodges, S. D., *Programming for Optimal Decisions*, Penguin, 1970. This book comprises a collection of papers ranging from a brief survey of the types of optimization procedures in existence, to case histories showing how actual problems were formulated and solved. Also provided are papers involved with non-linear programming, integer programming and a practical application of the Lagrange multiplier technique.

Specific texts

Allen, D. H., 'Linear programming models for plant operations planning', *British Chemical Engineering*, **16** (8), August 1971, pp. 685–691.

Allen, D. H., 'How to use mixed integer programming', *Chemical Engineering*, March 1976, pp. 114–120.

Bameson, R. A., Brannock, N. F., Moore, J. G. and Morris, C., 'Picking optimization methods', *Chemical Engineering*, July 1970, pp. 132–142.

Box, G. E. P., 'Evolutionary operation – a method for increasing industrial productivity', *Applied Statistics*, **6**, 1957, pp. 3–22.

Cooper, L. and Steinberg, D., *Methods and Applications of Linear Programming*, Saunders, 1974.

Hooke, R. and Jeeves, T. A., '"Direct search" solution of numerical and statistical problems', *Journal of the Association of Computing Machinery*, **8**(2), 1961, pp. 212–229.

Pontryagin, L. S., Boltyanskii, V. G., Gamkrelidze, R. V. and Mischenko, E. F., *The Mathematical Theory of Optimal Processes*, trans. Trirogoff, K. N. Interscience, 1962.

Symonds, G. H., *Linear Programming: The Solution of Refinery Problems*, Esso Publications, 1955.

Wilde, D., *Optimum Seeking Methods*, Prentice-Hall, 1964.

Williams, N., *Linear Programming and Non-linear Programming in Industry*, Pitman, 1967.

Zionts, S., *Linear and Integer Programming*, Prentice-Hall, 1974.

17.16   QUESTIONS

17.16.1   Coal fed to a power station must not contain more than 3.25 per cent of ash and 0.03 per cent of phosphorus. It can be blended from three different grades of coal with the properties and costs given below. How should these grades be blended to meet the power station quality restrictions at minimum cost?

Grade	% Ash	% Phosphorus	Cost (munits/tonne)
A	2.0	0.06	10
B	4.0	0.04	10
C	3.0	0.02	15

17.16.2   In a plywood factory, treated timber is sawn into thin sheets (veneer) which are subsequently stuck together to make plywood. Each plywood comprises three layers of veneer (one core and two faces). The factory produces $1000M$ sq.ft of usable veneer each month of the following qualities:

	M sq.ft.
Grade A (best quality)	200
Grade B (average quality)	400
Grade C (worst quality)	400

These veneers can be used to manufacture three grades of plywood to the following specifications and prices:

Plywood quality	Core veneer	Facing veneer(s)	Price ex-factory £/M sq. ft.
Grade 1	C	A	120
Grade 2	C	B	90
Grade 3	C	B & C	70

Formulate the appropriate linear programming problem to optimize the production of plywood. What would be your objective function and constraining equations? Write the initial simplex tableau, but do not solve the algorithm.

One of the strengths of the simplex LP is that it gives shadow prices. What are these? Where can they be found in the simplex algorithm?

17.16.3 An aromatic feed consisting of Benzene and Toluene is to be fractionated in a distillation column. The feed-pump and feed control valve will allow a feed rate up to 8 kg/min. The reboiler and condenser systems are designed to permit up to 4 kg/min of overhead product which for all economic purposes can be considered as pure Benzene. The reboiler section level control valve and bottoms product pump will permit up to 6 kg/min of bottoms product to be pumped away. For economic purposes, the bottoms product may be considered to be pure Toluene. The contribution to profit and overhead costs for the two products are 2 and 5 munits per kg for Benzene and Toluene respectively.

Using the LP simplex algorithm for your computations, decide the best feed composition for this distillation unit. How much would you be willing to pay to relax the flow constraints?

17.16.4 The Nateley Oil Company needs to produce regular and super grades of motor gasoline to the quality specifications described below:

| | Gasoline | |
	Regular	Super
Vapour pressure index not greater than	26	26
Composite performance number		
not greater than	62	No upper limit
not less than	61.4	62
Volume fraction distilled at 150°F not >	32%	40%
Volume fraction distilled at 200°F not <	45%	56%
Volume fraction distilled at 250°F not <	64%	No limit
Volume fraction distilled at 300°F not <	No limit	90%
Volume fraction distilled at 350°F not <	90%	

Eight different blendstocks are available for this purpose with the quality, quantity and economic characteristics given below:

| Blend-stock | Vapour pressure index | Composite performance number | Volume % distilled at | | | | | Quantity available (bls) | Contribution to overhead and profit £ per bl used |
			150°F	200°F	250°F	300°F	350°F		
C1	12	56	8	39	77	96	100	11 500	0.448
C2	24	58	20	54	88	100	100	5 000	0.464
C3	0	57	0	0	5	25	90	1 500	0.456
C4	28	66	91	100	100	100	100	5 500	0.528
C5	8	68	11	50	74	88	100	6 500	0.544
C6	0	66	0	3	6	20	52	4 750	0.528
C7	16	74	7	26	62	82	95	1 000	0.592
C8	140	74	100	100	100	100	100	limitless supply	0.592

Formulate this problem as a set of equations and set up the initial simplex tableau for its solution.

17.16.5   A company can manufacture two products using four different types of production process. The first and second processes yield items of Product A, and the third and fourth yield items of Product B. The inputs for each process are labour measured in man weeks, and materials S and T measured in kg.

Since each process varies in its input requirements the profit from each process differs even when producing the same product. Furthermore a week's production schedule is limited by the available amounts of man-power and both kinds of material. The full technology and input restrictions are given in the following table:

	Requirement per unit produced				Total availabilities (maximum)
	Product A		Product B		
Item	Process 1	Process 2	Process 3	Process 4	
Man weeks	2	2	2	2	30
Material S (kg)	14	10	6	4	240
Boxes of Material T (kg)	6	10	20	30	200
Unit profit (£/unit)	8	10	18	22	

What would be the maximum profit that could be made in one week?

How many units of product A would you produce and by which process would you produce them?

How many units of Product B would you produce and by which process would you produce them?

Up to what prices would you be willing to pay to remove the constraints by one unit each? (Use fractions, *not* decimals, when answering this question.)

17.16.6   The Ampoco Oil Refining Company owns an oil refinery which produces oil products from crude petroleum according to the data and flow sheet shown below.

Set out quality, quantity and yield restrictions in the form of linear constraints for this problem and check for degeneracy. Also set out the initial simplex tableau including cost and revenue data in the objective function of this tableau. Do *not* attempt to solve this tableau or perform any iterations. The physical and economic data are:

Reformer yields

	of T	of N	of M	of F	of B	Loss
1 unit input of V gives:	0	0.2	0.4	0.1	0.25	0.05
1 unit input of Q gives:	0.2	0.2	0.2	0.3	0.1	0

Wax remover yields

	of (W − P)	of L	Wastage
1 unit input of bottoms gives:	0.2	0.6	0.2

Polymer builder yields

	of (P − 4)	of (P − 5)	Wastage
1 unit input from any source gives:	0.3	0.6	0.1

Copper sweetener: output = input

Sulphur extractor yields
1 unit from any source gives: 0.8 unit of (E–5).

Quality restrictions
(a) At least 50 per cent of (D) must be (E–5).
(b) (2–P) must be not more than 75 per cent of the total
    input into the polymer builder (P).
(c) At least 30 per cent of G must be (3–4).
(d) At least 30 per cent, but not more than 40 per cent, of
    G must be (T).

Quantity restrictions
V must be less than 60 units.
Q must be less than 60 units.
The reformer must take less than 100 units of input.
The copper sweetener must take less than 10 units.
The sulphur extractor must take less than 25 units.
The polymer builder must take more than 25 units.
G must be greater than 25 units.
L must be less than 9 units.
D must be less than 40 units.
Tanks 2 and 4 together must not handle more than 30 units.

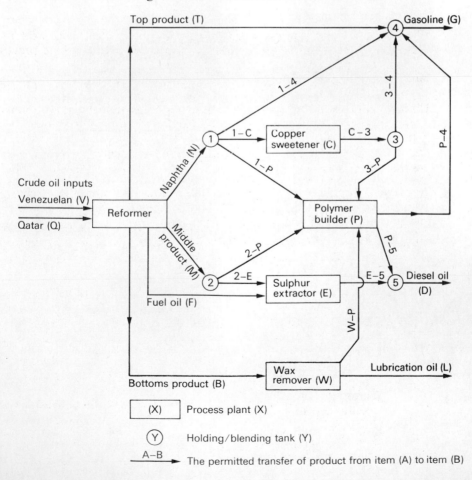

Material costs
V costs £10 per unit
Q costs £15 per unit

Selling prices
G fetches £30 per unit
D fetches £10 per unit
L fetches £100 per unit

Plant operating costs
Each unit of input into the reformer costs £2.
Each unit of input into the copper sweetener costs £4.
Each unit of input into the sulphur extractor costs £1.
Each unit of input into the wax remover costs £50.
Each unit of input into the polymer builder costs £4.

17.16.7 Three chemical feedstocks A, B and C, of the composition shown below can be fractionated to produce pure products X and Y. The estimated annual demand for Product X is 6 million lb at a price of 18 munits per lb, whereas the corresponding estimates for Product Y are 1.6 million lb and 13 munits per lb respectively. The overall yields of X and Y are 95 and 89 per cent respectively, losses being due to evaporation. The average process cost is 1 munit per lb of final product.

Feedstock	Composition (%)		Cost munits/lb
	X	Y	
A	80	20	10.5
B	90	10	12.0
C	75	25	9.0

What is the most profitable way of running the process?

17.16.8 A brewery produces two types of bitter beer – Keg and Best. It has available only a limited amount of labour, production capacity (measured in vat gallon hours) and warehouse capacity. These limitations and the profit per gallon for each beer are shown below:

Constraint	Maximum available per week
Labour (hours)	1 800
Production capacity (vat gallon hours)	15 000
Warehouse capacity (cubic feet)	3 000
Profit per gallon of Keg	£4
Profit per gallon of Best	£2

The resource requirements per gallon of Keg and Best are shown below:

Resource requirement per gallon	Keg	Best
Labour (hours)	1	2
Production capacity (vat hours)	20	40
Warehouse capacity (cubic feet)	6	6

To meet the needs of regular customers the firm must produce at least 100 gallons of Keg and 200 gallons of Best per week.

Using the information given, set out the firm's decision problem in terms of an LP formulation and determine the optimal production mix using the simplex algorithm. Discuss the significance of the shadow prices (opportunity costs) and show how these can be used to check the optimal solution.

17.16.9 A company has two factories, A and B, which produce three different products according to the following specifications:

Product	Hours per tonne Factory A	Factory B
1	0.25	0.20
2	0.40	0.25
3	0.35	0.40
Variable costs per hour:	£250	£300
Maximum availability (hours per week):	100	100

The corresponding market data are:

Product	Price (£ per tonne)	Maximum demand (tonnes per week)
1	100	310
2	120	300
3	150	125

An LP study has given the tableau shown below:

		37.5 X_{1A}	40 X_{1B}	20 X_{2A}	45 X_{2B}	62.5 X_{3A}	30 X_{3B}	0 W_A	0 W_B	0 W_1	0 W_2	0 W_3	W_0
0	W_A	0	0	0.0875	0	0	0.15	1	1.25	−0.25	−0.3125	−0.35	10
40	X_{1B}	0	1	−1.25	0	0	2	0	5	0	−1.25	0	125
37.5	X_{1A}	1	0	1.25	0	0	−2	0	−5	1	1.25	0	185
45	X_{2B}	0	0	1	1	0	0	0	0	0	1	0	300
62.5	X_{3A}	0	0	0	0	1	1	0	0	0	0	1	125
		0	0	21.875	0	0	3.75	0	12.5	37.5	41.875	62.5	33 250

(a) Prove that this tableau is the optimal solution tableau.
(b) What do the column headings X_{1A}, X_{1B}, X_{2A}, X_{2B}, X_{3A}, X_{3B}, W_A, W_B, W_1, W_2, W_3 and W_0 mean, and what are their units?
(c) What is the value of the optimal profit?
(d) What are the values of the shadow prices, and what precisely do these mean?
(e) Demonstrate how the values from (d) lead directly to the value from (c).
(f) What is the optimal production schedule?
(g) What is the slack capacity at each of the factories? Are the markets saturated?

17.16.10 A feed stream, F, is supplied to three separate processes, A, B and C. Each process has different yields of the two products P_1 and P_2. A flow diagram of the arrangement is:

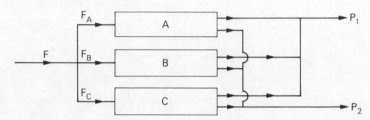

Find the optimum distribution of feed F to the three processes given the following information:

Flow streams		Process		
$F = 10\ 000$ kg/day	Yields	A	B	C
$F_A \leqslant 5\ 000$ kg/day	Wt % P_1	40	30	50
$F_B \leqslant 5\ 000$ kg/day	Wt % P_2	60	70	50
$F_C \leqslant 3\ 000$ kg/day				
$P_1 \leqslant 4\ 000$ kg/day	Prices			
$P_2 \leqslant 7\ 000$ kg/day	$F = 30$ p/kg			
	$P_1 = 40$ p/kg			
	$P_2 = 30$ p/kg			

Formulate as a linear programming problem assuming $F_A > 0$ at the optimum. Show graphically the feasible region in terms of F_B and F_C. Identify the extreme points and find the constraint which does not bound the feasible region. What is the optimum profitability?

17.16.11 Three collieries P_1, P_2 and P_3 produce 100, 125 and 75 tonnes per day of coal, respectively. This coal has to be delivered to five customers C_1, C_2, C_3, C_4 and C_5 requiring 100, 60, 40, 75 and 25 tonnes per week, respectively. The delivery costs, measured in munits per tonne, between the various collieries and customers are:

		Customers				
		C_1	C_2	C_3	C_4	C_5
	P_1	3	2	3	4	1
Collieries	P_2	4	1	2	4	2
	P_3	1	0	5	3	2

How should the coal be distributed to minimize the total distribution cost?

17.16.12 Devise a transportation layout for the following problem:

A fruit producer can sell fruit to retailers and canners according to the following seasonal restrictions (where X = an impossibility).

	May	June	July	Aug.	Sept.	Oct.	Nov.	Dec.
				Quantities (in tonnes)				
Amounts allowed								
To retailers	50	40	40	40	30	40	60	70
To canners	X	10	10	30	30	20	X	X
Possible production								
From greenhouses	15	20	25	25	25	20	10	X
From outside	5	20	40	50	60	20	10	X

His revenues and costs (£ per tonne) are given below:

	May	June	July	Aug.	Sept.	Oct.	Nov.	Dec.
Revenues								
To retailers	200	160	130	100	80	180	220	250
To canners	X	100	100	50	50	100	X	X
Costs								
From greenhouses	100	60	40	40	40	60	100	X
From outside	X	90	50	30	30	30	X	X

It is assumed that fruit can be sold during the month it is produced and that it can be stored. There is a storage cost of £10 per tonne when outside fruit is first put into store, and an equivalent cost of £5 per tonne for greenhouse fruit. There is an additional storage cost depending on the ambient temperature during the month of storage: this amounts to £1 per tonne per month for every degree above 45°F. A table of temperatures is given below:

May–June	June–July	July–Aug.	Aug.–Sept.	Sept.–Oct.	Oct.–Nov.	Nov.–Dec.
65°F	69°F	70°F	65°F	55°F	50°F	45°F

Fruit picked outside cannot be stored for more than a month. Fruit can be kept in store no longer than two months if it is being sent to retailers, or for three months if going for canning, and if grown in greenhouses. There is no penalty if there is either surplus capacity or if demand is not met.

On the tableau, state how you would deal with the amounts stored, shortages and surpluses.

17.16.13 Epco wishes to appraise the minimum distribution cost for delivering petroleum products from two of its refineries to three major customers. The distribution costs per tonne of product between the various refineries and customers are given in the following table, where the costs are in £ per tonne of product delivered.

Refinery	Customer A	B	C
1	10	8	12
2	10	15	8

The two refineries have the following capacities:

Refinery 1: 50 000 tonnes per annum

Refinery 2: 70 000 tonnes per annum

And the three customers' requirements are:

Customer A: 20 000 tonnes per annum

Customer B: 50 000 tonnes per annum

Customer C: 30 000 tonnes per annum.

Using the transportation linear programming MODI (opportunity cost–shadow price) technique, determine the optimal allocation of product between the refineries and the customers. What assumptions are inherent in your decision? What other factors would you need to consider before making a decision of this kind?

17.16.14 A firm produces animal feedstuffs at four manufacturing plants, W, X, Y and Z where output capacities in hundreds of tonnes per annum are 22, 20, 22 and 26, respectively.

The company possesses five regional depots A, B, C, D and E, which receive stock from the plants and store it prior to local distribution. The estimated demands on these depots for the forthcoming year are 20, 18, 12, 17 and 10 in units of hundreds of tonnes respectively. These demands must be met.

The unit transportation costs (in £ per tonne) for the various distribution schemes are:

			Depot		
Plant	A	B	C	D	E
W	7	5	6	8	4
X	10	9	10	8	5
Y	7	6	5	8	9
Z	3	2	4	4	7

Devise an optimal transportation scheme. (Do *not* use the Northwest Corner Rule.)

17.16.15 The Gas Council is looking at the economics of delivering gas to several of the Gas Boards. Two sources of gas are available: North Sea Gas (NSG) and Liquefied Petroleum Gas (LPG) from Libya. The NSG is landed at Tyneside by pipe-line, whilst the LPG is landed by bulk tanker at the Isle of Grain. The Gas Council has to decide on the best distribution of these gases between the Gas Boards. The landed price of both gases per therm is the same, whereas the distribution costs vary with the routing of each and depend primarily on the pumping costs. The table below gives the distribution costs (in £ per 1000 therms per annum) to the various Gas Boards:

	Midlands	North Eastern	Southern
North Sea Gas	10	8	12
Liquefied Petroleum Gas	10	15	8

The demand by each Gas Board is:

	Millions of therms per annum
Midlands	20
North Eastern	50
Southern	30

and the potential supply of NSG and LPG is 50 million and 70 million therms per annum, respectively.

What allocation of gas would you recommend and why? What assumptions are inherent in your decision? What other considerations are important?

17.16.16 The transport costs for moving tankers from depots X, Y and Z to factories at A, B, C, D and E are proportional to the numbers given in the table below. Nine tankers are available at X, six at Y and one at Z. Two tankers are required at A, two at B, four at C, four at D and three at E.

	A	B	C	D	E
X	90	60	170	70	110
Y	30	50	60	200	40
Z	95	200	10	45	120

Using a linear programming technique, determine the optimum allocation of tankers.

17.16.17 In a factory, a pay rise has been granted in return for an agreement with the trade unions concerning completely flexible working. The management are aware that not everybody has similar degrees of skill, and have decided to carry out a work study programme to determine average costs of various assignments of trades to tasks. Five trades (1–5) are involved and there are five tasks (A–E). The results of the work study are as follows:

Trade	Task	Cost £
1	A	14
	B	9
	C	13
	D	22
	E	15
2	A	18
	B	24
	C	13
	D	17
	E	19
3	A	9
	B	8
	C	10
	D	10
	E	11
4	A	22
	B	13
	C	16
	D	21
	E	19
5	A	20
	B	8
	C	16
	D	22
	E	12

Determine the optimal allocation of trade to task to minimize variable labour costs.

17.16.18 A personnel manager must provide additional staff at locations A, B, C, D and E. Staff are available at other locations P, Q, R, S and T. Bearing in mind all the costs involved in possible staff movements, the personnel manager has evaluated the relative cost factors. These are shown in the table below. The staff required at A, B, C, D and E are 2, 3, 3, 2 and 7 respectively, whilst the staff available at P, Q, R, S and T are 2, 3, 4, 3 and 5 respectively.

	A	B	C	D	E
P	5	3	27	9	19
Q	7	10	8	29	18
R	23	13	15	14	26
S	24	6	12	20	30
T	4	11	22	2	25

Use a linear programming method to determine how the personnel manager should allocate staff to satisfy staff requirements and determine the total minimum cost factor.

18. *Case Study I*

So far the substance of this book has been concerned with teaching points of principle, concepts and techniques and, with the exception of the economic decision making game in Chapter 12, the didactic technique employed to reinforce previous material has relied mainly on mathematically contrived examples and questions.

We shall now adopt a different tactic, and expose the reader to business case studies which allow us to develop our understanding of manufacturing systems economics in greater depth. Essentially, a business case is a statement of a set of circumstances which happened to a particular company in *reality*, except that fictitious names are used to retain its anonymity and the confidentiality of its commercial information. To allow the reader to understand the company's predicament within a reasonable time limit, and in the interests of script economy, it is usual for such cases to be brief but concise. As such, a case is not a complete account and usually does not emphasize the problem or opportunity facing the company; that is one of the main tasks for the reader. Likewise, all the data required to answer the case satisfactorily are not always provided; the reader must either find the appropriate information himself or make some reasonable assumptions which are fitting and can be justified, just as businessmen do.

The greatest benefit which can be derived from this pedagogical technique comes from the reader preparing a report on the case, as if he were a consultant hired by the company to recommend a decisive course of action. These reports should be prepared as professional documents, just as the consultant would do for his client, and should attempt to answer all of the different questions which the client is likely to ask. The report should be concise and to the point, and couched in business terms such as resources, opportunities and threats, cash flows, profits and costs, risk, morale, corporate image, etc., and should incorporate the following main features:

  (i) A *summary*: written after the main body of the report has been finalized, highlighting the important economic factors with their attendant risks and the non-economic factors too.
 (ii) An *introduction*: which places the problem and/or opportunity in context.
(iii) An *explicit statement of the problem and/or opportunity*, and any other issues which might also affect the company's performance.
 (iv) A *statement of the information and assumptions used to resolve the case.*
  (v) A *definition of the constraints imposed on the company*, affecting the resolution of the problem.
 (vi) *The recommended practical solution to the case.*
(vii) *The precise action plan* which must be implemented to resolve the problem, and
(viii) *Appendices*, incorporating the majority of calculations and graphs.

Having prepared and committed himself to his report, the next most beneficial way of reinforcing the major lessons of the case is for the reader to role-play an executive of such a firm – with 3–5 other readers if this is possible. By these means, each reader is exposed to his peers' point of view, which will either reinforce or modify his original concepts of the case.

In essence, therefore, the use of a business case study is a classroom simulation of a real business problem: it is the closest one can get in business studies to conducting a scientific or technological laboratory experiment.

The purpose of a case is the illustration of the principles, concepts and techniques learnt from reading *in application* permitting the reader to explore the relevance of his reading in a more meaningful, more complex and wider context.

Three case studies follow: one in this chapter, and two in Part IV. Their solutions, which are necessarily brief, are provided in Appendix D. It cannot be overstressed, however, that the greatest benefit to be realized from such cases comes from preparing a report and, if possible, a role-playing session, *prior to reading the solutions.*

Case study I   Branwell Plastics Limited*

The company 1962. Branwell Plastics Limited manufactures glass-reinforced boat hulls in three separate factories currently working on a two-shift basis and producing 700 hulls per annum. The factories have variable proportions of capital/labour and range from factory A which employs hand methods and little machinery, to factory C which is modern and highly mechanized. Factory B is in an intermediate position. These factories are located in a radius of 10 miles from Bradford in the West Riding of Yorkshire, England.

Problem 1962. The yearly profit statement has been submitted to the Board and the Managing Director, who advocated the policy of building factory C against the advice of his older colleagues is confronted with a lower profitability for his project than was expected. He has heard rumours that he may be called on to resign, and he calls in a team of industrial consultants and asks how the profitability of the company in general and the new factory in particular can be improved.

The basic facts. Facts immediately available to the investigators are restricted to the trading accounts which are as follows:

	Factory A	Factory B	Factory C
Sales (hulls)	100	200	400
	£	£	£
Sales revenue	10 000	20 000	40 000
Operating cost	7 500	12 500	20 000
Overhead cost	500	2 000	10 000
Total cost	8 000	14 500	30 000
Profit	2 000	5 500	10 000
Capital employed			
	£	£	£
Fixed	5 000	20 000	100 000
Working	10 000	20 000	40 000
Total	15 000	40 000	140 000
Profitability (profit/capital %)	13.3%	13.75%	7.14%

Note: It is assumed that all units are sold in the same year as they are produced. Operating costs are directly variable with output; items include wages, materials, factory expenses. Overhead costs are fixed for the year: items include salaries of staff, rent, rates, insurance, depreciation, etc.

* Reproduced by kind permission of Mr A.P. Hall, Bradford Management Centre, England.

The investigation. A detailed study of production potentials, prices and costs was made, resulting in the data shown in Appendix I.

Appendix I Data for optimization – facts available from investigation

---

1. Production per annum[a] (boat hulls):

Number of shifts	Factory		
	A	B	C
1	50	100	200
2	100	200	400
3	140	280	560
4	180	360	700

2. Costs per annum and per unit:

	Factory		
	A	B	C
Overhead cost per year	£500	£2 000	£10 000
Operating cost per unit			
(shifts 1 and 2)	75.0	62.5	50.0
(shift 3 marginal)	87.5	70.0	55.0
(shift 4 marginal)	100.0	87.5	75.0

3. Prices:

	Year		
	X	Y	Z
	(average quantities)	(good	bad)
		Market potential	
Market price per hull			
£75	1050	1150	950
£100	700	800	600
£125	350	400	300
£200	200	225	175

4. Working capital employed £100 per hull produced

---

[a] Divisibility between shift outputs may be achieved by working some machines only. Four shifts are necessary for working 24 hours per day throughout the year.

PART IV

The Disposal of
Manufacturing Assets

In Part IV we shall study the economic implications of plant replacement and retirement decisions using the life-cycle model developed in Part II as our underlying decision logic. To make profound replacement and retirement decisions, however, we need to supplement our previous knowledge of manufacturing systems economics with a proper understanding of the value and the economic life of an asset and the principle of sunk cost, the meanings of which are reinforced using two specially selected case studies.

Although Part IV represents the *finale* of the cradle-to-the-grave philosophy which we have promoted for *individual* projects throughout this book, it would be naïve in the extreme to consider corporate economics as having an identifiable end. Instead, it behoves each firm to develop new products and/or processes and/or manufacturing plants as an *ongoing activity* if it wishes to survive the contest which prevails in the market-place and it has to invent, appraise, select, implement, control and ultimately retire projects which fulfil or partially fulfil its profit gap requirements. In conclusion, therefore, we note that replacement and retirement decisions constitute only one critical link, in the realization of a manufacturing project according to our life-cycle philosophy, but we also recognize that the economic viability of a manufacturing firm is only as good as the weakest link in the life-cycle chain depicted by the following diagram.

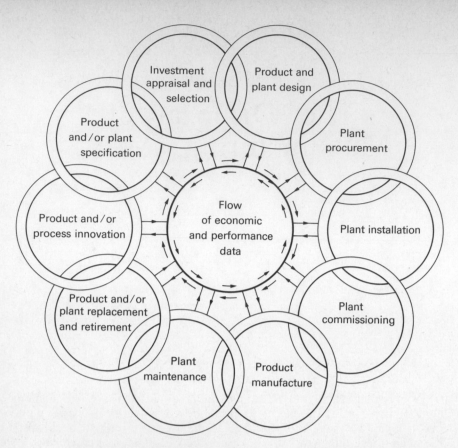

Critical links in the life-cycle performance of manufacturing assets.

19. *The Replacement and Retirement of Manufacturing Assets*

'*When to replace individual units of durable equipment by similar or improved units is one of the main problems upon which the success of industrial enterprise depends.*'
Gabriel Preinreich, 'The economic life of industrial equipment', *Econometrica*, **8**, 12, 1940

For the past 30 years or more, mass production of goods and services by the manufacturing and process industries has proved to be a most efficient means of satisfying human wants and needs. To achieve these ends, however, industry has shown a high propensity to consume vast quantities of capital resources, either due to physical impairment or because of the inevitable obsolescence experienced by capital assets. To remain competitive therefore necessitates the timely replacement of existing assets and their eventual retirement.

As many companies have discovered to their detriment, a firm's inability to upgrade its stock of capital plant as an ongoing part of its corporate strategy can be one of the routes to its eventual demise. Unfortunately, however, plant replacement and retirement decisions lack the glamour of capital expansion programmes, and experience shows that they are only too easily deferred, especially during times of severe cash rationing. While a firm's Board of Directors usually reserves the right to sanction capital expansion programmes, it is not unusual for replacement decisions to be delegated to lower echelons of management, so that replacement decisions do not normally experience the same degree of scrutiny and depth of economic analysis which befall business expansion projects. Despite these shortcomings, evidence suggests that firms spend about one-half of their capital on replacement projects and, generally speaking, it would appear that replacement analysis is more complicated than the investment analysis of business expansion projects.

In this chapter we shall examine the basic concepts and techniques involved in replacement and retirement decisions, only to find that the economic concepts developed in Part II need to be supplemented to make sense of replacement and retirement problems. In particular, we shall demonstrate that such analyses have to deal with three new concepts involving sunk cost, economic life and the so-called value of an asset.

19.1 THE FUNDAMENTAL OBJECTS OF REPLACEMENT AND RETIREMENT ANALYSIS

The term *replacement* can be rather ambiguous in its use so it is important to define what we mean when we use it. In the context of this book the term is used in its widest context. For example, replacement does *not* mean that an asset has to be

427

duplicated at the end of its economic life, nor does it imply a like-for-like substitution, indeed no resemblance between the present asset and its successor is necessary. Instead, replacement in this book is synonymous with *displacement*, which simply means that an existing asset is displaced by a more economic one. This implies that the end product or service involved with a replacement decision remains the same, but that the means (process, methods, systems, machines and tools) of accomplishing that objective can alter quite radically. Replacement, however, does not mean that the displaced asset is necessarily retired since it is quite conceivable that it could be put to some other, possibly less demanding, use.

The term *retirement* means that an asset is definitely disposed of. In some instances this might entail selling a group of assets as a going concern, in which case one is really concerned with divestment decisions. In other circumstances, however, assets are sold for their second-hand or scrap value. In some extreme conditions it is also conceivable that a company might have to *spend* money to dispose of certain assets, either because of some contractual agreement which was involved with their initial purchase, or because their disposal has certain social and/or legal implications.

The two basic reasons for replacing and ultimately retiring an asset are physical impairment and technological obsolescence. The first involves the condition of the asset itself, whereas the second concerns conditions in the environment which are external to an asset. These two effects can occur independently, or in concert. Physical deterioration can lead to a loss in the value of the service rendered by an asset and/or an increase in its consumption of resources needed to provide a prescribed level of service. For example, corrosion, erosion and general wear and tear can prevent a machine from manufacturing its specified output of product thereby causing its sales revenue to decline, whereas a specified production rate might possibly be attained if more monies were spent on its ordinary repairs and maintenance (OR & M). Obsolescence, however, is the change in the technical characteristics of new assets which enhances their value relative to older assets and it results from product, labour and process innovations. More often than not, this rate of enhancement is sufficiently large to warrant the replacement of existing assets which are still in good physical condition and *profitable*. In other cases, however, replacement is justified because a decline in a firm's sales renders its existing production capacity too large and expensive so that it is forced to retrench, at least temporarily, using smaller plant employing the same or more efficient technology.

The economy of replacing a functionally efficient asset, therefore, rests with the conservation of energy, effort, material and time, which is realized by its replacement, and the same holds true for retirement decisions. To appraise the economic merits of replacement/retirement decisions, we must answer four basic questions:

(i) Is it worth making any new investment to replace an existing asset? If the answer is no, possibly due to a deterioration in the competitiveness of the company's product or service, then the only remaining problem is to decide whether the present asset should be retired now or at some future date. If however the firm's existing business activity is sufficiently profitable, or can be made so by replacement investment, then the following fundamental questions also need answering.

(ii) What is the optimal life of the proposed investment?

(iii) What would be the economic advantage of the newly proposed asset (the challenger) if it were operated for its optimal economic life, compared with the economic merits of the existing asset (the defender)?

(iv) When would be the most economic moment to make the replacement?

We have met similar questions in Chapters 5, 6 and 11 when we considered 'Why make the investment in the first place, why make it now, and why do it this way?' but it will be noticed that these four questions are even more complicated. The first requires a forecast of the most advantageous way of using an existing asset in its existing business activity and a comparison of these costs and/or benefits against those realized by its most economic replacement which, of course, depends on the answers to questions (ii), (iii) and (iv).

Like most other decisions of economic choice, the replacement decision involves an economic trade-off. On the one hand a decision to prolong the operations of an existing asset means sacrificing the immediate benefits offered by new assets in order to postpone a capital outlay. On the other hand, the longer a replacement decision is postponed the greater becomes the probability that some other asset employing an even better technology than the present challenger will be made available.

The very nature of the replacement decision forces the decision maker to consider the consequences of sequential replacement decisions as a means of continuing an existing level of business activity. In addition one must also consider the possibilities of business expansion which might be forthcoming from the employment of new assets.

Since the economic merits of alternative replacement policies are usually highly sensitive to the assumed life for each asset, the central thesis of replacement analysis is that each alternative must be compared on its most economic basis, which means comparing its costs and/or benefit over its most economic life.

19.2   THE ECONOMIC LIFE OF AN ASSET

To demonstrate the meaning of the term economic life let us start by considering the following trivial example. Suppose the operating costs per unit of time of an asset increase monotonically with time t according to a functional relationship $C(t)$ which we have yet to define. If we denote the optimal replacement time by the symbol t_r, the operating costs would rise to a value $C(t_r)$ by the time a replacement occurred. Let us also suppose that the installed capital cost of each replacement is K including all incidental costs, that its scrap value net of all dismantling charges is zero, and that several replacements occur during the period of one year so there is little point allowing for the time value of money. Such a relationship as this is shown graphically in Figure 19.2.1.

If we also assume that the sales revenue is sufficiently greater than the operating costs to warrant the continuation of the business and the sales revenue is unaffected by the replacement strategy, then, in such circumstances, a reasonable objective would be *the minimization of the average total costs incurred per unit of time*, because such an objective would effectively maximize the wealth of the firm.

Since the average operating costs *increase* and the average capital cost *decrease* as the replacement interval is prolonged, we have to make a trade-off between these two opposing costs in some optimal fashion. Let the symbol $Z(t_r)$ denote the total costs incurred by an asset during the time period t_r so that:

$$Z(t_r) = \int_0^{t_r} C(t)\,\mathrm{d}t + K$$

The average total cost per unit of time $k(t_r)$ is therefore given by the expression:

$$k(t_r) = \frac{Z(t_r)}{t_r} = \frac{\int_0^{t_r} C(t)\,\mathrm{d}t + K}{t_r} \qquad (19.2.1)$$

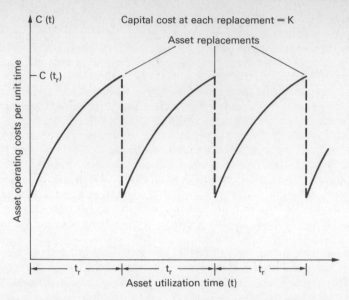

Figure 19.2.1   *The trend in operating costs and the systematic replacement of an asset.*

To discover the relationship which minimizes the average total cost per unit of time, all we need do is differentiate equation 19.2.1 with respect to the single independent variable t_r and set the first derivative equal to zero, in which case we find that:

$$C(t_r) = k(t_r) \qquad (19.2.2)$$

Put into words, equation 19.2.2 means that the optimal time to replace an asset, whose operating cost increases with use according to the assumptions of this case, is when its *current* operating cost per unit of time equals its average total cost per unit of time*. Providing we are able to discover the nature of the functional relationship $C(t)$, equation 19.2.2 provides a means for discovering the optimal replacement period t_r which is the economic life of the asset. If, for example, empirical evidence shows that the operating cost of an asset increases linearly with use according to the relationship:

$$C(t) = a + bt$$

where a and b are linear regression parameters, then, substituting this relationship into equation 19.2.2, we find that:

$$a + bt_r = \frac{\displaystyle\int_0^{t_r} (a + bt)\, \mathrm{d}t + K}{t_r}$$

which gives the simple solution:

$$t_r = \sqrt{\frac{2K}{b}}$$

For a capital cost of 200 munits per replacement and a value of b equal to 16 munits per week, we find that the optimal time to replace such an asset is every five weeks. This is the economic life of that asset.

---

* In the context of the theory of Chapter 2 this is equivalent to saying that the marginal (incremental) cost equals the average total cost when this cost is a minimum.

Table 19.2.1   *The costs of owning two types of industrial compressors*

Model	Installed capital cost (K) (munits)	Running cost per annum (C_i) (munits)	
A	5000	800	increasing by 200 per annum
B	2500	1250	

Regrettably, the identity given by equation 19.2.1 can only be solved for very simple functional relationships. Instead, the solutions to replacement problems usually have to be solved using numerical means similar to those adopted by the following example:

A firm is considering replacing an existing compressor, Model A, by a different type, Model B, which provides the same service at a lower capital cost, but which incurs higher annual running costs. These cost data are given in Table 19.2.1.

Using these data we discover from the results shown in Table 19.2.2 that the minimum cost of owning a Model A compressor is slightly *less* than that for a Model B compressor so, all other things being equal, we would *not* recommend the replacement of the current incumbent (Model A) by Model B. Instead we *would* recommend its replacement by another, brand new Model A compressor during the seventh year of its operation because such a strategy would minimize its life-cycle costs of ownership.

If, however, the roles of these two different types of compressor were reversed, so that a Model B compressor became the defender, then the converse of this argument would be valid, and we *would* recommend the substitution of a currently operated Model B compressor by a Model A compressor because we would reduce the overall cost of ownership by these means. Faced with this new set of conditions we would then have to decide the optimal time to make the substitution. Equation 19.2.2 provides the clue to this optimal replacement strategy and reinterpreted in the context of our existing problem it suggests that the replacement should proceed

Table 19.2.2   *Calculating the economic life of two alternative compressors*

	A (capital cost $K = 5000$)				B (capital cost $K = 2500$)		
Year (i)	Running cost (C_i)	Total costs $K + \sum_{i=1}^{n} C_i$	Average total cost $\dfrac{K + \sum_{i=1}^{n} C_i}{i}$	Year (i)	Running cost (C_i)	Total costs $K + \sum_{i=1}^{n} C_i$	Average total cost $\dfrac{K + \sum_{i=1}^{n} C_i}{i}$
1	800	5 800	5800	1	1250	3 750	3750
2	1000	6 800	3400	2	1450	5 200	2600
3	1200	8 000	2667	3	1650	6 850	2283
4	1400	9 400	2350	4	1850	8 700	2175
5	1600	11 000	2200	5	2050	10 750	2150
6	1800	12 800	2133	6	2250	13 000	2167
7	2000	14 800	2114	7	2450	15 450	2207
8	2200	17 000	2125	8	2650	18 100	2263
9	2400	19 400	2156	9	2850	20 950	2328
10	2600	22 000	2200	10	3050	24 000	2400

☐ = the minimum-average total costs per annum for operating each compressor.

when the *incremental* costs of running a Model B compressor just exceed the minimum average total costs of running a Model A compressor. In effect, Model B should be replaced sometime towards the end of its fifth year of operation. To postpone a replacement beyond this time would incur higher costs than necessary.

Although the previous example aptly illustrates the meaning of the term economic life, its results are only correct if the cost of capital is very small. In most real-life situations, however, this is not so and it is often found that a proper allowance for the cost of capital can significantly alter the results of an economic study. To cater for time value of money considerations we have to develop our understanding of replacement economics a little further. Given that the installed capital cost of some asset is K munits and its annual running costs C_i increase monotonically, it follows that the net present value *of costs*, incurred by the ownership of such an asset, is given by the expression:

$$\text{NPV}_c(n) = K + C_1 + \frac{C_2}{(1+r)} + \frac{C_i}{(1+r)^{i-1}} + \frac{C_n}{(1+r)^{n-1}} \qquad (19.2.3)$$

where $\text{NPV}_c(n)$ = the net present value of costs if an asset is operated for n years, C_i = the operating costs in a particular year i such that $(i = 0, n)$, it being assumed that the running costs occur at the beginning of a year, and r = the cost of capital measured as a decimal.

Based on the substance of Chapter 5, it will of course be realized that we can legitimately substitute the expression shown in equation 19.2.3 by that shown in equation 19.2.4

$$\text{NPV}_c(n) = A + \frac{A}{(1+r)} + \frac{A}{(1+r)^{i-1}} + \frac{A}{(1+r)^{n-1}} \qquad (19.2.4)$$

where the new identity A is defined as the effective annual cost of running an asset which gives the identical NPV of costs as a real asset over the same time horizon. Transposing equation 19.2.4 we get:

$$A = \frac{\text{NPV}_c(n)}{1 + X + \ldots X^{i-1} + \ldots X^{n-1}} \qquad (19.2.5)$$

where $X = (1+r)^{-1}$.

Substituting the expression given by equation 19.2.3 into equation 19.2.5 we get:

$$A = \frac{K + C_1 + C_2 X + \ldots C_i X^{i-1} + \ldots C_n X^{n-1}}{1 + X + \ldots X^{i-1} + \ldots X^{n-1}} \qquad (19.2.6)$$

Assuming that the revenue realized by an asset is unaffected by its replacement policy, it would therefore seem reasonable to replace such an asset when the value of the identity given by equation 19.2.6 is a minimum because such a strategy would *minimize* the *effective* annual cost of owning such an asset and, by the same token, it would *maximize* the NPV of the net cash inflows attributable to that asset*.

If we now analyse our previous compressor problem on the basis of equation 19.2.6 and an assumed cost of capital of 10 per cent per annum, we obtain the new set of results shown in Table 19.2.3. A quick glance at these results shows how they are significantly different from those given by Table 19.2.2. Most of the weighted costs of Table 19.2.3 are considerably larger than those of Table 19.2.2 as a result of the opportunity cost incurred by having money tied up in capital assets. Moreover the optimal life of compressor A is extended by one year, because of the time

---

* In Section 19.5 it will be shown that the tacit assumption of this model is that assets are perpetually replaced.

Table 19.2.3 *A review of the compressor problem using a 10 per cent per annum cost of capital*

Model A (capital cost $K = £5000$)

Year (i)	Annual running cost (C_i)	Discount factor (x^{i-1})	$C_i X^{i-1}$	$K + \sum_{i=1}^{n} C_i X^{i-1}$	$\sum_{i=1}^{n} X^{i-1}$	$\dfrac{K + \sum_{i=1}^{n} C_i X^{i-1}}{\sum_{i=1}^{n} X^{i-1}}$
1	800	1.000	800	5 800	1.000	5800
2	1000	0.9091	909	6 709	1.9091	3514
3	1200	0.8264	992	7 701	2.7355	2815
4	1400	0.7513	1052	8 753	3.4869	2510
5	1600	0.6830	1093	9 846	4.1699	2361
6	1800	0.6209	1118	10 964	4.7908	2289
7	2000	0.5645	1129	12 093	5.3553	2258
8	2200	0.5132	1129	13 222	5.8684	2253
9	2400	0.4665	1120	14 342	6.3349	2264
10	2600	0.4241	1103	15 445	6.7590	2285

Model B (capital cost $K = £2500$)

Year (i)	Annual running cost (C_i)	Discount factor (x^{i-1})	$C_i X^{i-1}$	$K + \sum_{i=1}^{n} C_i X^{i-1}$	$\sum_{i=1}^{n} X^{i-1}$	$\dfrac{K + \sum_{i=1}^{n} C_i X^{i-1}}{\sum_{i=1}^{n} X^{i-1}}$
1	1250	1.000	1250	3 750	1.000	3750
2	1450	0.9091	1318	5 068	1.9091	2655
3	1650	0.8264	1364	6 432	2.7355	2351
4	1850	0.7513	1390	7 822	3.4869	2243
5	2050	0.6830	1400	9 222	4.1699	2212
6	2250	0.6209	1397	10 619	4.7908	2217
7	2450	0.5645	1383	12 002	5.3553	2241
8	2650	0.5132	1360	13 362	5.8684	2277
9	2850	0.4665	1330	14 692	6.3349	2319
10	3050	0.4241	1294	15 986	6.7590	2365

☐ = the optimal replacement time and weighted average costs.

value of money effect. Lastly, but not least, one cannot help noticing that the results of this study *contradict* those given by Table 19.2.2 because compressor Model B is *now the cheaper*!

In effect, therefore, given that a Model A compressor is the current defender we would recommend its substitution by a Model B compressor during its eighth year of operation, and the subsequent replacement of Model B compressors every fifth year. By these means the total cost of owning these compressors would be minimized.

Although this example is academic and the data are contrived, it clearly demonstrates how important it is to include the cost of capital in studies of economic choice, always supposing, of course, that one is seeking the best decision!

19.3 THE VALUE OF AN EXISTING ASSET

To develop our understanding of replacement and retirement economics further, we need to define what we mean by the term the value of an existing asset. We could say that the price of an asset is a direct measure of its value, but such a definition would be rather narrow because it might not accommodate the economic implications arising from the functional loss of an existing asset. Instead the definition of value which we propose using is: 'The value of an existing asset is that lump sum of money which would just compensate for its loss for a precisely defined set of business conditions assuming that the firm would take the necessary action to mitigate the economic consequences of such a loss.'

This definition suggests that one must consider what would have been the firm's production and sales performance had the functional loss of the asset not occurred, and it also suggests that one must allow for the best possible means of maintaining that performance when faced with such a loss.

Three obvious ways of placing a value on an existing asset spring to mind – its replacement cost, its resale value, and its net present value (NPV). Providing a firm is willing and able to replace an existing asset, the *upper limit* to its value is its replacement cost if *instantaneous* replacement is possible. In these circumstances the purchase price of an asset which performs the *same* duty as the displaced asset, plus all delivery, dismantling, installation, testing and commissioning costs, constitute the replacement cost. If instantaneous replacement is not possible, however, some inconvenience factor reflecting the extent of the lost business resulting from the delay to the replacement, has to be added to the replacement cost previously suggested. The *lower limit* to the value of an asset is its resale value net of all incidental expenses.

The net present value concept of value is no stranger to this book. Unlike the other two concepts of value, however, the measurement of the NPV of an asset is not so clear cut because it relies on a forecast of the future cash flows which can be ascribed to an asset. Nevertheless, this meaning of value is profound and it offers an excellent method of assessing whether or not to replace or retire an existing asset. In practice, it is normally found that the NPV of the business which is attributable to a particular asset exceeds its replacement value for a large part of its *physical* life, providing its purchase was originally justified in economic terms. In these circumstances, the loss or failure* of the asset would justify its immediate replacement† and a proper valuation for that asset, which one might wish to indemnify by insurance cover, would be its *replacement cost.* For an older asset, however, it is conceivable that its replacement cost could exceed the NPV of its future business. In these circumstances one would not recommend its replacement if its functional performance were lost and a proper valuation for such an asset would be its net present value. With further ageing, an asset's NPV could decline to the lower limit set by its resale value. In these circumstances a replacement would not be economically justifiable if it failed. Instead, such an asset should really be retired before this condition is reached, and a proper valuation would be its *resale value.* In effect, therefore, there exist three different values for an asset which can be replaced. When an asset cannot be replaced, however, its NPV is its only measure of value providing that value exceeds its resale value‡.

The arguments of the preceding paragraph illustrate the importance of the NPV criterion as an economic decision-making tool. Admittedly, an accurate evaluation of the NPV of the business which can be attributed to an asset is not an easy matter because it relies on a forecast of the future cash flows of that business. Nevertheless, providing the magnitude of the NPV is sufficiently different from an asset's replacement cost or resale value, it can be used to trigger replacement and retirement decisions.

The inherent assumption here is that an asset would be replaced by a similar asset of a similar age using the same technology. With the inevitable march of technological progress, however, it is more than likely that the *loss* of an existing asset would

---

* What we have in mind here is a major collapse in the structure of an asset which does not justify repair.

† The suggestion here is that the asset could be replaced by a similar asset of similar age incorporating the same technology.

‡ A firm might be unable or unwilling to replace an existing asset for a variety of good reasons.

justify its replacement by a *new* asset embodying the latest, most cost-effective technology. Furthermore, it is quite conceivable that the lower cost structure of a new technological challenger could justify the replacement of an existing defender which is still in good condition and profitable. In these circumstances the measure of the value of an existing asset is the difference in the value of its business resulting from its retention compared with its immediate replacement.

To illustrate this point, let us consider a numerical example which was first demonstrated by Merrett and Sykes (1966) and later developed by Abrams (1971). Suppose it is definitely known that the services of an existing machine will stop in two years' time* and the cash proceeds attributable to its use are 300 munits per annum. Let us further assume that a new machine costing 3000 munits is available which provides the same service but at a lower operating cost. The net cash proceeds attributable to its use are 1300 munits per annum for a period of four years, which is reckoned to be its economic life. If we also assume that there is no further technological advance beyond this four-year period, the resale value of a machine is negligible, and that each new machine is replaced in turn, suggesting replacement to perpetuity, we obtain the two cash flow profiles shown in Rows A and B of Table 19.3.1. These represent the two alternative policies involved with the continued operation of the existing machine for two more years or, alternatively, its continued use for two years and its replacement by a string of replacement machines embodying the newer technology. However, these two policies are by no means the only ways of providing the service offered by the machine. Several other alternatives exist. The most obvious one which springs to mind is the immediate replacement of the existing machine by a string of new machines using the better technology. The cash flow profile representing this case is shown in Row C of Table 19.3.1.

If one plots graphs of the NPVs for these three alternatives against varying costs of capital on the assumption that replacements will continue indefinitely, one discovers that the economic preferences also vary according to the following decision rules:

(i)   If the cost of capital is less than 12.6 per cent per annum: Replace the existing machine immediately.

(ii) If the cost of capital is less than 26.5 per cent per annum but greater than 12.6 per cent: Replace the existing machine in two years' time.

(iii) If the cost of capital is greater than 26.5 per cent per annum: Continue operating the existing machine but do not replace it.

Since these decision rules reflect the value of the existing machine for a variety of business conditions, this trivial example demonstrates that we must extend the scope of our previous arguments concerning value to include the possibility of an immediate or delayed replacement of some asset by one providing the same output but using a more cost-effective technology.

To progress further we need to develop a formula which will allow us to calculate the value of an asset under the conditions just described. To do this however we need to employ the following notation: Let D_i = the end of year cash outflows for the Defender during the ith year of its *remaining* life such that $(i = 1, n)$, C_i = the end of year cash outflows for the Challenger during the ith year of its life such that $(i = 1, n)$, S_i = the end of year resale or scrap value of an asset which is retired in the ith year of its life or remaining life, k = the year when the defender is replaced, n = the economic life of a challenger, and K = the installed capital cost of a challenger.

---

* This might result from physical degradation, social pressures or legislation.

Table 19.3.1 *Cash flow profiles for alternative replacement strategies. Cash flows (munits)*

Strategy	Year end												
	0	1	2	3	4	5	6	7	8	9	10	11	12...etc.
A Operate existing machine for two years	0	+300	+300										
B Replace existing machine by new machine after two years	0	+300	−3000 +300	+1300	+1300	+1300	−3000 +1300	+1300	+1300	+1300	−3000 +1300	+1300	+1300
C Replace existing machine by new machine immediately	−3000	+1300	+1300	+1300	−3000 +1300	+1300	+1300	+1300	−3000 +1300	+1300	+1300	+1300	−3000 +1300

Table 19.3.2

Year	Number Symbol	0 0	1 1	2 2	...	4 n	5 $n+1$	6 $n+2$	...	8 $2n$	9 ... etc. $2n+1$
Net cash outflows due to a policy of *immediate* replacement		K	C_1	C_2		$(K+C_n-S_n)$	C_1	C_2		$(K+C_n-S_n)$	C_1

In the development of the following model we assume that the service provided by a machine is unaffected by its replacement policy, and we also assume there is no further technological advance beyond that offered by the immediate challenger, which is replaced by a string of challengers to perpetuity. Using these assumptions and notation, we find that the *costs* resulting from an *immediate* replacement of an existing asset are shown in Table 19.3.2.

Excepting the signs of these cash flows and the fact that this model allows for the cash receipts from the sale of retired machines, the close correspondence of the symbols of Table 19.3.2 with the numbers in Row C of Table 19.3.1 is apparent. In this particular case we have purposefully chosen the value $(n=4)$ to demonstrate this similarity. A careful examination of Table 19.3.2 shows a recurrence in the cash flows with the sequence $(C_1, C_2, \ldots C_n)$ and the single value (S_n) repeated every n years. If we denote the present values of the sequence $(C_1, C_2, \ldots C_n)$ by the symbol $C(n)$ such that:

$$C(n) = \sum_{i=1}^{n} \frac{C_i}{(1+r)^i}$$

and the present value of the single value S_n by the symbol $S(n)$ such that:

$$S(n) = \frac{S_n}{(1+r)^n}$$

the cash flows of Table 19.3.2 can be simplified and written in the form shown in Table 19.3.3, where we note that the recurrence relationship $[K+C(n)-S(n)]$ is periodic every nth year. It is quite an easy matter to prove (see Section 19.5) that the net present value $V(n)$ of this sequence of costs is given by the formula:

$$V(n) = \frac{K+C(n)-S(n)}{1-(1+r)^{-n}} \tag{19.3.1}$$

In a similar manner the profile of *costs* due to a policy of deferred replacement is shown in Table 19.3.4. But for the reversal of the signs of these cash flows and the allowance made for scrap values, this cash flow profile is very similar to that previously shown in Row B of Table 19.3.1 with the values $(n=4)$ and $(k=2)$. In part, Table 19.3.4 incorporates the same cash flows as Table 19.3.2, but delayed by k years. It follows therefore that the net present value $V(k)$ of this sequence of costs

Table 19.3.3

Year	Number Symbol	0 0	1 1	2 2	...	4 n	5 $n+1$	6 $n+2$	...	8 $2n$	9 ... etc. $2n+1$
Effective net cash outflows due to a policy of *immediate* replacement		$K+C(n)-S(n)$	0	0		$K+C(n)-S(n)$	0	0		$K+C(n)-S(n)$	0

Table 19.3.4

	Number	0	1	2	3	...	6	7	10	11 ... etc.
Year	Symbol	0	1	k	$k+1$		$k+n$	$k+n+1$	$k+2n$	$k+2n+1$

Net cash outflow due to a policy of *delayed* replacement		0	D_1	$(K+D_k-S_k)$	$C_1 \ldots (K+C_n-S_n)$	$C_1 \ldots (K+C_n-S_n)$	C_1

is given by:

$$V(k) = \frac{K+C(n)-S(n)}{1-(1+r)^{-n}} \cdot (1+r)^{-k} + D(k) - S(k) \qquad (19.3.2)$$

where the new identity $D(k)$ is given by:

$$D(k) = \sum_{i=1}^{k} \frac{D_i}{(1+r)^i}$$

It is very important to interpret properly the meanings of the two identities given by equations 19.3.1 and 19.3.2 as they represent the NPV of costs attributable to the two alternative policies of immediate and delayed replacement. They do not consider the cash receipts attributable to the business supported by an asset because these cash flows are assumed to be unaffected by any replacement policy*. If we denote the net present value of these cash receipts by the symbol V, it follows that the NPV of the *net* cash proceeds realized by the immediate replacement of an asset is given by $V-V(n)$. By the same reasoning, the NPV of the *net* cash proceeds realized by the delayed replacement of an existing asset is given by $V-V(k)$. Since the value of an asset to a company is obviously the *difference* between the NPV due to its retention *less* that resulting from its replacement, it follows that an asset of age j, where $(j=n-k)$, has a value $V(j)$ given by the identity:

$$V(j) = [V-V(k)]-[V-V(n)]$$
$$V(j) = V(n)-V(k)$$
$$V(j) = [K+C(n)-S(n)]\frac{[1-(1+r)^{-k}]}{[1-(1+r)^{-n}]} - D(k) + S(k) \qquad (19.3.3)$$

Equation 19.3.3 is a generalized model of the value of an existing asset of age j years assuming that it will ultimately be replaced.

If we represent the quotient $[1-(1+r)^{-k}]/[1-(1+r)^{-n}]$ by the symbol η, equation 19.3.3 can be rewritten in the following form:

$$V(j) = \eta K + [\eta C(n)-D(k)]-[\eta S(n)-S(k)] \qquad (19.3.4)$$

Using this expression it is quite an easy matter to see that if an existing asset is due for imminent replacement, the term η approaches zero so that the value of the asset approximates its *resale value*, $S(0)$. In a similar vein, if the asset has just been replaced by a brand new asset, the term η equals unity, and all the remaining terms of equation 19.3.4 cancel out because $C(n)=D(k)$ and $S(n)=S(k)$ by definition. In these circumstances the value of the newly replaced asset is its replacement cost, K. Between these two extremes the value of an asset declines at a rate governed by the

---

* In effect, therefore, the derivation of these valuation models assumes that the present value of the cash receipts from the business supported by an asset sufficiently exceeds the present value of its cash disbursements to justify the continuation of that business.

inferiority of its operating costs and resale price relative to those of a brand new asset incorporating the latest technology.

In conclusion, we see that the value of an existing asset which will definitely be replaced is bounded by the same conditions which we previously postulated, except that our emphasis now lies with the replacement cost associated with the most cost effective challenger.

The real values* of most assets decline over time due to the combined effects of physical deterioration and obsolescence. The first results in rising running costs and a diminution in the aesthetic appeal of the asset, the latter causes the productivity of an existing asset to decline relative to that of a new asset embodying the latest technology, coupled with the fact that the styling of new assets makes their forerunners seem out of date. We shall postpone a full discussion of the influence which technological innovation has on the replacement decision until Section 19.8. However it is instructive to demonstrate the influence which different patterns of operating costs and resale prices have on the value of an existing asset, using equation 19.3.3 for this purpose.

Suppose that an asset costing 2100 munits has an economic life of two years with a resale value of zero, and suppose that its annual operating costs are time invariable. Let us also assume that the cost of capital is 10 per cent per annum. According to equation 19.3.3 we find that:

(i) the value of the new asset, $V(0) = 2100$,
(ii) the value of an asset which is one year old, $V(1) = 1100$,
(iii) the value of an asset which is two years old, $V(2) = 0$

In effect, this very simple example demonstrates how the time value of money causes the decline in the value of an asset with constant operating costs and a negligible resale value to *accelerate* with age, and this effect becomes more pronounced the greater the cost of capital.

A positive resale value has the opposite effect. If we substitute an initial capital cost of 3310 munits into the previous example and assume that the asset's resale value is 1210 munits at the end of two years then equation 19.3.3 shows that:

(i) the value of the new asset, $V(0) = 3310$,
(ii) the value of an asset which is one year old, $V(1) = 2210$,
(iii) the value of an asset which is two years old, $V(2) = 1210$,

proving that the decline in an asset's value *decelerates* with age under these conditions.

The influence of rising operating costs on the value of an asset depends on the rate of change of those costs with time and their magnitude relative to the replacement cost of a new asset. It also depends on the magnitude of a firm's cost of capital. Usually the effect of a rising schedule of operating costs more than outweighs the time value of money effect and the rate of decline in the value of an asset decelerates with age.

Although the preceding material provides an indication of the effects of various economic factors on the value of an asset it does not allow for taxation considerations. We shall postpone our discussion of these matters until Section 19.5, but it is important to stress here that each factor of our generalized valuation equation should be enumerated on a net of tax basis. Needless to say, taxation can have a considerable effect on the value of an asset, although the precise effect depends on the particular details of the taxation system in force.

---

*This term suggests that the value of an asset should be assessed in terms of money with a constant purchasing power.

Three major conclusions can be drawn from this section. First, a proper valuation of an existing asset is much more complicated than accounting practice based on arbitrary depreciation methods would suggest. Secondly, the value of an existing asset which will definitely be replaced has no direct relationship with its original capital cost. Instead it is linked with its replacement cost which could be substantially different from its initial capital cost because of the influence of technological innovation. Thirdly, the value of an asset is inextricably linked with the economic life of its successors and the optimal moment for its replacement. In effect this means that the optimal life of a challenger is that value of n which minimizes the value of $V(n)$ in equation 19.3.1, whereas the optimal value of k is that value of k which minimizes the value $V(k)$ in equation 19.3.2. Of course, we had already demonstrated these principles with the example given in Table 19.2.3, so in this respect we have linked the theory of this section with the practice of the preceding section.

Finally, it should be noted that the derivation of equation 19.3.3 can be criticized as being academic on two counts. First, it assumes that the initial defender is replaced by an endless chain of challengers, and secondly it assumes that each of these challengers incurs the same life-cycle costs over identical economic lives. With regard to the first point, it will be appreciated that, conceptually at least, it is extremely difficult to select a time horizon which is correct for choosing between alternative replacement policies. Some advocate that the cessation of the business employing the asset should represent the time-span involved with a replacement decision. Unfortunately, time horizons which are connected to product life-cycles are notoriously difficult to forecast, besides it is quite conceivable that the assets relinquished from one business could be profitably employed by another. Furthermore, evidence suggests that the influence of discounting becomes so pronounced after a period of 50 years or more that the errors induced by the model are well within the tolerance of accuracy placed on the rest of the data employed by this model. Unless one can justify a different time horizon, it would appear that the assumption of an infinite time horizon is quite adequate. Furthermore, this assumption overcomes the problem encountered when one needs to compare the economic merits of alternative replacement strategies, where the economic lives of the alternatives are both different and large, thereby necessitating a study time horizon which is the least common multiple of their individual economic lives.

The second point concerns the difficulty of forecasting technological innovation or, more precisely, its economic impact on future generations of challengers. It is difficult enough to forecast the future costs incurred with an existing asset and its immediate successor let alone the cash flows of subsequent unknown challengers in the far distant future. For these reasons, our generalized valuation model assumes technological stagnation after the introduction of the first challenger, as do all the other models and examples in the preceding material of this chapter. The effect which a continuous change in the rate of technological advancement has on the economic life of an asset is discussed in more detail in Section 19.5 and is also covered by the writings of Terborgh 1958 and Connor and Evans (1972).

19.4 THE PRINCIPLE OF SUNK COST

It is an unfortunate fact of life that some people have personality traits, such as feelings of insecurity, which can prevent a firm taking sound and timely economic decisions, especially those involving replacement projects. For example, they derive a certain measure of security from owning and operating old assets which they are reluctant to dispose of especially if new replacement assets involve learning new skills and techniques. For them such assets become 'venerated friends'. Furthermore, the idea that one should replace an asset which is still in good condition is contrary to their concept of thrift. These kinds of attitudes can delay the timely replacement of assets causing a deterioration in a firm's productivity and profitability. A more damaging attitude where a replacement decision is concerned is the mistaken belief that a company should delay the replacement of assets until their book values have been written off. Indeed, it is not uncommon to hear managers say, 'We cannot replace existing assets until their book values have been *paid* for'. Of course, such an idea is preposterous on two counts. First, most assets are usually paid for during their initial procurement, so they cannot be paid for again! Secondly, it suggests a complete lack of understanding of accounting concepts and conventions and, more importantly, of the concept of value which we have studied in the preceding section. We have discussed the difficulties which result from the misunderstanding of accounting techniques before, both in general terms and specifically where depreciation expenses are concerned, but it is important to emphasize one particular point again. The book value of an asset is its initial purchase price (possibly including delivery and installation costs) less its accumulated depreciation expenses which are derived using an *arbitrary* allocation technique*. Although book values appear in a firm's balance sheet, and as such might be considered all important and possibly profound, they do not normally represent either the resale value, the replacement cost or the NPV of that asset. Unfortunately, managers are often reluctant to dispose of an existing asset which possesses a book value in excess of its resale value because this difference would be registered as an extraordinary loss in the firm's income statement. Although no actual loss of money would be involved in these paper transactions, it is conceivable that such a loss could be construed as an earlier error of judgement. For example, it might appear that the firm's previous depreciation policy had been lax, or that the rate of technological innovation had been poorly forecast when the asset was first purchased. Unfortunately, such a loss might be interpreted as proof of management's incompetence, especially if the initial purchase of the asset appeared unwarranted in retrospect. Faced with the possibility of criticisms of this kind, it is perhaps understandable that managers devise various ways of disguising their investment errors, which only come to light when replacement projects are considered. A most common way of doing this is to insist that the capital cost of the challenger should be burdened with the difference between the book value and the resale value of the defender when replacement investment appraisals are made†. If such an appraisal technique goes unchallenged, there is little chance that a previous investment error will be exposed. However, the unacceptable result of this deception is that, appraised in this way, some projects which are truly lucrative and warrant investment will be rejected because they are unable to bear this added, artificial financial burden. Such a practice cannot be defended; instead a more enlightened management should realize that the book value of the defender inevitably has to be written down to zero anyway and it must be remembered that depreciation expenses are only paper numbers, they are not cash flows. Indeed proof that writing off the book value of a defender has absolutely nothing to do with the economic merits of the challenger would be forthcoming if it were possible to leave an *idle* defender alongside its corresponding *active* challenger until such time as its normal depreciation expenses reduced its book value to zero, at which time it could be written off the company's books, but not necessarily sold or destroyed‡.

---

* Although accounting depreciation methods are arbitrary, they are neither random nor irrational. However they cannot yield the same results as our generalized valuation equation, except by chance.

† The mistaken belief is that the challenger should pay for the so-called loss in the book value of the defender.

‡ We are not suggesting that this should be done since the economic merits of such a policy would have to be properly appraised in economic terms.

As a point of logic, however, it is important to grasp the fundamental fact that money spent in the past or committed as a result of *past decisions* cannot be altered by *future decisions**. Indeed monies so spent can be considered sunk costs because they have been sunk into physical assets. Instead of expending energy, time and talent attempting to disguise past errors, it behoves management to learn from these errors to ensure that they are not repeated. In addition, given that a company possesses an asset (the defender) it is encumbent on management to use that asset to its best advantage. Whether it costs a fortune or whether it was made freely available is irrelevant where a future replacement decision is concerned†. What matters is the amount of wealth the company can generate from the future operation of that defender relative to the wealth created by a challenger. Since the NPV of a business, *net of all taxation considerations*, is the only way of measuring this wealth, the fate of a defender is decided, at least in economic terms, by the following decision rules:

	If	then
(i)	the NPV of future cash flows attributable to the defender is *too small* to warrant its continued use or it is *less* than its resale value‡	retire the defender.
(ii)	the NPV of future cash flows attributable to the defender is sufficient to warrant its continued use and it is *greater* than the NPV of future cash flows ascribed to the challenger,	retain the defender and do not substitute it by a challenger.
(iii)	if the NPV of future cash flows ascribed to the defender is *less* than the NPV of the future cash flows attributed to the challenger and these cash flows justify the use of the challenger,	replace the defender by the challenger.

Since the *historical* capital cost of a defender does *not* feature in the forecast of its *future* cash flows, it cannot feature in the NPV of an *existing* asset so it *must not* be taken into consideration when making decisions which affect future courses of action. Instead, the historical capital cost of an asset constitutes a sunk cost which is 'dead and gone'. If the replacement of an existing asset proves to be economically justified while that asset is still fairly new, then management should attempt to improve the accuracy of its future forecasting to ensure that future investments are put to the best economic advantage. Similarly, if the replacement of an asset is justified while its book value is still substantial, then management should question the suitability of its depreciation policy.

19.5 TAXATION EFFECTS IN REPLACEMENT ECONOMICS

As we demonstrated in Chapter 7.12, taxation has a significant effect on the cash flow attributes of a project. In certain circumstances these effects can either enhance

---

* We are not entertaining the possibility of a company defaulting on its instalment payments if the asset is being paid for by these means, since this could lead to its bankruptcy.

† This is not *absolutely* true, as we shall discover below, because certain taxation considerations involving the defender can have some impact, albeit small, on the economic merits of replacement.

‡ Its resale value could represent the price the company needed to pay to recruit a similar asset for some other line of business.

or diminish the economic merits of a project, so it is encumbent on management to consider the full implications of taxation when making decisions of economic choice. Possibly the most difficult application of taxation economics is that concerning capital replacement decisions. Indeed these taxation effects are sufficiently compli-cated to warrant the development of yet another economic model which will help us evaluate the relative economic merits of alternative replacement options.

In the formulation of the following model, we assume that the *net* cash receipts which are attributable to the service provided by a machine and its successors are sufficient to warrant the continuation of that service. In these circumstances it is appropriate to discover that replacement strategy which minimizes the NPV of costs incurred by the original machine and its string of replacements. To develop the replacement model we need to use the following notation:

$\text{NPV}_c(n)$ = the net present value of costs, after all taxation considerations have been taken into account, if a machine is operated for n years,

K = the capital cost of the machine, net of all taxation considerations,

C_i = the net of tax operating costs incurred by a machine during its ith year of operation such that $(i = 1, n)$,

n = the economic life of a machine such that the net present value of costs attributed to that machine *and* its replacements is minimized,

S_n = the resale value of a machine, net of all taxation considerations, when it is retired, and

$100 \cdot r$ = the after tax cost of capital (per cent per annum).

Using these symbols it follows that the net present value of costs incurred by the *original* machine in a continuous chain of replacements is given by the expression:

$$\text{NPV}_c(n) = K + \frac{C_1}{(1+r)} + \frac{C_2}{(1+r)^2} + \cdots \frac{C_n}{(1+r)^n} - \frac{S_n}{(1+r)^n}$$

The net present value of costs ascribed to the purchase and operation of the *first* replacement machine in a chain of replacements is given by the identical expression *except* this value occurs n years *after* the purchase of the original machine. In effect, therefore, the net present value of costs for a series of replacements, each occurring every n years is given by:

$\text{NPV}_c(n)$ at the beginning of Year 1 for the original machine,

$\text{NPV}_c(n)$ at the end of Year n for the first replacement,

$\text{NPV}_c(n)$ at the end of Year $2n$ for the second replacement, etc.

If we denote the sum of the net present values of a complete string of 'm' machines by the symbol $Z(n)$, it follows that:

$$Z(n) = \text{NPV}_c(n) + \frac{\text{NPV}_c(n)}{(1+r)^n} + \frac{\text{NPV}_c(n)}{(1+r)^{2n}} + \cdots \frac{\text{NPV}_c(n)}{[(1+r)^n]^{m-1}} \tag{19.5.1}$$

or:

$$Z(n) = \text{NPV}_c(n) \left[\frac{1 - (1+r)^{-mn}}{1 - (1+r)^{-n}} \right] \tag{19.5.2}$$

where m = the total number of machines which feature in the replacement sequence such that there is one original machine and $(m-1)$ replacements, and the economic life-cycle of the complete chain of replacements in mn years.

The economic interpretation of $Z(n)$ is that it represents the fund of money which one would need to invest at an interest rate of $100r$ per cent per annum after tax to generate just sufficient cash to finance the purchase and the operation of the entire series of machines for *mn* years. It is *not* suggested that a company would wish to embark on such a funding operation. However, a most reasonable objective would involve the selection of the variable *n* which *minimized* the value of $Z(n)$ because such a strategy would effectively *maximize* the NPV of the net cash inflows attributable to the business serviced by those machines.

At this juncture one cannot help noticing how complex this model is compared with its predecessors. Not only does it allow for the time value of money and the economic life of a machine, but it also allows for the total duration of the service provided by the machines, which could conceivably be the projected life-cycle of their manufactured product.

We shall postpone a full discussion of the implications of equation 19.5.2 until Section 19.6. However, one particular feature of this equation which concerns us here is the effect of allowing for a perpetual series of replacement machines, whereby the equation simplifies to the following form previously used in equation 19.3.1:

$$Z(n) = \mathrm{NPV}_c(n)\left[\frac{1}{1-(1+r)^{-n}}\right] \tag{19.5.3}$$

Using the identity:

$$k(n) = \left[\frac{1}{1-(1+r)^{-n}}\right]$$

where $k(n)$ = the present value to perpetuity factor, for which values are given in Table 19.5.1, we obtain the expression:

$$Z(n) = \mathrm{NPV}_c(n) \cdot k(n) \tag{19.5.4}$$

It will be noticed that, unlike equation 19.5.2, this expression does not include the variable *m*. Instead, the only variable in this equation is the economic life of the original machine and its replacements in perpetuity. An inspection of the values of $k(n)$ shown in Table 19.5.1 shows that, for a given cost of capital, $k(n)$ decreases monotonically for increasing values of *n*. However, the net present value of cost term $\mathrm{NPV}_c(n)$ increases monotonically for increasing *n*. In effect equation 19.5.4 incorporates the classic economic trade-off to which we have grown accustomed throughout this book.

If we reformulate the replacement problem previously given by Table 19.2.1 using equation 19.5.4, we obtain the results shown in Table 19.5.2. These show the identical optimal replacement periods to those shown by Table 19.2.3, proving that the two models given by equations 19.2.6 and 19.5.4 are equivalent. Unlike the results of Table 19.2.3, however, Table 19.5.2 does not help us evaluate the optimal time when substitution of the defender by a challenger should take place. To do this we have to commute the values of $Z(n)$ given by Table 19.5.2 into effective annual operating costs using the identity:

$$Z(n) = A + \frac{A}{(1+r)} + \frac{A}{(1+r)^2} + \dots \frac{A}{(1+r)^\infty} \tag{19.5.5}$$

where A = the effective annual cost of the series of replacements to perpetuity. It will be remembered that we first met a series of annuities such as this in Chapter 5.6. This time, however, the equation simplifies to the form:

$$Z(n) = \frac{A(1+r)}{r}$$

Table 19.5.1 *Values of the present value to perpetuity factor $k(n)$*

$$k(n) = \frac{1}{1-(1+r)^{-n}}$$

Replacement period n(years)	Cost of capital 100r% pa			
	8%	10%	12%	15%
1	13.500	11.000	9.333	7.667
2	7.010	5.762	4.931	4.101
3	4.850	4.021	3.470	2.920
4	3.774	3.155	2.744	2.335
5	3.131	2.638	2.312	1.989
6	2.704	2.296	2.027	1.762
7	2.401	2.054	1.826	1.602
8	2.175	1.874	1.678	1.486
9	2.001	1.736	1.564	1.397
10	1.863	1.628	1.475	1.328
11	1.751	1.540	1.404	1.274
12	1.659	1.468	1.345	1.230
13	1.582	1.408	1.297	1.194
14	1.516	1.358	1.257	1.165
15	1.460	1.315	1.224	1.140
16	1.412	1.278	1.195	1.120
17	1.370	1.247	1.171	1.103
18	1.334	1.219	1.150	1.088
19	1.302	1.196	1.131	1.076
20	1.273	1.175	1.116	1.065

or:

$$A = \mathcal{Z}(n) \cdot \frac{r}{1+r} \tag{19.5.6}$$

Using a cost of capital of 10 per cent per annum we find that $r/(1+r)$ in this equation is equal to 0.09091, and we also find that multiplying the values of $\mathcal{Z}(n)$ shown in Table 19.5.2 by this value we obtain identical results to those shown in Table 19.2.3. In effect we have proved that the essential tenet of our former model is the assumption that

Table 19.5.2 *A reformulation of the replacement problem of Table 19.2.3*

n	Model A NPV$_c$(n)	$k(n)$ 10% pa	$Z(n)$	n	Model B NPV$_c$(n)	$k(n)$ 10% pa	$Z(n)$
1	5 800	11.000	63 800	1	3 750	11.000	41 250
2	6 709	5.762	38 657	2	5 068	5.762	29 202
3	7 701	4.021	30 966	3	6 432	4.021	25 863
4	8 753	3.155	27 616	4	7 822	3.155	24 678
5	9 846	2.638	25 974	5	9 222	2.638	24 328
6	10 964	2.296	25 173	6	10 619	2.296	24 381
7	12 093	2.054	24 839	7	12 002	2.054	24 652
8	13 222	1.874	24 778	8	13 362	1.874	25 040
9	14 342	1.736	24 898	9	14 692	1.736	25 505
10	15 445	1.628	25 144	10	15 986	1.628	26 025

☐ = the optimal replacement for each alternative.

Table 19.5.3 *The schedule of operating costs and resale values for a replacement problem*

Age of machine (years)	Installed capital cost = 1600 munits	
	Operating costs (munits per year)	Resale value (munits)
1	50	900
2	100	800
3	150	600
4	200	400
5	300	200
6	400	0

replacements continue *indefinitely*. The advantage of our current model, given by equation 19.5.4, however is that it can readily cope with the intricacies of taxation which is our reason for developing it here.

To demonstrate the effect which taxation has on the replacement of capital assets, let us consider the following problem. Suppose a machine with an installed capital cost of 1600 munits incurs operating costs which increase with its age, whereas its resale value decreases with its age, according to the schedule presented in Table 19.5.3. Let us also assume that the following taxation particulars apply:

 (i) Rate of corporation tax payable one year in arrears = 45 per cent
 (ii) Initial capital allowance = 30 per cent
(iii) Annual capital allowance = 25 per cent

Our objective, therefore, is to discover the optimal replacement strategy for this machine taking into account the full effects of taxation. The basis for tax payments and allowances was described in Chapter 7.12, so only a few points need emphasizing here. Whereas we previously used corporation tax to reduce the net cash proceeds accruing to an asset, in this particular case the effect of such taxes is to reduce the net cash disbursements of a project. This applies because the accent of our analysis is on costs rather than on income*. In common with our previous treatment of taxes, the annual capital allowances are assumed to be computed on a reducing balance basis and so are related to the asset's written-down value *as interpreted by fiscal rather than by accounting means*. In addition, however, we have to apply a balancing adjustment when machinery or plant ceases to be used and is sold at a price which differs from its written-down value. If the money received from the sale of an asset is less than its written-down value the difference, which is interpreted as a loss, is treated as a balancing allowance similar to other tax allowances. If, however, the money received from the sale is greater than its written-down value, then the difference is treated as taxable income, and a balancing charge, known as a tax claw-back, is made by the Inland Revenue.

The initial step in our analysis is to compute the after tax allowances (tax shield) which alter from year to year. These are shown in Table 19.5.4.

The next step is to compute the balancing charges and allowances due to the different replacement options. These calculations are shown in Table 19.5.5.

The most critical step in the study involves the computation of the net costs incurred each year of the machine's life. These costs comprise a capital cost,

---

* The tacit assumption here is that the taxable net cash proceeds realized by an asset are sufficient to justify tax payments which, in turn, are sufficient to absorb all the capital allowances due to a capital project. Furthermore, we assume that the taxable cash receipts remain unaffected by any subsequent replacement policy.

Table 19.5.4　*The calculation of the tax shield resulting from operating cost and capital allowances*

End of year	Installed capital cost	Capital allowances Initial allowance	Annual allowance	Written-down value	Operating cost	Allowances before tax	Tax shield @ 45%
0	1600	480	400	720	0	880	
1			180	540	50	230	396
2			135	405	100	235	104
3			101	304	150	251	106
4			76	228	200	276	113
5			57	171	300	357	124
6			43	128	400	443	161
7							200

operating costs, resale values, a tax shield and a tax claw-back. Each step is shown in detail in Table 19.5.6.

To satisfy the needs of equation 19.5.4, the next step involves the calculation of the net present value of costs attributable to each replacement strategy, as shown by Table 19.5.7, and their translation into net present values of costs to perpetuity as shown in Table 19.5.8.

A careful examination of Table 19.5.8 shows that the value of $Z(n)$ declines rapidly as the replacement age of the machine increases, that it reaches a minimum value of 3363 munits at a machine age of five years, and then increases again. According to these results, we would advise that the machine should be operated for five years and then replaced by a brand new machine of the same type incurring the same costs and attracting the same taxes and tax benefits. (No allowance is made for technological innovation or uncertainty at this stage.) In this particular case the value of 3363 munits is the amount the firm would need to invest at an interest rate of 10 per cent per annum to be able to pay for the purchase, operation and replacement of new machines every five years in perpetuity. A practical application of this model involving the replacement of fork-lift trucks is given by Eilon et al. (1966).

Of course no manager worth his salt would accept the results of such a study at face value. As with all investment studies, the results of this study are only as good as the forecasts on which it is based. Instead, the prudent manager would wish to assess the sensitivity of the results of the study to possible changes and errors in its underlying assumptions to appraise the risks involved. In this respect, Chapter 9 is just as applicable to replacement investments as it is to any other kind of investment.

Table 19.5.5　*The calculation of the tax claw-back resulting from balancing charges and allowances*

End of year	Machine life (years)	Written-down value at end of life (munits)	Resale value (munits)	Balancing charge or allowance	Tax claw-back @ 45%
1	1	540	900	360	
2	2	405	800	395	162
3	3	304	600	296	178
4	4	228	400	172	133
5	5	171	200	29	77
6	6	128	0	−128	13
7	7				−58

Table 19.5.6 *The calculation of the net of tax costs attributable to each replacement option*

Year	Life	1	2	3	4	5	6
0	Installed capital cost	+1600	+1600	+1600	+1600	+1600	+1600
1	Operating cost resale value tax shield tax claw-back	50 −900 −396 +0 } −1246	50 0 −396 0 } − 346	50 0 −396 0 } − 346	50 0 −396 0 } − 346	50 0 −396 0 } − 346	50 0 −396 0 } − 346
2	Operating cost resale value tax shield tax claw-back	0 0 −104 162 } + 58	100 −800 −104 0 } − 804	100 0 −104 0 } − 4	100 0 −104 0 } − 4	100 0 −104 0 } − 4	100 0 −104 0 } − 4
3	Operating cost resale value tax shield tax claw-back		0 0 −106 178 } + 72	150 −600 −106 0 } − 556	150 0 −106 0 } + 44	150 0 −106 0 } + 44	150 0 −106 0 } + 44
4	Operating cost resale value tax shield tax claw-back			0 0 −113 133 } − 20	200 −400 −113 0 } − 313	200 0 −113 0 } + 87	200 0 −113 0 } + 87
5	Operating cost resale value tax shield tax claw-back				0 0 −124 77 } 24	300 −200 −124 0 } 24	300 0 −124 0 } + 176
6	Operating cost resale value tax shield tax claw-back					0 0 −161 13 } 148	400 −0 −161 0 } + 239
7	Operating cost resale value tax shield tax claw-back						0 0 −200 −58 } − 258

Table 19.5.7 *The calculation of the NPV for each replacement option*

Discount factor @ 10% pa	Year	1	2	Life 3	4	5	6
1.000	0	1600	1600	1600	1600	1600	1600
0.909	1	−1133	−315	−315	−315	−315	−315
0.826	2	48	−664	−3	−3	−3	−3
0.751	3		54	−418	33	33	33
0.683	4			14	−214	59	59
0.621	5				−29	−15	109
0.565	6					−84	135
0.513	7						−132
Net present values		515	675	878	1072	1275	1486

Table 19.5.8 *The calculation of the net present value of cost to perpetuity for each replacement option*

Machine life n (years)	1	2	3	4	5	6
Net present value of costs $\text{NPV}_c(n)$	515	675	878	1072	1275	1486
Present value to perpetuity factor $k(n) = \dfrac{1}{1-(1+r)^{-n}}$	11.00	5.762	4.021	3.155	2.638	2.296
Net present value of cost to perpetuity $Z(n) = \text{NPV}_c(n) \times k(n)$	5665	3889	3530	3382	3363	3412

19.6 A DYNAMIC PROGRAMMING APPROACH TO REPLACEMENT ANALYSIS

In the preceding section, we demonstrated how taxation details should be included in capital replacement studies using the net present value to perpetuity model as our underlying decision analysis tool. However the greatest difficulty with any replacement problem is in deciding the time horizon over which alternative replacement options should be compared. This is a conceptually difficult problem, especially when physical assets can manufacture several quite different products because, in these circumstances, their economic life is dictated by their own rates of technological obsolescence which are often extremely difficult to forecast. For example, process pumps have changed little over the past 50 years or more, and they are extremely versatile in their employ. What time horizon, then, would constitute a reasonable period to compare the economic merits and replacement policies of two different types of pumps, given that the choice between them is not intuitively obvious?

An alternative approach is provided by equation 19.5.2, providing one is willing to prescribe a *period* for the service required of an asset and its subsequent replacements. If we substitute the term $Z(m, n)$ for $Z(n)$ in equation 19.5.2 to show that the life-cycle costs of providing a service depend on the number of machines (m) in a

Table 19.6.1   *Values of $k(m, n)$ at 10 per cent per annum*

			n			
m	1	2	3	4	5	6
1	1.000	1.000	1.000	1.000	1.000	1.000
2	1.909	1.826	1.751	1.683	1.621	1.564
3	2.736	2.509	2.316	2.150	2.006	1.883
4	3.487	3.074	2.740	2.468	2.246	2.063
5	4.170	3.540	3.059	2.686	2.395	2.164
6	4.791	3.926	3.298	2.834	2.487	2.222
∞	11.000	5.762	4.021	3.155	2.638	2.296

replacement sequence as well as on their economic life (n), we get the expression:

$$Z(m, n) = \text{NPV}_c(n)\left[\frac{1-(1+r)^{-mn}}{1-(1+r)^{-n}}\right] \tag{19.6.1}$$

And if we substitute the expression:

$$k(m, n) = \left[\frac{1-(1+r)^{-mn}}{1-(1+r)^{-n}}\right]$$

into equation 19.6.1 we obtain the modified economic model:

$$Z(m, n) = \text{NPV}_c(n) \cdot k(m, n) \tag{19.6.2}$$

The factor $k(m, n)$ has to be interpreted as the present value of cost factor for a string of m machines operated for a life of n years each. Different values for this factor are given in Table 19.6.1 above.

To demonstrate the usefulness of this modified model, let us suppose a firm is contemplating using a machine according to the cost data provided by Table 19.5.3, and let us also assume that the services of such a machine are required for 12 years only. Quite obviously there are several ways of meeting this requirement. For example, the firm could replace a new machine after one year's service, in which case 12 consecutive machines would be required. Several other ways of satisfying a service life of 12 years are shown in Table 19.6.2 with the net present values of costs attributable to each replacement option. Although this list of options is by no means exhaustive, it does indicate that the cost of Option IV *may be* close to the cheapest possible means of providing this service. A close inspection of Table 19.6.2 shows that the cost $Z(m, n)$ declines monotonically as the age of the machine is increased to four years, but increases thereafter. Bearing in mind the results of our previous

Table 19.6.2   *The cost of alternative ways of providing a 12-year service*

Option	m	n (years)	$\text{NPV}_c(n)$ Table 19.5.7	$k(m, n)$ (Table 19.6.1)	$Z(m, n)$
I	12	1	515	7.495[a]	3860
II	6	2	675	3.926	2650
III	4	3	878	2.740	2406
IV	3	4	1072	2.150	2305
V[b]	2} 1}	5} 2}	1275} 675}	1.621} 0·386}	2067} 260} 2327
VI	2	6	1486	1.564	2324

[a] Derived by calculation.
[b] This assumes that two machines are run for five years each followed by one machine for two years.

study shown in Table 19.5.8, coupled with the fact that the value of $\mathcal{Z}(m, n)$ fast approaches that of $\mathcal{Z}(n)$ as the product $(m \times n)$ becomes large, this result is perhaps not surprising. However, it is conceivable that some other combination of replacement lives, which equals 12, could be cheaper than Option IV*.

This example clearly shows how we may assess the economic merits of different replacement strategies given that the decision maker is prepared to choose a time horizon for such replacement studies. However, it also demonstrates how the computational effort involved with such a study increases geometrically with the number of alternative ways of providing a service. Furthermore our ad hoc approach to this study has not assured us that an optimal solution has been found, so clearly we need some other means of resolving such replacement problems, especially when a vast number of alternatives exists.

A very well known technique for solving combinational and sequential problems of this kind is dynamic programming, which is equally useful for solving production and inventory scheduling problems, and which was pioneered by Bellman and Dreyfus (1962). Essentially, this technique accomplishes the same objective as the roll-back technique described in Chapter 10.3. The rationale of the algorithm of dynamic programming relies on the principle of optimality which states: 'An optimal policy must have the property that, regardless of the decisions taken in the past to arrive at some current predicament, all future decisions should constitute an optimal policy.' This is very similar to the principle of sunk cost.

Although this principle might appear to be quite straightforward, it is an unfortunate fact that the notation of dynamic programming (DP) is confusing to those who have not studied the technique before. To demonstrate the details of DP, let us assume that a firm requires the services of a machine whose cost structure is determined by Table 19.5.3 for a period of four years only. Furthermore, let us assume that a single machine is incapable of service after three years' operation. On the basis of these assumptions it is found that seven different combinations of machine-life exist which provide a four-year service, and these are shown below by the seven different paths of Figure 19.6.1. The nodes of this diagram represent the state of the replacement policy in force at any time. Node 1 represents the start of the four-year replacement project, whereas Node 16 represents the termination of that project. As an example of the seven different ways of meeting the four-year service requirements, the sequence of Nodes 1, 2, 5, 10 and 16 represents the operation and replacement of a machine every year, so in this respect the nodes represent the start, replacement or retirement of a machine. This does not apply to dissected nodes however. They represent the continued operations of an existing machine for a further year. In this respect the sequence of Nodes 1, 4, 9, 15 and 16 represents the operation of a machine for three years, followed by another machine for one year.

The numbers alongside the lines connecting each node represent the discounted net present value of costs attributable to that particular replacement strategy, according to the results of Table 19.5.7. For example, the NPV of costs incurred by a machine which is operated for one year only, starting at Node 1, is 515 munits, whereas starting one year later at Node 2 the present value of 515 would be 468 munits, at a cost of capital of 10 per cent per annum after tax. Unfortunately, the phenomenon of tax payments in arrears prevents one from allocating real annual costs to a machine whose service extends beyond one year†. To allow for this complication, artificial lettered costs are allocated to those paths incorporating

---

* The interested reader might like to experiment with these other options to determine whether Option IV is the optimal way of providing 12 years' service.

† We could overcome this problem by calculating the effective annual costs which would give the same NPVs using our annuity formula, but this seems unnecessarily complicated.

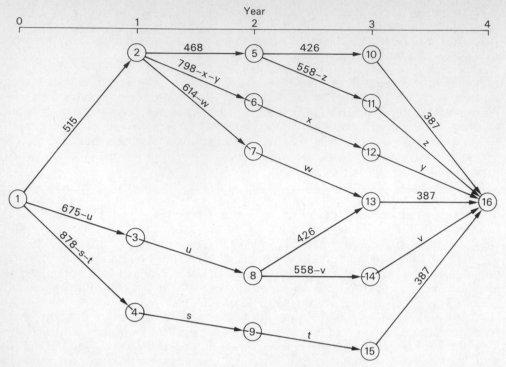

Figure 19.6.1 *The dynamic programming network for a replacement problem.*

dissected nodes. Since the sequence of Nodes 1, 4, 9 and 15 represents a machine which is operated for the maximum permissible period of three years, it follows, from Table 19.5.7, that the NPV of costs due to such a machine would be 878 munits over its three-year life. To overcome the tax problem we artificially allocate annual costs of s and t to its second and third years of operation in the certain knowledge that these artificial costs will not influence the final optimal decision.

To proceed, let the notation $C_n(S)$ represent the *minimum* net present value of costs which will be incurred if the service provided by the machine is currently in state S with n years of service *outstanding*. Since the nodes of our diagram represent the states of the replacement policy in force, it follows that the values of S for this particular problem range from 1–16. The symbol $C_1(10)$ therefore refers to the minimum cost which will be incurred if the service provided by the machines is currently in state 10 with one year of service outstanding. A quick inspection of Figure 19.6.1 shows that $C_1(10) = 387$ munits.

To discover the optimal route through the network of Figure 19.6.1 we must start at the extreme right-hand side of the diagram and work backwards to its point of origin, ruling out sub-optimal strategies as we go. At Node 5, for example, there are two alternative ways of meeting the outstanding two years' service. Quite obviously, faced with such alternative outcomes we would prefer to select the cheaper option represented by the sequence of Nodes 5, 11 and 16 rather than the more expensive alternative 5, 10 and 16. Using mathematical notation, this decision process can be represented in the following form:

$$C_n(S) = \min_J \left[C_{S,J} + C_{n-1}(J) \right] \qquad (19.6.3)$$

where $C_{S,J} =$ the annual cost incurred going from state S to state J, and $C_{n-1}(J) =$ the *minimum* costs which will be incurred if the service provided by the machines is currently in state J with $(n-1)$ years of service *outstanding*. Equation 19.6.3, therefore suggests that, starting at state S with n more years of service outstanding, we should select that route through state J which minimizes all future costs. Referring to Figure 19.6.1 we note that:

$$C_2(5) = C_{5,10} + C_1(10) = 426 + 387 = 813$$

and

$$C_2(5) = C_{5,11} + C_1(11) = 558 - z + z = 558$$

showing that the value for state J which minimizes future costs, is $J = 11$. Let us also use the notation $d_n(S)$ to represent the optimal decision which is made if the replacement strategy is currently in state S with n years of service outstanding. For example, $d_2(5) = 11$ means that, starting at state 5 with two years' service outstanding, we should go to state 11 rather than state 10 because this decision minimizes costs.

Having developed the model and defined the notation, we can now determine the optimal replacement strategy for our particular problem using this recursion algorithm. Table 19.6.3 gives the first iteration showing the six immediate routes and costs incurred, working backwards from state 16.

Table 19.6.3 *The first iteration of the dynamic programming problem*

$n = 1$
$C_{S,J} + C_0(J)$

	S	J Decision 16	$d_1(J)$	$C_1(S)$
	10	387	16	387
	11	z	16	z
Existing	12	y	16	y
state	13	387	16	387
	14	v	16	v
	15	387	16	387

To arrive at Nodes 10, 11, 12, 13, 14 and 15 shown in Table 19.6.3 we have to start at Nodes 5, 6, 7, 8 and 9 which are shown below in Table 19.6.4, and we notice that this second iteration involves the principle of optimality because several alternative ways for leaving state 5 and state 8 exist.

Tables 19.6.5 and 19.6.6 illustrate the third and final iterations of the algorithm, and Table 19.6.6 shows that the minimum cost incurred with the four-year service is 1233 munits. It also shows that the optimal route through the network is from Node

Table 19.6.4 *The second iteration*

$n = 2$
$C_{S,J} + C_1(J)$

	S	10	11	J Decision 12	13	14	15	$d_2(J)$	$C_2(S)$
	5	$426+387$	$558-z+z$	–	–	–	–	11	558
	6	–		$x \mid y$	–	–	–	12	$x \mid y$
Existing	7	–		–	$w+387$	–	–	13	$387+w$
state	8	–		–	$426+387$	$558-v+v$	–	14	558
	9	–		–	–	–	$t+387$	15	$387+t$

Table 19.6.5 *The third iteration*

$$n = 3$$
$$C_{S,J} + C_2(J)$$

S	5	6	J Decision 7	8	9	$d_3(J)$	$C_3(S)$
Existing 2	$468 + 558$	$798 - x - y + x + y$	$614 - w + 387 + w$	–	–	6	798
state 3	–	–	–	$u + 558$	–	8	$u + 558$
4	–	–	–	–	$s + t + 387$	9	$s + t + 387$

1 via Node 3. To determine the optimal strategy, we have to follow the decision sequence through all four tables and note that:

According to Table:	Starting at Node:	The next optimal node is:
19.6.6	1	3
19.6.5	3	8
19.6.4	8	14
19.6.3	14	16

In effect, the optimal replacement policy involves route 1, 3, 8, 14 and 16, which is equivalent to replacing a machine every two years in order to meet the four-year service requirement.

Although our trivial example does not really warrant using the dynamic programming algorithm with all its perplexing notation, it does demonstrate how one could resolve replacement problems given that the assumption of replacement in perpetuity is inappropriate, and providing one is willing to select a time horizon for the replacement study[*].

Excellent examples of replacement policies derived by these means are provided by Bellman (1955) and Jardine (1973). As a further point it should be noted that proprietary computer software for the computerized resolution of such problems is readily available.

Table 19.6.6 *The fourth iteration*

$$n = 4$$
$$C_{S,J} + C_3(J)$$

S	2	J Decision 3	4	$d_4(J)$	$C_4(S)$
Existing 1	$515 + 798$ $= 1313$	$675 - u$ $+ u + 558$ $= 1233$	$878 - s - t$ $+ s + t + 387$ $= 1265$	3	1233
state					

19.7   THE PROBLEM OF UNCERTAINTY IN REPLACEMENT ANALYSIS

Investment decisions concerning the replacement of physical assets are exposed to similar conditions of uncertainty and risk as decisions involving assets used for

---

[*] Of course the corollary to this requirement is that one should also be able to justify the choice of a time horizon for such a study.

business expansion purposes. These matters were discussed in depth in Chapter 9 and will not be repeated here. Of course, central to the whole problem of plant replacement and retirement decisions is the influence of technological innovation and the rate at which a firm's products and machines are made obsolete. These are special conditions of risk which receive proper attention in the following section. The particular point of focus here, however, concerns the problem of uncertainty arising from the unreliability of plant and machinery. The economic implications of reliability engineering are vast, and a considerable body of knowledge exists on the subject, and we are unable to do justice to the subject here because of limitations on space. However it would be wrong not to mention a few fundamental points, especially those which relate to the life-cycle costs of an asset and its replacements.

Some machines become more expensive to operate because their functional efficiency erodes with time. For example, heat exchangers used by the process industry lose their heat transfer capacities as foreign materials foul their heat transfer surfaces so they either require frequent cleaning and possibly overhauling to reduce their operating costs or else their functional deficiency is met by other means involving additional expenditure. In a similar vein, the tools of cutting and forming machinery gradually wear and either have to be refurbished or replaced. Increasing annual operating costs of this kind are properly allowed for in the NPV equations and models used in this chapter. By contrast, the optimal time to replace a machine which completely fails to perform its function because it suffers some catastrophic failure is not *properly* catered for by the models which we have studied to date, because they do not incorporate due allowance for the fact that the physical breakdown of machinery is a probabilistic process.

To demonstrate the effects which random failures have on the optimal replacement strategies of plant and equipment, let us first consider the problem involved with plant experiencing frequent failures, so that we do not have to consider the influence of the time value of money. Given this condition and the further assumption that the cost of replacing a broken machine is greater than its cost of replacement either by a new or reconditioned machine prior to failure, it follows that the principal uncertainty involved with a replacement policy is in knowing when the plant or machine will cease to function adequately. Providing sufficient historical failure data for similar machines working under similar conditions are available, this level of uncertainty can be reduced to a level which is acceptable to the decision maker, using well known and proven statistical techniques.

Numerous replacement models for plant and machinery experiencing complete functional failures are available in the literature, but the two best known involve the periodic replacement of plant irrespective of its age, and the age replacement model. To demonstrate these two models we first need to adopt some new notations:

C_p = the cost of a preventive maintenance replacement,

C_f = the cost of a failure replacement,

t_p = the time period between successive preventive maintenance replacements irrespective of the number of intervening failures,

t_p' = the time to the next preventive replacement based on the age of the equipment, which is assumed to be new if it is replaced or repaired,

$H(t_p)$ = the expected number of failures occurring during an interval t_p given that a periodic replacement policy is in force.

$F(t_p')$ = the cumulative probability of a failure occurring during an interval t_p',

$R(t_p')$ = the cumulative probability of an item not failing during a time period t_p' such that $R(t_p') = 1 - F(t_p')$ where $R(t_p')$ is known as the reliability of the item over the time interval t_p',

$M(t_p')$ = the mean time to failure of those items which fail before the scheduled replacement age t_p',

$C(t_p)$ = the mean average cost per unit of time due to a periodic replacement policy, and

$C(t_p')$ = the mean average cost per unit of time due to an age replacement policy.

Using these terms, it can easily be shown that the mean average replacement costs per unit of time for the two alternative strategies are given by the following expressions:

(i) periodic replacement:

$$C(t_p) = \frac{C_p + H(t_p) \cdot C_f}{t_p} \qquad (19.7.1)$$

(ii) age replacement:

$$C(t_p') = \frac{C_p R(t_p') + C_f[1 - R(t_p')]}{t_p' R(t_p') + M(t_p')[1 - R(t_p')]} \qquad (19.7.2)$$

To place the significance of these two models in perspective they have to be compared with the first model of this chapter, represented by equation 19.2.1, when their obvious differences arising out of their reliability terms become apparent. To discover the economic life of an asset subject to failure, one has to determine those values of t_p and t_p' which minimize the two costs $C(t_p)$ and $C(t_p')$ in these two equations. On the basis that one knows or is willing to forecast the reliability characteristics of a machine, several authors provide ready-reckoning methods to determine these economic lives. For example Woodman (1967) provides control limits on the ratio C_p/C_f to determine under what conditions a scheduled replacement is economically justified, and Glasser (1969) provides graphs to determine the economic scheduled replacement life of assets on the basis that equipment failures can be adequately modelled using the Weibull distribution function. All these models demonstrate that *two* conditions *must* be met for the replacement of a machine, which is subject to failure, to be justified. These two conditions are:

 (i) the total cost associated with a failure replacement must be greater than the total cost due to a scheduled preventive replacement, and
(ii) the plant or machine must exhibit a pattern of failures which, in reliability engineering terms, is known as wear out.

The first condition is normally met in practice since, for example, considerable disruption to the manufacturing process with high incidental costs could result from a machine failure, whereas with scheduled replacement lost production time could be kept to a minimum. The second condition introduces a dimension to replacement analysis which we have not previously encountered. It means that the probability of failure in successive and equal time intervals must increase with the age of the plant for planned replacement to be economically justified. The underlying danger of not understanding or appreciating this very subtle requirement is that economists, noticing that the costs attributable to the repair of a machine have risen over a period of time, will advocate its replacement on the basis of the economic models previously encountered in this chapter without realizing that the underlying causes for such increasing costs could be due to a random, non-ageing pattern of failures. In these circumstances scheduled preventive replacements would not be economically justified. Unfortunately, a proper appreciation of this subtlety requires an elementary understanding of reliability engineering which lies beyond the scope of this book. However such matters are well explained by Churchman et al. (1957) and Jardine (1973).

Reliability considerations also affect replacement strategies for another, quite different reason. Research shows that although repaired equipment might achieve the same functional performance as brand new equipment, there is a marked tendency for the reliability performance of repaired equipment to deteriorate with successive repair. The economic manifestation of this is that the maintenance costs of a machine increase with its age. In these circumstances the criterion for replacement is to select the exact number of repairs which a machine should receive prior to its replacement so that the life-cycle costs of providing its service are minimized. An example of industrial equipment replacement on the basis of research conducted by the University of Bradford is provided by de la Mare (1979).

The lesson of this section, therefore, is that a forecast of the likely future costs to be incurred by an asset should really consider the reliability characteristics of that asset if a truly optimal replacement strategy is to be implemented. Fortunately there is a growing body of knowledge about the reliability characteristics of plant and machinery which is now making such optimization studies possible.

19.8 THE INFLUENCE OF PROCESS INNOVATION ON PLANT REPLACEMENT DECISIONS

The optimal time to replace or retire any manufacturing asset is affected by three different types of innovation discussed in detail elsewhere in this book, namely:

(i) *Product innovation*, which is made manifest by the introduction of new and improved products into a market,
(ii) *Labour innovation*, which leads to productivity improvements brought about by better job organization and man management, and is sometimes known as learning, and
(iii) *Process innovation*, resulting from the exploitation of process improvements and inventions, and the economic advantages accruing to large-scale plants.

Quite clearly, the lifespan of any plant or machinery which is tailor-made to manufacture a particular product is *ultimately* limited by the first type of innovation, whereas this is not so for versatile assets. Product life-cycle effects therefore are the ultimate reason for the retirement of many assets. To some extent, this effect if it exists can be mitigated and the lifespan of those assets prolonged if a firm enjoys the benefits of labour innovation and a level of productivity which clearly distinguishes its performance from that of its competitors. However, this advantage is often short-lived because, outside of the constraints imposed by product life-cycle considerations, process innovation usually has the next most dominant effect on replacement and retirement decisions.

Examples of process innovation are ubiquitous, ranging from the substitution of manual production methods by robots and computerized machines at one extreme, to the extraordinary manufacture of plastic materials through biological fermentation and the creation of pharmaceutical products by genetical engineering at the other extreme. However the purpose of these innovations is identical – to manufacture cheaper and possibly better quality products. Furthermore, the economic advantages of large-scale plants are made obvious by the conspicuousness of such plants. As a result of the combined effects of these two forms of innovation there has been a dramatic decline in the production costs of many products during the last few decades, especially amongst those involved with high technology, such as microprocessors and organic chemical products. Indeed, a powerful negative relationship between cost and this form of productivity seems to be a well established empirical fact which has been studied in detail by Becker (1971) and de la Mare (1977).

Furthermore, the studies of Wragg and Robertson (1978) indicate that the benefits of innovation appear to go mainly to the customer by way of lower prices.

The exploitation of technological innovation which reduces the unit operating cost of new plants* has an interesting cascade effect. First, it enhances the immediate economic rewards realized by the innovator. Second, it often results in an expansion of aggregate supply as competitors build new capacity incorporating the same or an imitation technology. Third, the increase in supply diminishes the product price as firms compete for market share. And fourth, this results in the retirement of plants employing less efficient technology which are no longer economically viable. The withdrawal of obsolete production and distribution facilities and their replacement by more efficient systems is therefore the bedfellow of technological progress and a matter which is central to the whole business of corporate survival.

Several of the studies mentioned above have shown that the decline in product costs and prices can be *approximated* by exponential relationships of the following form:

$$P_t = P_0 e^{(a-b)t} \tag{19.8.1}$$
$$C_t = C_0 e^{(a-b)t} \tag{19.8.2}$$
$$C'_t = C_0 e^{(a+c)t} \tag{19.8.3}$$

where:

P_t = the unit price paid for a product at some time t,
C_t = the unit cost incurred by plants using the most efficient technology,
C'_t = the unit cost incurred by a plant with a fixed technological capability,
a = the general rate of cost inflation which, it is assumed, applies equally well to prices as costs (per cent per annum),
b = the rate of technological innovation (per cent per annum),
c = the rate of decline of production efficiency as a plant get older (per cent per annum),
t = the time since a plant was first installed and commissioned, and
e = the exponent which is the base of the natural and Napierian logarithms, such that $e = 2.71828$.

So defined, the rate of technological innovation implies that the unit cost, and subsequently the price of plants employing the most efficient methods of production and distribution, decline by a constant annual percentage b for different states of technology embodied in plants of different age. This situation is illustrated by Figure 19.8.1, where the unit cost of production has quite arbitrarily been set at 22 munits per 100 munits of capital employed and the parameters a, b, and c have been set as 2, 5 and $\frac{1}{2}$ per cent per annum respectively.

Ideally, one would expect a firm to continue operating an existing asset until its operating costs, represented by equation 19.8.3, equated the market price, represented by equation 19.8.1, because it would maximize the NPV of that asset and the capitalized value of the firm by these means†. Such a condition as this is

---

* This does not suggest that process innovation necessitates major capital investment or that the other two forms of innovation are unimportant.

† These considerations are properly covered by Chapter 8. In reality however it is quite conceivable that a firm might consider the continued operations of an existing asset, up to this point of equilibrium, unjustified in its use of scarce managerial talent.

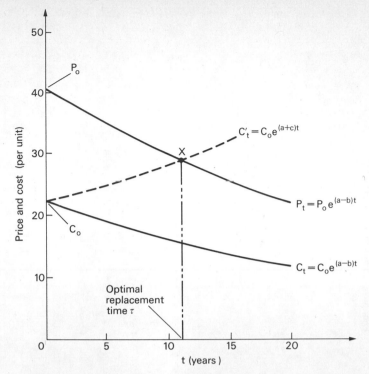

Figure 19.8.1 *Optimal replacement life for a manufacturing plant, subject to obsolescence. From de la Mare (1975), with kind permission of the Editor of* Chemical Engineer.

represented by point X in Figure 19.8.1 and the two relationships shown below:

$$P_0 e^{(a-b)\tau} = C_0 e^{(a+c)\tau} \tag{19.8.4}$$

$$\mathrm{NPV}(\tau) = P_0 \int_0^\tau e^{-(r+b-a)t}\, dt - C_0 \int_0^\tau e^{-(r-c-c)t}\, dt - K \tag{19.8.5}$$

where $\mathrm{NPV}(\tau)$ = the net present value realized by operating an asset for its optimal replacement life τ, and r = the nominal discount interest rate*. Both these relationships can be solved for τ and P_0 if the other factors are known by rearranging equation 19.8.4 to form:

$$\tau = \frac{\log_e (P_0/C_0)}{b+c} \tag{19.8.6}$$

and by integrating equation 19.8.5 to form:

$$\mathrm{NPV}(\tau) = P_0 \frac{1-e^{-(r+b-a)\tau}}{(r+b-a)} - C_0 \frac{1-e^{-(r-a-c)\tau}}{(r-a-c)} - K \tag{19.8.7}$$

Although these two equations cannot be solved analytically, they can be solved numerically, as one normally does with all discounting problems. To help us understand the salient lessons of such an analysis, we have calculated the values of τ, P_0 and P_t for the parametric values stated, and these results are depicted in Figures 19.8.2 and 19.8.3 where the values of r have been chosen so that equation 19.8.7

---

* It should be noticed that we use the discount factor e^{-rt} instead of the more conventional form $(1+r)^{-t}$. Our reason for so doing is that the mathematics are made simpler, but we would not normally recommend the use of such a relationship for the reasons given in Appendix F.

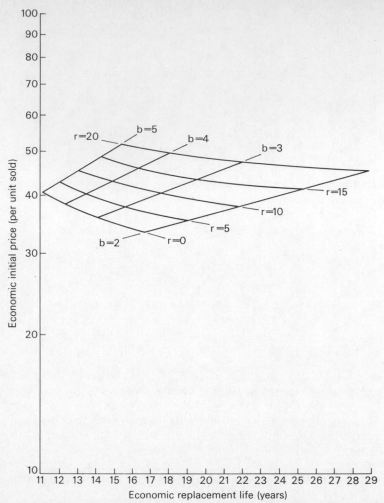

Figure 19.8.2 *Relationship between economic initial price and economic replacement life for varying rates of technological innovation and DCF rates of return on investment. From de la Mare (1975), with kind permission of the Editor of* Chemical Engineer.

equates to zero[*]. These graphs show the following results:

(i) for a constant rate of technological innovation it is necessary to keep plants operating longer as interest rates rise, and it is also necessary to charge higher prices to cover the higher interest charges; and

(ii) for a given cost of capital it is necessary to charge *higher initial prices* as the rate of technological innovation increases. This suggests a paradox which seems curious in light of the frequent assertion that improved productivity reduces rather than increases inflation. Supplementary evidence of this effect is given by the differentiation of equation 19.8.6 according to the relationship:

$$\frac{\partial P_0}{\partial b} = C_0 e^{(b+c)\tau}$$

---

[*] This means that the interest rate r is the highest rate a firm could afford to pay and yet break even economically by time τ. In essence, therefore r becomes the DCFRR. Although we would normally prefer to use the NPV criterion as a measure of economic efficiency, we are unable to do so here because this would necessitate three-dimensional graphs, which are impractical in this instance.

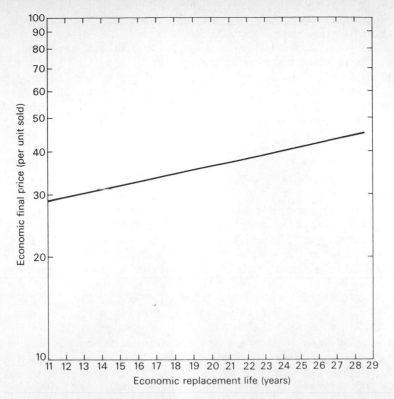

Figure 19.8.3 *Relationship between economic final price and economic replacement life. From de la Mare (1975), with kind permission of the Editor of* Chemical Engineer.

which shows that the initial price increases with an increasing rate of technological innovation. The reason for this peculiar effect is of course easy to understand if we consider the other factors affected by such a change. Figure 19.8.2 shows that the corollary to such a change entails shorter plant lives, proving that an increased rate of technological innovation hastens the obsolescence of manufacturing assets. Figure 19.8.3 shows that the *final* prices would also diminish accordingly. In essence, therefore, an increase in the initial price is needed to pay for the shorter plant life and the deteriorating final price as industry increases its rate of process innovation.

The effect of a decline in the production efficiency of manufacturing assets as they get older is best illustrated by the differentiation of equation 19.8.6 according to the relationship:

$$\frac{\partial \tau}{\partial c} = \frac{\log_e (C_0/P_0)}{(b+c)^2}$$

Since the numerator of this expression is negative, it follows that such a deterioration accelerates the replacement of older plants.

Although the inherent assumptions of this economic model are somewhat naïve* and the analysis seems somewhat academic, nevertheless its results reinforce what we might intuitively expect from a moment's careful reflection. In particular it shows

---

* It should be noted that this model does not explicitly cater for the effects of taxation, and it also assumes that the rates of price and cost erosion are equal.

that the economic life of any commercial asset is inextricably linked with the movement in its prices and costs, and the rate of technological innovation which applies to that particular type of business. It also shows that the economic viability of an asset is affected by all these issues, and that an ill-conceived price strategy or lack of awareness of likely future technological improvements could have a catastrophic impact on the economic merits of a new capital project. In effect, this simple model reinforces the need for technological forecasting (TF) as an ongoing corporate activity and, if it achieves nothing else, its presentation here is justified.

19.9   SOME COMMON ERRORS IN REPLACEMENT STUDIES

Observations of replacement decisions in practice indicate several major errors which are often made when dealing with replacement analyses. Perhaps the most serious error involves the addition of the excess of book value over the net realizable value of the defending asset to the estimated capital cost of the challenger. This is irrational and violates the principle of sunk cost discussed in Section 19.4. By stark contrast, some authors recommend that the net realizable value of the defender should not feature in the replacement economics because they believe that such a cash flow has nothing to do with the replacement, but depends only on the results of the past decision to finance the defender. They are most definitely wrong in this assertion, because in circumstances where replacement is economically justified the resale value of the defender is only realizable because of the existence of the challenger. In this respect the resale value of the defender enhances rather than diminishes the economic merits of replacement, and it is most important that estimates of the resale value of the defender and the challenger should both feature in the projected cash flows for each alternative course of action.

Another common error is the mistaken belief that one *must* replace a machine if the business of other assets is put in jeopardy by its failure. In many circumstances such a replacement would undoubtedly be justified and it is quite understandable why such decisions are often made in haste. However the logic of such decisions should never go unquestioned. In certain instances, for example, the economic life expectancy of the whole process containing the failed machine might be short-lived for reasons of product or process obsolescence. In these circumstances repair let alone replacement of the broken machine might not be economically justifiable. It is also most important to consider *all* the *future* cash flows which will accrue to the company as a result of a replacement because the failure of one machine might herald the incipient failures of others. Taken in aggregate, the capital cost of their subsequent replacements might not be warranted.

Inflation impinges on decisions of economic choice because it distorts the real worth of the future cash flows attributable to a business. Faced with rising costs, some studies might show that the replacement of assets is justified, but this might be false if the underlying reasons for the escalation of costs is predominantly the result of inflation. We have already discussed the problem of inflation and have resolved that the only logical way to select between economic alternatives is to compare their economic merits in *real, constant purchasing power* terms even though this necessitates forecasts of inflationary trends.

On the tacit understanding that the cash receipts from the sale of products are sufficiently larger than the cash disbursements of a business to warrant its continuation, and the added assumption that those cash receipts remain unaffected by any replacement policy, many books on engineering economy suggest that the economic merits of alternative replacement strategies should be compared over the same time horizon so that the same service is provided, and the effective annual costs* of running machines should be compared if their economic and/or physical life are different. In certain circumstances these assumptions might be valid, but they cannot go unchallenged. Since the whole economic purpose of investment is to create wealth, a prerequisite for all replacement decisions is that more wealth should result from a replacement than without it. The only sensible way to ascertain this fact necessitates a forecast of *all* the cash flows which will accrue to the company with and without the replacement, and a comparison of the economic merits of these cash flows using the techniques and criteria promulgated by this book. Notwithstanding risk and cash rationing considerations which we have already dealt with in detail, we strongly advise that the economic merits of replacement alternatives should be compared using the NPVs of their future net cash inflows. Such a criterion does *not* require the lifespan for each alternative to be identical because it is quite conceivable that they will be different. For example, a company might be able to continue producing and selling a product for longer with one replacement option than another because it would realize positive cash flows for longer. If, however, it appears that the life-cycle of the product of some machine is long lasting and much longer than the economic replacement life of alternative machines, then the time horizon for the economic replacement study could be made the same for each replacement option and their economic comparison could be based on their costs, providing their revenues are sufficient to warrant the continuation of that business. However, the economic replacement life of alternative machines, for example the defender and the challenger, will, in all likelihood, be quite different. To compare these costs on the basis of their effective annual costs is only correct if their economic life is identical or one is willing to assume that they could be replaced by identical machines to perpetuity. If these assumptions are not met then a comparison on this basis would be wrong. In these circumstances one should forecast the annual cash flows attributable to each alternative course of action which has been optimized, using dynamic programming means if necessary, to a common prescribed time horizon, and *then* compare their economic merits using NPV criteria.

19.10 SUMMARY

This chapter concludes the presentation of the theoretical aspects of this book and demonstrates that the net present value relationship, based on the discounted cash flows accruing to a project, is a sensible and realistic way to consider the life-cycle costs and benefits of a capital project, using a cradle-to-the-grave philosophy. To make proper economic sense of replacement and retirement problems however we demonstrate the need for three other economic concepts involving the value and the economic life of an asset and the concept of sunk cost. Without a proper understanding of these concepts optimal replacement and retirement decisions cannot be made. Although we do not repeat our previous presentation concerning matters of uncertainty and risk here, it goes without saying that the substance of Chapter 9 is equally pertinent where replacement and retirement decisions are concerned as it is for business expansion decisions. However we emphasize the point that reliability considerations are often at the heart of replacement problems and they bring to the economic analysis a special calculus of their own which, misinterpreted or overlooked, can result in wrong replacement decisions.

---

* Effective annual costs are those annuity costs which have the same NPV as a sequence of unequal actual costs.

19.11 BIBLIOGRAPHY

General texts

Both these books deal with the details of replacement analysis in their own special way, and both make allowance for the influence of technological innovation and obsolescence.

Connor, J. and Evans, J. B., *Replacement Investment*, Gower Press, 1972.

Terborgh, G. M., *Business Investment Policy*, Machinery and Allied Products Institute, 1958.

Specific texts

Abrams, H. J., 'The extended yield method and optimal replacement problems', *Journal of Business Finance*, **3**(2), 1971, pp. 26–34.

Becker, G. S., *Economic Theory*, Alfred A. Knopf, 1971.

Bellman, R. E., 'Equipment replacement policy', *Journal of the Society of Industrial and Applied Mathematics (SIAM)*, **3**, 1955, pp. 133–136.

Bellman, R. E. and Dreyfus, S. E., *Applied Dynamic Programming*, Oxford University Press/Princeton University Press, 1962.

Churchman, C. W., Ackoff, R. L. and Arnoff, E. L., *Introduction to Operations Research*, John Wiley & Sons, 1957.

de la Mare, R. F., 'Parameters affecting capital investment', *Chemical Engineer*, **296,** April 1975, pp. 227–247.

de la Mare, R. F., 'Chemical commodity price erosion', *Engineering and Process Economics*, **2,** 1977, pp. 295–304.

de la Mare, R. F., 'Optimal equipment replacement policies', *National Centre of Systems Reliability Research Report*, NCSR R. 21, April 1979.

Eilon, S., King J. R. and Hutchinson, D. E., 'A study of equipment replacement', *Operations Research Quarterly*, **17**(1), 1966, pp. 59–72.

Glasser, G. L., 'Planned replacement: some theory and its application', *Journal of Quality Technology*, No. 1, 1969, pp. 110–119.

Jardine, A. K. S., *Maintenance Decision Making*, unpublished PhD thesis, University of Birmingham, 1973.

Jardine, A. K. S., *Maintenance Replacement and Reliability*, Pitman, 1973.

Merrett, A. J. and Sykes, A., *Capital Budgeting and Company Finance*, Longman, 1966.

Woodman, R. C., *Industrial Replacement Theory*, unpublished PhD thesis, University of Birmingham, 1967.

Wragg, R. and Robertson, J., *Post-war Trends in Employment, Productivity, Output, Labour Costs and Prices by Industry in the United Kingdom*, Research Paper No. 3, Department of Employment, HMSO, 1978.

19.12 QUESTIONS

19.12.1   The Managing Director of a small jobbing machine shop company is in the process of buying a new multi-turreted lathe to replace several old single-chucked lathes. He has already extended the machine shop to accommodate the new lathe. However, he is becoming concerned because the project is going to cost more than the original £10 000 which was agreed by the Board. To date he has spent £2000 in preparing for the lathe. Moreover, due to the escalation in the price, it is now expected to cost £10 000. To make matters more complicated, the chief accountant now reckons that the cash flow savings which the lathe will realize over its useful ten-year life will be less than previously envisaged. He reckons that they will be £3000 per annum before tax. Taxes amounting to 50 per cent of the cash flow savings realized will be paid in the year that the saving is made. However, the company can claim an immediate 20 per cent tax free grant on the installed capital cost of the lathe. No other tax inducements are available. The depreciation system employed by the company is the traditional straight-line system. It is reckoned that the marginal cost of capital to the company is 10 per cent per annum after tax.

Would you recommend the Managing Director to continue with the project?

What considerations would you take into account when making your recommendation?

19.12.2　Due to physical impairment and increasing maintenance costs it is often economically justifiable to replace equipment by similar equipment which performs exactly the same function, deteriorates at exactly the same rate, and incurs the same capital cost and schedule of operating costs. In these circumstances prove that the optimal replacement strategy involves replacing equipment when $W(t)$ is a minimum and $W(t) = P(t)\left[\dfrac{1}{1-(1+r)^{-t}}\right]$

where $t =$ a variable denoting time (years), $W(t) =$ a function of time (t) and is defined as the present cost to perpetuity (infinity). It is the present value of all the costs incurred by the series of equipment replacements to infinity, $P(t) =$ a function of time (t) and is the present value of the costs incurred by the first piece of equipment, $r =$ the cost of capital. (Neglect salvage value and taxation considerations.)

19.12.3　Determine the best course of action for the ABC Company on the basis of the following conversation. Be precise, state any assumptions used in the assessment and show all your calculations.

MD (of ABC)	Well, Joe, six months ago you told us that the new lathe would cost £50 000 installed, including the cost of relocating some of the other machines, but I gather that you now wish to update that estimate.
Joe (estimator)	Yes, I'm afraid so. Due to inflation the capital cost of the lathe delivered will now be £30 000 instead of the previous estimate of £20 000. But we've already spent £10 000 in preparation for its installation. Will the Board approve the extra £10 000?
MD	Yes, I think so, provided that the economics are still OK. What do you think, Harry?
Harry (chief accountant)	I'll have to work the sums out again. Previously, the project showed a traditional accounting rate of return after tax and depreciation of 25 per cent per annum based on the company's normal practice of writing off assets over four years, even though the Inland Revenue only

allow a 10 per cent per annum annual allowance. This seemed quite good when compared with the company's cost of capital of 15 per cent per annum after tax, with corporation tax standing at 50 per cent.

19.12.4 Discuss the effect which technological progress has on the value of an existing asset and the frequency of plant replacement. Demonstrate how these effects could be accommodated by equation 19.3.3, which is a generalized model of the value of an existing asset.

19.12.5 In the Netherlands, reclaimed land is kept dry by pumping the sea water which seeps through the dykes back into the sea with very large pumps. These pumps have been highly developed and it is unlikely that there will be any further improvement in their design and performance which could be economically justified.

The costs associated with maintaining the pumps, their installed capital cost and their second-hand value are given in the table below. All costs are in real terms (having allowed for inflation) and are in units of thousands of Dutch Florins.

Installed capital cost = 400

Age of pump (years)	End of year maintenance costs	End of year second-hand values
1	0	225
2	20	200
3	30	150
4	20	100
5	80	50

The following tax allowances are claimable by those pump operators who pay tax:

(a) An immediate initial allowance (not a cash grant) of 30 per cent of the installed capital cost.
(b) An immediate annual allowance of 25 per cent of the installed capital cost, and thereafter end of year annual allowances of 25 per cent of the previously written-down value.
(c) A balancing allowance equal to the written-down value minus the second-hand value.

The corporation tax rate is 45 per cent and the real post-tax cost of capital is 10 per cent per annum.

What would be the optimal strategy for running the pumps?

19.12.6 A pump costs £1000 to purchase and install, and it incurs maintenance and lost production costs which vary with its age T according to the following relationships:

$$\text{Maintenance costs} = £100 \, T^2$$
$$\text{Lost production costs} = £200 \, T$$

where T = its age at the *beginning* of a year.

On the assumption that a pump can only be replaced at the beginning of a year, use the dynamic programming algorithm to determine the minimum life-cycle cost of providing a continued pumping service over a period of five years. (For the sake of simplicity, ignore the time value of money.)

19.12.7   An independent oil well operator is faced with the expensive problem of replacing his oil well pumps as they deteriorate. He currently uses a pump Model A of 5000 gallons per day capacity, but is contemplating using a bigger pump Model B of 10 000 gallons per day capacity which has recently come on the market. The installed capital costs of these pumps are:

Model A   £5000 each
Model B   £8000 each

The production rate of oil is dependent on market demand, but invariably ranges from 50 000–100 000 gallons per day. At these demand rates the oil reservoir is expected to last for centuries. If needed, the pumps could be operated for up to four years, but as they age they become more expensive to operate and maintain.

Taking into account the effects of taxation, the annual operating costs for these pumps are:

Model A

Year of net cash outflow	Pump life (years) 1	2	3	4
0	5000	5000	5000	5000
1	1000	1500	1500	1500
2		500	2000	2000
3			500	3000
4				500

Model B

Year of net cash outflow	Pump life (years) 1	2	3	4
0	8000	8000	8000	8000
1	1500	2000	2000	2000
2		1000	3000	3000
3			1000	4000
4				1000

The net cost of capital to the oil well operator is 10 per cent per annum after tax. Determine his optimal pump replacement strategy.

19.12.8   Using the example previously given in Table 19.5.3 and the economic results of that study, demonstrate the effect which different study time horizons have on the ensuing optimal replacement policy using dynamic programming as the method of analysis.

19.12.9   Process valves costing $100 each to purchase and install incur costs of $32 each time they are maintained. Historical evidence shows that the mean time to failure (MTTF) for these valves changes with their age according to the following data:

Failure number	MTTF (days)	Failure number	MTTF (days)
1	444	9	81
2	242	10	118
3	221	11	71
4	186	12	63
5	178	13	106
6	111	14	62
7	139	15	73
8	195	16	26

Using a 5 per cent per annum cost of capital and equation Fl.2.2 to convert nominal annual interest rates into effective daily interest rates, determine the optimal replacement policy for these valves assuming they will be replaced in perpetuity.

19.12.10 The following forecast is available for the number of manufactured units to be delivered by a company during each quarter of the coming year:

Quarter	Sales forecast (units)
1	5 500
2	20 000
3	8 000
4	19 000

At present the company has a fleet consisting of 60 wagons, each with a capacity for transporting 50 units/quarter, when working at full capacity. Their age profile is as follows:

Number of wagons	Age at 1 January (years)
10	New
10	1
30	2
5	3
5	4

The average time spent off the road for maintenance has been recorded for a number of years, and the following data are available. Average time off the road per annum:

1st year = 0
2nd year = 5 per cent
3rd year = 8 per cent
4th year = 8 per cent
5th year = 12 per cent

It costs £10 000 to buy a new wagon which has a useful life of five years, and a scrap value of £500 after that. Maintenance costs average out at £600 per annum per wagon, and drivers' wages are £8000 per annum.

Because of the forecasts of increased volume of business it is felt that the present fleet is inadequate. The company is undecided whether to buy more vehicles itself, or to lease identical vehicles complete with drivers for £3000 per quarter, inclusive.

It is not company policy to hire and fire, so any extra drivers taken on would be retained at least for the complete year. Leasing contracts, however, can be negotiated on a quarterly basis. Ignoring the cost of borrowing money, what strategy would you advise?

20. *Case Study II. Capital Budgeting at Marvelene Limited**

1. THE PRODUCT

Marvelene Limited is a company manufacturing a synthetic fibre with the trade name *Maron*. The product is supplied to the textile industry mainly for industrial end-use applications. Raw material used for the process is based mainly on oil by-products and the process is in two distinct stages: (i) polymer manufacture, and (ii) fibre manufacture. The product is then despatched to the customers' works.

2. THE PEOPLE

The company was started nine years ago by the present Chairman, Alister Marvel, a Scot in his late fifties who had previously worked in the oil refining industry. The Managing Director is James Hollis, a PhD with considerable experience in the chemical field. Hollis is a contemporary of Marvel's and has been heavily relied on for his technical and economic judgements. The Technical Director is Andrew Lee-Johnson, a Cambridge physicist in his mid-thirties. Lee-Johnson is often in conflict with Hollis when he presents new ventures which Hollis believes to be too revolutionary. The newly appointed Finance Director, Lionel Chamberlin, finds himself increasingly between the devil and the deep blue sea in relation to financial controversies on new projects between Hollis and Lee-Johnson. In the ordinary way, Chamberlin – who is in his late forties – uses all his skill in parrying and side-stepping such encounters, but on this occasion he is pinned down.

3. THE POLYMER PROCESS

A new project has just been tabled by Lee-Johnson for the manufacture of *Maron* polymer by a continuous process. It is contended that the installation of this process will considerably reduce the cost of *Maron* fibre which is meeting strong competition from other man-made fibres in industrial applications. The existing polymer process was pioneered by Hollis in the early days of the company and has generally proved to be sound and reliable. A £40 000 extension to the polymer plant was carried through by Hollis five years ago. With a remaining life of five years the net asset value of this plant is £200 000. Lee-Johnson now proposes that this plant should be written off and replaced by a new and much more simple continuous process with lower operating costs and the same capacity. The plant for the new process would only cost £100 000 and is expected to save £15 000 per annum in operating cost, taking into account depreciation of the new plant over ten years.

---

* Reproduced by kind permission of Mr A. P. Hall, Bradford Management Centre, England.

4. FINANCIAL RULES

There are no written rules explicitly stating under what circumstances capital projects will or will not be accepted by the Board. However, customarily it is understood that the proposer of a new venture should be able to convince his colleagues that the project will achieve net savings (before taxes, but after depreciation and all other costs) equal to or greater than 15 per cent.

5. INTERPRETATION OF RULES

Lee-Johnson's case is that the project is viable from an economic standpoint in that the return on investment is:

$$\frac{£15\,000}{£100\,000} \times 100\% \text{ pa} = 15\% \text{ pa}$$

where the annual savings are £15 000 per annum, and the capital cost of the new project is £100 000.

Hollis, on the other hand, strongly contests the project on economic grounds. In his submission, as the existing plant has a five-year span to run before it is written off, the residual capital value should be added to the new capital required when assessing the new project's profitability. Hollis contends that the proposed project only shows a return on investment of:

$$\frac{£15\,000}{£100\,000 + £200\,000} \times 100\% \text{ pa} = 5\% \text{ pa}$$

where the net asset value of the existing plant is £200 000 as per the company's balance sheet.

6. THE ARGUMENTS

After an inconclusive argument between Hollis and Lee-Johnson, a private meeting is convened by Marvel in an attempt to reach an acceptable settlement before the next Board meeting. Marvel calls in Chamberlin to advise in his official capacity. Each argument is then put forward.

Lee-Johnson: 'We have a new process which will make polymer more cheaply and which will save Marvelene Limited £15 000 per annum, after allowing for depreciation on the new plant over a ten-year life. What we have spent in the past is dead and gone – it is the future decision which is important. Only new capital must be set against real savings when considering the validity of the project. No money spent in the past can now be saved. Even if we have to write off twice the amount on the existing process, the new project will still pay.'

At this point Hollis quickly interrupts: 'That is the essence of your folly. We are here to safeguard the shareholders' money. If we are irresponsibly to write off the capital we are safeguarding on their behalf, we deserve to be out of business. If you delay the project for a few years, however, you might be nearer the mark.'

'Now, gentlemen, let us get down to the basic facts,' interjects Marvel. 'I charge you to go away and bring back your respective cases by 5.00 p.m. today. You, Chamberlin, will take these away tonight with you and have the right answer on my desk by 9.30 a.m. tomorrow or we shall be needing a new Finance Director! But before you go, just let us satisfy ourselves we have *all* the facts we need.'

At this stage Marvel summons the Production Director, Evan Thomas, a Welshman in his late forties. Thomas has been developed over the past five years from a driver of subordinates to a respected leader of a sophisticated team including a small OR group.

Marvel: 'Now, Evan, your OR team have had a few weeks looking at Lee-Johnson's polymer scheme. Can you tell us what their conclusions are?'

Thomas: Indeed we can. The draft report should be available tomorrow, but in essence their conclusions point to two factors that have so far been hidden. In the first place, we consider that Lee-Johnson's polymer will not be quite so reliable in terms of yield as the existing process. This wastage of material might in fact lose us between £500 and £5000 per annum depending on whether we value the scrap at input material cost or at the polymer transfer price. On the other hand, Lee-Johnson's process is a continuous one and considerable savings can be anticipated in the polymer plant inter-process stocks. My boys reckon that compared with the existing process there will be £50 000 less working capital needed to support the new process if it is accepted.'

Hollis: 'Sounds like six of one and half a dozen of the other so far as I can judge, gentlemen.'

Marvel: 'Not so fast. Let us weigh the basic facts, and if you are satisfied you now have said your respective pieces, then Chamberlin is to count them and see how the scales read. Understood?'

7.   THE PROBLEM

The unhappy Chamberlin resigns himself to working late at home on the problem. First he sets out some basic questions. These are:

  (i) Is it correct to compare the operating cost of the new process with the equivalent operating cost of the existing process and then declare the net savings as a ratio of only the new capital required?

 (ii) If the new process is economically viable and capital has to be written off, how should we explain this to the shareholders?

(iii) As there has been one sharp technological change in the method of making polymer, how can we ensure that the new polymer plant, if approved, is written off on a realistic basis, assuming another breakthrough is possible?

(iv) Hollis claims that if we delay the new project until the capital on the existing plant has been written off the new plant may be economically viable at some future date. Will delay help in the circumstances?

 (v) How should I convince either Lee-Johnson or Hollis that he is in error without losing their future confidence?

(vi) The information produced by Thomas from his OR team study throws new light on the problem. How significant is this information, and how should it be related to that already in our possession?

(vii) What lessons should I learn from this controversy to help me in the future in my job?

(viii) In the light of all the information available, what is the correct calculation for setting out the economics of this case?

At 5.00 p.m. Chamberlin collects the promised memoranda in preparation for his late night vigil.

Memorandum I

To: Company Chairman
From: J. Hollis, Managing Director
Re: Proposed *Maron* polymer plant

I set out below my interpretation of the scheme presented to you by Lee-Johnson which in my view should be rejected forthwith.
The facts are:

	Item 1 cost of existing process pa	Item 2 cost of proposed process pa	Item 3 estimated difference pa
	£'000	£'000	£'000
Operating cost	40	15	25
Overhead cost	10	10	–
Depreciation	–[a]	10	10
	50	35	15

Capital to be written off 200[b], New capital 100, Total capital 300

$$\text{Project return as a ratio of capital} = \left\{ \frac{15}{300} \times 100 \right\} = 5\% \text{ pa}$$

[a] I have ignored future depreciation on the existing plant on the assumption that the net value of the existing assets is to be written off and included with capital to be offset against the new scheme.
[b] Assuming the new scheme is rejected (since its return on investment is only one-third of the norm usually acceptable) I should point out that in five years' time the existing plant will be fully written off and there may then be a case for considering an alternative.

Memorandum II

To: Company Chairman
From: A. Lee-Johnson, Technical Director
Re: Proposed *Maron* polymer plant

The figures requested by you are as follows:

	Cost pa (£'000)
Operating cost of existing plant	40
Operating cost of proposed plant	15
Operating cost difference	25
Less depreciation on proposed plant	10
Net potential saving (due to building and operating new plant)	15

	Capital item (£'000)
New capital required for proposed plant	100

$$\text{Prospective return on capital} = \left\{ \frac{15}{100} \times 100 \right\} = 15\% \text{ pa}$$

Other items:
Transfer value of polymer = £120 000 per annum
Overhead cost = £10 000 per annum
Raw materials cost = £13 200 per annum

As these other items are common to *both* existing and new processes they have been omitted from the calculations.

Memorandum III

To: Company Chairman
From: E. Thomas, Production Director
Re: OR investigation into likely operational effects on quality and stocks; proposed polymer plant

Summary of essential facts:

1. Quality

$$\text{Polymer yield} = \frac{\text{Polymer weight output}}{\text{Raw material weight input}} \times 100\%$$

	Existing plant	Proposed plant	Difference
Input (million kg per annum)	1.32	1.37	0.05
Output (million kg per annum)	1.20	1.20	–
Value of polymer output at 10p per kg	£120 000	£120 000	–
Value of polymer scrap at transfer price	£12 000	£17 000	£5 000
Value of polymer scrap at raw material price of 1p per kg	£1 200	£1 700	£500

2. Polymer Stocks (million kg)

	Existing plant	Proposed plant	Difference
Raw material	100 000	100 000	–
Inter-process	600 000	100 000	500 000
Finished stock	100 000	100 000	–
Stock valuation of inter-process stock (at transfer value)	£60 000	£10 000	£50 000

21. *Case Study III. The Midland Hosiery Manufacturing Company Limited (MHM)**

In the Spring of 1964, Mr Albert Jay, the Chairman of the Albert Jay Group of Companies was examining the cost structure of stocking production at the Midland Hosiery Manufacturing Company, a knitwear and hosiery manufacturer and a member of the Albert Jay Group. He realized that the company must reduce costs for producing stockings if it were to remain in business in the face of severe competition from Italy.

The Group consisted of a marketing organization and eight manufacturing companies, and had grown from a small wholesaling firm into the present-day group of companies with an annual turnover of £3.5 million. Mr Albert Jay, although in his sixties, still took a lively interest in the management of the Group and was active in most policy decisions. His attitude towards MHM was summed up by his statement: 'We are in the women's hosiery business to stay. We may not be making money in this business at present, but some day the pendulum will swing the other way. The first function of a business is to survive. That is what we have to do now. The hosiery business is the only unprofitable section of the Group.'

Mr Jay described the United Kingdom hosiery industry as follows: 'There are seven large companies which produce advertised brands of stockings. Their products do not cost substantially more than ours to produce, but sell for ten to fifteen pence [Currency denomination: £1 = 100p (pence)] a pair more at the retail level. Then there are four other smaller companies of about our size which produce good middle-quality stockings. These companies have national distribution but do almost no advertising. Our company sells to chain stores and to small retailers through our own sales force, but we do not spend much on advertising our brand name. In addition to these companies there is a large number of small producers who sell primarily on price as opposed to brand name or quality. It is manufacturers from this group that are at present going out of business due to the low price prevailing in the UK market.'

THE MHM MACHINERY

MHM began manufacturing hosiery in 1931 and was an early producer of seamless hosiery in Great Britain. The company purchased most of its hosiery knitting machinery before the Second World War. This machinery consisted almost entirely of seamless stocking equipment. A seamless stocking knitting machine was a small, rather complicated machine which automatically took yarn from spools and knitted a tube. The tube, which was eventually to become the stocking, was produced with a

* Reproduced by kind permission from Cranfield School of Management and the Cranfield Case Clearing House.

reinforced section for the heel and a finished end at the top. The tube was next inspected and sent to a heat-treating machine where it was treated to prevent damage during handling. The toe was then closed up and the stocking sent to the dyers where it was coloured and shaped, and after another inspection, packaged. (See Exhibit 1 on p. 478.)

The knitting machines were arranged in banks in the plant. A bank consisted of a number of machines which one man (a knitter) would attend. The knitter was responsible for loading the yarn into the machines (each machine held enough yarn for about 24 hours' operation), for making minor repairs and adjustments to the machines, and for collecting and inspecting the stockings as they came out of the machines.

In the spring of 1964, the plant had 187 single-feed and 88 two-feed seamless machines, producing about 5000 dozen pairs of stockings per week. The number of feeds indicates the number of spools of yarn feeding into the machine and, for similar types of machines, was roughly proportional to the output of the machine. The machine arrangements in the plant are shown in Exhibit 2. Normally the single-feed machines were worked for one shift only, whereas the two-feed machines were operated round the clock for three shifts.

DEVELOPMENT OF THE PRESENT COMPETITIVE POSITION

Following the Second World War, when the most popular style was fully-fashioned hosiery (hosiery with a seam in the back) MHM produced seamless stockings and added a false seam at the end of the knitting process in order to utilize its machinery to meet the demand for fully-fashioned hosiery. As demand grew, the company added some fully-fashioned knitting machines.

In 1958–9, however, there was a sudden change in the style of women's stockings. The seamless stocking became, almost overnight, the only style acceptable. With the sudden change in fashion, MHM found itself in a good position to supply the market, as it was one of the few companies with seamless hosiery producing equipment. The company's profits in the period immediately after the fashion shift were very high since competitors were unable to get immediate delivery of seamless producing machinery. Machine producers in the United Kingdom were at that time quoting delivery times of two years because their production was committed to the export markets where the fashion shift to seamless stockings had occurred earlier.

By 1962, however, British competitors had obtained new seamless equipment and the capacity of the industry had reached about double the demand, according to MHM's estimates. The competitors had purchased new machinery which was much faster and more economical to operate than MHM's older equipment. However, MHM was still able to sell all its output.

In the autumn of 1962, during the ordering period for the Christmas rush, Italian-made stockings began to come into the country. The United Kingdom tariff on Italian stockings was 50p per dozen pairs. By autumn 1963, even after tariff payments, Italian stockings were being offered to the retailer at £1.175 per dozen pairs to be sold at retail for 15p per pair. MHM estimated its total factory cost at £1.30 per dozen pairs even for the cheapest grade of stocking. MHM executives, therefore, in concert with other stocking manufacturers considered that the Italians were dumping their excess stockings at an uneconomic price, and they could not continue for long to sell at this knock-down price. (See Exhibit 3 for breakdown of price.) However, as a result of the over-capacity in the industry and the influx of Italian stockings the prices of stockings fell to the levels shown in Exhibit 3.

Mr Jay concluded that total overhead expenses could not be substantially reduced, and that little could be done in the way of reducing raw material costs. Consequently, he thought the only answer to be a reduction of direct labour costs through purchasing faster action machinery and, at the same time, persuading the unions to change their existing attitude to what was considered an acceptable workload.

UNION NEGOTIATIONS

In the summer of 1964, under the threat of lost jobs as a result of competition from cheap Italian imports, the trade union agreed to the new work rules shown in Exhibit 4. Company negotiators had secured an unofficial agreement to perform the workloads shown in this Exhibit. The union, however, demanded a severance pay for any knitters laid off by modernization or by increased workloads. The demands for severance pay were for one week's salary at the highest rate the worker had received during his employment with the company multiplied by his total number of years with the company. Mr Jay hoped that this demand could be reduced. If the worker were retained, he could be put on another job but must receive pay at the old rate if it were higher than the rate for the new job. The knitters, who were the workers who would be made redundant by the new machinery and new rules, were the highest paid workers in the plant (average wage £22 per week). Their average time with the company was 12 years.

MR SUTTON'S INVESTIGATION

Mr Jay thought that labour costs under these new work arrangements and with the availability of faster multi-feed machines, might be substantially reduced. He therefore assigned his assistant, Mr David Sutton, a student at a well known Midlands management school, the task of investigating the purchase of new machinery.

Mr Sutton found that possible choices were limited to the machines described in Exhibit 5. He discovered that the company was paying approximately 50 per cent tax on profits. Divisions other than the stocking division were profitable and losses in one division could be written off against profits in another. The cash position of the Group was very good.

Capital allowances on new machinery, of both British and foreign manufacture, which could be set against taxes were:

> Investment allowance: 30 per cent
>
> Initial allowance: 10 per cent
>
> Annual allowances: 15 per cent

For internal calculations, the machinery would be depreciated by the straight-line method over five years. The equipment was considered to have a life of ten years, although new developments could make the machines obsolete much sooner, often within five years. An example of the taxation allowances on a new hosiery machine is shown in Exhibit 6.

Mr Sutton also found that a bank of machines would be manned in a variety of different ways:

(i) By the existing method each machine dropped the finished stockings into a bucket underneath. The knitters would then collect the stockings and examine them.

(ii) An alternative would be to have an examiner-collector (average wage £20 per week) for each bank who would collect and examine the stocking output, thus relieving the knitter of these tasks.

(iii) A further variation would be to have a collector (£10 per week) collect the buckets for 300 machines and bring them to examiners (£18 per week), each of whom could examine the output of one bank.

(iv) Another method would be to install a downstream system. The machines would then feed directly into a vacuum system which moved the stockings to an examining point at the end of the bank. The system cost about £2000 for each bank and would last about five years. An examiner (£18 per week) could examine the output of the bank.

Exhibit 4 gives the maximum number of machines a knitter was expected to operate under each system, and his wage. There was sufficient space available in the existing plant for the installation of any of these arrangements, or for adding more machines.

Mr Jay was willing to assume, as a first approximation of costs and savings, that the overhead figure of £68 000 per year for the plant would not change, except for the added depreciation. Overheads consisted of:

Needles:	Consumption would probably be slightly reduced with the new machines.
Power:	No significant change expected.
Repairs and conversions:	The number of mechanics could probably not be reduced, although their work load would be lighter with new machines.

Staff
Depreciation
Telephones, etc.,

The old seamless machines could not be converted for other uses and had almost no scrap value. Their book value is shown in Exhibit 7.

Discussion with Mr Jay indicated that a return on new investments of 10 per cent after tax would meet the company's requirements for the use of capital.

MR SUTTON'S RECOMMENDATIONS

In a brief report Mr Sutton suggested that the company should purchase 20 four-feed Bentley Knitting Machines for £30 000, a downstream system for £2000, scrap all 187 single-feed machines, and retain the 88 two-feed machines.

His calculations are summarized in Exhibit 8 and indicate a potential labour cost reduction from 14.65p to 10.72p per dozen pairs of stockings. Mr. Sutton accepted the majority opinion of MHM executives that the American S & W machine was unsuitable as it produced a patch heel.

Exhibit 1 *A schema of the hosiery manufacturing process*

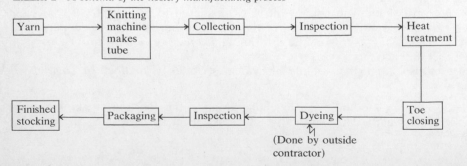

(Done by outside contractor)

Exhibit 2 *Hosiery plant arrangements – Spring 1964*

Single feed machines   Total machines
8 Banks of 16 machines   128
3 banks of 15 machines   45
1 bank of 14 machines   14
                              ———
                               187

Knitting time = 15 minutes per stocking
Maximum output per = 20 dozen pairs (assuming 3 shifts)
  machine per week   (=3740 dozen pairs)
Normal output per = 1250 dozen pairs (1 shift)
  week

Double feed machines
3 banks of 16 machines   48
1 bank of 14 machines   14
2 banks of 13 machines   26
                              ———
                               88

Knitting time = 8 minutes per stocking
Maximum output per = 37 dozen pairs (assuming 3 shifts)
  machine per week   (=3256 dozen pairs)
Normal output per = 3256 dozen pairs (3 shifts)
  week

Summary

	Total machines	Maximum (three shifts)		Normal working (single: 1 shift) (double: 3 shifts)	
		Operators	Output/wk (dozen prs)	Operators	Output/wk (dozen prs)
Single feed	187	36	3740	12	1250
Two feed	88	18	3256	18	3256
	275	54	6996	30	4506

Exhibit 3 *Prices and costs of stockings – spring 1964*

Type of stocking	Retail price per pair (pence)	Price to retailer per dozen pairs	Price ex-factory (i.e., price to wholesalers) per dozen pairs	MHM's factory cost per dozen pairs[a]	% of MHM's sales (by volume)
Advertised	35	£2.775	£2.25		
brands	30	£2.40	£1.975		
MHM's	25	£1.875–£1.525	£1.475	£1.425	40
stockings	20	£1.625	£1.40	£1.375	50
	15	£1.20	£1.20	£1.30	10
Italian	15	£1.175	£1.10		
stockings			(inc. import duty of 50p)		

[a] Mr Sutton estimated costs for the mix (at present volume and with previous labour arrangements) as follows:

	(pence per dozen pairs)		
Yarn	36.25	42.00	47.00
Labour (toe closing and mending)	10.00	11.25	11.25
	46.25	53.25	58.25
Labour (knitting and examining)	15.40	15.40	15.40
Finishing (sub-contracted)	40.80	40.80	40.80
Overheads (based on 5000 dozen pairs per week)	28.00	28.00	28.00
Total cost	130.45	137.45	142.45

Exhibit 4 *Union agreements on workloads and wages*

Old agreement		New official agreement (Summer 1964)		New unofficial union agreement (Summer 1964)	
Number of feeds on machine	Number of machines allowed per operator	Number of feeds on machine	Number of machines allowed per operator	Number of feeds on machine	Number of machines allowed per operator
1	16	1	60	1	60
2	16	2	40	2	40
		4	30	4	40
		6	20	6	30
		8	20	8	20

Old agreement	New official agreement (Summer 1964)	New unofficial union agreement (Summer 1964)
Wages = £22 per week for a knitter who collects and examines	Allowed only with downstream collection system (cost = £2000 for each bank) Wages = £27 per week for a knitting worker, and £18 per week for an examiner for each bank (no collector)	Allowed with bucket collection either by an unskilled examining collector, or by a collector who brings the stockings to the examiner Wages = £30 per week for knitter and either £20 per week for an examiner-collector (one required for each bank of machines) or £18 for an examiner (one required for each bank) and £10 for a collector who collects for 300 machines

Exhibit 5 *New knitting machines available*

Number of feeds on machine	Machine make	Price	Output (dozen of pairs per 24 hours per machine)	Other factors
4	Zodiac (Italian)	£1464	15	Six months' delivery time; believed difficult to obtain spare parts; one machine tested and found to be not very reliable.
6	Maxima (Italian)	£1500	25–30	Six months' delivery time; no test machine available, but a machine in another Leicester plant was rumoured to be having considerable troubles. Sample stockings from Maxima machine showed defects, and in the opinion of MHM executives and store buyers were unsaleable.
4	Uniplet J4Dc34 (Czech)	No quote available	15	MHM could find nobody with experience of this machine.
4	Lonati (Italian)	£1400	20	Output of 15 with conventional heel; not sure if one could sell type of heel produced with higher output. Experience with Lonati twin-feed showed them to be unreliable.
6	Sawo (Italian)	£1400	30	Test machine worked well. Requires more yarn, adding $1\frac{1}{2}$p per dozen to cost.
4	Bentley (English)	£1500	20–22	Bentley factory one mile from MHM plant; service quickly available; delivery from five months. Test machine satisfactory.
8	S & W (American)	£2200	80	Produced a patch heel which executives thought could not be sold in UK.

Exhibit 6 *Example of capital allowances for taxation purposes on new hosiery machines*

Cost = £1000
Technical life = 10 years
Probable economic life = 5 years

		£	WDV (£)	Taxation allowance (£)
Purchase cost			1000	
Year I investment allowance	30%	300		300
initial allowance	10%	100		100
annual allowance	15%	150	250	150
			750	550
Year II annual allowance	15%		112	112
			638	
Year III annual allowance	15%		96	96
			542	
Year IV annual allowance	15%		81	81
			461	
Year V annual allowance	15%		69	69
			392	
Year V balancing allowance if machine is scrapped			392	392
			–	461

Notes:

		Gross	Tax shield @ 50%
Summary of allowances	Year I	£550	£275
	Year II	112	56
	Year III	96	48
	Year IV	81	40
	Year V	461	231
		£1300	£650

Under tax regulations of 1964 the investment allowance is not deducted from the resulting balance. The company is therefore credited with a £1300 allowance for a £1000 investment.

Exhibit 7 *Purchase price and book value of machines in use in spring 1964*

Number of feeds	Machine makes	Number of machines	Total purchase price (£)	Total book value (£)
2	Bentley	32	31 334	26 239
2	Lonati	14	16 207	5 118
2	Lonati	14	16 587	11 635
2	Lonati	28	36 926	32 126
1	Brayson	2	NA[a]	40
1	S & W	6	NA	203
1	S & W	4	NA	108
1	Various	175	NA	175
		275		£75 644

[a] = Not available.

Exhibit 8   *Summary of calculations in Mr Sutton's report of July 1964*

Machines. Scrap the 187 single-feed machines and install 20 four-feed machines, keeping the 88 two-feed machines.

Arrangements. Arrange the machines as follows (all on three shifts, five-day week; assume working five × 7 1/2 hours shift):

Two-feed machines:
2 banks of 40 machines
Knitting time = 8 minutes per stocking
Output = 2960 dozen pairs per week
Four-feed machines:
1 bank of 20 machines with a downstream collection system
Output at $3\frac{1}{4}$ minutes per stocking = 1800 dozen pairs per week
Total proposed output 1800 + 2960 = 4760 per week
Cost saving
Weekly labour cost of present machines:
18 banks of machines, 18 knitters serving as knitters, collectors and examiners
Cost of knitters = £22 × 30 knitters = £660 per week
Output per week = 4506 dozen pairs
Labour cost per dozen pairs for knitting, collection and inspection = 14.65p
Weekly labour cost under proposed system:
3 banks of machines, 9 knitters
Cost = 9 knitters at £27 per week   = £243
Cost = 9 examiners at £18 per week = £162
Cost = 1 collector at £10 per week = £ 10
                                              ————
                                              £415
Output per week = 4760 dozen pairs
Labour cost per dozen pairs for knitting, collection and inspection = 8.72p
Extra depreciation: Calculated as straight line after first year's allowances of 55% × tax rate of $53\frac{1}{2}$% (standard rate of 38 1/2% + excess profits tax of 15%).

$$\frac{20 \text{ machines} \times £1060/\text{machine} + £1410 \text{ (for downstream system)}}{5 \text{ years}}$$

$$= 1.83\text{p per dozen pairs (say, 2p per dozen pairs)}$$

∴ Labour savings less depreciation = 3.93p per dozen pairs

Appendix A. Opportunity Costs and Lagrange Multipliers

The Lagrange multiplier technique is a method for optimizing the solutions to continuous linear and curvilinear functions subject to constraints. This method involves developing a compound function, known as the Lagrange function, comprising the original function to be optimized and the constraining equations. To demonstrate the mechanics of this technique, let us reconsider the optimization problem given in Section 2.10.

The objective function for this problem is to maximize profits according to equation 2.10.3:

$$TP(x) = 80x - 0.5x^2 - 70$$

subject to the constraint that the total cost should not exceed 3070 munits. Since the total cost is given by equation 2.10.2:

$$TC(x) = 0.5x^2 + 20x + 70$$

the following relationship becomes the constraining equation:

$$0.5x^2 + 20x + 70 \leqslant 3070$$

which can be rewritten in the following form and given the identity $\phi(x)$:

$$\phi(x) = 3000 - 0.5x^2 - 20x \geqslant 0$$

When only *one* constraining equation exists, the Lagrange multiplier technique involves the definition of *one* multiplier (λ) such that:

$$\lambda = 0 \quad \text{when} \quad \phi(x) > 0$$

$$\lambda > 0 \quad \text{when} \quad \phi(x) = 0$$

Although these two identities might at first appear formidable, their meaning is quite straightforward and can be likened to the operation of a switch. The former expression suggests that when the constraint is inactive (i.e., $\phi(x) > 0$) then the value for λ is zero, the analogy being that the switch is off. The latter equation suggests that when the constraint is active (i.e., $\phi(x) = 0$) then λ assumes a positive value, the analogy being that the switch is on.

It will be noticed that the multiplicand $\lambda \cdot \phi(x)$ is always zero. If we add this expression to both sides of equation 2.10.3 we get:

$$TP(x) + \lambda \cdot \phi(x) = 80x - 0.5x^2 - 70 + \lambda[3000 - 0.5x^2 - 20x]$$

The left-hand side of this equation is the compound function previously referred to, and is known as the Lagrange function. Since it is a function of two variables, x and λ, it can be represented mathematically by the following symbolic notation:

$$L[x, \lambda]$$

where the L = the fact that we are dealing with a Lagrange function.

Using classic differential calculus we can differentiate this equation to obtain the two following relationships:

$$\frac{\partial L[x, \lambda]}{\partial x} = 80 - x - \lambda x - 20\lambda \qquad (A.1)$$

$$\frac{\partial L[x, \lambda]}{\partial \lambda} = 3000 - 0.5x^2 - 20x \qquad (A.2)$$

The condition which provides the maximum profit, subject to the constraint, is discovered when both equations A.1 and A.2 equal zero*. Hence from equation A.2 we get

$$0.5x^2 + 20x - 3000 = 0$$

Using the normal method of solving quadratic equations we discover that $x = 60$ items per month, which confirms the result given in Table 2.10. Putting equation A.1 to equal zero however provides the following interesting result:

$$\therefore \lambda = \frac{80 - x}{x + 20} \tag{A.3}$$

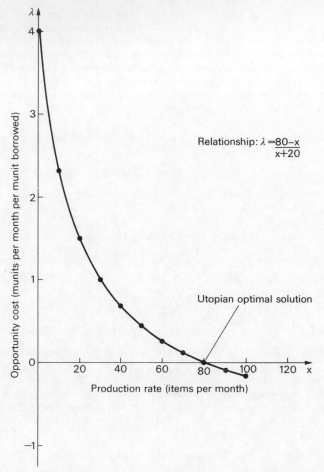

Figure A.1 *Relationship between the opportunity cost and the level of production for a hypothetical problem.*

To interpret this equation properly we need to reconsider the profit relationship for our firm, given by equation 2.10.3:

$$TP(x) = 80x - 0.5x^2 - 70$$

Differentiating this equation with respect to x we find that:

$$\frac{dTP(x)}{dx} = 80 - x \tag{A.4}$$

---

* Providing some important second derivative conditions are met, which are too complex to study here.

which is the numerator of equation A.3. Likewise, if we return to equation 2.10.2 we find that:

$$TC(x) = 0.5x^2 + 20x + 70$$

Differentiating this equation with respect to x we find that:

$$\frac{dTC(x)}{dx} = x + 20 \qquad (A.5)$$

which is the denominator to equation A.3.

Dividing equation A.4 by equation A.5 we arrive at the identity:

$$\lambda = \frac{dTP(x)}{dTC(x)} = \frac{80 - x}{x + 20}$$

By definition, therefore, λ measures the rate of change in the profit of our hypothetical firm with a change in the constraint (in this case the total cost of financing the production of products prior to their sale). In other words λ measures the firm's opportunity cost – the benefit forgone by having limited resources constrain the realization of extra profits. Figures A.1 and A.2 represent two ways of plotting this relationship for λ, and they show the

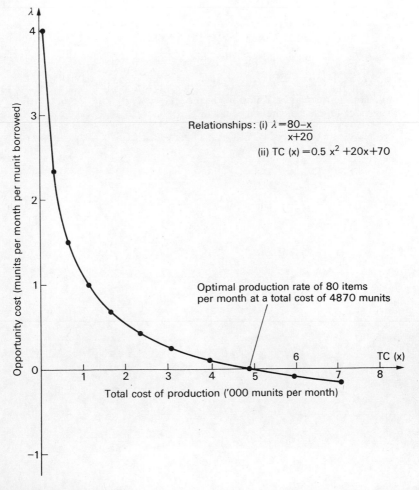

Figure A.2 *Relationship between the opportunity cost and the total cost of production for a hypothetical problem.*

following interesting points:

(i) If the restriction on available cash is so severe as to preclude any production, then, initially, our hypothetical firm should be willing to borrow money and pay up to, but no more than, 4 munits per month per munit borrowed to relax such a severe restriction.
(ii) As the availability of money increases permitting a greater level of production, so the firm should be willing to borrow more money, but pay less interest on it.
(iii) At a production rate of 80 items per month and a total budget of 4870 munits, the firm would no longer be willing to borrow money since this production rate represents the global optimal solution with the greatest possible profit.
(iv) At a production rate in excess of 80 items per month the opportunity cost would be negative, demonstrating that it would be in the firm's interests to reduce production rather than increase it.
(v) With a cash constraint of 3070 munits restricting total production to 60 items per month, the firm should be willing to pay up to 0.25 munits per month per munit borrowed (i.e., 25 per cent per month) to relax the cash constraint.

It should also be noted that this technique applies to other types of optimization problems and can accommodate more than one constraint. For example, if the production rate of our hypothetical firm were also constrained by the availability of 20 skilled workers, each capable of producing two items of product per month, then the following additional constraining equation would apply:

$$\psi(x) = 20 - 0.5x \geq 0$$

so that the Lagrange function would now become:

$$L[x, \lambda_1, \lambda_2] = 80x - 0.5x^2 - 70 + \lambda_1[3000 - 0.5x^2 - 20x] + \lambda_2[20 - 0.5x]$$

and the optimal solution would be found in the normal way, by differentiating the Lagrange function with respect to each of the variables in turn.

Appendix B. The Rudiments of Accounting

Throughout this book we liberally use accounting terminology which might be unfamiliar to some readers and obscure to others unacquainted with the concepts and conventions which form the basis of accounting theory. However, a proper understanding of the terminology is essential to all readers who are, or may be, involved with an investigation of the life-cycle economics of a project, whether it involves a new capital budgeting decision, the optimization of an existing asset or the replacement/retirement of an old asset. This need can only be properly met by studying a text book or by attending an introductory course on accounting. What follows, therefore, is but an attempt to bridge this need by introducing some of the most basic principles and conventions of accountancy.

In most countries, joint stock, limited liability corporations are legally required to publish annually two documents: a statement of their net earnings, and a statement of how their wealth is apportioned between their assets and to whom that wealth is attributable (their liabilities). The first of these documents is known as the profit and loss account, the second is known as the balance sheet. Collectively, they report the historical monetary transactions of the firm in a systematic way. Whenever a receipt, an expenditure of money or the supply or distribution of some product or service is incurred either one or both of these documents incorporates the information of that transaction. As such they constitute the foundation of the information system of any firm, and the logical starting point for anyone wishing to learn about accounting theory and practice.

B.1 THE FORMS OF BUSINESS ENTERPRISE

We have used the word corporation extensively without explaining its meaning, so its definition is now warranted. In legal terms a corporation is taken to be a collection of people associating together for some common purpose, and it is treated in law as though it comprises a *person in its own right*, quite separate from its membership. Whilst having no physical existence as such, corporations have a legal status which permits them to perform legal acts just like real people. With this point in mind, it is important to realize that it is the corporation, not its membership, which owns the property attributable to its name. Indeed, the members have no direct claim to any part of its property by way of their corporation membership.

Three different categories of corporations exist:

(i) Chartered corporations – such as charitable organizations, universities and local government councils,
(ii) Statutory corporations – which are created by the government, and involve, for example, regulatory authorities and nationalized industries, and
(iii) Corporations – created by registration as companies under an Act of Parliament.

Within category (iii) there exist limited and unlimited companies. Unlimited means that the creditors' rights of repayment go beyond the liquidated value of the assets of that company and extend into the private property of its owners. Because of this, such registered corporations are usually confined to organizations involving family estates and other forms of private property holding. The main reason in forming limited liability companies is to permit the owners to limit their personal liability to a controllable amount, possibly with the idea of attracting others to invest in the business also. Two forms of limited liability companies exist.

those limited by guarantee, and those limited by share capital. Examples of the first often involve private schools, in which case the promoters of such a company agree to contribute to its debts up to a limited sum in the event of that firm being liquidated. By contrast, the owners of companies limited by their share capital cannot be called upon to pay more than the *nominal amount* of their shares or so much thereof as might remain outstanding. Once the owners' shares are fully paid up, they bear no further liability in the event of that firm being liquidated.

It is this second category with which we are mostly concerned and it is this category with which one associates the title Registered Joint Stock Company. Two further special features are attributable to such companies whether they are private or publicly quoted. The first concerns the fact that they have to pay corporation tax* and the second that they are obliged by law to publish their balance sheets and profit and loss accounts annually.

Two further points need mentioning. First, only publicly quoted companies have their shares bought and sold on a stock exchange. Second, a company is not permitted to transact business outside the scope stipulated in its Articles of Association. Frequently, such Articles specify quite categorically an upper limit to the debt/equity ratio within which the managers of the company are obliged to work.

B.2   THE BALANCE SHEET

In most countries, any company borrowing money from shareholders is legally required to account for the use to which it puts all borrowed money in the running of its business and in the purchase of assets. The balance sheet is one of the principal documents which serves this purpose. It lists all the company's liabilities and balances their total value against a list of the values† of the firm's assets, at some predetermined moment in time which constitutes the end of the company's financial year. The total value of the firm's assets and liabilities must equate (balance) because the list of assets represents the value of the firm, and any excess in this value over and above its borrowed funds represents the retained profits not distributed to the shareholders as dividends. A skeleton balance sheet listing the more important categories of assets and liabilities, but by no means *all* possible categories, is shown in Table B.2.1 below. Since this information pertains to just one moment in time, it is common practice for companies to quote their equivalent records for the preceding year to give those interested some means of comparison. The well known double-entry book-keeping convention suggests that the assets of the firm should be entered to the left, and the liabilities to the right-hand side of the balance sheet and providing this convention is rigorously applied then accounting book-keeping becomes a very straightforward matter.

A brief description of the entries to this balance sheet follows:

Assets:
 (i) Current assets are those assets normally turned into cash during the process of a year and comprise:
    (a) ready cash, permitting the firm to conduct its business properly, any surplus to requirement possibly being invested on a short-term basis;
    (b) inventories – raw materials, goods-in-progress and finished goods inventories, and
    (c) accounts receivable (trade debtors) – these represent the money owed by customers as a consequence of the firm allowing them trade credit (time to pay their debts).
 (ii) Fixed assets involve those which are not normally liquidated during the process of a year and they include land, buildings, plant, machinery, tools, vehicles, fixtures and fitments and are usually shown at their *original historical cost* (but sometimes at a revaluation) *less* their total accumulated depreciation expense to date.
 (iii) Intangible assets (not shown in Table B.2.1), involving goodwill, trade marks, licensing agreements and patents.

---

* By contrast sole traders and partnerships, which do not constitute corporations but are personal enterprises, are liable for the payment of personal income tax at rates which differ significantly from corporation tax.
† In this context the word value is used loosely, as we shall discover in a while, and must not be confused with the NPV or resale value of such assets.

Table B.2.1 *A skeleton balance sheet*

Current assets (munits)		Current liabilities (munits)	
Cash	100 000	Accounts payable	800 000
Inventories	3 500 000	(trade creditors)	
Accounts receivable		Short-term debt	700 000
(trade debtors)	2 400 000	Taxes payable	600 000
		Dividends payable	400 000
Fixed assets			
Plant, machinery,		Long-term debt	4 000 000
buildings less		Share capital and	
accumulated de-		reserves	
preciation to		800 000 ordinary	
date	9 000 000	shares at 10 munits	
Land	1 000 000	each, fully paid	8 000 000
		Accumulated retained	
		earnings (revenue	
		reserve)	1 500 000
Total assets	16 000 000	Total liabilities	16 000 000

Liabilities:

(iv) Current liabilities – these involve liabilities which require payment during the process of a year and include accounts payable (trade credit received from suppliers), short-term debt (such as bank loans and overdrafts), taxes payable (due to the fact that taxes are usually paid partly in arrears) and dividends payable.

(v) Long-term debt – this involves long-term loans and debentures, which are discussed in Chapter 8.

(vi) Share capital and reserves – these involve ordinary share capital at par (nominal) value* and sometimes preference shares too (although these are less popular nowadays). In addition, this category involves accumulated retained earnings (revenue reserves) arising out of undistributed profits, and sometimes features capital reserves too (these are not shown in Table B.2.1 but they result from selling shares at a price in excess of their nominal value, and from selling assets at a capital gain).

Two special features need mentioning where the construction of a firm's balance sheet is concerned. The first concerns the fact that accounting practice has several different ways of depreciating the value of an asset†, each being valid but equally arbitrary, so every firm has to decide which depreciation policy will best serve its purpose. Accounting depreciation expenses are usually quite different from the capital allowances which are permitted by tax authorities (a matter which is discussed in more detail in Chapter 7.11).

The second point concerns the valuation of a company's inventories (stocks). In the case of raw materials stocks these are normally reported at their original (historical) cost or market value, whichever is the lower. But here again there exist optional ways of dealing with movements in stock levels, the main variants being FIFO, LIFO and AVCO‡. In times of significant price inflation these different variants can have a substantial effect on the ultimate year-end valuation of a company's stocks, thereby affecting the value of its assets and the calculation of its profits.

Although every effort is made to give the shareholders as accurate an account of the value of the company as possible, inevitably much of the balance sheet relates to historical costs.

---

* This means that the shares are fully paid up, but this need not always be the case. Sometimes firms elect to have their shares paid for by instalments.

† These comprise the straight-line, declining balance, sum-of-the-years'-digits, double-declining balance, and the sinking fund methods.

‡ FIFO = first-in-first-out. This is the traditional method which assumes that stock is consumed in the same order it arrives. LIFO = last-in-first-out, and is the complete opposite to FIFO. AVCO = average cost, meaning that the value of the stock in hand and that consumed is taken as the mean average value of the initial stock and all subsequent purchases.

This is a very important point to bear in mind when considering the market value of the firm as a whole or some part thereof. Such a value can be substantially different from the resale value or the valuation based on discounted cash flow principles.

B.3 THE PROFIT AND LOSS ACCOUNT

This is the other principal document legally required from a corporation and it shows the net earnings arising from the running of the business and how such earnings are distributed between the suppliers of debt, the different classes of equity shareholders and the tax authorities. It comprises the following principal entries:

(i) The annual net sales revenue defined as:

Net sales revenue = Gross sales revenue − trade discounts − goods returned − bad debts.
where the gross sales revenue of a single product = the quantity of product sold × its price.

(ii) The cost of materials used – in most industrial situations companies do not consume the exact quantities of their purchased raw materials or component parts each year, but instead their end-of-year inventories reflect any surplus of deficit in usage. Since the stocks in hand at the end of a year represent a part of the wealth of a firm it is very important that such values should nöt be included as expenses in the calculation of a firm's profit, otherwise this would be tantamount to double counting. In effect, therefore, the cost of raw materials used is given by the expression:

Cost of raw materials used = Opening stock value + cost of purchases − closing stock value.

The same situation exists in relation to the work-in-progress and finished stocks, although the cost of goods sold also includes the labour, services and utilities costs needed to translate the raw materials into finished products, along with the overhead costs involved throughout the year.

(iii) Depreciation expenses – this is one overhead expense which must be explicitly stated on the profit and loss account. It represents a notional allowance for the wear, tear and obsolescence involved with the ownership of assets in the realization of revenue. Depreciation expenses do not involve any money transactions, and they are most definitely *not* cash flows. In some circumstances depreciation expenses can realistically represent the deterioration in the resale value of assets, but in others such a relationship is often quite tenuous.

(iv) Interest – in all forms on loan capital. This is not really a part of the cost of manufacture but rather the cost of servicing the money borrowed by a firm. However, for taxation purposes, companies are permitted to deduct such interest charges (not the capital repayment) from their revenue before tax is levied.

(v) Taxation – in many countries tax payments during a particular year are based in whole or in part on profits earned in the preceding year, so the current net of tax cash flow for that company cannot be computed from its profit and loss account. In most industrialized countries the rate of corporation tax approximates 50 per cent, but some countries offer taxation incentives to manufacturers to build new factories to help alleviate unemployment. In these circumstances the calculation of a company's tax liability can be quite complicated (see Chapter 7.11).

(vi) The profit and loss account – this also states the balance of the after-tax profits retained by the company from previous years and the dividends currently payable. Technically speaking, the dividends which a firm can pay in any particular year can exceed its current net after-tax profits by drawing on past retained earnings. Of course, dividends can only be paid if there is money available for that purpose.

The profit and loss statement shows, or at least gives an indication of, the increase/decrease in a firm's wealth during the accounting period. However, it does not show the form in which that change in wealth was made manifest: that comes from a comparison of the firm's balance sheet for the year in question. Furthermore, since the profit and loss account is based on the

Table B.3.1 *A skeleton profit and loss statement*

		(munits)
Sales revenue (net)		
Less		
cost of goods sold		2 500 000
		1 500 000
Operating Profit		1 000 000
Less		
Directors' fees	25 000	
Debenture and loan interest	75 000	
Depreciation on fixed assets	100 000	
	200 000	200 000
Profit before tax		800 000
Less		
corporation tax		300 000
Profit after tax		500 000
Plus		
undistributed profits from previous years		1 500 000
Total revenue reserve available		
for dividend distribution		2 000 000
Less dividend payment		600 000
Accumulated retained earnings		1 400 000

realization of revenues, allowing for trade credit and arbitrary depreciation expenses, it does not represent an account of the firm's cash flow over the accounting period. Instead, the firm's Funds (Cash) Flow Statement is a quite separate document often used for internal management control purposes only.

A simplified example of a profit and loss account is given in Table B.3.1.

B.4 THE RELATIONSHIP BETWEEN THE BALANCE SHEET AND THE PROFIT AND LOSS ACCOUNT

Although the profit and loss account indicates the change in a firm's wealth over the accounting period, it does not necessarily explain the full difference between two sequential balance sheets. For example, if a firm raised more capital, then both the asset and the equity sides of the balance sheet would increase in equal amount quite independently of any trading operations. By the same token, if some debt were repaid then both sides of the balance sheet would decrease in equal amount. As a final example, if some machine was purchased for cash, then the asset cash would decrease and the asset equipment would increase by the same amount, leaving the balance sheet exactly counter-balanced. None of these transactions would affect the computation of the firm's profit and loss account. Only when some resource is consumed in the process of realizing revenues is there a direct link between the assets of the balance sheet and the profit and loss account. Examples in this category involve the payment of cash as wages, the consumption of raw materials, and the depreciation expenses. Furthermore, the only direct connection between the liabilities of the balance sheet and the profit and loss account arises from the fact that retained after-tax earnings constitute the *liability* revenue reserve which is matched by an equal value distributed amongst the firm's various assets. The double-entry book-keeping method of tracing the effects of different transactions through these two quite different yet connected accounts is given in Chapter 13, where it is used to determine the costs of manufacturing a product.

B.5 ACCOUNTING RATIO ANALYSIS

The main sources of loan capital to a company are institutional lenders such as merchant banks, pension funds and assurance firms. To safeguard their interests they normally require rigorous standards of credit worthiness from prospective borrowers, as measured by certain balance sheet cum profit and loss account ratios. To this end a firm is obliged to arrange its financial structure and economic performance to give ratios which fall within prescribed limits if it wishes to obtain a high credit rating which is conducive to borrowing funds for capital expansion. The major ratios of interest are given below:

(i) *The current ratio:* This is the ratio of the firm's current assets to its current liabilities. It is a measure of how readily a firm can meet its short-term obligations if called upon to settle its accounts quickly. Consequently, such a statistic is of special concern to short-term lenders, such as those providing trade credit, banks providing overdrafts, and discount houses lending on trade bills. However, it is also of interest to long-term suppliers of capital because the inability of a firm to meet its short-term debt obligations can result in its bankruptcy, the liquidation of its assets, and the possibility of financial loss to the shareholders and unsecured creditors. Such a situation can occur even when a firm is profitable, and especially when it is fast growing and limited for funds. To ensure against these dangers, it is customary for firms to regulate their current ratios within the range 1.5–2.5 : 1. The preferred ratio depends on the speed with which a firm can convert its short-term assets into cash (i.e., its liquidity). As a firm's current assets become more liquid, so a lower ratio becomes acceptable.

(ii) *The quick or acid test ratio:* This ratio is an extreme case of the previous ratio and recognizes the fact that some of a firm's short-term assets might not be readily convertible into cash at short notice. For example, investment in a subsidiary company cannot be considered a liquid asset because a sudden offering of a large block of its shares would depress its market capitalization considerably. Similarly, stocks of finished goods and raw materials might well be sold, especially at a knocked down price, but such sales might take some considerable time to arrange, and stocks of goods-in-progress might not be saleable at all.

By contrast cash and quoted stocks and shares (not constituting a substantial proportion of some other firm) are highly liquid forms of assets. A less obvious form of liquid asset is the debt outstanding with a firm's customers (its accounts receivable). Quite obviously it is impracticable to expect immediate payment of such debts but they may, of course, be sold to a factor at a discount, thereby realizing liquid funds.

In effect, therefore, the liquid assets of a firm are its cash, securities and the larger part of its accounts receivable and a quick ratio, defined as the quotient of its liquid assets to its current liabilities greater than one would be an indication of its solvency, whereas a ratio of less than one would be tantamount to a declaration of insolvency.

(iii) *The long-term debt to equity ratio:* As the name implies, this is the ratio of a firm's long-term loan and debenture commitments to its total equity, comprising the sum of its ordinary and preference capital and its capital and revenue reserves. It is a measure of the apportionment of risks between the two long-term sources of finance; it is also an indication of the extent to which a firm could fail to realize the book value of its assets in the event of its liquidation and yet be able to honour its debt obligations. For UK and US companies this ratio often approximates 1 : 2, whereas for some Japanese companies the ratio is often higher than 2 : 1. In financial parlance this ratio is referred to as the gearing or leverage ratio.

(iv) *Ratio of long-term interest coverage:* Often referred to as the ratio of times covered, this ratio measures the extent to which a firm's income could fall without jeopardizing the payment of its debt interest charges. Several variants of this ratio exist, some based on total debt, others on long-term debt only, some before tax, others after tax. As a general example, a ratio of 4 : 1 of profits to loan interest would mean that a firm's profits could fall by 75 per cent and still permit the payment of its debt interest obligations. The exact standards required of a firm obviously depends on the variability of its income, and the magnitude of the loan interest.

Several other accounting ratios are also used by the financial world, not so much as means of regulating loans to firms but as measures of their management and economic efficiency.

These ratios include:

(i) Return on capital $= \dfrac{\text{Annual trading profit} \times 100\%}{\text{Total capital employed}}$

(ii) Profit margin $= \dfrac{\text{Annual trading profit} \times 100\%}{\text{Annual sales revenue}}$

(iii) Rate of capital turnover $= \dfrac{\text{Annual sales revenue} \times 100\%}{\text{Total capital employed}}$

(iv) Trade credit given $= \dfrac{\text{Accounts receivable} \times 365 \text{ days}}{\text{Annual sales revenue}}$

(v) Trade credit taken $= \dfrac{\text{Accounts payable} \times 365 \text{ days}}{\text{Annual sales revenue}}$

(vi) Stock cover $= \dfrac{\text{Inventory values} \times 365 \text{ days}}{\text{Annual sales revenue}}$

Several different variants for each of these ratios exist depending on how taxes, depreciation, interest, bad debt, and the various means of valuating stocks are taken into account. These ratios allow one to compare the performance of companies which are considered sufficiently similar to justify such a comparison.

Appendix C. Solutions to the Capital Budgeting Game of Chapter 12

DOCUMENT 1

DCF worked example – expected sales volume

	Year	1	2	3	4	5	6	7	8	9	10	11	12
Sales volume	kt/y	0	0	2.8	5.5	8.7	11.7	14.3	16.3	17.7	18.8	19.9	20
Sales income	$£k$	0	0	700	1375	2175	2925	3575	4075	4425	4700	4875	5000
(=sales volume×250)													
Variable expenditure	$£k$	0	0	398	781	1235	1661	2031	2315	2513	2670	2769	2840
(=sales volume×142)													
Fixed plant capital	$£k$	580	580	–	–	–	–	–	–	–	–	–	–
Overhead capital	$£k$	87	87	–	–	–	–	–	–	–	–	–	–
(=15% plant capital)													
Capital related fixed costs	$£k$	–	–	116	116	116	116	116	116	116	116	116	116
(=10% plant capital/year)													
Operating labour costs	$£k$	–	–	60	60	60	60	60	60	60	60	60	60
Other annual fixed costs	$£k$	–	–	50	50	50	50	50	50	50	50	50	50
Commissioning expenditure	$£k$	–	–	100	–	–	–	–	–	–	–	–	–
Total expenditure	$£k$	667	667	724	1007	1461	1887	2257	2541	2739	2896	2995	3066
Net cash flow	$£k$	−667	−667	−24	368	714	1038	1318	1534	1686	1804	1880	1934
Cumulative net cash flows	$£k$	−667	−1334	−1358	−990	−276	762	2080	3614	5300	7104	8984	10918
Present values at 10% pa	$£k$	−667	−607	−20	276	486	643	738	782	792	758	733	677
NPV at 10% pa	$£k$	−667	−1274	−1294	−1018	−532	111	849	1631	2423	3181	3914	4591

☐ = the overall NPV for this project.

DOCUMENT 2

Parameter values in Document 2:

a	b	c	S	V	T	A	LM	F	$U\ldots$
5.6	1.02	1.73	250	142	20	50	60	1160	0.3, 0.6 or 0.9

$$N = 5.6[(250 - 1.02 \times 142)20U - 110] - 1.73 \times 1160$$
$$N = 11778U - 2623$$

The corresponding answers required for Document 2 are therefore:

$$U = 0.3, 0.6, 0.9$$
$$N = 910, 4444, 7977$$

According to this equation we would need a capacity utilization factor greater than 0.22 to make such a project economically viable. It should also be noted that the NPV for $U = 0.6$ is very close to that calculated by the traditional discounted cash flow analysis shown in the solution to Document 1. In other words, $U = 0.6$ is a good estimate of the particular capacity utilization realized by the expected sales forecast.

494

DOCUMENT 3

Using the relationship:

$$N = a[(S-bV)TU - LM - A] - cF$$

we can explore any change to the project's NPV knowing the change to each of the equation's factors. For example, if the fixed battery limits capital cost F were to change by an amount ΔF, all the other economic factors remaining the same, then the corresponding change to the net present value, denoted ΔN, would be given by:

$$\Delta N = -c\Delta F$$

According to Document 3 the firm could invest in one of two options – a plant constructed of mild steel or one incorporating special materials. We need to assess both to determine the most economic alternative:

Alternative 1 – Use more resistant materials
$\Delta F = 340$, ∴ $\Delta N = -c\Delta F = -1.73 \times 340 = -588$ (independent of U)
Alternative 2 – Replace MS parts when necessary
$\Delta A = 30$, ∴ $\Delta N = -a\Delta A = -5.6 \times 30 = -168$ (independent of U)

Since both options are independent of the yet unresolved value of U, it follows that investment in the plant constructed solely from mild steel would be £420k cheaper than switching to the more expensive plant.

DOCUMENT 4

Comparison of plant alternatives in the light of Document 4

(a) Effect of extra raw materials usage:

$$\Delta V = 4.7$$

$$\Delta N_V = -ab\Delta VTU$$

$$= -5.6 \times 1.02 \times 4.7 \times 20U = -537U$$

(b) Extra clean up stage:

$$\Delta F = 130$$

$$\Delta N_F = -c\Delta F = -1.73 \times 130 = -225 \text{ (independent of } U)$$

Capacity utilization pattern (u)	Poor $u = 0.3$	Medium $u = 0.6$	Good $u = 0.9$
Mild steel plant			
$\Delta N_V = -537U$	−161	−322	−483
$\Delta N_F = -225$	−225	−225	−225
$\Delta N_A = -168$	−168	−168	−168
$\Delta N \ (=\Delta N_V + \Delta N_F + \Delta N_A)$	−554	−715	−876
More resistant materials			
$\Delta N \ (=\Delta N_F)$	−588	−588	−588
Advantage in using more resistant materials	−34	127	288

Conclusion: more resistant materials are preferable providing $U > 0.37$.

DOCUMENT 5

In view of the marketing department's forecast, we shall build in corrosion-resistant materials. In addition to the quantifiable economic advantage, use of resistant materials of construction avoids unpredictable breakdowns, interruptions in production, loss of product, distortion of the maintenance load and, possibly, the need to build up stocks of product.
Parameter values after Document 5:

a	b	c	S	V	T	A	LM	F	U
5.6	1.02	1.73	250	142	20	50	60	1500	0.6

$$\therefore N = 4444 - 588$$
$$= 3856$$

DOCUMENTS 6 AND 7

Consider the value of the extra sales to USA. In this case no extra labour is involved, so LM and F are zero. The appropriate parametric values are therefore:

a	b	c	S	V	T'	U	A	LM	F
3.5	1.02	1.48	160	142	5	0.9	20	0	0

$$N \text{ (export)} = 3.5[(160 - 1.02 \times 142)5 \times 0.9 - 20]$$
$$= 169$$

So the extra business appears profitable, despite the much lower selling price of £160/tonne.

But Document 7 brings the sad news that freight charges would decrease the net selling price by £20/tonne i.e., the contribution $(S - bV)$ would drop from £15/t to $-£5/t$, and the extra NPV would fall from £169 to $-£146$. In view of these extra charges, this export business is no longer profitable. Faced with this situation we would ask marketing department either to test the USA market at £170+/tonne, or explore ways of reducing the export charges. We would also ask them to consider exporting to other markets.

DOCUMENT 8

In light of the conversion optimization we now have the following parametric values:

a	b	c	S	V	T	U	A	LM	F
5.6	1.02	1.73	250	126	20	0.6	50	60	1460

So the NPV would increase to $5022k$ if such an R & D innovation were built into the design of the process.

We now need to re-evaluate the economic merits of exporting to the USA, with the following values:

a	b	c	S	V	T'	U	A	LM	F
3.5	1.02	1.48	140	126	5	0.9	20	0	0

We see that the NPV due to the export business is now £111k because of the considerable decrease in the unit variable production costs. We shall refer to this as the marginal business to be pursued *only if* the investment project is economically justified *as a whole*.

DOCUMENTS 9, 10 AND 11

Prior to this news, the forecast NPV of Project 'UNOWAT' was £5022k.

Alternative ways of countering the threat

Through R & D project. The NPV will decrease due to the intended capital modification costing £100 000 by $c\Delta F$ i.e., by £173k. So the expected value (EV) of the project is given by:

$$EV = EV \text{ (given success)} + EV \text{ (given failure)}$$
$$= (5022 - 173) \times 0.9 + 0 \times 0.1 = £4364k$$

To obtain this expected value we would have to spend up to £40 000 on a pilot plant, so that the life-cycle costs of the pilot plant would be $c\Delta F$ (pilot plant) i.e., £69k, and we would also have to spend £45 000 on three chemists. Whether or not Project 'UNOWAT' should bear their cost is a moot point since effectively they are already paid for. However, they represent an opportunity cost, so their cost must be included in the economics for Project 'UNOWAT'.

The overall expected value of the R & D alternative with a 90 per cent chance of success is therefore:

$$4364 - 69 - 45 = £4250k$$

With an 80 per cent chance of success, however, it is

$$(5022 - 173) \times 0.8 - 69 - 45 = £3765k$$

Reduction in selling price to meet threat. The export section of the marketing department predict a £30/t reduction in NSP will hold market $\Delta N_S = -aTU\Delta S$.

$$\therefore \Delta N_S = -5.6 \times 20 \times 0.6 \times 30 = -2016,$$
$$\therefore N_2 = 5022 - 2016 = 3006$$

Buy licence from West German firm. This is likely to cost:
(a) £50k for licence,
(b) £200k for plant modifications,
(c) £5/t royalty, and
(d) £4/t increase in variable cost.
$$\Delta N_L = -50$$
$$\Delta F = 200$$
$$\Delta N_F = -1.73\Delta F = -346$$
$$\Delta V = 9$$
$$\Delta N_V = -abTU\Delta V = -5.6 \times 1.02 \times 12 \times 9 = -617$$
$$N_3 = 5022 - 50 - 346 - 617 = 4009$$

Abandon the project now. If done before the construction gets underway then $N_4 = 0$.

Abandon the project after four years' operation. Since $U = 0.6$, we can use the expected sales forecast of Document 1. The only difference between current information and that used for Document 2 is that the variable costs have dropped to £126, and the capital cost is now £1460k.

Reworking the calculations of Document 2 we now get:

Year	1	2	3	4	5	6
Sales (k tonnes)	0	0	2.8	5.5	8.7	11.7
Sales income (£k)	0	0	700	1375	2175	2925
Variable costs (£k)	0	0	353	693	1096	1474
Fixed capital	730	730	–	–	–	–
Overhead capital	110	110	–	–	–	–
Capital related fixed costs	–	–	146	146	146	146
Annual fixed costs	–	–	50	50	50	50
Labour	–	–	60	60	60	60
Commissioning expenditure	–	–	100	–	–	–
Net cash flow	−840	−840	−9	426	823	1195
Cumulative net cash flow	−840	−1680	−1689	−1263	−440	775
Present Values at 10% pa	−840	−764	−7	320	560	741
NPV at 10% pa	−840	−1604	−1611	−1291	−731	10

This table shows that the project would just provide a discounted breakeven after four years' operation.

Conclusion

The best of the currently available courses of action would therefore appear to lie with our own R & D effort providing we can get greater than 90 per cent success.

DOCUMENTS 12 AND 13

Change in factor b

Reference to Table 1 shows that due to seasonality, factor b increases from 1.02–1.09, if the appropriate interest rate (cost of capital) is 10 per cent per annum.

Change in factor a

Since we are now measuring the NPV from the beginning of Year 2 (not Year 1) the revenues from the sale of UNOWAT are closer by one year, so the discount factors are now too small. We need to increase these factors by $(1+r) = (1.1)$. Since a was 5.6 (Table 1), it now becomes $5.6 \times 1.1 = 6.2$ (not in Table 1).

Change in factor c

This is much more difficult to determine. Let us look carefully at the values of c given in Table 3:

The values of c_1 are readily explained, 1.18 being the undiscounted factor and the other values of c_1 being calculated by the expression:

$$c_1 = \frac{0.59}{(1+r)^{0.5}} + \frac{0.59}{(1+r)^{1.5}}$$

The values of c_2 are given by the expression:

$$c_2 = 1.18 \times \frac{d}{100} \times \sum_{i=2}^{n+1} \frac{1}{(1+r)^i}$$

Hence if $d = 10$, $n = 10$ years and $r = 0\%$ pa then

$$c_2 = 1.18 \times \frac{10}{100} \times 10$$

$$= 1.18$$

If $d = 10$, $n = 10$ years and $r = 10\%$ pa then

$$c_2 = 1.18 \times \frac{10}{100} \sum_{i=2}^{11} \frac{1}{(1.1)^i}$$

$$= 1.18 \times \frac{10}{100} \times \begin{bmatrix} 0.83 + 0.75 + 0.68 + 0.62 + 0.56 + 0.51 \\ + 0.47 + 0.42 + 0.39 + 0.35 \end{bmatrix}$$

$$= 0.118 \times 5.58$$

$$= 0.66$$

Likewise, if $d = 10$, $n = 5$ years and $r = 10\%$ pa then

$$c_2 = 1.18 \times \frac{10}{100} [0.83 + 0.75 + 0.68 + 0.62 + 0.56]$$

$$= 0.118 \times 3.44$$

$$= 0.41$$

If half the capital cost of the plant has already been spent (i.e., is a sunk cost) then the new value of c_1 (undiscounted) is given by:

$c_1 = 0.5$ (for the half of the capital expenditure still to be spent)

$\quad +0.05$ (for the half of the overhead cost yet to be spent)

$\quad +0.08$ (for the commissioning expenditure).

Therefore c_1 (undiscounted) $= 0.63$.

As c_2 is given by:

$$c_2 = 1.18 \times \frac{10}{100} \begin{bmatrix} 0.91 + 0.83 + 0.75 + 0.68 + 0.62 + 0.56 \\ + 0.51 + 0.47 + 0.42 + 0.39 \end{bmatrix}$$

$$= 0.118 \times 6.14$$

$$= 0.72$$

Therefore $c = \dfrac{0.63}{(1.1)^{0.5}} + 0.72$

$$= 0.60 + 0.72$$

$$= 1.32$$

As a consequence of Documents 12 and 13, the capital cost of Project 'UNOWAT' is now £1700k i.e.,

$$F = 1460 + 150 + 90 = 1700$$

The relevant factors for the project, as of the beginning of Year 2 are therefore:

a	b	c	S	V	$A + LM$	F	T	U
6.2	1.09	1.32	250	132	120	1700	20	0.6

$\therefore N = 4907.$

Hence the NPV has risen despite the increase in costs. This has occurred because half the capital cost has already been spent.

If instead of developing our own R & D, we had opted for the West German process, the relevant factors would have been:

$$V = 126 + 5 + 4 = 135$$

$$F = 1460 + 200 = 1660$$

so that with the following values:

a	b	c	S	V	$A + LM$	F	T	U
6.2	1.09	1.32	250	135	110	1660	20	0.6

we would get $N = 4779$.

It would appear that we made the right decision in not opting for the West German process, providing we can sell the forecast sales volumes at the stated prices and costs.

DOCUMENT 14

(i) The passage of another year has further increased a (from 6.2 to 6.8) and further reduced c (from 1.32 to 0.8).
(ii) To evaluate the opportunity to export to the EEC:

Without export:

a	b	c	S	V	$A + LM$	F	T	U
6.8	1.09	0.8	250	132	120	1700	20	0.6

$\therefore N = 6483$

With export:

a	b	c	S	V	$A + LM$	F	T	U
6.8	1.09	0.8	250	132	220	1700	20	0.9

$\therefore N = 10133.$

Hence we would wish to develop the EEC market despite the rather high sales cost.
(iii) To evaluate the possible purchase of intermediate product C:
At £135 per tonne against £132 per tonne the purchase of Intermediate C looks uneconomic, but it would allow us to sell off the first section of our plant and thereby save maintenance expenses.
The reduction in NPV due to an increase in material cost would be:

$$\Delta N_V = -ab\Delta VTU = -400$$

But savings on the capital related annual costs would be:

$$\Delta N_{FR} = 0.8 \times 840 = 672$$

and the scrap value of the plant would be £20k.
The net effect of buying C = $672 + 20 - 400$
$$= £292k$$

Hence, it is marginally attractive to purchase Intermediate C from 3I's, so we would recommend to our Board that we seek a long-term contract with 3I's. However, not wishing to be completely dependent on one supplier for the basic raw material for a new product, we would ask our purchasing department to investigate the world situation on Intermediate C. We would also ask the marketing department whether we should compete with 3I's in the Intermediate C market.

DOCUMENT 15

Factor U cannot be more than 0.1 for the sale of Intermediate C because it is already 0.9 for the sale of Product 'UNOWAT'. Hence the factors for this case are:

a	b	c	S	V	T	U	A	LM
6.8	1.09	0.8	101	95.9	22	0.1	0	0

$\therefore N = -53$

This business would be unprofitable so we would not recommend manufacturing Intermediate C for sale but have still to decide whether or not to make or buy Intermediate C for our own internal use.

Appendix D. Solutions to the Case Studies

To maintain the size of this book within reasonable bounds, the following solutions have *not* been prepared according to the format suggested on page 421. Instead, only their major highlights are given. It should also be realized that there exist no right or wrong solutions to such cases, although there do exist resonable and unreasonable ones. Only the most reasonable solutions follow.

I BRANWELL PLASTICS

Definition of the problem

In this case the most fundamental problem currently facing the firm is how best to deploy its existing resources.

Definition of the issues

Several major issues are involved here:

(i) What type of firm does Branwell want to be – a mass producer or a specialist producer of boat hulls?
(ii) What is the company's corporate policy regarding the use of different types of technology?
(iii) What is its labour policy regarding different forms of shift working and forced redundancy?
(iv) What future threats and/or opportunities could develop in the market which would force Branwell to change its strategy?

Assumptions

To answer this case satisfactorily we need to make the following assumptions:

(i) Branwell intends to stay in the boat building business in the foreseeable future.
(ii) Although seasonal in nature, nevertheless there exists a strong secular increase in the sales of small family boats. (This was certainly true in 1962.)
(iii) Branwell employees and their respective union(s) would accept working anti-social shifts if they were paid the appropriate wage differential.
(iv) Likewise, such employees and their union(s) would accept redundancies if the severance conditions were fair and reasonable.
(v) Branwell's market research and industrial engineering data is reasonably accurate.

Solution

The basic reason for the lower than expected profitability of Factory C results from its under-utilization and the restriction of a two-shift production policy. If we accept that a reasonable objective for any firm is to make as much profit as possible then it follows that such a profit is given by the relationship:

Total profit = Total sales revenue − total overhead costs − total operating costs

At a sales price of £100 per hull, Branwell's total sales revenue is £70 000 per annum, and the total overhead costs for all three factories is £12 500 per annum. The following profit relationship therefore holds:

Total profit = 57 500 − total operating costs.

At its current market price of £100 per hull it therefore follows that maximizing profit is synonymous with minimizing total operating costs. The optimal division of the present output level is therefore realized by allocating output to those factories and shifts with the cheapest marginal cost, in which case the following allocation, total profit and profitability prevail:

Factory	Shifts	Output (hulls per annum)	Unit price or marginal cost (£ per hull)	Factory operating costs (£pa)	Total revenue (£pa)
B & C		700	100	–	70 000
C	1 & 2	400	50	20 000	
C	3	160	55	8 800	
B	1 & part of 2	140	62.50	8 750	
		Total operating cost		37 550	37 500
		Total contribution to profit and o/h cost			32 450
		Total profit			19 950
		Total fixed capital			125 000
		Total working capital			70 000
		All capital			195 000

$$\% \text{ profitability} = \frac{19\,950 \times 100\%}{195\,000} = 10.2\% \text{ pa}$$

By these means Branwell could raise its overall profit by £2450 per annum, and its overall profitability by 1.2 per cent per annum.

The natural outcome of such a redistribution in shift working would be job severance. We do not really know how many jobs are at risk, but based on an estimated wage and fringe benefit allowance of £1500 per operative, a conservative estimate would be 4–5 jobs. We have no way of knowing what resistance there would be to such forced redundancies since the attitudes of the operatives and any union representatives would depend very much on Branwell's industrial relations record and the competence of its management, as well as on other factors such as the desire by some operatives for early retirement or the chance of starting up their own private business financed in part or whole by redundancy payments. Quite obviously Branwell's management would need to consider this matter closely before embarking on any decisive action. They would need to balance the risks involved, possibly by hostile industrial action and the strategic benefits accruing from a successful implementation of such a scheme. On the basis of the evidence provided, it would seem reasonable for such a scheme to meet with approval, especially if Branwell's management were willing to forgo the next few years' extra profits in order to finance a generous severance agreement.

Exactly what should be done with Factory A is quite another matter which very much depends on Branwell's R & D and product strategy. If it were decided to produce other plastic and/or fibreglass products, either for the marine industry or otherwise, then Factory A could be ideal for such R & D work and prototype developments. In this respect the building could be of strategic importance, and if such opportunities existed then it would be prudent to deploy some of the otherwise redundant operatives on such work. Effectively, therefore, the extra profit of £2450 would be seen as a possible means of financing much needed R & D work thereby helping to secure the company's long-term future. Alternatively Branwell could lease out Factory A or even sell it, and in both cases the monies realized could be put to profitable use.

The re-allocation of production would also involve other strategic implications, especially if Factory A were sold. It would marginally reduce the firm's production potential by 15 per cent, but this would still permit a 50 per cent increase over and above its existing sales level. Furthermore, it would reduce flexibility and possibly increase the risk of a production stoppage due to fire, explosion or sabotage. On the other hand, it would permit the company to concentrate its managerial talents on the proper professional control of its major capital asset.

The results of the firm's market research survey are shown by the three demand curves of Figure D1.1. Due to the paucity of data it is obvious that such demand curves have to be used cautiously, especially as they suddenly become quite price inelastic above £125 per hull. The corresponding total sales revenue curves are shown by Figure D.2.1, along with the total variable cost profile for Factories C and B only, it being assumed that production of hulls would cease at Factory A. The distance between the total sales revenue curves and the total variable cost curve gives the contribution to profit and overhead costs and it will be noticed that this is maximized according to the following sales–price relationships:

| | Production (hulls per annum) | | |
Factory	Average year	Good year	Bad year
B	52	140	0
C	560	560	560
B & C	612	700	560
Optimal price	£106.50	£106	£103.50

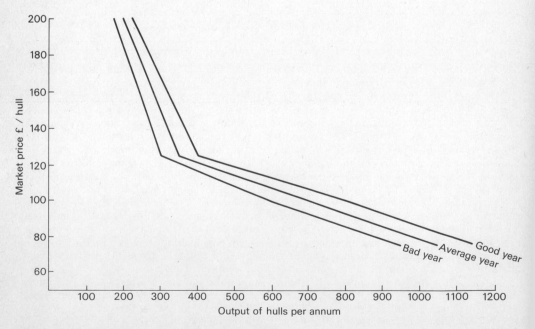

Figure D.1.1 *Demand curves for Branwell boat hulls.*

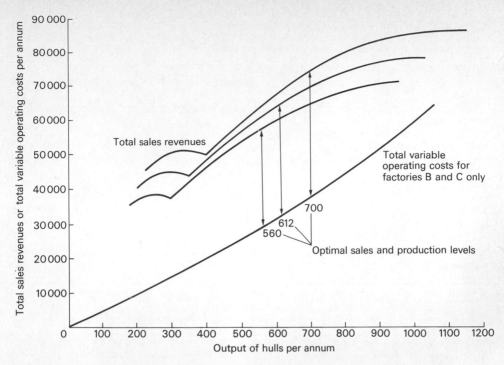

Figure D.2.1 *Evaluating Branwell's marketing strategy.*

From this evidence, it would therefore appear that the firm's market strategy is not quite optimal, and a small price increase of between £3–6 per hull is justified. Although some readers might consider such an analysis unfounded, nevertheless its elegance lies in the fact that such a pricing policy would be truly optimal and little affected by vacillating sales. Furthermore, such a small range of optimal prices is sufficiently close to its existing price structure to be easily accommodated and accepted by wholesalers and dealers.

The general philosophy of this solution therefore has been one of galvanizing the company's assets into a form well suited for profitable *expansion*. By stark contrast a mechanical treatment of the data could recommend the closure of both Factories A and C, and an increase in the price per hull to £200. Such a strategy could realize profits of £25 500 and a profitability quotient of 62.5 per cent per annum. Such a possibility is not seriously considered here for several reasons:

  (i) It does not reflect the fact that the majority of Branwell's £12 500 per annum overhead costs are fixed by factors outside of the number of factories employed, so this profit statistic could be in error by £5000–10 000 per annum.
 (ii) Such a price change would be quite traumatic and unsettling to traders and dealers.
(iii) Such a strategy could be tantamount to retrenchment, which might well be justified in a dying market or if the company decided to specialize production and differentiate its product from that of other manufacturers, but without these factors such a strategy could put the company at risk.

II MARVELENE COMPANY

Definition of the problem

In this particular case the problem is relatively simple, Should the company install the new polymer plant and, if so, when?

Definition of the issues

There are several major issues involved with this case:

(i) Should Marvelene remain in the fibre business?
(ii) What will be the future influence of competitive pressure on sales of *Maron* and its profits?
(iii) At what rate, and with what effect, will technological innovation occur which could affect *Maron* sales?
(iv) What is the firm's corporate profit objective, and what criterion is best suited to measure the profit contribution of alternative projects?
(v) Are there any legal, ethical, moral or social implications involved with the proposed project which could cause its rejection?
(vi) Are there any synergistic benefits accruing from the proposed new project?

Besides these major strategic issues there are a host of tactical issues, many of which Chamberlin has already reflected upon.

Assumptions

As with all case studies, not every conceivable piece of background information is provided in order to restrict the size of the case to reasonable limits, and to concentrate our attention on main points of principle. In this case we need to make the following assumptions:

(i) Marvelene intends staying in the fibre market so long as it remains profitable in the long term and to that end would contemplate subsidizing a possible loss from *Maron* production for a year or two, either from its other businesses or by way of a bank overdraft, if necessary.
(ii) Consistent with (i) above, Marvelene will continue to operate the polymer plant provided it can make an adequate profit at the transfer price of 10p per kg, which is the price Marvelene reckons it could readily buy in polymer from other manufacturers.
(iii) It is also assumed that the downstream fibre plant produces an adequate profit at a transfer price of 10p per kg of polymer.
(iv) The new polymer plant can be built adjacent to the existing plant and its operations phased into the existing process without undue disruption in the production of *Maron*. Furthermore, it is assumed that such a project would meet all regulatory requirements and trade union and employee approval.
(v) Funds of £100 000 can be raised, and the cost of capital to the company is either known or can be calculated.

Solution

Existing cash flow. The net cash inflow of the existing polymer plant before tax and depreciation is £56 800 per annum derived from:

		£pa
Sales revenue		120 000
Operating costs	40 000	
Raw materials costs	13 200	
Overhead costs	10 000	
	63 200	
		£56 800

It should be noted that both Hollis and Lee-Johnson omitted the raw materials costs on the incorrect assumption that such costs would be common to both the existing and the proposed plants.

Since we have no further information regarding tax payments and allowances, we have to assume that this annual cash flow is sufficient to warrant Marvelene's continued production of polymer. According to the statement '*Maron* fibre is meeting strong competition from other man-made fibres in industrial application', *Maron* might have to sustain a price reduction in the near future. A 10 per cent reduction in price of polymer would reduce the annual cash inflow by £12 000, bringing about a 21 per cent reduction in the polymer plant's annual cash flow. This demonstrates how price sensitive this business is to competitive pricing, and it emphasizes why the firm should minimize its costs to withstand such pricing pressures.

Net asset value. The £200 000 net asset value is the value of the existing polymer plant as written down in the company's balance sheet. This is a notional value derived through the use of conventional accounting practice using the concept of depreciation explained in Appendix B. This value will eventually reduce to zero if the polymer plant remains in existence, even if it is shut down. According to Hollis, we are led to believe that a zero net asset value will be realized in five years' time, suggesting that the annual constant rate of depreciation for this plant is £40 000 per annum. However, this £200 000 bears no relationship to the real value of the plant as dictated by market forces. Excepting some taxation implications which are discussed in detail in Chapter 19.5, the current plant's value is decided by the greater of two sums – its resale price or the amount of money it generates producing polymer. The original capital cost of the polymer plant is a sunk cost which is irretrievable and as such is completely irrelevant to any future decision outside of the taxation considerations.

The real value of the existing polymer plant. The existing plant could be sold either as scrap or to other firms wishing to buy it in whole, or part. Usually, such process plants, especially if they are relatively old, are of little use other than as scrap material and their scrap value is usually only just sufficient to cover their dismantling charges.

However the plant is currently generating a net cash flow of £56 800 per annum. We do not know how long this will last since this will depend on competitive pressures and the effects of technological innovation. The net present value criterion is the best means of evaluating these future cash flows. If we assume that the cost of capital to this company is 10–15 per cent per annum and these cash flows will prevail for the next 5–10 years, then the net present value of this plant is given by the expression:

$$\text{NPV}(r, n) = 56\,800 \sum_{i=1}^{n} \frac{1}{(1+r)^n}$$

with the following results:

	NPV (munits)	
	100r (% pa)	
n (years)	10% pa	15% pa
5	215 317	190 402
10	349 011	285 066

Since all these values are considerably greater than any conceivable scrap value it would seem reasonable to continue operating the existing plant providing there is no better process.

The economics of replacement. Outside of the implications of reduced working capital, the projected net annual cash flow accruing to the new process would be £81 300 derived from:

Sales Revenue		120 000
Operating Costs	15 000	
Raw Materials Costs	13 700	
Overhead Costs	10 000	
	38 700	
		£81 300

The corresponding NPVs to those given above and allowing for the £100000 capital investment (but again neglecting all taxation effects) are given by the following expression:

$$\text{NPV}'(r, n) = -100\,000 + 81\,300 \sum^{n} \frac{1}{(1+r)^n}$$

with the following results:

	NPV (munits)	
	100r (% pa)	
n (years)	10% pa	15% pa
5 years	208 190	172 530
10 years	399 553	308 025

On this basis it would appear that the following economic preferences apply:

	Best plant	
	100r (% pa)	
n (years)	10% pa	15% pa
5 years	Existing plant	Existing plant
10 years	New plant	New plant

In this particular case we would find ourselves *indifferent* between these two projects on an economic basis if they both only operated for 5.5 years (if the cost of capital was 10 per cent per annum) or 6.8 years (if the cost of capital was 15 per cent per annum).

One vital question which has to be answered therefore is, How long could both projects operate and still make adequate profits? It is conceivable that the costs of maintaining the existing plant could accelerate relative to the proposed plant within the next few years, and a time could arrive when it would become too expensive to operate, in which case investment in the new plant now could be justifiable. However, such ideas are speculative. What is needed here is expert opinion not guesses!

The effects of working capital. One way of realizing the value of the capital locked up in the existing inter-process stocks is to cease purchasing raw material for $4\frac{1}{2}$ months prior to commissioning the new project. Alternatively, one could reduce such purchases over a longer period depending on the attitude of suppliers and the technical feasibility of operating the existing plant with less inventory for a while. Such a diminution in stock would reduce cash outflow by £5000 and operating costs by approximately £8000 in a calendar year. In effect, therefore, the working capital released could reduce the capital cost of the project to £87 000 at best, making us indifferent between the two projects if their economic life was 4.4 years (at a cost of capital of 10 per cent per annum) and 5.5 years (at a cost of capital of 15 per cent per annum).

A partial solution. Since the preceding comparative analysis is effectively based on the differences between the economic merits of the two projects, it follows that the results will hold true even if competitive pressures forced down the price of *Maron* into a loss-making position, at which point Marvelene would have to consider abandoning its production. The advisability of the new process therefore hinges on:

(a) the likely rate of technological innovation and the possibility that another more economic alternative will be made available to Marvelene within the next 4–5 years,
(b) the nature, effect and timing of competitive pressure,
(c) product strategy considerations, such as the importance of fibre production in itself as well as its importance to Marvelene's portfolio of products, and
(d) R & D strategy considerations, such as the need to develop products and processes continually to reduce their costs and improve their qualities in the long term.

On the basis of the evidence provided, it would therefore appear that investment in the new project is marginally justified, providing no other more lucrative project exists which would compete for the company's limited cash resources. Any positive cash flow accruing from the sale of the old plant would favour investment in the new plant since it would increase the NPV of the replacement alternative. Likewise the new project *could* benefit from taxation considerations as previously described in Chapter 19.5.

If the old plant were replaced this matter would need reporting to the shareholders. The explanation would be that an economic alternative had been found which would increase the firm's wealth, as measured by its NPV, with the promise of dividends greater than would otherwise be forthcoming in the future. However, the firm would need to write down the net asset value of the old plant to zero, thereby reducing its assets and retained earnings at the stroke of a pen.

The major lessons. The central theme of this case study concerns the principle of sunk cost and the need to compare economic alternatives using proper appraisal techniques and criteria. In this respect, therefore, it would appear that Chamberlin is not doing his job properly. If he laid down a proper procedure for evaluating projects it is conceivable that the friction between his colleagues might be reduced.

III   MIDLAND HOSIERY MANUFACTURING (MHM) COMPANY

Definition of the problem

The basic problem facing MHM is how best to reduce its manufacturing costs, possibly using more flexible manning schemes and investment in more productive machinery.

Definition of the issues

The most fundamental issue concerned with any investment in capital plant involving the fashion industry is the expected lifespan of its products, there being a strong tendency for short but recurring fashion life-cycles. MHM must be acutely aware of such a problem in that seamless stockings have already spent five years of their cycle, suggesting, perhaps, that another competitive fashion is imminent.

Assumptions

The only assumption which needs to be made is that the MHM Group's tax payments are large enough to absorb the tax shield accruing from any investment in new plant and machinery. Otherwise, most of the other important points of policy have already been made explicit by Mr Albert Jay.

Solution

Defining the base case. Besides some errors and inconsistencies in his economic calculations, the single most glaring error inherent in Mr Sutton's study is his failure to define the standard means for comparing the various alternatives available to MHM. In his calculations he compares one alternative producing 4506 dozen pairs of stockings per week (abbreviated here to dps/week) with another producing 4760. This is quite unacceptable. Alternatives must be compared on some common standard – a base-case must be defined. Two pieces of evidence point to such a basis. According to Jay, the firm produces approximately 5000 dps/week. Furthermore, the fact that the labour (knitting and examining) cost is 15.4p/dp (Exhibit 3) as opposed to 14.65p/dp (Exhibit 8) corroborates this point, since their basic difference lies in the premium rate MHM pays for overtime. This can be calculated as follows:

£ per annum

(a) Total labour (knitting and examining) cost of producing 5000 dp/wk
    @ 15.4p/dp for 50 weeks.   38 500
(b) Standard cost of producing 4506 dp/wk is £660 (30 knitters @ £22 per week).   33 000
(c) Therefore additional 494 dp/wk are produced during overtime working and cost   5 500
(d) The overtime premium rate is therefore given by:

$$\frac{5500 \times 100}{494 \times 50 \times 14.65} = 1.5$$

or 50 per cent more than the standard rate.

The base-case, therefore, is defined by a production rate of 5000 dp/wk, an overtime premium rate of 50 per cent over the standard wage rate, and a total knitting and examining cost of £38 500 per annum.

The new unofficial agreement. Although it might seem illogical to consider the unofficial agreement when there already exists an official one, we really need to expose the separate effects of flexible working and investment. This is made possible only by the unofficial agreement, in which case the following costs are incurred:

	Standard weekly cost (£)	Standard[b] production (dps/wk)	Annual cost (£) to produce 5000 dps/wk
Single-feed machines 180[a]-off, single shifts;			
3 knitters @ £30	90⎫	1203	7 500
3 examiners @ £20	60⎭		
Double-feed machines 80[a]-off, three shifts;			
6 knitters @ £30	180⎫	2960	15 000
6 examiners @ £20	120⎭		
Totals	450	4163	
		Standard working cost	22 500
		Overtime working cost	6 786
		Total cost	29 286

[a] The extra seven single-feed and eight double-feed machines could be used as standby spares.

[b] $1250 \times \dfrac{180}{187} = 1203$; $3256 \times \dfrac{80}{88} = 2960$.

It should be noticed that this economic analysis does not consider the possibility of a separate collector service, since such an option is uneconomical.

It naturally follows that the unofficial agreement could reduce MHM's knitting and examining costs from £38 500 to £29 286 per annum, realizing a saving of £9214 per annum without any investment in machinery. To achieve this, however, the company would need to lay off 12 knitters at a total, once-and-for-all, severance payment of £3168. Such a rationalization would appear justified provided such redundancies could be achieved in a humane way and provided, of course, that the unofficial agreement can be made official.

Annual labour cost with incremental investment. The next logical step in this analysis is to appraise the economic merits of the smallest possible investment in plant and machinery, which comes from investing in the downstream collection system. Such a scheme would cost £10 000 for five such machines and would result in annual knitting and examining costs of £26 357, giving rise to annual savings of £2929 over those brought about by the unofficial manning agreement. The basic question therefore is, Does this additional saving justify this capital expenditure? To undertake such an analysis we must define the economic lifespan of such machines, and are forced to state quite explicitly how long we believe MHM can continue to produce its existing product. In the absence of any market research data this is quite impossible, so we have to make do with guesswork and then test the results to see just how sensitive they are to change in our guesses. First, we shall assume that MHM's market will survive the next five years, in which case the following economic appraisal applies:

Year	Capital investment	Tax shield (after 50% tax)	Cost savings (after 50% tax)	Net cash flow	Discounted cash flow @ 10% pa	@ 12% pa
0	10 000	–	–	−10 000	−10 000	−10 000
1		2 750	1 465	4 215	3 831	3 763
2		560	1 465	2 025	1 674	1 614
3		480	1 465	1 945	1 461	1 384
4		400	1 465	1 865	1 274	1 185
5		2 310	1 465	3 775	2 344	2 142
Totals	10 000	6 500	7 325	3 825	585	89

This analysis demonstrates that such a project would be marginally acceptable with a DCFRR slightly greater than 12 per cent per annum compared with a cost of capital approximately 10 per cent per annum. However, it should be noted that such a return would only be realized if the following conditions prevail:

(a) the economic life of the project is five years,
(b) the savings are time invariant, and
(c) the tax shield can be absorbed by tax payments elsewhere in the company.

Major re-investment. Several alternative purchasing strategies are available to MHM but perhaps the most reasonable one is to consider replacing the single-feed machines with four-feed Bentley machines, according to Mr Sutton's study. To avoid any complication arising from the possible use of downstream collection systems and to keep the analysis truly incremental we are obliged to reconsider the unofficial agreement to test the economic implications of new machine investment. To replace the 187 single-feed machines and yet employ the maximum flexibility offered by the labour agreement would suggest the purchase of 20 Bentley machines costing £30 000, resulting in the following production levels and costs:

	Standard weekly cost (£)	Standard production (dps/wk)	Annual cost (£) to produce 5000 dps/wk
Double-feed machines 80-off, three shifts:			
6 knitters @ £30	180⎱	2 960	15 000
6 examiners @ £20	120⎰		
Four-feed machines 20-off, three shifts:			
3 knitters @ £30	90⎱	1 800	7 500
3 examiners @ £20	60⎰		
Totals	450	4 760	
		Standard working	22 500
		Overtime working	1 702
		Total cost	24 202

This scheme would therefore realize savings of £5084 per annum over those realized by the more flexible manning arrangements and the following economic analysis would apply:

Year	Capital investment	Tax shield (after 50% tax)	Cost savings (after 50% tax)	Net cash flow	Discounted cash flow @ 2% pa
0	30 000	–	–	−30 000	−30 000
1		8 250	2 542	10 792	10 580
2		1 680	2 542	4 222	4 058
3		1 440	2 542	3 982	3 752
4		1 200	2 542	3 742	3 457
5		6 930	2 542	9 472	8 579
Totals	30 000	19 500	12 710	2 210	426

In this case we see that the DCFRR is only slightly in excess of 2 per cent per annum which is quite unacceptable.

General results of the economic appraisal. Although several other machine purchasing strategies should be evaluated by the reader, nevertheless, it would appear that the following conclusions prevail:

(a) the new manning arrangements should be implemented at a pace which will cause the least production interference and yet maintain harmonious labour relations.
(b) MHM should further consider the risk implications involved with investment in the downstream collection system and, should it decide that the risk is worth taking, then there would be no need to further develop the unofficial agreement.
(c) it would appear that investment in new knitting machines is not justified *unless* there exists a tacit agreement that such new machinery forms the basis for the more flexible manning schemes, in which case investment in new machines would be both necessary and economically justified.

Other possible means of realizing economies. Reference to Exhibit 3 shows that approximately 30 per cent of all MHM's production costs result from the contract dyeing and shaping of stockings. It is felt that this area should be explored in much greater depth for possible economies prior to investing in new capital plant and machinery. Furthermore, MHM's sales force should consider the possibility of a greater market penetration into the higher-priced stocking market because its lowest priced product is currently making an accounting loss, albeit that a positive contribution to profit and overhead cost is realized.

Appendix E. Answers to Odd-Numbered Questions

CHAPTER 2

2.13.1   The maximum total profit of 34 000 is obtained when the price and sales are 150 and 400 units respectively. The maximum sales revenue of 62 500 is obtained when the corresponding price and sales are 125 and 500 units respectively, and the profit is 31 500.

2.13.3   (i) $Q_{opt} = 20$ tonnes per day
    (ii) Breakeven occurs at 10 and 30 tonnes per day.
    (iii) $AVC = \$10/$tonne, $AFC = 300/Q$, $ATC = 10 + 300/Q$.
    (iv) $MC = \$10/$tonne.
    (v) $AR = 50 - Q$; $MR = 50 - 2Q$.

2.13.5   (i) $X_{opt} = 9$ tonnes per hour; hence the current policy is sub-optimal.
    (ii) Using the Lagrange multiplier technique we find that the opportunity cost (λ) for additional operatives is £16.50.

2.13.7   (i) The current sales policy is sub-optimal.
    (ii) The optimal policy obtains when $Q_{opt} = 62\,500$ tonnes per year at $P_{opt} = £2/$tonne.
    (iii) The optimal policy would increase the profit from £30 000 to £52 500 per annum.

2.13.9   (i) The unconstrained optimal sales policy calls for $Q_{opt} = 25$ tonnes/week with a profit of ¥525 per week.
    (ii) The constrained optimal sales policy calls for $Q_{opt} = 20$ tonnes/week and the opportunity cost (λ) per cubic metre of storage space is ¥1.00.

CHAPTER 5

5.14.1   DCFRR = 14.51 per cent per annum.

5.14.3   (i) The ROC for each of these four projects is 20 per cent per annum.
    (ii) The DCFRR for the four projects A, B, C and D are 29, 22, 39 and 19 per cent per annum respectively, showing that Project C is the superior project.

5.14.5   Proof of the identity DCFRR = 100A/K is given in Section 5.7. Using this relationship we get:

Project	I	II	III	IV
DCFRR on total investment	12.5	14.5	14.1	13.3
DCFRR on incremental investment	–	25.4	12.5	9.2

The preferred choice is therefore Project III since it yields a DCFRR on total and incremental capital which is greater than the cost of capital. Uncertainty, risk, the possibility of better alternative projects, the company's cash position and its cash requirements would also affect this decision.

5.14.7 NVP @ 10% pa = 4591
NVP @ 20% pa = 1881

5.14.9 $\text{NPV}(n) = -K + \dfrac{V(P-C)}{(1+r)} + V(P-C)\dfrac{(1+g)}{(1+r)^2} + \ldots V(P-C)\dfrac{(1+g)^{n-1}}{(1+r)^n}$

The minimum economic price is that price which makes $\text{NPV}(n) = 0$. Therefore:

$$K = \sum_{i=1}^{n} V(P-C)\frac{(1+g)^{i-1}}{(1+r)^i} = \frac{V(P-C)}{(1+r)} \frac{\left[1 - \left(\frac{1+g}{1+r}\right)^n\right]}{\left[1 - \left(\frac{1+g}{1+r}\right)\right]}$$

Rearranging and substituting $X = (1+g)/(1+r)$ we get:

$$P = C + \frac{K(1+r)}{V}\left[\frac{1-X^n}{1-X}\right]$$

CHAPTER 6

6.8.1 The incremental cost of capital at which one would be indifferent between these two projects is approximately $12\frac{1}{2}$ per cent per annum. Below this rate one would finance the larger project providing there were no other projects available yielding a higher incremental return.

6.8.3

	(units £k)			
Project	A	B	C	D
NPV @ 12% pa	17.9	38.5	123.2	65.7
NPV @ 17% pa	−29.8	1.9	28.0	35.6
DCFRR (% pa)	13.5	17.5	19	24

Hence Projects C and D are the best, although C is more sensitive to the possible errors in the interest rate.

6.8.5

	(units £k)			
Project	A	B	C	D
NPV @ 10% pa	167.3	375.4	375.0	308.9
NPV @ 15% pa	−129.6	−37.8	−325.0	9.0
DCFRR (% pa)	12–13	14–15	12	17

Project D seems the best, but we would need to confirm the cost of capital.

6.8.7

Project	A	B	C	D	E	F
Payback period (years)	6.5	5.0	3.0	10.0	2.5	6.1
Accounting ROC (% pa)	10.3	10.3	13.3	40.0	20.0	9.75
NPV @ 16% pa	−15 740	−3 340	19 180	24 300	15 480	−36 960
Approximate						
DCFRR (% pa)	13	15	20	17	29	12

CHAPTER 9

9.15.1

Case		DCFRR (% pa)
Base case (no change)		20
±10% change	in capital cost	∓2
	in operating level	±2
	in price	±5
	in variable cost	∓3

9.15.3

Decision rule	Option selected
Laplace	4
Maximin	2 or 5
Maximax	3
Hurwicz ($\alpha = 0.2$)	2
Minimax Regret	4

9.15.5   Expected NPV(A) − 11 700

Expected NPV(B) = 13 500

Therefore, recommend Project B.

9.15.7   Expected sales revenue = 228 000

Expected costs   = 150 000

Expected profit   =   78 000

Probability of making a loss is 18.68 per cent, so we would reject the project.

9.15.9   (i) Expected total profit according to both sets of data equals 151.
(ii) Assuming independence the variance of the total profit is 224.
(iii) Assuming dependence the variance of the total profit is 364.

CHAPTER 10

10.8.1   Recommended course of action:

(i) Invest £10 000 in the first R & D project on the basis of an expected NPV of £327 200.
(ii) If that R & D programme is successful and if the economics of the sequential capital investment decision warrant capital investment of £50 000, implement the capital project.
(iii) If this R & D programme is unsuccessful, invest in the subsequent R & D project with an expected NPV of £318 000.
(iv) If the second R & D project is successful and the sequential capital investment project warrants investment, implement that capital project.

10.8.3   Based on the expected value criterion, the recommendation would be:

(i) Finance a medium-sized pilot plant, because it gives the optimal expected NPV of £494k.
(ii) If the test market is medium-sized, then build a large, full-scale plant if its capital cost is still justified.
(iii) If the test market is small, then build a small, full-scale plant if its capital cost is still justified.

CHAPTER 13

13.12.1

Cash budget

	Jan. (£)	Feb. (£)	March (£)	April (£)	May (£)	June (£)
Opening balances	3 000	2 600	2 100	(400)	1 000	5 500
Cash receipts	42 000	41 000	45 000	49 000	52 000	54 000
	45 000	43 600	47 100	48 600	53 000	59 500
Cash payments:						
Materials	16 000	18 000	20 000	20 000	22 000	20 000
Labour	9 000	10 500	10 500	11 000	11 000	11 500
Manufacturing	4 700	6 200	6 200	6 700	6 700	7 200
overheads	900	–	–	900	–	–
Admin. overheads	3 800	3 800	3 800	5 500	4 300	4 300
Selling and distribution	3 000	3 000	3 000	3 500	3 500	3 500
Tax	5 000	–	–	–	–	–
Capital	–	–	4 000	–	–	8 000
	42 400	41 500	47 500	47 600	47 500	54 500
Closing balances	2 600	2 100	(400)	1 000	5 500	5 000

13.12.3

Meteng Ltd
Profit and loss account for the year ended 31 December 1977

		(£)		(£)
Cost of sales			Sales	70 000
Raw material	14 000			
Labour	21 000	35 000		
Gross profit c/d		35 000		
		70 000		70 000
			Gross profit b/d	35 000
Depreciation expenses		5 900		
Building maintenance		1 000		
Advertising expenses		4 000		
Miscellaneous office expenses		900		
Interest charge		1 600		
Net profit c/d		21 600		
		35 000		35 000

Meteng Ltd
Balance sheet as at 31 December 1977

		(£)			(£)
Fixed assets:			Capital:		
Land & buildings	92 000		Authorized £100 000		
Less depreciation	15 000	77 000	Issued		72 000
Plant & equipment	16 900		Retained profit	22 750	
Less depreciation	3 900	13 000		21 600	44 350
Current assets			Long-term liability:		
Stock		14 000	Loan secured on property at 8%		20 000
Debtors		19 400			
Cash in bank		26 500	Current liability:		
Cash in hand		450	Creditors		14 000
		150 350			150 350

13.12.5   Profit and Loss Account–February

		(£)
Sales revenue 4700×0.70		3290
Less materials	4000×0.09 = 360	
	800×0.11 = 88	
labour	250×1.10 = 275	
overheads	= 800	1523
	Profit	£1767

Standard cost and variance analysis

Standard sales revenue 5000×0.8		4000
Sales price variance 47 000 (0.70–0.80)		(470)
Sales volume variance 0.8 (5000–4700)		(240)
	Actual sales revenue	3290
Standard Cost*: 4700×0.35		1645
Standard profit before cost variance		1645

Production cost variances

			(£)
Materials price variance	448–480	=	(32)
Materials usage variance	0.10 (4800−4700)	=	10
Labour rate variance	0.10×250	=	25
Labour efficiency variance	1.0 (250−235)	=	15
Overheading spending variance		=	(200)
Overhead volume variance	1000−0.2×4700	=	60
Total overall production variance		=	(122)

Total profit = 1645 + 122

  = £1767

13.12.7   Profit and loss statement for January

		(£)
Sales revenue 1100 units @ £7.35		8085
Expenses:		
Materials 3201 kg @ £1.62	5185	
Labour 1100 @ 0.982 @ £1.50	1620	
Overheads	330	7135
Net operating profit		950

Standard cost statement

Standard sales revenue 1000 @ £7.50	7500
Sales volume variance 100 batches @ £7.50	750
Sales revenue expected due to volume variance	8250

Standard cost for 1100 batches

Materials 1100 @ 3kg @ 1.50	4950	
Labour 1100 @ 1hr @ £1.20	1320	
Overheads	300	6570
Expected profit at standard cost		1680
Actual profit		950
Total variance loss		730

---

* Product standard cost (1lb bags)

Materials 1lb @ 10p	0.10
Labour 1/20 @ £1	0.05
Overheads £1000/5000	0.20
	0.35/lb

This variance loss is due to the following reasons:

	Gain (£)	Loss (£)
Sales price variance:		
Actual quantity (actual price less standard price)		
1100 (7.35–7.50)	–	165
Materials usage variance:		
Standard cost (actual less standard quantity)		
1.50 (3201–3300)	149	–
Materials price variance:		
Actual quantity (actual less standard price)		
3201 (1.62–1.50)	–	384
Labour rate variance:		
Actual quantity (actual price less standard price)		324
1080 (1.5–1.2)		
Labour efficiency variance:		
Standard cost (actual less standard quantity)		
£1.20 (1080–1100)	24	
Overhead cost variance		30
Totals	173	903
		730

Total profit variance loss
Hence all of the variances are explained.

CHAPTER 15

15.12.1   (i) Optimal tank capacity = 125 tonnes.
        (ii) Minimum total incremental cost = \$2500 per annum.
        (iii) Number of tank fillings per annum = 500 times.

15.12.3   The opportunity cost (λ) of extra storage capacity is given by the relationship:

$$\lambda = \frac{c_1 r(1 - r/q)}{X^2} - \frac{c_2}{2}$$

where c_1 = pump set-up cost (£ per time), c_2 = average hire cost (£ per bl pa), X = available storage capacity (bls), r = rate of consumption (bls pa), and q = rate of production (bls pa).

It follows that the oil well operator should be willing to pay up to £6 per barrel per annum for the next incremental barrel of storage capacity, but this value will change as the average hire cost changes. Ideally, the operator would like to hire 1000 barrels of ullage at a price of £4 per barrel per annum.

15.12.5   EOQ (phosphate) = 120 tonnes.
        EOQ (sulphite) = 67 tonnes.

15.12.7   The warehouse keeper would ideally like to stock 30 deep-freezers, but space constrains this quantity to 15. The EOQ is, therefore, 15 and the opportunity cost (λ) is £0.15 per cubic metre for the next incremental cubic metre of space.

15.12.9   By drawing a graph of the cdf on the basis of the data provided we discover that the value:

$$F_X(Y) = (P + G)/(P + G + L) = 0.821$$

corresponds with the optimal restocking quantity of 189 kg/week of drug.

CHAPTER 17

17.16.1   The three coals A, B and C, should be blended in the ratio 1:4:7 to give the optimal power station feed costing £12.92/tonne

17.16.3 The optimal feed composition for the distillation unit is 2 kg and 6 kg per minute of Benzene and Toluene respectively, giving the maximum possible contribution of 34 munits per minute. The opportunity costs are:

(i) for the feed rate to the distillation tower: 2 munits per kg/min.
(ii) for the bottoms product flow rate: 3 munits per kg/min.

17.16.5 (i) £397.1, (ii) 14.3, (iii) 15.7, (iv) £3.7 to remove the man weeks constraint, and £5/7 to remove the material Z constraint.

17.16.7 The optimal combined rates of feedstocks B and C are 1.537×10^6 and 6.576×10^6 lb per annum respectively, giving an annual profit of $43.565 + 10^6$ munits.

17.16.9 (a) The values of the bottom row are the values of the solution indicators. Since these are all either zero or positive this means that an optimal solution has been found.

(b) All the $X_{i,j}$ column headings for ($i = 1, 2, 3$ and $j = A, B$) are the numbers of tonnes of product i produced at Factory j during the week.
W_A = hours of slack capacity at Factory A,
W_B = hours of slack capacity at Factory B,
Wi for ($i = 1, 2, 3$) = the numbers of tonnes of product i which are not met during the week,
Wo = the values of the variables in the solution tableau.

(c) £33 250.

(d) The values of the shadow prices are: 0, 12.5, 37.5, 41.875 and 62.5. This means:

(i) that we would not be willing to pay anything to remove the availability restriction on Factory A,
(ii) that we would be willing to pay *up to* £12.50 per extra hour of plant availability to remove the production restriction on Plant B,
(iii) that we would be willing to pay *up to* £37.50, £41.875 and £62.50 per tonne each to remove the market restrictions on the sale of Products 1, 2 and 3 respectively.

(e) $0 \times 100 + 12.5 \times 100 + 37.5 \times 310 + 41.875 \times 300 + 62.5 \times 125 = 33\,250$.

(f) Produce:

185 tonnes of 1 at Factory A
125 tonnes of 3 at Factory A
125 tonnes of 1 at Factory B
300 tonnes of 2 at Factory B

(g) The only slack capacity is ten hours per week at Factory A.
The markets for all three products are saturated.

17.16.11 The optimal solution tableau is:

	C_1	C_2	C_3	C_4	C_5	Totals
P_1	25	–	–	50	25	100
P_2	–	60	40	25	–	125
P_3	75	–	–	–	–	75
Totals	100	60	40	75	25	300

Units = tonnes per day.

17.16.13 The optimal solution tableau is:

	A	B	C	Slack	Totals
1	–	50 000	–	–	50 000
2	20 000	–	30 000	20 000	70 000
Totals	20 000	50 000	30 000	20 000	120 000

Units = tonnes per annum.

17.16.15 The optimal solution tableau is:

	MGB	NEGB	SGB	Slack	Totals
NSG	–	50	–	–	50
LPG	20	–	30	20	70
Totals	20	50	30	20	120

Units = millions therms per annum.

17.16.17 The optimal assignment is:

Trade	Task	Cost(£)
1	A	14
2	C	13
3	D	10
4	B	13
5	E	12

Minimum total cost of tasks   £62

CHAPTER 19

19.12.1 Several aspects of this question are designed to test the reader's grasp of economic fundamentals. The £2000 already spent is a sunk cost and should not feature in the subsequent economic analysis. Also the depreciation policy is irrelevant as it does not affect the economics of the problem. The NPV for the *future* cash flows involved with this project is given by:

$$\text{NPV} = -10\,000 + 2000 + 1500 \sum_{t=1}^{10} \frac{1}{(1+0.1)^t} = £1217$$

The firm would therefore be advised to continue the project providing the unspent monies cannot be better deployed elsewhere, and providing it is of a risk class suitable to the firm.

19.12.3   (i) The capital outstanding for this project is £40 000.
(ii) If X denotes the forecast gross cash inflows then:

$$\frac{(X-10\,000)\times0.5}{40\,000} = 0.25$$

Therefore $X = 30\,000$
(iii) The after-tax and allowance annual cash flows are therefore £17 000 per annum, and

(iv) the NPV is £30 500. Providing the project does not necessitate unusual risks and no better use can be found for the capital outstanding, the project should continue.

19.12.5 The net present values of costs to perpetuity $Z(n)$ for different replacement options are:

Pump life (years)	1	2	3	4	5
$Z(n)$ (Dutch Florins)	1342	928	832	770	783

The recommended optimal replacement period is therefore every four years.

19.12.7 The economic life and the minimum life-cycle costs for these two pumps are:

Model	Economic life (years)	$Z(n)$
A	4	33 500
B	4	50 250

Since Pump B has twice the capacity of Pump A, the operator should replace existing Model A pumps by Model B pumps to reduce the life-cycle costs of the pumping service.

19.12.9 The optimal replacement strategy calls for the replacement of these valves at their *sixth* failure.

Appendix F. Some Technical Problems with the Discounted Cash Flow Technique

F.1 DIFFERENT DISCOUNTING METHODS

F.1.1 Introduction

Throughout this book we have proceeded on the basis that the cash flows of a project occur as lump sums at discrete, end-of-period moments in time. This convention enjoys a certain business appeal in that it is similar to financial accounting practice which also uses end-of-period reporting. In most circumstances it is assumed that these end-of-period moments occur at yearly intervals, so that the net present value of a project is computed by the following equation:

$$\text{NPV} = \sum_{t=0}^{n} \frac{C_t}{(1+r)^t} \tag{F.1.1}$$

where NPV = net present value, C_t = a lump sum cash flow realized at the end of year t, r = the nominal interest rate (written as a decimal), and t = the end-of-year when the cash flows C_t are assumed to be realized, so that $t = 0, 1, 2, \ldots n$ (years)

In reality, several of the cash flows of a manufacturing project do not conveniently occur as lump sums at the ends of years. For example, the capital cost of building a project can extend over several years, especially in such cases as the building of a steelworks or a petrochemical complex. Furthermore, the building contractor would normally expect to be paid in instalments during the year for the work done, and one would expect the contract to specify the frequency of such payments. As a further example, cash receipts from customers for the purchase of goods or services normally occur on a continuous basis*. Obviously further examples of project cash flows which contradict the use of this lump sum, end-of-year convention exist, but we shall not labour the point here. What is important is the extent to which the myopic adherence to such a convention could lead to erroneous decision making. Most books and articles on the subject of capital project selection give scant treatment to the possibility of such a problem, whereas others have developed mathematical models which supposedly resolve the problem, when in fact they do not! From a pedagogical viewpoint it is important that we recognize the possibility for erroneous decision making on the basis of such a convention, even if the conditions for such errors seldom occur in practice.

F.1.2 Compounding more frequently than once a year

Using the nomenclature developed in Chapter 5, we know that the relationship between the present and future values of a sum of money can be computed according to the relationship shown by equation F.1.2.1 below:

$$F = P(1+r)^t \tag{F.1.2.1}$$

---

* Although the regularity of cash receipts from customers will undoubtedly be governed by the number of customers, the extent of business transacted, the terms of trade and the method of payment, it is conceivable that payments could be realized throughout the day from early morning to late afternoon. Such a system of payment could be regarded as being almost continuous.

where the interest is assumed to be compounded on an annual basis. When interest is compounded on a more frequent basis, it is necessary to develop a further convention in order to make sense of the results. If an interest rate of, say, 6 per cent per annum is paid quarterly or semi-annually, the 6 per cent per annum rate is known in banking circles as the nominal rate. This is the rate which would be realized if interest were compounded only once at the end of a year.

For a nominal interest rate of 6 per cent per annum with interest compounded semi-annually, the appropriate interest rate for the first half-year would be 3 per cent, and the future value of 1 munit in half a year's time would be 1.03. If this sum were reinvested for a further half-year, the future value of this investment would be

$$1.03 \times 1.03 = 1.0609$$

which is greater than the corresponding value of 1.06 munits had the compounding been done only once at the year-end. The reason for this difference lies in the fact that with more frequent compounding, the interim interest, as well as the original principle, attracts further interest in subsequent time periods. To differentiate investments which attract interest only once a year from those which attract interest more frequently, bankers and economists have devised an effective annual interest rate, which is defined as: 'the total interest which is compounded over the period of one year as a percentage of the principle at the beginning of the year. In our previous example, the effective annual interest rate would equal the nominal interest rate of 6 per cent per annum when compounding is done annually. However, when compounding is done semi-annually the effective interest rate is 6.09 per cent per annum. Table F.1.2.1 gives the effective annual interest rates at a nominal rate of 6 per cent per annum for a variety of compounding schemes and it will be noticed that the more frequently interest is compounded the greater becomes the effective annual interest rate. The relationship between any nominal and effective interest rate can be established algebraically using equation F.1.2.1:

For annual compounding: $\qquad F = P(1+r)^t$
For semi-annual compounding: $\qquad F = P(1+r/2)^{2t}$
For compounding m times a year: $F = P(1+r/m)^{mt}$

If r_{eff} = the effective annual interest rate, then we get:

$$F = P(1+r_{\text{eff}})^t = P\left(1+\frac{r}{m}\right)^{mt}$$

so that:

$$r_{\text{eff}} = \left[1+\frac{r}{m}\right]^m - 1 \qquad\qquad (\text{F.1.2.2})$$

At this stage the reader might like to use equation F.1.2.2 to verify the results given in Table F.1.2.1.

Table F.1.2.1 *Effective annual interest rates for a variety of compounding periods at a nominal interest rate of 6 per cent per annum*

Compounding frequency	Number of compounding periods per annum	Effective interest rate per period (%)	Effective annual interest rate (%)
Annually	1	6.0000	6.0000
Semi-annually	2	3.0000	6.0900
Quarterly	4	1.2500	6.1364
Monthly	12	0.5000	6.1678
Weekly	52	0.1154	6.1797
Daily	365	0.0164	6.1799
Continuously	∞	0.0000	6.1837

F.1.3 Compounding and discounting on a continuous basis

If compounding is done so frequently that it can be assumed continuous then:

$$F = P \lim_{m \to \infty} \left[\left(1 + \frac{r}{m}\right)^{mt} \right]$$

This can be rewritten as:

$$F = P \lim_{m \to \infty} \left[(1 + r/m)^{m/r \cdot rt} \right]$$

In mathematics it is well known that the relationship:

$$\lim_{m \to \infty} \left[(1 + r/m)^{m/r} \right] = e = 2.17828$$

where e = the exponential, which is the base of the natural, Napierian and hyperbolic logarithm. Hence:

$$F = Pe^{rt} \tag{F.1.3.1}$$

and conversely:

$$P = Fe^{-rt} \tag{F.1.3.2}$$

Using the relationship* given by equation F.1.3.1, the corresponding effective annual interest rate when compounding is done continuously is given by:

$$F = P(1 + r_{eff})^t = Pe^{rt}$$

or:

$$r_{eff} = e^r - 1 \tag{F.1.3.3}$$

Table F.1.2.1 also gives the corresponding effective annual interest rate for a 6 per cent per annum nominal interest rate when compounded continuously.

Many engineers and economists fallaciously use equations F.1.3.1 and F.1.3.2 in the belief that they incorporate continuous cash flows which overcome the criticism which was previously made about the end-of-year convention. Regrettably they are most definitely wrong in this assumption! A careful study of equations F.1.3.1 and F.1.3.2 shows that the cash flows

---

* The relationship given by equation F.1.3.1 can be more easily derived using calculus. An infinitesimally small change in a principle (P) invested for an infinitesimally short period of time (dt) is given by the relationship:

$$dP = P \cdot r \cdot dt$$

hence:

$$\frac{dP}{P} = r \cdot dt$$

Integrating between the limits set by $P = F$, when $t = t$ and $P = P$, when $t = 0$, we get:

$$\int_P^F \frac{dP}{P} = \int_0^t r \cdot dt$$

Therefore

$$|\log_e P|_P^F = |rt|_0^t$$

Hence:

$$\log_e (F/P) = r \cdot t$$

and simplifying:

$$F = Pe^{rt}$$

Table F.1.3.1 *Comparison of the DCFRRs, based on end-of-year discounting and continuous discounting, for the previous example*

Year	Cash flow	End-of-year discounting @ 35% pa		Continuous discounting @ 30% pa	
		Discount factor	Discounted cash flow	Discount factor	Discounted cash flow
0	−11 100	−1.000	−11 100	1.000	−11 100
1	5 000	0.741	3 705	0.741	3 705
2	5 000	0.549	2 745	0.549	2 745
3	5 000	0.406	2 030	0.406	2 030
4	5 000	0.301	1 505	0.301	1 505
5	5 000	0.223	1 115	0.223	1 115
Net present value			=0		=0

Source: *Journal of Business Finance and Accounting,* **2** (2), Summer 1975. Reproduced by kind permission of Basil Blackwell, Oxford.

still appear as lump sum, end-of-year entities and do not cater for continuous cash flows. The fact of the matter is that continuous compounding/discounting and continuous cash flows are two quite different phenomena which have to be treated separately.

Besides this confusion, however, the adoption of more frequent compounding also results in another problem concerning the proper interpretation of the results of a DCFRR study. Suppose we were instructed to appraise the economic merits of a project giving the following cash flow profile:

Year	0	1	2	3	4	5
Cash flow	−11 100	5000	5000	5000	5000	5000

Such a project would give a DCFRR of 35 or 30 per cent per annum depending on whether we used the conventional end-of-year method or the continuous method of discounting. These results are shown in Table F.1.3.1.

In this example the discounted cash flows for the discrete, end-of-year case were calculated on the same basis as described in Chapter 5.3, using the discount factors given in Appendix G. For the continuous discounting case, the discount factors given by e^{-rt} were evaluated using tables of exponential functions which are normally found in most books containing logarithms. No separate tables for such values are given in this book because they are not warranted. The reason for the difference between the two DCFRRs of 35 and 30 per cent results from the difference of the discounting techniques and, of course, these two rates are equivalent. This can be verified using the relationship given by equation F.1.3.3. If we substitute a nominal interest rate of 30 per cent per annum into this equation we get:

$$r_{eff} = e^{0.30} - 1$$
$$= 1.349859 - 1$$
$$= 0.349859$$
$$= 0.35$$

The fundamental problem however is that business executives usually express their interest requirements in nominal terms, so the DCFRR of a project can be compared with the cost of capital needed to finance that project. As might be expected, the discount factors associated with continuous discounting are considerably smaller than end-of-year discount factors at the same interest rate as Figure F.1.3.1 shows, so the corresponding DCFRR on a continuous basis will be less than on a discrete, end-of-year basis. Unless the significance of this difference is brought to the attention of the decision maker and understood, it is conceivable that the wrong decision could be made. The fact that people confuse continuous discounting with continuous cash flows only goes to reinforce the point that such errors could be made.

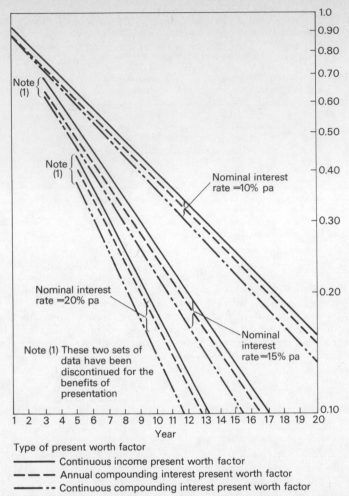

Figure F.1.3.1 *Present worth factors compared. Source:* Journal of Business Finance and Accounting, **2** (2), *Summer 1975. Reproduced by kind permission of Basil Blackwell, Oxford.*

The one virtue which continuous discounting does possess is that it facilitates the building of fairly complex and readily tractable mathematical models on the basis that the relationship e^{-rt} can be easily differentiated and allows optimal solutions to be found. In the context of real economic decision making however this small virtue is insufficient to counter the considerable disadvantages which accrue from its use.

F.1.4 Allowing for continuous cash flows

We must now decide how best to deal with continuous cash flows in our calculations, and then decide if the greater complexity involved justifies the extra computational refinement.

As a basis, we shall continue with the suggestion of Section F.1.3 that executives prefer to think of interest rates in annual terms. If 1 munit was received over one year at a continuous and steady rate then the number of munits received over an infinitesimally short period of time (dt) would be $1 \cdot dt$. Furthermore, if this money was realized at some time t in the future the present value of this infinitesimally small receipt would be:

$$\frac{1 \cdot dt}{(1+r)^t}$$

Table F.1.4.1 *Values of the multiplication factor K for correcting lump sum discount factors into continuous income discount factors, with annual discounting*

Interest rate (% pa)	K	Interest rate (% pa)	K
1	1.005	26	1.125
2	1.010	27	1.130
3	1.015	28	1.134
4	1.020	29	1.139
5	1.025	30	1.143
6	1.030	31	1.148
7	1.035	32	1.153
8	1.039	33	1.157
9	1.044	34	1.162
10	1.049	35	1.166
11	1.054	36	1.171
12	1.059	37	1.175
13	1.064	38	1.180
14	1.068	39	1.184
15	1.073	40	1.189
16	1.078	41	1.193
17	1.083	42	1.198
18	1.088	43	1.202
19	1.092	44	1.207
20	1.097	45	1.211
21	1.102	46	1.216
22	1.106	47	1.220
23	1.111	48	1.224
24	1.116	49	1.229
25	1.120	50	1.233

If this 1 munit was received (say) between the beginning of year $(n-1)$ and the beginning of year (n), the present value of this 1 munit would be given by the following relationship:

$$\int_{n-1}^{n} \frac{1\,dt}{(1+r)^t} = \frac{(1+r)^{-n}-(1+r)^{-(n+1)}}{\log_e (1+r)^{-1}}$$

This expression is the discount factor for 1 munit received at a continuous and steady rate throughout year $(n-1)$, at an interest rate of $100r$ per cent per annum. Despite its apparent complexity, its values are obtained by multiplying the conventional end-of-year discount factors, given in Appendix G, by the correction factors given in Table F.1.4.1.

It will be noticed that these correction factors get progressively larger as the interest rate increases and they are consistently greater than unity. This suggests that the value of 1 munit received continuously and steadily throughout a year is worth more than 1 munit received at the end of the year, as we would expect. The difference between these two discount factors is also shown in Figure F.1.3.1.

Critics of this continuous income discount factor point out that in the DCFRR range 10–15 per cent per annum, which is typically the critical accept–reject range for many capital investment proposals, this discount factor is only 5–7 per cent greater than the orthodox discount factor and, considering the likelihood of much greater inaccuracies in the forecast project cash flows, the extra accuracies brought about by this new method are unwarranted. An example will show the possibility of errors in this way of thinking. Suppose we were asked to appraise the economic merits of a project with the following cash flows:

Year	0	1	2	3
Cash flows	−5500	3000	2000	1500

then according to the calculations shown by Table F.1.4.2 we would arrive at a DCFRR of

Table F.1.4.2 *Comparison of the DCFRR computed on the basis of the continuous income discount factor and the lump sum, end-of-year discount factor, both with annual discounting*

Year	Cash flow	End-of-year discounting @ 10% pa		Continuous income discounting @ 14.5% pa	
		Discount factor	Discounted cash flow	Discount factor	Discounted cash flow
0	−5500	1.000	−5500	1.000	−5500
1	3000	0.909	2725	0.935	2805
2	2000	0.826	1650	0.816	1630
3	1500	0.751	1125	0.712	1065
Net present value			=0		=0

Source: *Journal of Business Finance and Accounting*, **2** (2), Summer 1975. Reproduced by kind permission of Basil Blackwell, Oxford.

14.5 per cent per annum on the basis of the new method of discounting, but only 10 per cent per annum on the basis of the orthodox method.

The outcome of this trivial example shows that the original 5–7 per cent difference in the discount factors has been magnified by the cash flows to produce a 45 per cent difference in the resultant DCFRRs. If such errors can result from the use of different economic models when the same raw data are used then surely it is imperative that the proper models should be used. For many companies the difference between the two results of Table F.1.4.2 could be highly significant and lead to the rejection of the proposed investment on the basis of the more conservative and orthodox method of discounting, whereas the project would be marginally acceptable on the basis of the continuous income discount factors. The fact that the cash flow forecasts might be difficult to predict with anything like the required degree of accuracy is quite another matter, dealt with in Chapter 9, and such matters must not be allowed to confuse the issue at hand, namely the relevance of the various discounting techniques.

In many – indeed most – circumstances the indiscriminate use of the orthodox discount factors $(1+r)^{-t}$ is technically wrong because most manufacturing projects comprise many cash flows which are realized almost on a continuous basis. Typical examples are the cash receipts from sales, cash expenditures on raw materials, fuel and services, maintenance, transport, salaries and wages, and indirect labour costs. Admittedly some project cash flows do occur on a discrete, lump sum basis and they should be discounted using the conventional discount factors of Appendix G.

Two commonly used methods of overcoming the errors involved with the orthodox discounting method when applied to continuous cash flows assume that the cash flows in any year t are approximated by either:

(i) the same valued lump sum cash flow realized at the middle of year t, or
(ii) half the cash flow is realized at the beginning and half at the end of year t.

Both of these results give answers which are quite close to those given by the more rigorous continuous income discounting method discussed. Since both require more calculation than the proposed technique it would seem logical to use the correct continuous income discount factors.

Before we leave this point, it should be mentioned that engineering economists have also devised a discount factor on the basis of continuous income and continuous discounting. The formula for this special discount factor is:

$$\frac{e^r - 1}{re^{rt}}$$

Outside of its possible use in mathematical models, however, this formula cannot be recommended because it suffers from the disadvantage of continuous discounting, discussed in Section F.1.3.

F.1.5 Dealing with continuous but uneven cash flows

Traditional practice assumes that the capital cost of a project is realized at the commencement of a project (Year 0). However, we have already noted that the capital cost is likely to be paid on a more frequent basis and, depending on the number of contractors and the method of payment, could be assumed to be almost continuous for certain large-scale projects. In these circumstances it is most unlikely that these cash flows would be even. Instead, one would expect them to follow the S-shaped pattern which typifies capital expenditure in most manufacturing projects. In this case the assumption that the full capital cost is realized at the beginning of the project is unduly pessimistic. Much of this problem could be overcome if the capital expenditures in the various years of the construction period could be forecast with moderate accuracy. This information is needed before the construction phase starts anyway because the company needs to arrange the appropriate financing. A means for overcoming this problem has been devised by de la Mare (1979) and it has been shown that the orthodox discount factors based on the formula $(1+r)^{-t}$ are usually too high by approximately 10 per cent.

Here again, the traditional method of discounting results in DCFRRs which are unnecessarily conservative.

F.1.6 Bibliography

de la Mare, R. F., 'Modelling capital expenditure', *Engineering and Process Economics*, **4**(4), December 1979, pp. 467–477.

F.2 THE PROBLEM OF MULTIPLE DCFRRs

F.2.1 Introduction

In Chapter 5 we developed the DCFRR criterion which we defined as 'that interest rate which we could afford to pay on the debt outstanding in a project such that the net cash inflows would be just sufficient to pay back the debt and the interest charges by the end of the project'. We also saw that it was the interest rate at which the project's NPV was equal to zero. Unfortunately, the computational method involved with DCFRR calculations can suffer certain deficiencies which we must understand if we are to continue using this criterion sensibly.

F.2.2 Differentiating between borrowing and lending opportunities

The first deficiency of the DCFRR criterion results from the fact that it cannot distinguish between borrowing and lending opportunities. For example, the two projects shown in Table F.2.2.1 have the same DCFRR of 10 per cent per annum and yet, according to the convention we decided to use at the outset, the first is an investment whereas the second constitutes a loan.

Under certain conditions, the inability to discriminate between these two types of opportunity can lead to problems of interpretation as we shall see. This difficulty can be partly

Table F.2.2.1

End-of-year cash flows	Year 0	Year 1
Project A	−100	110
Project B	100	−110

overcome by imposing the condition that the initial cash flow *for an investment* must be negative. To ensure that a project is an investment all the time – a pure investment – money must be outstanding in the project right up to (but not including) the end of the project, *when the DCFRR is used to discount its cash flows.* Hence, any project with a cash flow profile symbolized by:

$$C_0, C_1, C_2, \ldots C_n$$

throughout the n years of its economic life can be defined as a pure investment if there is a solution to the equation:

$$C_0 + C_1(1+r)^{-1} + C_2(1+r)^{-2} + \ldots C_n(1+r)^{-n} = 0$$

such that:

$$C_0 \qquad\qquad\qquad\qquad\qquad\qquad\qquad\qquad\qquad < 0$$
$$C_0 + C_1(1+r)^{-1} \qquad\qquad\qquad\qquad\qquad\qquad < 0$$
$$C_0 + C_1(1+r)^{-1} + C_2(1+r)^{-2} \qquad\qquad\qquad < 0$$

$$C_0 + C_1(1+r)^{-1} + C_2(1+r)^{-2} + \ldots C_{n-1}(1+r)^{-n+1} < 0$$

Where r = its DCFRR.

Properly interpreted, this set of conditions means that a pure investment requires its cumulated discounted cash flow (CDCF) to be negative right up to (but not including) the terminal cash flow, when discounted at its DCFRR. Conversely, a pure lending opportunity requires all these conditions to be met with the inequality signs reversed. If *any* of these conditions is not met then we have a project which is a mixture of investment and lending opportunities. The DCFRR for such a project cannot be defined in the orthodox way. Furthermore, such projects can result in multiple DCFRRs which tend to confuse the use of this criterion as a decision-making tool.

F.2.3   The existence of multiple DCFRRs

Multiple DCFRRs *can* result when there is more than one reversal in the signs associated with a project's cash flows. Tables F.2.3.1 and F.2.3.2 give examples of projects with three such sign reversals. However, only the first example gives rise to multiple DCFRRs.

The reason for this phenomenon lies in the fact that, when discounted at its DCFRR, the CDCF of the first becomes positive and as such no longer meets the requirements of a pure investment. The second example does not suffer the same fate. To understand this somewhat complicated matter we must use two sets of mathematical conditions which define the necessary and sufficient circumstances for multiple DCFRRs to exist.

Table F.2.3.1

Year	0	1	2	3
End-of-year cash flows	−1000	4700	−7200	3600

Table F.2.3.2

Year	0	1	2	3	4	5	6	7	8	9
End-of-year cash flows	−3209	500	500	500	500	−3390	1500	1500	1500	1500

Writing the net present value equation in its polynomial form we get:

$$NPV = C_0 + C_1 k + C_2 k^2 + \ldots C_j k^j + \ldots C_n k^n = 0$$

where $k = (1+r)^{-1}$. We know that the $NPV = C_0$, when $r = \infty$, and

$$NPV = \sum_{j=0}^{n} C_j,$$

when $r = 0$, and $j = (0, 1, 2 \ldots n)$

The first set of conditions, the continuity rule, states that there will be an even number of positive DCFRRs if C_0 and $\sum_{j=0}^{n} C_j$ are of the same sign, but an odd number if they are of different sign. The second set of conditions is governed by Descartes' rule for the signs of an nth degree polynomial. This rules states that the number of real positive roots (the values of k which make the $NPV = 0$) of an nth degree polynomial with real coefficients (the values of C_j in the above equation) is never greater than the number of changes of sign in the sequence of its coefficients and, if less, always by an even number. It must be realized, however, that a positive value of k in this polynomial equation can result from *negative* values of the DCFRR.

Most investment projects have a negative value for C_0, a positive value for $\sum_{j=0}^{n} C_j$ and only one reversal in the signs associated with their cash flows. According to these two rules, therefore, such projects have an odd number of DCFRRs and one value for $(1+r)$. In other words they have a single unique DCFRR as we have come to expect.

However, some projects have the same qualities as this category but also feature negative cash flows towards the end of their project life. These negative cash flows feature contractual or moral obligations, such as the payment of taxes after the project has terminated, the cost of removing an unsightly and obsolete plant, or the cost of refurbishing the landscape when a factory site is no longer required. Such projects usually have an even number of values to the root $(1+r)$, according to Descartes' rule. In other words, they have one positive and one negative DCFRR. This suggests that such projects are mixed borrowing/lending opportunities. The example of Table F.2.3.3 demonstrates this.

Table F.2.3.3

Year	0	1	2	3	4	5	6	7	8	9	10
End-of-year cash flow	−8554	2000	2000	2000	2000	2000	2000	2000	2000	2000	−4000
CDCF @ 15%	−8554	−6814	−5302	−3986	−2884	−1848	−986	−228	+420	+990	0000

This example shows that the project is almost a pure investment but for the fact that its CDCF becomes slightly positive in years 8 and 9. The plot of the NPV for this project as a function of all *positive* discount rates yields a graph of the same shape as we became accustomed to in Chapter 5. This is always the case for projects with two reversals in sign provided that C_0 is negative, and $\sum_{j=0}^{n} C_j$ is positive. The basic problem with such projects is that we need to explain their positive CDCFs and reinterpret the meaning of their DCFRRs. We shall delay this however until we have reviewed the more general case for multiple DCFRRs.

It is an easy matter to construct cash flow profiles which exhibit multiple DCFRRs, all that is required is to multiply those factorial equations which produce such results. For example, if we want a project to have two DCFRRs of 10 and 20 per cent per annum respectively, all we have to do is to multiply the two factors $[(1+r)-1.1]$ and $[(1+r)-1.2]$ and set their multiplicand to zero thus:

$$[(1+r)-1.10][(1+r)-1.20] = 0$$

Simplifying this we get:

$$1.00(1+r)^2 - 2.30(1+r) + 1.32 = 0 \qquad \text{(F.2.3)}$$

The coefficients of equation F.2.3 are the lowest common multiples for projects of two years' duration possessing dual DCFRRs of 10 and 20 per cent per annum. If we multiply these

Table F.2.3.4 *An example of a two-year project exhibiting dual DCFRRs of 10 and 20 per cent per annum*

Year	0	1	2
End-of-year cash flows	−1000	2300	−1320

coefficients by 1000 then one such project would have the cash flow profile shown in Table F.2.3.4.

According to the continuity rule, this cash flow profile has an even number of positive DCFRRs, since both C_0 and $\sum_{i=0}^{n} C_i$ are of equal sign and according to Descartes' rule we expect two values for the root $(1+r)$, since there are two sign reversals. Such a project has a most unusual NPV graph, shown by Figure F.2.3.1, and it will be noticed that it has a negative accounting profit, because $\sum_{i=0}^{n} C_i$ is negative. It follows that this project would only increase wealth if its cost of capital was in the range of 10–20 per cent per annum.

A project with DCFRRs of 20, 50 and 100 per cent per annum could be derived from the following relationship:

$$[(1+r)-1.20] \cdot [(1+r)-1.50] \cdot [(1+r)-2.00] = 0$$

and such a project could exhibit the following cash flows, −1000, 4700, −7200 and 3600 for Years 0–3.

According to the continuity rule this project has an odd number of positive DCFRRs, since C_0 and $\sum_{i=0}^{n} C_i$ are of opposite sign, and either three or one positive values to the root $(1+r)$ according to the Descartes' rule. The NPV graph for this example is shown in Figure F.2.3.2.

This example shows that the project would only increase wealth if its cost of capital was in the region 0–20 per cent per annum or 50–100 per cent per annum. Here we have an example

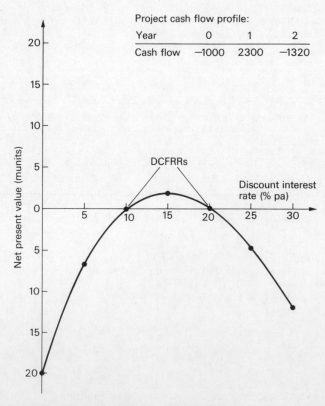

Figure F.2.3.1 *An example of a project exhibiting dual DCFRRs.*

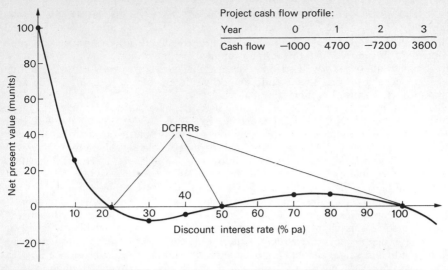

Figure F.2.3.2 *An example of a project exhibiting three DCFRRs.*

of a well mixed borrowing/lending opportunity where the CDCF becomes positively quite large, as shown by Table F.2.3.5.

Table F.2.3.5

Year	0	1	2	3
End-of-year cash flow	−1000	4700	−7200	3600
CDCF at 20% pa	−1000	2917	−2083	0
CDCF at 50% pa	−1000	2133	−1066	0
CDCF at 10% pa	−1000	1350	−450	0

By contrast the following cash flow profile, which we mentioned at the outset of this section, also has three sign reversals, but only one unique DCFRR of 9 per cent per annum:

$$-3209, 500, 500, 500, 500, -3390, 1500, 1500, 1500, 1500$$

The reason for this fundamental difference lies in the fact that this is an example of a pure investment. Discounted at 9 per cent per annum, the CDCF never becomes positive throughout the entire project, despite the large negative cash flow in Year 6. This project can be regarded as two separate projects, A and B, which collectively yield the same overall cash flow profile as the original example, as demonstrated by Table F.2.3.6, each project having a DCFRR of 9 per cent per annum. Projects of this type do occur in reality; one example could be a project requiring a large-scale expansion at some future date to take advantage of an expanding market demand.

Table F.2.3.6

Year		0	1	2	3	4	5	6	7	8	9
End-of-year cash flows	Project A	−3209	500	500	500	500	0	628.5	628.5	628.5	628.5
	Project B	0	0	0	0	0	−3390	871.5	871.5	871.5	871.5
	Project A and B combined	−3209	500	500	500	500	−3390	1500	1500	1500	1500

F.2.4 A realistic assessment of the problems associated with the DCFRR computation

From the discussion so far, it is obvious that certain investment projects can feature multiple DCFRRs and/or be impure investment opportunities. We now know the way to test for both. The fundamental questions which arise in these circumstances are, How can we use multiple DCFRRs as decision making tools? and How do we interpret the meaning of the DCFRR when the project is an impure investment?

On their own, multiple DCFRRs are of little use since they do not define those ranges of interest rates where the NPV is positive or negative. In this predicament, the wise decision maker would require the complete graph of the NPV plotted as a function of the discount rate and a reasonable estimate of the cost of capital before he would be willing to make a decision either on the basis of DCFRRs or NPVs. Moreover, he would need to test the sensitivity of such a curve to possible changes and errors in the original cash flow estimates.

In the case of multiple DCFRRs, the definition of the DCFRR reduces to its lowest level of significance, namely that discount rate which makes the NPV equal zero. *The same result follows when a project gives only one DCFRR, but is also an impure investment.* In most of the examples studied in this chapter we saw that the CDCF becomes positive at some inter- mediate stage in the project's life. Properly interpreted this means that the project has repaid the initial debt by this stage, and had accumulated a cash flow surplus which it needs to lend at the same rate in order to generate just sufficient funds to pay off some subsequent contractual liability (negative cash flow). In such circumstances the notion of the DCFRR being the interest rate on the *outstanding debt* is no longer appropriate, and the DCFRR means nothing more than the interest rate which makes the NPV equal zero.

Fortunately, most manufacturing projects are pure investments and do not exhibit multiple DCFRRs. The problem of multiple roots can arise when comparing the economic merits of two mutually exclusive projects on the basis of their incremental DCFRR, although here again such problems are rare where manufacturing projects are concerned.

Appendix G. Tables of Discount Factors

Discount Factors Present value of 1 at 100r per cent per annum $\{P/F_{r,t} = (1+r)^{-t}\}$
(all numbers are after the decimal point)

Yrs	1/2%	1%	2%	3%	4%	5%	6%	7%	8%	9%	10%	11%	12%	13%	14%	15%	16%	17%	Yrs
1/4	9988	9975	9950	9927	9902	9878	9855	9832	9810	9787	9765	9742	9721	9699	9678	9656	9636	9615	1/4
1/2	9975	9950	9901	9853	9806	9759	9713	9667	9623	9579	9535	9491	9449	9407	9336	9325	9285	9245	1/2
1	9950	9901	9804	9709	9615	9524	9434	9346	9259	9174	9091	9009	8929	8850	8772	8696	8621	8547	1
2	9901	9803	9612	9426	9246	9070	8900	8734	8573	8417	8264	8116	7972	7831	7695	7561	7432	7305	2
3	9851	9706	9423	9151	8890	8638	8396	8163	7938	7722	7513	7312	7118	6931	6750	6575	6407	6244	
4	9802	9610	9238	8885	8548	8227	7921	7629	7350	7084	6830	6587	6355	6133	5921	5718	5523	5337	4
5	9754	9515	9057	8626	8219	7835	7473	7130	6806	6499	6209	5935	5674	5428	5194	4972	4761	4561	5
6	9705	9420	8880	8375	7903	7462	7050	6663	6302	5963	5645	5346	5066	4803	4556	4323	4104	3898	6
7	9657	9327	8706	8131	7599	7107	6651	6227	5835	5470	5132	4817	4523	4251	3996	3759	3538	3332	7
8	9609	9235	8535	7894	7307	6768	6274	5820	5403	5019	4665	4339	4039	3762	3506	3269	3050	2848	8
9	9561	9143	8368	7664	7026	6446	5919	5439	5002	4604	4241	3909	3606	3329	3075	2843	2630	2434	9
10	9513	9053	8203	7441	6756	6139	5584	5083	4632	4224	3855	3522	3220	2946	2697	2472	2267	2080	10
11	9466	8963	8043	7224	6496	5847	5268	4751	4289	3875	3505	3173	2875	2607	2366	2149	1954	1778	11
12	9419	8874	7885	7014	6246	5568	4970	4440	3971	3555	3186	2858	2567	2307	2076	1869	1685	1520	12
13	9372	8787	7730	6810	6006	5303	4688	4150	3677	3262	2897	2575	2292	2042	1821	1625	1452	1299	13
14	9326	8700	7579	6611	5775	5051	4423	3878	3405	2992	2633	2320	2046	1807	1597	1413	1252	1110	14
15	9279	8613	7430	6419	5553	4810	4173	3624	3152	2745	2394	2090	1827	1599	1401	1229	1079	0949	15
16	9233	8528	7284	6232	5339	4581	3936	3387	2919	2519	2176	1883	1631	1415	1229	1069	0930	0811	16
17	9187	8444	7142	6050	5134	4363	3714	3166	2703	2311	1978	1696	1456	1252	1078	0929	0802	0693	17
18	9141	8360	7002	5874	4936	4155	3503	2959	2502	2120	1799	1528	1300	1108	0946	0808	0691	0592	18
19	9096	8277	6864	5703	4746	3957	3305	2765	2317	1945	1635	1377	1161	0981	0829	0703	0596	0506	19
20	9051	8195	6730	5537	4564	3769	3118	2584	2145	1784	1486	1240	1037	0868	0728	0611	0514	0433	20
21	9006	8114	6598	5375	4388	3589	2942	2415	1987	1637	1351	1117	0926	0768	0638	0531	0443	0370	21
22	8961	8034	6468	5219	4220	3418	2775	2257	1839	1502	1228	1007	0826	0680	0560	0462	0382	0316	22
23	8916	7954	6342	5067	4057	3256	2618	2109	1703	1378	1117	0907	0738	0601	0491	0402	0329	0270	23
24	8872	7876	6217	4919	3901	3101	2470	1971	1577	1264	1015	0817	0659	0532	0431	0349	0284	0231	24
25	8828	7798	6095	4776	3751	2953	2330	1842	1460	1160	0923	0736	0588	0471	0378	0304	0245	0197	25
26	8784	7720	5976	4637	3607	2812	2198	1722	1352	1064	0839	0663	0525	0417	0331	0264	0211	0169	26
27	8740	7644	5859	4502	3468	2678	2074	1609	1252	0976	0763	0597	0469	0369	0291	0230	0182	0144	27
28	8697	7568	5744	4371	3335	2551	1956	1504	1159	0895	0693	0538	0419	0326	0255	0200	0157	0123	28
29	8653	7493	5631	4243	3207	2429	1846	1406	1073	0822	0630	0485	0374	0289	0224	0174	0135	0105	29
30	8610	7419	5521	4120	3083	2314	1741	1314	0994	0754	0573	0437	0334	0256	0196	0151	0116	0090	30
35	8398	7059	5000	3554	2534	1813	1301	0937	0676	0490	0356	0259	0189	0139	0102	0075	0055	0041	35
40	8191	6717	4529	3066	2083	1420	0972	0668	0460	0318	0221	0154	0107	0075	0053	0037	0026	0019	40
45	7990	6391	4102	2644	1712	1113	0727	0476	0313	0207	0137	0091	0061	0041	0027	0019	0013	0009	45
50	7793	6080	3715	2281	1407	0872	0543	0339	0213	0134	0085	0054	0035	0022	0014	0009	0006	0004	50
Yrs	1/2%	1%	2%	3%	4%	5%	6%	7%	8%	9%	10%	11%	12%	13%	14%	15%	16%	17%	Yrs

Discount Factors   Present value of 1 at 100r per cent per annum $\{P/F_{r,t}=(1+r)^{-t}\}$
(all numbers are after the decimal point)

Yrs	50%	45%	40%	35%	30%	29%	28%	27%	26%	25%	24%	23%	22%	21%	20%	19%	18%	Yrs
1/4	9036	9113	9193	9277	9365	9384	9401	9420	9438	9457	9476	9496	9515	9535	9555	9574	9594	1/4
1/2	8165	8305	8452	8607	8770	8804	8839	8874	8909	8945	8980	9016	9054	9091	9129	9167	9206	1/2
1	6667	6897	7143	7407	7692	7752	7813	7874	7937	8000	8065	8130	8197	8264	8333	8403	8475	1
2	4444	4756	5102	5487	5917	6009	6104	6200	6299	6400	6504	6610	6719	6830	6944	7062	7182	2
3	2963	3280	3644	4064	4552	4658	4768	4882	4999	5120	5245	5374	5507	5645	5787	5934	6086	3
4	1975	2262	2603	3011	3501	3611	3725	3844	3968	4096	4230	4369	4514	4665	4823	4987	5158	4
5	1317	1560	1859	2230	2693	2799	2910	3027	3149	3277	3411	3552	3700	3855	4019	4190	4371	5
6	0878	1076	1328	1652	2072	2170	2274	2383	2499	2621	2751	2888	3033	3186	3349	3521	3704	6
7	0585	0742	0949	1224	1594	1682	1776	1877	1983	2097	2218	2348	2486	2633	2791	2959	3139	7
8	0390	0512	0678	0906	1226	1304	1388	1478	1574	1678	1789	1909	2038	2176	2326	2487	2660	8
9	0260	0353	0484	0671	0943	1011	1084	1164	1249	1342	1443	1552	1670	1799	1938	2090	2255	9
10	0173	0243	0346	0497	0725	0784	0847	0916	0992	1074	1164	1262	1369	1486	1615	1756	1911	10
11	0116	0168	0247	0368	0558	0607	0662	0721	0787	0859	0938	1026	1122	1228	1346	1476	1619	11
12	0077	0116	0176	0273	0429	0471	0517	0568	0625	0687	0757	0834	0920	1015	1122	1240	1372	12
13	0051	0080	0126	0202	0330	0365	0404	0447	0496	0550	0610	0678	0754	0839	0935	1042	1163	13
14	0034	0055	0090	0150	0254	0283	0316	0352	0393	0440	0492	0551	0618	0693	0779	0876	0985	14
15	0023	0038	0064	0111	0195	0219	0247	0277	0312	0352	0397	0448	0507	0573	0649	0736	0835	15
16	0015	0026	0046	0082	0150	0170	0193	0218	0248	0281	0320	0364	0415	0474	0541	0618	0708	16
17	0010	0018	0033	0061	0116	0132	0150	0172	0197	0225	0258	0296	0340	0391	0451	0520	0600	17
18	0007	0012	0023	0045	0089	0102	0118	0135	0156	0180	0208	0241	0279	0323	0376	0437	0508	18
19	0005	0009	0017	0033	0068	0079	0092	0107	0124	0144	0168	0196	0229	0267	0313	0367	0431	19
20	0003	0006	0012	0025	0053	0061	0072	0084	0098	0115	0135	0159	0187	0221	0261	0308	0365	20
21	0002	0004	0009	0018	0040	0048	0056	0066	0078	0092	0109	0129	0154	0183	0217	0259	0309	21
22	0001	0003	0006	0014	0031	0037	0044	0052	0062	0074	0088	0105	0126	0151	0181	0218	0262	22
23	0001	0002	0004	0010	0024	0029	0034	0041	0049	0059	0071	0086	0103	0125	0151	0183	0222	23
24	0001	0001	0003	0007	0018	0022	0027	0032	0039	0047	0057	0070	0085	0103	0126	0154	0188	24
25	0000	0001	0002	0006	0014	0017	0021	0025	0031	0038	0046	0057	0069	0085	0105	0129	0160	25
26	0000	0001	0002	0004	0011	0013	0016	0020	0025	0030	0037	0046	0057	0070	0087	0109	0135	26
27		0000	0001	0003	0008	0010	0013	0016	0020	0024	0030	0037	0047	0058	0073	0091	0115	27
28		0000	0001	0002	0006	0008	0010	0012	0015	0019	0024	0030	0038	0048	0061	0077	0097	28
29		0000	0001	0002	0005	0006	0008	0010	0012	0015	0020	0025	0031	0040	0051	0064	0082	29
30			0000	0001	0004	0005	0006	0008	0010	0012	0016	0020	0026	0033	0042	0054	0070	30
35				0000	0001	0001	0002	0002	0003	0004	0005	0007	0009	0013	0017	0023	0030	35
40					0000	0000	0001	0001	0001	0001	0002	0003	0004	0005	0007	0010	0013	40
45							0000	0000	0000	0000	0001	0001	0001	0002	0003	0004	0006	45
50										0000	0000	0000	0000	0001	0001	0002	0003	50
Yrs	50%	45%	40%	35%	30%	29%	28%	27%	26%	25%	24%	23%	22%	21%	20%	19%	18%	Yrs

Present value of annuity of 1 at 100r per cent per annum $\left\{ P/A_{r,t} = \dfrac{1-(1+r)^{-t}}{r} \right\}$

Yrs	1/2%	1%	2%	3%	4%	5%	6%	7%	8%	9%	10%	11%	12%	13%	14%	15%	16%	17%	Yrs
1	0.9950	0.9901	0.9804	0.9709	0.9615	0.9524	0.9434	0.9346	0.9259	0.9174	0.9091	0.9009	0.8929	0.8850	0.8772	0.8696	0.8621	0.8547	1
2	1.9851	1.9704	1.9416	1.9135	1.8861	1.8594	1.8334	1.8080	1.7833	1.7591	1.7355	1.7125	1.6901	1.6681	1.6467	1.6257	1.6052	1.5852	2
3	2.9702	2.9410	2.8839	2.8286	2.7751	2.7232	2.6730	2.6243	2.5771	2.5313	2.4869	2.4437	2.4018	2.3612	2.3216	2.2832	2.2459	2.2096	3
4	3.9505	3.9020	3.8077	3.7171	3.6299	3.5460	3.4651	3.3872	3.3121	3.2397	3.1699	3.1024	3.0373	2.9745	2.9137	2.8850	2.7982	2.7432	4
5	4.9259	4.8534	4.7135	4.5797	4.4518	4.3295	4.2124	4.1002	3.9927	3.8897	3.7908	3.6959	3.6048	3.5172	3.4331	3.3522	3.2743	3.1993	5
6	5.8964	5.7955	5.6014	5.4172	5.2421	5.0757	4.9173	4.7665	4.6229	4.4859	4.3553	4.2305	4.1114	3.9975	3.8887	3.7845	3.6847	3.5892	6
7	6.8621	6.7282	6.4720	6.2303	6.0021	5.7864	5.5824	5.3893	5.2064	5.0330	4.8684	4.7122	4.5638	4.4226	4.2883	4.1604	4.0386	3.9224	7
8	7.8230	7.6517	7.3255	7.0197	6.7327	6.4632	6.2098	5.9713	5.7466	5.5348	5.3349	5.1461	4.9676	4.7988	4.6389	4.4873	4.3436	4.2072	8
9	8.7791	8.5660	8.1622	7.7861	7.4353	7.1078	6.8017	6.5152	6.2469	5.9952	5.7590	5.5370	5.3282	5.1317	4.9464	4.7716	4.6065	4.4506	9
10	9.7304	9.4713	8.9826	8.5302	8.1109	7.7217	7.3601	7.0236	6.7101	6.4177	6.1446	5.8892	5.6502	5.4262	5.2161	5.0188	4.8332	4.6586	10
11	10.6770	10.3676	9.7868	9.2526	8.7605	8.3064	7.8869	7.4987	7.1390	6.8052	6.4951	6.2065	5.9377	5.6869	5.4527	5.2337	5.0286	4.8364	11
12	11.6189	11.2551	10.5753	9.9540	9.3851	8.8633	8.3838	7.9427	7.5361	7.1607	6.8137	6.4924	6.1944	5.9176	5.6603	5.4026	5.1971	4.9884	12
13	12.5562	12.1337	11.3484	10.6350	9.9856	9.3936	8.8527	8.3577	7.9038	7.4869	7.1034	6.7499	6.4235	6.1218	5.8424	5.5831	5.3423	5.1183	13
14	13.4887	13.0037	12.1062	11.2961	10.5631	9.8986	9.2950	8.7455	8.2442	7.7862	7.3667	6.9819	6.6282	6.3025	6.0021	5.7245	5.4675	5.2293	14
15	14.4166	13.8651	12.8493	11.9379	11.1184	10.3797	9.7122	9.1079	8.5595	8.0607	7.6061	7.1909	6.8109	6.4624	6.1422	5.8474	5.5755	5.3242	15
16	15.3399	14.7179	13.5777	12.5611	11.6523	10.8378	10.1059	9.4466	8.8514	8.3126	7.8237	7.3792	6.9740	6.6039	6.2651	5.9542	5.6685	5.4053	16
17	16.2586	15.5623	14.2919	13.1661	12.1657	11.2741	10.4773	9.7632	9.1216	8.5436	8.0216	7.5488	7.1196	6.7291	6.3729	6.0472	5.7487	5.4746	17
18	17.1728	16.3983	14.9920	13.7535	12.6593	11.6896	10.8276	10.0591	9.3719	8.7556	8.2014	7.7016	7.2497	6.8399	6.4674	6.1280	5.8178	5.5339	18
19	18.0824	17.2260	15.6785	14.3238	13.1339	12.0853	11.1581	10.3356	9.6036	8.9501	8.3649	7.8393	7.3658	6.9380	6.5504	6.1982	5.8775	5.5845	19
20	18.9874	18.0456	16.3514	14.8775	13.5903	12.4622	11.4699	10.5940	9.8181	9.1285	8.5136	7.9633	7.4694	7.0248	6.6231	6.2593	5.9288	5.6278	20
21	19.8880	18.8570	17.0112	15.4150	14.0292	12.8212	11.7641	10.8355	10.0168	9.2922	8.6487	8.0751	7.5620	7.1016	6.6870	6.3125	5.9731	5.6648	21
22	20.7841	19.6604	17.6580	15.9369	14.4511	13.1630	12.0416	11.0612	10.2007	9.4424	8.7715	8.1757	7.6446	7.1695	6.7429	6.3587	6.0113	5.6964	22
23	21.6757	20.4558	18.2922	16.4436	14.8568	13.4886	12.3034	11.2722	10.3711	9.5802	8.8832	8.2664	7.7184	7.2297	6.7921	6.3988	6.0442	5.7234	23
24	22.5629	21.2434	18.9139	16.9355	15.2470	13.7986	12.5504	11.4693	10.5288	9.7066	8.9847	8.3481	7.7843	7.2829	6.8351	6.4338	6.0726	5.7465	24
25	23.3456	22.0232	19.5235	17.4131	15.6221	14.0939	12.7834	11.6536	10.6748	9.8226	9.0770	8.4217	7.8431	7.3300	6.8729	6.4641	6.0971	5.7662	25
26	24.3240	22.7952	20.1210	17.8768	15.9828	14.3752	13.0032	11.8258	10.8100	9.9290	9.1609	8.4881	7.8957	7.3717	6.9061	6.4906	6.1182	5.7831	26
27	25.1980	23.5596	20.7069	18.3270	16.3296	14.6430	13.2105	11.9867	10.9352	10.0266	9.2372	8.5478	7.9426	7.4086	6.9352	6.5135	6.1364	5.7975	27
28	26.0677	24.3164	21.2813	18.7641	16.6631	14.8981	13.4062	12.1371	11.0511	10.1161	9.3066	8.6016	7.9844	7.4412	6.9607	6.5335	6.1520	5.8099	28
29	26.9330	25.0658	21.8444	19.1885	16.9837	15.1411	13.5907	12.2777	11.1584	10.1983	9.3696	8.6501	8.0218	7.4701	6.9830	6.5509	6.1656	5.8204	29
30	27.7941	25.8077	22.3965	19.6004	17.2920	15.3725	13.7648	12.4090	11.2578	10.2737	9.4269	8.6938	8.0552	7.4957	7.0027	6.5660	6.1772	5.8294	30
35	32.0354	29.4086	24.9986	21.4872	18.6646	16.3742	14.4982	12.9477	11.6546	10.5668	9.6442	8.8552	8.1755	7.5856	7.0700	6.6166	6.2153	5.8582	35
40	36.1722	32.8347	27.3555	23.1148	19.7928	17.1591	15.0463	13.3317	11.9246	10.7574	9.7791	8.9511	8.2438	7.6344	7.1050	6.6418	6.2335	5.8713	40
45	40.2072	36.0945	29.4902	24.5187	20.7200	17.7741	15.4558	13.6055	12.1084	10.8812	9.8628	9.0079	8.2825	7.6609	7.1232	6.6543	6.2421	5.8773	45
50	44.1428	39.1961	31.4236	25.7298	21.4822	18.2559	15.7619	13.8007	12.2335	10.9617	9.9148	9.0417	8.3045	7.6752	7.1327	6.6605	6.2463	5.8801	50
Yrs	1/2%	1%	2%	3%	4%	5%	6%	7%	8%	9%	10%	11%	12%	13%	14%	15%	16%	17%	Yrs

Present value of annuity of 1 at $100r$ per cent per annum $\left\{ P/A_{r,t} = \dfrac{1-(1+r)^{-t}}{r} \right\}$

Yrs	50%	45%	40%	35%	30%	29%	28%	27%	26%	25%	24%	23%	22%	21%	20%	19%	18%	Yrs
1	0.6667	0.6897	0.7143	0.7407	0.7692	0.7752	0.7813	0.7874	0.7937	0.8000	0.8065	0.8130	0.8197	0.8264	0.8333	0.8403	0.8475	1
2	1.1111	1.1653	1.2245	1.2894	1.3609	1.3761	1.3916	1.4074	1.4235	1.4400	1.4568	1.4740	1.4915	1.5095	1.5278	1.5465	1.5656	2
3	1.4074	1.4933	1.5889	1.6959	1.8161	1.8420	1.8684	1.8956	1.9234	1.9520	1.9813	2.0114	2.0422	2.0739	2.1065	2.1399	2.1743	3
4	1.6049	1.7195	1.8492	1.9969	2.1662	2.2031	2.2410	2.2800	2.3202	2.3616	2.4043	2.4483	2.4936	2.5404	2.5887	2.6386	2.6901	4
5	1.7366	1.8755	2.0352	2.2200	2.4356	2.4830	2.5320	2.5827	2.6351	2.6893	2.7454	2.8035	2.8636	2.9260	2.9906	3.0576	3.1272	5
6	1.8244	1.9831	2.1680	2.3852	2.6427	2.7000	2.7594	2.8210	2.8850	2.9514	3.0205	3.0923	3.1669	3.2446	3.3255	3.4098	3.4976	6
7	1.8829	2.0573	2.2628	2.5075	2.8021	2.8682	2.9370	3.0087	3.0833	3.1611	3.2423	3.3270	3.4155	3.5079	3.6046	3.7057	3.8115	7
8	1.9220	2.1085	2.3306	2.5982	2.9247	2.9986	3.0758	3.1564	3.2407	3.3289	3.4212	3.5179	3.6193	3.7256	3.8372	3.9544	4.0776	8
9	1.9480	2.1438	2.3790	2.6653	3.0190	3.0997	3.1842	3.2728	3.3657	3.4631	3.5655	3.6731	3.7863	3.9054	4.0310	4.1633	4.3030	9
10	1.9653	2.1681	2.4136	2.7150	3.0915	3.1781	3.2689	3.3644	3.4648	3.5705	3.6819	3.7993	3.9232	4.0541	4.1925	4.3389	4.4941	10
11	1.9769	2.1849	2.4383	2.7519	3.1473	3.2388	3.3351	3.4365	3.5435	3.6564	3.7757	3.9018	4.0354	4.1769	4.3271	4.4865	4.6560	11
12	1.9846	2.1965	2.4559	2.7792	3.1903	3.2859	3.3868	3.4933	3.6059	3.7251	3.8514	3.9852	4.1274	4.2784	4.4392	4.6105	4.7932	12
13	1.9897	2.2045	2.4685	2.7994	3.2233	3.3224	3.4272	3.5381	3.6555	3.7801	3.9124	4.0530	4.2028	4.3624	4.5327	4.7147	4.9095	13
14	1.9931	2.2100	2.4775	2.8144	3.2487	3.3507	3.4587	3.5733	3.6949	3.8241	3.9616	4.1082	4.2646	4.4317	4.6106	4.8023	5.0081	14
15	1.9954	2.2138	2.4839	2.8255	3.2682	3.3726	3.4834	3.6010	3.7261	3.8593	4.0013	4.1530	4.3152	4.4890	4.6755	4.8759	5.0916	15
16	1.9970	2.2164	2.4885	2.8337	3.2832	3.3896	3.5026	3.6228	3.7509	3.8874	4.0333	4.1894	4.3567	4.5364	4.7296	4.9377	5.1624	16
17	1.9980	2.2182	2.4918	2.8398	3.2948	3.4028	3.5177	3.6400	3.7705	3.9099	4.0591	4.2190	4.3908	4.5755	4.7746	4.9897	5.2223	17
18	1.9986	2.2195	2.4941	2.8443	3.3037	3.4130	3.5294	3.6536	3.7861	3.9279	4.0799	4.2431	4.4187	4.6079	4.8122	5.0333	5.2732	18
19	1.9991	2.2203	2.4958	2.8476	3.3105	3.4210	3.5386	3.6642	3.7985	3.9424	4.0967	4.2627	4.4415	4.6346	4.8435	5.0700	5.3162	19
20	1.9994	2.2209	2.4970	2.8501	3.3158	3.4271	3.5458	3.6726	3.8083	3.9539	4.1103	4.2786	4.4603	4.6567	4.8696	5.1009	5.3527	20
21	1.9996	2.2213	2.4979	2.8519	3.3198	3.4319	3.5514	3.6792	3.8161	3.9631	4.1212	4.2916	4.4756	4.6750	4.8913	5.1268	5.3837	21
22	1.9997	2.2216	2.4985	2.8533	3.3230	3.4356	3.5558	3.6844	3.8223	3.9705	4.1300	4.3021	4.4882	4.6900	4.9094	5.1486	5.4099	22
23	1.9998	2.2218	2.4989	2.8543	3.3254	3.4384	3.5592	3.6885	3.8273	3.9764	4.1371	4.3106	4.4985	4.7025	4.9245	5.1668	5.4321	23
24	1.9999	2.2219	2.4992	2.8550	3.3272	3.4406	3.5619	3.6918	3.8312	3.9811	4.1428	4.3176	4.5070	4.7128	4.9371	5.1822	5.4509	24
25	1.9999	2.2220	2.4994	2.8556	3.3286	3.4423	3.5640	3.6943	3.8342	3.9849	4.1474	4.3232	4.5139	4.7213	4.9476	5.1951	5.4669	25
26	1.9999	2.2221	2.4996	2.8560	3.3297	3.4437	3.5656	3.6963	3.8367	3.9879	4.1511	4.3278	4.5196	4.7284	4.9563	5.2060	5.4804	26
27	2.0000	2.2221	2.4997	2.8563	3.3305	3.4447	3.5669	3.6979	3.8387	3.9903	4.1542	4.3316	4.5243	4.7342	4.9636	5.2151	5.4919	27
28	2.0000	2.2222	2.4998	2.8565	3.3312	3.4455	3.5679	3.6991	3.8402	3.9923	4.1566	4.3346	4.5281	4.7390	4.9697	5.2228	5.5016	28
29	2.0000	2.2222	2.4999	2.8567	3.3317	3.4461	3.5687	3.7001	3.8414	3.9938	4.1585	4.3371	4.5312	4.7430	4.9747	5.2292	5.5098	29
30	2.0000	2.2222	2.4999	2.8568	3.3321	3.4466	3.5693	3.7009	3.8424	3.9950	4.1601	4.3391	4.5338	4.7463	4.9789	5.2347	5.5168	30
35	2.0000	2.2222	2.5000	2.8571	3.3330	3.4478	3.5708	3.7028	3.8450	3.9984	4.1644	4.3447	4.5411	4.7559	4.9915	5.2512	5.5386	35
40	2.0000	2.2222	2.5000	2.8571	3.3332	3.4481	3.5712	3.7034	3.8458	3.9995	4.1659	4.3467	4.5439	4.7596	4.9966	5.2582	5.5482	40
45	2.0000	2.2222	2.5000	2.8571	3.3333	3.4482	3.5714	3.7036	3.8460	3.9998	4.1664	4.3474	4.5449	4.7610	4.9986	5.2611	5.5523	45
50	2.0000	2.2222	2.5000	2.8571	3.3333	3.4483	3.5714	3.7037	3.8461	3.999	4.1666	4.3477	4.5452	4.7616	4.9995	5.2623	5.5541	50
Yrs	50%	45%	40%	35%	30%	29%	28%	27%	26%	25%	24%	23%	22%	21%	20%	19%	18%	Yrs

Name Index

Abrams, H. J., 435
Allen, D. H., 252, 404
Allen, D. H. and Page, R. C., 156
Ansoff, H. I., 69
Ansoff, H. I. and Stewart, J. M., 65
Argenti, J., 48
Ayres, R. U., 260

Baker, D. J., 252
Baker, N. R. and Pound, W. H., 252
Bameson, R. A. et al., 410
Baumol, W. J. and Quandt, R. E., 114
Becker, G. S., 457
Bell, D. C. et al., 253
Bellman, R. E. and Dreyfuss, S. E., 451
Beranek, W., 202
Bierman, H. and Smidt, S., 119
Bowman, E. H. and Fetter, R. B., 359
Box, G. E. P., 410
Box, G. E. P. and Jenkins, G., 135
Brech, R., 261
Brichter, A. M. and Sharp, E. M., 248
Bridgewater, A. V., 166, 169
Bright, J. R., 63, 258
Bromich, M., 119
Brown, R. G., 361
Buffa, E. S., 373
Buffa, E. S. and Taubert, W. H., 361, 366

Caudle, P. G., 139
Centre of Interfirm Comparison, 170, 179
Chambers, J. C. et al., 135
Chernoff, H. and Moses, L. E., 241
Churchman, C. W. R. et al., 366, 456
Clark, C. E., 338
Collcutt, R. H. and Reader, R. D., 253
Connor, J. and Evans, J. B., 441
Cooper, A. C., 651

Cooper, L. and Steinberg, D., 409
Cyert, R. M. and March, J. G., 48

Danø, S., 409
Dantzig, G. B., 114, 409
Dean, J., 143
de Bono, E., 67
de la Mare, 134, 146, 181, 269, 457, 529
Dewhurst, H. A., 247
Disney, R. L., 372
Disney, R. L. and Solberg, J. J., 372

Earley, F., 142
Edey, H. C., 317
Edwards, W., 237
Eilon, S. et al., 464
Enos, J. L., 248, 257
Erlang, A. K., 366

Feldstein, M. A., 89
Fidgett, M., 171
Fisher, L., 131
Fisher, L. and Lorie, J. H., 195
Forrester, J., 360
Fulkerson, D. R., 334

Gates, M. and Scarpa, A., 181
Gershuny, J., 3
Gilfillan, S. C., 257
Gilman, J. J., 248
Glasser, G. L., 456
Gordon, W. J. J., 67
Grant, E. L. et al., 90
Grayson, J. C., 241
Green, P. E., 241
Griliches, Z., 248
Grubbs, F. E., 334
Grumer, E. L., 170
Guthrie, K. M., 165

Hall, A. P., 422, 470
Hall, R. L. and Hitch, C. J., 142
Harrison, P. J. and Pearce, S. F., 132
Hayes, R. H., 240
Hayes, W. W. and Solomon, M. B., 271
Haynes, W. W., 142

Helmer, O., 258
Hertz, D., 232
Hess, S. W., 253
Hirschmann, W. B., 165
Hirshleifer, J., 94
Hitchcock, F. L., 392
Hodge, H. P., 148
Holland, F. A. et al., 82
Hooke, R. and Jeeves, T. A., 409
Hutchinson, A. C., 87

Isenson, R. S., 247
Istvan, D. F., 90

Jantsch, E., 257
Jardine, A. K. S., 176, 456, 464
Jewkes, J. et al., 65

Kahn, H. and Wiener, A. J., 261
Kaplan, A. D. H. et al., 142
Kay, S. R., 150
Kelly, A. and Harris, M. J., 176
Klammer, T., 90
Krishnamoorthi, B., 372
Kyburg, H. E. and Smokler, H. E., 237

Lang, J., 156
Lentz, R. C., 260
Leontief, W., 132
Le Page, N., 278
Levy, F. K. et al., 338
Liversey, F., 143
Lockyer, K. G., 337
Lorie, J. H. and Savage, L. J., 110

MacCrimmon, K. R. et al., 334
Magee, J. F. and Boodman, D. M., 361
Mahmoud, M. A. M., 171
Malloy, J. B., 146, 207, 235
Markowitz, H. M., 199, 241
Maroney, M. J., 216
Martino, J. P., 140
Mathur, S. S. and Padley, H., 171
McKinley, D. H. et al., 126
Menon, K. A. P. and Bowander, B., 140

541

Merrett, A. J. and Sykes, A.,
    50, 90, 195, 202, 435
Miller, C. A., 165
Modigliani, F. and Miller, M.
    H., 198
Moore, P. G. and Hodges, S.
    D., 409
Morse, P. M., 367, 373
Mossin, J., 199
Mueller, W. F., 66
Mumford, L. S., 225

Naylor, T. H. et al., 373
Nicholson, R. L. R., 260

Pavitt, K., 10
Pearce, I. F., 143
Pearson, A. W. and Topaling,
    A. S., 252
Peck, L. G. and Hazelwood,
    R. N., 372
Perry, R. H. and Chilton, C.
    H., 150
Pontryagin, L. S. et al., 410
Popper, H., 166
Prest, A. R. and Turvey, R.,
    89

Robinson, C., 142

Rockley, L. E., 90
Rosenberg, N., 12
Rothwell, R., 10
Ruberstein, A. H., 252
Ruberstein, M. G., 199
Russo, J. G. and Cowles, H.
    A., 180
Ryan, R. R., 199

Saaty, T. L., 372
Samuelson, P. A., 12, 127
Sasieni, M. et al., 367
Savage, L. J., 227
Sciberras, E., 10
Scott, R., 167
Schlaifer, R., 227
Schmookler, J., 247
Sharpe, W., 199
Smith, A., 13
Solomon, E., 197
Souder, W. E., 253
Stobaugh, R. B., 138
Stout, D., 10
Swalm, R. O., 242
Symonds, G. H., 409

Taylor, J. H. and Craven, P.
    J., 144
Terborgh, G. M., 441

Thuesen, H. G. et al., 119
Tietzen, K. H., 248
Tiles, S., 70
Tocher, K. D., 373

Van Arnum, K. J., 136, 138
von Neumann, J. and
    Morgenstern, O., 237

Wagle, B., 220
Walsh, M. J., 308
Weingartner, H. M., 114
Wessel, H. E., 171
Wierst, J. D., 271
Wild, N. H., 82
Wild, R., 338
Wilde, D., 410
Wilkes, R. E., 141
Williams, N., 410
Wills, G. et al., 70, 258
Wilson, D. C., 169
Wilson, R. M. S., 166
Woodman, R. C., 456
Wright, T. P., 144
Wragg, R. and Robertson, J.,
    458

Zionts, S., 409

Subject Index

Accelerator principle, 125
Accounting—
  allocating overhead costs, 310–14
  data used in economic studies, 295–317
  depreciation expenses, 87–8, 314, 489–90
  double entry book keeping, 309–14, 488
  rudiments, 487–493
Algorithms, 380
Alternatives—
  choice between, 95–119
  mutually exclusive, 100–108
  search for, 59–69
  with unequal economic lives, 449–454
Analogy—
  costing, 151
  forecasting, 136, 260
Annuities, 82–4, 432, 444–5
Assets—
  current, 488
  fixed, 488
  replacement, 427
  value, 182, 433–40, 489
Average—
  physical product, 26
  total costs, 31
  variable costs, 31, 308

Balance sheet, 301, 488–90
Bills of exchange, 191
Bonds, 192
Book value, 184, 447
Breakeven analysis, 34, 315–16
Budgeting, 299–305
Building programme, 180–1
Business cycles, 124–7
Business forecasting, 124–40

Capability analysis, 65–6, 148
Capital Asset Pricing Model (CAPM), 199
Capital—
  budgeting, 71, 273, 305
  cost estimating, 149–65, 169–72
  cost-capacity ratios, 155
  fixed, 281
  grants, 184
  rationing, 106–19
Case studies, 421, 470, 475
Cash flow—
  budget, 304
  continuous, 526–9
  definition, 80
  diagram, 81
  fixed, 280

incremental, 80, 104
  variable, 279
Challenger, 435
Chance nodes, 254
Chance pattern of failures, 454–57
Check lists, 67, 148, 162–3, 249–52
Comparison of alternatives—
  basis for, 462, 509
  mutually exclusive, 100–106
  with unequal economic lives, 449–54
Competitive advantage, 6–11
Compound interest, 72
Continuous compounding/discounting, 524–6
Constraints, 37, 106, 355, 376
Contracts, 181
Corporate—
  control, 297–8
  planning, 46
  objectives, 47, 194
  strategy, 45, 59–64, 275–6
Cost benefit analysis, 89
Cost control, 295
Cost of capital, 190–201
Cost of equity finance, 193–6
Costing—
  absorption, 142
  analogy, 151
  detailed, 164
  exponential, 151
  factorial, 156–66
  job, 309–14
  marginal, 315–17
  responsibility, 298–9
  standard, 305–9
Costs—
  capital, 149–65
  direct, 170, 296
  distribution, 393
  effective annual, 432–3
  energy, 171
  first, 101–4
  fixed, 30
  incremental, 345
  indirect, 296
  inventory, 339–61
  holding, 345
  labour, 171
  life-cycle, 178–80
  marginal, 31
  marketing, 302
  operating, 169–72
  opportunity, 37–41, 399, 483–6
  overhead, 172

Cost (*Continued*)
  queueing, 370–1
  production, 30–1
  research/development, 246–8
  restocking, 345
  set up, 341
  stockout, 342–9
  sunk, 173, 440–2, 507
  variable, 30, 314–16
Critical path method (CPM)—
  diagrams, 323–334
  economic aspects, 334–7
Current assets, 301, 488–9
Current liabilities, 301, 488–9
Curves—
  demand, 14–25
  indifference, 17–21, 95–117
  supply, 14–15, 24–9

Debentures, 199, 489
Debt–equity ratio, 196, 268, 488, 492
Decision—
  criteria, 68, 71
  pay-off matrix, 211–14, 253–6
  theory, 237
Defender, 431
Degeneracy, 401
Delphi technique, 137, 227, 258
Demand—
  cross elasticity of, 23–5
  curves, 14–25
  factors of, 60, 137
  income elasticity of, 23–5
  price elasticity of, 23–5
  utility of, 16–22
Depreciation, 86, 88, 314, 488, 490
Decartes' rule of signs, 531
Design—
  economic consequences of, 175
  life-cycle cost considerations, 178
  specifications, 174
Diminishing returns to scale, 26–8, 404
Direct costs, 170, 296
Discount factors—
  annual, 74–89
  continuous income, 527
Discounted cash flow (DCF), 75
Discounted cash flow rate of return (DCFRR),
    76–89, 96, 118, 272, 525
Distributions—
  continuous, 223, 233–4
  discrete, 222, 233–4
Dividend—
  cover, 50
  payout ratio, 268
  policy, 193–5
  yield, 49
Diversification, 61–3
Dynamic programming, 449–54

Economic life, 88, 429
Economic growth, 6
Economic order quantity (EOQ), 347
Economics—
  micro, 13–41

  macro, 124–37
Effective interest rate, 524
Efficiency, 25, 307–8, 404
Elasticity of demand, 22–4
End of period convention, 72
End use analysis, 130, 137
Entrepreneur, 35, 236
Engineering design considerations, 174–5
Equity, 193–6, 268
Equivalence, 74
Errors, allowing for, 164, 462
Estimating, 149, 169
European Economic Community (EEC), 5
Expected value criterion, 219
Experience curves, 144
Exponential cost factors, 151

Factors—
  of production, 14
  efficient use of, 37
  limiting, 299
Feasibility study, 150, 274
Financial ratio analysis, 86, 491–3
Financing—
  effect on cost of capital, 196
  methods, 190
First cost, 101–4
Fiscal policy, 36, 126, 182
Fixed cost, 30, 316
Forecasting—
  econometric, 131
  models, 123
  profit gap, 51–6
  technological, 257

Gain on asset disposal, 446
Gearing, 196–9
General Agreement of Tariffs and Trade (GATT),
    5
Gompertz function, 133–5
Government policy, 36, 128, 182
Gross domestic (national) product, 7, 131
Growth—
  capitalization value, 50
  dividend, 194
  market sales (share), 132, 148

Health and safety legislation, 36
Heuristic, 271
Historical analogy, 136, 258
Human behaviour, 13–14, 293
Hungarian assignment method, 406–8
Hurwicz rule, 214–5

Income—17–25
  statement, 310
  tax, 181, 442
Incremental costs, 345
Increasing returns, 26–8, 404
Independence, 219
Indices, 29, 132, 155, 201
Indifference curves, 17–22
Inferior products, 24
Inflation, 199–201
Information feedback, 175, 275, 317
Innovation, 8–11, 457–62

Input–output analysis, 132
Insurance, 272, 434
Interest rates—
  continuous, 522
  effective, 52
  nominal, 523
Inventiveness, 63, 246–8
Inventory cost control, 339–61
Investment criteria, 71–89, 275
Investment on a mortgage basis, 73

Judgement—
  in decision making, 147, 272, 462
  in estimating, 235

Knowledge of techniques, 65, 88, 389

Labour costs—
  direct, 170, 296
  indirect, 296
Lagrange multiplier, 110, 357, 483
Laplace rule, 214
Law of diminishing returns, 28
Learning theory, 25, 144, 165
Leverage, 196–9
Liabilities, 489
Life-cycle benefit/cost concept, 3, 11, 88
Life-cycle equation, 88–9
Limiting factors, 299
Liquidity, 85, 492
Linear programming, 114, 375–92
Loans—
  limits on borrowing, 488
  medium–long-term, 191–2
  short-term, 191–2
Loss—
  economic, 34
  on disposal of fixed assets, 440, 446
Lot size, inventory, 347

Maintenance, 173, 281
Make or buy decisions, 317
Management by objective (MBO), 299
Management information system (MIS), 317
Management science, 294
Marginal costs, 31
Marginal physical product, 27
Market—
  forecasting, 127–40
  leader, 48, 62, 149
  price, 14, 141–7
  research, 128
  share, 4, 147–8
  strategy, 59–63
Marketing, 44
Materials costs, 296, 385
Mathematical models, 123, 344, 368, 375
Maximin rule, 212
Maximax rule, 213
Minimax regret rule, 213
Minimum cost analysis, 385–8, 429
MODI. technique, 399
Monetary policy, 36, 126
Monte Carlo simulation, 228–36
Morphological forecasting, 260

Mortality curves, 180–1, 455–7
Mortgage, 73
Multiple rates of return, 529–34
Multiplier principle, 125
Mutually exclusive projects, 100–6

Net cash flows, 75, 498
Net present value (NPV), 79, 278, 435, 443
Network analysis, 323–37
Nominal interest rates, 523
Non-linear programming, 404–6
Northwest corner rule, 393

Objective function, 111, 376
Objectives, 47, 194
Obsolescence, 428
Operating cost estimation, 169–72
Opinion sampling, 136
Opportunities for—
  borrowing, 97–9
  lending, 97–9
  marketing, 59–69
  technology, 63
Opportunity cost, 37–41, 399, 483–6
Optimization, 35, 336–7, 349
Optimum reorder quantity, 347
Optimum replacement period, 88, 429
Organization, 273
Overhead costs, 172

Par value, 489
Payback time, 84–6
Pareto effect, 344
Patents, 144–6
Pay-off matrix, 211–4, 253–6
PERT, 323
Physical behaviour of queues, 367–8
Physical product, 26
Planning, 46, 55, 59–69, 293
Post audits, 298
Power rule, 152
Present values, 74–82
Price—
  earnings ratio, 195
  elasticity of demand, 22–4
  equilibrium, 15
  shadow, 379, 384, 399
  strategy, 45, 59–69, 275
Principle of sunk cost, 440–2
Probability—
  of success, 253
  subjective, 226–8
  theory, 216–26
Product—
  design, 174
  life cycle, 52–3
  planning, 59
  price, 15–40
  strategy, 59–63
Production—
  effect on inventory costs, 351
  factors of, 14
  function, 25
  multiple batch, 353–5
  scale of, 26

Productivity, 6–8, 164–5
Profit—
  excess, 36
  gap, 51–6
  maximization, 33–7, 376
Profit and loss account, 490–1
Profitability index, 109
Project—
  duration, 180–1
  optimization, 187–8
  ranking, 106–9
Quality, 174
Quantitative techniques, 294, 323, 339, 365
Queueing theory, 365–73

Ranking of projects, 109, 248
Ratio analysis, 491–3
Recession, 125
Reinvestment, 106–8
Reliability, 175–8, 180
Repairs, 455–7
Replacement theory, 427–63
Resale value, 434, 439, 446
Research and development—
  costs and benefits, 246–8
  strategy, 63–5
Responsibility costing, 298–9
Return on investment—7, 87, 196, 268
  DCFRR, 76
  incremental, 98, 104
  IRR, 76
Returns to scale, 26–8, 152
Revenue from sales—
  average, 33
  marginal, 34–5
  total, 32
Risk, 164, 205, 272
Risk analysis, 226–42
Roll-back technique, 254
Rules of thumb, 108–9

Salvage (scrap) value, 186, 462, 509
Scale of production, 26–8
Scenario writing, 261
Sensitivity analysis, 209–11
Sequential decision making, 253–7
Shadow prices, 37–41, 399, 483–6
Share capital, 193, 489
Shares, 49, 193

Simplex algorithm, 385
Simulation, 231–6, 361, 373
Social welfare, 35–6
Standard deviation, 220
Standardization, 174, 299
Stockouts, 349
Strategy, 59–69
Substitute products, 25
Supply, demand and price, 14–16
Sunk cost, 173, 440–2, 507
Synergy, 54, 61

Taxation effects in DCF analysis, 181–7, 442–9
Technical returns to scale, 151
Technological innovation, 8–11, 66–9, 261–2
Technical forecasting, 257–61
Terotechnology, 173–4
Time—
  preference for money, 94–100
  trend analysis, 132–6, 258–60
  value of money, 76
Total costs of production, 30
Total physical product, 25
Total systems approach, 267
Trade credit, 190
Trade off, 347, 429
Transportation linear programing (TLP), 393
Two-thirds power rule, 151

Uncertainty, 203–42, 454–7, 333–4, 358–61
Unequal lives, 449–454
Utility theory, 236–42

Value, 433–40, 489–90
Variable cost, 30, 314–16
Variance—
  cost, 305
  statistical, 219
Vogel's approximation method, 397–9

Waiting lines, 365–73
Working capital, 166–9, 340
Work in progress, 168
Written-down value (WDV), 184, 447, 481

Yield—
  bond, 192
  material, 404–5
  share, 49, 194